AFRICAN AMERICAN URBAN EXPERIENCE

AFRICAN AMERICAN URBAN EXPERIENCE: PERSPECTIVES FROM THE COLONIAL PERIOD TO THE PRESENT

EDITED BY JOE W. TROTTER
with Earl Lewis and Tera W. Hunter

palgrave
macmillan

First published 2004 by PALGRAVE MACMILLAN™
175 Fifth Avenue, New York, N.Y. 10010 and
Houndmills, Basingstoke, Hampshire, England RG21 6XS.
Companies and representatives throughout the world.

PALGRAVE MACMILLAN is the global academic imprint of the Palgrave
Macmillan division of St. Martin's Press, LLC and of Palgrave Macmillan Ltd.
Macmillan® is a registered trademark in the United States, United Kingdom
and other countries. Palgrave is a registered trademark in the European
Union and other countries.

ISBN 0-312-29464-6 hardback
ISBN 0-312-29465-4 paperback

Library of Congress Cataloging-in-Publication Data

The African American urban experience : perspectives from the colonial period
to the present / [edited by] Joe W. Trotter, Earl Lewis, Tera W. Hunter.
        p. cm.
    A product of several conferences, seminars and lecture series sponsored
by the Center for Africanamerican Urban Studies and the Economy (CAUSE)
and the Midwest Consortium for Black Studies (MCBS).
    Includes bibliographical references and index
    ISBN 0-312-29464-6 (hc)—0-312-29465-4 (pbk.)
      1. Sociology, Urban—United States. 2. African Americans—Social
Conditions. I. Trotter, Joe William, 1945- II. Lewis, Earl. III. Hunter, Tera W.

HT123.A66168 2004
307.76'089'96073—dc21   2002041739

A catalogue record for this book is available from the British Library.

Design by Kolam

First edition: March 2004
10 9 8 7 6 5 4 3 2 1

Printed in the United States of America.

In memory of

W. E. B. Du Bois
E. Franklin Frazier
Charles S. Johnson
St. Clair Drake
Horace R. Cayton

CONTENTS

PREFACE

This volume is based upon research at Carnegie Mellon's Center for Africanamerican Urban Studies and the Economy (CAUSE). An interdisciplinary center for historical, social scientific, and policy research, CAUSE is committed to building bridges between Carnegie Mellon and other institutions of higher education. In 1996, our collaboration with other institutions gained sharp expression with the founding of the Midwest Consortium for Black Studies (MCBS). Comprised of African American Studies programs at Michigan State University, the University of Michigan, the University of Wisconsin at Madison, and Carnegie Mellon, the MCBS aims to deepen the presence of black studies at member schools and chart new directions for African American Studies as a multi-disciplinary field of study. Thus, the essays in this volume not only highlight the interdisciplinary character of research on the African American urban experience, but accent the transformation of scholarly debates and policy discussions of race, cities, and social change in U.S. history.

The collection of essays that comprise *African American Urban Studies* is a product of several national conferences, graduate seminars, and public speakers series organized by CAUSE and the MCBS. In 1995, CAUSE opened with a conference called Race, Workers, and the Urban Economy: Recent Trends in Scholarship. This conference took advantage of *Labor History*'s special 25th anniversary issue titled "Race and Class." Under the editorship of labor historians Alan Dawley and Joe Trotter, this volume commemorated the 25th anniversary of the journal's groundbreaking volume, "The Negro and the American Labor Movement: Some Selected Chapters." Published in the summer of 1969, "The Negro and the American Labor Movement" highlighted the gradual emergence of black labor and working class history as a field of serious scholarly inquiry. Twenty-five years later, however, the commemorative volume not only emphasized changes in research on the experiences of black workers, but included essays on Latino/Latina and Asian American workers, noting the varieties of paths that studies of race and class had taken by the closing decades of the twentieth century.

As a means of announcing the creation of CAUSE, we brought the contributors to the special *Labor History* volume to Carnegie Mellon for a one-day conference on urban workers. Supplemented by James R. Barrett's essay on ethnic and racial fragmentation of the U. S. labor movement, the essays from our founding conference have been updated and published in this volume as "Part III, Comparative Perspectives." These articles include Chris Friday's assessment of Asian American labor history; Camille Guerin-Gonzales's review of Latino/Latina working class experiences; and Alan Dawley's critique of racial interpretations in U. S. labor and working class history. Moreover, perspectives from both Earl Lewis's keynote address on the changing meaning of race in U.S.

history and Joe Trotter's essay on new directions in African American urban and labor historiography have been synthesized in the introduction to this volume (with Tera Hunter).

In 1997–98, CAUSE hosted the second of two graduate seminars and public lecture series funded by a grant from the Ford Foundation to the Midwest Consortium for Black Studies. While the first seminar, under Professor Stanlie James of the University of Wisconsin, focused on black women's studies, history, and social policy, Carnegie Mellon's year-long seminar focused on "African American Urban Studies: History, Work, and Social Policy." The seminar unfolded in three interconnected parts: 1) an assessment of changes in research on the African American urban experience from the early twentieth century through recent times; 2) a close examination of recent historical case studies of black life in particular cities; and 3) an exploration of social scientific and policy-oriented studies of contemporary black urban life.

During the fall of 1997, guest presenters included historians James Oliver Horton, George Washington University; Ronald L. Lewis, West Virginia University; Brenda Stevenson, University of California-Los Angeles; Thomas Buchanan, Carnegie Mellon University (now at the University of Nebraska-Omaha); and Tera Hunter, Carnegie Mellon University. Winter and spring guests were an interdisciplinary mix of historians and social scientists (including economists, urban planning scholars, and urban geographers): Quintard Taylor, University of Oregon (now at the University of Washington in Seattle); Alice O'Connor, University of California-Santa Barbara; Karen Gibson, Carnegie Mellon University (now at Portland State University); William A. Darity, University of North Carolina-Chapel Hill; Susan McElroy, Carnegie Mellon University (now at the University of Texas-Dallas); James Johnson, University of North Carolina-Chapel Hill; and Richard Walter Thomas, Michigan State University. With the exception of two papers, essays presented by these visiting scholars appear in Parts I and II of this volume. Chapters by Horton, Lewis, Buchanan, Hunter, and Taylor provide historical perspectives on black urban history from the colonial era through the mid-twentieth century, while essays by O'Connor, McElroy, Darity (with Patrick Mason), Gibson, and Thomas illuminate transformations in black urban life since World War II and the advent of the modern civil rights and black power movements.

As part of our most recent Ford Foundation-funded activities (2000–2002), CAUSE conducted a semester long graduate seminar, titled "African Americans in the Post-Industrial City." This seminar also brought together scholars from other Midwest Consortium schools for a one-day conference (26–27 October 2001) on black life during the second half of the twentieth century. The conference featured a keynote address by civil rights scholar Charles M. Payne of Duke University and presentations by leading specialists on black urban life—Kenneth Kusmer, Temple University; Thomas Sugrue, University of Pennsylvania; Arnold Hirsch, University of New Orleans; Venus Green, City University of New York; and Ronald Bayor, Georgia Institute of Technology. Along with Kusmer and others, presenters included emerging young scholars, Robert Self, University of Michigan (now at the University of Wisconsin-Milwaukee) and Karl E. Johnson, Temple University. Together, papers from this conference helped to shape our critique of the literature in the introduction to this volume, where we call attention to the need for more systematic case studies of black urban life in the period since World War II.

For helping to make this volume possible, we are indebted to numerous institutions and people. First, we wish to thank Carnegie Mellon University, the Ford Foundation, the Mellon Financial Corporation, and the Maurice Falk Medical Fund for their generous financial support. Such support not only enabled us to strengthen contacts with scholars across the country and bring this volume to fruition, but facilitated exceedingly fruitful interchanges between the university and the larger Pittsburgh metropolitan community.

Almost from its beginnings, CAUSE has benefited from the support of colleagues in the Midwest Consortium for Black Studies. Nellie McKay, Stanlie James, and Craig Werner at the University of Wisconsin; Darlene Clark Hine and Curtis Stokes at Michigan State University; James Jackson and his colleagues at the University of Michigan, all represent models of collegiality and friendship. Their presence and participation at CAUSE conferences and speakers series not only enhanced the intellectual value of our activities, but broadened the comparative scope of our work. For his support, we are also grateful to historian Frederick Douglass Opie of Morehouse University (now at Marist College, New York).

In addition to the contributors to this volume and those listed above, we extend gratitude to numerous other presenters. We thank Sharon Harley, University of Maryland-College Park; Kenya C. Dworkin, Carnegie Mellon University; Daniel J. Leab, then editor of *Labor History;* Laurence Glasco, University of Pittsburgh; Seth Sanders, Carnegie Mellon University (now at the University of Maryland); Stephen Appold, Carnegie Mellon University (now at the National University of Singapore); Pauline Abdullah, Braddock, PA; Fernando Gapasin, Penn State University-New Kensington; and Henry Louis Taylor, State University of New York-Buffalo.

Postdoctoral fellows played an important role in both CAUSE and MCBS seminars and conference activities. In addition to Karen Gibson, the center's first postdoctoral fellow, these include Yevette Richards, University of Pittsburgh (now at George Mason University) John Hinshaw, Lebanon Valley College; Richard Pierce, University of Notre Dame; Eric Brown, Cornell University; and Lisa Levenstein, University of North Carolina-Greensboro.

Current and past graduate students have been perhaps the most important ingredient in helping us to sustain the activities of the center. At Carnegie Mellon, the center benefited from the thoughtful input of Charles Lee, Robin Dearmon Jenkins, Matthew Hawkins, Jesse A. Belfast, Alex Bennett, Steve Burnett, Geoffrey Glover, C. Evelyn Hawkins, Lisa Margot Johnson, Lindsay McKenzie, Patricia Mitchell, Mary L. Nash, Lewis W. Roberts, Delmarshae Sledge, Cornell Womack, Susan Spellman, Tywanna Whorley, Jonathan White, and Germaine Williams.

Graduate students at other MCBS schools offered similar input: Eric Duke, John Wess Grant, Julia M. Robinson, Marshanda Smith, and Matthew Whitaker of Michigan State University; Jerome Dotson, Michele Gordon, Rhea Lathan, and Michael Quieto of University of Wisconsin-Madison; and Charlene J. Allen, Aqueelah Cowan, Marya McQuirter, Shani Mott, Ebony Robinson, Shawan

Wade, and Umi Vaughan of University of Michigan. Other undergraduate and graduate student participants included: Keona Ervin (Duke University); Claudrena Harold (University of Notre Dame); Latonia Payne (University of Michigan), and Zachary Williams (Bowling Green State University). We wish to extend a special thanks to Carnegie Mellon Ph.D.s who witnessed, encouraged, and aided the creation and development of CAUSE and the Midwest Consortium for Black Studies—Ancella Livers, John Hinshaw, Donald Collins, Liesl Orenic, Trent Alexander, and Susannah Walker.

For its ongoing counsel, support, and advice, we are especially indebted to the center's steering committee: Philip B. Hallen, Maurice Falk Medical Fund; the late Jeffrey Hunker, Carnegie Mellon University; Mark S. Kamlet, Carnegie Mellon University; Barbara B. Lazarus, Carnegie Mellon University; John P. Lehoczky, Carnegie Mellon University; James P. McDonald, Mellon Financial Corporation; Susan Williams McElroy, University of Texas-Dallas; Kerry O'Donnell, Maurice Falk Medical Fund; Steven Schlossman, Carnegie Mellon University; and Everett L. Tademy, Carnegie Mellon University.

Indispensable to the day-to-day operation of the center are business manager Gail Dickey and administrative assistant Nancy Aronson. For their hard work on behalf of the center we are most grateful. CAUSE has also benefited from the able assistance of undergraduate assistants, most notably in recent years Mavis Burks. In addition to such staff support, we are grateful to colleagues in the department of history and members of the larger Pittsburgh metropolitan region. Their regular attendance at public speakers series and conference presentations has been greatly appreciated. Such collegial support and critical engagement with the issues facing African American urban studies have helped to make both the center and this volume a reality.

As always, we owe our greatest debt of gratitude to family members and friends. Earl Lewis and Joe Trotter, respectively, extend a special thanks to their wives Susan and LaRue, in addition to the authors' friends. They have not only made work on this book enjoyable, but helped us to keep in view the larger meaning of our labor—that is, to create a more humane world in which to live. Finally, as a small token of appreciation to our forbears, pioneers in black urban studies, we dedicate this volume to the memory of W. E. B. Du Bois, E. Franklin Frazier, Charles S. Johnson, St. Clair Drake, and Horace R. Cayton.

Introduction

Connecting African American Urban History, Social Science Research, and Policy Debates

Joe W. Trotter, Earl Lewis, and Tera W. Hunter

Open any newspaper, listen to most news reports, catch the words of many politicians bemoaning the decline of the central city, and for years the images used to accompany the message pictured a black face. Since the 1960s, against the backdrop of race riots and general despair, the words black, inner city, ghetto and problems became connected and at times interchangeable. Oftentimes the stories produced appear as if blacks inhabit the inner cities alone. In this world there are no Asians, Latinos and Latinas, Native Americans, or whites. In this world the central cities are divided from power structures, businesses, labor unions, politics, and adjacent suburbs. In this world race and racism exist within a tightly bound space divorced from the larger society. Why is this? And just as important, how do we add a historical perspective to the long list of policy recommendations that have captivated public discourse for more than four decades?

This books attempts to answer these and other questions. It also seeks to uncover the multiple histories of urban life in America. It centers on the history and lived conditions of African Americans, and places them in proximity and interactions with the broad spectrum of others who peopled this nation.

It is a volume that seriously explores the multiple meanings of race in the past by focusing on the aforementioned broad spectrum. It seeks to understand how several generations of immigrants from Europe, Latin America, Africa, and Asia came to see and experience the city, especially by the second half of the twentieth century, as a place dominated by blacks. Therefore this is a study about history, policy, and intergroup relations. To understand that history and the attendant relations, special attention is paid to labor matters, cross-ethnic coalition building, and the usefulness of racial difference for a range of social actors.

The transformation of rural blacks into a predominantly urban people is a twentieth century phenomenon. Only during World War I did African Americans move into cities in large numbers, and only during World War II did more blacks reside in cities than in the countryside. By the early 1970s, African Americans had not only made the transition from rural to urban settings, but were almost evenly distributed by region. Before they could anchor in the nation's urban industrial economy, however, blacks faced the onslaught of deindustrialization, high unemployment, residential segregation, and new forms of community, institutional, cultural, and political conflict. Adding new and more complex dimensions to class and race relations were new waves of immigrants. For the first time in the nation's history, the majority of newcomers came from countries in Latin America and Asia. By the 1990s, about 25 percent of the U.S. population were people of Asian, Latin American, Native American, and African descent (including people from the English speaking Caribbean and Africa).[1]

After nearly a century of black population movement from South to North, blacks turned southward again. Until the 1970s, only about 15,000 African Americans who had moved North returned to the South. During the last third of the twentieth century, the return migration of blacks rose to nearly 50,000 each year. The Great Migration of southern blacks to the North and West had reversed itself. As anthropologist Carol Stack puts it, growing numbers of southern-born northern and western blacks and their children answered "The call to Home."[2] At the same time, African Americans made the trek from inner city neighborhoods to predominantly white suburbia, especially in northern and western cities. Indeed, by the turn of the twenty-first century the magnitude of black migration to the suburbs had surpassed the Great Migration to American cities.

Scholars from a variety of disciplines have examined the urban transformation of African American life, but few studies bring these disparate perspectives together in a single interdisciplinary volume. In order to help bridge this gap in our understanding, this book connects historical, social scientific, and comparative perspectives on African American and U.S. urban and social history. Connecting these myriad lines of intellectual inquiry not only requires an interdisciplinary assessment of research on the black urban experience, but an examination of the ongoing interplay between scholarship, race, and public policy, from the emergence of black urban studies at the beginning of the twentieth century through recent times. Thus, in this introduction, we take up in turn the rise of black urban studies at the turn of the twentieth century; the increasing confluence of social scientific and historical studies under the influence of the modern civil rights and Black Power movements; and the ways that the essays in this volume promise to address significant theoretical, methodological, temporal, and substantive lacunae in our knowledge of the interrelationship of race, class, cities, and social change in American life.

ORIGINS OF BLACK URBAN STUDIES

During the early to mid-twentieth century, sociological and social anthropological studies established the intellectual foundations for the emergence of black urban studies as a scholarly field. Focusing on black life in large northern cities, mainly Chicago, New York, and Philadelphia, W. E. B. Du Bois, Charles S. Johnson, E. Franklin Frazier, St. Clair Drake, and Horace R. Cayton adopted the urban community study format and used a race contact theoretical framework for understanding the urban-industrial transformation of African American life.[3] But their work was by no means monolithic in approach, argument or conclusions. E. Franklin Frazier, for example, emphasized the loosening of racial or caste constraints as African Americans made the transition from farm to city during World War I and the 1920s.

Frazier took his cue from the race relations cycle theory of University of Chicago sociologist Robert E. Park. According to Park and his Chicago colleagues, African Americans were making the transition from a racial caste to an ethnic minority, which meant that their experiences would parallel the pattern of prior immigrants from south, central, and eastern Europe. As such, Park, Frazier, and others believed that blacks should be considered the most recent of the immigrant groups. Conversely, Drake and Cayton and their colleagues were less convinced that blacks would follow the path of European immigrants. They accented the persistence of racial barriers and the ways that only dire national emergencies like the Great Depression and World War II promised to initiate more equitable social policies and remove barriers to the upward mobility of African Americans.

During World War II, the Swedish economist Gunnar Myrdal sought to synthesize the caste and class models of African American life. Myrdal appreciated both change and continuity in the barriers that blacks faced in American society. On the one hand, a variety of forces suggested that blacks were gaining a footing in the urban political economy—the resurgence of black rural to urban migration, African American employment in the nation's defense industries, and their vital role in Franklin Delano Roosevelt's New Deal coalition. On the other hand, the segregationist order (in its de facto and de jure forms) persisted and undermined the impact of these changes on the socio-economic status of blacks. Myrdal and his contemporaries also noted the role of spatial concentration, class formation, and the changing status of black men and women within the urban environment, but they gave insufficient attention to the historical dimensions of these important developments in African American life. As we will see below, post-World War II scholars would call attention to these lacunae in our understanding and give prominence to the process of historical change in their assessments of the black urban experience.

BLACK URBAN HISTORY, THE GHETTO, AND THE RISE OF THE MOYNIHAN THESIS

Black urban history fully emerged and flourished as a field of scholarship during the 1960s and 1970s. Like early twentieth century social scientific studies, the first wave of historical scholarship focused almost exclusively on African American life in large northern cities. In studies of New York, Chicago, and Cleveland, respectively, historians Gilbert Osofsky, Allan Spear, and Kenneth Kusmer adopted the urban community study format, but used the "ghetto" as the primary lens for understanding black life in cities. They took sharp issue with immigration historian Oscar Handlin and the emerging cold war revival of the "last of the immigrants" thesis—that is, that blacks, no less than a variety of European immigrant groups, would eventually find a solid footing on the urban occupational ladder and move into the mainstream of urban industrial society. On the contrary, historians of the black urban experience argued that the city forever marked blacks by their color and offered them "no escape" from a severely restricted ghetto society.[4]

Social scientific and policy studies reinforced the theoretical and substantive orientation of the ghetto studies. During the 1950s and 1960s, as the Civil Rights Movement escalated, social scientists and policy experts turned increasingly toward a victimization model to justify federal social welfare appropriations for poor families. Such research culminated in the publication of Daniel Patrick Moynihan's *The Negro Family: The Case for National Action* in 1965. Building upon the earlier ideas of sociologist E. Franklin Frazier, as well as 1950s slavery studies, Moynihan concluded that the "deterioration of the Negro family" stood at "the heart of the deterioration of the fabric of Negro society." In his view, the institution of slavery and its successor the Jim Crow system initiated the destruction of black families, which urban migration heightened. Echoing the emerging "culture of poverty" idea (advanced by social anthropologist Oscar Lewis), Moynihan emphasized what he called "the tangle of pathology," that is, that blacks suffered from the absence of mainstream values of monogamy, hard work, thrift, and frugality. Rather than a product of external forces (for example, class and racial exploitation) that artificially limited opportunities for group mobility, poverty was a product of deeply entrenched group norms and social practices. Moynihan suggested that blacks exhibited a range of so-called "deviant behavior" that seemed likely to persist long after the conditions (like Jim Crow) that gave rise to it had passed away.[5]

As certain social scientists and policy experts honed the ghetto-slum interpretation of black urban life, others dissented somewhat but supported its central thrust. In 1966 and 1967, for example, two social-anthropological studies countered aspects of the Moynihan thesis of cultural disorganization among poor and working class blacks. In *Tally's Corner,* a study of twelve black street corner men in Washington, D. C., Elliott Liebow concluded that the behavior of black men did not reflect a "culture of poverty." According to Liebow, these men did not inhabit a "self-contained, self-sustaining system or even subsystem with clear boundaries marking it off from the world around it." Liebow noted a pattern of "serial monogamy" among the men and argued that their values paralleled those of the larger middle class society in which they lived.[6]

Other social anthropologists also rejected the "culture of poverty" concept, but emphasized the development of a distinct African American culture, rather than affinities to middle class values. Studies by Roger Abrahams, Ulf Hannerz, and Charles Keil approvingly underscored the ways that African American culture diverged from aspects of predominantly white middle class ideas and social practices. In his study of black male blues singers, for example, Charles Keil forcefully argued that these men did not conform or necessarily hope to conform to white middle class mores. In his words, the blues men were "the ablest representatives of a long cultural tradition—what might be called the soul tradition—and they are all identity experts, so to speak, specialists in changing the joke and slipping the yoke."[7] Nonetheless, as anthropologist Carol Stack noted, these studies did not go far enough. They "tended to reinforce popular stereotypes of the lower class or black family—particularly the black family in poverty—as deviant, matriarchal, and broken."[8] Similarly, historian Robin Kelley recently concluded that such studies ignored what "black expressive cultures" meant for the practitioners themselves. In other words, few of these scholars attempted to analyze black culture primarily from the vantage point of the black poor and working class.[9]

AFRICAN AMERICAN URBAN HISTORY, CULTURE, AND THE "UNDERCLASS DEBATE"

Under the impact of emerging class and gender perspectives on African American and U.S. history, historians moved beyond ghetto formation studies during the 1980s and 1990s. Studies by the authors of this volume, Darlene Clark Hine, and others, pinpointed certain limitations of the ghetto model and expressed increasing sensitivity to the dynamics of migration, working class formation, the role of black women, politics, and cultural issues. Late twentieth century studies also focused attention on the centrality of the South for understanding the socioeconomic, cultural, and political transformation of black life in the nation.[10]

Focusing on Cleveland's black community during the inter-World War years, Kimberly Phillips' *Alabama North* (1999) documents what she calls "the varieties of individual and collective struggles" that southern blacks developed around "wage work." Key to the maturation of Cleveland's black industrial working class, she argues, was the Great Migration of southern blacks to the city during World War I and the 1920s. Under the impact of the Depression and World War II, Phillips demonstrates how southern black working men and women led rather than followed the militant demands for defense industry jobs in firms with government contracts. Buttressing their demands was the rapid expansion of black churches, fraternal organizations, social clubs, and leisure time pursuits. In an extraordinary discussion of black gospel choirs and the community building activities of black women, Phillips accents the "racial, personal and religious experiences" of southern blacks in the northern urban environment. According to Phillips, many migrants, especially women, arrived in the North with as much experience building communities and associational life as they had "piecing together wage work." In short, as she puts it, black workers rebuilt "Alabama North."[11]

Rather than focusing on the South to North migration, other studies focused on rural to urban migration within the South itself. Among other southern cities, these included studies of Norfolk, Louisville, and Atlanta. As Earl Lewis noted, "more blacks migrated to southern cities between 1900 and 1920 than to northern cities." In her study of Atlanta's black working-class women, Tera Hunter not only illuminated the dynamics of black rural to urban population movement within the Jim Crow South, but documented the shifting role of black household workers within the context of Atlanta's larger political economy. By analyzing the interplay of work, residence, leisure, and politics in the lives of black household workers, Hunter also highlighted the impact of black working women on the interrelated processes of urbanization and industrialization. As such, she exposed deep class, race, and gender contradictions in the rise of Atlanta as a symbol of the so-called New South, which prided itself for embarking upon a new era of progress.[12]

The new working class, women, and cultural studies found early support among contemporary social scientists. Between 1970 and the early 1990s, a rich body of ethnographic research emerged. This research reinforced emphases on the development of a cohesive culture among poor and working class blacks. As early as 1974, anthropologist Carol Stack published *All Our Kin: Strategies for Survival in a Black Community*. Based upon extensive interviews with black residents as well as the case files of AFDC families in the poorest section of a midwestern city near Chicago, Stack offered a sharp critique of prevailing 1960s ethnographic, sociological, and policy studies. In her view, such studies downplayed the interpretations that poor and working class blacks gave to their own ideas, beliefs, and behavior.[13]

In order to counteract biases found in previous studies, Carol Stack developed a research strategy designed to illuminate the internal dynamics of black kinship and community networks. She convincingly argued that poor black families developed "a resilient response to the social-economic conditions of poverty." More specifically, she concluded that the "distinctively negative" characteristics—fatherlessness, matrifocality, instability, and disorganization—were not general features of black families living substantially below the subsistence line in urban America. As she put it, "Within the domestic networks women and men maintain strong loyalties to their kin, and kin exert internal sanctions upon one another to further strengthen the bond."[14] During the 1980s and 1990s, studies by social anthropologists John Langston Gwaltney, Dan Rose, and Mitchell Duneier reinforced research on the inner lives of poor and working class black urbanites.[15]

Even as historical, social science, and cultural studies affirmed the vitality of the African American community, certain changes in late twentieth century class and race relations helped to erode this interpretation among social researchers. Between 1965, the year of the controversial Moynihan Report, and 1980, out-of-wedlock black births increased from 25 to 57 percent; black female-headed families rose from 25 to 43 percent; and violent crimes and unemployment likewise increased as the nation's urban economy underwent a dramatic reorientation from durable goods or mass production firms to new computer driven service and information industries. During the late 1970s and early 1980s, as the incidence of inner city African American poverty increased, a variety of social scientists, policy experts, and journalists adopted the notion of underclass to describe and explain what they called the new urban poverty. According to these analysts, the "urban underclass"—defined as those families and individuals who existed outside the mainstream of the American occupational structure—was a new phenomenon.[16]

The underclass thesis gained its most forceful expression in the scholarship of sociologist William J. Wilson. In Wilson's view, the underclass signaled several overlapping transformations in black urban life. First, although Wilson and others recognized poverty as a persistent problem in black urban history, they emphasized relatively low levels of unemployment, crime, and welfare dependency before the emergence of the modern civil rights era. Since class and racial discrimination limited housing opportunities for all blacks during the Jim Crow era, the residences and lives of poor and elite blacks remained closely intertwined. Middle and working class blacks, they argue, not only shared the same space with the urban poor, but also provided social stability and leadership. Well-off blacks spearheaded the development of a broad-range of community institutions— churches, fraternal orders, and mutual benefit societies—to deal with class and racial inequality.[17]

Under the influence of new civil rights legislation and social protests during the 1970s and 1980s, substantial numbers of middle- and working-class blacks moved into racially and ethnically integrated neighborhoods outside the inner-city. At the same time, deindustrialization undercut the position of black men in heavy industries and left a growing number of workers permanently unemployed. According to underclass analysts, the intensification of urban poverty undercut the earlier pattern of multi-class communities and precipitated the rise of single-class black neighborhoods. The collapse of class integrated black communities deprived inner-city poor and working class black neighborhoods of vital leadership and social stability. Making matters worse, according to sociologist Elijah Anderson, "if those who are better off do remain . . . they tend to become disengaged, thinking their efforts as instructive agents of social control futile."[18]

Impressed by changing social conditions and growing emphasis on the segregated underclass, some historians turned their sights back toward the ghetto model. In 1986, Roger Lane published his study of violence in black Philadelphia. Lane's book sought to resuscitate the notion of a "culture of poverty." Lane concluded that the emergence of a black criminal "subculture" ("the product of a peculiar and bitter history") explained the long-term persistence of black crime, at the same time that violent crime decreased for "the white population as a whole." Similarly, though in more subdued tone, in his study of Philadelphia's AME Church and southern black migrants, Robert S. Gregg concluded that ghettoization best explained the migrants' experience in the northern city. As Gregg put it, "It is this anvil of oppression [the ghetto] that needs to be transformed, not the people whose sparks [supposedly] burn out in the ghettos." Still, at the level of community-building and institutions, Gregg employed the ghetto as his "fundamental conceptual and theoretical framework."[19]

Underclass scholarship did not go unchallenged. In 1993, historians registered their discontent in a collection of essays, The 'Underclass Debate': Views from History, edited by social historian Michael Katz.[20] According to these historians, the magnitude, scope, and configuration of urban poverty changed over the past two decades, but such urban problems were not entirely new. They characterized black life in the past. By linking the growth of the urban underclass to developments of the last two decades, Katz and his colleagues argued that underclass social science and policy studies provided inadequate insights into the historical development of the black community, its changing class structure, and the early

twentieth century roots of contemporary urban black poverty. *The "Underclass"*
Debate: Views from History reveals more connections between the past and present than the social science literature on the urban underclass would have us
believe. Moreover, as suggested by late twentieth century ethnographic studies,
poor and working class blacks forged new cultural forms under the impact of
deindustrialization.[21]

Published since the mid-1990s, a new wave of historical scholarship emphasizes changes in the politics and economics of African American work, residence,
and levels of poverty.[22] Building upon but moving well beyond the pioneering
work of historian Arnold Hirsch, these studies focus mainly on the first three
decades of the postwar years. They accent "white flight" (including people, jobs,
and capital) from the central cities to the suburbs; the rise of predominantly black
and poor inner city neighborhoods; the collapse of liberal civil rights and labor
coalitions; and the intensification of interracial conflict between blacks and
whites, within and between central cities and suburbs. In short, much of this
scholarship revolves around efforts to understand what historian Thomas Sugrue
describes as the "contemporary urban crisis." In his book, *Origins of the Urban*
Crisis, Sugrue defines the "urban crisis" as the process by which the city of
Detroit lost its position as "home to the highest-paid blue-collar workers" in the
country during the industrial era, and became, by the 1990s, a city wracked by
joblessness, concentrated poverty, physical decay, and rising levels of segregation
by race.

Although *Origins of the Urban Crisis* is not a systematic community study of
black Detroit, it nonetheless advances key propositions that should inform historical work on a broad range of black communities across the country.
Dissatisfied with the limited historical perspective of sociological and policy studies of the so-called "urban underclass," Sugrue grounded his study of post-war
Detroit in a close analysis of the industrial era. Based on his assessment of socioeconomic change during the late nineteenth and early twentieth centuries,
Sugrue concludes that contemporary poverty, residential segregation, and social
conflict were not entirely unique to the late twentieth century city. Such experiences not only characterized the plight of urban blacks during the era of the
Great Migration, but the lives of millions of south, central, and eastern European
immigrants during the industrial age. Nonetheless, according to Sugrue, in the
past, poor people did not experience the same level of segregation and isolation
as they do today, and "most poor people were active, if irregular, participants in
the labor market."[23]

Post-World War II studies not only pay close attention to the dynamics of
change over time, but pinpoint the need for broader metropolitan rather than
simply inner city perspectives on black urban life. In his book, *American Babylon:*
Class, Race, and Power in Oakland and the East Bay, 1945–1977, historian
Robert Self examines the working class suburbs of Milpitas and San Leandro as
well as Oakland's central city neighborhoods. According to Self, the metropolitan area produced new "spaces and politics" between the end of World War II
and the late 1970s. Drawing upon the theoretical insights of Marxist geographer
David Harvey, Self argues that these contests not only gave rise to new kinds of
racial spaces, but "reconfigured the meaning and political significance of both the

ghetto and the suburb." More precisely, Self concludes that urban-suburban "property relations" and social conflict supplanted an earlier pattern of "labor relations" as the key "mediator of class and racial power in the post-war city." Although *American Babylon* suggests that struggles over property rights in Oakland and East Bay were part of larger, racialized, urban-suburban battles throughout postwar America, we need many more systematic historical studies of such changes in other metropolitan areas.

Recent studies not only document the obstacles that blacks faced, but the strategies that they employed to expand their foothold in the political economy and geography of the city. In his forthcoming book, *Place of Their Own: African American Suburbanization Since 1916*, historian Andrew Wiese persuasively argues that the African American struggle for space on the edge of the city transcended a dream of middle class status among blacks; it was an act of resistance against the confines of Jim Crow (in both its de facto and de jure forms). African American strategies for suburban home ownership not only included the heroic individual acts of the so-called "pioneers" (i.e., the first black occupants of housing in previously all-white neighborhoods) but the collective civil rights and political activities of central city and emerging black suburban communities as well.[24] Although Wiese does not elaborate sufficiently on this phase of the process, black suburbanization was closely linked to transitions from the integrationist rhetoric of the modern civil rights movement to the era of Black Power and the forging of new forms of collective identity and strategies of resistance. The Black Power movement placed a great deal of emphasis on reclaiming the distinctive aspects of African American history from the clutches of the integrationist phase of the black freedom struggle. According to political and historical anthropologist Steven Gregory, African Americans in Corona (Queens), New York, recollected and reworked their past through "social practices of memory" and brought the meanings of the past to bear on the creation of new identities in the post-industrial city.[25] Again much more work is needed on these important processes in different cities.

The late twentieth century unleashed a series of changes that led to both convergence and divergence in the experiences of urban blacks across regions. Recent scholarship deepens our understanding of these regional differences in urban class, race, and ethnic relations during the transition from industrial to post-industrial capitalism. According to urban historian Kenneth Kusmer, areas of convergence included residential segregation or "ghettoization"; increasing participation in electoral politics; and the spread of de facto forms of institutional segregation, in the South as well as the North, in the wake of new civil rights legislation during the 1950s and 1960s.[26] Another area of convergence was the rapid suburbanization of the black population. By the 1990s, suburbanization had supplanted the Great Migration of southern blacks from farms and small towns to central cities of the North, South, and West. Conversely, areas of divergence included relatively lower levels of white resistance to the desegregation of public accommodations in the North than in the South; more violence (mainly against inner city property) in the urban North than in the South; and the deindustrialization of the northern urban economy compared to the economic expansion of the southern sunbelt, which attracted rising numbers of blacks from the urban North and West.[27]

Emerging research on the postwar years also enables us to see more clearly certain differences and similarities in the African American transition from industrial to post-industrial communities over time. In his forthcoming book, cited above, Andrew Wiese concludes that the African American struggle for suburban space represented substantial continuity as well as discontinuity over time. Real estate firms, private homeowners, and banks developed a variety of strategies for blocking African American access to suburban property, but working class blacks dominated the process of African American suburbanization during the early 20th century, while middle class, well-educated, and propertied blacks dominated the process from the early post-World War II years through recent times.

Pre-World War II blacks envisioned suburban home-ownership as relief from the insecurity of wage-earning industrial jobs. The suburbs offered an opportunity to invest one's own labor (that is, "sweat equity") into the building of a house; vegetable gardens; and a few livestock to supplement the family's diet. In the wake of the civil rights era, however, as more blacks gained access to higher incomes, their perception of suburban homeownership gradually shifted to issues of safety, better education for their children, and various amenities associated with prevailing white middle class notions of suburban living. Still, even as intraracial class distinctions intensified, the experience of neighborhood decline exposed the black residents "to wider structures of racial exclusion and injustice."[28] In other words, while the move to suburbia accented substantial class and status distinctions and tensions within the black metropolitan community, racist ideas and social practices prevented blacks from envisioning their move to suburbia in exclusively class terms. Moreover, despite Wiese's persuasive argument about middle class blacks in recent suburbs, a full understanding of the class dynamics of recent suburban change will require many more case studies of particular metropolitan areas.

Current research not only reveals more clearly regional differences and similarities in the shift from industrial to postindustrial communities, but changes in the comparative experiences of blacks and other ethnic groups over time. Existing scholarship reveals significant differences in the experiences of African Americans and immigrants from diverse nationality backgrounds. Until the mid-twentieth century, American born whites sought to define America as a white nation despite its ethnic and racial diversity. Although African Americans and immigrants developed their own unique visions of citizenship and waged vigorous struggles for equal treatment, efforts to define America as a white nation hampered the development of multiracial movements for social justice. Nonetheless, diverse movements for full citizenship rights resulted in the rise of the new industrial unions, the New Deal state, and the gradual growth of the modern civil rights and Black Power movements. Under the influence of these movements, U.S. social policy not only resulted in the demolition of the Jim Crow system, it also loosened immigration restriction legislation and facilitated the increasing ethnic and racial diversification of the nation's population. By the late twentieth century, more immigrants entered the nation from Asia and Latin America than from Europe.[29]

As the nation forged a more democratic and diverse polity, its economic under-pinnings eroded under the onset of deindustrialization and the rise of new and more conservative political regimes. U.S. workers lost millions of jobs through plant closings, movement of companies overseas, and the adoption of new com-puter-based technologies during the 1980s and 1990s. At the same time, African Americans faced increasing attacks on the social welfare gains of the civil rights movement. In 1980, the election of Republican Ronald Reagan symbolized white resistance to the fruits of the civil rights movement, but the Democratic party also played a role in undermining social welfare and affirmative action employment and education programs. In the presidential election of 1992, for example, the Democrat William Jefferson Clinton pledged to end welfare as we know it and later signed into law the Republican Personal Responsibility Act of 1994. The Personal Responsibility Act severely curtailed aid to poor families and established programs designed to move recipients rapidly from welfare to work, usually in low-wage jobs in the service sector of the economy.[30]

The 1980s and 1990s have received far less historical treatment than the ear-lier decades of the postwar years. Thus, the last two decades offer perhaps the most fruitful opportunities for the next generation of scholarship. Such research is crucial for a fuller understanding of social conflict, cooperation, and alliance building in the postwar era. In her recent book on postwar Detroit, his-torian Heather Thompson gives substantial attention to the changes of the 1980s. Her book challenges us to rethink a series of propositions in existing post-war studies. According to Thompson, by accenting the loss of inner city white residents, the decline of interracial labor and civil rights coalitions, and the triumph of racial conservatism in the politics of cities and the nation, his-torical studies of the postwar years overstate the role of conflict and understate the extent of interracial and interethnic cooperation at different points along the political spectrum. Even as groups of blacks and whites fought pitched bat-tles at work and in public spaces, Thompson convincingly argues that other blacks and whites built political bridges to each other and formed alliances on the left, right, and center.[31] In order to gain a more comprehensive under-standing of the postwar years, more research on the 1980s and 1990s is imperative.

Coupled with the foregoing critique of existing scholarship, the essays in this volume establish an intellectual foundation for interdisciplinary research on African Americans and their interactions with diverse ethnic and racial groups. *African American Urban Studies* shows how black urban life had its origins and development within the larger context of global economic, social, and political changes. African Americans participated in shifting modes of economic pro-duction and consumption during the overlapping eras of commercial, indus-trial, and, recently, post-industrial capitalism. Each of these epochs in the nation's political economy not only witnessed profound changes within the black community, but brought African Americans into conflict as well as coop-eration with diverse racial and ethnic groups. In succession, urban blacks encountered Irish and German immigrants during the antebellum years; Jews, Italians, Poles, and other south, central, and eastern Europeans during the industrial era; and, more recently, increasing numbers of immigrants from Latin

America, Asia, the Caribbean, and to some extent, Africa. While movements for racial solidarity and unity based on a shared sense of history were recurring themes in black history, African Americans gradually broadened their under-standing of black urban culture and politics beyond expressions of racial con-sciousness to include notions of class, nationality, and gender diversity. Our volume not only acknowledges that our understanding of these processes remain incomplete, but encourages new historical, social scientific, and com-parative research on the subject.

THE ESSAYS

HISTORICAL

Part I, comprised of five essays, presents both nineteenth and twentieth century historical perspectives on black urban life. By including selections on both the nineteenth and twentieth century experience, this section acknowledges the slav-ery roots of black urban life. In his essay, James Horton examines the develop-ment of what he calls "race-based populism—an alliance built around race and working class status." Focusing on the urban North between about 1750 and the 1820s, Horton persuasively argues that pre-Revolutionary whites from the "underside of colonial society"—general day laborers, indentured servants, and dock workers—often made common cause with their enslaved black and exploited Native American counterparts. As such, the so-called underside not only fueled slave revolts and plots to revolt, but colonial resistance to British tyranny that resulted in the birth of the new republic.

While some blacks gained their freedom under the impact of the Revolution and gradual abolition thereafter, they were soon disfranchised under the onslaught of race-based populism during the early post-Revolutionary years of the new nation. The upsurge of populist politics and the enfranchisement of white workers went hand in hand with the racist exclusion of free blacks. African Americans were now more likely to find allies among white elites than among whites of similar class backgrounds. Interracial working class alliances had become the exception rather than the rule. Thus, it was white elites who helped to fuel the antebellum abolitionist movement, while working class whites, including new immigrants from Germany and Ireland, fueled the deeds of antiabolitionist and anti-black mobs. According to Horton, this racist legacy helps to explain certain contemporary all-white populist movements, which proclaim "The future of America, Red Necks and White Skins."

Ron Lewis explores the place of industrial slavery within the larger context of rural plantation slavery in antebellum America. Although urban and industrial slaves represented only 5 to 10 percent of the enslaved labor force, they repre-sented a disproportionate number of workers in southern cities and industrial enterprises. Moreover, since most industrial slaves worked in rural rather than urban environments, their lives blurred the lines between industrial and rural, plantation and urban, free and unfree labor. As Lewis notes, industrial slaves often lived and labored alongside nearly a half million free blacks and some poor and working class whites.

Lewis forcefully argues that "the structures of slave work" as well as geography influenced the conditions of life "for industrial slaves." Coal, iron and mine workers gained substantial opportunities to use their skills to negotiate "extra provisions and payment" for extra work, while the geographical expanse of the turpentine camps "exposed slaves who worked in them to a life of isolation and misery." Finally, Lewis offers a detailed analysis of human bondage in the southern Appalachian region, often treated by scholars as "a unified, homogeneous region" whose residents were hostile to slavery by egalitarian temperament, its rugged terrain, and the severity of its climate.

Focusing on antebellum steamboats, Thomas Buchanan accents the racialization of work in early industrial America. Boat owners and captains entirely excluded enslaved and free blacks from the most favored positions as officers, pilots, captains, engineers, clerks, and mates. While American-born whites occupied nearly 90 percent of these favored jobs, various immigrant groups comprised the remainder. Although white officers frequently segregated black and white work crews, Buchanan nonetheless demonstrates how black steamboat workers occupied a variety of jobs that became even more diverse when small single-deck steamboats gave way to larger double-deck boats.

Partly because black workers shared certain hazardous and exploitative working conditions and forms of labor discipline with all workers, they developed both unified as well as distinctive forms of resistance. Unique forms of resistance included refusing to answer to the name "boy," using river life to learn to read and write, and the preservation and extension of plantation-based black music. Finally, Buchanan convincingly argues that riverboat men and women played a key role in linking blacks in the North and South, city and country, slavery and freedom to "a broader African American world."

Based upon her study of working class black women in postbellum Atlanta, Georgia, Tera Hunter critiques Du Bois's *The Philadelphia Negro*. According to Hunter, Du Bois recognized the importance of black women's labor during the transformation of capitalist labor relations with the onset of industrialization, but he hoped "to make the occupation more efficient" by improving "the behaviors and attitudes" of the workers themselves. Hunter concludes that Du Bois gave insufficient attention to working class people's own culture, values, and modes of collective resistance to inequality, including their use of urban space "for respite and recovery from wage work." In her view, black working class women "creatively built sustaining neighborhoods in the urban North and South, drawing from a rich heritage and resilient culture that they continually reconstituted to meet the exigencies of urban life." Hunter's essay is not only a critical review of Du Bois's ideas about race, women, and work, but a closely argued substantive comparison of working women's lives in two cities.

Drawing upon his groundbreaking study of blacks in the West, Quintard Taylor examines a hundred years of black western urbanization, work, and race relations. Taylor decries the usual scholarly neglect of the black urban experience in the western United States. He asks to what extent was the West different for African Americans compared to other groups, Latinos, Asian– and Anglo–Americans? Did the West represent a racial frontier where black people could expect freedom and opportunity? While blacks often celebrated life in the urban West, where they often met less hostility than their non-white counterparts, Taylor concludes that they soon discovered that life and labor under that "open sky" did not translate into an egalitarian racial frontier.

SOCIAL SCIENTIFIC

Part II, also comprised of five essays, provides a series of social scientific assessments of contemporary black urban life. Alice O'Connor explores the connection between past and present perspectives in research on urban poverty, race, and social policy. Building upon her recent book on the subject, O'Connor pinpoints the relationship between the "underclass" concept and "an older tradition of social scientific research and ideological debate" about race and poverty—that is, the ideas of the "Chicago School" of sociology during the 1910s and 1920s. O'Connor persuasively argues that the Chicago School accented "cultural breakdown and social disorganization" among the migrants themselves as the principle source of urban poverty. According to O'Connor, the Chicago School not only influenced the conceptualization of Daniel Patrick Moynihan's study of the black family in 1965, but William J. Wilson's prolific research on the subject of black urban poverty during the 1970s and 1980s.

Drawing upon her ongoing research on the relationship between the earnings of black women and educational attainment, economist Susan McElroy probes factors behind the decline of black women's relative income gains by the 1980s. As such, she moves beyond optimistic reports that race and gender differences closed between World War II and the late 1970s. She readily acknowledges that black women have lower marriage, higher divorce, and lower remarriage rates after divorce than white women. In her view, however, scholars from E. Franklin Frazier to Moynihan to Wilson perhaps overemphasized the degree to which differences in marriage, childbearing, and family patterns contributed to racial differences in economic status. Noting that few economists have analyzed these issues empirically, McElroy pinpoints key sociological and economic models used "to explain why educational choices are made and in turn how these choices effect earnings" differences by race and gender, and concludes with a sharp discussion of why and how economists invariably treat race as a "dummy variable"—a factor impervious to precise measurement.

For their part, economists William Darity and Patrick L. Mason examine empirical data on contemporary discrimination by race and gender. They conclude that "discrimination by race has diminished somewhat, and discrimination by gender has diminished substantially. However, neither employment discrimination by race or by gender is close to ending." Civil rights legislation and affirmative action "purged" most overt forms of discrimination from American society, but "covert and subtle forms of discrimination persist." Furthermore, they conclude that such discrimination is masked and rationalized by widely-held presumptions of "black inferiority."

Similar to McElroy, Darity and Mason provide a useful critique of human capital and labor market discrimination models of economic inequality. They conclude that such models "are forced by their own assumptions to the conclusion that discrimination only can be temporary." Hence, Darity and Mason propose a model that reevaluates "the neoclassical theory of competition" and advances a "classical" or "Marxist approach" to competition—one that treats wage differences or discrimination as "the norm for competitive labor markets" rather than an anomaly related to insufficient information about the "real" characteristics of workers.

In her essay on the social dynamics of race, class, and space, urban planning scholar Karen Gibson counters William J. Wilson's emphasis on the role of class and economic transformation in the expansion of black urban poverty during the 1970s and 1980s. According to Gibson, the underclass research overlooks "race" as "the key factor explaining the racial disparity in labor market attachment," that is, employment rates. On the other hand, Gibson calls attention to the non-Hispanic white poor, emphasizing the need to recognize poverty as a multi-racial phenomenon.

Based upon 1990 census data for the Detroit and Pittsburgh metropolitan areas, Gibson offers a comparative assessment of poverty in black and white neighborhoods classified as low, medium, and high poverty areas. While poverty rates were higher for whites in Pittsburgh than Detroit, Gibson found that blacks faced disproportionately higher levels of poverty in both cities. Even in low poverty black neighborhoods, middle class blacks had double the unemployment rates of whites. Consequently, Gibson concludes "Race affects life chances. It plays a strong role in creating and maintaining the 'underclass' and marginalizing working and middle class African Americans from the labor market."

In his essay, historian Richard Walter Thomas extends his notion of the community-building process, developed in his study of Detroit's black community during the inter-World War years, to what he calls the "post-urban disorder" period in Detroit's recent past, 1967–1997. Thomas defines the community-building process as "the sum total of the historical efforts of black individuals, institutions, and organizations to survive and progress as a people and to create and sustain a genuine and creative communal presence." Thomas carefully documents the responses of black Detroit to the urban violence of 1967, the economic downturn of the 1970s and 1980s, and the rise of black youth on youth violence of the 1980s and early 1990s.

Thomas argues that neither moderates nor militants were prepared to address the upsurge of teenage violence during the mid 1980s. Thus, a new organization, Save Our Sons and Daughters (SOSAD), emerged at the center of the community-building process. Under the leadership of Clementine Barfield, the mother of a slain 16-year-old black male, SOSAD addressed "building community at the deepest, most wounded and fractured level. . . . Each year SOSAD went deeper into the trenches of killing, despair and mourning, lifting spirits and building community."

COMPARATIVE

Part III offers comparative perspectives on race, class, and ethnicity in twentieth century America. Chris Friday analyzes the transformation of scholarship on

Asian American workers. Until the onset of the modern civil rights and social history movements, Friday shows how scholars of Asian American history accented "anti-Asian activities" and neglected what Asians had done on their own behalf. By the late 1970s and 1980s, growing numbers of scholars charted the broad range of jobs that Japanese and Chinese workers performed; documented the specific strategies that Asian workers developed to counteract labor exploitation, including some cases of labor solidarity with black and white workers; and gradually incorporated the diverse experiences of Asian American women.

Friday's essay not only allows us to address certain similarities in the transformation of Asian and African American labor and working class history, but enables us to see substantial differences in the experiences of the two groups. Although the Asian population was much smaller than the black population, their communities absorbed far more ethnically diverse populations than African Americans. The diplomatic activities of Asian countries—Korea, the Phillipines, China, and Japan—also had greater influence on the fortunes of Asians in the U.S. than did the actions of African states until the independence movements of the 1950s and 1960s.

Historian Camille Guerin-Gonzales examines the complicated development of Latino/Latina labor and working class history from the first generation of scholarship during the 1920s through recent times. Similar to early twentieth century black labor historians, early twentieth century writers counteracted racist portrayals of Mexicans as workers and as a people. These scholars produced their studies as tools in the struggle for social justice for Latino workers, including the elimination of discriminatory immigration laws and repressive labor practices. During the 1960s and 1970s, growing numbers of scholars applied the insights of the new social and labor history to the experiences of Latino workers and their communities. By the early 1990s, Guerin-Gonzales notes that women's historians like Vicki Ruiz; cultural historians like George Sanchez; and regional historians like Neil Foley had helped to transform Latino and Latina labor studies into a more gender– and culture–conscious field of scholarship. Some of these scholars, notably Neil Foley, had also built bridges between southern and African American history on the one hand and southwestern and Chicano history on the other.

Focusing on the development of Chicago's multiethnic and multiracial labor force during the early twentieth century, labor historian James Barrett reinterprets the role of racial and ethnic fragmentation in the decline of the city's organized labor movement. Despite the emergence of an extraordinarily diverse working class, the labor movement experienced considerable success in organizing workers across ethnic and racial lines, from about the turn of the century through the immediate aftermath of World War I. South, central, and eastern European immigrants and, to some extent, African Americans were active participants in these campaigns.

Although each of Chicago's interracial working class campaigns ultimately failed, Barrett argues that racial and ethnic fragmentation of the working class facilitated but did not "cause" the downfall of Chicago's labor movement.

Despite the horrors of the 1919 race riot, Barrett accents the impact of class rather than race war as the determinant factor in the decline of organized labor in the years after World War I. In his view, it was the onslaught of the "Red Scare" and the intensification of corporate resistance activities that undermined working class solidarity.

Finally, Alan Dawley analyzes shifting definitions of race in U.S. society. Dawley argues that the defeat of "racial Darwinism" ushered in two different approaches to race or "diversity" by the 1960s. One reduced racial classifications into two categories—one white and the other nonwhite, mainly black. A second classification scheme rejected the notion that white ethnics had melted down into one homogenous white social group. Immigration historians led the way in resuscitating the view that Euro-Americans were not merely whites, but Poles, Italians, and Jews, and so on. Dawley also analyzes the emergence of studies focusing on the "social construction" of race as an idea, historical category, and phenomenon that changed over time and under particular circumstances.

Above all, Dawley decries approaches to racial inequality that lets international corporate wealth, elite control, or upper class privilege off the hook, and treats the U.S. as an exception. Instead, he suggests that, "European powers, too, have their own versions of race-based inequality owing to the legacy of slavery and colonialism." As a means of drawing attention to the multi-ethnic and global nature of class formation under capitalist expansion, Dawley suggests that we build upon the ideas of borderland scholars like David Montejano and others to illuminate the "racialization" of a variety of group experiences—southern and eastern European, Asian-American, and Latino as well as African American.

NOTES

1 Earl Lewis, "To Turn as on a Pivot: Writing African Americans into a History of Overlapping Diasporas," *The American Historical Review* 100, no. 3 (June 1995), pp. 765–787; Alferdteen Harrison, ed., *Black Exodus: The Great Migration from the American South* (Jackson: University Press of Mississippi, 1991); Daniel M. Johnson and Rex R. Campbell, *Black Migration in America: The Black Man Comes to the City* (Chicago: Nelson-Hall, 1972); Joe W. Trotter, *The African American Experience* (Boston: Houghton Mifflin Company, 2001); Joe W. Trotter, ed., *The Great Migration in Historical Perspective: New Dimensions of Race, Class, & Gender* (Bloomington: Indiana University Press, 1991); Henry Louis Taylor and Walter Hill, ed., *Historical Roots of the Urban Crisis: African Americans in the Industrial City, 1900–1950* (New York: Garland Publishing, Inc., 2000).

2 Carol Stack, *Call to Home: African Americans Reclaim the Rural South* (New York: Basic Books, 1996).

3 Joe W. Trotter, "African Americans in the City: The Industrial Era, 1900–1950," in Kenneth W. Goings and Raymond A Mohl, ed., *The New African American Urban History* (Thousand Oaks, CA: Sage Publications, 1996), pp. 299–319; Kenneth Kusmer, "The Black Urban Experience in American History," in Darlene Clark Hine, ed., *The State of Afro-American History: Past, Present, and Future* (Baton Rouge: Louisiana State University Press, 1986); Martin Bulmer, *The Chicago School of Sociology: Institutionalization, Diversity, and the Rise of Sociological Research* (Chicago:

University of Chicago Press, 1984); Alice O'Connor, *Poverty Knowledge: Social Science, Social Policy, and the Poor in Twentieth-Century U.S. History* (Princeton, NJ: Princeton University Press, 2001); Michael B. Katz and Thomas J. Sugrue, *W. E. B. DuBois, Race and the City: The Philadelphia Negro and Its Legacy* (Philadelphia: University of Pennsylvania Press, 1998); Vernon J. Williams, Jr., *From a Caste to a Minority: Changing Attitudes of American Sociologists Toward Afro-Americans, 1896–1945* (New York: Greenwood Press, 1989).

4 Kusmer, "The Black Urban Experience in American History"; Trotter, "African Americans in the City"; Lewis, "To Turn as on a Pivot;" Trotter, ed., *The Great Migration in Historical Perspective.*

5 Lee Rainwater and William L. Yancey, ed., *The Moynihan Report and the Politics of Controversy* (Cambridge, MA: Massachusetts Institute of Technology, 1967); Lee Rainwater, "Crucible of Identity: The Negro Lower-Class Family," *Daedalus* 95(2): 172–216.

6 Elliott Liebow, *Tally's Corner: A Study of Negro Streetcorner Men* (Boston: Brown and Company, 1967).

7 Charles Keil, *Urban Blues* (Chicago: The University of Chicago Press, 1966); Ulf Hannerz, *Soul Side: Inquiries into Ghetto Culture and Community* (New York: Columbia University Press, 1969); Roger Abrahams, *Deep Down in the Jungle: Negro Narrative Folklore from the Streets of Philadelphia* (Harboro, PA: Folklore Associates, 1963).

8 Carol B. Stack, *All Our Kin: Strategies for Survival in a Black Community* (New York: Harper Colophon Books, 1974).

9 Robin D. G. Kelley, *Yo' Mama's Disfunktional!: Fighting the Culture Wars in Urban America* (Boston, MA: Beacon Press, 1997).

10 Trotter, "African Americans in the City," pp. 299–319; Lewis, "To Turn as on a Pivot"; Kusmer, "The Black Urban Experience in American History."

11 Kimberly Phillips, *Alabama North: African-American Migrants, Community, and Working-Class Activism in Cleveland, 1915–45* (Urbana: University of Illinois Press, 1999).

12 Earl Lewis, *In Their Own Interests: Race, Class, and Power in Twentieth-Century Norfolk, Virginia* (Berkeley: University of California Press, 1991); George Wright, *Life Behind a Veil: Blacks in Louisville, Kentucky, 1865–1930* (Baton Rouge: Louisiana State University Press, 1985); Tera W. Hunter, *To 'Joy My Freedom: Southern Black Women's Lives and Labors After the Civil War* (Cambridge: Harvard University Press, 1997).

13 Stack, *All Our Kin*, pp. 124–126.

14 *Ibid.*

15 John Langston Gwaltney, *Drylongso: A Self-Portrait of Black America* (New York: Vintage Books, 1981); Dan Rose, *Black American Street Life: South Philadelphia, 1969–1971* (Philadelphia, PA: University of Pennsylvania Press, 1987); Mitchell Duneier, *Slim's Table: Race, Respectability, and Masculinity* (Chicago: The University of Chicago Press, 1992). Cf. Melvin D. Williams, *On the Street Where I Lived* (New York: Holt, Rinehart and Winston, 1981).

16 Joe W. Trotter, "Blacks in the Urban North: The 'Underclass Question' in Historical Perspective," Michael B. Katz, "The Urban 'Underclass' as a Metaphor of Social Transformation," "Reframing the 'Underclass' Debates"; Thomas J. Sugrue, "The Structures of Urban Poverty: The Reorganization of Space and Work in Three Periods of American History"; Jacqueline Jones, "Southern Diaspora: Origins of the Northern 'Underclass' "; Kathryn M. Neckerman, "The Emergence of 'Underclass' Family Patterns, 1900–1940," all in Michael B. Katz, ed., *The "Underclass" Debate: Views from History* (Princeton, NJ: Princeton University Press, 1993).

17 William Julius Wilson, *When Work Disappears: The World of the New Urban Poor* (New York: Alfred A. Knoff, 1996); *The Truly Disadvantaged: The Inner City, the Underclass, and Public Policy* (Chicago: The University of Chicago Press, 1987); *The Declining Significance of Race: Blacks and Changing American Institutions* (Chicago: The University of Chicago Press, 1978); Elijah Anderson, *Streetwise: Race, Class, and Change in an Urban Community* (Chicago: University of Chicago Press, 1990); Douglas S. Massey and Nancy A. Denton, *American Apartheid: Segregation and the Making of the Underclass* (Cambridge, MA: Harvard University Press, 1993); Bill E. Lawson, *The Underclass Question* (Philadelphia, PA: Temple University Press, 1992); Christopher Jencks & Paul E. Peterson, *The Urban Underclass* (Washington, D.C.: The Brookings Institution, 1991); William A. Darity, Jr. and Samuel L. Myers, Jr. with Emmett D. Carson and William Sabol, *The Black Underclass: Critical Essays on Race and Unwantedness* (New York: Garland Publishing, Inc., 1994); Douglas G. Glasgow, *The Black Underclass: Poverty, Unemployment and Entrapment of Ghetto Youth* (New York: Vintage Books, 1981).

18 Quote in Anderson, *Streetwise*, p. 57.

19 Roger Lane, *Roots of Violence in Black Philadelphia, 1860–1900* (Cambridge: Harvard University Press, 1986) and *William Dorsey's Philadelphia & Ours: On the Past and Future of the Black City in America* (New York: Oxford University Press, 1991); Robert Gregg, *Sparks from the Anvil of Oppression: Philadelphia's African Methodists and Southern Migrants, 1890–1940* (Philadelphia: Temple University Press, 1993).

20 See essays by Michael Katz, Jacqueline Jones, Thomas Sugrue, Joe W. Trotter, and Kathryn Neckerman, in Katz, *The "Underclass" Debate*. See also, Jacqueline Jones, *The Dispossessed: America's Underclasses from the Civil War to the Present* (New York: Basic Books, 1992), and *American Work: Four Centuries of Black and White Labor* (New York: W. W. Norton & Company, 1998).

21 See n. 15 above.

22 Thomas J. Sugrue, *The Origins of the Urban Crisis: Race and Inequality I Postwar Detroit* (Princeton, NJ: Princeton University Press, 1996); Robert O. Self, *American Babylon: Class, Race, and Power in Oakland and the East Bay, 1945–1977* (Princeton, NJ: Princeton University Press, forthcoming); Andrew Wiese, *Places of Their Own: African American Suburbanization Since 1916* (Chicago: The University of Chicago Press, forthcoming); Steven Gregory, *Black Corona: Race and the Politics of Place in an Urban* Community (Princeton, NJ: Princeton University Press, 1998); Ronald H. Bayor, *Race and the Shaping of Twentieth-Century Atlanta* (Chapel Hill: The University of North Carolina Press, 1996); Heather Ann Thompson, *Whose Detroit? Politics, Labor, and Race in a Modern American City* (Ithaca: Cornell University Press, 2001). See also Arnold R. Hirsch, *Making the Second Ghetto: Race and Housing in Chicago 1940–1960* (Chicago: The University of Chicago Press, 1983, 1998).

23 Sugrue, p. 4.

24 Wiese, *Places of Their Own*.

25 Gregory, p. 13.

26 Kenneth Kusmer, "African Americans in the City Since World War II: From the Industrial to the Post-Industrial Era," *Journal of Urban History* 21, no. 4 (May 1995), pp. 458–505.

27 For a useful beginning, see Stack, *Call to Home*.

28 Gregory, p.65.

29 Joe W. Trotter, "The Great Migration, African Americans, and Immigrants in the Industrial City," in George Fredrickson and Nancy Foner, ed., *Not just Black and White* (New York: Russell Sage Foundation, 2004).

30 Joe W. Trotter, *The African American Experience* (Boston: Houghton Mifflin Company, 2001).

31 Thompson, pp. 9–27, 217–23.

PART I

HISTORICAL PERSPECTIVES

Chapter 1

Urban Alliances: The Emergence of Race-Based Populism in the Age of Jackson

James Oliver Horton

On a cold January day in 1987 civil rights marchers moved in chanting columns toward the court house square in Forsyth county, Georgia, a place where, even in the mid-1980s, no black person could live, or even visit safely after dark. As the marchers reached the court house itself they were met by the jeers of counter-protesters, white supremacists shouting racial insults and carrying a sign which read, "The future of America, Red Necks and White Skins."

This essay seeks to provide a historical context for that sign. It is not enough simply to say that racial intolerance has a long history in Georgia, the South, and America, although surely that is true. I want to argue that the particular kind of race-based populism—an alliance built around race and working class status—that is implicit in the words of that sign and that most Americans, by now, take for granted—developed in the years after the Revolution and as a partial response to the broadening political democracy of that period. Further, these changes are instructive for considering the dynamics of interracial alliance building in America. In discussing these dynamics I will focus on American northern urban communities from the mid-18th century to the rise of the abolition movement during the Jacksonian period.

Before the Revolution British North America was a society built on the principle of social and political deference. Colonial ladies and gentlemen were easily distinguishable by their dress, their carriage and their associates. Their numbers grew smaller and ever more economically and politically powerful as the eighteenth century progressed. They occupied the top ranks of American society, above the "middling" classes of yeoman farmers, small merchants, and artisans, and far from the "mean" and "vile" masses at the very bottom. Among the elites this social structure was thought to be the natural order of things, set by a higher power who, "hath Ordained different degrees and orders of men, some to be high and Honorable, some to be Low and Despicable . . . "[1] The underside of colonial society was occupied by common day laborers, sailors, dock workers, farm hands, indentured servants, and slaves. They shared a similar, though not identical, social and economic circumstance, and their ranks were the most mul-tiracial in America. White servants often found themselves at the mercy of over-bearing masters who, except in theory, were largely unrestrained by colonial authority. While not reduced to the level of slaves, indentured servants, regard-less of color, experienced similar degradation. As one complained, white servants were often "subject to the same laws as the Negroes and have the same coarse food and clothing." This perception among many whites, blacks, and Indians, that those at the bottom of society, regardless of race, shared unjust and brutal treatment at the hands of their "betters," provided a basis for interracial cooperation.[2]

Colonial elites formed a self conscious social and political group which, by their words and actions, often inadvertently encouraged interracial alliance among the lower classes. They frequently lumped those at the bottom of society together, labeling them "the herd" or the "mean and vile classes." But when alliances formed by the lowest of society threatened the social order and the priv-ileged positions of those above them, colonial elites acted to discourage these associations. In the 1670s, a popular uprising in Virginia that began as an attempt by poor whites to appropriate Indian lands evolved into a full-scale interracial rebellion against colonial authority when black servants and slaves joined in. Initially led by Nathanial Bacon, a wealthy Virginia planter, the rebels attacked Jamestown and drove the governor from the colony. Bacon died before the vio-lence ended and his forces were defeated, but among those who held out longest were eighty blacks and twenty whites. After the rebellion the white aristocracy, fearing the implications of such a concerted effort, instituted policies designed to obscure underlying tensions in colonial class relations and to discourage class-based interracial alliances. Virginia authorities were particularly concerned that black slaves and white servants had continued to fight against the colonial mili-tia long after Bacon had died. Such a band of "degraded rabble" was viewed as especially dangerous and unpredictable without proper leadership from members of the better classes. Colonial elites were right to fear such alliances, for although race was always a factor in determining group loyalties, throughout the colonial period, a common social position could obscure the potential divisions of race and unite the poor against the wealthy.[3]

During the early eighteenth century, New York officials attempted to discour-age alliances between blacks and Indians by passing laws that restricted slave travel into the Indian territory north of Saratoga. Further, Indians were forced into treaties that prohibited their sheltering of fugitives and attempted to sepa-rate them from African Americans as completely as possible. These efforts gener-ally proved ineffective, in part, because of the long-standing associations between blacks and Indians and because the enforcement of such provisions would have separated many families. Throughout the colonial period, whereever blacks and Indians came into contact, alliance was always a possibility.[4] Thus, in 1712 sev-eral Indians and a few whites joined with slaves in a plot to burn parts of New York City to "revenge themselves for some hard usage . . . from their masters." Before the colonial militia restored order the rebels had killed nine and wounded six others. Many of the slaves and their allies escaped to the woods for a time but finally they were captured. The rebels paid a horrific price for their rebellion. Several were tortured and hanged; others were burned at the stake, starved to death or broken on the wheel. Two Indians were executed for their part in the conspiracy, and repressive laws were enacted against blacks and Indians.[5]

Such interracial cooperation was not surprising to observers of eighteenth century urban society. In community celebrations, in individual social interaction, as in direct action and political protest, whites, blacks, and Indians often traversed the color line, as practical circumstances demanded. Africans in America often bent conventional European festivals to their own purposes, celebrating "General Election Day," on which slaves elected ceremonial leaders, and "Pope's Day," or Pinkster celebrations, with food, drink, sporting events, music, and dancing, in the tradition of African or West Indian carnival. Although these celebrations were distinctively African in style, they often included nonblacks. Cultural anthropological research has confirmed that Pinkster celebrations in Albany were "multi-ethnic (including Germans, Yankees, Scots, Irish, Welsh, and English), multi-regional (including French Canadians and Vermonters), multi-racial (including blacks, Indians, and whites), and multi-occupational (including jack tars [sailors] and politicians)."[6] Sometimes colonial elites amused themselves by joining their slaves in celebration, but their role was generally superficial and very limited. White indentured servants, Indians, and lower class white workers, on the other hand, were likely to take part as the friends and associates of slaves and free blacks. One poem, written in 1760, described those who attended these festivals as ". . . a motley crew Of Whites & Blacks & Indians too."[7] Another expressed the distinctly class basis of such gatherings, saying at one point, "Tho' hard and humble be our lot, The rich man's spleen we envy not."[8]

Their public denunciations and the passage of ordinances in several colonies, evidence the discomfort that most colonial elites felt about these interracial associations. Some of the earliest colonial regulations were calculated to maintain racial distance. In Virginia, interracial marriage was deemed illegal in 1660. Other southern colonies followed suit and even in Massachusetts, where the numbers of blacks was relatively small, laws forbade interracial marital unions as early as 1705. New England colonies discouraged interracial associations in a variety of ways. In 1708 Rhode Island forbade the entertainment of any slave in the home of any free person without the presence of the slave's master. In New York complaints about the gathering of blacks and whites in private homes or public drinking houses sparked calls for strict regulation. Such interracial contacts were viewed by many in authority as dangerous to the maintenance of order and "destructive to the morals of servants and slaves." It was believed to be "the principle bane and pest of the city," as one newspaper reported.[9]

Despite efforts to discourage it, however, interracial association remained common. In the South, where the black population was largest, the results of sexual associations were most evident. One Virginian confirmed this observation remarking, "The country swarms with mulatto bastards." While not as numerous as in the South, mulattoes accounted for between 20 percent and one-quarter of the black population in some northern colonies. The percentages rose dramatically during the late eighteenth and into the nineteenth century so that in the decades before the Civil War Cincinnati's free black population, most of which had migrated from the South, was 60 percent mulatto. Gender imbalance seemed to correlate with substantial numbers of mulattoes, but even in the middle Atlantic colonies, where there was relative parity among white males and females, there was a significant mulatto population. Despite all efforts to the contrary, interracial relationships bound blacks, whites, and Indians in ties of friendship and family throughout the colonial period.[10]

Nor did restrictions eliminate interracial protest action precipitated by the harsh conditions of colonial poverty. When a combination of inflation and rising unemployment in Boston during the 1730s weighed heavily on the city's poor workers, they reacted. In 1738 after some "general murmurings against the government and the rich people, young People, Servants and Negroes" resorted to full-scale rioting in order to force colonial officials to adopt measures that finally diminished the economic crisis.[11]

There were many situations in which African Americans, European Americans, and Native Americans found themselves allied in opposition to extreme circumstances as, for example, when "press gangs" entered a community to forcibly remove young able-bodied men to serve in the British Navy. None was immune, save those whose family or political connections acted to protect them from what often amounted to little more than legalized kidnapping. For those without such connections, the only protection was group resistance. In 1745 and again in 1747, Boston men, angered by the appearance of "press gangs," mounted what one report called a "riotous, tumultuous assembly of foreign seamen, servants, Negroes and other persons of mean and vile condition" in violent resistance. They turned their rage on colonial troops who attempted to subdue the mob which also apparently included several men from the middling classes.[12]

Violent resistance to perceived oppression was not unique to Boston. Throughout the mid 18th century, impressment sparked interracial resistance in the major port cities. In Newport, Rhode Island during the summer of 1765 five hundred "seamen, boys and Negroes" took direct action against press gangs that had operated in the city for more than a month.[13] Resistance was not limited to New England. Protest also exploded in New York City and Norfolk, Virginia.

Given the similarity in their circumstances and the frequency of their social interaction, interracial alliances among eighteenth century urban working people is not surprising. And because much of this interaction took place in the colonial underworld, some of these alliances involved criminal activity. In the 1740s in New York City, John Romme, a white saloon owner, operated a notorious establishment. Most knew, or at least suspected, that it was a clearing house for stolen goods supplied by several urban gangs. The Geneva Club, a black gang, was one of the most well known, but there were other gangs, some white and some interracial. Romme's saloon was a gathering place for these groups, a place where blacks and whites at the lowest end of New York's society came together to share a common economic and social position, and to express common complaints about the city's elites. From the vantage point of Romme's regulars, the bosses, creditors, and masters of indentured servants and slaves seemed unduly repressive and unfairly advantaged.[14]

Romme's was but one of New York's dens and saloons of concern to city authorities. John Hughson, a shoemaker, was another white underworld character who operated an interracial bar. New York officials had strong evidence that his establishment was in fact a front for a sophisticated fencing operation serving the city's criminals, free blacks, slaves, and poor whites. Like Romme's saloon, Hughson's pub attracted an interracial crowd to transact underworld business and to socialize. They were entertained by Margaret (Peggy) Sorubiero, "the Newfoundland Irish beauty," who entertained male patrons, blacks as well as whites. On weekends, slaves, customarily allowed Saturday nights and Sundays to themselves, joined whites and free blacks to dance and enjoy the music and good food, from goose and mutton to fresh baked bread and strong rum and cider. On occasion, even off-duty British soldiers joined in what was often a lively, interracial urban social scene.[15]

It was in Hughson's tavern, and with the assistance of Romme and his associates, that blacks and whites hatched a plot that seemed to confirm the worst fears of colonial elites and urban authorities. Courtroom testimony revealed their plan to consolidate New York's criminal activity and to divert attention from widespread thievery by burning parts of the city. Official response was swift and extreme. Thirteen blacks were burned at the stake, sixteen other blacks and four whites were hanged and more than seventy blacks and seven whites were banished from the British colonies.[16] This plot was further evidence of the dangerous potential of concerted interracial, class-based action.

Yet, as the eighteenth century wore on, British colonial tax policy angered Americans of all classes and emphasized a common condition. Colonial elites began to find the mob a handy instrument of political policy. After the passage of the universally unpopular Stamp Act in 1765, "respectable Americans" were likely to accept the riotous actions of those formerly regarded as "dissolute persons," as justifiable protests against British disregard for American rights. Now mobs that took to the streets in Boston, New York, Newport, and other colonial towns to demonstrate against the Stamp Act and other regulations included the middling classes and some elites as well black and white sailors and laborers. New York City's fashionable Queen's Head tavern at Broad and Pearl Streets operated by "Black Sam" Fraunces, a West Indian mulatto, became the staging ground for violent opposition to the Stamp Act and remained a notorious revolutionary center throughout the 1770s.[17]

Thus, as the economic pressures of British regulation confronted both the fiscal and the political independence of colonial merchant and planter classes, American protest took on inter-class as well as interracial characteristics. American tolerance diminished as British military presence in the colonies, especially in colonial cities, grew. A broadening coalescence of diverse Americans increasingly used the derisive term "Lobster backs" to refer to red coated British troops who came to symbolize the threat to colonial legal, economic and political rights. In Boston for example, merchants resented the commandeering of their warehouse space for the quartering of British troops who enforced hated taxes and duties on trade. Working people suffered from rising prices and job competition from British soldiers who undercut wages by taking part-time work at reduced wages.[18]

Many of the colony's wealthy were beginning to agree with men like fugitive slave Chrispus Attucks, who held British officials to blame for American woes. Attucks, a mulatto of African and Natick Indian parentage, was 27 years old when he escaped from slavery in Framingham, Massachusetts and went to sea. He worked on interracial crews aboard coastal vessals and signed on to a whaler for a time. Like most laborers and sailors in the 1770s Attucks felt the financial pinch of British colonial tax policy and of the labor market competition from British troops whose off duty part-time employment depressed wages. Tensions exploded in March of 1770 when Attucks and several stone-throwing, club-wielding working men, described as a group of 20 or 30 "saucy boys, negroes and mulattoes, Irish teagues and outlandish jack-tarrs" taunted the guard at Boston's Custom House on King Street. This confrontation was precipitated by a violent encounter between three soldiers and "some young lads" on a Boston street and a chance meeting in a tavern between a group of under-employed Boston workers and a soldier seeking part-time employment. Attucks was among those in the tavern angered by the moonlighting soldier who symbolized the British threat to American jobs. In the assault on the custom house that followed, he took the lead. "The way to get rid of these soldiers is to attack the main-guard," he asserted; "strike at the root: this is the nest." After a few moments hesitation, the troops opened fire on what had become a large and angry mob, killing Attucks and two of his comrades and fatally wounding two others.[19]

Although some colonial elites were concerned by the violence of the mob and John Adams even acted as defense council for the British troops, many celebrated this interracial confrontation as the Boston Massacre and Crispus Attucks as the first martyr of the American Revolution.[20] Adams apparently changed his mind about Attucks, acknowledging his role as a freedom fighter for American liberty and honoring his courage in a curious manner. Three years after the Boston Massacre Adams wrote in his diary a strong letter scolding Governor Hutchinson for his role in the injustices visited on the people of Massachusetts. "You acted, coolly, deliberately, with all that premeditated Malice, not against Us in Particular but against the People in general . . . " And then he added, "You will hear from Us hereafter." Adams signed the letter, "Crispus Attucks."[21] A century later, in 1888, Massachusetts erected a monument to Crispus Attucks on the Boston Commons.

The interracial alliances that had developed during the colonial period pro-vided a fitting context for the deployment of continental troops during the Revolutionary War. Although General George Washington and the Continental Congress refused to induct African Americans into the army at first, black Minutemen had stood at Lexington Green, charged up Bunker Hill and served as sailors in the fledgling American Navy. When the necessities of war made black recruitment into the army inevitable, many units were integrated. The Navy was integrated from the start of the war. Significantly, this was the last time black and white Americans would serve in integrated military units until the Korean War in the 1950s.[22]

The Revolution profoundly affected slavery and the meaning of race in America. From the standpoint of many slaves, the Revolution was a war of liber-ation, bringing freedom to tens of thousands who escaped to British lines and eventually left America with the withdrawing British Army, and to the thousands who served in the American forces winning emancipation as a result. The liberal ideals of the Revolution also encouraged the northern states, where slave labor was less economically critical than in the South, to abolish slavery either outright or through gradual emancipation measures. Talk of liberty as the basis of a new society held out hope that the interracial alliances struck earlier in the century might continue and broaden in this new democratic nation. As one group of slaves announced in a petition for their freedom, "We expect great things from men who have made such a noble stand against the designs of their fellow men to enslave them."[23] African American poet Phillis Wheatley was less optimistic, predicting the difficulty of abolishing slavery, achieving human equality, and convincing Americans "of the strange Absurdity of their Conduct whose Words and Actions are so diametrically opposite."[24]

Wheatley's doubts were well founded. Although America wrote into its founding Constitution the principles of individual freedom and civil rights, in the generations after independence, race divided its people more completely than ever before, making interracial alliances more difficult. American citizenship under the Constitution bore no relation to class, as it had under the Articles of Confederation, which denied citizenship to paupers and vagabonds. Women could be citizens, although their rights were assumed to be folded into those of their husbands or fathers, seen as their "virtual" representatives. Directly or indirectly, white men and women meeting the criteria of American birth or naturalization could meet the test of citizenship. Race, however, was critical as a factor in the assumption of citizenship. State law considered slaves to be property, not persons eligible for citizenship. The status of free blacks was not clear. They were deprived of most citizenship rights like voting, serving on juries and testifying in courts of law. Black people were prohibited from carrying the U.S. mail and from becoming naturalized citizens by a 1790 federal law that limited naturalization to "free white persons." As historian Linda Kerber has observed, "by racializing the qualifications for newcomers, the first naturalization statue recalibrated the relationship to the political order of the free black and free whites who were already in it and set strict limits on future access to citizenship."[25]

The nature of the democracy created in the United States and the racial restrictions placed on citizenship worked to bind white Americans to one another and to separate blacks and whites who shared a similar economic status at the bottom of society. This racial separation was reinforced by a growing dissimilarity in political status during the early decades of the nineteenth century. Toleration of the expression of politics through mob action, often referred to as "out-door politics," so common during the colonial period, was beginning to wane as white workingmen gained access to other forms of political participation. Party politics was becoming the only legitimate political vehicle through which plain people could address their political grievances. Citizens of increasingly diverse economic levels participated in this more organized form of politics. Urban workers transformed fraternal organizations into political action groups through which they exercised power in the economic life and the politics of the city. As workingmen organized, the number of voters doubled in Philadelphia in the 1790s. In Massachusetts, New Hampshire, New York, and New Jersey, where colonial assemblies had been largely the preserve of the economic elite before the Revolution, the number of yeomen farmers and mechanics in the legislatures increased dramatically in the early years of nationhood.[26]

For eighteenth century elites concerned about the dangers of mob action, especially the threat of interracial "out door politics," the emerging racially restricted political democracy was comforting. Yet, at the turn of the nineteenth century, most states required property holding as a prerequisite to the vote and since urban workers possessed very little property, they generally were denied the franchise. The growth of republicanism and a democratic spirit in most states resulted in demands for the removal of property qualifications and the extension of the franchise. This extension was, however, largely limited to white males. During the first generation of the nineteenth century one state after another democratized American politics by removing property requirements for voting, enfranchising virtually all adult white males by the late 1820s.

The expansion of the franchise for white men was often accompanied by the restriction or elimination of the franchise for blacks. The New Jersey Constitution did not limit the vote by race. Only property was required until 1807, when state law added racial restrictions. African Americans could vote in Connecticut until an 1814 law, incorporated into the state constitution four years later, disenfranchised them. In 1822 Rhode Island's legislature restricted black voting in that state for the first time.[27]

The spread of American democracy and the extension of full citizenship widened the distance between the social and political circumstances of blacks and whites erecting barriers to class based interracial alliances that had been common in colonial America. Ironically, by the end of the eighteenth century African Americans were less likely to find allies among whites with whom they shared a common economic position than among some of the wealthy, well-situated members of the urban elite. Many were Federalist. Men like John Jay and Alexander Hamilton, helped establish the New York Manumission Society. Benjamin Franklin was a member of the manumission society in Pennsylvania. Dr. Benjamin Rush from Philadelphia, an active reformer, believed that Africans were the moral and intellectual equal of whites. In New England the list of elite Federalist reformers was long, including Massachusetts' James Otis, who argued that, "all men . . . white or black" were "by the law of nature free born."[28] Quakers were also a source of support for northern blacks in their struggle for freedom and civil rights. From before the Revolution until the Civil War, Quakers stood against slavery and often assisted African Americans by providing education and welfare services and aiding fugitive slaves. Always an important element in the abolition movement, many of these highly educated and often comfortably positioned Quaker reformers financed and otherwise supported black institutional and community development. Yet these interracial alliances differed from many of those in the colonial period, as they were struck between economically disparate partners.[29]

By the 1820s important political changes had decreased the effectiveness of the Federalists as advocates of African American rights and submerged Quaker support into a broader interracial alliance. The rhetoric of the Jeffersonian Republicanism championed the independent yeoman farmer against the Federalists, seen as the party of special privilege. Yet the racist assumptions of these "liberal" Republicans often dismissed the rights and even the humanity of yeomen blacks, in favor of promoting democracy and equality of opportunity for yeomen whites. In New York, for example, the constitution of 1777 guaranteed all men, including free blacks who could meet the property requirements, the right to vote. New York Republicans struggled to disenfranchise black voters throughout the early years of the nineteenth century, while Federalists defended black voting rights and foiled several attempts to institute racial restrictions. The War of 1812 was a turning point for Federalist political power in New York, as elsewhere. Discredited by their opposition to the war, Federalists lost control of state politics and were unable to stop Republicans first from limiting the black vote in New York City in 1814, then changing the state constitution in 1821. Property qualifications for white males were removed, but any black man seeking to vote was required to have lived in the state for three years and possess more than $250 in property. This so limited the number of qualified black voters that by 1825 only 298 of the state's almost 30,000 blacks and only 16 of New York City's more than 12,000 blacks held the property needed for voting.[30]

This then, was the context for the rise of Andrew Jackson's populist approach to presidential politics in this "age of the common man." Establishing a network of local newspapers to spread his message of equality and democracy, and his opposition to undeserved economic and social privilege, Jackson failed in his presidential campaign of 1824 but succeeded in 1828. In speeches delivered on the stump and reprinted in these newspapers, Jackson spoke the language of the emerging independent American individualist. This was a country, he argued, that recognized no "artificial distinctions" and no limits for those willing to expend energy in exchange for opportunity. As one historian reported, Jackson believed that the government "must serve as a referee among all classes in society and prevent any one from gaining an advantage over the others." Yet even as he called for a "people's government" and railed against the rich man's bank, Jackson was clearly speaking to, for, and about white people.[31] A slaveholder and staunch white supremacist, Jackson reflected the mood of his times with its drive towards the emerging middle class values of equal opportunities for self-made men, and its fixed racist assumptions. He would remove Native Americans from the path of "progress" and destroy any who resisted. He would war against the alliance of Seminoles and fugitive slaves in Florida in the name of protecting southern planters from raids during which red and black guerrilla units liberated slaves. He would attack the burgeoning abolition movement as dangerous to good order and property rights—all this in the name of promoting democratic society. His was the age of the common man of pale complexion.

Thus, Jacksonianism arose from and encouraged a populist politics characterized by white mobs that attacked blacks in Boston, New York, and Philadelphia in the 1820s and 1830s and invaded the black sections of Cincinnati in 1829, driving hundreds of African Americans out of the city. It reflected the sentiment that denied most northern free blacks decent jobs and a public education, and placed black institutions and communities at constant risk of white violence. Even as African Americans found new allies in the emerging national antislavery movement and among the Garrisonian militant abolitionists, white workers, increasingly Irish immigrants during the 1840s, filled the ranks of anti-abolitionist mobs.

Clearly the interracial alliances of poor people that existed in the eighteenth century were more difficult, perhaps even impossible to form in the decades before the Civil War.

The new interracial alliances, like those struck during the early nineteenth century, brought wealthy, or at least comfortably middle class whites into association with largely poor, uneducated blacks. There were African Americans of considerable wealth and/or education, to be sure. Philadelphia minister Richard Allen; businessman James Forten; international entrepreneur and Massachusetts ship's captain Paul Cuffe; Canadian newspaper editor Mary Ann Shadd Cary; and New York businesswoman Freelove Slocum were only a few of those who stood level with most white abolitionists in financial achievement. Yet, in the racial context of nineteenth century America, no black person, regardless of personal achievement, could really stand as an equal in white society. Most often, paternalism was the best that African Americans could expect from their white allies. Eighteenth-century interracial alliances, in which all shared similar economic levels and social status, had followed a different pattern.[32]

The early years of the nineteenth century were critical in the formation of American class and race relations. During that period patterns emerged that continued, with few interruptions, for the rest of that century and well into the next. Assumptions about racial prejudice and the potential for racial violence as predominant among the white working classes were shaped by the political and economic forces that developed in the wake of the Revolution. They brought Andrew Jackson to the presidency in 1828 and although they ebbed and flowed over the post-Civil War decades and through the twentieth century, they helped to sweep George Wallace into the Alabama State House and on to the center stage of national politics in the 1960s. They also serve as a partial explanation for the emergence of former Ku Klux Klansman David Duke into the mainstream of 1990s American politics. Yet it is important to understand that the race-based populism upon which these politicians depended was not always the natural state of American politics. Interracial alliances such as those of the 1950s and 1960s Civil Rights Movement, the American labor movement during the 1930s, and the Populist Movement during the 1890s, have important antecedents. There was a time when unfree and oppressed people, black, white, and red, stood together, perhaps not in perfect agreement, but as an acknowledgement of shared circumstance, similar enough to warrant common action. "Red Necks and White Skins" may have described the race-based alliances of urban workers in antebellum America. It may have described the class politics of twentieth century Forsyth county, Georgia. But demographers suggest that it may not represent the future of America. This makes all the more critical our understanding of the interracial alliances of America's past.

NOTES

I thank Denise D. Meringolo for reading and commenting on an early draft of this essay.
1 For an explanation of the colonial social hierarchy, see Gordon S. Wood, *The Radicalism of the American Revolution* (NY: Alfred A. Knopf, 1992). John Saffin, *A brief and Candid Answer to a Late Printed Sheet. . .* (Boston, 1700), quoted in Gary

Nash, *The Urban Crucible: Social Change, Political Consciousness, and the Origins of the American Revolution* (Cambridge, MA: Harvard University Press, 1979), 7.

2 Bernard Bailyn and Barbara DeWolfe, *Voyagers to the West* (New York: Vintage Books, 1986), 324. Although it may be true, as Gordon Wood argued in *The Radicalism of the American Revolution* that class consciousness based on occupation and wealth as we might define it today did not exist in eighteenth century colonial America, there was a sense of shared disadvantage among those at the bottom of American society. Likewise there was a shared feeling of advantage among those at the top.

3 For an extended version of this argument see, James Oliver Horton and Lois E. Horton, *In Hope of Liberty: Culture, Community and Protest Among Northern Free Blacks, 1700–1860* (New York: Oxford University Press, 1997).

4 Roi Ottley and William J. Weatherby, eds., *The Negro in New York: An Informal Social History, 1626–1940* (New York: New York Public Library, 1967).

5 Kenneth Scott, "The Slave Insurrection in New York in 1712," *New York Historical Society Quarterly* 45 (1961): 43–74.

6 David Steven Cohen, "In Search of Carolus Africanus Rex: Afro-Dutch Folklore in New York and New Jersey," *Journal of the Afro-American Historical and Genealogical Society* 5, 3&4 (Fall & Winter, 1984): 147–162, 154.

7 Samuel E. Morrison, "A Poem on Election Day in Massachusetts about 1760," *Proceedings of the Colonial Society of Massachusetts* 18 (February, 1915): 54–61.

8 Absalom Aimwell, *Pinkster Ode* (Albany: Absalom Aimwell, Esq., 1803), quoted in Cohen, "In Search of Carolus Africanus Rex": 154.

9 Robert Cottrol, *The Afro-Yankee* (Westport, CT: Greenwood Press, 1982),19; *New York Weekly Journal*, August 9, 1742, quotation in Edgar J. McManus, *A History of Negro Slavery in New York* (Syracuse, NY: Syracuse University Press, 1966), 87.

10 Gary Nash, *Red, White, and Black: the Peoples of Early America* (Inglewood Cliffs, NJ: Prentice-Hall, Inc., 1974), 285.

11 Howard Zinn, *Twentieth Century: A People's History* (New York: Harper, 1998), 51; Nash, *Urban Crucible*, 134–136; Benjamin Colman to Mr. Samuel Holden, Boston, May 8, 1737, Colman Papers, unpublished papers, v. 2, Massachusetts Historical Society.

12 Jesse Lemisch, "Jack Tar in the Streets: Merchant Seamen in the Politics of Revolutionary America," *William and Mary Quarterly* 25 (1968): 371–407; Zinn, *People's History*, 51; Nash, *Urban Crucible*, 221–223.

13 Lemisch, "Jack Tar in the Streets": 379.

14 Daniel Horsmanden, *The New York Conspiracy*, Thomas J. Davis, ed. (Boston: Beacon Press, 1971). Also see Davis' *Rumor of Revolt: The Great Negro Plot in Colonial New York* (New York: Free Press, 1985).

15 Davis, *Rumor of Revolt*.

16 Horsmanden, *The New York Conspiracy*.

17 Ottley and Weatherby, eds., *Negro in New York*, 36–37.

18 Horton and Horton, *In Hope of Liberty*.

19 Benjamin Thatcher, *Traits of the Tea Party Being a Memoir of George R. T. Hewes* (New York: 1835), 103–104; George Washington Williams, *History of the Negro Race in America, 1619–1880* (New York: G. P. Putnam's Sons, 1883, reprinted, New York: Arno Press, 1968), 332. See also William Cooper Nell, *The Colored Patriots of the American Revolution* (Boston: Robert F. Wallcut, 1855)

20 See the *Boston Gazette*, March 12, 1770 for an eye-witness account of this event.

21 Adams' letter, which he signed "Crispus Attucks," is included in Sidney Kaplan, *The Black Presence in the Era of the American Revolution, 1770–1800* (Washington, D.C.:

Smithsonian Institution Press, 1973). I thank Anthony Hill for bringing this letter to my attention and for alerting me to the fact that it was not written by Attucks.

22 Although more than 5,000 African Americans served in the Continental Army and the southern colonies where slaveholding was largest, refused to enlist black troops. See Horton and Horton, *In Hope of Liberty*.

23 Letter "in behalf of our fellow slaves in this Province and by order of their committee," April 20, 1773, New York Historical Society.

24 David Grimsted, "Anglo-American Racism and Phillis Wheatley's 'Sable Veil,' 'Length'ned Chain,' and 'Knitted Heart,' " in Ronald Hoffman and Peter J. Albert, ed., *Women in the Age of American Revolution* (Charlottesville: University Press of Virginia, for the U.S. Capitol Historical Society, 1989), 443.

25 Linda K. Kerber, "The Meaning of Citizenship," *The Journal of American History* (December 1997):833–854,841. Also see Kerber, *No Constitutional Right to Be Ladies: Women and the Obligations of Citizenship* (New York: Hill and Wang, 1998).

26 Gordon S. Wood, *The Radicalism of the American Revolution* (New York: Alfred A. Knopf, 1992); also see Henretta, *The Evolution of American Society, 1700–1815: An Interdisciplinary Analysis* (Lexington: D.C. Heath Company, 1973).

27 Phyllis F. Field, *The Politics of Race in New York* (Ithaca: Cornell University Press, 1982); Leonard P. Curry, *The Free Black in Urban America 1800–1850* (Chicago: University of Chicago Press, 1981); Paul Finkelman, "Prelude to the Fourteenth Amendment: Black Legal Rights in the Antebellum North," *Rutgers Law Journal* 17, 3 & 4 (Spring and Summer, 1986): 415–482.

28 James Otis, *The Rights of British Colonies Asserted and Proved* (Boston: Edes & Gill, 1765), 37.

29 For an extensive argument on these points see Horton and Horton, *In Hope of Liberty*.

30 Phyllis F. Field, *The Politics of Race in New York*. Under New York's first constitution, the property requirements for voting were a $50 freehold to vote for an congressmen, or a $250 freehold to vote for a senator or governor.

31 Robert V. Remini, *The Revolutionary Age of Andrew Jackson* (New York: Harper & Row, Publishers, 1976), 15.

32 Horton and Horton, *In Hope of Liberty*.

CHAPTER 2

INDUSTRIAL SLAVERY: LINKING THE PERIPHERY AND THE CORE

RONALD L. LEWIS

INTRODUCTION

Industrial slavery seems destined to forever occupy a place at the periphery of the discourse on American slavery. The Old South was, after all, overwhelmingly a rural, plantation economy, and industry is generally associated with urban places. The fact that only about 5 percent of the region's slave population labored in industrial pursuits at any given time is sufficient to understand why industrial slavery has generated relatively little scholarship. Non-specialists are generally unaware that industrial slavery existed at all. Similarly, few scholars or laymen are aware that slavery was a significant institution in the southern Appalachians. Both industrial and Appalachian slavery existed at the periphery of the South's staple agricultural economy, but we can learn much about the South and slavery from studying the role played by this one-half million slaves in the region's economy.

Even though the antebellum South was dominated by the plantation system and slave-owning oligarchy, it was nevertheless a diverse region with a complex social hierarchy. By 1860 the South's free population totaled eight million whites. Just below the planters on the social hierarchy was a middle class, about two-thirds of which was composed of white yeomen farmers, craftsmen, mechanics, professionals, and commercial interests. Near the bottom of the pyramid were nearly one million poor whites. In addition, four million slaves were compressed into the lowest social category reserved for them alone. About one-quarter of a million free blacks occupied the ambiguous ground between slaves and poor whites. Slave-owning was widespread, engaging nearly four hundred thousand families; about two million people had direct property interest in slaves. The typical slave owner was a farmer who owned one or two slave families and a few hundred acres of land, but ownership was concentrated among elite planters who owned more than 20 slaves each; collectively this small elite controlled more than one-half of the slave population and possessed the best land. Slaves were concentrated in the staple-producing areas, and they raised 90 percent of the cotton in the Black Belt, and even more of the tobacco in Virginia, rice in Carolina, and sugar in Louisiana.[1]

Urban development was limited in this plantation economy. By 1860 only eight southern cities skirting the periphery of the region claimed populations of greater than 22,000 residents: Baltimore, Richmond, Charleston, Savannah, Mobile, New Orleans, St. Louis, and Louisville. Washington, D.C. had a population of sixty thousand. Few interior towns had developed in the region, and North Carolina, Florida, Mississippi, Arkansas, and Texas lacked a city of more than ten thousand people. Most southern cities were commercial and residential; Richmond had emerged by the 1840s as the only truly industrial city. These urban centers provided port facilities necessary for agricultural exports, and served the commercial, financial, and social needs of the plantation society. Factors, bankers, lawyers, shop-keepers, and slave dealers dominated the urban economy. Backcountry towns that had served as rural crossroads of politics and trade, and where commodities were transshipped to the core, soon became nascent industrial locations,[2] particularly along the expanding railroad lines that penetrated and linked the backcountry to the larger markets.

Slaves represented a substantial portion of the urban population, 50 percent in Charleston in 1850. About seventy thousand slaves lived in the 8 leading southern cities in 1850, about 25,000 of whom were industrial bondsmen. Two-thirds of the urban slaves were involved in domestic service or in commercial occupations as artisans and craftsmen, draymen, or laborers. Industrial slaves formed only a minority of the urban bondsmen.[3] In fact, historian Robert Starobin writes, "The typical industrial slave lived in a rural, small-town, or plantation setting, where most industry was located, not in a large city."[4] Moreover, being close to the fields, agricultural slaves often doubled as industrial workers as need demanded, a fact that greatly enlarges the number of slaves who labored in industrial pursuits, and hence the influence of industrial enterprise on the lives of slaves in the Old South.

SCALE OF INDUSTRIAL SLAVERY

The distinctive qualities of industry in the Old South have been obscured by the long shadow cast by the plantation. Much less specialized than their northern peers, southern factory owners often blended their careers with those of planter and politician. This propensity constituted one of the most striking characteristics of industrial development in the South. Since they owned a disproportionate share of the region's surplus wealth, planters who themselves did not become businessmen often invested capital in industrial expansion. Whether managed and financed by planters, businessmen, or both, however, established social and economic imperatives determined that slaves would be relied on to turn the wheels of industry just as surely as they were to pick cotton. In fact, slavery became one of the characteristic features of southern industry.

Most southern cotton and woolen factories utilized a slave workforce, either exclusively or alongside poor white workers. The first southern textile mill was probably established in South Carolina during the American Revolution, but by the 1840s, Georgia's remarkable expansion in productive capacity distinguished it as the "New England of the South." The textile industry followed a unique employment pattern. Piedmont factories generally utilized poor whites rather than blacks, while lowland mills almost universally employed only slave labor. This practice is at least partially explained by the fact that poor whites predominated in the Carolina uplands; their well-known class antagonism toward the institution of slavery and the relatively scant number of slaves in the district precluded reliance on bonded factory operatives. On the other hand, lowland slaves often outnumbered whites by a wide margin and political and economic necessity dictated that slaves be employed in the lowland mills. Unlike William Gregg's famous experiment with poor white workers at the Graniteville cotton mills, most antebellum factories followed the example of South Carolina's Saluda mill, which employed 158 bondsmen in 1851. Even though owners of southern textile factories began to shift from slave to free white operatives during the 1850s, in 1860 they still employed more than five thousand factory slaves.[5]

By contrast, in the Virginia and North Carolina tobacco district most tobacco factory slaves were hired hands, although the employers always owned a sizable portion of their operatives. Whether owned or hired, however, the number of slave hands at tobaccories was always large, and by 1860 totaled 12,843. The most successful Richmond tobacconist, James Thomas, Jr., utilized 150 bondsmen who produced over one million pounds of chewing tobacco annually.[6]

Hemp production represented another leading industry of the Old South. During the eighteenth century, Virginia hemp became a major staple from which osnaburg, linsey-woolsey, linen, rope, and sail were manufactured. Many Virginia planters, such as Robert Carter of Nomini Hall, erected small establishments for the commercial production of cloth and, even in these first small transitional shops between the homespun and factory stages, slaves spun and wove the finished products. During the Revolutionary War, numerous slaves worked at Virginia's ropewalk and at other establishments erected during the period to produce hemp products. By the turn of the nineteenth century, the center of the American hemp industry had shifted westward to Kentucky, where the fiber became a staple of major importance. In fact, according to the preeminent authority on the topic, James F. Hopkins, "without hemp, slavery might not have flourished in Kentucky, since other agricultural products of the state were not conducive to the extensive use of bondsmen."[7] By the Civil War, nearly two hundred Kentucky hemp factories utilized five thousand bondsmen. At the same time, another twenty-five hundred slave operatives toiled in the hemp factories of Missouri.[8]

The large representation of slaves in the various skilled crafts grew out of the colonial period, when there was a chronic shortage of free artisans in the southern colonies. Many slaves became sawyers, carpenters, blacksmiths, coopers, tanners, shoe-makers, cabinet-makers, wheelwrights, weavers, and worked in a wide range of other trades. During the nineteenth century, slaves not only continued to practice traditional crafts but learned new ones as well. Bondsmen became machinists, cobblers were grouped into shoe factories, and slaves operated the innumerable tanneries, bakeries, and printing presses. They also labored by the hundreds in southern brick yards, and by the thousands in the small local gristmills that ground flour throughout the South. Similarly, commercial mills, such as the Gallego and Haxall mills (the world's largest at the time) of Richmond,

Virginia, were operated with slave manpower. Throughout the South Carolina and Georgia tidewater hundreds of slaves labored in rice mills, and in Louisiana and Texas sugar mills bonded labor was used exclusively.[9]

The South's fisheries yielded a very important protein supplement to the diet of slaves and masters alike, and provided a significant volume for export as well. The famous traveler and landscape architect Frederick Law Olmsted observed that fishing constituted an important branch of industry and a "source of considerable wealth." Like most industries, fisheries also employed "mainly negroes, slave and free."[10] An estimated twenty thousand fishery slaves plied southern waters by 1861.[11] Unlike the textile, tobacco, hemp, and many other kinds of industrial employment that utilized men, women, and children, the South's extraction industries relied on male slaves almost exclusively. Out of the Mississippi and Louisiana swamps black bondsmen chopped, trimmed, and rafted cypress to New Orleans and Natchez, where still other slaves operated the steam-powered saw mills that could be found in most southern cities. Some of these mills became sizable operations that frequently employed more than one hundred slaves. Many bondsmen disappeared into southern swamps for months at a time to cut wooden shingles and barrel staves. On the eve of the Civil War, most of the sixteen thousand men who labored in the region's forest products industry were slaves.[12]

Although the South lagged far behind the North in internal improvements, the region's turnpikes, bridges, canals, levees, railroads, city sewers, and waterlines all were built by male slave labor. Probably a total of twenty thousand bondsmen toiled on southern railroads alone during the antebellum period. Numerous blacks also worked at shipyards, the most famous being Frederick Douglass, the runaway ship caulker from Baltimore. They also piloted the many boats, large and small, which negotiated southern waterways; they operated the ferries and manned canal boats; they labored on steamboats as deckhands, porters, firemen, and engineers; and they performed countless other tasks which had nothing to do with picking cotton.[13]

Few nonagricultural occupations in the Old South made use of slaves so universally, and over such an extended period of time, as the production of iron and the mining of coal. For a half century prior to the American Revolution, Maryland and Virginia iron dominated the colonial exports market. Although the Chesapeake region lost its American preeminence after the Revolution, within the South it remained the most important single center for the production of iron. Also, the eastern Virginia coal field near Richmond provided the major supply of coal for homes and industries along the Atlantic Coast from the development of the first commercial mine in the 1760s until the 1840s when railroads made it economically feasible to develop the enormous reserves of bituminous coal in western Virginia and Pennsylvania. Until the late 1850s, however, when the Alabama and Tennessee fields assumed a minor degree of importance, commercial coal mining in the South was almost exclusively a Virginia enterprise. During the eighteenth century, at least 65 ironworks were erected in Maryland and Virginia which employed 4,500 hands at any given point in time. By the nineteenth century, slave-operated ironworks increased to about 80 and collectively utilized a slave force of approximately seven thousand workers. Starobin estimates the iron industry for the South as a whole numbered ten thousand.[14] Between the American Revolution and the Civil War, a minimum of forty coal companies operated in the Richmond Coal Basin of eastern Virginia, and employed about two thousand miners at peak production in the 1830s and 1840s.[15]

Too often historians write about "slavery," when they really mean the slavery that they know. Slavery by whatever name is slavery, of course, but the conditions of slave life varied with a diversity that makes it difficult to generalize along the traditional interpretative axis of accommodation versus oppression. Richard Wade's 1964 study, *Slavery in the Cities,* argued that urban and industrial slaves enjoyed greater liberties than did their plantation counterparts. Focusing on the conspicuous examples of Richmond's tobacco and iron factories, Wade claimed that the slaves who worked in these factories became famous for demonstrating that slavery was feasible in complex industrial settings, but not without compromises in discipline and slave control that the fluidity of city and industrial life forced upon masters. The hiring-out system greatly relaxed the rigidity of slavery by constantly reallocating slave labor to meet shifting demand. In the process, however, masters lost direct, daily control over their property. Industrialists often chose to own key production workers to ensure control of the manufacturing process, but contracted with other slave owners to hire their surplus hands. Some masters allowed their slaves, usually slave craftsmen, to hire out their own time so long as the owners received the rent. Such slaves held a "quasi-free" status as long as they stayed out of trouble, and enjoyed much better conditions than did plantation slaves who were under the constant gaze of overseers. Moreover, payment for extra work allowed slaves to enjoy sundry food, clothing, or leisure activities which were denied to other plantation hands. Wade believed that these features demonstrated that slavery in the cities was gradually being accommodated and that, left to historical evolution, slavery eventually would have withered away.[16]

In his revisionist study, *Industrial Slavery in the Old South* (1970), Robert Starobin saw in the hiring out system evidence for a very different kind of slave existence. He claimed that the conditions endured by industrial bondsmen usually were worse than for slaves engaged in agriculture. For one thing, industrial slaves labored longer, harder, and at more hazardous occupations than their agricultural brothers and sisters. They bore the hazards associated with early industrialization, when machines and tools themselves were dangerous, and mistakes could readily cost one's life or limbs. The restraints imposed by ownership of valuable slave workers might have encouraged care for some, Starobin argued, but if the hiring-out system provided more freedom of movement for slaves it also separated the slave from the master who protected his property, and exposed the slave to hard-driving industrialists interested more in wringing a profit out of slaves than preserving their well-being. Starobin saw in the same sources examined by Richard Wade evidence that the conditions of daily life were worse than on the plantation. Urban slaves lived in shanties or tenements attached to or near the factories, and sometimes in the plant itself. Quarters for rural industrial slaves, the majority of industrial bondsmen, were more primitive than those for urban slaves.[17] Starobin also challenged the view that payments to slaves for extra work was evidence that slavery was evolving toward freedom for slaves, and pointed out that the incentive system was an eighteenth-century invention, not a nineteenth-century concession to freedom.[18] Masters approved money payments to slaves because they improved discipline and the willingness to work; extra cash was the carrot, but the lash was readily available to provide the stick if discipline broke down. For Starobin, incentives and accommodation were merely devices to extract even more labor, and demonstrated the adaptability of slave labor to an expanding economy rather than as a sign of its decline.

This Wade-Starobin debate dramatizes how current politics shape our view of the past. Coming as it did between 1960 and 1970, during the civil rights and then black power revolutions, the issue of whether slavery would have withered away without the Civil War mirrored the civil rights question of whether Jim Crow was going to succumb to its own irrationality, or had to be destroyed root and branch by any means necessary. At this propitious moment one scholar, Eugene Genovese, almost single-handedly redirected the thrust of slavery studies by developing an interpretation that satisfied radicals by portraying the planters as precapitalistic paternalists already badly outdated in the antebellum period. Their world was being antiquated by an emergent capitalist order, but their paternalism had allowed for a vibrant African American culture to take form. Thus in one stroke the leftists were satisfied and so were the cultural nationalists. Genovese's focus on culture recharted the course of slavery studies for the rest of the twentieth century. Since the early 1970s the search for the autonomous world of African American culture has dominated slavery studies.

The Structures of Work and Slave Life

In their book on slavery in the Americas, published in 1993, Ira Berlin and Philip P. Morgan called for a redirection of slavery studies back toward the importance of work, and reminded us that slavery was first and foremost a labor system. "Slaves worked," they wrote, and "when, where, and especially how they worked determined, in large measure, the course of their lives." So central was labor to the existence of slavery that recent studies have ignored the obvious, focusing instead on current popular themes of slaves' social organization, domestic arrangements, religious beliefs, music, cuisine, and language in analyzing the congealing of a distinctive African American culture. The quest for this culture has led into the quarters, family, and church, but seldom to the worksite. Although these perspectives have generated a rich and important history of slave life and culture, "work necessarily engaged most slaves, most of the time." Indeed, it seems that slave autonomy has replaced slave resistance as the dominant motif in the current historiography of slavery. Peter Kolchin's survey, *American Slavery,* places the emphasis squarely on the internal struggle among slaves to wrest as much autonomy as possible from their masters, and identifies this continuous struggle as the fulcrum of African American culture.[19]

In a post-modern world, Berlin and Morgan seem to be calling for a correction in the historical scholarship that would reacknowledge some of the strengths of a now discarded functionalism.

Exactly how slaves worked for their owners depended most vitally upon the requirements of particular crops and crafts, which shaped the nature of the work force, the organization of production, and the division of labor. These, in turn rested upon the geography, the demographic balance of slave and free and black and white, the size of slave holding units, the character of technology, and the management techniques prevalent at different times and in different places. Any systematic study of slave work must also consider the knowledge and skills of individual slave men and women, the slaves' origins, and those of their owners. The complex matrix of circumstances that determined the slaves' labor, moreover, changed over time and differed from place to place.[20]

Whatever the theoretical underpinnings of the redirection they call for, it seems obvious that the conditions of slave life and labor depended on the structure, nature, and scale of the work itself.

STRUCTURE OF WORK

The underlying premise of this chapter is that the structures of work influenced the conditions of life for African American slaves. Time-tested strategies led most planters to organize agricultural labor into gangs. Depending on the scale of operations, masters either developed a managerial hierarchy to control the process, as on large plantations, or worked alongside their slaves as on smaller farms. Slaves, organized by gangs, labored in groups from dawn to dusk, often defined by age and sex, under the close supervision of overseers. The gang system was generally most suitable for large plantations, but the task system was more readily adaptable to other work environments. The organization of slaves under the task system, which defined the slaves' labor according to the work to be accomplished, left much more latitude to slaves in governing the pace of their work. Slave owners relinquished some direct daily control of the gang for the task system in part because the task system enabled them to measure the slaves' work performance precisely against a fixed standard. Industrial slaves generally labored under this form of organization. The system offered slaves the incentive to complete their task as quickly as possible, for once they satisfied their daily production quota their time was their own to take in leisure or to continue to produce for pay.[21] Experience generally taught slave masters how high to set the quota in order to get a full day's labor from slaves; the incentive, generally in the form of cash or credit, was to encourage them to produce beyond a hard day's work.

Extensive studies of the coal and iron industries have shown that slaves in the mines and forges challenged and succeeded in modifying the masters' theoretically absolute power over them.[22] Slave miners and ironmakers improved their quality of life by negotiating extra provisions and payment for work performed beyond their normal tasks, gaining more autonomy over their work and daily lives. In the struggle to control that ambiguous middle ground between absolute power and absolute submission, skilled slave iron and coal operatives forced their masters to yield some degree of control in return for a more reliable workforce. The structures of iron making and coal mining determined and organized work processes and relations. Clearly, work in the underground coal mine dictated the use of a young male workforce. It was often difficult to hire slaves for such dangerous employment because masters understandably feared the loss of their valuable property. Iron manufacture and coal mining also called for certain skills generally unfamiliar to slaves. Therefore, there was often an integrated workforce composed of a few very skilled white workers in positions of judgement vital to production and slaves performing the less skilled functions. Nevertheless, coal and iron operators often preferred that their own slaves learn the most skilled job whenever possible in order to achieve stability at key steps in the production process.[23]

GEOGRAPHY AND ENVIRONMENT

Geography and the environment also played a major role in shaping the conditions and organization of labor. While iron and coal slaves found advantage in the task system, and the overwork payment incentives enhanced their ability to provide extras for their families, these were viable inducements only because the slaves were close to their loved ones. Such was not the case in the naval stores industry. Centered in North Carolina, where 90 percent of the nation's tar and turpentine was produced, at least fifteen thousand slaves labored at southern distilleries in 1860.[24] Work in the naval stores industry was organized on the task basis because workers fanned out into the forests to perform their tasks individually. In the long leaf pine forests of the South environmental factors imposed conditions on slaves that made the gang labor of plantations seem idyllic by comparison.

The geographically expansive turpentine orchards covered thousands of acres, and exposed slaves who worked in them to a life of isolation and misery. Physical strength was a prerequisite for work in the woods; therefore men dominated the industry. Turpentine orchards were marked off in continuous grids and workers were assigned to specific sections. A "woods rider" served as overseer, but the distances were so great that one rider could not effectively manage more than 12 slaves. While naval stores slaves may have had more independence, responsibility, and sense of satisfaction from the individuality of their work, they suffered far more than did plantation slaves from harsh living conditions. By the mid-nineteenth century, railroads enabled naval stores manufacturers to move their distilling operations into the depths of the virgin pine forests. Far from the plantations, their families, and without female companionship, male turpentiners were isolated geographically and psychologically. The overseer's performance was judged by production, so he pushed the slaves hard, cash and time incentives were offered for those who exceeded the high task requirements, and physical punishment faced those who lagged.

In his study of slavery in the naval stores industry, Robert Outland found that, unlike industrial slaves in Virginia, bondsmen in the Carolina pineries were treated much more harshly, and were too isolated to negotiate between the competing interests of their owners and hirers. Once slaves had made the difficult adjustment to such a life, masters were reluctant to risk their replacement by a novice, so naval stores slaves tended to be committed for long periods if not the duration of their work lives. The isolated setting, the environment of a semi-tropical forest, and the migratory nature of the industry all conspired to ensure a comparatively miserable life for naval stores slaves, irrespective of the masters' motives. Turpentine operations lasted no more than ten years; therefore housing, and everything else, was temporary. Like with other occupations that were transitory, such as shingle making, fisheries, and lumber camps, most of the buildings were crude. Slave housing consisted of little more than shanties or lean-tos. Pinery slaves were clothed poorly, too. Even if they received the same issue as plantation slaves, and there is evidence that they did not, the resin from the trees soon ruined their clothing and shoes. Food was generally purchased by the operator and sent into the woods, and since it represented the largest cost of supporting a woods slave, rations were kept at subsistence levels. The slaves had no opportunity to raise their own food, pilfer it from the storehouses, or otherwise acquire it from the underground or "slave economy."[25]

A host of health problems were associated with naval stores work. Drinking water was often scarce in the piney woods, and slaves carried straws with them to drink water from the turpentine boxes after rains. Turpentine is a local irritant and a central neural depressant, so its ingestion was probably the cause of dysentery, abdominal pain, inflammation of the intestine, and other maladies commonly found among turpentine workers. The resin (raw sap), an extremely sticky substance, caused dermatitis and considerable annoyance. Fumes from the stills resulted in asthma, neurological damage, and intellectual impairment. The primitive living conditions endured by naval stores slaves were further aggravated by the constant presence of wild animals, poisonous snakes, malarial mosquitoes, ticks and chiggers, and the ever-present danger of becoming lost in the woods.[26] Beyond being chattel slaves, the lives of the Virginia iron founders and the North Carolina "tar heels" could not have been more different.[27]

If iron and turpentine represented the range of possibilities in industrial slavery for being isolated from an adjacent agricultural slave community, tobacco represented a mix of both types of labor. Tobacco was Virginia's, indeed the South's, first cash crop. From its early beginnings in the seventeenth century, tobacco culture grew to become the dominant crop in eastern Virginia by the nineteenth century. Richmond was the leading tobacco manufacturing center, but smaller centers were found in Petersburg, Lynchburg, and Danville, near the North Carolina state line. In the Dan Basin of Virginia and North Carolina, nearly every planter who raised tobacco also was a manufacturer. Some, however, made a business of purchasing loose tobacco from neighboring farmers and planters.[28]

By the 1840s tobacco manufacturing had become the basis of Southside Virginia's economy. Throughout Virginia the workforce in tobacco manufacturing was almost entirely black. The major difference between Richmond and Danville, however, was scale and the organization of local industry. Richmond tobacco factories were the largest and have come to represent the urban tobacco factory model. Danville, however, represented the more prevalent diffused model, in which planters and manufacturers were nearly inseparable. The factories in Danville itself were directly tied to the surrounding plantations. The tobacco interests were integrated from countryside production through city manufacturing, and slave labor circulated within a close, often overlapping, network of planters, manufacturers, and merchants. The integration of rural and urban labor markets within these networks was facilitated by the local slave hiring agency. The practice of joint hiring, therefore, became prevalent in Danville, with manufacturers and planters hiring slaves to be shifted from field to factory, according to seasonal demand. Slaves were both agricultural and industrial workers, components in an integrated system that linked field and factory, the gang system and the task system. With a population of only 3,689 people, only 8 percent of whom were white males 21 or over, Danville tobacco factory slaves did not experience the "freedoms" found in the urban environment of Richmond. On the other hand, they were not perennially chained to the hoe,[29] nor did they suffer the physical and psychological isolation or the environmental hazards of slaves who toiled in the naval stores industry.

ROLE OF FREE LABOR

The role of free white labor in a slave society is another structural determinant that affected where and how slaves would be employed. Planters held the reins of power in the antebellum South, and any threat to their hegemonic control met with swift and firm resistance. But their elitism was built on an inherent contradiction: Maintenance of a distinctive South independent of the North required the development of urban industrial centers, which most planters distrusted. Cities threatened their control, for slavery required, in Richard Wade's phrase, "a high degree of order, the careful regulation of Negro affairs, and a fixed status for bondsmen. On the other hand, the city demanded fluidity, a constant reallocation of human resources, and a large measure of social mobility."[30] The planters viewed the prospect of a fluid and open society as inimical to their control, and throughout the 1830s and 1840s, such a prospect motivated their vigorous opposition to measures, such as internal improvements, that would foster such a trend. By the late 1840s, however, the hostility of planters toward industrialists had diminished, and by 1850 the southerners were conscious of their dependency on the manufactured products. If the South were to control its own destiny, then surely an expanded manufacturing base was essential. Once the necessity was admitted, the issue confronting southern elites focused on what kind of labor force southern industry should employ, rather than whether or not the South should have industry at all.[31]

The planters had long feared the rise of an economically independent and politically powerful urban middle class. Even more troublesome, during the late antebellum era an explosive debate erupted over which form of industrial labor was preferable, black slaves or free whites. Fired by a growth in manufacturing of such items as tobacco products, textiles, coal, and iron, the debate did not center on the profitability of slave versus free labor. Southern white leaders had already convinced themselves that slavery was not only profitable but also absolutely essential in a biracial society. Instead, the debate pivoted on the question of whether it was in the region's interest to foster the growth of either a slave or free white industrial working class. Both could prove fatal to the region's traditional social system.[32]

Proponents of slave labor usually maintained that bondsmen were most economical and, since they lacked mobility, also provided more stability than whites on a seasonal basis. Furthermore, whites wasted time by drinking or by engaging in meetings, musters, elections, and similar activities closed to slaves. Moreover, bondsmen did not strike or demand wage increases, manufacturers did not have to educate them, nor did they go off on binges and engage in otherwise unruly behavior. Even though antebellum manufacturers often encountered difficulty persuading planters to invest in industry, they found slave owners willing to lease their excess slaves. This diverted an unproductive surplus of hands from agriculture into industry and guaranteed against a labor surplus and declining slave prices. On the other hand, when agricultural prices were up, slaves could be retained on the plantations. The economic advantages were apparent to planters, and they realized that it left them in full control.[33] At the same time, planters were unnerved when they saw blacks in the Richmond tobacco industry hiring themselves to the highest bidder, acquiring their own food and lodging, and earning wages for overwork,[34] or when they saw Tredegar Ironworks slaves who lived "pretty much on the basis of free labor" as long as they did their jobs as expected.[35]

In 1849 James H. Hammond, a leading planter of South Carolina, summed up the fears created by the specter of industrial slavery: "Whenever a slave is made a mechanic he is more than half freed, and soon becomes, as we too well know, and all history attests, with rare exceptions, the most corrupt and turbulent of his class."[36] In Richmond, the authorities attempted to curb the relative freedom of movement, and consequent loss of control, over slaves who worked in the city. In 1852 the *Richmond Daily Dispatch* reported that some slaves, especially those who worked in the tobacco factories, received between 75 cents and one dollar per week to provide for their own board and that the city council was considering legislation restricting the practice. By 1859 Richmond had passed a city ordinance that stipulated that every "hirer, owner or other employer of slave labor" must provide food and lodging for slave workers "upon his own premises, or by engaging board and lodging for them with some free person."[37]

Proponents of white factory labor based their primary arguments on the assumption that it was the social responsibility of self-respecting leaders to bring poor whites into the mainstream of southern life. Industrial expansion, therefore, should be based on white labor, with industry absorbing and uplifting the multitudes of poor whites by providing them with the "proper supervision" and "moral instruction." In the process, the entire cultural life of the region would ultimately be elevated.[38] James H. Hammond clearly expressed the reasoning behind this approach:

> It has been suggested, that white factory operatives in the South would constitute a body hostile to our domestic institutions. If any such sentiments could take root among the poorer classes of our native citizens, more danger may be apprehended from them, in the present state of things, with the facilities they now possess and the difficulties they have now to encounter, than if they were brought together in factories, with constant employment and adequate remuneration. It is well known, that the

abolitionists of America and Europe are now making the most strenuous efforts to
enlist them in their crusade, by encouraging the exclusive use of what is called 'free
labor cotton,' and by inflammatory appeals to their pride and their supposed interests.
But all apprehensions from this source are entirely imaginary. The poorest and hum-
blest freeman of the South feels as sensibly, perhaps more sensibly than the wealthiest
planter, the barrier which nature, as well as law, has erected between the white and
black races. . . . Besides this, the factory operative could not fail to see here, what one
would suppose he must see, however distant from us, that the whole fabric of his own
fortunes was based on our slave system.[39]

Had the planters not been so paranoiac about maintaining the traditional
social and political status quo, they would have realized that the industrialists
constituted no fundamental threat to southern society. Joseph R. Anderson
clearly revealed this in his reaction to a strike by white workers at his Tredegar
Iron Works in 1847. Anderson not only perceived a menace to his authority and
profits in their attempt to block the employment of slaves in skilled rolling mill
positions, but he also believed that the white strikers threatened the principle of
slave ownership and hence slave society itself. Anderson therefore fired them. "It
must be evident," he declared, "that such combinations are a direct attack on
slave property; and, if they do not originate in abolition, they are pregnant with
evils." The *Richmond Times and Compiler* stated that the principle behind the
strike attacked "the root of all the rights and privileges of the master, and if
acknowledged, or permitted to gain foothold, will soon wholly destroy the value
of slave property."[40]

Planters might have seen that industrial slaves also were used to restrain the
white proletariat, the class that the planters most feared would create turmoil and
demand the abolition of slavery. Essentially, industrialists and planters alike used
black slaves to control white workers, and reactionary elites employed the economic and political means at their disposal to crush all challenges to established
class relations. In 1851 James Hammond pointed out that "in all other countries,
and particularly manufacturing states, labor and capital are assuming an antago-
nistical position. Here it cannot be the case; capital will be able to control labor,
even in manufactures with whites, for blacks can always be resorted to in case
of need."[41]

Operators of southern textile mills certainly agreed that slave labor was the
most desirable, but the marketplace also entered the equation that determined
their response. The availability of slave and free workers was determined by the
local labor pool, price of slaves, migratory patterns of whites, and the willingness
of workers to enter the mills at prevailing wages. These were important consid-
erations that lay beyond the control of both mill operators and slaves, but certainly had a direct effect on the lives of African Americans. The issue of slave
versus free labor probably was discussed most heatedly in the context of the textile industry. Most of the early southern mills were owned and managed by
planters. They were generally small, and organized at the cottage industry level
on the plantation. As the industry grew, the planter ran his expanded factory as
an extension of the plantation, shuttling slaves back and forth between demands
of field and factory.[42]

Textile manufacturers found it increasingly difficult to purchase or hire slaves by the 1850s, as cotton prices rose and owners found it more productive to put them to work in the fields. In many places in the Deep South slaves were unavailable at any price. Unable to compete with cotton planters, textile mill operators shifted to white workers. By 1860 only one mill in South Carolina still used slaves, and in North Carolina white labor had displaced them completely. Most studies of the antebellum textile industry agree that free white labor might have been available, but it did not necessarily conform to the standards desired by mill operators. Unaccustomed to organizing their lives according to the demands of machine production, rural white workers prompted complaints from mill operators over absenteeism and a lack of discipline. William Gregg's famous experimental mill village of Graniteville, South Carolina, was plagued by white workers who constantly violated his rules on sobriety, promptness, and industry. The only reason Gregg did not shift to slave labor was the fact that so many poor whites in his Piedmont neighborhood were in need of the work.[43]

Hoping to demonstrate that textile manufacturing was worthy of economic and political support, southern operators argued that their mills would provide wage labor for large numbers of poor whites and, as Hammond suggested, would link the interests of this potentially troublesome class to those of the slave regime. Growing criticism from southern white workers about unfair competition with slaves grew primarily out of the unrest of urban artisans, but spread among the rest of the white working class in the South, heightening the racial consciousness of all southern white wage earners in the 1850s. Racial mixing on the job was a bogey that the elites could hardly support in principle, and white workers used it to gain class advantage. Free whites and black slaves working together in one Georgia textile mill prompted the local newspaper to snort: "Negroes, slaves, and White men, and White Women, co-operating in a cotton factory! What an association! Disgusting!"[44] The shift to white labor was confined mainly to the eastern seaboard states where there was a surplus of white labor. Elsewhere in the antebellum South, however, textile mills continued to rely on slave labor.[45]

Southern Appalachian Periphery

Although industrial slavery operated at the margins of the region's staple economy, the Appalachian highlands of the Old South were a true economic periphery supplying raw materials to the core manufacturing centers. If industrial slavery has been marginalized in the scholarship, slavery in the mountains has been all but ignored. Indeed, popular generalizations would lead us to believe that Southern Appalachia was a unified, homogeneous region hostile to slavery by the egalitarian temperament of its people, rugged terrain, and the severity of climate. Disinformation claiming the incompatibility of slavery in a mountainous context was already popular by the turn of the twentieth century. In 1899, William Goodell Frost, the president of Berea College, wrote that "mountain people owned land, but did not own slaves," and this fact "soon separated them from their fellow citizens of the surrounding lowlands." The widely read Smoky Mountain outdoors writer, Horace Kephart, linked the mountaineers with the anti-aristocratic followers of Oliver Cromwell, when he declared in 1913: "These roundheads had little or nothing to do with slavery."[46] The prominent African American historian Carter Woodson published an article on slavery in Appalachia in 1916, which presented a more critical perspective, but nevertheless underscored the commonly held idea that mountain residents were opposed to slavery. That Woodson's short piece is still a standard reference on the subject is a commentary on the sorry state of historical research on the topic of slavery in Appalachia.[47]

"Appalachia" is a socially constructed region, and therefore its boundary depends on the criteria. Assuming that the census data is correct, a problem in itself, the region can fluctuate enormously depending on which counties are included. Maps of Appalachian counties range from the Appalachian Regional Commission's 397 counties, to an earlier map that included only 189 counties. As might be expected, the black population also varies widely from 153,133 to 338,600 (see Table 2.1). Determining completely reliable figures on the number of African Americans in the region during the antebellum era therefore is nearly impossible.[48]

Based on the most conservative, restrictive definition of the region, however, Appalachian slavery was far more significant than popularly assumed. A national growth rate of 23.4 percent between 1850 and 1860 provides stark evidence that slavery was not a dying institution on the eve of the Civil War, and that southern Appalachia was not exceptional in this regard. Excluding Appalachian Kentucky and Virginia, where there was zero-growth during the decade before the war, the rate of slave increase in the other Appalachian sections was a robust average of 37 percent. Tennessee's 23 percent growth equaled the national average, and North Carolina's was a modest 13.2 percent, but the number of slaves in Georgia exploded by 68.7 percent, and neighboring Alabama nearly equalled that at 64.7 percent. This is particularly impressive since most of the Appalachian highlands were not suited to a plantation economy.[49]

By 1860 there were 6,019 industrial enterprises in southern Appalachia, employing 23,357 laborers. As is generally the case in peripheral regions, industrialization in Appalachia resulted in a stunted and distorted development of the economy. Capital investment was only one-half the national average, and

Table 2.1   Appalachian Slave Population by State, 1860

State:	Number of Slaves and % of Population:	African Americans and % of Population:
Alabama	6,740 (13.1)	6,868 (13.4)
Georgia	25,308 (18.8)	25,527 (19)
Tennessee	28,352 (9.1)	31,660 (10.2)
North Carolina	12,793 (10.2)	14,395 (11.5)
Virginia	61,289 (10.7)	69,334 (12.6)
Kentucky	4,314 (3.1)	5,349 (3.9)
Appalachian Total:	138,796 (10.4)	153,133 (11.5)

Source: Adapted from U.S. census figures cited in James B. Murphy, "Slavery and Freedom in Appalachia: Kentucky as a Demographic Case Study," *Register of the Kentucky Historical Society* 80 (Spring 1982): 153-81, 157-58.

below the average for the South as a whole. Therefore, most firms were small; only 15 percent were large firms as measured by capitalization and production. Moreover, industrialization proceeded unevenly throughout the region, which resulted in enclaves of concentration and few spinoff enterprises. While the region lagged behind national and southern averages, industrial enclaves developed in western Maryland and West Virginia, which led the region in manufacturing capital and production. Six counties in the region had industrialized to levels that exceeded national averages (Fannin County, Georgia; Marion and Polk Counties, Tennessee; Allegheny County, Maryland; and Kanawha and Ohio Counties, West Virginia.).[50] Moreover, a recent study claims that, far from being a land of subsistence farmers, large surpluses of farm commodities were in fact exported from Appalachia in the late antebellum era, particularly wheat, corn, and livestock.[51] Appalachian enterprises also concentrated primarily on processing agricultural commodities and raw materials for export, enterprises which did not stimulate sustained, diversified economic development. Agricultural processing in southern Appalachia was concentrated in flour and cornmeal milling, distilling grains into liquor, packing beef and pork, finishing livestock hides into leather goods, manufacturing tobacco products, and cotton and woolen cloth.[52] Three-fifths of the region's manufacturing investment went into extractive industries, such as salt, coal, iron, timber, gold, and other mineral exports, such as copper, lead, saltpeter, and alum. These industrial enterprises tended to be concentrated in industrial enclaves located on strategic rivers, canals, and later, railroads, which carried these commodities to distant markets.

Knowledge of slave labor in these industries remains almost a complete void. For the sake of brevity this essay focuses on three distinctly different industrial enclaves in the region to demonstrate larger patterns of employment: extraction and processing of salt and coal in southwestern Virginia, eastern Kentucky, and West Virginia; the railroad-driven commercialization of agriculture in the Great Valley of Southwest Virginia and East Tennessee; and the mixed livestock-gold-tourist economy of western North Carolina.

Salt was one of the first extraction industries to be organized for export. Salt furnaces in West Virginia, southwestern Virginia, and eastern Kentucky led the nation in the production of this vital commodity for export to regional and distant markets of the world. Appalachia's largest salt exporters were located in Kanawha County, West Virginia. By 1828, 65 salt wells and 20 furnaces were in operation along the Kanawha River near Charleston. At the industry's peak in the 1840s, more than three million bushels of salt were exported primarily down the Kanawha River to meatpacking firms along the Ohio and Mississippi Rivers, or on to New Orleans for transshipment to the markets of the world.[53]

The industry's organization, capital, investors, and reliance on slave labor was directly influenced by its connections with the eastern Virginia model of slave-run manufacturing. Kanawha County had 12,001 white residents in 1850, and the highest slave population in trans-Allegheny Virginia at 3,140. Over half of these slaves were either owned or controlled by the salt firms. As in eastern Virginia, the number of slaves engaged in salt manufacturing is not absolute. The actual number of slaves involved in the industry far exceeded those accounted for in the census because more than 50 percent of the slaves were hired in any given year and were, therefore, transients who toiled for a time at the saltworks and then moved on to other kinds of labor.[54]

Like manufacturers back east, Kanawha salt producers employed slaves in all phases of the production process, from the most skilled to the common laborer. One salt furnace in 1853 deployed its slave force in the following manner: fourteen coal diggers, five wheelers, four haulers, three kettle tenders, one or two cleaners, six steam engineers, two salt lifters-wheelers, seven general laborers and packers, two blacksmiths, one cook, and one "negro man sort of manager."[55] Saltworks operated around the clock, six days a week, and manufacturers organized the labor force around the task system, supplemented by monetary incentives to encourage slaves to work during periods when they would otherwise be at rest. Despite the task system, a managerial hierarchy was maintained to oversee operations. White men usually occupied the supervisory positions such as general overseer, boss kettle tender, coal-bank manager, and occasionally a well manager, but slave managers were not unheard of. In one company inventory, for example, Simon, a 33-year old slave, was described as "keen, stout; salt well tuber, engine repairer, salt-maker and overseer—experienced, skillful, and industrious."[56]

Slave families did exist in the industry among workers owned by the companies, especially those held by the larger, better-financed companies. Some salt masters combined industrial and agricultural enterprises. Dickinson & Shrewsbury, for example, effectively integrated an extensive industrial enterprise with equally developed agricultural operations that included some of the most fertile land in the Kanawha Valley, and required the work of many slaves. The company achieved great flexibility by shifting its slaves from factory to farm as need required,[57] but also maintained a social structure under which slave families were possible. Slave family life at the southern mountain periphery is another of the many related topics that remain unexplored.

Most occupations associated with the manufacture of salt were dangerous, coal mining being the most hazardous. Coal mining was almost completely integrated into salt manufacturing, which used coal to fire the evaporation furnaces. In one year's time the Kanawha saltworks consumed 5.6 million bushels of coal. Only two coal companies in the county were independent operators in 1850.[58] Many, probably most, of the hired slaves came from eastern Virginia, and living so far from their masters, leases often stated that the hired slave was not to work in the mines. The multitude of court suits to recover damages for injured or killed slaves is stark testimony that many salt makers disregarded leases restricting the use of slaves in the coal mines. Danger lurked at every turn near the furnaces, too, where steam machinery and hot brine exacted a heavy toll for mistakes. Another danger confronting the owner of slaves hired to the Kanawha saltworks was the loss of their property by absconding. Flight to freedom was a real possibility, as the slave coffles trekked their way over the sparsely populated and rugged Appalachians; others waited until they arrived to run away. The Kanawha salines were a short overland flight from freedom in Ohio; some slaves stowed away on the many riverboats which plied the Ohio River watershed.[59] Hired bondsmen from the Piedmont, in particular, might have further reason for lighting out for freedom: Although by all accounts food was not strictly controlled, and ample food was provided to keep up the energy levels for these hard working laborers, the major study of this industry contends that separation from their master translated into harsher use by salt manufacturers.[60] Antebellum Kanawha salt manufacturers and coal mine operators faced a constant shortage of labor, but they generally agreed with their eastern counterparts that slaves were preferred to white workers.[61]

The comparatively small slave population in the mountains is a demographic fact, but that does not mean that slavery can be shrugged off as peripheral to Appalachian society. In fact, nothing better illustrates that southern Appalachia was indeed southern, than its reflexive adoption of southern values and readiness to shift to slave labor whenever the opportunity presented itself. Railroads demonstrate this inclination clearly, for in nearly every part of the southern mountains that was penetrated by railroads before the Civil War, commercial agriculture, towns, industry, and slavery soon followed. In fact, the railroads themselves were built by slaves.

Railroads first entered Appalachia in the 1850s, linking the remote backcountry with the urban commercial-industrial centers. When the Virginia and Tennessee Railroad (V&T) reached Bristol, Tennessee in 1856, for example, it precipitated the commercialization of regional agriculture, and spawned dramatic town and commercial development in the southwestern Virginia countryside. Bristol is perched at the northern end of the Great, or Tennessee, Valley which runs in a northeastern and southwestern direction between the Smoky Mountains and the Cumberland Mountains. Bristol also became the eastern terminus of the East Tennessee and Virginia Railroad, which provided through connections not only to the markets of the South, but also for its institutions and ideology.[62]

Appalachia generally is thought to have been settled by small yeoman farmers whose Jeffersonian republicanism made them hostile to slavery and antagonistic toward the planter elite. Recent studies examining landownership in the mountains, however, conclude that fewer than 50 percent of those defining themselves as farmers in the 1850s actually owned their own land, that a relatively small minority owned a disproportionate share of the land and wealth, and that tenants and laborers made up a group of landless poor nearly equal to the yeomen, anywhere from a third to one half of the population. Hardly the Jeffersonian ideal.[63]

In Southwest Virginia completion of the V&T stimulated a significant 23.5 percent rate of increase in the white population between 1850 and 1860. In making eastern markets accessible, tidewater and piedmont planters, who already owned much of the land, were encouraged to relocate to Southwest Virginia's fertile valleys, bringing with them their families and slaves. Seeds of the institution had been planted earlier, and now southwestern slavery sprouted like a virile weed. When planters put land into cultivation in the 1850s, poor white tenants were replaced by slaves. A dramatic rise in property values and taxes, which increased 62.6 percent during the 1850s, sparked another migration: retreat of the landless and poor farmers deeper into the rugged plateau, outmigration to the west, or abandonment of the land for wage labor.[64]

African Americans had been present in southwestern Virginia since the founding of the nation, but by 1860, after the arrival of the V&T, the number of slaves in Southwest Virginia had grown to 19,026, or 10.3 percent of the population. Conversely, Northwest Virginia also received a railroad in the 1850s, the Baltimore & Ohio, but it connected Wheeling to Baltimore and the Midwest rather than Richmond and the South, and the number of slaves in that section declined from nearly 20 percent in 1850 to only 2.5 percent of the population in 1860. Slavery in the mountains expanded with the penetration of the railroads linked to the South because that is where market-related activity was concentrated, particularly in the valleys, where slave-based agriculture was possible.[65] The railroad also stimulated industrial growth in Southwest Virginia, such as the copper industry in Carroll County, which prompted a spurt in the number of slave workers during the 1850s. Slaves toiled in a greater diversity of tasks in addition to farming, such as various service jobs associated with the numerous hot spring resorts, as skilled artisans, in commerce, as well as in the mines and foundries. For the railroads they laid track, and worked as train crewmen, freight hands, and brakemen. In 1856, 435 of the V&T's 643 workers were hired slaves who worked alongside European immigrants.[66]

The diversity of mountain slavery suggested by the Southwest Virginia case is amplified by the slave experience in western North Carolina where, unlike Southwest Virginia, agriculture simply was not a viable means for acquiring wealth. Mountain elites there combined farming with business or the professions; they were the 10 percent of the population who were slave owners. In these 15 counties slaves made up 10.2 percent of the total population in 1860.[67] Appalachia was a major livestock-raising region of antebellum America, and an entire economy grew up around getting livestock to market. The major north-south valley between the Smoky Mountains and the Blue Ridge Mountains was still without railroad service in the 1850s, so stock were driven on the hoof over the turnpike that followed this valley south into South Carolina and Georgia. Professional drovers collected herds of livestock at strategic gathering points in the valley system and followed the turnpikes to market. Along the way, every ten miles or so, "drover stands" were established to provide food and lodging for the drovers, and food and water for the stock. On the Buncumbe Turnpike hundreds of thousands of stock passed annually, perhaps more. One stand reportedly fed ninety thousand hogs in a single month.[68] Stock from western North Carolina were sent primarily to the plantation world of South Carolina and Georgia. Like residents of Southwest Virginia whose ideology and economic fate were tied to the South by the railroad, western North Carolinians were tied to the plantation world of the Deep South by mountain turnpikes.

Although Appalachian residents preferred union to secession, they were generally prompted by their belief that states' rights were more likely to be achieved through the constitution rather than secession. Only in a few localized sections was slavery ever seriously challenged. The demands of small holders in the mountains of Carolina meant that slaves were occupied in a wide variety of activities. A breakdown of the economic activities of western North Carolina slave holders in 1860 suggests this diversity: professional, 32 percent; merchant-commercial, 68 percent; real estate/mining, 24 percent; hotel management/tourism, 12 percent; agriculture alone, 3 percent. Most slave owners combined another profession with farming.[69] Slaves also worked in brick yards, ironworks, and at carriage, furniture, and tobacco factories. Mining engaged the largest number of nonagricultural slaves after gold was discovered in 1828 and the ensuing rush saw a dramatic growth of bondsmen in the gold district. Burke County, the center of the gold rush, alone had five thousand slaves in 1833, twice its slave population prior to the strike, as eastern masters and local masters sent their slaves to work sinking shafts and along the streams.[70] From the 1830s through the 1850s gold and copper mining in the western North Carolina and eastern Tennessee mountains employed thousands of slaves.[71]

CONCLUSION

Even though scholarship on slavery in the mountains is seriously limited, we can come to some generalizations based on the few studies that are available. Slavery at the periphery was less restrictive, and master-slave relationships were more relaxed. Frederick Law Olmsted reported that slaves in the mountains lived more like free laborers than slaves of the plantation South, and enjoyed much greater freedom of movement.[72] To the extent this was true, the reasons, according to historian John Inscoe, lie in the same demographic and economic factors that set slavery apart from its lowland equivalent. Slave work involved diverse nonagricultural tasks; small slave holdings led to more intimacy and personal association between master and slave; the low proportion of slaves in the general population posed less of a threat to whites; flexible work assignments were necessary, and it was necessary for slaves to move about more freely in order to make the system work.[73] Again, the deeper structures of labor had a dramatic impact on slave life.

Competition between slave and free white labor in the factories of the core regions of the South undoubtedly exacerbated race relations and intensified racism among white workers. On the issue of racism among white mountaineers, however, interpretations seem to be directly contradictory. Carter Woodson, for example, maintained that there was more social harmony between the races than elsewhere in the South, but W. J. Cash argued that the "lack of contact" between white mountaineers and blacks intensified their hostility toward African Americans to such extremes that "it was worth a black man's life to venture into many mountain sections."[74] These extremes suggest that racism in the mountains probably ran the full spectrum, but it seems reasonable to assume that racism and attitudes toward slavery were no more enlightened in the mountains than elsewhere in the South. White mountain farmers who condemned slavery generally did so because it enabled lowland planters to dominate the state government at the expense of the highlanders. Belief in the sanctity of property rights, however, generally prevented Appalachians from condemning slave owning and demanding abolition. In fact, the opinion was widespread that slavery was an acceptable system of race control. Both in western North Carolina and southwestern Virginia the predominant factor shaping favorable attitudes toward slavery among many mountaineers was their dependency on the South for economic prosperity. Farm and industrial products from the Appalachian periphery were dependent on the slave regime, and this dependency forged their regional identity as southerners.[75]

Notes

1   Robert S. Starobin, *Industrial Slavery in the Old South* (New York: Oxford University Press, 1970), 4–5.
2   Ibid., 8.
3   Ibid., 9.
4   Ibid., 11–12.
5   E. M. Lander Jr., "Slave Labor in South Carolina Cotton Mills," *Journal of Negro History* 38 (April 1953): 161–73; Clement, Eaton *The Growth of Southern Civilization, 1790–1860* (New York: Harper & Row, Publishers, 1961), chap. 10.
6   Joseph Clarke Robert, *The Tobacco Kingdom: Plantation, Market, and Factory in Virginia and North Carolina, 1800–1860* (Gloucester, Mass.: Peter Smith, 1965, originally 1938), 197; Starobin, *Industrial Slavery,* 17; Richard, C. Wade *Slavery in the Cities: The South, 1820–1860* (New York: Oxford University Press, 1964), 22, 33–35; Eaton, *The Growth of Southern Civilization,* 229–30.
7   James F. Hopkins, *A History of the Hemp Industry in Kentucky* (Lexington: University of Kentucky Press, 1951), 4.
8   G. Melvin Herndon, "A War-Inspired Industry: The Manufacture of Hemp in Virginia during the Revolution." *Virginia Magazine of History and Biography* 74 (July 1966), 301–11; Louis Morton, *Robert Carter of Nomini Hall: A Virginia Tobacco Planter of the Eighteenth Century* (Charlottesville: University Press of Virginia, 1941), chap. 7; Eaton, *The Growth of Southern Civilization,* 239–40.
9   Marcus Wilson Jernegan, *Laboring and Dependent Classes in Colonial America, 1607–1783* (Chicago: University of Chicago Press, 1931), 13, 23; Starobin, *Industrial Slavery,* 19–21; *DeBow's Review and Industrial Resources, Statistics, etc., of the United States and More Particularly of the Southern & Western States* (New York: Augustus M. Kelly, 1966), 1846, 331 and 1853, 611.
10   Frederick Law Olmsted, *A Journey in the Seaboard Slave States* (New York: Dix & Edwards, 1856), 351.
11   Starobin, *Industrial Slavery,* 27.
12   Ibid., 25–26; Olmsted, *Journey,* 149–156; John Hebron Moore, "Simon Gray, Riverman: A Slave Who Was Almost Free," *Mississippi Valley Historical Review* 49 (December 1962): 472–84; Jeffrey A. Drobney, *Lumbermen and Log Sawyers: Life Labor, and Culture in the North Florida Timber Industry, 1830-1930* (Macon, Ga.: Mereer University Press, 1997); Nollie Hickman, *Mississippi Harvest: Lumbering in the Longleaf Pine Belt, 1846-1915* (University, Miss.: University of Mississippi Press, 1962).
13   Ronald L. Lewis, *Coal, Iron, and Slaves: Industrial Slavery in Maryland and Virginia, 1715–1865* (Westport, Conn.: Greenwood Press, 1979), 10.
14   Starobin, *Industrial Slavery,* 15.
15   Lewis, *Coal, Iron, and Slaves,* 6–7.
16   Wade, *Slavery in the Cities,* chaps. 2 and 5.
17   Starobin, *Industrial Slavery,* chap. 2.
18   Ibid., 100–01.
19   Ira Berlin and Philip D. Morgan, eds. *Cultivation and Culture: Labor and the Shaping of Slave Life in the Americas* (Charlottesville: University Press of Virginia, 1993), 1; Peter Koichin, *American Slavery, 1619-1877* (New York: Hill and Wang, 1993).
20   Berlin and Morgan, *Cultivation and Culture,* 3–4.

21 Ibid., 14–15.
22 Kenneth M. Stampp, *The Peculiar Institution: Slavery in the Ante-Bellum South* (New York: Alfred A. Knopf, 1956); Stanley M. Elkins, *Slavery: A Problem in American Institutional and Intellectual Life* (Chicago: University of Chicago Press, 1959); Charles B. Dew, *Bond of Iron: Master and Slave at Buffalo Fo,* (New York: W.W. Nov. 1994).
23 Lewis, *Coal, Iron, and Slaves,* 31–34, 67, 192; Dew, Bond of Iron, passion.
24 Starobin, *Industrial Slavery,* 26; Olmsted, *Journey,* pp.338–51.
25 Robert B. Outland, II, "Slavery, Work, and the Geography of the North Carolina Naval Stores Industry, 1835–1860," *Journal of Southern History* 62 (February 1996): 27–56.
26 Ibid.,
27 Ibid.,
28 Frederick F. Siegel, *The Roots of Southern Distinctiveness: Tobacco and Society in Danville, Virginia, 1780–1865* (Chapel Hill: University of North Carolina Press, 1987), 123.
29 Ibid., 130–132.
30 Wade, *Slavery in the Cities,* 262.
31 Lewis, *Coal, Iron, and Slaves,* 223.
32 Ibid; Eugene D. Genovese, *The Political Economy of Slavery: Studies in the Economy and Society of the Slave South* (New York: Random House, 1965), 181, 221.
33 Lewis, *Coal, Iron, and Slaves,* 224; Thomas P. Jones, M.D., "The Progress of Manufactures and Internal Improvements in the United States and Particularly on the Advantages to be Derived from the Employment of Slaves in the Manufacturing of Cotton and Other Goods." originally published in *American Farmer* 9 (30 November 1827): 290–91, and reproduced in *Textile History Review* 3 (July 1962), 156; Genovese, *Political Economy,* 222. For an assessment of the profitability of slavery by two economists, see Fred Bateman and Thomas Weiss, *A Deplorable Scarcity: The Failure of Insustrialization in the Slave Economy* (Chapel Hill: University of North Carolina Press, 1981).
34 Lewis, *Coal, Iron, and Slaves,* 224; Genovese, *Political Economy,* 224–225, 231, 233; Robert, *The Tobacco Kingdom,* 203.
35 Lewis, *Coal, Iron, and Slaves,* 224; Kathleen Bruce, *Virginia Iron Manufacture in the Slave Era* (New York: Augustus M. Kelly, 1960, originally 1930), 252 n. 89.
36 *DeBow's Review and Industrial Resources,* 1850, 518.
37 *Charters and Ordinances of Richmond* (Richmond: Virginia State Library, 1859) 196–97.
38 *DeBow's Review and Industrial Resources,* 1852, 42–49; Genovese, *Political Economy,* 227–28.
39 *DeBow's Review and Industrial Resources,* 1850, 519–520.
40 Lewis, *Coal, Iron, and Slaves,* 231; Patricia A. Schechter, "Free and Slave Labor in the Old South: The Tredegar Ironworkers' Strike of 1847," *Labor History* 35 (Spring 1994): 165–86; *Richmond Times and Compiler,* May 28, 1847.
41 *DeBow's Review and Industrial Resources,* 1851, 130.
42 Randall M. Miller, "The Fabric of Control: Slavery in Antebellum Southern Textile Mills." *Business History Review* 55 (Winter 1981): 473–74.
43 Ibid., 477–79.
44 Ibid., 479–80.
45 Ibid., 480.
46 William G. Frost, "Our Contemporary Ancestors in the Southern Mountains," *Atlantic Monthly* 83 (March 1899): 313; Horace Kephart, *Our Southern Highlanders* (New York: Macmillan, 1913), rev. ed. 1941, 439.

47 Carter G. Woodson, "Freedom and Slavery in Appalachian America," *Journal of Negro History* 1 (April 1916): 132–50. A recent addition to the literature is John C. Inscoe, ed., *Appalachians and Race: The Mountain South from Slavery to Segregation* (Lexington: University Press of Kentucky, 2001). A forthcoming book on Appalachian slavery by Wilma A. Dunaway will go far toward redressing this lack of scholarship.

48 James B. Murphy, "Slavery and Freedom in Appalachia: Kentucky as a Demographic Case Study," *Register of the Kentucky Historical Society* 80 (Spring 1982): 153–54; William H. Turner and Edward J. Cabbell, eds., *Blacks in Appalachia* (Lexington: University Press of Kentucky, 1985), 238.

49 Murphy, "Slavery and Freedom," 156.

50 Wilma A. Dunaway, *The First American Frontier: Transition to Capitalism in Southern Appalachia, 1700–1860* (Chapel Hill: University of North Carolina Press, 1996), 157–64.

51 Ibid., 136–42.

52 Ibid., 145.

53 Ibid., 175–77; John E. Stealey III, *The Antebellum Kanawha Salt Business and Western Markets* (Lexington: University Press of Kentucky, 1993), chap 12–13. For an excellent study of slavery and the salt industry in Clay County, Kentucky, see Dwight B. Billings and Kathleen M. Blee, *The Road to Poverty: The Making of Wealth and Hardship in Appalachia* (Cambridge: Cambridge University Press, 2000).

54 Stealey, *Salt Business*, 133–34, 141.

55 Ibid., 134–35.

56 Ibid., 136.

57 Ibid., 141.

58 Dunaway, *American Frontier*, 181; James T. Laing, "The Early Development of the Coal Industry in the Western Counties of Virginia, 1800–1865," *West Virginia History* 27 (January 1966): 144–55; Otis K. Rice, "Coal Mining in the Kanawha Valley to 1861: A View of Industrialization in the Old South," *Journal of Southern History* 31 (November 1965): 393–416.

59 Dunaway, *American Frontier*, 181; Stealey, *Salt Business*, 142–46.

60 Stealey, *Salt Business*, 150.

61 Ibid., 156.

62 Kenneth W. Noe, *Southwest Virginia's Railroad: Modernization and the Sectional Crisis* (Urbana: University of Illinois Press, 1994), 59.

63 Noe, *Southwest Virginia's Railroad*, 31–52; Dunaway, *American Frontier*, 87–121.

64 Noe, *Southwest Virginia's Railroad*, 31–52; W. Todd Groce, "The Social Origins of East Tennessee's Confederate Leadership," in *The Civil War in Appalachia: Collected Essays*, 30–54, edited by Kenneth W. Noe and Shannon H. Wilson, 34–43.

65 Noe, *Southwest Virginia's Railroad*, 69–70.

66 Ibid., 82.

67 John C. Inscoe, *Mountain Masters, Slavery, and the Sectional Crisis in Western North Carolina* (Knoxville: University of Tennessee Press, 1989), 62.

68 Ibid., 48.

69 Ibid., 62.

70 Ibid., 70–72; David Williams, *The Georgia Gold Rush: Twenty-Niners, Cherokees, and Gold Fever* (Columbia: University of South Carolina Press, 1993), 84–88.

71 Inscoe, *Mountain Masters*, 70–72, 79.

72 Frederick Law Olmsted, *A Journey in the Back Country in the Winter of 1853–54* (New York: Mason Bros., 1860, rpt. ed., G. P. Putnam, 1907), 226–227; Inscoe, *Mountain Masters*, 89, 107–8.

73 Inscoe, *Mountain Masters*, 104–5. Characterizing the severity of slavery in Appalachia varies according to the kinds of work in which slaves were employed. Billings and Blee found that slavery in the Kentucky salt industry was "extremely brutal," and there is "little evidence that Clay County's slaves actually fared better than southern plantation slaves" (*Road to Poverty*, 210–11).

74 Woodson, "Freedom and Slavery," 132–50; for the full quotation see W. J. Cash, *The Mind of the South* (New York: Knopf, 1941), 219.

75 Inscoe, *Mountain Masters*, 110, 114; Noe, *Southwest Virginia's Railroad*, 7–8.

CHAPTER 3

BLACK LIFE ON THE MISSISSIPPI: AFRICAN AMERICAN STEAMBOAT LABORERS AND THE WORK CULTURE OF ANTEBELLUM WESTERN STEAMBOATS

THOMAS C. BUCHANAN

For African American men the attraction of Mississippi River steamboat work was intense. The slave Josiah Henson remembered that working on the Mississippi was a "sunny spot" in his life and was "one of his most treasured recollections."[1] William Wells Brown found work in a steamboat cabin "pleasant" especially when compared to work on shore.[2] Sella Martin "very much desired" river work while Madison Henderson "preferred" to work on Mississippi steamers.[3] Free blacks such as Amos Warrick, James Seward, and Charles Brown all sought the benefits of steamboat labor.

For most African Americans, however, working on these technological marvels was not possible. Women were nearly entirely excluded. A few slave and free black women found employment as chambermaids on the boats, but for the most part the steamboat workforce was a male world. But even most slave and free black men could only dream of steaming the western rivers on the spectacular wooden boats that dominated the landscape of the Old South. While hundreds of thousands of slaves worked in the states of Mississippi, Louisiana, Arkansas, Tennessee, and Missouri, only three or four thousand worked at any one time on riverboats. Most steamboat jobs were filled by native whites, Irish, and Germans—though in the deep South slaves and free blacks often dominated crews. Thus black rivermen's distinctive identity was based on a very unusual experience. But the envious gaze from field hands, domestic servants, farmers, and urbanities, suggests the broader importance of this small occupational group.

For urban slaves and free blacks the chances of working on a steamboat were much greater than for rural African Americans. Steamboat workers were part of the urban economy; they lived in cities, got jobs in cities, and enjoyed leisure time in cities. Steamboat owners found that time spent docked along urban levees was an ideal opportunity to hire laborers. It was in cities that they could find both the necessary quantity of labor and the specialized skills necessary to run their businesses. In this way steamboats became an important extension of African American urban communities along the Mississippi River system.

The urban-based river industry fostered a variety of affirmative identities and resistant actions among its black workers. Personal movement transformed urban slaves into cosmopolitan inland maritime workers with opportunities for independence and freedom. Steamboats allowed slaves and free blacks to move across hundreds of miles of territory, thereby defying the master classes' attempts to control slaves' mental horizons. Slaves often lived in virtual freedom, paying their masters a monthly fee for the right to hire. This mobility allowed river hands to achieve various elements of both white working-class and middle-class ideals of manhood while allowing for distinctive expressions of black masculinity as well. Steamboats gave slaves opportunities to make and spend money, for public cultural expression, for illicit communication, for informal trade, and for escapes. This chapter will pay particular attention to how African Americans claimed manhood by using the river to maintain touch with family members over long distances. But these opportunities and gender identities came at a severe cost: harsh conditions and physical abuse. Black life on the Mississippi was created in this juxtaposition of extreme exploitation and the opportunities of African American workers.

By analyzing the neglected work culture of antebellum steamboats this chapter broadens our understanding of African American work environments in the antebellum period. In particular it provides further insight into the ways in which the maritime world shaped the world of slavery and black identity. W. Jeffrey Bolster has rightly pointed out the ways in which Atlantic ships were crucial to the formation of black masculinity. But the importance of these workers to black communities was not restricted to port cities on the ocean. St. Louis, Memphis, Nashville, Baton Rouge, and Cincinnati were just a few of the places in the growing West that were intimately tied to the maritime river world. Black men in these cities, and in southern plantation districts, viewed the rivers much as African American men on the eastern seaboard viewed the oceans. They were places of opportunity. But as Marcus Rediker reminds us, shipping has long been the sight of pronounced class conflict and struggle.[4]

The racial and gender identities African Americans created on riverboats contrasted considerably with those they were able to fashion on plantations. Outside the confines of the slaves' quarters, bondsmen had limited ability to assert the dominant ideals of patriarchal manhood. Slave men were uable to achieve independence from other men or to maintain control over their domestic lives, powers that were broadly associated with dominant constructions of masculinity in the period. Free black Americans, as James Oliver Horton demonstrates, had only slightly more opportunity to assert an affirmative masculine identity.[5] Free blacks were denied the political rights of manhood, were relegated to the lowest class of menial jobs, and were unable to free black women from work outside the home. While slave and free black men found numerable ways to assert themselves within the constraints that surrounded them, and were far from stripped of their manhood, the opportunity to assert their masculinity was of considerable importance in their overall struggle to resist exploitation.

Both the opportunities and the oppression of the African American experience on Mississippi riverboats were intimately rooted in the labor process. There were two basic types of male steamboat workers: those who worked in the cabin and those who worked on deck. African Americans were excluded from officers' positions, which were held nearly entirely by native whites or European immigrant labor. On deck they filled jobs as roustabouts, deckhands, and firemen. In the cabin they worked as waiters, cooks, stewards, barbers, and porters. Cabin workers cultivated middle-class identities and distinguished themselves from the rough culture of masculinity that flourished on deck. Black stewards and barbers, in particular, were some of the most esteemed men in African American western communities and they often aspired to a refined sensibility. While boundaries between the deck and cabin crews were far from rigid, and men did move between these crews, steamboats reflected two different classes of black labor and thus two distinct variations of black masculinity.

Deck workers were movers of commodities. Their tasks varied depending upon whether they were steaming along the rivers, when there was less to do, or docked at a levee landing, when excruciating physical labor filled their jobs. Firemen's tasks required heroic bursts of energy. Hired or leased by engineers, who supervised them on board, their job consisted of two related processes: carrying wood or coal onto the boat from shore or adjacent flatboats and then, once underway, feeding the fuel into the mouths of the furnaces.[6] During refueling, firemen walked ashore, under the driving eyes of officers, climbed the levee embankment, picked-up logs four or five feet in length, and then hustled back across the narrow boat staging. They then deposited the wood crossways in piles surrounding the fire pits at mid-boat. When steamboats were at full capacity these piles surrounded the boilers and often rose high up onto the guards.[7] Firemen sometimes piled twenty to forty cords of wood on deck during a single stop. Men "firing" would throw logs into the furnaces, making sure to stir the embers to increase efficiency. Traveler Frederika Bremer watched as blacks "naked to their middle" hurled with "vigorous arms" wood into boat furnaces.[8] Charles Latrobe watched as "with a thousand grimaces" African American firemen "grasped the logs and whirled them into the brazing throat of the furnace."[9] In addition to these main tasks, engineers also required firemen to haul away ashes and to clean out the boilers which frequently became filled with river sediment.[10]

Deckhands were similarly bound to backbreaking tasks, though slaves and free blacks on Mississippi steamers typically filled fewer of these jobs. Under the direct supervision of the mate, and on call at every landing, they spent considerable time in the unusually small holds of western Steamboats.[11] One captain claimed that the deckhands' job was "to store the freight, and take care of it in the hold" and also believed that it was "their duty to get it out of the hold, and then help the roustabouts carry it about the deck. . . ."[12] "Cutting cotton," a term used by African Americans to describe loading and packing bales of cotton on southern rivers, was a particularly important part of deckhands' work.[13]

Until the late 1840s this work was done without the help of steam powered lifts. Considering that many steamboats had holds that could store produce weighing one hundred tons or more, the amount of lifting involved in the job was truly prodigious.[14] In addition to these main tasks, deckhands also cleaned the deck, pumped leaking water out of the hold, called out "soundings" to the pilot and took turns as night watchmen.

Roustabouts labored as freight pickers. Slaves, particularly on deep South steamers, frequently filled these jobs. Under the supervision of the mate, their tasks consisted almost entirely of carrying freight on and off steamers. Mates generally instructed them to load from the "inside-out" and unload in the reverse pattern. In performing their duties, roustabouts frequently worked alongside both dock stevedores, whom officers sometimes contracted with to help load and unload in the major western cities, and plantation slaves, who hauled produce down to rural levees and sometimes helped in loading the boats as well. As one deep South plantation slave recalled, "We lived clos' to a boat landin' an' my father helped to unload de supplies from de boats when we wuz not workin' in de fiel's."[15]

These duties required varying work rhythms. On smaller boats with fewer workers and less cargo, roustabouts were frequently on duty at each landing. On larger boats the crew was divided into two watches. These were organized either by time (six hours on, six hours off) or task (one watch for each side of the boat). All roustabouts were "on call" for large loads. Whatever the specific arrangement, the work was nearly continuous as boats frequently stopped to load and unload on their way up and down river. One traveler reported that the "negro boatmen" were "hardly ever . . . permitted to sleep undisturbed upon their own beds, the cotton bales, and at all times are they summoned by the perpetually ringing bells to their severe labor."[16] Another watched them run ashore "like so many ants" at each landing.[17]

While the work of roustabouts was predominantly physical labor, the specific knowledge necessary to complete it varied as much as the products they had to load. The labor was collective. Loading cotton bales, which often weighed five hundred pounds apiece and totaled thousands of bales when fully loaded, required the labor of two men, each with the help of cotton-hooks that one traveler labeled "the unmistakable badges of their profession."[18] Making sure not to wet the cotton, which doubled its weight, the men rolled the bales across the gangway, and pushed them into place—often high over the guards—to locations assigned by the mate. Roustabouts reflected on this process when they sang that "we gwine to roll de cotton way up ten tiers high."[19] From another perspective, up high in the cabin, one passenger commented that while it "was a great bore" to the traveler in a hurry "to those who can take pleasure in witnessing athletic feats, or have a taste for the picturesque, it is full of interest."[20]

Using labor processes distinct to each product roustabouts stored other commodities on board. Barrels of molasses were rolled on assembly-line style. One at a time, huge sacks of cotton seed were lifted by two men onto a third man's back who then carried the sack on board. Boxes of dry goods were heaved onto the boats. Hogs were slung over the shoulder, while teams of roustabouts drove larger animals on board. One traveler watched as roustabouts slowly persuaded mules, by pushing and pulling them, to cross a narrow plank bridging the boat and the embankment.[21] Such tasks epitomized the difficulty of steamboat work. One slave who worked in the deck crew recalled that it took two or three years before he mastered such tasks.[22]

A more refined, middle-class masculine ethos pervaded black cabin crew workers. These service positions were predominately held by free blacks and native whites—a marked contrast to the mix of European immigrants and slaves who filled out deck crews. Black cabin workers were often members of the antebellum black elite. Working as they did in the elite culture of the steamboat cabin, amidst ornate stairways and well-appointed main cabins, they held some of the best jobs open to African Americans in the period. Free black stewards, waiters, and barbers were often leaders in their home communities. They were what historians have called "masculine achievers," men who focused on advancement and success in the growing market economy. While cabin work was also associated with the feminine laborers of black chambermaids, men succeeded in forging an assertive masculine identity on steamboats, based upon their considerable earnings and refined deportment. With their respectable clothes and their propensity to earn wages, tips, and other money, cabin workers were the envy of many people on shore. These qualities made them desirable marriage partners, a fact that further bolstered their manly status.

Waiters had jobs similar to those held by African Americans in the dining rooms of the West's finest hotels. William Wells Brown stated the job's requirements simply enough when he wrote, "my employment on board was to wait on gentlemen."[23] Under the immediate supervision of the steward, who generally hired between two and five "cabin boys," waiters did numerable tasks. They filled drinks, served food, prepared the table, filled the coal stoves that heated the cabin, erected cots for cabin passengers when staterooms were overbooked, ran errands for provisions or other goods, and helped cooks with washing dishes or slaughtering game. They were also expected to keep the cabin immaculate.[24]

Passengers frequently commented on the details of slave and free black waiters' jobs. Charles Latrobe watched two "supple-limbed black boys" perform some of these tasks. He watched as they drew out the long 20-foot folding table and covered it with cloth and silver, a task that took nearly an hour to complete. After waiting on passengers during the meal, they cleared the dishes, and then placed the sliding table together again "straining with might and main till the ends met." Latrobe commented that "before you could have believed it possible" the two were at it again for the next meal.[25] A. Oakey Hall also watched African American waiters work. Early in the morning he saw "a heavy-eyelided negro" sweeping the cabin and another "shaking the large cabin bell," an activity, Hall complained, which was "intended to diminish a passenger's quota of sleep."[26] He also saw "other sleepy waiters" emerging "from unknown parts of the boat" who worked on the "complicated machinery of the table." Minutes later the passengers crowded around watching "with stomachic [sic] interest the evolutions of the waiters. They anathematize the laziness of this one, or commend the briskness of that one." They watched as one "cabin boy" put bread on each plate using a fork and a "dexterous" forefinger, as another came with a coffee urn and as still others followed with more beverages and main courses. After the waiters placed all dishes on the table passengers slowly "edged up" and the meal began.[27]

On the larger boats African Americans often filled jobs as cabin watchmen. Watchmen worked all night. Mates required watchmen to walk inside through both the ladies' and gentlemen's areas of the cabin, and also to walk outside on the guards which ran along the edges of the boiler deck. In making these rounds they watched for fires and other hazards while the officers slept. In addition to these duties, boat watchmen were also sometimes required to wake during the daytime meals to trim the lamps in the cabin. Watchmen who shipped under such an agreement were able to sleep for only a few hours between meals.[28]

Porters were responsible for all baggage checked on board. Under the direction of the clerk, porters were the roustabouts of the cabin. They received baggage from passengers, forwarded nonpassenger freight to the clerk for entering into the boat's freight book, stored baggage in the lobby at one end of the cabin, issued baggage claim tickets, and assisted passengers in carrying baggage off steamboats. Like their deck crew counterparts, their job was often momentarily finished when the boat was in motion. They had to be on call, however, at each country landing as steamers made their way up and down river.[29]

In cramped kitchens, often tucked behind the stairwell on the main deck, African American cooks performed the onerous tasks of planning, preparing, and cooking three meals a day for the cabin passengers and crew.[30] While the rich and varied cuisine of steamboats was a distinguishing characteristic of western travel, producing it took long, tedious hours. Working sometimes 18 hours a day in searing heat, cooks labored in slightly staggered shifts from three o'clock in the morning, at the start of breakfast prep, to mid-evening, when the final dinner pan was washed. On smaller vessels the first and second cook completed these tasks while on the larger vessels three or four cooks were employed. In all cases the first cook managed meal preparation and worked with the steward to obtain provisions. He also hired, fired, and paid—from wages given to him by the captain—the rest of the kitchen crew. On the larger boats, the kitchen crew was expanded to include a cook specializing in baking bread and pastries and a third cook, or "slush," who was given the most menial tasks. Third cooks lighted the fires, washed the pans, and created the pool of leftovers that were given to the crew to eat.[31]

While first cooks were esteemed members of the African American community, the most sought after job among African Americans was the steward's post. A supervisory job, but one that still held the crucial classification of "service," this was the most prestigious position that African Americans could hope to obtain. African American waiters often labored for years in the cabin, hoping to earn the favor the captain and be hired as steward—the "captain of the cabin."[32] Historian Carter G. Woodson called them the "fortunate few" among river laborers.[33]

The job was multifaceted and required a broad range of skills. Captains required stewards to procure necessary foodstuffs from port cities as well as to coordinate the purchase of additional foodstuffs during trips. These tasks took them off the boat and into a variety of settings. Well-networked stewards knew wholesale grocers and rural planters as well as foodstuff providers within the slave community. When underway, stewards' responsibilities changed. They managed waiters and cooks and to a lesser extent they supervised the other cabin workers. Stewards watched over meals, planned leisure activities, made sure passengers adhered to the cabin rules, and booked travelers. Free black riverhand James Thomas commented that "the colored Steward was told to spread himself and spare neither pains nor money to make them [the passengers] comfortable."[34]

African Americans filled most of the jobs as barbers on the larger river packets. Four of the five barbers that census taker Ed Mulligan recorded on St. Louis's docked steamboats in 1850 were free blacks.[35] This job differed from other types of African American cabin labor in that barbers were independent proprietors and were not on the clerk's payroll. They worked in small rented shops, generally at one end of the cabin, where they cut hair for fees and tips. James Thomas, who often shipped as a steamboat barber, recalled "in antebellum times, when the large number of steamboats needed barbers, the shop keepers had hard work getting men to stick."[36] William Johnson, the famous free black barber and diarist from Natchez, often lost workers to steamboats. In 1850, he remarked "my force at present in the shop is myself, Edd and Jim, for Jeff has left and taken the Shop on the S. B. *Natchez* and he is starting now for New Orleans." In another instance he wrote "Claiborne leaves the Trade today to take a Birth on a Steam Boat."[37] Working on a steamboat was a way for young journeymen barbers to see the world while saving money to start a riverside shop.[38]

Whether African Americans worked on deck or in the cabin, they faced dangerous, abusive conditions—often worse than other antebellum workers. Steamboat labor combined the dangerous elements of maritime and early industrial labor in one harrowing workplace. Together boat snags, collisions, and fires killed or injured hundreds of workers a year on the antebellum western rivers.[39] Boiler explosions posed an even greater danger. These explosions became a national issue because so many passengers died. But workers were particularly vulnerable. Newspaper accounts of explosions illustrate that the casualties included a range of workers including members of both the deck and cabin crews.[40] Altogether Robert Starobin estimated that several thousand slave workers lost their lives on riverboats during the antebellum period.[41]

Individual workers faced additional dangers that did not involve the sinking of the entire vessel. On deck, all workers had to endure cold winter weather with less than adequate clothing and no shelter—conditions that often led to frostbite. In other instances, deckhands were injured by slipping into boat holds or were crushed once in them by falling cargo.[42] Unsafe walkways made drowning a continual danger. Roustabouts and firemen commonly slipped on narrow loading planks or on wood piled too close to the guards and then fell into the river.[43] Once in the river many drowned because they could not swim. For the cabin crew, conditions were less dangerous, but mishaps sometimes killed them as well. In one case a cook drowned trying to draw water for his pots.[44]

Disease similarly affected workers. Unrelenting work, primitive medical supplies, constant exposure to the elements, and contact with a variety of unsanitary urban environments led to recurrent illness among river workers. Boat workers spread cholera, which became an increasingly common disease in the Mississippi Valley after the 1830s, as they traveled up and down the western rivers.[45] Other diseases such as measles, malaria, yellow fever, influenza, and colds frequently struck workers and kept them from their jobs for extended periods of time. One steamboat agent wrote to a master that "all of them [the slave workers] were out of health—all had colds and looked badly."[46] Slaves remembered losing considerable time to illness. One slave steamboat worker remembered that "I have been working . . . for more than two years—all the time when I wasn't sick."[47] The slave Judy Taylor remembered losing two months "to sickness" in her last year working on a steamer.[48] The slave Joseph Jackson recalled that "all the time that he wasn't sick" he worked on the *Louisville*."[49] Another slave remembered that "if some disease broke out an' git a heap o' de crew sick we would have a time."[50] While many workers no doubt used the excuse of sickness to avoid labor, such testimony also reflects the grim reality of prevalent sickness among commercial laborers.

Physical coercion was also central to the work culture of steamboats. Slaves faced beatings from officers, passengers, and masters on shore. Mates and engineers used a variety of techniques to discipline the deck crew. Incessant cursing frequently gave way to kicking, pushing, and hitting—often with a piece of lumber picked up from a wood pile. Watching a predominantly African American crew on the upper Mississippi, Arthur Cunynghame remarked that the "general demeanor of the chief mate . . . appeared the reverse of benevolent."[51] Another traveler felt that treatment of slave deckhands on his steamer "lacked humanity."[52]

Cabin workers received less physical abuse from officers than did deck crew members but were more vulnerable to passengers' attacks. One traveler, for instance, witnessed several passengers beat a black porter for accidentally bumping them with a piece of baggage.[53] Being told that he could not sit at the officers' table, another passenger struck an African American steward on the head with his cane. The man yelled, "No black bastard can tell me where to sit!" He then knocked the steward to the floor.[54] In another case, a steward entered a white woman's cabin, which he believed to be unoccupied and nearly started a gunfight.[55] Chambermaids may have received more physical abuse than male workers. Isolated in a male work environment, chambermaids were vulnerable to sexual assault.[56]

Of course, just as their counterparts did on the riverbanks on the Mississippi, African American cabin and deck river workers used a variety of cultural expressions, mostly notably music, to redeem the drudgery of their labor. Officers used cabin workers' musical abilities to entertain passengers and often sought out workers whose skills included musical talents. The former slave Will Long remembered "effen he could, de Cap'n allers hire deck hands an' cabin boys dat could play some kind ob insterment, dat how he git me."[57] One observer remembered "the upstairs band was composed of the barber, the head waiter and one of his subordinates. Laying aside their white jackets and aprons . . .

these gentlemen assumed garments more appropriate to the evening, and an hour or two after the tables had been cleared away took their places in the cabin and struck up a lively tune."[58] Of roustabouts, Charles Latrobe observed that "their ordinary song might be strictly be said to be divided into a rapid alteration of recitative and chorus—the solo singer uttering his part with great volubility and alertness, while the mass instantly fell in with the burden, which consisted of a few words and notes in strictly harmonious unison."[59] African American firemen sang as they loaded wood into the furnaces and African American roustabouts sang while they loaded freight. "The labor . . . is generally performed amid bursts of boisterous merriment, jests, and songs," Latrobe noted.[60] "The loud and plaintive singing of the negroes,"Charles Lanman commented, "gives animation and cheerfulness to all whose lot it is to toil."[61] Lanman no doubt misunderstood the intentions of many of these singers. As one former slave recalled "if they [roustabouts] liked or disliked a boat their song expressed their feelings."[62]

Such expressions of resistance were also evident during moments of leisure. Drinking and gambling were rampant expressions of a culture that remained insulated from middle-class respectability and religious sentiment. Many officers freely gave their slave workers alcohol as an incentive to work thus openly violating laws forbidding such practices.[63] The practice of paying workers in western city saloons further suggests their general tolerance of the habit.[64] One observer of roustabouts claimed he "saw a bottle, out of which the negroes drank."[65] In other cases, African American workers bought alcohol directly from cabin barkeepers. When all else failed, African Americans, like other common laborers, opened kegs of whiskey.[66] Steamboat workers played cards, craps, and other games of chance with abandon. One Kentucky slave, who ran away from his master to work on the river, recalled "I got me a job and worked as a roustabout on a boat where I learned to gamble wid dice. I fought and gambled all up and down de Mississippi River. . . . "[67]

Another important attraction to the steamboat culture for African Americans was the ability to earn money. All black workers—slave and free—earned wages of various kinds. While precise comparison is impossible with existing data, steamboat wages were likely comparable or higher than similar types of riverside labor. With room and board paid during work, free blacks stood to make a relatively decent wage compared to other types of employment. Shipping out on a steamboat generally meant at least two weeks of work and frequently more. This represented a considerable opportunity for free black men who often struggled to find steady work in western cities.[68]

Wage levels varied by position. In the cabin, stewards and first cooks often bargained for wages that were three or four times those procured by common waiters, porters, second cooks or chambermaids. It was not uncommon at mid-century, for instance, for waiters to earn 20 dollars a month while first cooks and stewards earned 50 dollars a month or more. On deck there was less wage variation. Deck workers generally made more wages than common members of the cabin crew but not as much as stewards and skilled cooks. Firemen often earned about 35 dollars a month at mid-century. Roustabouts and deckhands generally contracted for about 30 dollars a month.[69]

In most cases vigilant riverside masters prevented their slaves from keeping the bulk of these wages. In the 1850s, Richard Rudd meticulously recorded the wages paid to him by various boat clerks for each of his leased steamboat slaves.[70] Another traveler near St. Louis reported that masters "called every Saturday evening upon the clerk of the vessel to obtain their wages, amounting to the sum of one dollar per day for the services of each."[71] In other cases, however, slaves received wages themselves and were responsible for giving wages to masters—a practice that encouraged deceptive bargaining with masters.[72] Louis Hughes, a slave who worked near Memphis, commented that "it was common for slaves to be permitted to hire themselves out for wages that they were required to return, in whole or in part, to their masters."[73]

Steamboat workers labored seven days a week. While the extent to which slaves were able to keep regular wages varied, it was fairly common for steamboat slaves to bargain for and retain Sunday wages. Steamboat slaves received Sunday wages either from boat officers during the voyage or from their masters after the boat returned. In an example of the former practice, Frederick Law Olmsted witnessed officers paying slaves a dollar for each Sunday they were on board.[74] In contrast, James Rudd preferred to pay his slaves a lump sum when they returned to port. During the 1850s, for instance, he paid his slaves as much as ten dollars apiece for Sunday wages when they returned to Louisville, following extended periods of steamboat work.[75] Sunday work placed additional burden on black workers, yet it assured that small amounts of cash ended up in the pockets of slave workers.

Tips were an important way in which masculinity was affirmed. Tips allowed slaves and free black cabin workers a measure of financial autonomy—often completely unregulated by masters—that enabled them to participate in the growing American consumer economy. The free black boatmen James Thomas claimed that "at the end of the trip the steward, the waiter, and all who attended the passengers were compensated"[76] Moses Grandy's slave narrative refers to passengers giving from twenty-five cents to a dollar for good service at the end of a trip.[77] Before leaving the boat gentlemen "would call up the steward, press a piece of currency or a gold piece in his hand, call for the cook and do the same. In like manner the boys who had waited on him and his family at the table."[78] A traveler recalled the "universal panacea of a dollar" in effecting good service.[79] Frederick Law Olmsted, traveling in a crowded boat, secured a cabin room cot by tipping. "A waiter, whose good will I had purchased at the supper-table," he recalled, "gave me a hint to secure one of them [a cot] for myself, as soon as they were erected, by putting my hat in it."[80]

Steamboat money translated into considerable consumptive power and status in western cities. Slaves joined free blacks in purchasing a range of personal items. Steamboat slaves reportedly bought their own clothes, shoes, and food when in port.[81] Others spent money on liquor.[82] Much of the rest went to rent. Census returns from Pittsburgh, St. Louis, and New Orleans illustrate that most free black river workers lived in nuclear households. In many cases they were the main wage earners. Cyprian Clamorgan's *The Colored Aristocracy of St. Louis* reveals the importance of steamboat wages to the wealthy free blacks in that city.[83] Slaves spent money on housing as well. While most steamboat slaves lodged with their masters in or near western cities some lived apart from their masters and contracted their own living arrangements. The slave Madison Henderson reportedly spent considerable time living at "Leah's," a black boardinghouse.[84] A slave steamboat barber from Louisville reported that he lived with free people and that "it was just as though I was free."[85] While masters sometimes permitted living out, in other cases masters were frustrated by their slaves' ability to receive steamboat wages and then disappear for months at a time into the urban landscape.[86]

Some steamboat slaves and free blacks also purchased their freedom and the freedom of family members, thus asserting their control over their personal lives. A man known as Cox told the American Freedmen's Inquiry Commission: "I bought myself about thirteen years ago for $2100. I was a steward on the river, and brought them good wages, and that is why they charged me so much. I paid $250 for myself when I hired my time. . . . I have two nephews, one I paid $1200 for, and the other $900."[87] Considering that river stewards often received forty-five dollars a month or more for their services and that Cox paid two hundred and fifty dollars a year to his master, he likely kept part of his wages which, along with tip money, he then used to liberate his family. Another slave recalled "I went to work as steward of a steamboat. At first, I got $35 a month, which raised till I got $100 a month. I paid off Guard [his master] six or seven years after. . . . "[88]

Perhaps the most important elements of the masculine identity of African American steamboat workers stemmed from their multifaceted use of their mobility. While this had various elements, family communication was a particularly important component. While slaves and free blacks actively maintained relationships on shore during their periods of employment in the industry, the river offered many workers the opportunity to reclaim family members torn away by the internal slave trade.[89]

Milton Clarke's narrative provides an example of one river slave who used the river to connect family members. For Clarke, reclaiming family ties was a watershed moment in his life. Until his steamboat lease, his narrative focuses on his Lexington, Kentucky master's cruel treatment and on his relentless toil in a local tannery. Central to Clarke's description of these early years was his poignant discussion of the loss of his sister Dela, who was sold downriver to New Orleans in the early 1830s. Her transport, "chained to a gang of a hundred and sixty slaves," punctuated a series of cruelties inflicted on Milton's family by his master.[90] Clarke's reunion with Dela was made possible by his 1838 lease to a steamboat that ran between Louisville and New Orleans. Knowing she had been sent to New Orleans, he searched the city in the off time he had at the end of each downriver trip. His efforts were not immediately successful. He recalled that "I was at New Orleans three or four times" before he discovered any news.[91] When he did find news it was through an "old acquaintance" who knew Dela and gave Milton her address.[92] The reunion itself—some thousand miles away from their childhood slave experiences—was no doubt typical of many such incredulous and joyful encounters. Milton recalled that "I went to the house, but I was so changed by the growth of seven or eight years, that she did not know me."[93] Milton's sister made him prove his identity by having him identify a piece of clothing she still had from her Kentucky days. Soon, however, they were anxiously talking about family news, and rapidly catching up with each other's lives.[94]

While some boat laborers came to steamboat work with hopes of finding their own loved ones, in other cases they served as links between non-river slaves in disparate parts of the western slave economy. Slave and free black boat workers carried notes, as well as more informal news, between family members. The narrative of Aunt Sally provides the best example of the role of boat workers using their mobility to reconnect separated families. In her narrative, African American boat workers are constructed as heroic carriers of information who allow Aunt Sally's family a glorious and triumphant reunion.[95] In his study *Free People of Color*, about the experience of northern free blacks, James Oliver Horton provides several examples of African American boat workers shuttling information between families.[96] These accounts reveal the geographic breadth of boat workers' influence. Not only did they shuttle information within the slave economy, they also provided crucial links to families separated between the North and the South. In particular, boat workers connected northern fugitives with their families left behind in bondage. In Cincinnati, an African American community in which most free blacks had southern roots, such connections were particularly important.[97]

Such activities confirmed the masculinity of boat workers. The manhood of river workers was not simply a product of their association with a heavily male workforce, the public performance of tough physical labor, or their ability to earn significant compensation. It also stemmed from their efforts to assert their rights as fathers and family members outside the industry. On the Mississippi River system whatever paternalism existed on large plantations was left far behind. In a complex river economy that linked southern cities and plantations with the North, black workers found significant opportunity to assert their interests and reclaim manhood that was constantly threatened by slavery. The histories of black masculinity and the Mississippi River were intimately linked.

NOTES

1 J. Passmore Edwards, *Uncle Tom's Companions: Facts Stranger than Fiction. A Supplement to Uncle Tom's Cabin: Being Startling Incidents in the Lives of Celebrated Fugitive Slaves* (London: Edwards and Company, 1852), 92.

2 Gilbert Osofsky, ed. *Puttin on Ole Massa: The Slave Narratives of Henry Bibb, William Wells Brown, and Solomon Northrup* (New York: Harper and Row, 1969), 187, 189.

3 John W. Blassingame, ed., *Slave Testimony: Two Centuries of Letters, Speeches, Interviews and Autobiographies* (Baton Rouge: Louisiana State University, 1977), 727; *Trials and Confessions of Madison Henderson, alias Blanchard, Alfred Amos Warrick, James W. Steward, and Charles Brown, Murderers of Jacob Weaver: As Given By Themselves and Likeness of Each, Taken in Jail Shortly After Their Arrest* (St. Louis, MO: Chambers and Knapp, Republican Office, 1841), 8.

4 W. Jeffrey Bolster, *Black Jacks: African American Seamen in the Age of Sail* (Cambridge: Harvard University Press, 1997); Marcus Rediker, *Between the Devil and*

the Deep Blue Sea: Merchant Seamen, Pirates and the Anglo-American Maritime World, 1700–1750 (Cambridge: Cambridge University Press, 1987).

5 James Oliver Horton, *Free People of Color: Inside the African-American Community* (Washington, D.C.: Smithsonian University Press, 1993).

6 Herbert and Edward Quick, *Mississippi Steamboatin'* (New York: Henry Holt, 1926), 235. Coal was loaded from riverside barges which sold to passing steamboats. Firemen loaded coal into and out of large wooden boxes known as coal hoppers, which sat near the fires. See Sophie Pearson, Unpublished Manuscript "The Man -His Boats -the River," chapter eight, Box three, Sophie Pearson Collection, Special Collections, Hill Memorial Library, Louisiana State University.

7 Quick and Quick, *Mississippi Steamboatin'* (1926), 179. Firemen on the lower Mississippi checked wood piles for snakes before loading.

8 Frederika Bremer, *Homes of the New World: Impressions of America*, Vol. II, (New York: Harper and Brothers, 1854), 174.

9 Charles Latrobe, *The Rambler in North America, 1832–1833* (New York: Harper and Brothers, 1835), 299. Alex Mackay noted the "frantic pace" of African American firemen. See Alex Mackay, *The Western World: or, Travels in the United States in 1846–7* (London: Richard Bentley, 1849), 48.

10 For descriptions of firemen's work process see Louis C. Hunter, *Steamboats on the Western Rivers : An Economic and Technological History* (Cambridge, MA: Harvard University Press, 1949), 453; George Byron Merrick, *Old Times on the Mississippi River: Recollections of a Steamboat Pilot from 1854 to 1863* (Cleveland, OH: Arthur H. Clarke, 1909), 59–63; John Gleason, et. al. v. Steamboat *Urilda*, No. 1519, (1868), United States District Court Records, Eastern District of Missouri, National Archives Great Plains Region (NAGPR), Kansas City, Missouri; McKinney v. Steamboat *Yalla Busha*, No. 602, Unreported (1848), Records of Louisiana Supreme Court, Special Collections, University of New Orleans (UNO); Mackay, *The Western World; or, Travels in the United States in 1846–7* (1849), 46–48.

11 John Habermehl, *Life on the Western Rivers* (Pittsburgh, PA: McNary and Simpson, 1901), 87. Atlantic deep sea merchant ships had very different hull designs than did western steamboats. While Atlantic ships stored their cargo and shipped their passengers in large holds below water level, steamboats were designed for the shallow western rivers. They had flatter, broader-based hulls that split cargo between the deck and small, six- to seven-foot-high holds.

12 Testimony of Captain Kinney, Henry James v. Steamboat *Cora*, No. 1162, Unreported (1866), United States District Court Records, Eastern District of Missouri, NAGPR.

13 Testimony of Berry Smith, George Rawick, ed., *The American Slave: A Composite Autobiography*, Mississippi Narratives, Supplement, Series 1, Volume 10, Part 5 (1977), 1981–82.

14 A complete record of a western river steamboat cargo, including individual shipments and their weight, is contained in the complete bills of lading for several runs of the Missouri River steamer *Evening Star* in 1867. See Records of the *Evening Star*, Box 2, Folders 37–47, Trail Collection, State Historical Society of Missouri, Columbia, Missouri.

15 Testimony of William Waymen, Rawick, ed., *The American Slave*, Texas Narratives, Supplement, Series 2, Volume 10, Part 9 (1979), 4144. For other reports of plantation slaves working with steamboat hands see Rice v. Cade, 10 La 288 (1836), UNO; Charles Lanman, *Adventures in the Wilds of the United States* (Philadelphia: John W. Moore, 1856), 210.

16 Lanman, *Adventures in the Wilds of the United States* (1856), 167. Olmsted found "negroes lying asleep, in all postures, upon the freight." Frederick Law Olmsted, *The Cotton Kingdom: A Traveler's Observations on Cotton and Slavery in the American Slave States, 1853–1861* (Arthur Schlesinger, ed. New York: Da Capo Press, 1996), 273.

17 Charles Beadle, *A Trip the United States in 1887* (London: J. S. Virtue and Co., nd.), 65.

18 Lanman, *Adventures in the Wilds of the United States* (1856), 167.

19 Quick and Quick, *Mississippi Steamboatin'* (1926), 252.

20 Lanman, *Adventures in the Wilds of the United States* (1856), 167.

21 [Mrs Houstoun, *Hesperos: or, Travels in the West* (London: John W. Parker, 1850), 54.] For other descriptions of roustabout work see Hunter, *Steamboats on the Western Rivers* (1949), 454. See also Sophie Pearson, Unpublished Manuscript "The Man the Boats -the River," chapter 8, Box 3, Louisiana State University Archives; "The River-Boatmen of the Lower Mississippi," *Annual Reports of the Supervising Surgeon General* (Marine Hospital Service, 1873); Williams v. *Jacob*, No. 1773, Unreported (1870), United States District Court Records, Eastern District of Missouri, NAGPR; Bennet v. Steamboat *Nashville*, No. 5210, Unreported (1854), UNO; Rice v. Cade, 10 La 288 (1836).

22 Testimony of Peter Barber, in Ronnie W. Clayton, ed., *Mother Wit: The Ex-Slave Narratives of the Louisiana Writers' Project* (New York: Peter Lang, 1990), 25.

23 Osofsky, ed., *Puttin' on Ole Massa*, 187. See also Barbara Leigh Smith Bodichon, *Barbara Leigh Smith Bodichon: An American Diary 1857–8*. Joseph W. Reed, Jr., ed. (London: Routledge and Kegan Paul, 1972), 112–13. Workers generally had to purchase their own clothes. This cost cabin laborers more than deck workers. See Habermehl, *Life on the Western Rivers* (1901), 28. Charles Rosenberg, "Sexuality, Class and Role in Nineteenth Century America," in Elizabeth Pleck and Joseph E. Pleck, eds., *The American Man* (Englewood Cliffs, NJ: Prentice Hall, 1980), 219–57. For further discussion of this ideal and the African American community see James Oliver Horton and Lois E. Horton, "Violence, Protest, and Identity: Black Manhood in Antebellum America," in Darlene Clark Hine and Earnestine Jenkins, eds., *A Question of Manhood: A Reader in Black Men's History and Masculinity*, vol. 1 (Bloomington: University of Indiana Press, 1999), 382–99.

24 For an example of the difficulty of meeting passenger demands see Frederick Law Olmsted, *A Journey to the Seaboard Slave States* (New York: Mason Bros., 1861), 569; Blair et. al. v. Steamboat *Aunt Letty*, No. 183, Unreported (1857), United States District Court Records, Eastern District of Missouri, NAGPR.

25 Latrobe, *The Rambler in North America* (1835), 296.

26 A. Oakey Hall, *The Manhattaner in New Orleans; or, Phases of "Crescent City" Life* (New York: J. S. Redfield, 1851), 179.

27 Hall, *The Manhattaner in New Orleans; or Phases of "Crescent City" Life* (1851), 179–180.

28 Testimony of Joseph Jones, Mary Johns v. Henry Brinker, No. 5399, 30 La Ann. 241 (1878), Supreme Court Records of Louisiana, Special Collections, Earl K. Long Library, UNO.

29 Block v. Steamboat *Trent*, No. 855, 18 La Ann 664 (1866), UNO.

30 Habermehl, *Life on the Western Rivers* (1901), 153. Deck passengers generally carried their own provisions.

31 Habermehl, *Life on the Western Rivers* (1901), 59–63; Hunter, *Steamboats on the Western Rivers* (1901), 400–2; Blair et. al. v. Steamboat *Aunt Letty*, No. 183, Unreported (1857), United States District Court Records, Eastern District of Missouri, NAGPR.

32 This term was occasionally used to describe stewards. See Wm. Patterson v. Steamboat *Great Republic*, No. 1563, Unreported (1869), United States District Court Records, Eastern District of Missouri, NAGPR.

33 Carter G. Woodson, "Negroes of Cincinnati Prior to Civil War," *Journal of Negro History* 1 (January 1916). This article has been reprinted in Wendell Phillips Dabney, *Cincinnati's Colored Citizens; Historical, Sociological and Biographical* (New York: Negro University Press, 1970), 38.

34 James Thomas, *From Tennessee Slave to St. Louis Entrepreneur: The Autobiography of James Thomas,* Loren Schweninger, ed. (Columbia: University of Missouri Press, 1984), 107.

35 See steamboat crew lists, Manuscript, Seventh Population Census of the United States, Reel 417, City of St. Louis, National Archives. Barbers would have been among the workers least likely to be present on board during landings—a fact that was probably responsible for the small number of barbers the census taker recorded in his riverside enumeration of boat workers. For more on how barbering was considered "nigger work" in the South see Ira Berlin, *Slaves Without Masters: The Free Negro in the Antebellum South* (New York: Vintage Books, 1976), 235–36.

36 Thomas, *From Tennessee Slave to St. Louis Entrepreneur: The Autobiography of James Thomas,* Schweninger, ed. (1984), 85.

37 William Ransom Hogan and Edwin Adams Davis, eds. *William Johnson's Natchez: the Antebellum Diary of a Free Negro* (Baton Rouge: Louisiana State University Press, 1993), 508, 743.

38 For barbers' work process, and the shifting of workers between riverside barbershops and steamboats, see Hogan and Davis, eds., *William Johnson's Natchez: The Antebellum Diary of a Free Negro* (Baton Rouge: Louisiana State University Press, 1993); Testimony of Isaac Throgmorton, Blassingame, ed., *Slave Testimony* (1977), 432–33.

39 Hunter, *Steamboats on the Western Rivers* (1949), 272.

40 Hunter, *Steamboats on the Western Rivers* (1949), 290–98. For examples of African Americans killed in boiler explosions see *New Orleans Picayune*, April 26, 1859; *New Orleans Picayune*, November 16, 1849; Rountree v. Brilliant Steamboat Company, No. 2804, 8 La Ann 289, (1853).

41 Robert Starobin, *Industrial Slavery in the Old South* (New York: Oxford University Press, 1970), 43–44.

42 *New Orleans Picayune*, September 7, 1844; *New Orleans Picayune*, September 11, 1844; *New Orleans Picayune*, February 11, 1849; *Missouri Republican*, November 29, 1847.

43 When slaves died their masters sometimes sued for negligence see Johnstone v. *Arabia*, No. 3, Box 584, 24 Mo 86 (1853), Missouri Supreme Court Records, Missouri State Archives, Jefferson City, Missouri; Rice v. Cade, 10 La 228 (1836); Morgan's Syndics v. Fiveash, No. 1700, 7 Mart (n.s.) 410 (La, 1829); Lacoste v. Sellick, No. 6101, 1 La Ann 336 (1846); Poree v. Cannon, No. 6006, 14 La Ann 501 (1859); England v. Gripon, No. 6316, 15 La Ann 304 (1860); Howes v. *Red Chief*, Nos. 5944, 6487, 15 La Ann 321 (1860); Huntington v. Ricard, No. 2288, 6 La Ann 806 (1851); Barry v. Kimball, No. 3500, 10 La Ann 787 (1855) and No. 4684, 12 La Ann 806 (1851).

44 *Missouri Republican*, October 17, 1846. For an African American steward's drowning death see *New Orleans Picayune*, December 4, 1849.

45 Hunter, *Steamboats on the Western Rivers* (1949), 430–35.

46 Quoted in Robert Starobin, *Industrial Slavery in the Old South* (1970), 65. In this case the master thought the sickness of his slaves' was caused by damp below deck sleeping quarters.

47 Testimony of Joseph Jackson, United States v. *Louisville*, No. 346, Unreported (1863), United States District Court Records, Southern District of Illinois, National Archives Great Lakes Region (NAGLR), Chicago, Illinois.

48 Testimony of Judy Taylor, United States v. *Louisville*, No. 346, Unreported (1863), United States District Court Records, Southern District of Illinois, NAGLR.

49 Testimony of Joseph Jackson, United States v. *Louisville*, No. 346, Unreported (1863), United States District Court Records, Southern District of Illinois, NAGLR. Slave rivermen received different treatment on shore from other workers. Federally funded marine hospitals, founded to help address the public health threats posed by maritime workers, covered only free workers. While there may have been exceptions, slave workers generally remained in the care of masters and private physicians. In some cases officers took them to urban slave hospitals, though in these instances masters were responsible for treatment costs.

50 Testimony of Elmo Steele, Rawick, ed., *The American Slave*, Mississippi Narratives, Supplement, Series 1, Volume 10, Part 5 (1977), 2027.

51 Lieut-Col Arthur Cunynghame, *A Glimpse at the Great Western Republic* (London: Richard Bentley, 1851), 143.

52 Lanman, *Adventures in the Wilds of the United States* (1856), 167.

53 Rev. Robert Everest, *A Journey Through the United States and Part of Canada* (London: John Chapman, 1855), np. For more on the racial fears passengers see, Entry for 5 June n.y., Diary of Sallie Diana Smith, Trail Collection, Box 1, Folder 11, State Historical Society of Missouri.

54 Shields McIlwaine, *Memphis Down in Dixie* (New York: E. P. Dutton, 1948), 192.

55 Lient.-Col. Arthur Cunynghame, *A Glimpse at the Great Western Republic* (London: Richard Bentley, 1851), 142. For an example from the immediate postwar period see Entry for 5 June n.y., Diary of Sallie Diana Smith, Box 1, Folder 8, Trail Collection, State Historical Society of Missouri.

56 The privacy of cabin rooms gave travelers and officers ample opportunity for sexual advances. See Osofsky, ed., *Puttin' On Ole Massa* (1969), 194.

57 Testimony of Will Long, Rawick, ed., *The American Slave*, Texas Narratives, Supplement, Series 2, Volume 6, Part 5 (1979), 2409.

58 *St. Louis Globe-Democrat*, January 8, 1893.

59 Latrobe, *The Rambler in North America* (1835), 299.

60 Latrobe, *The Rambler in North America* (1835), 299.

61 Lanman, *Adventures in the Wilds of the United States* (1856), 167.

62 Testimony of William H. McCarthy, Rawick, ed., *The American Slave*, Mississippi Narratives, Supplement, Series 1, Volume 9, Part 4 (1977), 1373.

63 Habermehl, *Life on the Western Rivers* (1901), 87; England v. Gripon, No. 6316, 15 La Ann 304 (1860), UNO.

64 Lafcadio Hearn, *Children of the Levee*, O. W. Frost, ed. (Lexington: University of Kentucky Press, 1957), 81.

65 Rice v. Cade, et. al., 10 La 288 (1836).

66 Testimony of Isole Darcole, Barry v. Kimball, No. 4684, 12 La Ann 372 (1857), UNO; M. De Grandfort, *The New World*, Edward C. Wharton, trans. (New Orleans, LA: Sherman, Harton, and Co., 1855), 81.

67 Testimony of Ben Lawson, T. Lindsay Baker and Julie P. Baker, eds., *The WPA Oklahoma Slave Narratives* (Norman: University of Oklahoma Press, 1996), 245.

68 Hunter, *Steamboats on the Western Rivers* (1949), 466.

69 Hunter, *Steamboats on the Western Rivers* (1949), 465–66.

70 Account book of James Rudd, 1830–1860, James Rudd Papers, 1789–1867, Filson Club, Louisville, Kentucky.

71 Cunynghame, *A Glimpse at the Western Republic* (1851), 143.

72 Testimony of Judy Taylor, United States v. *Louisville*, No. 346, (1863), United States District Court Records, Southern District of Illinois, NAGLR.

73 Louis Hughes, *Thirty Years a Slave: From Bondage to Freedom* (Milwaukee, WI: South Side Printing Company, 1897), 103.

74 Frederick Law Olmsted, *Journey in the Seaboard Slave States* (New York: Mason Brothers, 1861), 564.

75 Account book of James Rudd, 1830–1860, James Rudd Papers, 1789–1867, FC.

76 Thomas, *From Tennessee Slave to St. Louis Entrepreneur: The Autobiography of James Thomas*, Schweninger, ed. (1984), 108.

77 Moses Grandy, *Narrative of the Life of Moses Grandy, Late a Slave in the United States of America* (Boston: Oliver Johnson, 1844), 30.

78 Thomas, *From Tennessee Slave to St. Louis Entrepreneur: The Autobiography of James Thomas*, Schweninger, ed. (1984), 119. For another account of the custom of tipping see Eliza Potter, *A Hairdresser's Experience in High Life* (New York: Oxford University Press, 1991), 158.

79 Judge William Pope *Early Days in Arkansas: Being for the Most Part the Personal Recollections of An Old Settler* (Little Rock, AK: Frederick Allsopp, 1895), 7–8. John Habermehl wrote that "those who gave tips" were "sure to get the warmest buckwheat pancakes and the nicest fried eggs." See Habermehl, *Life on the Western Rivers* (1901), 48, 155.

80 Olmsted, *The Cotton Kingdom* (1996), 272.

81 Testimony of Daniel Tucker, McMaster v. Beckwith, No. 2017, 2 La 329 (1831), UNO.

82 Testimony of John Eaton, Emmerling v. Beebe , No. 3642, 15 La 251 (1840), UNO.

83 Cyprian Clamorgan, *The Colored Aristocracy of St. Louis* (St. Louis, MO: S.N., 1858), 17–22.

84 *Trials and Confessions of Madison Henderson, alias Blanchard, Alfred Amos Warrick, James W. Seward, James W. Seward, and Charles Brown, Murderers of Jesse Baker and Jacob Weaver: As Given by Themselves and Likeness of Each, Taken in Jail Shortly After Their Arrest* (1841), 20–22.

85 Blassingame, ed., *Slave Testimony* (1977), 432.

86 Tyson v. Ewing, 3 J.J. Marsh. 185 (Ky, 1830).

87 Blassingame, ed., *Slave Testimony* (1977), 389–90.

88 Drew, *A North-Side View of Slavery* (1969), 190. William Anderson reported saving 500 dollars during his 11 years of service as a cook and steward on steamboats. See Drew, *A North-Side View of Slavery* (1969), 178.

89 Osofsky, ed., *Puttin' On Ole' Massa* (1969), 188.

90 Lewis and Milton Clarke, *Narratives of the Sufferings of Lewis and Milton Clarke, Sons of a Soldier of the Revolution, During a Captivity of More Than Twenty Years Among the Slaveholders of Kentucky, One of the So Called Christian States of North America* (Boston: Bela Marsh, 1846), 74.

91 Clarke and Clarke, *Narratives of the Sufferings of Lewis and Milton Clarke* (1846), 81.

92 Ibid.

93 Ibid.
94 Ibid.
95 *Aunt Sally; The Cross the Way of Freedom* (Cincinnati, OH: American Reform Tract, 1862).
96 James Oliver Horton, *Free People of Color: Inside the African-American Community* (Washington, D.C.: Smithsonian Institution Press, 1993), 69.
97 Ibid.

CHAPTER 4

"The 'Brotherly Love' for Which This City Is Proverbial Should Extend to All" The Everyday Lives of Working-Class Women in Philadelphia and Atlanta in the 1890s

TERA W. HUNTER

In 1871, an anonymous "colored woman" wrote a letter of rhetorical inquiry to the *Philadelphia Post*. "I take the liberty of asking you to explain to me why it is that when respectable women of color answer an advertisement for a dressmaker, either in families or with a dressmaker, [they] are invariably refused." In lieu of preferred jobs they are offered "a place to cook or scrub, or to do house work," she stated. She described the subterfuge used by shop owners and garment and textile manufacturers to rebuff the employment of African American women. Despite the advertisements in newspapers publicizing openings, black women were turned away repeatedly with advice to call again" or to "return later" at some illusory time when they would be needed. "There are many respectable women of color competent to fill any of the above named positions," she reiterated. Yet these women "eke out a scanty livelihood sewing at home," wait for a more receptive job market in vain, or resort to domestic work. "The 'brotherly love' for which this city is proverbial should extend to all, irrespective color, race or creed," she insisted.[1]

This letter, though written during the era of Reconstruction, could have easily been written twenty-five years later as W. E. B. DuBois began his landmark social science study, *The Philadelphia Negro*. DuBois documented the thwarted ambitions of black women in a city that locked them out of the relatively diverse enterprises that employed native-born white and immigrant women. Even fifty years later the situation had improved little. The major difference was that by 1920 not only did most black women perform domestic work; nearly half of the women in domestic labor were black—a trend moving toward long-standing patterns in southern cities like Atlanta.[2]

This paper focuses on the everyday lives of working-class women, most of whom engaged in household work, in Philadelphia and Atlanta in the 1890s.[3] DuBois recognized the importance of these women's labor in the context of the transformation of capitalism, which changed from a preindustrial help system into a wage system in the industrial era. He discussed domestic work in the main body of his study and attached an appendix written by Isabel Eaton, a graduate student at Columbia University awarded a fellowship to collaborate with him. Eaton's "Special Report on Negro Domestic Service in the Seventh Ward" coincided with the publication of another pioneering book, Domestic Service (1897), written by her mentor and friend Lucy Maynard Salmon. Salmon's was the first social scientific study on the topic, though it treated black women only minimally. Salmon, Eaton, as well as DuBois conducted their research not simply as scholars, but also as Progressive reformers, settlement house leaders, and potential, if not actual, employers of domestic workers. Like other middle-class professionals in the Progressive era, they were preoccupied with the "servant problem"—how to make the occupation more efficient and how to improve the behaviors and attitudes of the workers.[4] The present chapter reexamines the mostly poor women who were the subjects of investigation and objects of social reform. It analyzes the everyday experiences and conditions of working-class women who frequented the pages of DuBois's study and reconsiders DuBois's own values that influenced his attitudes on working-class culture and women in particular.

The similarities and the differences in the lives of Philadelphia and Atlanta African Americans offer insight for broadening our understanding of urban women. Philadelphia, an inland port city sandwiched between the Schuylkill and Delaware Rivers, was a leading center of commerce dating back to the colonial era. Atlanta, an inland city, originated in the antebellum period as a tiny railroad depot but grew to maturity during the Civil War. The railroads were critical enterprises in both cities. Philadelphia was home to Jay Cooke, the railroad entrepreneur and owner of the Pennsylvania Railroad, the largest corporation in the United States, whose business tactics went awry and triggered the national depression of 1873. Atlanta was a child of the railroad and owed its sudden and spectacular growth during and after the Civil War to the steam locomotive. The Confederate Army favored the city's strategic location in shipping goods throughout the region and made the city a pivotal distribution and manufacturing center. Philadelphia was an industrial city heavily invested in iron, steel, and coal plants, as well as in sugar and oil refineries. Textile factories were the city's largest and biggest employers. At the turn of the century, Philadelphia was the largest producer of wool, silk, and cotton enterprises like clothing and carpet production were spread out in small workshops and tenements occupied by European immigrants. Atlanta's textile industry was largely limited to cotton in an agricultural economy where cotton was king. The textile factory bore an ideological as well as economic burden of regenerating a new South and providing jobs to displaced white yeoman farmers. It was the central symbol in an aggressive public relations campaign spearheaded by local entrepreneurs, politicians, and journalists determined to make Atlanta the prototype for regional economic development. Heavy industry ruled the northern city's economy, but there were a variety of other economic enterprises—foundries and rolling mills, as well as cigar, wagon, box, broom, soap, and candy manufacturers. Atlanta, unlike most of the South, also developed a diversified economy—foundries, metalworks, and rolling mills, as well as wagon, book, paper goods, furniture, patent medicine, straw hat, and piano manufacturers.[5]

The character of the population of the two cities diverged in significant ways. Compared to other northern cities, Philadelphia was dominated by native-born whites. Foreign-born residents in 1880 made up only 24 percent of the population—half the proportion in the populations of New York and Chicago. But compared to Atlanta, with less than 4 percent foreign-born people, there were significantly more Irish, English, German, Italian, and Jewish immigrants in Philadelphia.[6] By 1890, the absolute number of African Americans in Philadelphia exceeded those in Atlanta, though they constituted only 4 percent of the population in the former and 40 percent in the latter.

The physical development of the two cities also differed but overlapped. Neither ghettos nor de jure segregation were apparent in the last two decades of either city. In Philadelphia, a city in which ethnic groups were clustered but dispersed, blacks were mainly concentrated in the inner city's Seventh Ward, though they also lived throughout the entire metropolitan area. Some wards of the city were heavily white or black, but none excluded either race entirely. In Atlanta, the city's wealthy residents and businesses dominated the urban core. Most African Americans lived in neighborhoods in outlying areas—close enough to walk to work within the urban core, but far enough to be out of sight of upper-class homes. They too were spread throughout the metropolitan areas.

Despite these characterizations Jim Crow was clearly not just on the horizon but already operative in both places. Philadelphia had a reputation for being a city of homes. Rows of modest one-family houses lined the streets, unlike in other northern cities, which were dominated by overcrowded multifamily dwellings. Yet poor people of different ethnic groups lived in the worst areas of the inner city—in dark courtyards and narrow alleys, in substandard and over-crowded houses. Blacks as well as poor whites in Atlanta tended to live in the worst areas of the city as well, on low-lying areas subject to floods and sewage spills where waste products from the hilly middle- and upper-class residents literally poured down into the valleys below. Whites tended to live fronting streets, blacks in the rear or in alleys. In both cities the political and economic elites controlled the distribution of municipal services that were important to health and sanitation of the entire citizenry. Resources allocated for water supply, sewage disposal, and road and street construction and repair were mostly directed to the areas dominated by businesses and the residences of the elites. Atlanta did not implement its residential segregation laws until 1922, but the pattern had already been fixed in practice decades before.[7]

Philadelphia had the largest number of African Americans in the North at the time of DuBois's publication of *The Philadelphia Negro*. The majority of the black residents in this city, as in most other cities either in the North or South, were women. Nearly half of all black females were gainfully employed, and their families relied in part, and too often entirely, on their meager wages. Seventy percent of black families were headed by two parents in 1880, and 25 percent were headed by women. Similarly, 80 percent of white families were headed by two parents and 14 percent were headed by women. Blacks, however, were more likely to live in households with three generations or other extended kin, which was an important cultural adaptation for the survival of people of West African descent in the New World.[8]

The slightly higher percentage of female-headed households among African Americans, then as now, was judged derisively. According to the statistics DuBois collected, the rate of marriages of most black and white Philadelphians was virtually the same; the proportion of single (never married) women over age fifteen across the races was nearly identical. Despite this, DuBois insisted that the "greatest weakness of the Negro family is still lack of respect for the marriage bond," which he attributed to sexual immorality.[9] But the data available to DuBois indicated that the most significant difference in marital status across race was the relatively higher number of black widows. Extraordinarily high mortality rates of black men wreaked havoc on potential and actual marital relationships in diminishing the prospects of long-term survival.[10] Black women with living spouses were also more likely to be separated from their husbands than were white women, quite frequently because black men were forced to leave home in order to find work. Black family structure and conjugal relations were also more fluid and complex than DuBois understood, or was willing to accept, and could not be easily measured against standards of morality that failed to respect the distinctive history and culture of African Americans. DuBois criticized female-headed households because he believed they created other social problems, such as a disproportionate share of members of the "submerged tenth"—the most socially and economically debilitated among the lowest class (*Philadelphia Negro*, pp. 55, 66–68, 311–19).[11]

DuBois's conception of the "submerged tenth" bears a striking resemblance to recent constructions of the "underclass," which defines working class people more by behavioral and moral infractions and deficiencies than by their economic conditions. Although *The Philadelphia Negro*'s detailed analysis of the structural roots of poverty and racism exceeded the narrow aims established by the white reformers in the College Settlement Association who sponsored it, DuBois shared their paternalism toward the poor. DuBois's pioneering work became one of the most influential sociological studies in the twentieth century, inspiring a body of insightful urban history, sociology, and ethnography. His condemnatory moralizing about black working-class deviations from presumed cultural norms, however, has also been recapitulated and ultimately rendered less multifarious by some social scientists who have followed him. His reproach of female-headed households sowed the seeds of the "black pathology" thesis that would be taken up by E. Franklin Frazier and Daniel Patrick Moynihan, and elaborated by a host of social scientists and policymakers in extended debates about the "underclass" problem in the late-twentieth century.[12]

DuBois's attitudes toward female-headed households also reflected his sympathy toward women who bore the burden of earning a disproportionate share of family income, compared to white women, regardless of marital status.[13] Black men were paid relatively higher wages than women, but even the combination of both spouses' wages was often insufficient for establishing a comfortable standard

of living. Nor was marriage a guarantee of two steady incomes. Unemployment
was a common experience for male common laborers; separation or death of a
partner could reduce a family's resources unexpectedly to below the minimum
standard of living. Ironically, though black women entered and remained in wage
labor significantly longer than did their white counterparts in order to support
their families, they had 20 percent fewer children. Black and white women gave
birth to roughly the same proportion of children, but poor health, disease, and
poverty created extraordinarily high rates of stillbirths and mortality of African
American children under five. There is some evidence that black urban women
also practiced contraceptive methods to limit the number of children they bore
(pp. 150, 151, 158, 164–68).[14]

Nearly all the women wage earners who contributed to the coffers of black
families were household workers. In the 1890s, at least 90 percent of all black
female wage earners in both cities were domestics. The most obvious difference
between women in the two cities was that black women monopolized domestic
work in Atlanta, whereas they constituted only a minority and competed with
whites for jobs in Philadelphia. By the end of the century, as European immigration climbed, black Philadelphians faced increasing competition from English
and Swedish servants considered more fashionable by elite employers. Blacks
were relegated to the bottom of the bottom of the labor market in the "plainer
establishments" (p. 448).

Another significant difference that profoundly affected the experiences of
domestic work was the preponderance of live-in workers in Philadelphia. The
majority of black women in Philadelphia lived in isolation from their families and
communities in the homes of their employers, though they lived-in less often
than white women did. While 61 percent of single women lived-in, only 28 percent of married women did so. More single women may have preferred to live-
in their own homes, but given the competition for jobs, they had to
accommodate employers' demands. This pattern differed from domestic service
in the antebellum period when the majority of free blacks working as domestics
lived in their own homes (pp. 141, 448).[15] In Atlanta, the pattern of late-
nineteenth-century Philadelphia was reversed. The overwhelming majority of
black women desired to physically distance themselves from erstwhile masters
and were able to exercise this preference because of their leverage in a labor market that employers incessantly claimed was in short supply. The workers perceived
few advantages from live-in arrangements, material or otherwise. "Free" accommodations and food were usually meager, especially when added to isolation
from family and friends and the lack of privacy. In Philadelphia, Eaton suggests
that live-ins may have had a slight advantage in net income by saving money on
room and board, since there was little variation between the wages of those who
lived-in compared to those who lived at home (pp. 453–54).[16]

Women in Atlanta entered the occupation between the ages of ten and sixteen
and remained within it most of their lives. Women in Philadelphia, however,
tended to enter service work as adults, because employers rarely hired black children. Very few black women wage earners found options outside domestic work,
but some were able to make choices about particular jobs, which they often did
according to changes in their life cycles. In Atlanta and the South, younger and

single women tended to become general housemaids and child nurses, while older and married women, especially those with children, chose cooking and washing. Younger women concentrated in general service positions contributed to their parents' income. But once they married or began giving birth to children of their own, they made occupational choices, like laundry work, that gave them more time and flexibility for their new responsibilities. In Philadelphia, black women faced more constraints in meshing wage labor and child rearing. Employers often preferred to hire women unencumbered by children, especially those who lived-in. This put mothers at a disadvantage in finding employment and safe, affordable child care. When no other options were available, some women sent their offspring to "baby farms" during the week—expensive institutions that absorbed their wages and put their young ones at risk. The most destitute mothers were forced out of jobs onto the streets, fired by employers who discovered their offspring, and were unable to find suitable work.[17]

Most women in both cities found jobs through casual networks or by knocking on doors of potential employers. But employment agencies were notorious for luring young and unsuspecting women in the South to move North under false pretenses of lucrative job offers. Itinerant agents offered advances in the form of transportation, for those who could not afford the fee, and promised good wages, nice jobs, and desirable living conditions. Agencies propagated deceitful claims on billboards, like one DuBois noticed on the streets of Norfolk, Virginia, that enticed black women to believe there were plentiful jobs as stenographers and clerks in the North. Once they reached their destination, however, many migrants discovered they had been duped and were forced to take undesirable jobs at wages lower than promised. Some of the employment agencies were actually procurers for brothels furtively searching for prostitutes. Women migrants often arrived in the city indebted to these agencies for the cost of transportation and other fees and their personal effects were held hostage in order to coerce them into accepting substandard domestic work or prostitution. To counter these tactics, the Association for the Protection of Colored Women was formed in Philadelphia in 1905 to meet women migrants at the docks and train stations and escort them to decent boardinghouses and legitimate employment agencies (p. 118).[18]

Once hired, Philadelphia domestics made up for the loss of independence that accompanied live-in service by insisting on time off at least on Thursday afternoons and alternating Sundays. Black women demanded time off for themselves more often than white women did. They worked long hours, however, and were paid on average four to sixteen dollars per month. Cooks, laundresses, and janitors commanded the highest average wages in Philadelphia, while chambermaids, errand girls, and general domestics received the lowest. Their counterparts in Atlanta worked seven days a week, with the exception of laundresses, who usually worked six. Whatever time off they acquired was achieved by manipulating the perpetual "shortage" in the labor market by quitting and moving around. Their wages on average were half that of the workers in the North. The more remarkable characteristics of these rates was that they changed so little over time and across occupations. When variations existed, cooks tended to command the highest wages per hour and kitchen sculleries the lowest. Laundresses could increase their earnings by adding on clients and seeking help from family members (447–48). Domestic work in general, however, was poorly paid work, which made survival difficult for women; no wages made it even harder. Some employers were notorious for cheating their workers of rightful earnings on spurious grounds. Workers could be deprived of wages when employers decided that they had overspent their household budgets. Live-in workers were especially vulnerable to real or imagined financial shortfalls because they could be expected to weather such periods without compensation. Any worker could face deductions for behavioral infractions such as lost time or impudence or for the replacement of missing, broken, or consumed objects. Sometimes employers would substitute perishables or durable goods in lieu of cash for remuneration without the worker's consent.[19]

There were distinct, if overlapping, skills and talents involved in household labor. But no matter what job they chose, African American women were assured arduous work. Even as the expectations of good housekeeping dovetailed with changes in the economy and family life, very little changed in the actual labor processes of housework in the nineteenth century. Technological advances hardly ever reached individual homes, and the few that did made limited improvements.[20] Housework was a full-time job, which meant double duties for women working for wages and taking care of their own families' housekeeping chores.

The specific duties and work conditions of general domestics varied according to the economic means of employers and the number of other servants hired. Hauling water and tending fires consumed a large part of the daily routine. The work of servants in wealthy families was facilitated by their access to gas and indoor plumbing. This advantage, however, was offset by the ostentatious surroundings and lavish objects that required extra care. Servants working in more modest homes might have fewer articles to maintain, but the work was harder if they lacked amenities such as piped-in water.

Any number of a dizzying array of chores were required of general domestics. Their work could require cooking, helping with preparing and preserving foodstuffs, and maintaining the kitchen. Women hired to perform general duties would sometimes do the laundry, ironing, mending, and caring for children. Servants who lived with employers faced the added encumbrance of having to respond to unpredictable intrusions at any hour that diminished time off for themselves. Domestics not only performed physical labor, but also pomp and circumstance in signifying the hosts' social rank. In the South, hiring a black servant was itself a mark of racial privilege; in the North, employers were more likely to hire specialized workers, usually men and European immigrants to signify social caste.

Child nurses would arrive early in the day to keep children occupied and protected while their parents engaged in other remunerative and social activities. In the South, many girls were hired at a young age to perform tasks from rocking cradles to the full range of caretaking responsibilities for charges not much younger than themselves. An older nurse described the litany of her duties as follows: "I not only have to nurse a little white child, now eleven months old, but I have to act as playmate or 'handy-andy,' not to say governess, to three other children in the home, the oldest of whom is only nine years of age."[21] She washed, fed, and bedded the children, which required round-the-clock work according to the infants' and children's needs. But even when the children demanded little attention, the work did not end there. The women were also expected to perform other household tasks between their child-care duties.

Cooking required the most skill and creativity among household occupations, though constantly working around a hot stove was fatiguing. Cooking was the only household chore to benefit from technological advances in this period. The cast-iron stove, common by the late-nineteenth century, was the most important improvement, replacing the open fireplaces that had reigned in earlier kitchens. Cast-iron stoves required less fuel, worked more efficiently and safely, and were built high enough off the ground to prevent constant bending by the cook. But the lack of built-in thermostats forced cooks to gauge the level of heat through trial and error—arranging dampers and drafts or placing foods in strategic spots according to estimates of the time and degree of heat required. In other respects, food preparation remained virtually the same in the 1890s as it had been in 1800.[22] Most cooks developed improvisational styles of food preparation that defied emergent notions of scientific housewifery. Black women were cognizant of the cerebral aptitude required for cooking. As one cook described her work: "Everything I does, I does by my head; it's all brain work."[23]

In addition to food preparation, cooks also washed dishes, mopped floors, and cleaned and maintained the stoves, pots, pans, and utensils. The degree of autonomy they enjoyed varied, but they generally planned the meals and marketed for groceries. In the South cooks took on additional emotional roles. The comfort and intimacy evoked by the warmth and pleasant smells of the kitchens made them a prime social space, especially for children of the employing household in search of comfort and treats.[24] Black cooks conjured the stereotype of "Mammy" perhaps as much as child nurses did in the minds of white southerners.

If cooking required the most inventiveness, laundry work was the most difficult job of all. Unlike cooking, laundry work became more demanding as a result of industrialization. Manufactured cloth expanded individual wardrobes and the wider availability of washable fabrics such as cotton increased the need for washing. Laundry work was the single most onerous chore in the life of a nineteenth-century woman and the first chore she would hire out whenever the slightest bit of discretionary income was available. Even some poor urban women sent out at least some of their wash. In the North, white women who lived in tenements and lacked the proper equipment might send their dirty clothes to commercial laundries.[25] In the South, however, where the adoption of technology lagged and manual labor predominated, many poor whites sent out part or all of their wash to black women.[26]

Atlanta, and the urban South more generally, had the highest concentration of domestic workers per capita in the nation. This regional disparity is accounted for not only by the cultural significance of domestic service as a racial signifier, but also by the large number of laundresses.[27] In marked contrast to the stereotype of the obsequious "Mammy" faithfully wedded to white families, the independent washerwoman was the archetype laborer in Atlanta. In Philadelphia, the general domestic working in isolation in a one-servant home was the typical black female laborer. Most of the laundresses hired in Philadelphia worked in the homes of employers, as did other domestics, though they were usually hired by the day. Eaton counted only thirty-one independent laundresses in the Seventh Ward, and they faced competition from businesses run by whites, and Chinese, as well as by a few African Americans (pp. 102–3, 143, 504).[28]

In Atlanta, the work of the washerwoman began on Monday morning and continued throughout the week until she delivered clean clothes on Saturday. Hundreds of pounds of water had to be toted from wells, pumps, or hydrants for washing, boiling, and rinsing clothes. Many women made their own soap from lye, starch from wheat bran, and washtubs from beer barrels cut in half. They supplied washboards, batting blocks or sticks, workbenches, fuel, and cast-iron pots for boiling. Different fabrics required varying degrees of scrubbing and then soaking in separate tubs with appropriate water temperatures. When the weather permitted, the preference was to perform the work outdoors under the shade of trees and to hang saturated garments on clotheslines, plum bushes, or barbed wire fences—to be marked by the telling signs of three-pronged snags on freshly cleaned fabric. When inclement conditions moved the work inside, clotheslines were hung across the main room. Once the clothes were dry, several heavy irons were heated on the stove and used alternately. After each use, the irons were rubbed with beeswax and wiped clean to minimize the buildup of residue, and, one by one, items were sprayed or dampened with water or starch and pressed into crisp form.[29]

Flexibility marked the main advantage of laundry work, especially for women with children. They could intermingle washing with other obligations and incorporate help from family members. Male relatives or hired draymen sometimes picked up dirty clothes in wheelbarrows or wagons. Children could also help with pickup and deliveries, assist with maintaining the fire, or beat the clothes with sticks. Laundry work was the best alternative among job options available to most black women in the urban South.

No matter what particular domestic job black women occupied, they fought to use whatever leverage and resources available to make wage labor fit their needs as mothers, wives, sisters, and daughters. The predominance of domestics who lived and worked in their own homes in Atlanta was the result of concessions they won. While some employers undoubtedly welcomed the absence of live-ins, many resented the loss of control that resulted from domestics returning to their own communities at night.[30]

DuBois criticized domestics who lived in their own homes because of the temptations it offered them after work. In his view, it was better for them to be cloistered in middle-class homes to avoid the temptations of "vice" that awaited them in their own neighborhoods. Living outside of the watchful eye of employers left black women "free at night to wander at will, to hire lodgings in suspicious houses, to consort with paramours, and thus to bring moral and physical disease to their place at work" (p. 141). DuBois's protestations ignored his own acknowledgment that white households were not necessarily safe havens for black women vulnerable to sexual exploitation by white men; he reinforced the fears of white employers already predisposed to seeing black domestics as profligate and contagious. The fear that black domestics were fecund with disease led the medical establishment to take note of black health issues, especially as migration increased after the turn of the century. Similar sentiments in Atlanta, however, aroused a more pejorative public health campaign that scapegoated black domestics as the primary carriers of tuberculosis infecting the white populace.[31]

African American women devised a number of other strategies to maximize autonomy and relief from poorly rewarded work. In Atlanta, where most workers were not given time off, quitting work was a routine method of usurping time and expressing discontent. Though quitting did not usually assure better wages and conditions, it expressed a refusal to submit to unfair treatment. Women also quit work for temporary periods, to take care of sick family or to participate in social activities. When church groups or secret societies sponsored train "excursions" as fund-raising and social events, employers were guaranteed sudden departures of their household help. In Philadelphia, seasonal departures occurred during the spring and summer as wealthy northerners headed for coastal resorts. Black Philadelphians, and some competitors from the upper South, took advantage of this opportunity to find temporary work outside of the city. Employers often complained of the "migratory turn of mind" of black servants predisposed to quit work at will (pp. 135, 488).[32]

Quitting was a thriving strategy for resisting onerous aspects of domestic work precisely because it was not easily defeated in a free labor system. Though some workers may have openly confronted their employers before departing, quitting did not require open or direct antagonism. Workers who had the advantage of living in their own homes could easily make up excuses for leaving, or leave without notice at all. These small and fleeting victories of individuals accumulated into bigger results as workers throughout Atlanta repeatedly executed this tactic, frustrating the nerves of employers.[33]

Household workers sometimes reappropriated the material assets of their employers for their own use. The "pan-toting" custom of taking away table scraps or dry goods presents a microcosm of the competing expectations of workers and employers and the encroachment of the wage system. Household laborers expected employers to acknowledge openly their obligation to insure their workers basic subsistence by supplementing wages with leftover foodstuffs, or else they literally reclaimed the fruits of their labor without the employers' consent. DuBois and Eaton did not perceive "pantoting" as customary vails or perquisites dating back centuries, nor did they recognize the retribution sought by workers who often had few, if any, legal remedies to redress grievances. Instead, they emphasized pilfering as theft—pure and simple matters of dishonesty among workers (pp. 260–6 1, 485–86).[34]

For black women in the South, pan-toting helped to alleviate some of the onerous consequences of low-wage labor. Some employers conceded to the practice, openly admitting that they paid low wages with table scraps in mind. Even though domestics sometimes used pan-toting to counter employers' dishonest tactics, critics attacked the custom as theft. Conflict over this matter was often resolved to the benefit of employers, who called for the police to arrest black women. Domestic workers, however, had no such recourse when duped by employers, who too frequently defined "free" labor as their right to expropriate labor without compensation. Outright refusals to pay wages, the use of coercion to pawn off extraneous articles in lieu of cash, bilking workers of wages for trivial "offenses," and assessing "insurance fees" were common occurrences.[35]

"Stealing" breaks, feigning illness, and sloughing off at work were other strate-gies used by discontented workers. Child nurses scheduled walks or outings with their charges in order to conveniently pass through their own neighborhoods to conduct business they would otherwise neglect. Feigning illness was a popular tactic, especially for live-in workers, who had less control over their time during or after work. On the spur of the moment, a dispute resolved without satisfac-tion to a cook or general maid could lead her to take action immediately by per-forming her job poorly. Even servants who were considered "well-raised" and "properly" trained by their employers would show "indifference" to their work if they felt unduly provoked. As one employer explained: "Tell them to wipe up the floor, and they will splash away from one end of the room to the other; and if you tell them that is not the way to do it, they will either be insolent or per-haps give you a vacant stare as if they were very much astonished that you thought that was not the way to do it, and they will keep right on."[36] These everyday tactics of resistance brought moments of relief and satisfaction to domestic workers who had few other outlets for recourse.

Despite the constraints of the urban occupational structure that limited black women's access to jobs outside private white homes, some managed to find other kinds of employment. The options in Philadelphia were more varied than in Atlanta. Some black women worked as janitors, office maids, waiters, and public cooks; while these were jobs very similar to domestic work in private homes, they offered better wages and more distance from the vicissitudes of intense personal relations. The largest number of women outside domestic work were dressmak-ers and seamstresses, often independent artisans; a few owned their own shops and others worked at home. Despite the array of clothing manufacturers in the city, the jobs available for seamstresses in factories were limited, just as the anony-mous "colored woman" cited earlier lamented. When Jewish women immigrants at a local factory struck in 1890, Gabriel Blum, spokesmen for manufacturers, promised to open the industry to black women. After announcements in churches and newspapers, five hundred black women eagerly lined up at the fac-tory at the crack of dawn the next day, hoping for the break they had long awaited. Most were turned away empty-handed, except for a few who were given piecework to take home.[37] Though relatively few in number, seamstresses doing piecework were the largest group of home workers and were afforded the auton-omy similar to that of Atlanta's washerwomen. A few dozen other women ran their own businesses in undertaking, hairdressing, and catering, and ran gro-ceries, employment agencies, and hardware stores. Most cigar stores, which often included bicycle rentals, bootblack stands, and pool rooms, were operated for and by men, but a few women entered the businesses. There were several candy and notion stores that were primarily female-run enterprises. A few dozen women worked in the professions, as teachers and nurses; a smaller number earned a living as musicians, actors, and artists (pp. 97–123).

In Atlanta, black women were hired as domestics in boardinghouses, brothels, and hotels. Others established à la carte meal services or lunch carts—dozens of these six-by-nine-foot shacks were erected on busy streets. As in Philadelphia, the largest number of nondomestics were dressmakers, seamstresses, and milliners. And here too, some were skilled artisans and business owners, while most did piecework at home on sporadic contracts. Just as Atlanta was becoming a thriving manufacturing center for white women, black women were locked out of industries. Black women were more likely to work in sales and clerical work in the small but growing blackowned insurance companies and retail stores. A small number worked as schoolteachers and nurses.[38]

A nascent underground economy supplied black women with alternative sources of income and employment as gamblers, bootleggers, and prostitutes. In Philadelphia, "policy playing" was a popular betting sport among women as well as men (p. 265).[39] In Atlanta, some women found they could maximize their options and evade detection by the police if they maintained a semblance of legal employment in domestic labor. Games of chance offered fun and recreation as well as the potential to earn extra cash. Similarly, bootlegging granted women a way to evade laws prohibiting their entry into Atlanta saloons and gave them access to profits that accrued from peddling liquor in alleys and side streets. Prostitution could range from casual trading of sex for favors between people of acquaintance to street and brothel trafficking. Women who sold their bodies assumed risks of arrest and disease, but they earned more money than they could accumulate as domestic and other wage workers.[40]

Prostitution in Atlanta, at least for white women, was a thriving business at the end of the century as the city attracted large numbers of transient men doing business, visiting conventions, or passing through on the railroad. White women entrepreneurs controlled the brothels and tied their trade to the fortunes of real estate companies, landlords, police officers, and politicians who took a cut of the profits. There is no way to know how many African American women worked as prostitutes, but most of the available evidence from the period enumerates a small number of black women compared to whites. The most visible women could be found streetwalking on Decatur Street, the city's red-light and amusement district, and in a few brothels.[41]

Though DuBois found only fifty-six black prostitutes in 1896, he estimated that there were probably twice as many practicing in the sex trade. He spotted them inhabiting the slums with the "criminal class" in alleys, back streets, and courtyards. He noticed their presence as next door neighbors to laundresses and as "well-dressed and partially undetected prostitutes" intermingling with some "estimable families." It was this kind of contamination by the "submerged tenth" with more respectable members of the working and middle-classes that disturbed DuBois most. DuBois was also bothered by what he saw as a misguided materialism in Gilded Age America that led some women into prostitution to support worldly desires and to buy fancy clothes for their idle men (pp. 61, 192–93, 313–14). DuBois expected to find more evidence of prostitution given his belief that common law marriages, cohabitation between unmarried couples, and moral laxity were widespread, yet he did not. Though later estimates would suggest that DuBois had undercounted prostitutes by a much wider margin than he anticipated, there are no reliable data on the number in the Seventh Ward or in greater Philadelphia.[42]

African American women pieced together livelihoods by wage work, casual jobs, and illegal endeavors, if necessary. They also engaged in non-remunerative labor in their own homes and neighborhoods that was life-sustaining. The significance of laundry work and the stark disparity between the number of independent washerwomen in Atlanta and Philadelphia is thrown into greatest relief in this context. Laundry work was critical to the process of community building because it encouraged women to work together in communal spaces within the neighborhoods, fostering informal kinlike networks of reciprocity that sustained them through health and sickness, love and heartaches, birth and death.[43] This support system also facilitated the management of child care; laundresses watched the children of neighbors left at home or in the streets to fend for themselves as their parents worked away. The intimacy of laundry work inspired unity, but it could also produce friction between women. Gossip cut both ways. Individuals used it to pass on vital—literally life-saving—information, but as rumor and innuendo it could evoke jealousy or rouse ill will. Sharing did not occur indiscriminately, for one's past actions determined one's reputation for adherence to social expectations. Nor did women redistribute scarce resources simply on the basis of abstract or sentimental principles; they anticipated reciprocity. Public brawls and street fights, not uncommon in working-class neighborhoods, were used as a method of airing grievances, seeking support, and obtaining resolution, with the sanction of the wider community when there were disagreements about conduct or the violation of social rules.

Communal labor also made it possible for women to use time during the day to salvage resources from nearby merchants. Early in the mornings, before the business day commenced in Atlanta, women and children rummaged through the garbage pails of groceries, restaurants, and fruit stands and in the public domain. Everything from discarded cinders to generate fuel for cooking or for doing laundry, to food, clothing, and furniture were refurbished for use, trade, or resale in neighborhood pawnshops in exchange for cash. Sometimes children were sent out on their own to collect items for their mothers.

Shopping for fresh foods and dry goods was a luxury that working-class women could not always afford. Backyard gardens and chickens spotted in Atlanta were evidence of rural migrants continuing to produce some of their own food once they arrived in the city. Chickens in bedrooms and goats in cellars were familiar to working-class immigrant communities in Philadelphia as well. Livestock and fertile plots supplied food to caretakers and also enabled them to share the fruits, vegetables, and meats that fostered sociability among family, friends, and neighbors.[44] When able to purchase foods, they bought what they needed in small quantities from street vendors, peddlers, and grocery stores near their homes. This meant, of course, they could not obtain volume discounts, which raised their food costs. Hardly a disregard for economy, as some of their contemporaries decried, minimal shopping prevented food spoilage and permitted budgeting of small, irregularly paid wages.[45]

Renting rooms to boarders also provided a source of income for working-class families to help defray living expenses. Commercial boardinghouses as well as bedding and meal services in private households were necessary in cities where hotels were still scarce and the performance of routine household chores was not a customary habit of single men. The sudden population explosion and influx of migrants in Philadelphia during the last few years of the century made such services imperative. Three to four times more black families in Philadelphia rented rooms to boarders than did in Atlanta. Many of these boarders were young, single women who not only provided extra income, but sometimes helped with baby-sitting and household production. DuBois pointed out the perils of renting rooms to strangers, especially for girls left unattended by their mothers and exposed to the predatory acts of designing men, such as waiters who often returned to their lodging places between meals. DuBois objected to boarding because it violated sacred family norms: "the privacy and intimacy of home life is destroyed, and elements of danger and demoralization admitted" (pp. 194, 164–67, 271).[46]

Subsistence strategies and wage labor consumed most of working-class women's lives, but women found ways of replenishing their spirits through activities that gave them joy and pleasure. Recreation and personal gratification, of course, could serve multiple purposes. Lunch carts generated income and meeting places on the streets. Bootlegging, gambling, and prostitution could satisfy emotional and social desires, as well as bring in cash.

Churches were central to the social lives of black urban working-class women in both cities. Aside from the regular church service on Sunday, rituals like funerals, weddings, and baptisms were important life-affirming events. Churches offered social and spiritual activities throughout the week. Though DuBois thought the "noisy missions" frequented by the working class were marred by illiterate preachers and ecstatic worship, he gave credit to churches for the social services they provided to the larger community. Thursday afternoon events such as concerts, solo musicals, receptions, reading circles, and literary recitations were designed especially for domestic workers in Philadelphia. Given these women's relatively high literacy rate, reading and literary events were popular activities. Church-sponsored night schools added to personal enrichment, and kindergartens provided safe havens for children while their mothers worked (pp. 197–221, 469–72).[47]

Mutual aid societies rivaled the influence of the church in the lives of the working class. These benevolent associations provided benefits for the sick, widows, orphans, and unemployed workers in exchange for regularly assessed fees. Some of the organizations owned halls that served as meeting places for education, political, and social events. In Atlanta, domestic laborers were active and visible members and leaders in such societies as the Daughters of Bethel, Daughters of Zion, Sisters of Friendship, and Sisters of Love. In Philadelphia, they joined the Sons and Daughters of Delaware, the Female Cox Association, and the Sons and Daughters of Moses. The groups proved indispensable to urban survival, race advancement, and personal enrichment and offered formal mechanisms for weaving together a tightly knit community. DuBois, however, questioned the benefits of working-class investments in dues and fees in some unscrupulous or "doubtful societies" that may have been better saved in banks or invested in property (pp. 185, 173, 221–30).[48]

Household workers in the South demonstrated their commitment to these organizations by taking leave from work to carry out their various membership duties and obligations. Despite the six- to seven-day a week schedule, many domestic workers were devoted to fulfilling their community obligations, even if it meant missing work. Moreover, organized mutuality offered group protection by bolstering their ability to quit work with confidence when their rights were violated. As one employer regretfully acknowledged, secret society membership "makes them perfectly independent and relieves them from all fear of being discharged, because when they are discharged they go right straight to some of these 'sisters.' "[49] Domestic workers often used secret societies to blacklist or boycott employers who violated their rights, transforming individual grievances into collective dissent.[50]

Other loci of urban leisure included alleys, side streets, front porches, dance halls, theaters, saloons, and gambling dens. Commercial entertainment centers in both cities were located downtown in and near black neighborhoods, where legal and illegal activities often overlapped. Atlanta had Decatur Street, known as the "melting pot of Dixie" because of the conspicuous interracial and ethnic commerce and social intercourse that stood in marked contrast to that of the rest of the city. African Americans gathered there to share news, purchase fish from the market, hang out at barbershops, exchange sundry items for cash at pawnshops, play cards, drink, gamble, and dance. Philadelphia had Seventh and Lombard Streets, as well as many other locations in the Seventh Ward, where similar activities were carried out in pool rooms, private houses, and on the streets. Theaters and travel excursions were also popular among working-class people. DuBois singled out balls and cakewalks as "the most innocent amusements," in contrast to many of the other activities listed above, which he discerned to be of questionable character and doubtful value to the advancement of the race (pp. 319, 61, 192, 265–67, 309–21).[51]

Working-class women pieced together their livelihoods through wage labor and a variety of nonremunerative consumption strategies described here that were critical both materially and socially. Scavenging, borrowing, and "pan-toting" increased provisions of poor people. Domestic workers transformed raw products into consumable goods in their own families, the same labor that they performed in the homes of their employers, albeit under austerity. They conducted much of this activity at the level of neighborhoods, creating informal social networks in communal laundry spots, on the streets, at lunch carts, and in dance halls and saloons. The casual mechanisms of mutual aid, in turn, facilitated the development of more formal institutions such as churches and mutual aid societies, which provided other outlets for social, spiritual, and political expression, as well as economic cooperation. Churches and secret societies, in turn, strengthened the ties that bound people together as family, friends, and neighbors.

DuBois recognized the structural problems of racial discrimination that perpetuated underemployment and unemployment of African Americans and constrained their human potential generation after generation. He acknowledged the burdens on black family life when women were forced into the labor market, locked into positions as servants, and kept in poverty. He substantiated the double obstacle of women confined to domestic labor as the occupation was declining due to industrialization, yet denied access to the best paid positions by competition from recent immigrants. Yet DuBois coupled his dissection of the restrictions of the racist political economy with attributions of black volition for existing conditions. He blamed the intolerant practices, attitudes, and institutions of white employers and workers alike, and he criticized African Americans for making wrong choices within the structural limitations imposed on them. Women who took in boarders to defray living expenses or those who were forced to work without the benefit of safe child care were criticized for imperiling their unsupervised children. Yet domestics who chose to live with their own families, rather than with employers, were chastised for exposing themselves to temptations of the flesh. Even within the context of otherwise wholesome religious institutions, DuBois argued, there was "a tendency to let the communal church and society life trespass upon the home." He believed that African American churchgoers diminished the primacy of the nuclear family ideal by participating in too few "strictly family gatherings" (pp. 194–96).

An underlying assumption running throughout *The Philadelphia Negro* is a bifurcation between the private "home" and the public "street." DuBois privileged the sanctity of nuclear, private homes—black and white—over and above working-class neighborhoods and collective public culture. He attributed multiple signs of communal life outside the private family sphere to intractable "traces of plantation customs" brought by southern migrants and immoral proclivities of untrained newcomers and old-timers alike. DuBois constructed the "street" or "neighborhood life" as sites of danger and vice. Women and men seen "loafing and promenading" on the streets, in his view, demonstrated the absence of "home life." But DuBois singled out young domestic servant girls who skirted the margins of respectability by roaming the streets unsupervised or unescorted by proper men. He viewed the heterosexual sociability and casual mingling between strangers or acquaintances as open invitations to engendering a number of social ills: deemphasis on the nuclear family and emphasis on sex outside of marriage, illegitimacy, crime, and the pursuit of short-term pleasures that ultimately impaired the progress of the race (pp. 191–95, 249, 320–21, 391). In effect, DuBois condemned a broad range of everyday cultural practices that working-class women relied on to survive the racially circumscribed job market, daily insults at work, low wages, no wages, and unemployment. He derogated the ways they looked for moments of joy and pleasure in their workaday lives. What he often defined as antisocial behavior or maladjustment of rural peasants to city life were, on the contrary, highly social and rational adaptations by migrants with prior urban experiences.[52]

DuBois's attitudes and assumptions were not unique, however; they reflected the Victorian sensibilities of middle-class America. DuBois subscribed to the idea of "uplifting" the race by reforming the masses. Racial uplift was partly a critique of notions of black inferiority, partly an expression of hope in the capacity of the poor to improve their circumstances through proper training, and partly a faith in a meritocracy wherein blacks as a group could demonstrate and achieve standards of "civilization," they could overcome racism and be granted full citizenship rights. Middleclass spokespersons of racial uplift often assumed a position of moral superiority that inevitably denigrated the habits, traits, and behaviors they associated with the masses. Improving the home, protecting the nuclear family, and encouraging monogamous legal marriages were inextricably tied to the advancement of the race as much as was the advocacy of civil rights. Thus, DuBois's condemnation of cultural practices that appeared to him to devalue the family was consistent with the ideas of many middle-class people of the period.[53]

DuBois was also a product of the Progressive reform movement. Like other educated professionals inspired to use the tools of new academic disciplines such as sociology to improve society, DuBois set out to collect empirical data that would not only expose the inequities in Philadelphia, but would also prompt social change.[54] His formula for reform surpassed mainstream proposals of the era in advocating for the transformation of institutions and practices that were impediments to democracy in the labor market, politics, and society. He sent a prescient and pointed warning to politicians and industrialists that "Negro prejudice costs the city something." He argued that dire consequences could result from "the atmosphere of rebellion and discontent that unrewarded merit and reasonable but unsatisfied ambition make" (p. 351).

DuBois, like other middle-class reformers, however, also wished to reshape the behavior and values of the masses to fit them to fulfill their lot, however unfairly it may have been assigned to them, in urban industrial America. In this regard, he failed to fully appreciate working-class people's own values and tactics, which emphasized autonomy and collective life and savored social spaces for respite and recovery from wage work. Wage labor in itself was not virtuous, not by the estimates of the people who labored by their hands and sought to minimize its degradations. Though African Americans worked hard by necessity, conforming to standards of chaste, disciplined, hard-driving workers granted them few rewards. African American working-class women devised strategies within the constraints of inequality in fin de siècle America that made the difference between starvation and subsistence, enduring indignities and preserving self-respect. They creatively built sustaining neighborhoods in the urban North and South, drawing from a rich heritage and resilient culture that they continually reconstituted to meet the exigencies of urban life.

NOTES

1 *Philadelphia Post,* November 1, 1871, in *We Are Your Sisters: Black Women in the Nineteenth Century,* ed. Dorothy Sterling (New York: W. W. Norton, 1984), pp. 423–24.

2 Joseph A. Hill, *Women in Gainful Occupations* (Washington, D.C.: U.S. Government Printing Office, 1929), p. 115.

3 For an in-depth analysis of women in Atlanta, see Tera W. Hunter, *To 'Joy My Freedom: Southern Black Women's Lives and Labors After the Civil War* (Cambridge, Mass.: Harvard University Press, 1997).

4 For an important critique of Salmon's flawed methodology and the influence of Progressive thinking on her book and the subsequent literature on domestic work, see Bettina Berch, " 'The Sphinx in the Household': A New Look at the History of Household Workers," *Review of Radical Political Economics* 16 (Spring 1984): 105–21.

5 Nathaniel Burt and Wallace E. Davies, "The Iron Age, 1876–1905," in *Philadelphia: A 300-Year History,* ed. Russell F. Weigley (New York: W. W. Norton, 1982), pp. 471–83; Roger Lane, *The Roots of Violence in Black Philadelphia, 1860–1900* (Cambridge, Mass.: Harvard University Press, 1986), pp. 7–13; James Michael Russell, *Atlanta, 1847–1890. City Building in the Old South and the New* (Baton

Rouge: Louisiana State University Press); Don Doyle, *New Men, New Cities, New South: Atlanta, Nashville, Charleston, Mobile, 1860–1910* (Chapel Hill: University of North Carolina Press, 1990), pp. 1–21, 136–58; Jonathan McLeod, *Workers and Workplace Dynamics in Reconstruction Era Atlanta* (Berkeley and Los Angeles: University of California Press, 1989).

6   Burt and Davies, "Iron Age," pp. 488–94; Russell, *Atlanta*, pp. 152–53; Doyle, *New Men*, pp. 11–14.

7   Burt and Davies, "Iron Age," pp. 491–92; Lane, *Roots of Violence*, pp. 20–21; James Michael Russell, "Politics, Municipal Services, and the Working Class in Atlanta, 1865–1890," *Georgia Historical Quarterly* 66 (Winter 1982): 467–91; Doyle, *New Men*, 143–47; Jerry Thornbery, "The Development of Black Atlanta" (Ph.D. diss., University of Maryland, 1977), pp. 7–12; Dana F. White, "The Black Sides of Atlanta: A Geography of Expansion and Containment, 1870–1970," *Atlanta Historical Journal* 26 (Summer/Fall 1982–83): 199–225; John H. Ellis, "Businessmen and Public Health in the Urban South During the Nineteenth Century: New Orleans, Memphis, and Atlanta," *Bulletin of the History of Medicine* 44 (May-June 1970): 197–371; John H. Ellis and Stuart Gallishoff, "Atlanta's Water Supply, 1865–1918," *Maryland Historian* 8 (spring 1977): 5–22; Michael Leroy Porter, "Black Atlanta: An Interdisciplinary Study of Blacks on the East Side of Atlanta, 1890–1930" (Ph.D. diss., Emory University, 1974).

8   Frank F. Furstenberg, Jr., Theodore Hershberg, and John Modell, "Origins of the Female-Headed Black Family: The Impact of the Urban Experience," in *Philadelphia: Work, Space, Family, and Group Experience in the Nineteenth Century, Essays Toward an Interdisciplinary History of the City*, ed. Theodore Hershberg (New York: Oxford University Press, 1981), pp. 438–46; Herbert Gutman, *The Black Family in Slavery and Freedom, 1750–1925* (New York: Random House, 1976); Andrew Miller, "Social Science, Social Policy, and the Heritage of African-American Families," in *The "Underclass" Debate: Views from History*, ed. Michael B. Katz (Princeton, NJ.: Princeton University Press, 1993), pp. 254–92; Antonio McDaniel, "The Power of Culture: A Review of the Idea of Africa's Influence on Family Structure in Antebellum America," *Journal of Family History* 15,2 (1990): 225–38.

9   The proportion of white single women was 38 percent and black women 37.8 percent. *Philadelphia Negro*, pp. 71–72.

10 It is important to stress here the assessment DuBois made of his own data. Recent scholars, however, have questioned the reliability of census statistics on black widows. The extremely high rate of black male mortality notwithstanding, it appears that the number of black widows was overreported by women or that errors were made by census enumerators. I thank Antonio McDaniel for calling this issue to my attention. See Samuel H. Preston, Suet Lim, and S. Philip Morgan, "African American Marriage in 1910: Beneath the Surface of Census Data," *Demography* 29 (February 1992): 1–15.

11 Furstenberg, Hershberg, and Modell, "Origins of the Female-Headed Black Family," 435–54; Miller, "Social Science," pp. 254–92; Stewart Tolnay, "Black Fertility in Decline: Urban Differentials in 1900," *Social Biology* 27 (Winter 1980): 256–57; Michael B. Katz, "The Urban 'Underclass' as a Metaphor of Social Transformation," in *"Underclass" Debate*, pp. 3–26.

12 On DuBois's influence on Frazier and Moynihan see the following: Elliot Rudwick, "W. E. B. DuBois as a Sociologist," in *Black Sociologists: Historical and Contemporary Perspectives*, ed. James E. Blackwell and Morris Janowitz (Chicago: University of Chicago Press, 1974), p. 25; David Levering Lewis, *W. E. B. DuBois: Biography of a Race* (New York: Henry Holt, 1993), pp. 209–10; Anthony M. Platt, *E. Franklin*

Frazier Reconsidered (New Brunswick, N.J.: Rutgers University Press, 1991), pp. 111–20,133–42.

13 Furstenberg, Hershberg and Modell, "The Origins of the Female-Headed Black Family," pp. 439–42; Kathryn M. Neckerman, "The Emergence of 'Underclass' Family Patterns, 1900–1940," in Katz, *"Underclass" Debate*, p. 200. Southern black women were three times mote likely to participate in the labor force than southern white women, and married black women were nearly six times more likely than married white women. See Claudia Goldin, "Female Labor Force Participation: The Origin of Black and White Differences, 1870 and 1880," *Journal of Economic History* 37 (March 1977): 94; Janice L. Reiff, Michael R. Dahlin, and Daniel Scott Smith, "Rural Push and Urban Pull: Work and Family Experiences of Older Black Women in Southern Cities, 1880–1900," *Journal of Social History* 16 (Summer 1983): 39–48; Thornbery, "Black Atlanta," p. 34; Jacqueline Jones, *Labor of Love, Labor of Sorrow. Black Women, Work, and the Family from Slavery to Freedom* (New York: Basic Books, 1985), p. 113; Gutman, *Black Family*, pp. 442–50,624–42.

14 Tolnay, "Black Fertility Decline," pp. 249–60. For a misinterpretation of low fertility to bolster a black family "pathology" thesis, see Roger Lane, *Roots of Violence*, p. 158. Lane concluded that the small family size can be attributed to a large percentage of black women prostitutes and infertility caused by gonorrhea. This claim is made without providing any evidence of the incidence of gonorrhea, by exaggerating the number of prostitutes and by ignoring live birth, stillbirth, and infant mortality rates. Lane dismissed other factors for low fertility, such as the possibility that black women had fewer children voluntarily, either through birth control or abstinence. For an explicit rejection of the correlation between low fertility and venereal disease, see Tolnay, "Black Fertility in Decline." Lane continued this line of thought, slightly modified, in a subsequent study. He argued that low rates of marriage, high rates of infant mortality, and diseases from prostitution accounted for small black family sizes—except for "the most distinguished" black Philadelphians. The small family sizes of the elite can be attributed "not as the result of disease or desperation but of decision." See Lane, *William Dorsey's Philadelphia and Ours: On the Past and Future of the Black City in America* (New York: Oxford University Press, 1991), p. 305. According to Tolnay's data from the 1900 census, better-off families had fewer children than did the poor among black urbanites. If Lane accepts this data, his conclusions are inconsistent, since poor women had more children and he associates infertility, prostitution, and venereal disease with poor women. DuBois's conclusions concur with Tolnay. See *Philadelphia Negro*, p. 319.

15 Faye Dudden, *Serving Women: Household Service in Nineteenth-Century America* (Middletown, Conn.: Wesleyan University Press, 1983), p. 64; Nash, *Forging Freedom*, pp. 146, 150; Lane, *William Dorsey's Philadelphia*, pp. 77–80.

16 Hill, *Women in Gainful Occupations*, pp. 334–36; David Katzman, *Seven Days a Week: Women and Domestic Service in Industrializing America* (New York: Oxford University Press, 1978), pp. 87–91.

17 Lane, *William Dorsey's Philadelphia*, 88.

18 Frances A. Kellor, *Out of Work: A Study of Employment Agencies, Their Treatment of the Unemployed, and Their Influence upon Homes and Business* (New York: G. P. Putnam's Sons, 1905); Dorothy Salem, *To Better Our World: Black Women in Organized Reform, 1890–1920* (New York: Carlson Publishing, 1990), pp. 45–46; Charles Ashely Hardy III, "Race and Opportunity: Black Philadelphia During the Era of the Great Migration, 1916–1930" (Ph.D. diss., Temple University, 1989), p. 450; Ruth Rosen, *The Lost Sisterhood: Prostitution in America, 1900–1918* (Baltimore: Johns Hopkins University Press, 1982), p. 81.

19 See for example entries for 1880–99, Edwin Edmunds Account Book, 1838–92, Southern Historical Collection, University of North Carolina, Chapel Hill; Berch, "Sphinx in the Household," pp. 114–15; Dudden, *Serving Women*, pp. 87–93.

20 Susan Strasser, *Never Done: The History of American Housework* (New York: Pantheon, 1982).

21 A Negro Nurse, "More Slavery at the South," *New York Independent* 72 (January 25, 1912): 196.

22 Strasser, *Never Done*, pp. 36–46; Kathleen Ann Smallzried, *The Everlasting Pleasure. Influences on America's Kitchens, Cooks, and Cookery, from 1565 to the Year 2000* (New York: Appleton-Century-Crofts, 1956), pp. 93–102.

23 Quoted in Elizabeth Ross Haynes, "Negroes in Domestic Service in the United States," *Journal of Negro History* 8 (October 1923): 411.

24 See for example, Polly Stone Buck, *The Blessed Town: Oxford, Georgia, at the Turn of the Century* (Chapel Hill: University of North Carolina Press, 1986), p. 16.

25 Strasser, *Never Done*, pp. 105–2 1; Ruth Schwartz Cowan, *More Work for Mother: The Ironies of Household Technology from the Open Hearth to the Microwave* (New York: Basic Books, 1983), pp. 65,98.

26 Katzman, *Seven Days a Week,* pp. 185–87; Ray Stannard Baker, *Following the Color Line: American Negro Citizenship in the Progressive Era* (1908; reprint, New York: Harper and Row, 1964), p. 53; Walter L. Fleming, "The Servant Problem in a Black Belt Village," *Sewanee Review* 8 (January 1905): 14, W. E. B. DuBois, "Negroes of Farmville, Virginia," *Bulletin of the Department of Labor* 14 (January 1898): 21; Dolores Janiewski, *Sisterhood Denied: Race, Gender, and Class in a New South Community* (Philadelphia: Temple University Press, 1985), pp. 43–44,127–29.

27 Katzman, *Seven Days a Week*, pp. 60–62; U.S. Department of Commerce and Labor, Bureau of the Census, *Special Reports: Occupations at the Twelfth Census* (Washington, D.C.: U.S. Government Printing Office, 1904), pp. 486–89.

28 It is difficult to calculate the number of laundresses in Philadelphia. DuBois and Eaton referred to laundresses working in employers' homes as "day workers" and included housewives and seamstresses in this category.

29 For descriptions of laundry work, see Sarah Hill, "Bea the Washerwoman," Federal Writers Project, Southern Historical Collection, University of North Carolina, Chapel Hill (hereinafter FWP, SHC); Jasper Battle, "Wash Day in Slavery," in *The American Slave: A Composite Autobiography* (Westport, Conn.: Greenwood Press, 1972–79), vol. 2, pt. 1, p. 70; Buck, *Blessed Town*, pp. 116–20; Katzman, *Seven Days a Week*, pp. 72, 82, 124; Daniel Sutherland, *Americans and Their Servants: Domestic Service in the United States from 1800 to 1920* (Baton Rouge: Louisiana State University Press, 1981), p. 92; Dudden, *Serving Women*, pp. 224–25; Patricia E. Malcolmson, *English Laundresses: A Social History, 1850–1930* (Urbana: University of Illinois Press, 1986), pp. 11–43; Strasser, *Never Done*, 105–21.

30 See Don L. Klima, "Breaking Out: Streetcars and Suburban Development, 1872–1900," *Atlanta Historical Journal* 30 (Summer-Fall 1982): 67–82; Testimony of Albert C. Danner, in U.S. Senate Committee on Education and Labor, *Report upon the Relations Between Labor and Capital* (Washington, D.C.: U.S. Government Printing office, 1885), 105 (hereinafter *Labor and Capital*).

31 David McBride, *Integrating the City of Medicine. Blacks in Philadelphia Health Care, 1910–1965* (Philadelphia: Temple University Press, 1989), pp. 34–35; Hunter, *To 'Joy My Freedom*.

32 Lane, *William Dorsey's Philadelphia*, p. 8 1.

33 *Atlanta Journal*, March 3, 1883; Testimony of Mrs. Ward, *Labor and Capital*, pp.
   328,343; Katzman, *Seven Days a Week*, 195–97; Tera W. Hunter, "Domination and
   Resistance: The Politics of Wage Household Labor in Atlanta," *Labor History* 34
   (Spring-Summer 1993): 208–11.

34 For comparison of vails and customary rights in seventeenth- and eighteenth-century
   London, see Peter Linebaugh, *The London Hanged: Crime and Civil Society in the
   Eighteenth Century* (Cambridge: Cambridge University Press, 1992), pp. 250–55;
   Roger Lane argues that black domestics had some legal recourse when falsely accused
   of stealing in Philadelphia or when employers invaded their privacy by opening their
   mail, though he also acknowledges that only a few who were mistreated made formal
   complaints. *William Dorsey's Philadelphia*, p. 79.

35 For the controversy on pan-toting see Negro Nurse, "More Slavery at the South," p.
   199; "The Negro Problem: How It Appeals to a Southern White Woman,"
   Independent 54 (September 18, 1912): 22–27; Fleming, "Servant Problem," p. 8;
   Haynes, "Negroes in Domestic Service," pp. 412–13; Testimony of Mrs. Ward, *Labor
   and Capital*, p. 343; Elizabeth Kytle, *Willie Mae* (New York: Knopf, 1958), pp.
   116–17; E. P. Thompson, "The Moral Economy of the English Crowd in the
   Eighteenth Century," *Past and Present* 50 (February 1971): 76–135. For an insightful discussion of "social wages" see Marcus Rediker, *Between the Devil and the Deep
   Blue Sea: Merchant Seamen, Pirates, and the Anglo-American Maritime World,
   1700–1750* (Cambridge: Cambridge University Press, 1987), pp. 116–52.

36 Testimony of Mrs. Ward, *Labor and Capital*, p. 343. On resistance see Hunter,
   "Domination and Resistance," pp. 205–20; James C. Scott, *Domination and the Arts
   of Resistance: Hidden Transcripts* (New Haven, Conn.: Yale University Press, 1990).

37 Lane, *William Dorsey's Philadelphia*, 78.

38 U.S. Department of the Interior, Bureau of the Census, *Report of the Population of
   the United States at the Eleventh Census: 1890* (Washington, D.C.: U.S. Government
   Printing Office, 1897), pt. 2, p. 634; McLeod, *Workers and Workplace*, pp. 41, 100;
   Gretchen Maclachlan, "Women's Work: Atlanta's Industrialization and Urbanization,
   1879–1929" (Ph.D. diss., Emory University, 1992), pp. 13–20.

39 Lane, *Roots of Violence*, pp. 116–22.

40 See *Atlanta Constitution*, May 15 and June 18, 1900, November 30,1902; *Atlanta
   Journal*, April 12 and August 12, 1901; *Atlanta Independent*, September 22, 1906;
   "Condition of the Negro in Various Cities," *Bulletin of the Department of Labor 2*
   (May 1897): 257–359.

41 Maclachlan, "Women's Work," 203–25; "Reports of the Martha Home," 1913–15,
   in Christian Council Papers, Men and Religion Forward Movement, Atlanta History
   Center; Minute Book, 1908–18, Neighborhood Union Papers, Robert W. Woodruff
   Library, Clarke Atlanta University; Ruby Owens, tape-recorded interview by Bernard
   West, January 23, 1976, Living Atlanta Collection, Atlanta History Center.

42 Though Roger Lane acknowledged that there are no direct figures on black women
   prostitutes, he made questionable calculations nonetheless. He derived the estimate of
   2,000 to 2,500 black prostitutes (20 to 25 percent of the total presumed number) by
   arguing that black women accounted for 29 percent of prosecutions for infanticide, 40
   percent of known deaths from abortion, and 20 percent of official deaths caused by
   syphilis. How all of these morbidity and mortality measures, problematic in themselves,
   are linked to prostitution and prostitution alone is never substantiated or explained.
   Lane overreached his evidence even further to claim that "perhaps" as many as 25 percent of all black women in Philadelphia (e.g., over 5,000 women in 1890), by the end
   of their childbearing years "had at some time had exposure to the disease and habits
   associated with prostitution." There is no evidence presented here or elsewhere to

sustain this conjecture—he cites two newspaper articles from 1863 and 1880. See *Roots of Violence*, pp. 107–9, 122–33, 159.

43 See "Bea the Washerwoman," p. 4; Julia. Campbell Buggs, Mary Campbell, and Dinah Campbell, "Three Sisters," pp. 5, 9, FWP, SHC.

44 See Thornbery, "Black Atlanta," 210; Strasser, *Never Done*, 16–31.

45 On women's neighborhood networks and subsistence strategies see Neckerman, "Emergence of 'Underclass' Family Patterns," pp. 197–205; Christine Stansell, *City of Women: Sex and Class in New York, 1789–1860* (New York: Alfred A. Knopf, Inc., 1986), pp. 41–62; Ellen Ross, "Survival Networks: Women's Neighborhood Sharing in London Before World War I," *History Workshop* 15 (spring 1983): 4–27; Jeanne Boydston, "To Earn Her Daily Bread: Housework and Antebellum Working-Class Subsistence," *Radical History Review* 35 (1986): 7–25.

46 Maclachlan, "Women's Work," 163–85; Neckerman, "Emergence of 'Underclass' Family Patterns," 197–205.

47 DuBois, ed., *Efforts for Social Betterment Among Negro Americans* (Atlanta: Atlanta University Press, 1898), pp. 11–16; Porter, "Black Atlanta," pp. 68–75; Thornbery, "Black Atlanta," pp. 147–69.

48 U.S. Department of Treasury, Register of Signatures of Depositors in the Branches of the Freedmen's Savings and Trust Company, Atlanta Branch, 1870–74 (microfilm) National Archives, College Park, Maryland; DuBois, *Efforts for Social Betterment; American Missionary* (October 1889): 292; Porter, "Black Atlanta," 75–76.

49 Testimony of Mrs. Ward, *Labor and Capital*, p. 344; Ma [Margaret Cronly] to darling Rob [Cronly], June 29, 1881, Cronly Family Papers, William R. Perkins Library, Duke University.

50 This tactic of resistance evoked much controversy among employers in Atlanta as demonstrated by the attention it received in Joseph E. Brown's antiblack and antilabor U.S. Senate campaign in 1914. See 1914 campaign literature, Joseph M. Brown Papers, Atlanta History Center; *Atlanta Constitution*, March 31, 1910. Brown vowed to ease the burdens of "helpless" white housewives by eradicating domestic workers' organizations.

51 *Atlanta Constitution*, July 20, 1881; Porter, "Black Atlanta," pp. 254–61; Lane, *Roots of Violence*, 109–25.

52 Recent literature on black migration indicates that more African Americans had prior urban experiences than previously assumed. Blacks usually migrated incrementally from rural areas to southern cities, rather than moving directly from the rural South to the urban North. DuBois discussed the urban origins of many migrants from the upper South in *The Philadelphia Negro*, but his descriptions of southern migrants as a group usually depicted them as rural peasants inexperienced in urban life. See Peter Gottlieb, *Making Their Own Way: Southern Blacks' Migration to Pittsburgh, 1916–1930* (Urbana: University of Illinois Press, 1987), pp. 23–30; Joe William Trotter, ed., *The Great Migration in Historical Perspective: New Dimensions of Race, Class, and Gender* (Bloomington: Indiana University Press, 1991); James R. Grossman, *Land of Hope: Chicago, Black Southerners, and the Great Migration* (Chicago: University of Chicago Press, 1989); Carole Marks, *Farewell—We're Good and Gone. The Great Black Migration* (Bloomington: Indiana University Press, 1989).

53 See for example, Robert Gregg, *Sparks from the Anvil of Oppression: Philadelphia's African Methodist and Southern Migrants, 1890–1940* (Philadelphia: Temple University Press, 1993), pp. 3–5, 109–11; Willard B. Gatewood, *Aristocrats of Color. The Black Elite, 1880–1920* (Bloomington: Indiana University Press, 1990); Evelyn Brooks Higginbotham, *Righteous Discontent: The Women's Movement in the Black Baptist Church, 18801920* (Cambridge, Mass.: Harvard University Press, 1993);

Claudia Tate, *Domestic Allegories of Political Desire: The Black Heroine's Text at the Turn of the Century* (New York: Oxford University Press, 1992); Lewis, *DuBois*, pp. 189, 205. Too little research has been done on how the working class defined, challenged, or embraced "racial uplift" ideology. "Uplift" ideals were not necessarily limited to the black middle or upper classes, as many working-class people participated in the popular discourse about race advancement by attending public lectures, debates, and sermons, and by reading and discussing novels and serialized fiction and nonfiction in newspapers, such as the *AME Church Review*, published in Philadelphia.

54 *The Philadelphia Negro* makes explicit DuBois's many recommendations for changing policies, institutions, and individual behaviors. As Rudwick argued, DuBois enthusiastically embraced the double role of social scientist and social reformer. See Rudwick, "W. E. B. DuBois as a Sociologist," pp. 28, 38; Lewis, *DuBois*, pp. 183–210; Mary Jo Deegan, "W.E.B. DuBois and the Women of Hull-House, 1895–1899," *American Sociologist* 19 (Winter 1988): 301–11.

CHAPTER 5

URBAN BLACK LABOR IN THE WEST, 1849-1949: RECONCEPTUALIZING THE IMAGE OF A REGION

QUINTARD TAYLOR

In April 1992, South Central Los Angeles exploded in anger and rage. Although Los Angeles is the largest metropolis in the west, those scenes of carnage, no less than the city itself, undermine the regional self-image most westerners prefer: placid valleys or broad vistas populated by proud, self-reliant citizens jealously guarding their individual rights and freedom, "under an open sky."

Yet black western history, much like the Los Angeles uprising, intrudes itself onto our sensibilities and forces a reexamination of the imagined West. That history, with its examples of resistance, conflict and cooperation between African Americans and other westerners can be celebrated or critiqued but it can no longer be ignored.

Unlike Asian American, Chicano or much of Native American history, which are automatically "western" in orientation, black history in this region continues to be viewed by western regional historians and historians of African America as an interesting footnote to a story focused elsewhere. Indeed historian Walter Prescott Webb in 1957 described the West as the American region without—"water, timber, cities . . . or Negroes."

This paucity of black western scholarship is particularly surprising considering the size of the black population at certain times in the history of the region. If we define the West as beginning with the states that straddle the 98th meridian and stretching to the Pacific, then as early as 1870 African Americans comprised 12 percent of the region's population. Put another way, some 284,000 black people resided in every state and territory in the West. By 1910 there were slightly fewer than a million black westerners, about 6 percent of the regional population. That figure had grown to 6 million by 2000, or 6 percent of the regional total.

The Los Angeles Riot of 1992 made the nation aware of the complex relationships among peoples of color in the modern urban West. Yet the multiple sources of that relationship are rooted in five centuries of encounter of racially and culturally diverse peoples both as individuals and distinct populations. Was the West significantly different for African Americans? Was there a western racial "frontier" beyond which black people could expect freedom and opportunity? Perhaps one answer can be found in the employment of black urban westerners.

An examination of black labor in the West can explain much not only about black workers but as well the social and cultural conditions of African American communities in the region. As Milton P. Webster, vice president of the Brotherhood of Sleeping Car Porters declared in a 1929 interview, "Race workers are the backbone of the race, and upon their welfare . . . depends the progress of all phases of our life, whether religious, social, fraternal, civic or commercial."[1]

The first black urban workers in the West were the 6,000 slaves who resided in the Texas cities of Austin, San Antonio, Galveston, and Houston. Although only 6 percent of Texas bondspeople, they nonetheless formed a distinct population. Galveston and Houston, the largest cities in antebellum Texas, each had over one thousand black slaves, while several hundred lived in Austin and San Antonio. The urban black slave population grew proportionately with the cities while their work followed the occupational patterns of the region. The majority of these slaves were house servants, but others worked as cooks, teamsters, hotel waiters, carpenters, bricklayers, and boatmen. A small number of skilled slaves worked in flour mills, sawmills, and brickyards. The growth of the skilled slave artisan class prompted white groups such as the Houston Mechanics Association to adopt a resolution in 1858 declaring their opposition to "the practice adhered to by some of making contracts with the negro mechanics to carry on work, as a contractor."[2]

Most white urban Texans worried about the social latitude black people assumed in the cities because of their occupations. One Austin ordinance enacted in 1855 granted the "city marshal and his assistants . . . control and supervision of the conduct, carraige [sic], demeanor and deportment of any and all slaves living, being, or found within the city limits" and another forbade "any white man or Mexican" from "making associates" of black slaves. City laws called for slave patrols, the regulation of assemblies, and the prohibition of gambling or the possession of liquor and weapons. Yet some urban slaves openly flouted these bans, prompting one Austin newspaper editor in 1854 to declare in disgust that he "almost imagines himself in the land of amalgamation, abolition meetings, and woman's rights conventions."[3]

Other slaves challenged the limits of their servile status by openly defying whites. Urban slaves commonly disregard the groveling courtesies demanded by "polite" racial etiquette and instead engaged in insubordination and disorderly conduct. one bondsman was quoted in an Austin paper as declaring "let any white man tell him to stop his mouth, and see if he would not give him hell."[4]

California's antebellum black population comprised the first voluntary African American migrants to the West and the first significant free African American population in the region. In an 1854 letter to Frederick Douglass, black San Franciscan William H. Newby, described his new city of 35,000 inhabitants. "San Francisco presents many features that no city in the Union presents. Its population is composed of almost every nation under heaven. Here is to be seen at a single glance every nation in miniature." Newby depicted the entire population but his words applied equally to the diverse array of African Americans gathered in the Golden State. In 1850 California had nearly one thousand blacks from north and south of the Mason-Dixon line as well as a foreign-born population of Afro-Latin Americans from Mexico, Peru, and Chile, and a significant population of Jamaicans.[5]

Antebellum urban California blacks pursued a range of occupations similar to those available in eastern cities, although the gold-enriched economy provided significantly higher wages for the most menial positions. Black stewards on river steamers earned $150 a month during the 1850s. At the top of this employment hierarchy stood the cook. Of the 464 blacks in San Francisco in 1852, 67 were cooks. Sacramento, with 338 black residents had 51 African American cooks. The designation cook, however, obscured the vast range of incomes African Americans received in this occupation. Mary Ellen Pleasant's reputation as a cook preceded her when she arrived in the city in 1852, and she was besieged at the wharf by men anxious to employ her. Pleasant ultimately selected an employer who promised 500 dollars a month, a gold miner's average income. Next came barbers and stewards. San Francisco in 1852 had 22 black stewards and 18 black barbers, Sacramento 8 and 23, respectively. Yet most African American men and women worked at unskilled positions—"whitewashers," porters, waiters, maids, and servants—in businesses and private homes.[6]

A few fortunate African Americans in San Francisco became wealthy business owners. Mary Ellen Pleasant, perhaps the most celebrated black property-owner in antebellum California, owned three laundries and was involved in mining stock and precious metals speculation. John Ross operated Ross's Exchange, a used-goods business, while James P. Dyer, the West's only antebellum black manufacturer, began the New England Soap Factory in 1851. Former slave George Washington Dennis managed a successful livery business in the city. Mifflin W. Gibbs arrived in San Francisco in 1850 with ten cents and initially worked as a bootblack. In 1851 he formed a partnership with fellow Philadelphian, Peter Lester, the Pioneer Boot and Shoe Emporium, a store that eventually had "patrons extending to Oregon and lower California." By 1854 black San Francisco could proudly boast of "two black-owned joint stock companies with a combined capital of $16,000, four boot and shoe stores, four clothing stores, two furniture stores, two billiard saloons, sixteen barbershops, and two bathhouses . . . 100 mechanics, 100 porters in banking and commercial houses, 150 stewards, 300 waiters, and 200 cooks."[7]

African American San Franciscans created the first permanent community in the Far West. Between 1849 and 1855 most African American residents settled near the waterfront and expanded slowly from there. The eastward-facing slope of Telegraph Hill was home to most blacks and was situated in a larger mixed community of color that evolved in a section derisively termed "Chili Hill" because of the concentration of Latin Americans. Occupying the same neighborhood of tents, shacks, saloons, hotels, and gambling houses, Mexican American, Chilean, and African American sailors, miners and laborers pooled resources in one of the earliest examples of cooperation among people of color. In 1854, for example, Mexican Americans and African Americans organized a pre-Christmas masquerade ball.[8]

Kansas had the only other significant concentration of free black urban west-erners prior to 1865. Black Kansas was virtually created by the Civil War itself. The late 1850s battle for "bleeding Kansas" ended in a victory for free state partisans. Yet the territory by 1860 attracted only 627 African Americans. By 1865, however, over 12,000 blacks resided in Kansas, 9 percent of the popula-tion. This population explosion came from a combination of politics and geog-raphy. "Free" Kansas posed an enticing destination to the large Missouri slave population.

The Civil War influx swelled the black population in Kansas cities which had 56 percent of the total black population. Two Kansas towns, Leavenworth with 2,400 blacks and Lawrence with nearly a thousand, contained 72 percent of the state's urban black population. From the beginning of the war, Kansas Senator James H. Lane and other abolitionists envisioned an exchange of black labor for black freedom. The Senator even employed contrabands to grow cotton on his Douglas County farm.[9]

But urban refugees depended upon work in towns and cities. The type of labor they performed and the skills they brought from their slave experience guaran-teed that they were never far from their previous condition. The state census of 1865 showed 349 employed blacks in Lawrence. Ninety-five men were listed as soldiers. Eighty-five were day laborers, the second largest occupational category. Of the 92 female workers, 49 were domestics, 27 were washerwomen, and 7 worked as housekeepers, 6 as servants, and 3 as cooks. Overall, some 270 blacks, 77 percent of the town's total, worked in various capacities as unskilled laborers. Of the 23 percent who were skilled, 23 were teamsters, 8 were black-smiths, and 4 barbers. Lawrence also had one black saloonkeeper, one carpenter, one shoemaker, one printer, and one preacher.[10]

Leavenworth, the oldest and largest town in Kansas during the Civil War, also had a sizeable African American population, some 2,455 in 1865, 16 percent of the city's population. Like most black newcomers to Kansas, Leavenworth's African Americans were mostly fugitives who had arrived "wholly destitute of the means of living." Leavenworth African Americans found employment in a vari-ety of occupations. Some worked on farms during the spring and summer but a much larger number were employed as teamsters, hotel waiters, porters, cooks, maids, and manual laborers. The Emancipation League's Labor Exchange and Intelligence Office, located in the drugstore of Dr. R. C. Anderson, became an informal employment agency for local blacks. Yet the rapid influx of fugitive slaves, their few skills, and the small size of the town insured that their employ-ment prospects remained circumscribed.[11]

With full emancipation in 1865, larger numbers of African Americans migrated west. The popular image of this migration is of homesteaders trekking toward the setting sun to build upon the foundation established earlier by black cowboys or buffalo soldiers. The image is incomplete rather than untrue. In 1885, as black cowboys trailed cattle from Texas to Dodge City, or black homesteaders grew wheat from west Kansas soil, far more black women and men moved to Denver, San Francisco, Seattle, and Los Angeles in search of the jobs available in the urban economy. These contrasting images of black cowboys, homesteaders, and urban workers remind us that "multiple" Wests often existed side by side.

The nineteenth century black urban community expanded in the region's larger cities and in smaller towns such as Salt Lake City, Utah; Topeka, Kansas; Virginia City, Nevada; Helena, Montana; Yankton, South Dakota; and Pocatello, Idaho. In large and small cities, churches, fraternal organizations, social clubs, even fledgling civil rights organizations established the pattern of community life. Black urban populations in Helena and Yankton did not survive into the twentieth century but Houston, Dallas, Oakland, Denver, and Los Angeles, became the final destination for tens of thousands of hopeful migrants.[12]

The combined African American population of the five largest Western cities in 1910, San Francisco, Los Angeles, Seattle, Denver, and Portland, totaled only 18,008, slightly-more than one-fifth the total of the largest black urban community at the time, Washington, D.C. Such small numbers, however, did not prevent western urban blacks from organizing a rich social and cultural life, or battling against racial injustice.[13]

Western black urban communities shared numerous characteristics. Local and sub-regional economies might differ, but African Americans in every western city performed surprisingly similar work; both men and women were personal servants for wealthy households, while black males worked as hotel waiters, railroad porters, messengers, cooks, and janitors. Some entrepreneurial blacks operated barbershops, restaurants, and boarding houses.[14]

San Francisco had the oldest black urban community in the west. Following the Gold Rush influx of one thousand African Americans, the number of blacks in the city did not appreciably increase and, in fact, declined between 1890 and 1910, as numerous African Americans moved to the city's first suburb, Oakland. Most of those who remained in the city survived on the margin of the urban economy. San Francisco in 1910 offered the same types of service jobs as in 1860. Most black workers were coachmen, butlers, cooks, maids and porters. If sailors, ship stewards, and dock workers, their meager wages did little to raise overall prosperity.[15]

Postbellum African American San Franciscans had few employment options. One of them was in food service. San Francisco's booming economy, with its multitude of hotels, restaurants, saloons, and private clubs, should have offered numerous opportunities. But black workers were challenged even in this arena. In 1875 San Francisco's most exclusive luxury hotel, known simply as the Palace, offered nearly two hundred service positions to black workers. Besides the good wages and prospect for handsome tips, these workers basked in the prestige of employment in the most elegant hotel west of the Mississippi River. That pride showed in an 1875 banquet honoring General Philip Sheridan. The staff for the evening were portrayed by one spectator as "an army of waiters in swallow-tailed coats and white . . . gloves, flitting noiseless to and fro."[16]

Fourteen years later, however, all of the black Palace waiters were abruptly replaced by whites, a move that presaged the elimination of most African Americans from the city's hotel and restaurant industry. The genesis of this change could be traced to July 1883, when white waiters formed the Cooks and Waiters Union of the Pacific Coast and went on strike, demanding that black and Asian waiters be fired and barred from future hotel and restaurant employment. The strike did not eliminate black workers but the CWU gained the support of allied labor groups such as the bakers and confectioners unions. By 1888 the San Francisco local again struck and succeeded in eliminating all nonunion labor in "the places were colored help is employed." One of those places was the Palace. Many black San Franciscans shared the conclusion of an editorial in one of the city's major newspapers, the Daily Alta California, "The object of this movement is to do away with colored help altogether and to have only white men in the kitchen and dining room."[17]

The San Francisco example described above held true for every other major city in the West through 1940. Excluded from most jobs, African American workers had little contact with most white workers, including obviously, most union members. Such exclusion created a vicious cycle of mutual hostility and recrimination. White workers, claiming that blacks were antiunion, adamantly refused to lower color bars, while black workers, and much of the African American community leadership, embraced strikebreaking to forcibly open restricted jobs.[18]

Colorado's African Americans were concentrated in Denver where as early as 1870 they comprised 56 percent of the state's black population. These mostly male settlers included Barney Ford, a Virginia native who worked as a Chicago barber and a steward on a Nicaragua steamer in the 1850s before coming to Denver in 1860. After brief periods as a successful restaurant and boarding house owner, Ford in 1874 built the Inter-Ocean Hotel, which "for some years . . . was the aristocratic hostelry of Denver." Later in the decade Ford accepted the invitation of Cheyenne businessman to build a second hotel in the Wyoming territorial capital.[19]

A number of other African Americans followed Ford's initial trade, barbering, because it offered both status and relative financial independence. The 1870 census reported that Denver area black barbers comprised 65 percent of the Territory's barbers. By the 1880s fast-growing Denver attracted far more laborers and construction workers. These mostly single black Denverites lived throughout the city in its earliest decades. By the 1890s, however, a small number of middle class African American families began to concentrate in the Five Points district, creating a stable, if increasingly segregated community northeast of the city's downtown core.[20]

Despite the limited job prospects, black Denver evolved into a permanent community. Three African American newspapers, the *Star,* the *Argus,* and the *Colorado Statesman,* were published during the late nineteenth century. By 1900 the community supported nine churches, one hotel, various restaurants, saloons, a funeral home, and drugstore. Its professional class included two doctors, three lawyers, and numerous musicians. Moreover, a number of women were involved in dressmaking, catering, storekeeping, and mining. The Bonita Silver and Gold mining Company, founded in 1896, was controlled by two women, president Mary E. Phelps, and secretary, Mrs. L. K. Daniels. By 1906 the community also included an enterprising former Louisianian, Sarah Breedlove, who married a local newspaper reporter, Charles J. Walker. Mrs. or "Madame" C. J. Walker marketed hair care products door to door and in 1907 opened a business and manufacturing headquarters in Denver while promoting her "Walker System" throughout the East. Madame C. J. Walker eventually became the most successful African American cosmetics manufacturer in the United States.[21]

In 1910, Omaha's blacks comprised the third largest African American population among the major cities in the West. Most Omaha blacks worked as janitors, maids, and porters, but at least some held jobs in railroad construction, the city's stockyards, and meat packing industry. Major firms used African American workers as part of the "reserve army" of strikebreakers following the Union Pacific's example in the 1877 railroad strike. In 1894 the major packing companies, Swift, Hammond, Cudahy, and Omaha, used blacks to break a strike. Not all African Americans were antiunion however. Black Omaha barbers, for example, organized the first African American labor union in the city in 1887 and went on strike because they deemed it "unprofessional" to work beside white competitors. In a city where race and ethnicity defined worker solidarity as much as class, such a development is not surprising.[22]

Unskilled labor was the prospect for the vast majority of late nineteenth and early twentieth century black Los Angeles residents. Many newcomers found jobs as construction and repair workers for the Southern Pacific and Santa Fe railroads, or as porters, cooks, waiters and maids. Pio Pico, California's last Mexican-era governor, for example, recruited one hundred black workers for his Pico House Hotel in the mid-1880s. In 1903 the Southern Pacific Railroad brought nearly 2,000 black laborers to break a strike by Mexican American construction workers in 1903, doubling the size of the community and initiating intense interethnic rivalry among the largest non-Anglo groups in the region that would continue long after the strike. Harrison Gray Otis, the powerful antiunion founder of the *Los Angeles Times*, exploited organized labor's antiblack bias by encouraging African American workers to come to the region and financing organizations such as the local Afro-American League. These new workers and their families supported a vibrant commercial district along Central Avenue, which eventually became known as Harlem of the West.

The Texas cities—San Antonio, Houston, Dallas, and Fort Worth—constitute an anomaly in the discussion of the black urban West. In 1910 none exceeded 100,000 inhabitants and thus were not among the region's largest urban centers. Yet the Texas cities combined African American populations totaled 65,949. Houston's 23,929 residents exceeded the combined black population of the five largest cities in the West.[23]

Nineteenth-century black urban Texas emerged in the shadow of slavery. The first significant numbers of blacks to arrive in post-Civil War Texas cities were newly freed slaves from nearby plantations who began an intrastate rural-to-urban migration in the summer of 1865 that continues to this day.[24] The ex-slaves who settled in Houston's Freedmantown or Dallas' Deep Ellum, usually found work as domestic servants, manual laborers for railroads, or on numerous building construction projects, and in Houston, as dockworkers.[25]

By 1910 the parameters of black urban settlement in the West were fixed. African American communities existed in all of the cities of the region and were poised to grow with the general population. These African American communities in the region differed nearly as much from each other as they did from communities east of the Mississippi River. Black Houston, a segregated "city within a city," for example, grew from the nearby rural population, while black San Francisco evolved from a population of globally diverse origins. Yet, as the twentieth century progressed, such differences receded as Western urban blacks fought for greater economic opportunity, political influence, and educational access.

In 1913 W. E. B. Du Bois embarked on a promotional tour for the newly founded National Assciation for the Advancement of Colored People (NAACP) through Texas, California, and the Pacific Northwest. Du Bois's tour signalled the growing recognition of western urban African American communities. By the second decade of the twentieth century the center of black life in the West was urban. African American urbanites outnumbered rural residents in every Western state except Texas and Oklahoma. Even there the political, economic, and cultural center of black life lay in Houston, Dallas, Oklahoma City, and Tulsa long before most black Oklahomans or Texans became urbanites. The fate of the average twentieth century black western worker would be determined in the city.[26]

Black San Francisco, Omaha, Denver, and Los Angeles continued to grow. Indeed the southern California city had the largest black population by 1940. But African Americans moved to other western cities, notably Seattle and Portland in the Pacific Northwest; Phoenix, Tucson, and San Diego in the far Southwest; and Wichita, Oklahoma City, and Tulsa on the Southern Plains. Black Tulsa's rapid growth during World War I, prompted by oil discoveries in the region, gave rise to an enterprising, successful population that chafed under Southern-inspired racial restrictions. Their success heightened black-white tensions and sparked the Tulsa Race Riot of 1921, an orgy of white violence on June 1, which took 30 lives and destroyed 1,100 homes and most businesses in "Deep Greenwood," Tulsa's fabled African American district.[27]

Despite the continued growth of black urban communities, nineteenth-century urban employment patterns continued virtually unchanged until World War II. In 1930 most African American males in San Francisco, Oakland, Denver, Portland, and Seattle worked as servants. Only in Houston did male workers in manufacturing outnumber those in domestic service. For black women in the largest western cities, domestic service dominated with percentages ranging from a low of 83 percent in Seattle to a high of 93 percent in Dallas. This employment concentration prompted the *Northwest Enterprise,* Seattle's black newspaper, to declare in 1927, "Colored men should have jobs as streetcar motormen and conductors. [Black women] should have jobs as telephone operators and stenographers. . . . Black firemen can hold a hose and squirt water on a burning building just as well as white firemen. We want jobs, jobs, after that everything will come unto us."[28]

C. L. Dellums, Vice President of the Brotherhood of Sleeping Car Porters, recalled work opportunities soon after he came to the San Francisco Bay area from Texas in 1923. "I had been around here long enough to realize there wasn't very much work Negroes could get." African American workers could either "go down to the sea in ships or work on the railroads." Fourteen years later Kathryn Bogle, discovered similar limitations when she began to search for employment after graduating from a Portland high school. "I visited large and small stores . . . I visited the telephone company; both power and light companies. I tried to become an elevator operation in an office building. I answered ads for inexperienced office help. In all of these places I was told there was nothing about me in my disfavor except my skin color." Bogle then described how several employers who refused to hire her downtown nonetheless offered her work "as a domestic . . . where her color would not be an embarrassment."[29]

The Great Depression ravaged western black communities throughout the 1930s. Houston's black unemployment approached 40 percent in 1931 compared to 17 percent for white workers. One of every three black workers in Los Angeles was unemployed in 1931 and one of every four in Denver and Seattle. The unemployment burden African American workers assumed prompted the *Colorado Statesman* to declare in 1933, "Is [the Negro] not an American citizen and entitled to share and share alike. . . . Although he is perfectly willing to take his chances, he is not given a chance . . . He is, in truth and deed, the forgotten man."[30]

Statistics cannot completely convey the sense of loss and despair. Seattleite Sara Oliver Jackson remembered that during the early 1930s "there wasn't any particular jobs you could get, although you knew you had to work. So, you got a domestic job and made $10.00 a month, cause that was what they were paying, a big 35 cents a day" William Pittman, a San Francisco dentist, unable to continue his practice, worked for $80 per month as a chauffeur. Pittman's wife Tarea, a 1925 University of California graduate, concluded that discrimination compounded the family's declining economic fortunes. "I am unable to find work," wrote Tarea Pittman, "on account of my race." One unidentified Portland woman remembered, "We were without work for well over a year. I did a number of things to help bring in money, and my husband worked for fifty cents a day shoveling snow down at the [Portland] Hotel just trying to make it."[31]

War followed Depression, and World War II changed forever the African American West. The region's black population grew by 443,000 (33 percent) during the war decade and redistributed itself toward the west coast. Oklahoma lost 23,000 African Americans, 14 percent of its black population, while California alone gained 338,000 a 272 percent increase. The three Pacific Coast states and Nevada led the nation in the percentage of black population growth. Most of these newcomers concentrated in five major metropolitan regions: Seattle-Tacoma, Washington, and Portland, Oregon-Vancouver, Washington, in the Pacific Northwest; the San Francisco Bay area comprising San Francisco, Oakland, and smaller cities such as Berkeley and Richmond; the Los Angeles-Long Beach area; and San Diego. These metropolitan regions saw black population increases ranging from 798 percent for San Francisco to 168 percent for Los Angeles. Las Vegas, although 200 miles inland, grew much like the coastal cities. Between 1940 and 1950 its African American population exploded from 178 to 2,888, a 1,522 percent increase. The numbers were less dramatic in Denver, Omaha, Phoenix, Tucson, and Honolulu but these cities also saw surging black populations.[32]

If expanding populations indicated change, so did expanding work opportunity. After decades of menial labor, thousands of black workers entered the region's factories and shipyards, a process historian Joe Trotter has described as the proletarianization of the black work force. Thousands more African American military personnel stationed in the West ended their enlistments at western bases, sent for family members, and settled permanently in the region. Marilyn Johnson's conclusion that World War II era migration made the East Bay area population "younger, more southern, more female, and noticably more black" than ever before, applies equally to western communities from Omaha to San Diego.[33]

African Americans working in defense industries had to overcome the bias of many employers and union leaders. Worker shortages, however, and pressure from the Fair Employment Practices Committee (FEPC) soon opened numerous Western workplaces previously closed to African Americans as well as white women and other people of color. The FEPC proved a powerful ally. Although black leaders criticized its caution, many African Americans recognized the FEPC as the one federal agency sympathetic to their grievances. As Katherine Archibald remarked in her wartime study of Bay Area shipyards, "There was a feeling that the law, at least—if not . . . justice—was on the side of the black man. . . ."[34]

Black wartime migration to the West occurred within a larger white influx to the region. Eight million people moved west of the Mississippi River in the 1940s; nearly half came to the Pacific Coast. California received 3.5 million new-comers who accounted for the single largest addition to a state's population in one decade in the nation's history. The entire West grew by 26 percent during the 1940s. Since blacks were a segment of a much larger migration, resentment toward newcomers did not apply exclusively to African Americans. When Portland Mayor Earl Riley warned, "Undesirables—white or colored—are not wanted and if they fail to obey our laws, will be unceremoniously dealt with," he articulated concerns that transcended the race of the newcomers.[35]

Even so, race became a powerful component of that opposition. The possibility of racial violence prompted Seattle Mayor William F. Devin in February 1944, to form the Seattle Civic Unity Committee. The Mayor set the tone of urgency in a speech at the University of Washington in July, 1944, when he announced: "The problem of racial tensions is . . . going to affect us not only during the War, but also after the War, and it is our duty to face the problem together. If we do not do that, we shall not exist very long as a civilized city or as a nation."[36]

The five West Coast metropolitan areas, Seattle, Portland, San Francisco-Oakland, Los Angeles, and San Diego, that collectively absorbed 70 percent of the increase in the region's African American population during the decade were heavily affected by rapidly expanding defense industries. San Diego became an aircraft production center. Portland and San Francisco Oakland developed ship-building facilities. Los Angeles and Seattle excelled in both categories. Black migration, however, was not consistent throughout the decade or proportionately divided among the cities. Los Angeles attracted half the West Coast bound migrants between 1940 and 1943, receiving a record 12, 000 in June of the latter year. Black Los Angeles, which had seen its population double each decade between 1900 and 1940, was accustomed to huge population increases. The same could not be said for the other Pacific coast metropolitan areas. Between 1943 and 1945 other West Coast cities saw influxes that overwhelmed their prewar populations.[37]

Migrants came west for work in shipbuilding and aircraft production. Three Los Angeles shipbuilders, Consolidated Steel, California Ship (Cal Ship), and

Western Pipe and Steel employed over 60,000 workers at the height of wartime production in 1944. Cal Ship, the largest, had 7,022 black employees at the end of 1944, 15 percent of the work force. African Americans found work in seven Bay Area shipbuilding facilities: Marinship near Sausalito, Moore Drydock and Bethlehem-Alameda in Oakland, and four Kaiser Company shipyards in Richmond. At peak production the Kaiser-Richmond yards employed 90,000 people including 18,000 African Americans. Kaiser also had three shipbuilding facilities in the Portland area. Two yards, Oregon Shipbuilding and Kaiser-Swan Island were in the city; a third, Kaiser-Vancouver, was built on the north bank of the Columbia River in neighboring Vancouver, Washington. The Portland area shipyards eventually employed over 7,700 African Americans in 1944. They comprised 9 percent of the overall workforce but 96 percent of all the black workers in the city. No single shipbuilding employer dominated production in Seattle. Twenty-nine yards in the city and neighboring Bremerton employed 4,000 African Americans.[38]

By 1944, 7,186 African Americans worked at four Los Angeles area aircraft companies: Lockheed-Vega in Santa Monica, Douglas in Long Beach, North American Aviation in Inglewood, and Consolidated-Vultee in Los Angeles. These black employees comprised from 3.2 to 7.2 percent of the workers in the various firms. By 1945, 1,200 black Boeing workers comprised 3 percent of the Pacific Northwest's largest workforce. Consolidated Aircraft employed 1,000 of the 1,200 black San Diego aircraft employees at the height of war production in 1945.[39]

Local African Americans fought to obtain defense plant jobs long after President Franklin Roosevelt issued Executive Order 8802 to prevent employment discrimination. Leaders of the Aero-Mechanics Local 751, which represented the Boeing workforce, voiced their displeasure with the opening of jobs even temporarily to African Americans. "We rather resent that the war situation has been used to alter an old established custom," declared IAM representative James Duncan, "and do not feel it will be helpful to war production." By 1942 acute labor shortages in the west coast cities required the mobilization of all able-bodied workers—women as well as men, Asian Americans, Native Americans, Latinos and blacks, even prisoners and the handicapped. A boilermakers' union publication claimed that the new Kaiser recruits represented "a bottom of the barrel" assortment of "shoe clerks, soda jerks, professors, pimps, and old maids." Nonetheless, continuing labor shortages forced the shipbuilders to turn eastward to tap the national labor pool.[40]

With War Manpower Commission (WMC) assistance, defense employers began to recruit workers. Kaiser's efforts were typical. The company targeted dozens of Southern and Midwestern cities with "surplus" labor, dispatching 170 recruiters to the East. Between 1942 and 1943 Kaiser brought nearly 38,000 workers on "liberty" trains that originated as far away as New York City. Another 60,000 paid their way to the West Coast. "There's a job of vital importance to your country waiting for you in the Richmond shipyards," declared one Kaiser pamphlet. "You can learn a trade, get paid while you're learning, and earn the highest wages for comparable work anywhere in the world." Wartime migration soon assumed a momentum independent of Kaiser's recruiting efforts. Black workers wrote home describing the high wages, the mild climate, and greater freedom. A 1943 War Manpower Commission survey indicated that nearly 75 percent of the black migrants to the Bay Area came west without any direct contact with recruiters.[41]

Four states (Arkansas, Louisiana, Texas and Oklahoma) contributed a disproportionate number of newcomers, more than half of whom were women. Getting to the Pacific coast was the first task. Many migrants followed hot, dusty stretches of U.S. Highways 80, 60, and Route 66, made famous by the Dust Bowl migration a decade earlier, across Texas, New Mexico, and Arizona. They came with their "mementos, histories and hope, all tied to the top of a car." Since few hotels along the route accommodated black people, migrants took turns driving and camped by roadsides. On occasion they stayed in African American homes along the route in Amarillo, Santa Fe, Albuquerque, Flagstaff, Phoenix, or Barstow.[42]

Train travelers faced three to four days on crowded, uncomfortable cars. Edwin Coleman accompanied his parents on their 1943 journey from El Dorado, Arkansas to Alameda, California. Even segregated seating for blacks was unavailable, since white soldiers and passengers filled the "colored" section. Coleman, his mother, and his sister, stood in the vestibule of the train, including practically all the way to Salt Lake City. Bertha Walker, who left Houston in October 1943, rode "out of Texas on the Jim Crow car . . . packed with military people." In El Paso, Bertha changed trains and shortly afterward a soldier and who rose to give her his seat said, "you can relax now, because we're at the end Mason-Dixon line."[43]

"Getting there" proved relatively easy compared to challenges of the new workplace. All shipyard workers had to adjust to assemble the regimen of prefabricated shipbuilding. West Coast shipbuilders used techniques developed in building Boulder Dam. Whole sections of a ship's structure, including boilers, double bottoms, and deckhouses were preassembled elsewhere and lifted into place by workers using huge cranes. This technique allowed the yards to assemble vessels in record time. The *Robert E. Peary* was built in four days in November 1942 in a Richmond shipyard. Since workers performed specific, repetitive tasks, training went rapidly. But these workers faced a bureaucratized environment: for the first time in their lives they used security badges, got company-sponsored health care, reported to timekeepers, and received their paychecks (with income tax withheld) from pay windows. The Richmond yards were laid out in a grid system of numbered and lettered streets. One worker described the 900 acres of shipyards: "It was such a huge place. . . . People from all walks of life, all coming and going and working, and the noise. The whole atmosphere was overwhelming to me."[44]

West Coast shipyards pioneered new production techniques and labor management relations but they also embraced old stereotypes. The Chinese performed detail-oriented electrical work considered suitable for their skills. White women held welding jobs, considered the easiest position on the yards, while black women were relegated to scaling (cleaning), sweeping, and painting ship hulls. Portland shipyard worker Beatrice Marshall described her job as a painter's helper: "We had to crawl on our hands and knees and carry our light on an extension cord . . . because it was pitch dark. We . . . scraped the rust off the bottom of the boat where they had to paint. . . . We had to wear masks, there [was] so much rust in there . . . you could hardly breathe."[45]

War time labor demands guaranteed black women and men would work; they did not guarantee equitable treatment. Throughout the war black workers, shipyard managers and union officials engaged in a triangular negotiation over workplace segregation and worker assignments. In the bewildering order of job allocation by the shipyard unions and managers, black workers could build ships but not repair them; clean ships, but not paint them; and weld steel plates but not pipes. Doris Mae Williams, originally a Kaiser Vancouver shipyard welder, took a job as a laborer rather than suffer continued abuse from her supervisor and coworkers who refused to accept her credentials. "I am now scaling. [It is] hard labor," Williams wrote to the FEPC. "Our crew is mixed, we are all treated alike. Why couldn't the same be said for skilled workers?" Eventually labor shortages and production demands broke down this arcane racial classification, but most black workers remained in unskilled work categories for the rest of the war.[46]

Two barriers were rarely broached. Black women and men, regardless of education or experience, did not become clerical workers or supervisors. Katherine Archibald recounted the story of an unidentified African American schoolteacher from Texas who worked at Oakland's Moore Dry Dock as "matron of a women's rest room." Despite clerical experience, the woman was denied the office job she sought, "because of my race." We don't know why the woman refused a more lucrative position in the yards, but according to Archibald, "She bore herself with the dignity of a duchess at her tea table." Shipyard managers allowed African Americans to head all-black crews but never to supervise whites. One Bay Area shipyard personnel director declared, "We wouldn't ask white people to work under a Negro and we shouldn't expect them to."[47]

African American workers, native and migrant alike, concluded that the International Brotherhood of Boilermakers (AFL) accounted for much of their difficulty. Until 1937 the boilermakers excluded black workers. However, facing escalating CIO competition, and the prospect that shipyards would eventually hire black workers, the union at its 1937 convention reversed its policy and created all-black "auxiliary" locals. Had the Boilermakers remained one of a number of unions competing for shipyard jurisdiction, their impact on black workers would have been minimal. The rival CIO-affiliated Industrial Union of Marine and Shipbuilding, for example, was racially integrated. But in 1941 the Boilermakers negotiated a closed shop agreement with the Kaiser Company. Other shipbuilders followed giving the Boilermakers jurisdiction over 65 percent of the U.S. shipyard workers and all of those in West Coast yards except Seattle. By 1944, 32,000 black employees were forced into A-26 in Oakland, A-32 in Portland, A-92 in Los Angeles, and A-41 in Sausalito.[48]

Membership in an auxiliary entailed restrictions not faced by white union members. Once hired, black employees had to secure approval of white locals before they could seek promotion. Furthermore, an auxiliary, unlike a regular local, could be abolished at any time by International officials. Testifying before a Congressional Committee, Fred Jones, a member of A-92, demonstrated the absurdity of auxiliary unions when he initially claimed to be Hindu and was granted full membership; however, when he told union officials he was African American, they immediately reassigned him to the auxiliary union. "We pay our dues but what do we get?" declared Joyce R. Washington, a Cal Ship worker in 1943, "Nothing but to be discriminated against and segregated."[49]

Most West Coast African Americans adamantly disagreed with a Boilermaker official's view of auxiliary unions as an "internal union matter." Shipyards were by far the largest employers of African Americans on the Pacific coast. Boilermaker policies directly affected these workers from Portland to San Diego. FEPC representative James H. Wolfe, chief justice of the Utah Supreme Court, reached that conclusion after a 1943 west coast fact-finding visit when he declared, "The problems presented by the West Coast situation are national in import and must be solved on the national level . . . "[50]

That solution came in the summer of 1943, when west coast shipyards, at Boilermakers's insistence, fired black workers for protesting the auxiliary scheme. In rapid succession 200 workers were dismissed at Marinship in Sausalito, 100 at Moore Drydock in Oakland, 300 workers at Cal Ship in Los Angeles, and 350 at the three Kaiser shipyards in Portland. Among the dismissed Marinship workers was Joseph James, president of the San Francisco NAACP. Shipyard workers in each community immediately mounted legal challenges. In Portland and Los Angeles black workers requested FEPC action on shipyard discrimination. In response, the federal agency held its first West Coast hearings in Portland on November 15-16 and in Los Angeles on November 19-20. On December 9 the FEPC directed the Boilermakers and shipbuilders to end discrimination and abolish the auxiliary system. Shipyard companies complied with the ruling but the Boilermakers resisted, arguing that the FEPC's directives "alienate[d] the goodwill of organized labor and its support of the war effort."[51]

Black workers, emboldened by the FEPC ruling, filed lawsuits against the union in Portland, Los Angeles, and San Francisco. Joseph James's suit against Marinship near San Francisco reached the California Supreme Court in 1944. The court ruled in *James v. Marinship* that the union's "asserted rights to choose its own members does not merely relate to social relations; it affects the fundamental right to work for a living." It ordered the Boilermakers to dismantle their auxiliary structure in the state. A U.S. District court in Portland ruled much the same, and in 1946 the California Supreme Court in *Williams v. International Brotherhood of Boilermakers* reaffirmed and extended the earlier James opinion. Following the James decision the union abolished auxiliaries but retained other discriminatory practices until 1946. Such questions of discrimination appeared moot when thousands of workers—black and white—were laid off at the end of the war. Even so, the legal challenges affirmed Katherine Archibald's 1946 assessment that "the white worker . . . may still come to the table first and take the best seat, but now the Negro sits there too."[52]

West Coast aircraft makers were the second largest employer of African American labor during the war. Like the shipbuilders, they at first resisted hiring black workers. In 1940 W. Gerald Tuttle, Director of Industrial Relations at Vultee Aircraft in southern California, wrote the National Negro Congress stating, "I regret to say that it is not the policy of this company to employ people other than of the Caucasian race . . ." The president of North American Aircraft in Inglewood, California, was equally blunt. "Regardless of their training as aircraft workers, we will not employ Negroes in the North American plant. It is against company policy."[53]

By 1942 Executive Order 8802, severe labor shortages, and occasional public pressure ended the exclusion. In July 1942 several hundred black women marched on the Los Angeles office of the U.S. Employment Service, vowing to make the room look like "little Africa," until the agency opened aircraft production jobs. One protester, Mrs. Lou Rosser, declared, "This is our war [but] we cannot win it in the kitchen, we must win it on the assembly line." Their demonstration was unnecessary. Aircraft companies were already moving to employ black workers. Boeing hired its first African American production worker, Dorothy West Williams, a sheet metal worker, in May 1942. By July 1943, 329 blacks worked at Boeing. That number peaked at 1,600 by 1945. In June Consolidated Aircraft in San Diego and Lockheed-Vega in Los Angeles began placing black workers. By August, 1942, Lockheed-Vega employed 400 blacks, including 50 women among their 41,000 workers. One year later the company had 2,500 black workers.[54]

The West Coast aircraft industry thus quickly rose above its past. One Watts resident recalled those days. "Man, we were all there the first day. We didn't know what we were applying for or what kind of job they had; some of us . . . had jive-time jobs as porters [or] janitors . . . and some of us hadn't worked in months. . . . Man, I didn't know what a P-38 or a B-17 was, but I wanted to learn, I wanted an opportunity. When the personnel officer asked me if I had ever worked on an assembly line or as a technician to produce a B-17, I was honest and I told him I didn't know if he were talking about a gun, a battleship, or a plane."[55]

Once in West Coast aircraft plants African American employees encountered individual problems—an unwarranted pay deduction or transfer, antiblack remarks by supervisors or coworkers, or social segregation, as recalled by Fanny Christina Hill. "They did everything they could to keep you separated," declared Hill. "They just did not like for a Negro and a white person to get together to talk." But black workers in west coast plants were not relegated to auxiliary unions, work in segregated buildings, or lunch in separate cafeterias. Nor did any west coast plant label jobs "white" and "colored" in advertisements as happened in Texas and Oklahoma. For thousands of black women and men hired in skilled jobs, wartime aircraft factory work changed the quality of their lives. As Fanny Christina Hill, who worked at North American Aviation in Inglewood from 1943 until her retirement in 1980, recalled, "The War made me live better . . . Hitler was the one that got us out of the white folks' kitchen."[56]

Western African Americans shared the nation's joy on V-E Day, 1945. Yet the celebration soon turned to anxiety. By war's end the federal government and Western industrialists were scaling back war-related production and employees. Kaiser shipyards in Richmond shrank employment from 47,000 workers in December 1944 to 9,000 by March 1946, a pace matched by other defense plants and shipyards. By 1947 thousands of African Americans who two years earlier had been "essential workers" now roamed the streets of Los Angeles, Oakland, and Portland. Two years after the end of the war Black Oaklanders comprised half those applying for indigent relief although they were only 10 percent of the city's population. Nearly half of the 4,000 blacks in Vallejo, California were unemployed. The prospects for post-war employment in Portland were so dismal that the black population declined by 50 percent (11,000) between 1944 and 1947.[57]

Other black Westerners prospered in the post-war period. In San Francisco black representation in unions, and in the skilled occupations organized labor controlled, grew appreciably between 1945 and 1950. By the later date 9,000 black unionists comprised 9 percent of the membership of 76 San Francisco locals. Large numbers of black males entered the construction trades and transportation, and a few men obtained white-collar jobs in banks, insurance firms, and utilities such as Pacific Gas and Electric. Progress was slower for black women. By 1950, nearly 53 percent remained concentrated in domestic service (down from 65 percent in 1940). But a few black women began to work as clerks, stenographers and secretaries.[58]

Postwar black Seattle suffered no economic downturn. Boeing's workforce continued to grow due to the emerging Cold War dependence on air power and growing demand for commercial airplanes. Thus the city proved attractive to blacks drawing another 5,000 persons between 1945 and 1950. By 1948 the median income of African American families in Seattle was $3,314, 53 percent above that of blacks nationally and only 14 percent below that of white Seattle families. Black Seattle median income was only 4 percent below that of white families nationally.[59]

During the century between 1849 and 1949 African Americans, like other Americans, pursued their dreams of economic prosperity westward toward the setting sun. Whether railroad porter, hotel maid or aircraft worker, they believe the words of African American gold miner Peter Brown who wrote in 1851, "California is the best country in the world to make money. It is also the best place for black folks on the globe. All a man has to do is work, and he will make money." Seventy-four years later James Weldon Johnson, NAACP national secretary declared much the same to a Denver reporter when he said, "Your West is giving the Negro a better deal than any other section of this country. . . . There is more opportunity for my race . . . than anywhere else in the United States."[60]

A close examination of the history of the region suggests that such statements were overly optimistic. Western employment opportunity for African American women and men was limited by the beliefs and traditions many white employers and workers brought from the East. As black workers sadly discovered, work in the in the West was not beyond the racial frontier.

NOTES

1 Quoted in Quintard Taylor, *The Forging of a Black Community: Seattle's Central District from 1870 through the Civil Rights Era* (Seattle: University of Washington Press, 1994), p. 49.

2 Quoted in Susan Jackson, "Slavery in Houston: The 1850s," *Houston Review* 2:2 (1980): 81. See also Paul D. Lack, "Urban Slavery in the Southwest," *Red River Valley Historical Review* 4:2 (Spring 1981):14; and Alwyn Barr, *Black Texans: A History of Negroes in Texas, 1528–1971* (Austin, TX: Jenkins Publishing Company, 1973), pp. 24–25.

3 See Lack, "Slavery and Vigilantism in Austin, Texas, 1840–1860," *Southwestern Historical Quarterly* 85:1 (July 1981):2, 12, and "Urban Slavery in the Southwest," pp. 9, 16. See also Haygood, "Use and Distribution of Slave Labor," pp. 35–38; Barr, *Black Texans,* p. 25; and Rudolph B. Campbell, *An Empire for Slavery: The Peculiar Institution in Texas, 1821–1865* (Baton Rouge: Louisiana State University Press, 1889), pp. 125–26.

4 *Ibid.*

5 Newby's letter to Douglass appears in C. Peter Ripley, ed., *The Black Abolitionist Papers,* Volume IV, (Chapel Hill: University of North Carolina Press, 1991), p. 235. See also Rudolph Lapp, *Blacks in Gold Rush California* (New Haven, CT: Yale University Press, 1977), p. 49. Lapp's study represents by far the most comprehensive survey of African Americans in antebellum California.

6 See Lynn M. Hudson, "A New Look, or 'I'm Not Mammy to Everybody in California': Mary Ellen Pleasant, a Black Entrepreneur," *Journal of the West* 32:3 (July 1993): 36; Douglas Daniels, *Pioneer Urbanites: A Social and Cultural History of Black San Francisco* (Philadelphia: Temple University Press, 1980), p. 20, and Lapp, *Blacks in Gold Rush California,* pp. 96–99.

7 The report on black businesses appeared in the *Daily Alta Californian,* April 7, 1854, p. 2. See also Mifflin W. Gibbs, *Shadow and Light: An Autobiography* (New York: Arno Press and the *New York Times,* 1968), pp. 44– 45; and *Proceedings of the First State Convention of the Colored Citizens of the State of California* (Sacramento: Democratic State Journal Printer, 1855, p. 18.

8 See Lapp, *Blacks in Gold Rush California,* pp. 103–4.

9 The quotations are from Richard B. Sheridan, "From Slavery in Missouri to Freedom in Kansas: The Influx of Black Fugities and Contrabands into Kansas, 1854–1864," *Kansas History* 12:1 (Spring, 1989): 39. See also Albert Castel, "Civil War Kansas and the Negro," *Journal of Negro History* 51:2 (April 1966): 129–30.

10 See Richard Cordley, *Pioneer Days in Kansas,* (New York: Pilgrim Press, 1903), pp. 137–38, and Kathe Schick, "The Lawrence Black Community, 1860–1866," (Unpublished manuscript, Watkins Community Museum, Lawrence, Kansas, n.d.), pp. 13–17.

11 Sheridan, "From Slavery in Missouri to Freedom in Kansas," pp. 42–43.

12 For a general discussion of the network of Western cities see Lawrence H. Larsen, *The Urban West at the End of the Frontier* (Lawrence: The Regents Press of Kansas, 1978), Chapters 1–2.

13 See U.S. Census, *Twelfth Census of the United States,* 1900, *Population,* Part I, (Washington: U.S. Government Printing Office, 1901), pp. cxix-cxxi, and Willard B. Gatewood, *Aristocrats of Color: The Black Elite, 1880–1920* (Bloomington: Indiana University Press, 1990), pp. 129–138. For a discussion of one 19th century western urban community see Taylor, *Forging,* Chapter 1.

14 For a detailed examination of the occupational and social structure of two 19th century black western community see Thomas C. Cox, *Blacks in Topeka, Kansas, 1865–1915: A Social History* (Baton Rouge: Louisiana State University Press, 1982), Chapter 4, and Taylor, *Forging,* chapter 1. See also Willard Gatewood's appraisal of elites in Western cities in *Aristocrats of Color,* p. 138.

15 See Daniels, *Pioneer Urbanites,* pp. 15–17, 31, 106–7.

16 Quoted in Daniels, *Pioneer Urbanites*, p. 36.

17 San Francisco *Daily Alta California*, November 9, 1889, p. 1. See also Daniels, *Pioneer Urbanites*, pp. 36–39.

18 For a description of this pattern in one western city see Taylor, *Forging*, chapter 2.

19 For a brief account of Barney Ford see Frank Hall, *History of the State of Colorado*, 4 vols. (Chicago: The Blakely Printing Company, 1895), volume 4, pp. 440–41. The quote appears on p. 441. See also Lionel Dean Lyles, "An Historical-Urban Geographical Analysis of Black Neighborhood Development in Denver, 1860–1970," (PhD. Dissertation, University of Colorado, 1977), p. 58.

20 See Lynda Faye Dickson, "The Early Club Movement Among Black Women in Denver: 1890–1925" (Ph.D. Thesis, University of Colorado, 1982), pp. 72–84; Moya Hansen, "Pebbles on the Shore: Economic Opportunity in Five Points, 1920–1950" (Unpublished paper in author's possession), p. 7; and Brian R. Werner, "Colorado's Pioneer Blacks: Migration, Occupations and Race Relations in the Centennial State" (M.A. Thesis, University of Northern Colorado, 1979), pp. 9–10, 27. See page 57 for an occupational chart of black Denver between 1870 and 1885. See also Lyle W. Dorsett, *The Queen City: A History of Denver* (Boulder: Pruett Publishing Company, 1977), pp. 104–5, and Lyles, "An Historical-Urban Geographical Analysis," p. 64–67.

21 On Walker see her entry in Edward T. James, Janet Wilson James and Paul S. Boyer, eds., *Notable American Women, 1607–1950. A Biographical Dictionary* 3 vols. (Cambridge: Harvard University Press, 1971) 3:533–35. For a discussion of black leisure activities in Denver see Moya Hansen, "Entitled to Full and Equal Enjoyment: Leisure and Entertainment in the Denver Black Community, 1900 to 1930," *University of Colorado at Denver Historical Studies Journal* 10:1 (Spring 1993): 57–71.

22 See Lawrence H. Larsen and Barbara J. Cottrell, *The Gate City: A History of Omaha* (Boulder, CO: Pruett Publishing Company, 1982), Chapter 3, pp. 121–23; Nebraska Writers' Project (Works Progress Administration), *The Negroes of Nebraska* (Lincoln, NE: Woodruff Printing Company, 1940), pp. 10, 24.

23 The Texas quote appears in Lawrence B. de Graaf, "The City of Black Angels: The Emergence of the Los Angeles Ghetto, 1890–1930," *Pacific Historical Review* 39:3 (August 1970): 330. For the Rydall quote see E. H. Rydall, "California for Colored Folk," *The Colored American Magazine* 12:5 (May 1907): 386. For the interview of Tennessee migrants see Bond, "The Negro in Los Angeles," p. 65. See also pp. 14–15, and De Graaf, "City of Black Angels," p. 330, 334–35. On Harrison Gray Otis and black Los Angeles see Mikel Hogan Garcia, "Adaptation Strategies of the Los Angeles Black Community, 1883–1919," (Ph.D. Dissertation, University of California, Irvine, 1985), pp. 33–36.

24 See Cary D. Wintz, "The Emergence of a Black Neighborhood: Houston's Fourth Ward, 1865–1915," in Char Miller and Heywood T. Sanders, ed., *Urban Texas: Politics and Development* (College Station: Texas A&M University Press, 1990), pp. 97–100. See Kenneth Mason, "Paternal Continuity: African Americans and Race Relations in San Antonio, Texas, 1867–1937," (Ph.D. dissertation, University of Texas, Austin, 1994), chapter 2, for a discussion of post-Civil War migration to San Antonio.

25 See Robert Prince, *A History of Dallas From a Different Perspective* (Dallas, TX: Nortex Press, 1993), pp. 31–41, and Howard Beeth and Cary D. Wintz, eds., *Black Dixie: Afro-Texan History and Culture in Houston* (College Station: Texas A & M University Press, 1992), pp. 21–25, 74–75.

26 See *Crisis*, 6:3 (July 1913): 130–32, 6:4 (August 1913): 192–95, and 6:5 (September, 1913):237–240. For a discussion of the local response to DuBois's visit

in Los Angeles, San Francisco, and Seattle see Lonnie G. Bunch, "A Past Not Necessarily Prologue: The Afro-American in Los Angeles," in Norman M. Klein and Martin J. Schiesl, eds., *20th Century Los Angeles: Power, Promotion, and Social Conflict* (Claremont, CA: Regina Books, 1990), p. 101; Albert Broussard, *Black San Francisco: The Struggle for Racial Equality in the West, 1900–1954* (Lawrence: University Press of Kansas, 1993), p. 76; and Taylor, *Forging,* pp. 79, 88.

27 On the Tulsa riot see Scott Ellsworth, *Death in a Promised Land: The Tulsa Race Riot of 1921* (Baton Rouge: Louisiana State University Press, 1982), pp. 15–16, 57–70. Black Los Angeles's eclipse of Northern California communities is described in James Adolphus Fisher, "A History of the Political and Social Development of the Black Community in California, 1850–1950" (Ph.D. dissertation, State University of New York at Stony Brook, 1972), pp. 161, 170–173.

28 *Northwest Enterprise,* July 21, 1927, p. 4. See also Taylor, *Forging,* p.61.

29 Dellums is quoted in Broussard, *Black San Francisco,* p. 40. The Bogle quotes are from E. Kimbark MacColl, *The Growth of a City: Power and Politics in Portland, Orecron, 1915 to 1950* (Portland, OR: The Georgian Press, 1980), p. 536.

30 Quoted in Colorado *Statesman,* November 18, 1933, p. 1. See also U.S. Bureau of the Census, *Census of Unemployment, 1937. Final Report on Total and Partial Unemployment,* (Washington, D.C.: Government Printing Office, 1938), Vols. I-III, Table 1; Randy J. Sparks, " 'Heavenly Houston' or 'Hellish Houston'? Black Unemployment and Relief Efforts, 1929–1936," *Southern Studies* 25: (Winter 1986): 355, and Lawrence P. Crouchett, Lonnie G. Bunch, III, and Martha Kendall Winnacker, *Visions Toward Tomorrow: The History of The East Bay Afro-American Community, 1852–1977* (Oakland: Northern California Center for Afro-American History and Life, 1989), p. 35.

31 Quoted in Elizabeth McLagan, *A Peculiar Paradise: A History of Blacks in Oregon, 1788–1940* (Portland, OR: The Georgian Press, 1980), pp. 126–27. The Pittman quote appears in Broussard, *Black San Francisco,* p. 118. See also pp. 117, 119. The Jackson quote appears in Taylor, *Forging,* p. 64.

32 In 1940, Texas, Oklahoma, and Kansas accounted for 86 percent of the West's blacks. Ten years later their share dropped to 67 percent. Conversely, the Pacific Coast states, California, Oregon, and Washington, jumped from 10 percent to 28 percent. For specific population increases see U.S. Bureau of the Census, *Sixteenth Census of the United States, 1940 Population,* Vol. II, *Characteristics of the Population* (Washington, D.C.: U.S. Government Printing Office, 1943), Table 35; U.S. Bureau of the Census, *Seventeenth Census of the United States, 1950, Census of the Population,* Vol. II, *Characteristics of the Population* (Washington, D.C.: U.S. Government Printing Office, 1952), table 53.

33 The quote appears in Marilynn S. Johnson, *The Second Gold Rush: Oakland and the East Bay in World War II* (Berkeley: University of California Press, 1993), p. 58. Trotter posits that proletarianization first occurred in World War I with the waves of Southern black migrants lured to Northern industrial centers. For a full discussion of his thesis see *Black Milwaukee: The Making of an Industrial Proletariat, 1915–45* (Urbana: University of Illinois Press, 1985), chapters 2, 7.

34 The Archibald quote appears in Katherine Archibald, *Wartime Shipyard: A Study in Cultural Disunity* (Berkeley: University of California Press, 1947), p. 92. For a discussion of Executive Order 8802 and the Fair Employment Practices Committee it spawned, see Jervis Anderson, *A Philip Randolph: A Biographical Portrait* (New York: Harcourt Brace Jovanovich, 1972), pp. 241–61; and Richard M. Dalfuime, "The 'Forgotten Years' of the Negro Revolution," *Journal of American History* 55:1 (June 1968): 92–100. See Alonzo Nelson Smith, "Black Employment in the Los Angeles

Area, 1938–1948," (Ph.D. dissertation, University of California at Los Angeles, 1978), chapter 4, for the impact of the FEPC in one western city.

35 The quote appears in Robert E. Colbert, "The Attitude of Older Negro Residents Toward Recent Negro Migrants in the Pacific Northwest," *Journal of Negro Education* 15:4 (Fall 1946): 699. On western population statistics see Shirley Ann Moore, "The Black Community in Richmond, California, 1910–1963" (Ph.D. dissertation, University of California, Berkeley, 1989), p. 76.

36 Quoted in Taylor, *Forging*, pp. 167–168.

37 For figures on overall black migration see U.S. Department of Labor, *Negroes in the United States: Their Employment and Economic Status* (Washington, D.C. : Bureau of Labor Statistics, December 1952) Bulletin 1119, pp. 5–9; Keith E. Collins, *Black Los Angeles: The Maturing of the Ghetto, 1940–1950* (Saratoga, CA: Century Twenty One Publishing, 1980), p. 18; and Lawrence B. DeGraaf, "Negro Migration to Los Angeles, 1930–1950" (Ph.D. dissertation, University of California, Los Angeles, 1962), pp. 261–63.

38 See Collins, *Black Los Angeles,* p. 18; Johnson, *The Second Gold Rush,* pp. 32–33. On Portland employment figures see FEPC Headquarters Records, Reel 13, Documents. Micro film No. 16335E, National Archives, Record Group 228; and Gerald D. Nash, *The American West Transformed: The Impact of the Second World War* (Bloomington: Indiana University Press, 1985), p. 103. Shirley Ann Moore, *To Place Our Deeds: The African American Community in Richmond, California, 1910–1963* (Berkeley: University of California Press, 2000), chapter 2. On Seattle see Taylor, *Forging,* p. 161.

39 See de Graaf, "Negro Migration to Los Angeles," p. 269; LeRoy E. Harris, "The Other Side of the Freeway: A Study of Settlement Patterns of Negroes and Mexican Americans in San Diego, California" (Doctor of Arts dissertation, Carnegie-Mellon University, 1974), p. 64; and Taylor, *Forging,* p. 161.

40 The Duncan quote appears in Taylor, *Forging,* p. 164. The second quote appears in Moore, *To Place Our Deeds,* p. 53. See also Johnson, *The Second Gold Rush,* pp. 37, 55–56.

41 The quote is from Johnson, *The Second Gold Rush,* p. 38. See also pp. 52– 54, and Moore, *To Place Our Deeds,* pp. 42–47.

42 The quotation appears in Lynell George, *No Crystal Stair: African Americans in the City of Angels* (London: Verso Press, 1992), p. 1. See also Gretchen Lemke-Santangelo, *Abiding Courage: African American Migrant Women and the East Bay Community* (Chapel Hill: University of North Carolina Press, 1996), p. 66; Johnson, *The Second Gold Rush,* p. 52; Moore, *To Place Our Deeds,* pp. 47–52; and Paul Spickard, "Work and Hope: African American Women in Southern California During World War II," *Journal of the West* 32:3 (July 1993): 71–72.

43 Quoted in Lemke-Santangelo, *Abiding Courage,* p. 65. For the Coleman account see Delores Nason McBroome, "Parallel Communities: African-Americans in California's East Bay, 1850–1963" (Ph.D. dissertation, University of Oregon, 1991), pp. 124–25.

44 Quoted in Johnson, *The Second Gold Rush,* p. 63.

45 The Marshall quote appears in Amy Kesselman, *Fleeting Opportunities: Women Shipyard Workers in Portland and Vancouver During World War II and Reconversion* (Albany: State University of New York Press, 1990), p. 43. See also Johnson, *The Second Gold Rush,* p. 65.

46 The Williams quote appears in Kesselman, *Fleeting Opportunities,* p. 43. See also pp. 41–42; Archibald, *Wartime Shipyard,* pp. 60–61, 83–84; and Johnson, *The Second Gold Rush,* pp. 63–65, 75.

47 The personnel director is quoted in Broussard, *Black San Francisco*, p. 157. See also Archibald, *Wartime Shipyards*, p. 88.

48 See William H. Harris, "Federal Intervention in Union Discrimination: FEPC and West Coast Shipyards During World War II," *Labor History* 22:3 (Summer 1981): 325–47; Herbert Hill, *Black Labor and the American Legal System*, Vol. I, *Race Work and the Law* (Washington, D.C.: Bureau of National Affairs, Inc., 1977) pp. 192–95, 200. For a full discussion of the Boilermakers discriminatory practices in Portland and Los Angeles, see Alonzo Smith and Quintard Taylor, "Racial Discrimination in the Workplace: A Study of Two West Coast Cities During the 1940's," *The Journal of Ethnic Studies* 8:1 (Spring 1980): 35–54. On Richmond see Moore, *To Place Our Deeds*, pp. 54–62.

49 The Washington quote appears in FEPC Headquarters Records, Reel 14. See also Harris, "Federal Intervention," pp. 327–328; and Hill, *Black Labor*, p. 187.

50 Quoted in Harris, "Federal Intervention," p. 332.

51 Quoted in Archibald, *Wartime Shipyard*, p. 99. See also *Tames, et. al., v. Marinship Corporation*, 25, 2nd California Reports, 721 (1944), *Williams, et, al., v. International Brotherhood of Boilermakers, Iron Shipbuilders and Helpers of America*, 28, 2nd California Reports, 568 (1946), and William H. Harris, *The Harder We Run: Black Workers Since the Civil War* (New York: Oxford University Press, 1982), pp. 120–21. See FEPC Headquarters Records, Reel 14, Documents, for a list of black workers in various auxiliary unions across the nation. See also Smith and Taylor, "Racial Discrimination," pp. 39–40, 43–45; Hill, *Black Labor*, 204, Moore, "The Black Community in Richmond," p. 96.

52 *Ibid.*

53 The Tuttle quotation appears in Robert C. Weaver, "Negro Employment in the Aircraft Industry," *Quarterly Journal of Economics* 59:4 (August 1945): 598. The quote from the North American Aviation President appears in de Graaf, "Negro Migration," p. 168.

54 On the demonstration by black women see *California Eagle*, July 16, 1942, pp. 1–A, 8–B. For a general discussion of the transition to black labor among the companies see Weaver, "Negro Employment," pp. 608–13; de Graaf, "Negro Migration to Los Angeles," p. 173; and Taylor, *Forging*, pp. 163–165.

55 The quotation appears in Collins, *Black Los Angeles*, pp. 60–61.

56 The two Christina Hill quotations appear in Sherma Berger Gluck, *Rosie the Riveter Revisited: Women, The War and Social Change* (Boston: Twayne Publishers, 1987), pp. 43, and 23, respectively. Comparative figures for the percentage of African Americans in the local population and percentages of employees in individual plants bear out de Graaf's argument of perceived opportunity outside the South. For example, Vultee Aircraft in Nashville in 1944 had a 4.9 percent black workforce in a city that was 30 percent African American, while its plant in Los Angeles had a 3.2 percent workforce when blacks comprised 7.1percent of the city's population. North American Aviation's workforce in its Inglewood plant was 7.2 percent black in 1944 in contrast with its Dallas facility which was 6.5 percent in a city where African Americans comprised 18 percent of the population. See Robert Weaver's 1945 national survey of the aircraft industry. See Weaver, "Negro Employment," pp. 616, 620–622, and de Graaf, "Negro Migration to Los Angeles," pp. 208–11.

57 See Wilson Record, "Willie Stokes at the Golden Gate," 11 *Crisis* 56:6 (June 1949): 177. On Portland's declining African American population see Portland *Oregonian*, June 16, 1947, p. 8.

58 Broussard, *Black San Francisco*, pp. 206–208.
59 See Taylor, *Forging*, p. 175.
60 The quotes appear in Quintard Taylor, *In Search of the Racial Frontier: African Americans in the American West, 1528–1990* (New York: W.W. Norton, 1998), pp. 84 and 17, respectively.

Part II

Social Scientific, Cultural, and Policy Perspectives

CHAPTER 6

RACE AND CLASS IN CHICAGO-SCHOOL SOCIOLOGY: THE UNDERCLASS CONCEPT IN HISTORICAL PERSPECTIVE

ALICE O'CONNOR

For well over a decade beginning in the mid-1980s, social scientific discussion of urban poverty was dominated by the concept of the "underclass" formulated by William Julius Wilson and expanded upon in a large-scale research project on "underclass" neighborhoods surrounding the University of Chicago. With support from foundations and government agencies, the "underclass" idea spawned a substantial research industry, featuring empirical investigation, training fellowships, conferences, and near-continuous debate, much of it devoted to scrutinizing, testing, and criticizing Wilson's central hypotheses.[1] By the early 1990s, European scholars had been drawn to the underclass concept as a way of understanding new forms of "social exclusion" in their own countries. Although the attraction seems to have passed, this debate subjected the concept to a new round of scrutiny, stirring some scholars to warn against the temptation to "Americanize" European poverty research by imposing concepts borrowed from the more radically racialized urban setting in the United States.[2]

Ironically, one reason Wilson's concept proved so influential on this side of the Atlantic was that it purported to de-racialize the urban poverty debate—even as poverty in segregated black neighborhoods was growing more visible and politically volatile. Although racially "neutral" on the surface, "underclass" was already in circulation as a term for the ghettoized black urban poor when Wilson began to develop the concept in a series of articles in the early 1980s.[3] Accompanied in the popular press by images suggesting rampant crime, willful joblessness, and uncontrolled sexuality, it tapped into deep-seated racial fears and stereotypes. The black "underclass" was also becoming a stalking horse for the conservative right in the crusade to roll back the civil rights revolution and undermine the liberal welfare state. Charles Murray, in his conservative manifesto *Losing Ground*, characterized the black "underclass" as an immoral, pathological subculture nurtured by permissive Great Society social policies.[4]

Wilson's concept, in contrast, deliberately downplayed the salience of race and social policy to treat the underclass as largely an economic and sociological phenomenon, the product of structural shifts in the economy and the social isolation of poor inner-city neighborhoods. In his book *The Truly Disadvantaged* (1987), Wilson traced the roots of what he later called "ghetto poverty" to the combination of urban deindustrialization and middle-class out-migration that had occurred in major rustbelt cities since the 1970s, leaving central city residents without either the job opportunities or the social capital to anchor stable community life. The underclass represented a new form of urban poverty, he argued, characterized by spatial concentration, social isolation, almost complete detachment from the legitimate labor force, and the breakdown of family and other social institutions. Unlike mere income shortfalls, this new kind of poverty operated as an all-encompassing "cycle" of joblessness, welfare dependency, teenage pregnancy, crime, juvenile delinquency and social "disorganization" that constituted a "tangle of pathology" in ghetto neighborhoods. Relying heavily on indicators of economic and social "dislocation" in highly segregated black communities, Wilson minimized the role of racial discrimination in sustaining ghetto poverty, arguing that inner city blacks were more "truly disadvantaged" by the presumably race-neutral forces of structural economic and spatial change.

Appearing amidst a rising tide of urban poverty and conservative backlash against the welfare state, Wilson's views quickly caught the attention of liberal foundation officials. Here, after all, was a respected black sociologist willing to take on issues that had been subject to "benign neglect" in policy and scholarship for much of the past two decades, and to talk about ghetto "pathology" from a structural point of view. Wilson was invoking the popular imagery of the underclass to reconstruct rather than demolish progressive social policy. At the same time, he was offering a critique of liberal "race-targeted" civil rights programs that, in contrast to Murray's *Losing Ground* (1984), still envisioned a positive role for the state. By 1985, even before *The Truly Disadvantaged* had appeared, Wilson and several colleagues at the University of Chicago were beginning to get large amounts of foundation support for an ambitious program of survey and ethnographic research in surrounding poor neighborhoods.

But Wilson's project was not just a response to a conservative, postindustrial, post-civil rights moment. In shifting the focus from race to class and culture as the source of ghetto deprivation, the Chicago Urban Poverty and Family Life Study resonated with an older tradition of social scientific research and ideological debate about race and poverty in urban America. Associated with the "Chicago school" of the 1910s and 20s, this tradition grew out of two important developments in the history of social science and in its role in the struggle for racial equality. The first was the sociological "discovery" of the slum and the ghetto as laboratories for academic research. While by no means the first to conduct social research in poor neighborhoods, Chicago-school sociologists played an important part in transforming the earlier, more reform-minded inquires associated with the settlement house movement into the detached, academic "social ecology" of modern social science.[5] As the Chicago school gained preeminence in the interwar years, so, too, did its naturalistic, apolitical view of urban social processes—a view that minimized the political or racial economy of inequality and instead explained poverty as a reflection of economic inevitabilities combined with cultural breakdown and social "disorganization" among unassimilated urban migrants.

Second was the emergence and evolution of racial liberalism in twentieth-century social science, in the first instance as an alternative to the biological racism in American science and culture, but also to counter more radical analyses of "the race problem" based on Marxist, Afro-centric and, later, black feminist ideas. Chicago-school sociology, with its ultimately affirmative, assimilationist understanding of industrial capitalism and race relations, was highly influential in mapping out the ideological middle ground: Suffering as much from poverty and cultural deprivation as racial oppression, blacks could look to urbanization, industrial job opportunity, and cultural assimilation as the avenues to racial equality. In this, their experience could be likened to that of other immigrant groups. But the ever-contested middle ground of racial liberalism was also influenced by a rival school of thought, which characterized American race relations as an all-pervasive caste system devoted to maintaining white supremacy and keeping blacks "in their place." In what came to be known as the "caste and class" analysis, racial equality would not be achieved through economic and cultural assimilation alone; it required a more explicitly race-targeted reform agenda, to end institutionalized racial oppression and the poverty it caused.

In formulating and developing a research agenda around the idea of a socially disorganized, culturally isolated, economically deprived *underclass*, Wilson was at once reviving the older Chicago-school tradition and staking out what proved to be a highly controversial position in a debate that had since been reformulated, in artificially polarized shorthand, as the "race vs. class" debate. He was also resurrecting a notion of lower-class pathology that had been generated within both strands of racial liberalism—and that underscored its limitations as a reform ideology.

THE CHICAGO SCHOOL

The Chicago school of the 1920s has rightly been noted for its singular impact on sociological theory and method.[6] In a host of theoretical and empirical studies published between the wars, members of the sociology department provided the grounding for an empirical science of society that took the processes of urbanization, assimilation, and ethnic interaction as its central themes. They also played a leading role in distinguishing sociology as a scientific, primarily academic endeavor rather than an instrument of social reform, in part by endowing their theories of social process with the logic and language of natural scientific law. At the same time, they worked to establish a more scientific relationship between knowledge and social policy, both in writing and in collaborations with social service and policy agencies. Most of all, the Chicago sociologists built a formidable research and training institution, underwritten with generous foundation support, which enabled them to exercise leadership in the discipline and to place their students in research institutes and academic departments throughout the country. Among these students were Charles S. Johnson and E. Franklin Frazier, unquestionably the most pre-eminent black sociologists of their day.[7]

Chicago sociology gained renown for its innovations in social research with such publications as W. I. Thomas and Florian Znaniecki's *The Polish Peasant* (5 vols., 1918–20). In that study Thomas and Znaniecki developed the concept of "social disorganization" that Chicago-trained sociologists would use to explain the high rates of poverty, family break-up, delinquency, and crime among recent immigrants, and that future generations would use more generically to describe conditions in poor neighborhoods. Social disorganization, in this perspective, was a kind of institutional disintegration symptomatic of the traumatic but inevitable cultural break-down experienced by traditional peasant groups under the atomizing influences of the modern industrial metropolis. A temporary stage in the larger process of ethnic assimilation, disorganization would eventually lead to cultural reorganization as immigrants adapted to urban demands, developed new cultural mechanisms for maintaining social cohesion, and, eventually, became fully assimilated into the dominant culture.

Thomas's ideas and methods formed the basis of an extensive program of field-work and theoretical training under the direction of Robert E. Park and Ernest W. Burgess, who together helped to make Chicago one of the most productive as well as the most influential sociology department in the country. They also set Chicago sociology—however obliquely—against the rising tide of nativist, anti-immigrant sentiment in post World War I politics, by challenging the idea of the unassimilable, ethnically "other" immigrant and by offering sociological explanations for ethnic patterns of poverty and crime.

At the core of the Chicago school program was an "ecological" model of social development that essentially incorporated Thomas's model of ethnic assimilation into a more all-encompassing scientific framework. The social order could be understood as an expression of an ecological cycle of human interaction, Park and Burgess explained in their introductory text, which moved naturally through the stages of competition, conflict, accommodation, and assimilation. Slavery, caste, segregation, and the division of labor could all be seen as "accommodations" to the laws of competition and conflict, acting as devices for achieving "equilibrium" and peaceful interaction among naturally competing groups. None of these accommodations was permanent, however. The equilibrium was constantly subject to disruption, from forces such as large-scale migration or technological advance, which would in turn rekindle the cycle of conflict, accommodation and assimilation. This process, which could be described as one of "succession," was natural, continuous and irreversible.[8] In the Chicago-school framework, urban social geography was devoid of political, institutional or even immediate human agency; the configuration of the city, like the social order itself, was attributable to the naturalistic forces of economic competition, intergroup relations, and residential succession.

As applied in a host of empirical studies, the ecological framework could be used to explain a wide range of urban social problems in the politically neutral terms of geography, urban growth, and the assimilation process. As newcomers, immigrants gravitated to the innermost "zone of deterioration," where, as Burgess noted, they experienced initial "disorganization," which was not "pathological" but "normal," a preliminary stage in the "reorganization of attitudes and conduct [that] is almost invariably the lot of the newcomer to the city." Poverty was part of the "natural, if not normal, life of a city," that for most would be a temporary condition. Similarly, segregation was part of an organic process, "which sifts and sorts and relocates individuals and groups by residence and occupation," and a necessary stage in the immigrant's assimilation into urban life.[9] Racial inequality, too, could be explained in terms of the assimilation cycle: blacks, the latest in a series of urban migrants, were a rural peasantry in the throes of adjustment to city life. Racial conflict, residential segregation, poverty, and social disorganization were all inevitable aspects of a process that would eventually result in assimilation.[10]

A great deal of subsequent research has underscored the inadequacies of the Chicago-school framework, both as a description of the immigrant experience and as a predictor of how black migrants would fare in the city. Its view of poverty and segregation as expressions of cultural (mal)adjustment virtually ignored the role of economic, political, or related institutional practices in shaping and maintaining inequality, and could be used as readily to rationalize as to promote change in the racial and economic status quo. The notion that racial conflict would give way to accommodation—as if of its own accord—vastly underestimated the amount or degree of native resistance to interaction with newcomers of any sort, and particularly blacks. And yet, these very same features made Chicago-school sociology compelling to an early generation of African American and white racial liberals, who used it to challenge then-standard theories of black biological inferiority and to provide scientific justification for an integrationist future. Equally important, Chicago-school theory, like the urban ecology it imagined, was malleable enough to accommodate revision and change, especially in the face of the increasingly volatile racial "laboratory" Chicago and other northern industrial cities would become.

Such was the case following the eruption of racial violence in the summer of 1919, when Chicago broke out into a five-day riot that ended in 38 deaths, hundreds of injuries, mass homelessness, and thousands of dollars in property damage, the vast majority of it in black neighborhoods. In response, Illinois Governor Frank O. Lowden appointed the biracial Chicago Commission on Race Relations to study the incident and make recommendations. The resulting report was drafted principally by staff member Charles S. Johnson, who had studied with Robert Park and was then research director for the Chicago Urban League, and was entitled *The Negro in Chicago* (1922). Following Chicago-school precepts, the report traced the origins of racial conflict to the great migration of African Americans from the rural South to Chicago during World War I, and in particular to the intense competition for residential and recreational space it had helped to set off. But the report also highlighted factors missing from Park's theoretical scheme: discriminatory economic practices, deep-seated racial animosities, state-sanctioned segregation and, especially, the profoundly political nature of racial inequality. Employers and labor unions routinely excluded blacks from industrial jobs, the commission concluded. Government agencies upheld a cynical double-standard in providing services and enforcing the law. The police were not only negligent in failing to protect black neighborhoods; they had, in some instances, actually participated in the riots. Politicians gave tacit sanction to the roving white "athletic clubs" that had been found responsible for so much of the violence. And the resentments fueled by prejudice and extremism had created a dangerous level of "race consciousness" among blacks as well as whites. Especially pernicious were the myths and misunderstandings that characterized public opinion, many of them perpetuated by the press. The race problem, then, was a product of policies, racial attitudes and economic practices that the naturalistic "cycles" of urban growth and human interaction would not wipe away. The Commission's report concluded with 59 recommendations to provide equal opportunities in employment, education, housing, services, and political representation, and to promote interracial understanding and cooperation.[11]

Yet the Commission report in many ways remained true to the principles of detachment and racial gradualism associated with the Chicago school. Damning as its findings were, it was objective in tone and measured about assigning responsibility—enough so to draw criticism for its overly cautious point of view. Race relations were a problem in Chicago, but they were rooted in an "inheritance of prejudice" that would make the remedy "necessarily slow." It also raised objections against efforts to stir race consciousness among blacks, warning that "thinking and talking too much in terms of race alone are calculated to promote separation of race interests and thereby to interfere with racial adjustment."[12] Black organizations would do better to promote interracial cooperation and help migrants adapt to urban demands, the Commission argued. Economic integration, not racial solidarity, would be the most effective avenue for advance.

Despite the prominence of the Commission report, it was not for another decade that the roots of what would prove to be the Chicago school's most lasting legacy to poverty research would be firmly planted. In studies that rivaled *The Polish Peasant* in ambition and scope, Chicago-trained sociologist E. Franklin Frazier told the story of black migration as that of an unacculturated rural peasantry slowly becoming assimilated into the "free competition" of the modern, urban industrial order. In his path breaking early studies *The Negro Family in Chicago* (1932) and *The Negro Family in the United States* (1939), Frazier emphasized recognizable Chicago-school themes. He explained widespread poverty in black inner-city neighborhoods as part of the "disorganization/reorganization" cycle experienced by all immigrant groups, and as such a "natural consequence" of the impact of "modern civilization" on traditional peasant folkways.[13] At the same time, he mapped the story of black progress through stages of residential mobility and absorption into the industrial working class. But Frazier also introduced something new to the Chicago-school framework by making a key distinction between blacks and other migrant groups. That distinction, which rested on the singular historical experience of an oppressed racial group, was captured in the Frazier's account of the emergence of the "matriarchal" black family and the "pathological" lower-class culture with which he associated it.

Like Charles S. Johnson, Frazier recognized that the Chicago-school model of ethnic assimilation did not adequately account for the persistent racism and racial discrimination blacks experienced in presumably more progressive northern cities.[14] At the same time, he used that model to condemn racism as an artificial barrier to the natural ecology of urban ethnic succession. But equally important, to Frazier, was the enduring legacy of slavery, and especially its impact on black family structure.

Contrary to subsequent characterizations, Frazier did not see the matriarchal family as inherently disorganized or pathological.[15] Although he rejected the idea that black family patterns reflected African cultural traditions, Frazier saw the matriarchy as an adaptive response to the dynamic of racial and economic oppression blacks had experienced since slavery. Enslaved blacks had established a matrilineal family system as an accommodation to the enforced separations of the slave trade. Similarly, the matrilineal bond became the basis of a post-Emancipation accommodation for a landless black peasantry, cut loose from the enclosed social system of the plantation, and unable to find stable work. Adaptive though it may have been to economic conditions that kept men wandering in search of work, Frazier's matriarchy also cultivated sexual practices and attitudes that, under the "disorganizing" influences of the city, became part of a pernicious cycle of delinquency, crime, welfare dependency, and poverty. At bottom, however, the preponderance of female-headed families in poor black neighborhoods was a matter of economics: Black men, facing labor market discrimination, could not assume their rightful places as heads of household; black women, in the meantime, enjoyed an unnatural economic independence thanks to welfare and domestic work. Thus, Charles Johnson concluded in a later study, the "real key to the organization of the Negro family . . . is found in the relative economic positions of men and women," which fostered "independence" in women complemented by 'irresponsibility' in the men."[16]

Despite their emphasis on economic factors, both Frazier and Johnson believed that family structure could play an independent role in perpetuating poverty as well. They also became increasingly preoccupied with family structure as the marker of class differentiation between lower- and middle-class blacks. Identified as the source rather than as a adaptation to economic deprivation, the black "matriarchy" became thoroughly pathologized. Thus, Frazier and Johnson concluded in separate studies on Negro youth commissioned by the American Council on Education, black children suffered from the burden of lower-class as much as racial status, and the socializing influence of the "disorganized" or matriarchal family was largely to blame. Lower-class children were exposed to instability, deviant "sex mores," and even violence from an early age. Equally important, they grew up isolated from the influences of middle-class culture and were taught to be resigned to their lot in life. Lacking the "security, affectional as well as economic, which children in the middle and upper classes enjoy," the lower-class youth sought "only the satisfaction of his individualistic impulses and wishes," Frazier wrote.[17] The disadvantages of class, he concluded, were as much psychological and cultural as material in nature, and would keep lower-class blacks from overcoming the disadvantages of race.

The Chicago-school vision of lower-class family disorganization would come under fire only later, when the "crisis" of the Negro family became the focal point for heated political debate after the public release of a policy report written by then Assistant Secretary of Labor Daniel Patrick Moynihan (1965). By then, however, Chicago-school theorists had developed a way of characterizing and explaining ghetto poverty that would prove remarkably resilient—even in the wake of the Moynihan debate. Anchored in notions of "disorganization," interlocking "pathologies," social "isolation," and cultural "deviance," the concept of the urban underclass echoed core Chicago-school theories. Like Frazier and Johnson, Wilson put more emphasis on class and culture than on racial discrimination as an explanation for persistent poverty. Like Frazier and Johnson, he lamented the proliferation of the female-headed family in poor black neighborhoods and put faith in industrial jobs to undo its cultural damage by providing black men with the wherewithal to take a "responsible place" in family life. In the dramatically deindustrialized context of the late twentieth-century city, however, the underclass concept would take on far more ominous connotations than Frazier's vision of the unassimilated lower class—which, for all its emphasis on pathology, was linked to a story of urban progress and assimilation."[I]n retrospect," Frazier wrote, "the waste of human life, the immorality, delinquency, desertions and broken homes which have been involved in the development of Negro family life in the United States . . . appear to have been the inevitable consequences of the attempt of a preliterate people, stripped of their cultural heritage, to adjust themselves to civilization."[18] Allowed to compete freely in the capitalist industrial economy, blacks would eventually succeed in their efforts to assimilate to the white, middle-class, patriarchal norm.

But well before the visible decline of the industrial city, the Chicago-School idea of cultural adaptation and assimilation came up against a much different analysis, of the dynamics of racial dominance and subordination, that challenged its optimistic premises and shifted the focus of social scientific racial liberalism to the problem of white racism.

CASTE AND CLASS IN THE BLACK METROPOLIS

Published just six years after the first printing of *The Negro Family in the United States*, St. Clair Drake and Horace Cayton's *Black Metropolis* bore the marks of a resurgent racial consciousness in late Depression and World War II social science. Race was once again prominent on the urban political agenda, fueled by the resumption of black migration, major incidents of racial violence in New York and Detroit, and the growing visibility of civil rights organizations demanding equality of opportunity in employment, the armed forces, and education. This was also a period of great ferment in the social science of race, culminating in Gunnar Myrdal's *An American Dilemma* and in the "triumph of liberal environmentalism" over biological theories of race.[19] With funding from liberal philanthropies such as Carnegie, Rockefeller, and the Julius Rosenwald Fund, social scientists had subjected the American Negro to the same detached scrutiny accorded to other social groups, treating the endeavor as a step in promoting racial equality as well as a new frontier in the human sciences. Although universally committed to the environmentalist perspective, liberal scholars offered widely divergent interpretations of black culture and experience, with important implications for the politics of racial equality.

Especially important as a challenge to the Chicago school was the "caste and class" framework developed in a number of anthropological studies set in the South. Initially spelled out by social anthropologist W. Lloyd Warner, this framework was more fully elaborated in community studies by John Dollard, Hortense Powdermaker, and Warner students Allison Davis and Burleigh Gardner, all documenting the impact of a rigid racial hierarchy on the psychological, socioeconomic and cultural development of blacks.[20] A permanent caste system regulated race relations in the South, in this view, maintained and reproduced by the political, economic, and social institutions of the dominant race, and dedicated to suppressing the appearance of mobility and class differentiation among blacks. An anomaly in the world's most advanced democracy, racial inequality would not disappear without major change in the attitudes and institutions perpetuating the caste system.

Written by collaborators trained in both of these "schools," *Black Metropolis* was in its own way an attempt to reconcile Chicago's process-driven view with the more structural orientation of social anthropology. It was also a response to the racial urgency of the day. St. Clair Drake, an anthropologist who had conducted fieldwork on one of the caste and class studies in the South, had recently arrived in Chicago to complete his doctoral degree. Horace Cayton had trained in sociology with Robert Park, but had subsequently spent four years as W. Lloyd Warner's research director for a large Works Progress Administration (WPA) study of urban social conditions in the black neighborhoods of Chicago's South Side. Commissioned to write a summary volume of the WPA research, Drake and Cayton combined the methods of Chicago school sociologists and social anthropologists, and expanded the scope of the research. What started as a report on research and methodology became a comprehensive narrative of the processes and the social structures shaping the black community, with conclusions explicitly directed to the newly invigorated Chicago Commission on Human Relations.[21]

Black Metropolis starts off as a Chicago school sociological analysis, mapping the black experience along the expected immigrant trajectory of economic and residential mobility and assimilation. And yet, contrary to assimilationist expectations, the analysis only highlighted the discrepancy between immigrants and blacks, with graphic illustrations of the "job ceiling," the "color line" and the segregationist residential practices that kept blacks "in their place." When Drake and Cayton turned to anthropology, to observe the black ghetto in daily life, the barriers of race seemed more caste-like and impenetrable than ever. Viewed from the inside, the inhabitants of "Bronzeville" were encircled by the "iron band" of segregation and denied full participation in the market economy. "Negroes," they wrote, "live in a state of intense and perpetual awareness that they are a black minority in a white man's world."[22] No black person could escape the impact of racial subordination, but its most obvious victims were the members of the black lower class. Subjected to "the double subordination of caste and class," they were relegated to irregular, low-paying employment, and unable to establish stable family lives. Here Drake and Cayton were fully in accord with Frazier and Johnson: economic marginalization was sustaining an isolated, culturally deviant way of life for the majority of the lower class, a life of "wandering men" and "forceful women," of "disorganized" families and delinquent children—a life that kept them at a distance from the world of their middle and upper class neighbors, and was beginning to take on a self-perpetuating dynamic of its own.

There was a great deal in *Black Metropolis*, then, to challenge and undermine the Chicago school point of view. Blacks were a subordinate racial minority, not just another ethnic group. Chicago's racial configuration was the product of human behavior, institutional practices, and political decisions, not of organic processes at work. Nevertheless, Drake and Cayton were not prepared to embrace the structural implications of the caste and class interpretation when it came time to draw policy conclusions: Chicago, they insisted, was not a caste system dependent on total racial subordination, but a dynamic, moving equilibrium. The "color line" was not "static" but "bends and buckles and sometimes breaks. This process results in tension, but the very existence of the tension—and even of the violence that sometimes results—is evidence of democracy at work."[23] There was hope, albeit limited, in the new, more racially integrated union movement and in the discovery by the Democratic party that the black vote could count. There was opportunity in the pragmatic reality that the war effort required mobilization of all available workers. Most of all, the war had transformed the "Negro Problem," "almost overnight," by drawing world attention to the moral hypocrisy of a democratic nation with a subordinate racial group. *Black Metropolis* ended by hearkening back to the Chicago school framework, with a call to push forward the "moving equilibrium" of race relations, with programs to prevent discrimination and segregation, and to educate whites about the needs and aspirations of blacks. What blacks needed most was unfettered access to the "free competition" of urban industrial life.[24]

In characterizing the "Negro Problem" as a moral dilemma, Drake and Cayton were articulating what was rapidly becoming a new liberal orthodoxy on race.[25] Developed as the central theme of Gunnar Myrdal's *An American Dilemma*, the liberal orthodoxy pointed to white attitudes and beliefs as the principal source of black subjugation, and called for education and interracial cooperation in response. It was premised on a belief that the American system was fundamentally democratic and a faith that participation in the "free competition" of a growing industrial economy would lead to greater equality for blacks. Minimizing the structural, systemic roots of racial subordination, the liberal orthodoxy adopted a gradualist program of guaranteeing civil rights and opening up individual access to mainstream opportunities, confident that racial equality could be achieved without more fundamental economic or institutional change. Black urban poverty was no longer sustained by an economic system dependent on racial subordination, as it had been in the South, but by the cultural deprivation that resulted from continued exclusion from the urban industrial economy. The problem of poverty would be resolved with policies to eliminate overt racial discrimination, change white attitudes, and open the door to cultural assimilation. Thus, while embracing aspects of the caste and class analysis, postwar liberal orthodoxy made it far more compatible with industrial capitalism and political gradualism than its structural emphasis would suggest.

Equally important from the standpoint of the later underclass concept, racial liberalism incorporated the idea of black lower-class cultural pathology into its understanding of poverty and race. And by invoking, as Myrdal famously did, the metaphor of the "vicious circle," it temporarily resolved the tension between the class-based analysis of Chicago-school ecology and the race-based analysis of social anthropology: Lower-class culture and white racism, that is, were mutually reinforcing pathologies in a circle that could be broken with targeted social interventions.

WILSON, RACE, AND THE UNDERCLASS

Several developments helped to sustain the liberal racial orthodoxy after World War II. Steady economic growth and continued northward migration had substantially expanded the ranks of the black working and middle classes, while social policies for black war veterans had put higher education and homeownership within reach for some. Gains in civil rights were slower and more painstaking, but continued to show signs of gradual progress. Revising their earlier tone of struggle and foreboding, Drake and Cayton issued a new edition of *Black Metropolis* in 1961, predicting that a decade of prosperity and increased racial integration would continue the trend toward racial equality. They noted, however, that the job ceiling and the black ghetto persisted, and expressed some frustration at the slow pace of change.

By decade's end, this tone of measured optimism had been replaced by one of dark foreboding, and the liberal orthodoxy was in complete disarray. The 1969 edition of *Black Metropolis* raised the spectre of racial violence, this time underscored by the racial "events" in major cities during every summer since 1964. Poverty was the source of black frustration, the new edition stressed, and gradual improvements in civil rights would not make it go away. Economic growth and integration had not, after all, meant much to the majority of the black labor force in Chicago, who continued to lag far behind their white counterparts in wages, and formed a vast "urban peasantry" with all the markings of a subordinated caste.[26] Drake and Cayton were by no means the only social scientists to sound the warning. The black inner city had once again become the focus of community study by social scientists with foundation and government backing. What they were describing was not, however, a growing, diversified metropolis, but an isolated and alienated "Dark Ghetto," segregated by poverty as well as race.[27] Daniel Patrick Moynihan, building on the interpretation by E. Franklin Frazier, used much of this research to make a "case for national action" to save the deteriorating black family. Racism had contributed to the "Negro Problem," these studies agreed, but it operated in a new, less visible way. Blacks no longer suffered from explicit, institutionalized racism, but from the self-hatred and cultural damage that centuries of racial oppression had created.[28] Poverty was the mainstay of the self-perpetuating "pathology" of family instability, criminal behavior, sexual deviance, and social isolation that engulfed ghetto neighborhoods. And it was the failure to address this "tangle of pathology" that was keeping the struggle for racial equality from moving ahead.

The looming threat of a pathological ghetto subculture marked a subtle shift in the social science of racial disadvantage. No longer was migration, assimilation, or the caste system the focus of inquiry; instead it was the culture and behavior of the poor. Hitherto widely accepted in liberal social science, the idea of black lower-class cultural pathology became the center of a bitter, polarized debate following the release of the Moynihan Report in the mid-1960s, which opened up the premises of "white" liberal social science to widespread attack.[29] Research on the black ghetto continued,[30] but in the political backlash against Great Society liberalism, social science and foundations followed the Nixon Administration's policy of intellectual retreat and "benign neglect."[31] Equally important, the ethnographic community studies tradition that had informed these earlier investigations was eclipsed by the quantitative, analytic "revolution" in poverty research brought about by the War on Poverty.[32]

Wilson thus stepped into a highly charged but stalemated debate a decade later when he first introduced his concept of the black underclass in *The Declining Significance of Race* (1980). As the title suggests, this was a plea to move beyond racial explanations for black disadvantage, and to recognize the growing importance of class. Pointing to changes in the black class structure since the 1940s, Wilson argued that class rather than race was the key determinant of life chances and called on social scientists and policymakers to "redefine" problems once considered racial as problems of class. Blacks had gained a solid foothold in the working- and middle-class occupational structure since the 1950s, Wilson argued, thanks to the combination of economic growth, public sector job opportunities, unionization, urbanization, and antidiscrimination legislation. And yet even as the prospects for working and middle class blacks were improving, the prospects for poor, uneducated, unskilled blacks were ever more bleak. Rising youth unemployment, labor force detachment, persistently high poverty rates, and the growing number of female-headed households were all evidence of a "semipermanent" underclass increasingly concentrated in ghetto neighborhoods. The economic "schism" among blacks was more consequential than the black/white racial divide, and policy would have to shift from its postwar focus on antidiscrimination to more direct economic intervention.[33]

The Declining Significance of Race stimulated a great deal of controversy, much of it focused on Wilson's claims about the extent of the political and economic gains made by the black middle class. In the meantime, however, the idea of a culturally deviant, dangerous black "underclass" was beginning to enjoy much broader circulation among conservative social critics and in the popular media, quite apart from the confines of academic debate.[34] Wilson thus had two related objectives when he set out to develop the underclass concept in greater depth. One was to challenge and reorient what he saw as the still-reigning orthodoxy of racial liberalism, from its postwar emphasis on combating racism and promoting civil rights to one on class, economic, and cultural uplift. Indeed, Wilson's argument, even more than its Chicago school predecessors, diminished the role of racial discrimination in contemporary ghetto poverty—claiming that "historic discrimination is more important than contemporary discrimination in understanding the plight of the ghetto underclass."[35] The other objective was to reclaim the ghetto for liberal social scientific research, in part by reclaiming the language and conceptual apparatus of ghetto pathology that, having originated in Chicago-school and related strands of liberal social science, had long since been appropriated by the right.

The black underclass, in Wilson's view, represented a new form of urban poverty brought about by the interaction of three processes that operated independently of race: economic restructuring, industrial decentralization, and residential mobility. The shift toward a more global, service-based economy put the predominantly low-skilled black population at a severe disadvantage in the labor market, he argued, while industrial decentralization had left inner-city residents without the ready access to jobs they once enjoyed. These skill and spatial "mismatches" were separating inner-city blacks from industrial opportunities, Wilson concluded, using the benign and neutral language favored by economists. Geographic isolation and low skills, not racism, were responsible for the high levels of joblessness among blacks. Ignoring a well-documented history of racially motivated policies and institutional practices, Wilson wrote about black economic dislocation as the product of impersonal, and inevitable, forces of structural economic change.[36]

Wilson similarly depicted the process of residential mobility as an apolitical, race-neutral process, arguing that middle-class outmigration had contributed to the growing social isolation of the poor. Ironically, this isolation had resulted in part from one of the major achievements of the civil rights movement: Having secured access to formerly restricted neighborhoods, middle- and working-class blacks were now free to move out of the ghetto, taking with them the small businesses, churches, social clubs, and other neighborhood institutions that had anchored the community. In ecological terms, upwardly mobile blacks were assuming normal patterns of ethnic succession, while leaving their neighbors in the "zone of deterioration" behind. Poverty, not race, was what prevented the inner city underclass from following this upward residential trajectory.

Wilson's depiction of a pathological underclass culture also proceeded along Chicago school-lines, beginning with the use of *underclass* as a cultural category marking off one segment of an impoverished lower class from another along behavioral lines. Taking a lead from Frazier, Wilson explained patterns of family "disorganization" in terms of the economic dislocation of black men. There had been a steady decline in the "male marriageable pool index"—calculated as the number of black men with steady jobs in the labor force—that was responsible for the declining marriage rates among blacks. This was in turn responsible for the high "illegitimacy ratio" in the black community, and the rising rates of female-headed households. Like Frazier's "matriarchy," this unstable family system had devastating consequences for the black urban poor, particularly when combined with the "concentration effects" of living in extreme deprivation, in a neighborhood without middle-class role models or social networks, faced with a job market with few opportunities for the low-skilled. Deviant behavior was a logical response to economic deprivation, but it was taking on the attributes of a self-perpetuating culture that only further isolated the underclass from middle class norms.

Wilson's underclass concept took the Chicago school parallel a step further when, as the focal point of a substantial and well-funded research enterprise, it helped to reshape the course of research on urban poverty. To some, this represented a positive development, opening up a field of inquiry that had been somewhat neglected for the past several years. Wilson's own research project, the Chicago Urban Poverty and Family Life Study, helped to generate renewed interest in urban ethnography and to revive the more contextualized type of community survey that had long since been eclipsed by the large-scale national survey. By linking the underclass to the problem of economic deindustrialization, Wilson had at least opened the door to a more structural analysis of the causes of poverty. And yet, the vast majority of the "new" underclass research was in fact dominated by the narrowly focused, detached, quantitative analysis that had come to characterize poverty research since the War on Poverty. Indeed, the first round belonged to the economists, who tested the idea by seeing whether they could measure it using the individualized data available from conventional national-level surveys. Others zeroed in on one or more of the concept's "testable hypotheses," again testing them with individual-level datasets that ignored the institutional and related contextual mechanisms through which inequality is reproduced. Race, with a few notable exceptions, was virtually ignored as anything other than an individual demographic attribute. In the course of translating the concept into empirical science, then, the underclass industry narrowed the focus to individual characteristics, culture and behavior, and treated it as a problem largely divorced from the trends generating inequality in the broader urban economy. Measured as a behavioral phenomenon, "underclass" poverty affected a small, socially isolated population that was sharply differentiated from the presumably more mainstream "working poor."

But Wilson's argument departed from Chicago-school tradition in important ways. One was in its considerably more pessimistic outlook. Seen through the lens of urban deindustrialization, underclass poverty was not a temporary condition in an ultimately regenerative process of urban growth and assimilation, but the permanent remnant of ineluctable urban decline. Even this assessment was informed by Chicago-school premises. The rise of the socially isolated underclass neighborhood, Wilson argued, was rooted in recent, post-1970s economic conditions, and marked a distinct departure from the more vertically integrated, institutionally stable black ghetto of the immediate postwar decades. The world did once work according to assimilationist assumptions, in this vision: A growing industrial economy acted as an engine of upward mobility, class as well as racial integration, and a stabilizing, "civilizing" force in black cultural life. It some senses, then, Wilson was taking up a new chapter in the Chicago school paradigm, applying its basic conceptual framework in an era of postindustrial decline.

Wilson's underclass concept also emerged from a deeply pessimistic, divisive moment in twentieth-century racial liberalism, when the strategies and achievements of the civil rights movement were being called into question from many different directions, along with the integrationist assumptions at their core. In this context, Wilson's "race-neutral" approach to the glaringly racial problem of ghetto poverty was welcomed by liberal philanthropists and neoliberal centrists as a way of neutralizing race as a political issue: Improving conditions for blacks would be "hidden" within a more "universalistic," class-oriented policy agenda that would appeal to majority white constituents as well.[37] Once again, Chicago-school sociology was playing a part in mapping out the middle ground of racial liberalism—this time, in the post-civil rights atmosphere of backlash against race-targeted social policies.

Wilson's reprise of ghetto pathology can also be understood as part of this neutralizing thrust. While acknowledging that racism was once a factor in ghetto formation, the idea of the self-perpetuating "cycle" or "tangle" of pathology keeps racism safely in the distant past: The underclass, in effect, is the victim of its own self-destructive behavior. Meanwhile, by locating the "pathology" in characteristically "underclass" behaviors, it makes the ghetto safe for liberal intervention. "Breaking the cycle" means changing poor people's behavior, through education, work training, and, with support from across a dramatically right-slanted ideological spectrum, legislation to end welfare and promote heterosexual marriage.

CONCLUSION

Despite—or, perhaps, because of—its emphasis on race neutrality, the underclass concept did not neutralize the social scientific debate about race and poverty. Alongside the considerable canon of underclass literature, an extensive counter-literature has emerged to show that race does indeed "matter"—in the broader distribution of opportunity and power in American society as well as in the maintenance of racially subjugated neighborhoods.[38]

Wilson himself has subsequently revised the arguments in *The Truly Disadvantaged* and, in reaction to the stigma associated with the term, dropped "underclass" in favor of "ghetto poor," and now writes of "jobless ghettos" rather than "underclass neighborhoods." Most notably, he has retreated from his earlier position on the "declining significance" of race to acknowledge the continued importance of discrimination in blocking opportunities for blacks. Government policy and employer practices contributed to the creation of the jobless, racially segregated ghetto, he acknowledged in *When Work Disappears*.[39]

But while the debate over the nature and "significance" of race continues, at least one strand of underclass thinking—and of social scientific racial liberalism—has become as stubbornly entrenched as the poverty it deigns to understand: the idea of the socially disorganized black ghetto with the pathologically matriarchal ("female-headed") family at its core.[40] And it is in perpetuating this cultural imagery that Chicago-school sociology, for all its intentions to the contrary, ultimately undermined its own assimilationist project. Far from making the case for the kinds of integrationist economic and educational interventions liberals have imagined, the idea of the pathological ghetto has itself become part of the "vicious cycle" of poverty: obscuring the structural roots of inequality and reinforcing the idea of an unassimilable racial minority in our midst.

NOTES

1 Paul E. Peterson and Christopher Jencks, *The Urban Underclass* (Washington D.C.: The Brookings Institution, 1991); Michael B. Katz (ed.), *The "Underclass" Debate: Views From History* (Princeton, NJ: Princeton University Press, 1993); Douglas S. Massey and Nancy A. Denton, *American Apartheid: Segregation and the Making of the Underclass* (Cambridge, MA: Harvard University Press, 1993).

2 Hartmut Haussemann, Martin Kronauer, and Walter Siebel (eds.), *An den Raendern der Staedte* (Frankfurt/M. Suhrkamp, 2003); Hillary Silver, "National Conceptions of the New Urban Poverty: Social Structural Change in Britain, France, and the United States," *International Journal of Urban and Regional Research* 17-3 (1993): 336–54; Margaret Weir, "Race and Urban Poverty: Comparing Europe and America." *The Brookings Review*, Summer, 1993.

3 Katz, *"Underclass" Debate*, Introduction, Herbert Gans, *The War Against the Poor: The Underclass and Antipoverty Policy* (New York: Basic Books, 1995), pp. 27–57; Alice O'Connor, *Poverty Knowledge: Social Science, Social Policy, and the Poor in Twentieth-Century U.S. History* (Princeton, NJ: Princeton University Press, 2001), pp. 265–67.

4 Charles Murray, *Losing Ground: American Social Policy, 1950–1980* (New York: Basic Books, 1984).

5 Mary Jo Deegan, *Jane Addams and the Men of the Chicago School, 1892–1918* (New Brunswick: Transaction Books, 1988); David Ward, *Poverty, Ethnicity, and the American City, 1840–1925: Changin Conceptions of the Slum and the Ghetto* (Cambridge: Cambridge University Press, 1989).

6 Andrew Abbott, *Department and Discipline: Chicago Sociology at One Hundred* (Chicago: University of Chicago Press, 1999); Martin Bulmer, *The Chicago School of Sociology: Institutionalization, Diversity and the Rise of Sociological Research* (Chicago: University of Chicago Press, 1984); Fred H. Matthews, *The Quest for an American Sociology: Robert E. Park and the Chicago School,* (Montreal: McGill-Queen's University Press, 1977); Stow Persons, *Ethnic Studies at Chicago: 1905–1945* (Chicago: University of Illinois Press, 1987).

7 Bulmer, *The Chicago School of Sociology*; Persons, *Ethnic Studies.*

8 Robert E. Park, Ernest W. Burgess, and Roderick D. McKenzie, *The City* (Chicago: University of Chicago Press, 1925); Dorathy Ross, *The Origins of American Social Science* (Cambridge: Cambridge University Press, 1991), pp. 359–60; Persons, *Ethnic Studies*, pp. 60–64.

9 Park et al, *The City*, pp. 50–56.

10 E. Franklin Frazier, "The Changing Status of the Negro Family," *Social Forces* 9 (1931): 386–93; Persons, *Ethnic Studies.*

11 Chicago Commission on Race Relations, *The Negro in Chicago: A Study of Race Relations and a Race Riot* (Chicago: University of Chicago Press, 1922).

12 Chicago Commission, quoted in St. Clair Drake and Horace R. Cayton, *Black Metropolis: A Study of Negro Life in a Northern City* (Chicago: University of Chicago Press, 1945), p. 71.

13 E. Franklin Frazier, *The Negro Family in the United States* (Chicago: University of Chicago Press, 1939), p. 487.

14 Persons, *Ethnic Studies*, 139–43.

15 Daryl Scott, *Contempt and Pity: Social Policy and the Image of the Damaged Black Psyche, 1880–1996* (Chapel Hill: University of North Carolina Press, 1997).

16 Charles S. Johnson, *Growing Up in the Black Belt: Negro Youth in the Rural South* (Washington, D.C.: American Council on Education, 1941), pp. 58–59.

17 E. Franklin Frazier, *Negro Youth at the Crossways.* Washington D.C.: American Council on Education, 1940, p. 52. Johnson, *Growing Up in the Black Belt*, pp. 224–25.

18 Frazier, *The Negro Family in The United States*, p. 367.

19 Gunnar Myrdal, *An American Dilemma: The Negro Problem and Modern Democracy* (New York: Harper and Brothers Press, 1949); Walter A. Jackson, *Gunnar Myrdal and America's Conscience: Social Engineering and Racial Liberalism, 1938–1987* (Chapel Hill: University of North Carolina Press, 1990); George M. Frederickson,

The Black Image in the White Mind: The Debate on Afro-American Character and Destiny 1817–1914 (Middletown, CT: Wesleyan University Press, 1987).

20 John Dollard, *Caste and Class in a Southern Town* (New Haven, CT: Yale University Press, 1937); Hortense Powdermaker, *After Freedom: A Cultural Study in the Deep South* (New York: Viking Press, 1939); Allison Davis, Burleigh B. Gardner, and Mary R. Gardner, *Deep South: A Social Anthropological Study of Caste and Class* (Chicago: University of Chicago Press, 1941).

21 St. Clair Drake and Horace R. Cayton, *Black Metropolis: A Study of Negro Life in a Northern City* (Chicago: University of Chicago Press, 1945), pp. xiii-xv.

22 *Ibid*, p. 390.

23 *Ibid*, pp. 275–86.

24 *Ibid*, pp. 755–67.

25 Jackson, *Gunnar Myrdal*, pp. 272–311; Stephen Steinberg, *Turning Back: The Retreat from Racial Justice in American Thought and Policy* (Boston: Beacon Press, 1995), pp. 21–49.

26 Drake and Cayton, *Black Metropolis*, pp. 828–29.

27 Kenneth B. Clark, *Dark Ghetto: Dilemmas of Social Power*, (New York: Harper and Row, 1965); Lee Rainwater and William L. Yancey, *The Moynihan Report and the Politics of Controversy* (Cambridge, MA: MIT Press, 1967); Elliot Liebow, *Tally's Corner: A Study of Negro Street-Corner Men* (Boston: Little, Brown, 1967).

28 Scott, *Contempt and Pity*, pp. 93–118.

29 Rainwater and Yancey, *The Moynihan Report;* Joyce Ladner, *The Death of White Sociology* (New York: Random House, 1973); Charles A. Valentine, *Culture and Poverty Critique and Counter Proposals* (Chicago: University of Chicago Press, 1968).

30 Ulf Hannerz, *Soulside*, (New York: Columbia University Press, 1969); Carol B. Stack, *All Our Kin: Strategies for Survival in a Black Community* (New York: Harper Torchbooks, 1974).

31 Steinberg, *Turning Back*, pp. 107–23.

32 O'Connor, *Poverty Knowledge*, pp. 196–210.

33 William J. Wilson, *The Declining Significance of Race* (Chicago: University of Chicago Press 1980), pp. 155–82.

34 Katz, *The "Underclass" Debate*.

35 Wilson, *Truly Disadvantaged*, p 141.

36 Arnold Hirsch, *Making the Second Ghetto: Race and Housing in Chicago, 1940–1960* (New York: Cambridge University Press, 1983); Massey and Denton, *American Apartheid*.

37 On the "race-neutral" as a "hidden" agenda, see Wilson, *Truly Disadvantaged*, pp. 140–64; and "Race-Neutral Politics and the Democratic Coalition," *The American Prospect* 1 (Spring 1990): 82–129. On its appeal to liberal philanthropy, see Alice O'Connor, "Foundations, Research, and the Construction of 'Race Neutrality,' " *Souls* 4:1 (Winter 2002): 54–62.

38 Among the works that explicitly counter the "race neutral" emphasis of the underclass idea are Massey, *American Apartheid*; Katz, *The 'Underclass' Debate*, Michael Omi and Howard Winant, *Racial Formation in the United States: From the 1960s to the 1990s* (New York, Routledge, 1994); Melvin Oliver and Thomas Shapiro, *Black Wealth/White Wealth: A New Perspective on Racial Inequality* (New York and London: Routledge, 1995; Thomas J. Sugrue, *The Origins of the Urban Crisis: Race and Inequality in Postwar Detroit* (Princeton, NJ: Princeton University Press, 1996); Alice O'Connor, Chris Tilly, and Lawrence D. Bobo, eds., *Urban Inequality: Evidence from Four Cities* (New York: Russell Sage Foundation, 2001).

39 William J. Wilson. *When Work Disappears: The World of the New Urban Poor.* (New York: Alfred A. Knopf Press, 1996).

40 Among the most trenchant recent criticisms of this imagery are Dorothy Roberts, *Killing the Black Body: Race, Reproduction, and the Meaning of Liberty* (New York: Pantheon, 1997); and Robin Kelley, *Yo' Mama's Dysfunktional* (Boston: Beacon Press, 1997), pp. 15–42.

CHAPTER 7

BLACK + WOMAN = WORK: GENDER DIMENSIONS OF THE AFRICAN AMERICAN ECONOMIC EXPERIENCE

SUSAN WILLIAMS MCELROY

DEFINING BLACK ECONOMIC PROGRESS AND EDUCATIONAL ATTAINMENT

The economic progress of black Americans has captured the attention of economists and sociologists since Gunnar Myrdal's *An American Dilemma* appeared in the early 1940s. More than half a century later, social scientists are still intrigued with the determinants of black economic status and how that status has changed over time. In 1989, the National Research Council published a major study entitled *A Common Destiny: The Status of Black Americans,* which served as a clear signal that interest in the economic progress of blacks was deeply entrenched in economic and sociological research. Even though there is considerable research on the economic progress of African Americans, there is no consensus regarding what factors best explain changes over time in the economic conditions of African Americans.[1]

The overwhelming majority of research by economists on black economic status has focused exclusively on black men, overlooking black women. Nevertheless, in order to understand the economic condition of black Americans, it is surely as crucial to understand the economic status of black women as it is to understand that of black men, for at least three reasons. First, black women account for more than half (53 percent) of all blacks in the labor force.[2] The comparable figure for white women is 46 percent of whites in the labor force.[3] Second, an increasingly large fraction of all black family households[4] are headed by a woman with no spouse present. In the year 2000, 44 percent of all black family households were headed by a female with no spouse present, as compared to 14 percent of all white family households.[5] Three decades earlier, in 1970, less than one third (29 percent) of all black family households were headed by a female with no spouse present. Finally, the number of black women in the labor force is increasing faster than the number of black men in the labor force is increasing. Between 1990 and 2000, the number of black women in the labor force increased by 30 percent, while the number of black men in the labor force increased by 17 percent.[6] Taken together, these three reasons clearly point to the increasing centrality of African American women to the recent African American economic experience.

The centrality of African American women to the African American economic experience becomes evident when the advancement of black women in the labor market is placed in historical perspective. From the late 1930s through the early 1970s black women made enormous wage and occupational gains relative to white women. Of the four race-gender groups—black males, black females, white females, and white females—black females made the largest occupational gains between 1940 and 1980.[7] The most salient aspect of black women's occupational change was the movement out of domestic and agricultural work primarily into clerical occupations, retail sales, and health care service occupations.[8] As Malveaux observes, "There is distance between 1940 and 1980. In 1940, the majority of [employed] black women worked as private household workers. . . . By 1980, black women worked in occupations (such as architects, accountants, managers in the public and private sector, computer specialists and others) where they were previously completely unrepresented."[9] By 1980 black and white women's occupational distributions were very similar.[10] Because of the importance of African American women to the historical and contemporary African American economic experiences, any analysis that claims to explain the African American economic condition but in fact excludes African American women is therefore inherently incomplete.

Numerous studies have documented the monumental improvements in black economic status since 1940, and more specifically, the increases in black incomes relative to those of whites. Each of these studies has identified education as a central factor, and often as *the* central factor, which accounts for the narrowing of the racial gap in incomes. Smith and Welch (1986), for example, estimate that education played the most important role in the narrowing of the black-white male wage gap between 1940 and 1980.[11] Both economists and sociologists who have studied black economic and social status recognize the central importance of education.[12]

Levy (1987) summarizes the principal factors that determined the rate of black men's relative economic gains during the 1960s: 1) economic prosperity of the 1960s, which resulted in "tight labor markets," 2) reduction of discrimination, and 3) narrowing of differences in educational attainment levels of younger black and white men.[13] Beginning in the early 1980s evidence began to mount that black economic progress had begun to stagnate. It became increasingly clear that the enormous progress blacks had made since 1940 had slowed considerably or perhaps even stopped.

Black Women's Educational Attainment and Earnings

As explained above, the majority of research by economists on black relative income has been limited to black *men's* relative income, that is, relative to white men. One result of this limitation is that much less is known about the factors that determine black women's incomes. In part because black women's relative economic status has received less attention than black men's relative status has received in the literature, there is still much to be learned about the role of education in the narrowing of the wage gap between black women and white women over time.

In trying to explain the persistent and growing income differentials between black and white women, researchers have asked some of the same questions they asked about income differentials between black and white men. During the postwar period, black women's occupational distribution changed much more rapidly than did those of either black men, white women, or white men. The rapid occupational change of black women in the postwar period accounts for much of the increase in black women's relative wages.[14]

Several explanations appear in the literature as to why black women's earnings are lower, on average, than white women's. Jones' (1986) study of black and white women's labor force participation stands out as one study that considers the differential returns (that is, the impact of schooling on income) for black and white women. Jones argues that black women have a lower return to schooling. While some economists argue that black women encounter double discrimination in the labor market, that is, race discrimination coupled with gender discrimination, others argue that black women receive preferential treatment.[15]

Freeman describes the increase in black-white income ratio for women between 1950 and 1972 as "extraordinary" and "especially large."[16] He notes that black women's progress relative to white women was faster than black men's progress relative to white men.[17] His explanation for this phenomenon is the reduction of labor market discrimination against black women.

The subject of black women's rapid occupational change in the postwar period dominated the literature on how black women's economic status changed in the 1960s. Both human capital increases and the rapid occupational change among black women workers received much attention. According to Freeman, "The most striking change for black females ages 35–44 in 1960 was the movement out of household services."[18] Most of the younger black women entering the labor force were clerical workers, whereas most older women leaving the labor force were domestics.[19]

The literature on black women's economic progress in the 1970s stresses black women's achievement of "wage parity" by the late 1970s, as well as the impact of equal employment opportunity legislation and antidiscrimination policies.[20] Wallace used 1970 Census data to assess a number of aspects of black women's labor force status, one of which was earnings, and concluded that while black women had made sizeable relative wage and occupational gains, they were still the lowest paid race-gender group. Smith attributed the narrowing of wage differentials between black and white women through the late 1970s, to a "vintage effect," that is the accumulated result of the narrowing of the educational attainment gap between younger black and white women. At the end of the 1970s, it appeared that black women's relative wage gains would continue. Was there any reason to think otherwise?

The literature on black women's relative gains in the post–1980 period reflects a slowdown in the rate of black women's progress. One measure of the stagnation in the relative earnings progress of black women is the average annual growth rate of black female relative median earnings. Black female relative median earnings for full-time workers grew at an average of 3.3 percent per year from 1965 to 1975, but declined at an annual rate of −1.2 percent from 1975 to 1985.[21] Cotton (1989) explains that while most studies on black relative economic status have focused exclusively on men, the decline in black women's relative economic status is also characteristic of the 1980s. Can human capital factors explain the slowdown in black women's relative wage gains? According to Figart and others, the answer as regards human capital in the form of education is no. As they posit, "We suspect that, although in recent years the schooling of black women has not increased as rapidly as before, changes in human capital differences between black and white women are not likely to account for the relative fall in black women's wages."[22]

Several social scientists have commented on the paucity of research on black women in the labor force.[23] Malveaux commented, "Discussions of black women in the workplace have usually been buried between discussions of blacks (usually men) and women (usually white)."[24] The literature on blacks in the labor force and the literature on women in the labor force *do not* combine to explain the economic status of black women.

In 1939 the median income of black women (age 25 years and over) employed full-time[25] was 38.9 percent of the median income of white women employed full-time. By 1979, black women's relative income[26] had risen to 88.5 percent of white women's income. Several factors account for black women's relative income gains between the late 1930s and the late 1970s. First, the movement out of domestic and agricultural work, primarily into clerical and service occupations played a major role in black women's wage gains. Second, the rapid increase in black women's educational attainment narrowed the educational attainment gap between black and white women. Third, migration of blacks from the rural South to the urban North was important since wage levels were higher in the North than in the South. For those blacks who stayed behind, the remarkable and rapid growth of the Sunbelt cities fostered improvement in black economic conditions. The fourth factor was the passage and enforcement of antidiscrimination regulations outlawing employer discrimination on the basis of such worker characteristics as race or gender.[27] One result of the changes described above was that by the late 1970s black women earned as much as white women, for a given age and level of education.[28]

Although black women made remarkable wage and occupational gains relative to white women through the late 1970s, at some point, black women's progress began to stall. Black women "hit a wall," losing ground to white women in terms of relative income for the first time since 1940. Black women's relative income rose only marginally between 1979 and 1987, from 88.5 percent in 1979 to 89.3 percent in 1987.

Table 1 below, based on income data from the U.S. Census Bureau, shows black women's relative median income for full-time workers[29] from 1939 to 1999 by education level for women aged 25 to 34 and 35 to 44. These age groups were selected because by age 25, most persons have completed their formal schooling. In addition, as Carnoy (1994) points out, relative incomes of

Table 7.1 Black Female Relative Median Income* by Education Level, Ages 25–34 and 35–44: 1939–1999 (Full-time Workers Only)

	1939	1949	1959	1969	1973	1979	1982	1987	1999
Ages 25–34									
All Education Levels	0.37	0.60	0.64	0.80	0.87	0.92	0.91	0.87	0.88
High School Dropout	0.46	0.65	0.62	0.77	0.86	0.97	1.11	0.86	1.08
High School Complete	0.49	0.75	0.73	0.84	0.94	0.95	0.92	0.92	0.89
Some College	0.53	0.74	0.78	1.02	0.96	0.99	0.97	0.94	0.98
College Complete	0.59	0.80	0.71	1.01	0.97	0.95	0.92	0.87	0.89
Ages 35–44									
All Education Levels	0.36	0.56	0.64	0.79	0.83	0.93	0.92	0.89	0.87
High School Dropout	0.51	0.65	0.63	0.72	0.81	0.93	0.88	0.95	1.05
High School Complete	0.46	0.66	0.74	0.91	0.87	1.02	0.98	0.97	0.86
Some College	0.47	0.70	0.84	1.04	0.93	1.01	1.00	0.87	0.88
College Complete	0.59	0.79	0.97	0.94	0.89	0.95	0.94	0.93	0.86

*Black female relative median income is defined as the median income of black females divided by the median income of white females.

Sources: U.S. Bureau of the Census, The 1/1000 Public Use Sample of the U.S. Census, Current Population Surveys, various years; *Educational Attainment in the United States: March 2000*, Detailed tables. Available at http://www.census.gov/population/ socdemo/education/p20–536/tab09.pdf Date accessed 13 January 2003, Last revised October 3, 2002.

NOTE: The educational attainment categories are based on Census and Current Population Survey data on the number of years of schooling completed by survey respondents. Each educational attainment category in the table is based on the highest grade completed, according to the table below.

Level of Education	Years of Schooling Completed
High school dropout	1 to 3 years high school
High school complete	4 years high school
Some college	1 to 3 years college
College complete	4 years college

workers in the 25 to 34 age group provide evidence of how workers who entered the labor market more recently are faring, and incomes of 35- to 44-year-olds show how "prime age" workers are faring, even though, in the case of women, this age group has many reentrants who left the paid labor force to have children and then returned.[30]

For both age groups represented in table 7.1 and figure 7.1, black female relative income increased dramatically across education levels between 1939 and 1979. Between 1979 and 1999, young black women actually lost ground relative to young white women. In this two-decade period, black women age 25 to 34 experienced a decline in relative income from 0.92 in 1979 to 0.88 in 1999. For black women in the 35–44 age group, relative income declined from 0.93 in 1979 to 0.87 in 1999. From 1979 to 1999, the general trend for black female high school graduates and higher (some college and college complete) was a decrease in relative income. The one exception was high school dropouts, for whom black female relative income actually increased from 0.97 in 1979 to 1.08 in 1999 (age 25 to 34). Black female high school dropouts in the 35–44 age group also experienced an increase in their relative income during this period.

Although black women made considerable wage gains relative to white women between the late 1930s and the late 1970s, the wage gains that they made relative to white men and black men were smaller. Even if black women's gains relative to white men were not as large as their gains relative to white women, black women still made remarkable progress in the labor market relative to white women for a considerable period of time. Then, after four decades of progress, black women began to experience stagnation in their relative wage gains, beginning in the late 1970s. As Carnoy explains, "The past half century tells a story of African-Americans' incomes beginning to catch up to whites' and then leveling off far short of equality, leaving many blacks still in poverty and most frozen economically."[31]

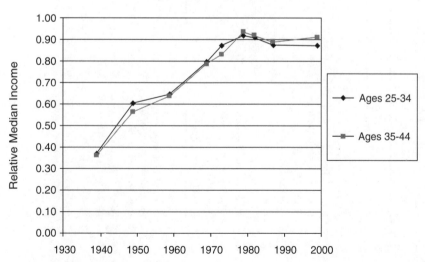

Black Female Relative Median Income, Ages 25 to 34
and 35 to 44: 1939 to 1999 (Selected Years)

Were the late 1970s a turning point for black women? Had black women come to the end of a period of wage gains relative to white women? Was there something inherently different about the 1980s that resulted in the stagnation of black women's wage gains relative to white women? We know from earlier research that college attainment became more important to earnings in the 1980s.[32] Research on men's wages in the United States indicates that during the 1980s the relative wages of more skilled workers rose relative to less skilled workers and that labor demand shifted toward more skilled workers.[33]

One frequently cited explanation for the low economic status of blacks, particularly relative to whites, is that blacks as a group have marital, family, and childbearing patterns that are very different from those of whites. For example, black women are less likely to marry, more likely to divorce, and less likely to remarry after a divorce.[34] In addition, black women are more likely to bear their first child during their teen years and more likely to bear children out of wedlock. Black women are also less likely to marry in order to legitimate a premarital conception.

The notion that economic status and family patterns are not only associated but causally linked dates back at least as early as 1939, with the publication of the first edition of E. Franklin Frazier's *The Negro Family in the United States* (1948). Frazier believed that the abolition of slavery through the Emancipation Proclamation created disorder in the Negro family. He attributed what he called the "breakdown" of the Negro family to the mass migration of the Negro population from the South to the urban areas of the North. According to Frazier, urbanization changed the character of black families, family life, and values. Frazier considered unwed motherhood a form of "social disorganization."[35] The mother-centered family was viewed as part of the legacy of slavery. Life in urban areas was associated with the breakdown of family ties. Many other social scientists considered the black family matriarchal, including Kenneth Clark and Jessie Bernard. Clark argued that the dominant position black women played in black families was a carryover from slavery because black men were relegated to menial jobs.[36]

Nearly three decades after the publication of Frazier's landmark study, the U.S. Department of Labor published its now well-known report on the Negro family, commonly referred to as "The Moynihan Report." Moynihan argued that the basic cause of poverty among Negroes was family structure, particularly the prevalence of families headed by women and the large proportion of births to black women were out of wedlock.[37] It is no surprise, then, that Moynihan cited Franklin repeatedly in his report.[38]

A clear connection developed in the literature between the urbanization of the black population and the increase in the number of families headed by women with no spouse present. Furthermore, the practice of interpreting black economic conditions solely in terms of *black men's* employment, to the neglect of *black women's* employment, continues today, evident in the works of such scholars as William Julius Wilson.[39] Wilson asserts that families headed by women make up an increasingly large proportion of the poverty population, but he does not examine the causes behind the link between poverty and female family headship.

Although racial differences in economic status are often attributed to differences in marriage, childbearing, and family patterns, surprisingly little research has analyzed the degree to which black-white differences in marital, family, and childbearing patterns actually account for the low relative economic status of blacks, especially black women, over time.

MODELS OF RACE AND ECONOMIC STATUS

There is a wide body of literature which consistently finds that earnings differ by race. The three dominant theoretical models which have been developed in order to explain why educational choices are made and in turn how these choices affect earnings are the human capital model, the status attainment model, and the labor market discrimination model, both from the economics literature, and from the sociology literature. These two perspectives—economic and sociological— dominate the empirical literature that attempts to explain racial and gender earnings differences.

THE HUMAN CAPITAL MODEL

Human capital theory, having its roots in the basic neoclassical microeconomic model, includes assumptions that firms maximize profits and that markets are perfectly competitive. In addition, the theory assumes that individuals maximize utility, that is, they make choices based on the objective of attaining the highest level of personal satisfaction or well-being possible. The human capital model is built on the concept of the marginal productivity of labor. The marginal productivity of labor is the change in the amount of product (or output) produced when an additional unit of labor is used in production. Workers are paid their marginal product, which implies that high-wage workers are more productive than low-wage workers. A basic tenet of the theory is that education makes people more productive, and this productivity is rewarded in the form of higher earnings in the labor market. It follows that individuals who have completed more education will have higher earnings on average.

Human capital theory borrowed basic concepts from the theory of investment in physical capital to develop a theory of investment in human beings. Therefore, a central concept in human capital theory is that of investment. The term "capital" is used because the individual in whom the investment is made will generate income in the future.[40] Human capital differs from physical capital in that human capital is embedded in the person.[41]

Investment in human capital, through education, on-the-job training, or experience, raises a worker's marginal productivity. By acquiring education, experience, or on-the-job training, workers are investing in themselves in order to raise their productivity. The level of investment is determined by the costs (the sum of direct costs and earnings foregone) and the benefits. Human capital theory includes a time component, since the investment takes place over a period of years.[42] Individuals forego consumption in the present with the expectation that they will have higher earnings in the future.

According to the reasoning of human capital theory, earnings differentials are the result of individual differences in innate ability and different levels of investment in human capital. According to Becker, earnings depend on the amount invested, which is itself determined by comparing costs and benefits.[43] Both the rates of return and the amounts of investment differ significantly across individuals.[44] Mincer's thesis is that the variance in income can be explained by the variance in human capital characteristics.

The implications of human capital theory for black-white earnings differentials are clear and straightforward. For example, human capital theory implies that whites earn more than blacks because they have more innate ability or because they invest more than blacks do in their human capital through education, experience, or on-the-job training. According to Becker, it is possible to infer an individual's ability from his or her level of investment in human capital. It is also possible that blacks could obtain a lower rate of return on their investment in human capital than whites.[45] If the quality of schooling provided to blacks is lower than that provided to whites, then for each additional year of schooling blacks may obtain a lower increment in earnings. Human capital theory predicts that, as the black-white gap in human capital narrows over time, earnings differentials between blacks and whites should also narrow.

Analyzing changes over time in the black-white male wage ratio, Smith and Welch conclude that improvements in black male relative standing are the result of changes over time in both the quantity and quality of schooling received by blacks. In their frequently cited 1986 study *Closing the Gap,* they attribute the narrowing of the black-white income gap for males between 1940 and 1980 to the reduction of black-white educational attainment gap. Smith and Welch, Freeman, Farley, and others claim that black men have made enormous progress relative to white men in terms of their individual incomes.[46] In his studies of black-white differences in the labor market through the 1960s, Freeman points to "dramatic economic progress for black Americans in a relatively short time."[47] He also notes that relative incomes of black men are higher at higher levels of education.

Two different explanations are offered by economists for black men's low relative earnings. One explanation is that white men have completed more education on average than black men have. In other words, white men have acquired more human capital than black men have. Evidence to support this notion would include higher rates of high school and college completion among white males. A second explanation for why black men have lower earnings than white men do is that black men receive a lower "payoff" to education than white men receive.

THE STATUS ATTAINMENT MODEL

Blau and Duncan (1967), viewing occupational mobility as the key indicator of social stratification, measured the effect of various background measures on occupational attainment. Using a five-variable model, which included father's occupation, father's occupational status, son's (respondent's) education, son's first job, and son's occupational status in 1962, Blau and Duncan were able to explain 26 percent of the variance in son's education, 33 percent of the variance in status of son's first job, and 43 percent of the variance in son's occupational status in 1962. The authors reached a number of conclusions regarding black-white differences in the occupational attainment process for males. They asked whether Negroes[48] and whites had the same chances for occupational mobility and concluded that Negro men had less educational opportunity than did white men. Furthermore, Negro men were disadvantaged in terms of the determinants of occupational status, such as father's occupation. Also, within the same occupation, Negroes had lower earnings than whites.

A key part of the Blau-Duncan conceptual framework is that the role of education is an intervening one, mediating the effect of social origins on occupational attainment. For both Negro and white men, education increases the probability that one moves up from his social origins, attaining an occupational status higher than that of his father. However, they write, "Education, a path to upward mobility for all, is not as effective a route for non-whites as it is for whites."[49] Education, while important for the social mobility of men of both races, did not influence mobility as profoundly for Negro men as it did for white men.

Opportunity and Change by Featherman and Hauser (1978) represented an early effort to incorporate race into the status attainment model. Designed as a replication of the research reported in *The American Occupational Structure,* the Featherman-Hauser study analyzed changes over time in the relationships between the same variables in order to determine whether the American social system had become more or less rigid between 1962 and 1973.[50] Their goal was to measure both the magnitude and the direction of the changes in social mobility which had taken place in this period corresponding to approximately a decade.

The main conclusions of *Opportunity and Change* are that during the period between 1962 and 1973, the American occupational structure was characterized by declining status ascription and increasingly universalistic status allocation. Interested in black-white differences in the status attainment process, Featherman and Hauser concluded that Negro fathers were more able over time to translate socioeconomic advantages to their sons. However, racial differences in socioeconomic status were still evident.[51]

The status attainment model also incorporates a "life-cycle view." That is to say, choices and circumstances in the individual's early life are studied in relationship to one's status and conditions in later life. Duncan summarizes this socioeconomic life-cycle view in an article on the relationship between race and poverty. In his words, "What factors, conditions, circumstances, and choices observable at one stage of the life cycle are determinative or prognostic of outcomes to be observed at later stages?"[52] The outcomes which he analyzes include educational attainment and income.[53]

Duncan's analysis is limited to males, and he carried out separate analyses for black and white men in order to determine the degree to which structural differences in the relationship between family background, on one hand, and educational attainment and income, on the other hand, may differ by race. He found that not only did Negroes tend to come from lower social class, or more disadvantaged backgrounds than did whites, but Negro men were also less able than whites to "translate" whatever advantage in social status they may have into their own higher educational attainment and income. Raising the question of whether

Negroes are poor as a result of the "inheritance of poverty" or whether the "inheritance of race" plays a larger role, he concludes that it is race which dominates the intergenerational status transmission process.

LABOR MARKET DISCRIMINATION

If the status attainment perspective is the dominant approach to explaining status differences in the sociological literature, then indeed labor market discrimination is the dominant approach to explaining earnings differences in the economics literature. Labor market discrimination constitutes yet another theoretical perspective on the black-white earnings gap. Proponents of such a view fall into two camps: 1) "pure discrimination" theorists and 2) "statistical discrimination" theorists. The neoclassical theory of "pure discrimination," a model based on the pioneering work of Gary S. Becker, centers on tastes and preferences. Becker defines the "market discrimination coefficient" as the relative wage differential between black and white workers, which is a quantitative measure of the intensity of the "taste for discrimination."[54] If employers dislike associating with blacks, they are willing to forego profits in order to limit the extent of their contact with blacks.

Arrow, also writing in the neoclassical tradition, extends Becker's "taste" model of labor market discrimination.[55] Arrow writes, "The notion of discrimination involves the additional concept that personal characteristics of the worker unrelated to productivity are also valued on the market."[56] Arrow concludes that even if blacks and whites are equally productive, the wage rate for white workers will be higher in equilibrium than the wage rate for nonwhite workers if employers have a taste for discrimination. The upshot of Arrow's argument is that employers with a taste for discrimination are willing to exchange a certain amount of profit in order to limit the number of blacks they employ.

Both Becker and Arrow make the key assumption that black and white workers are perfect substitutes in production, which means that black and white workers can be exchanged for one another without affecting productivity. This assumption implies that blacks and white have the same marginal products of labor. In the absence of discrimination, black and white workers would earn the same wage, but because blacks are paid less than their marginal product, and whites are paid more than their marginal product, blacks are paid less than whites in equilibrium.[57]

In contrast to the theory of "pure discrimination," "statistical discrimination" theory holds that under uncertainty and with incomplete information regarding potential workers' productivities, firms will pay blacks less on average than they pay whites because they assign the average characteristics of the group to individual workers.[58] That is, employers attribute to individual job applicants the average characteristics of the group (or groups) to which that individual belongs. For example, if the employer believes that black workers are less productive on average than white workers are, then presented with two applicants who are identical in every regard except race, the employer will tend to hire the white worker instead of the black worker. The employer will also pay the black worker a lower wage.

In her "crowding" model of occupational discrimination, Bergmann (1971) argues that blacks are restricted to a narrow range of occupations, which are generally low-wage occupations.[59] Such "crowding" lowers marginal productivity of blacks in those occupations. It is therefore possible for equally skilled occupations to have different wage rates, and racial wage differentials may be the result of occupational segregation rather than the result of discrimination based on tastes.[60] According to Bergmann's analysis, ending racial discrimination in jobs would have a negligible effect on white incomes.[61]

CONCLUDING THOUGHTS

Economists and sociologists have used a variety of models to analyze racial differences in economic status, including the human capital model, the labor market discrimination model, and the status attainment model. Each model presented in this chapter offers researchers a different perspective on race and economic progress. If these models are to prove fruitful in the study of race in the economy, underlying each model must be a conceptual framework which has at its most basic level a clear notion about how the world works and whether, how, and why race matters. Moreover, economic analysis of race differences, and in particular, analysis of the African American economic experience will remain incomplete until the gender dimension is recognized and included.

Acknowledgements: An earlier version of this chapter was presented at the Graduate Seminar in African American Urban Studies: History, Work, and Social Policy at Carnegie Mellon University, Department of History on April 23, 1998. I would like to thank the professors who served on my dissertation committee at Stanford University: Martin Carnoy, chair; Henry M. Levin (now on faculty at Columbia University), and Myra H. Strober. Thanks also to Leonard Stewart, Jr., who provided helpful comments and editorial assistance on this chapter.

NOTES

This chapter draws on my doctoral dissertation; Susan Williams McElroy, "The Effect of Teenage Childbearing on Young Black and White Women's Educational Attainment, Labor Force Participation, and Earnings." PhD dissertation. Stanford University, 1996.

1 Gunnar Myrdal, *An American Dilemma: The Negro Problem and Modern Democracy* (New York: London: Harper & Brothers, 1944); Gerald David Jaynes and Robin M. Williams, Jr., eds., *A Common Destiny: Blacks and American Society* (Washington, D.C.: National Academy Press, 1989).
2 According to the U.S. Bureau of Labor Statistics, in 2002, there were 7,794,000 black males and 8,787,000 black females age 16 and over in the civilian labor force.
3 These employment statistics are annual averages for 2002, and they correspond to workers age 16 years and over. U.S. Department of Labor, Bureau of Labor Statistics, *Handbook of Labor Statistics*, Bulletin 2340, 1989.
4 The Census Bureau defines a family household as follows: "A family household is a household maintained by a householder who is in a family (as defined above), and includes any unrelated people (unrelated subfamily members and/or secondary indi-

viduals) who may be residing there." "A family is a group of two people or more (one of whom is the householder) related by birth, marriage, or adoption and residing together; all such people (including related subfamily members) are considered as members of one family."

5 U.S. Bureau of the Census, *Statistical Abstract of the United States* (Washington, D.C.: U.S. Government Printing Office, 1993).

6 *Ibid.*

7 Frank Levy, *Dollars and Dreams: The Changing American Income Distribution* (New York: W.W. Norton, 1987).

8 Martin Carnoy, *Faded Dreams: The Politics and Economics of Race in America.* (Cambridge: Cambridge University Press, 1994); Richard B. Freeman, "Changes in the Labor Market for Black Americans, 1948–72," *Brookings Papers on Economic Activity* 1: (1973) 67–120, 1973; Julianne Malveaux, "Changes in the Labor Market Status of Black Women," prepared for the Education and Labor Committee, U.S. House of Representatives (A Report of the Study Group on Affirmative Action to the Committee on Education and Labor. U.S. House of Representatives. 100th Congress. 1st session. Serial No. 100–L, 1986); Phyllis A. Wallace, "A Research Agenda on the Economic Status of Black Women," *Review of Black Political Economy* 14 (Fall/Winter 1985–86): 293–95.

9 Malveaux, "Changes in the Labor Market," p. 214.

10 Jane Riblett Wilkie, "The Decline of Occupational Segregation Between Black and White Women," in Cora Bagley Marrett and Cheryl Leggon, ed., *Research in Race and Ethnic Relations: A Research Annual,* Vol. 4, (1985): 67–89; Najda Zalokar, *The Economic Status of Black Women: An Exploratory Investigation* (Washington, D.C.: U.S. Commission on Civil Rights, U.S. Government Printing Office, 1990).

11 James P. Smith and Finis R. Welch, *Closing the Gap: Forty Years of Economic Progress for Blacks* (Santa Monica, CA: RAND Corporation, 1986).

12 Reynolds Farley and Walter R. Allen, *The Color Line and the Quality of Life in America* (New York: Russell Sage Foundation, 1987); Gerald David Jaynes and Robin M. Williams, Jr., eds., *A Common Destiny: Blacks and American Society,* (Washington, D.C.: National Academy Press, 1989); James P. Smith and Finis R. Welch, "Black-White Male Wage Ratios: 1960–70," *American Economic Review* 67 (June 1977): 323–38; Smith and Welch, *Closing the Gap*; Smith and Welch, "Black Economic Progress After Myrdal," *Journal of Economic Literature* 27 (June 1989): 519–64.

13 Frank Levy, *Dollars and Dreams: The Changing American Income Distribution* (New York: W.W. Norton, 1987).

14 Levy, *Dollars*; Phyllis Wallace with Linda Datcher and Julianne Malveaux. *Black Women in the Labor Force* (Cambridge, MA: MIT Press, 1980); Wilkie, "Decline."

15 Allan G. King, "Labor Market Racial Discrimination Against Black Women," *Review of Black Political Economy* 8 (Summer 1978): 325–35; Malveaux, "Changes in the Labor Market"; Zalokar, *The Economic Status of Black Women*; Elizabeth M. Almquist, "Untangling the Effects of Race and Sex: The Disadvantaged Status of Black Women, *Social Science Quarterly* 56 (June 1975): 129–42.

16 Freeman, "Changes in the Labor Market," pp. 76, 111.

17 *Ibid*, p. 67.

18 *Ibid*, p. 115.

19 *Ibid*, p. 115.

20 James P. Smith, "The Convergence to Racial Equality in Women's Wages," in Cynthia B. Lloyd, Emily S. Andrews, and Curtis L. Gilroy, ed., *Women in the Labor Market*

(New York: Columbia University Press, 1979): pp. 173–215; Wallace, Datcher, and Malveaux, *Black Women in the Labor Force.*

21 Augustin Kwasi Fosu, "Trends in Relative Earnings Gains by Black Women: Implications for the Future," *Review of Black Political Economy* 17 (Winter 1988): 31–45.

22 Deborah Figart et al, "The Wage Gap and Women of Color," In *First Annual Women's Policy Research Conference Proceedings, May 19, 1989* (Washington, D.C.: Institute for Women's Policy Research, 1990), p. 30.

23 Almquist, "Untangling the Effects of Race and Sex"; Patricia A. Gwartney-Gibbs and Patricia A. Taylor, "Black Women Worker's Earnings Progress in Three Industrial Sectors," *Sage: A Scholarly Journal on Black Women* 3 (Spring 1986): 20–25; Gerda Lerner, ed., *Black Women in White America; A Documentary History* (New York: Pantheon Books, 1972); Zalokar, *The Economic Status of Black Women.*

24 Malveaux, "Changes in the Labor Force."

25 By age 25, most persons have completed their formal schooling. "Full-time" is defined as 35 or more hours per week.

26 Throughout this chapter, the terms "black women's relative income" or "black female relative income" will be used interchangedly to refer to black women's median annual income as a percent of white women's median annual income, unless otherwise indicated.

27 Carnoy, *Faded dreams*; Jaynes and Williams, *A Common Destiny.*

28 Smith, "The Convergence to Racial Equality."

29 This table includes full-time workers only because part-time workers have lower average earnings because they work fewer hours, and many women work part time.

30 Carnoy, *Faded Dreams.*

31 *Ibid*, p. 14.

32 Kevin M. Murphy and Finis Welch, "The Structure of Wages," *Quarterly Journal of Economics* 107 (Feb. 1992): 285–326.

33 Lawrence F. Katz and Kevin M. Murphy. "Changes in Relative Wages, 1963–1987: Supply and Demand Factors," *Quarterly Journal of Economics* 107 (Feb. 1992): 35–78; Murphy and Welch, "The Structure of Wages."

34 Neil G. Bennett, David E. Bloom, and Patricia H. Craig, "The Divergence of Black and White Marriage Patterns," *American Journal of Sociology* 95 (Nov. 1989): 692–722.

35 Edward Franklin Frazier, *The Negro Family in the United States.* (New York: Dryden Press, revised and abridged edition, 1948).

36 Kenneth Bancroft Clark, *Dark Ghetto: Dilemmas of Social Power* (New York: Harper and Row, 1965); Jessie Bernard, *Marriage and Family Among Negroes* (Englewood Cliffs, NJ: Prentice-Hall, 1966).

37 U.S. Department of Labor, Office of Policy Planning and Research, *The Negro Family: A Case for National Action* (Washington, D.C.: U.S. Government Printing Office, 1965).

38 Ludwig L. Geismar and Ursula C. Gerhart, "Social Class, Ethnicity, and Family Functioning: Exploring Some Issues Raised by the Moynihan Report," *Journal of Marriage and the Family* 30 (Aug. 1968): 480–87.

39 William Julius Wilson, *The Truly Disadvantaged: The Inner City, the Underclass, and Public Policy* (Chicago: University of Chicago Press, 1987).

40 Robert M. Solow, *Capital Theory and the Rate of Return* (Amsterdam: North-Holland, 1963); M. Woodhall, "Human Capital Concepts," in George Psacharopolous, ed., *Economics of Education: Research and Studies,* (Oxford: Pergamon Press, 1987), pp. 21–24.

41 Gary S. Becker, *Human Capital: A Theoretical and Empirical Analysis with Special Reference to Education*, 2d ed. (Chicago and London: University of Chicago Press, 1975).

42 Jacob Mincer, *Schooling, Experience, and Earnings* (New York: National Bureau of Economic Research, 1974); Becker, *Human Capital*.

43 *Ibid.*

44 *Ibid;* Mincer, *Schooling*.

45 Becker, *Human Capital*.

46 Smith and Welch, "Black-White Male Wage Ratios," *Closing the Gap*; and *Black Economic Progress After Myrdal;* Freeman, "Changes in the Labor Market"; Reynolds Farley, "Assessing Black Progress: Employment, Occupations, Earnings, Income, Poverty," *Economic Outlook USA* 13 (Third Quarter 1986): 14–19.

47 Freeman, "Changes in the Labor Market," p. 120.

48 The term "Negroes" is used in place of "blacks" in order to be consistent with the terminology used in the literature being reviewed here. Peter M. Blau and Otis Dudley Duncan, with the collaboration of Andrea Tyree, *The American Occupational Structure* (New York: John Wiley and Sons, 1967).

49 Blau and Duncan, *American Occupational Structure*, p. 210.

50 David L. Featherman and Robert M. Hauser, *Opportunity and Change* (New York: Academic Press, 1978).

51 *Ibid.*

52 Otis Dudley Duncan, "Inheritance of Poverty or Inheritance of Race?" in Daniel Moynihan, ed., *On Understanding Poverty* (New York: Basic Books, 1969).

53 *Ibid.*, pp. 88–89. Duncan also analyzes two other outcomes: the number of children in the family in which the man grew up and the man's occupational status as an adult.

54 Gary S. Becker, *The Economics of Discrimination*, 2d ed. (Chicago, Ill.: University of Chicago Press, 1971).

55 Kenneth J. Arrow, "Models of Job Discrimination," in Anthony Pascal, ed., *Racial Discrimination in Economic Life* (Lexington, Mass.: Lexington Books, 1972a), pp. 83–102.; "The Theory of Discrimination," in Pascal, ed., *Racial Discrimination in Economic Life*, pp. 187–203; "The Theory of Discrimination," in Orley Ashenfelter and Albert Rees, ed., *Discrimination in Labor Markets* (Princeton, N.J.: Princeton University Press, 1973), pp. 3–33.

56 Arrow, "*The Theory of Discrimination*," p. 3.

57 Becker, *The Economics of Discrimination*.

58 Dennis J. Aigner and Glen G. Cain, "Statistical Theories of Discrimination in Labor Markets," *Industrial and Labor Relations Review* 30 (Jan. 1977): 175–87; Edmund S. Phelps, "The Statistical Theory of Racism and Sexism," *American Economic Review* 62 (Sept. 1972): 659–61.

59 Barbara R. Bergmann, "The Effect on White Incomes of Discrimination in Employment," *Journal of Political Economy* 76 (March/April 1971): 294–212.

60 Ray Marshall, "The Economics of Racial Discrimination: A Survey," *Journal of Economic Literature* 12 (Sept. 1974): 849–71.

61 Bergmann, "The Effect on White Incomes."

CHAPTER 8

EVIDENCE ON DISCRIMINATION IN EMPLOYMENT: CODES OF COLOR, CODES OF GENDER

WILLIAM A. DARITY Jr. AND PATRICK L. MASON

There is substantial racial and gender disparity in the American economy. As we will demonstrate, discriminatory treatment within the labor market is a major cause of this inequality. The evidence is ubiquitous: careful research studies that estimate wage and employment regressions, help-wanted advertisements, audit and correspondence studies, and discrimination suits that are often reported by the news media. Yet, there appear to have been periods of substantial reductions in economic disparity and discrimination. For example, Donohue and Heckman provide evidence that racial discrimination declined during 1965–1975.[1] Gottschalk has produced statistical estimates that indicate that discrimination against black males dropped most sharply between 1965 and 1975, and that discrimination against women declined during the interval 1973–1994.[2] But some unanswered questions remain. Why did the movement toward racial equality stagnate and eventually decline after the mid-1970s? What factors are most responsible for the remaining gender inequality? What is the role of the competitive process in the elimination or reproduction of discrimination in employment?

The Civil Rights Act of 1964 is the signal event associated with abrupt changes in the black-white earnings differential.[3] Along with other important pieces of federal legislation, Leonard shows that the Civil Rights Act of 1964 also played a major role in reducing discrimination against women.[4] Prior to passage of the federal civil rights legislation of the 1960s, racial exclusion and gender-typing of employment was blatant. The adverse effects of discriminatory practices on the life chances of African Americans, in particular, during that period have been well documented.[5] Cordero-Guzman observes that "up until the early 1960s, and particularly in the south, most blacks were systematically denied equal access to opportunities [and] in many instances, individuals with adequate credentials or skills were not, legally, allowed to apply to certain positions in firms."[6] Competitive market forces did not eliminate these discriminatory practices in the decades leading up to the 1960s. They remained until the federal adoption of antidiscrimination laws.

Newspaper help-wanted advertisements provide vivid illustrations of the openness and visibility of such practices. We conducted an informal survey of the employment section of major daily newspapers from three northern cities, the *Chicago Tribune*, the *Los Angeles Times* and the *New York Times*, and from the nation's capital, *The Washington Post*, at five-year intervals, from 1945 to 1965. (Examples from southern newspapers are even more vivid.) Table 8.1 presents verbatim reproductions of some of these advertisements in 1960 that explicitly indicate the employers' preference for applicants of a particular race, far more often than not white applicants.

With respect to gender-typing of occupations, the help-wanted advertisements were structured so that whole sections of the classifieds offered job opportunities separately and explicitly for men and women. Men were requested for positions that included restaurant cooks, managers, assistant managers, auto salesmen, sales jobs in general, accountants and junior accountants, design engineers, detailers, diemakers, drivers, and welders. Women were requested for positions that included household and domestic workers, stenographers, secretaries, typists, bookkeepers, occasionally accountants (for "girls good at figures"), and waitresses.[7] *The Washington Post* of January 3, 1960 had the most examples of racial preference, again largely for whites, in help-wanted ads of any newspaper edition we examined. Nancy Lee's employment service even ran an advertisement for a switchboard operator—presumably never actually seen by callers— requesting that all *women* applying be white!

Advertisements also frequently included details about the age range desired from applicants, for instance, men 21–30 or women 18–25. Moreover, employers also showed little compunction about specifying precise physical attributes desired in applicants.[8]

Following the passage of the Civil Rights Act of 1964, none of the newspapers carried help-wanted ads that included any explicit preference for "white" or "colored" applicants. However, it became very common to see advertisements for "European" housekeepers (a trend that was already visible as early as 1960). While race no longer entered the help-wanted pages explicitly, national origin or ancestry seemed to function as a substitute. Especially revealing is an advertisement run by the Amity Agency in the *New York Times* on January 3, 1965, informing potential employers that "Amity Has Domestics": "Scottish Gals" at $150 a month as "mothers helpers and housekeepers," "German Gals" at $175 a month on one-year contracts, and "Haitian Gals" at $130 a month, who were "French speaking." Moreover, in the "Situations Wanted" section of the newspaper, prospective female employees still were indicating their own race.

The case of the help wanted pages of the *New York Times* is of special note because New York was one of the states that had a state law against discrimination and a State Commission Against Discrimination in place, long prior to the passage of the federal Civil Rights Act of 1964. However, the toothlessness of New York's State Commission Against Discrimination is well-demonstrated by the fact that employers continued to indicate their racial preferences for new hires

Table 8.1 Examples of Racial Preference in help Wanted Advertisement (Selected Newspapers and Years, 1960)

CHICAGO TRIBUNE	LOS ANGELES TIMES	NEW YORK TIMES	WASHINGTON POST
January 3, 1960	January 2, 1960	January 3, 1960	January 3, 1960
LABORATORY TECHNICIAN Experienced, Modern southside medical center. White. Salary open. Call Vincennes 6-3401	COMPANION. White. Lite hswk. for single lady. Must drive. Local refers. CR 1-7704	COOK, housekeeper, Negro preferred, experience essential, prominent family, permanent position, high salary, MA 7-5369	NURSE (practical) white, for small nursing home, Silver Spring area. Car nec. Good salary. EV 4-6161
WAITRESS–White. Good tips. 7611-15 Stoney Island RE 4-8837	GIRL, white, 25-40. Lite household duties. Rm, board, sal. Apply eves. after 5, 10572 S. Vermont Ave.	COOK-hswkr., fine position, top salary + bonus. Start Jan. Must be capable, white; ref. HU 2-7222	BOYS–WHITE Age 14 to 18. To assist Route manager full or part-time. Must be neat in appearance. Apply 1346 Conn. Ave. NW, room 1006, between 9 to 11 a.m. or 3:30 to 4:30 p.m.
WHITE-Firing (Stokers) and Manage Unf. Apt. Bldg.; Sal. $350 + Apt. Age to 50. D.P. accepted. Write MXB 152, Tribune	HOUSEKEEPER–European or Oriental–2 adults, pri. quarters, under 45. Ref. GR, 2-4891	COOK-HOUSEKEEPER European OWN ROOM AND BATH. FAMILY OF FOUR. LONG ISLAND HOME. $70 WEEKLY. 7-3212 TIMES.	DINING ROOM AND CLUB MANAGER AND ASSISTANT MANAGER OVERSEAS-FAR EAST ...White, married or single, 2-year contract...Call NA, 8-5189 Monday 8:30-12:00

Man. empl. White, for small mfg. hse. North. 4-rm. furn. apt. and sa. Write MXB 303. Tribune

WHITE married men who can furnish and opr. late air cond. Cadillac Limo.—Good opportunity. ID 2-4864

SINGLE, white man—work in first class tables. Room, board + $60 per month, CR 2-0299

HSKPR., white, 22-45, 2 school boys. Must live in. Refs. BR, 2-7041

COUPLE, $400-500, white for business couple with 2 adult children. Private home Forest Hills. Man to work in business. BO 3-2649.

HOUSEKEEPER-cook, European; must be honest, clean, reliable; own room & bath; other help; recent references; good salary; 70's East Side. RE 4-25581

HOUSEKEEPER, white, sleep out, 5 1/2 days. 10 thru dinner, experienced, must love children; recent references; East Side TR 9-6001

DRIVERS (TRUCK) Colored, for trash routes; over 25 years of age; paid vacation, year-around work; must have excellent driving record. Apply SHAYNE BROS.) 1601 W St., NE

PAINTER–White, for apts. in S.E. area; exp. Apply rm. 7, 140 Eye St., NW

MEN-COLORED $125 WEEK I will teach three men the selling profession. Earnings will start from the first day on the job. If you are ambitious you can earn as high as $250 a week after 30 days training. Apply 705 Park Rd., NW, 9:30 to 12 noon only. See Mr. Jackson.

Continued

Table 8.1 Examples of Racial Preference in Help Wanted Advertisements (Selected Newspapers and Years, 1960)

CHICAGO TRIBUNE	LOS ANGELES TIMES	NEW YORK TIMES	WASHINGTON POST
January 3, 1960	January 2, 1960	January 3, 1960	January 3, 1960
Brand new organization has openings in all departments for men 18 t 25, white, for immediate employment. Guaranteed weekly salary $95. Car furnished. Call Mr. Fulton, DE 2-0589, between 9:30 and 1.			AMBITIOUS MEN (WHITE) National concern requires services of 3 neat-appearing young men, 18-35, to work in the library dept. for executive position... For appointment call MR ALBRIGHT, ME, 8-1484, 9 a.m. 'til 2 p.m.
TOW TRUCK DRIVERS White, also work around station. See Carl, 530 N. La Salle St.			SERVICEMEN, OFFICE WORKERS, Etc. (White), EX 3-0397 8-6:30 Mon.
DOORMAN-WHITE age 30 to 45 married...Neat in appearance and at least 5'11" or taller in height...Address MEK 149, Tribune			STUDENTS Boys, white, 14 yrs. and over, jobs immediately available. Apply 3:30-4:30 p.m., Rm. 724 9th St., NW. See Mr. Faulkner

in help-wanted ads, as well as by descriptions of personal experience like that of John A. Williams in his semi-autobiographical novel, *The Angry Ones.*[9]

Help-wanted ads were only the tip of the iceberg of the process of racial exclusion in employment. After all, there is no reason to believe that the employers who did not indicate a racial preference were entirely open-minded about their applicant pool. How successful has the passage of federal antidiscrimination legislation in the 1960s been in producing an equal-opportunity environment in which job applicants are now evaluated on their qualifications? To give away the answer at the outset, our response is that discrimination by race has diminished somewhat, and discrimination by gender has diminished substantially. However, neither employment discrimination by race or by gender is close to ending. The Civil Rights Act of 1964 and subsequent related legislation have purged American society of the most overt forms of discrimination. However, discriminatory practices have continued in a more covert and subtle form. Furthermore, racial discrimination is masked and rationalized by widely held presumptions of African American inferiority.

STATISTICAL RESEARCH ON EMPLOYMENT DISCRIMINATION

Economic research on the presence of discrimination in employment has largely focused on black-white and male-female earnings and occupational disparities. The position typically taken by economists is that some part of the racial or gender gap in earnings or occupations is due to average group differences in productivity-linked characteristics (a human capital gap) and some part is due to average group differences in treatment (a discrimination gap). The more of the gap that can be explained by human capital differences, the easier it becomes to assert that labor markets function in a nondiscriminatory manner, and that any remaining racial or gender inequality in employment outcomes must be due to differences between blacks and whites or between men and women that exist outside the labor market.

One widely used approach is to estimate regression equations in which earnings levels or occupations are the dependent variable, to be explained by some combination of factors such as years and quality of education, experience, job tenure, region of country, and dummy variables for race and gender. If the coefficients on the race and gender variables are significant and negative, after controlling for other factors, that is taken as evidence of discrimination within the labor market.

A second widely used approach is to apply the Blinder-Oaxaca decomposition procedure. This procedure involves estimation of separate earnings or occupational status regressions for a reference group—for example, all males or all white males—and all other groups whose labor market outcomes are being compared against them. The Blinder-Oaxaca technique permits the researcher to sort between the extent to which the disparity in outcomes between the reference and the comparison group is due to differences in average group endowments (human capital) of income-generating characteristics and differences in treatment (discrimination) of given characteristics. The human capital gap is captured by isolating the effects of intergroup disparity in mean values of the constant term and coefficients in the regressions. Thus, the Blinder-Oaxaca decomposition identifies the presence of discrimination when there are palpable differences in the estimated structural equations producing economic outcomes for the reference and the comparison groups.

Our general expectation is the race-gender dummy variable approach and the Blinder-Oaxaca technique should lead to the same conclusions about the presence or absence of labor market discrimination. If a race or gender dummy is statistically significant or negative in the first approach, a Blinder-Oaxaca decomposition probably will reveal that the corresponding racial or gender group suffers a loss in economic outcome due to differential treatment of given characteristics. However, the first approach obviously constrains the coefficient estimates on the productivity-linked variables to be the same for all groups, while the Blinder-Oaxaca approach does not.

REGRESSIONS ON GENDER DIFFERENTIALS

The 1980s and 1990s saw a general narrowing of the wage differentials between men and women. In 1981 the annual earnings of women employed full-time and year-round were 59 percent of the annual earnings of men. By 1995 this ratio was 71 percent.[10] When adjustments are made in regression equations for education, job experience, and so on, the differential shrinks still further. There are at least three reasons for the narrowing of the wage gap. First, Gottschalk shows that from 1973 to 1994 men at or below the 78th percentile of the male wage distribution experienced absolute decreases in their real wage rate.[11] Simultaneously, the wages of women rose at all points along the female wage distribution, although women above the median received the most dramatic wage improvements.[12] Second, female-male gaps in human capital, especially the gap in actual market experience, have declined.[13] Third, legal pressure has succeeded in expanding the range of job opportunities for women; hence, the level of discrimination against women appears to have been reduced.[14]

However, two substantial issues remain: the "family gap," which is the lower level of wages received by women with children;[15] and the continued occupational segregation of women into lower-paid jobs. Both of these issues pose problems for the standard earnings regression framework. A respectable model of human capital must include job experience and education, but if the level of job experience and education are determined in part by social expectations of how much education women need and social patterns of who will need to take time off from work to look after children, then those variables may be embodying discrimination against women, rather than controlling for an exogenous variable. Similarly, if an earnings equation does not control for type of occupation, then it is open to the criticism that it does not compare equivalent jobs. However, if it does control for type of occupation, and society pushes women into particular jobs, then occupation becomes a variable that embodies discrimination against women, rather than control for an exogenous factor.[16]

There is strong evidence of a "family gap" in women's earnings, a gap between women with children and those without. This difference goes some way to explaining the remaining overall gender gap in earnings. Waldfogel reports that the consensus estimate of the family penalty is 10 to 15 percent. Women with children are systematically paid a lower wage than women without children (after adjusting for differences in productive attributes.)[17] On the other hand, married men (who are much more likely to have children than unmarried men) receive a wage premium. Waldfogel shows that among workers 24 to 45 years of age, women without children receive wage rates that represent 81.3 percent of men's pay, while women with children receive wage rates that represent only 73.4 percent of men's pay. Waldfogel's catalog of possible explanations for the family gap include: unobserved heterogeneity (mothers are less motivated or supply less effort for market work than non-mothers); discrimination (employers prefer women without children); and institutional barriers to labor force participation by mothers (anemic maternity leave and child care policies as well as workplaces that do not provide flexible workhours).

In addition, there continues to be strong evidence of occupational crowding by gender in the United States.[18] For example, the index of occupational dissimilarity was 53 percent in 1990,[19] which means that nearly one-half of women (or men) would have to change occupations in order to have equal gender representation in all occupations. This is lower than the 1970 value of 68 percent, but it indicates that substantial differences in occupational employment by gender. These differences cannot be explained well by human capital differences between men and women; women continue to be concentrated in lower-paying jobs than men with an equivalent level of education.

Intriguing evidence on gender inequality is developed by Blau and Kahn in a cross-national study that compares gender inequality in nine Organisation for Economic Cooperation and Development (OECD) countries—Australia, Austria, Germany, Hungary, Italy, Norway, Sweden, Switzerland, and the United Kingdom—with the United States.[20] Blau and Kahn report a seeming paradox: "1) U.S. women compare favorably with women in other countries in terms of human capital and occupational distribution; 2) the United States has had a longer and often stronger commitment to equal pay and equal employment opportunity policies than have most of the other countries in our sample; but 3) the gender pay gap is larger in the United States than in most countries."[21] From an international perspective, cross-national differences in human capital, occupation, and laws will fail to explain the cross-national variation in gender disparity in earnings.

Instead, the major explanatory factor appears to be differences in the overall degree of inequality in the national economy. For example, Blau and Kahn show that American and Australian women have two of the highest percentile rankings in the male wage distributions in their respective countries; in both cases, the average woman is at the 33rd percentile of the male wage distribution.[22] However, Australian women have an hourly wage that is 73 percent of the Australian male mean, a wage ratio that is second only to Sweden's 77 percent ratio among the 10 countries studied. In contrast, American women have an hourly wage rate that is only 65 percent of the USA male mean, which is among the lowest of the countries studied, with those of Hungary and Switzerland also at 65 percent and that of the United Kingdom at 61 percent. Wage-setting institutions in each country appear to have a profound impact of the extent of male-female economic inequality. Countries such as the United States and the United Kingdom, with their decentralized wage setting institutions and weaker trade unions, tend to have the greatest general levels of inequality. Since those in the lower half of the income distribution are more penalized in the United States and the United Kingdom than elsewhere comparatively, their gender inequality is worse relative to that of other countries as well.[23] For Australia, Austria, Germany, Italy, Norway, and Sweden, greater inequality of the male wage distribution can account for the higher gender gap.[24]

REGRESSION EVIDENCE ON RACIAL DISCRIMINATION

When we consider economic disparities by race, a difference by gender emerges. Using a Blinder-Oaxaca approach in which women are compared by their various racial and ethnic subgroups, based on U.S. Census data for 1980 and 1990, little evidence of systematic wage discrimination is found.[25] However, when males are examined using the same Census data, a standard result emerges. A significant portion of the wage gap between black and white males in the United States cannot be explained by the variables included to control for productivity differences across members of the two racial groups.

Black women are likely to have the same school quality and omitted family background characteristics as black men (the same is true for white women and men). Hence, it strains credibility to argue that the black-white earnings gap for men is due to an omitted labor quality variable unless one also argues that black women are paid more than white women conditional on the unobservables. The findings of Darity, Guilkey and Winfrey (1996) and Rodgers and Spriggs (1996) indicate that in 1980 and 1990 African American men in the United States suffered a 12 to 15 percent loss in earnings due to labor market discrimination.[26]

There is a growing body of evidence that uses color or "skin shade" as a natural experiment to detect discrimination. The approach of these studies has been to look at different skin shades within a particular ethnic group at a particular place and time, which should help to control for factors of culture and ethnicity other than pure skin color. Johnson, Bienenstock, and Stoloff looked at dark-skinned and light-skinned black males from the same neighborhoods in Los Angeles and found that the combination of a black racial identity and a dark skin tone reduces an individual's odds of working by 52 percent, after controlling for education, age, and criminal record![27] Since both dark-skinned and light-skinned black males in the sample were from the same neighborhoods, the study *de facto* controlled for school quality. Further evidence that lighter-complexioned blacks tend to have superior incomes and life chances than darker-skinned blacks in the United States comes from studies by Ransford, Keith and Herring, and Johnson and Farrell.[28]

Similar results are found by looking at skin color among Hispanics. Research conducted by Arce, Murguia, and Frisbie utilizing the University of Michigan's 1979 Chicano survey involved partitioning the sample along two phenotypical dimensions—skin color ranging from "very light" to "very dark" on a five-point scale and physical features ranging from "very European" to "very Indian" on a five-point scale.[29] Chicanos with lighter skin color and more European features had higher socioeconomic status. Using the same data set, Telles and Murguia found that most of the income differences between the dark phenotypic group and other Mexican Americans could *not* be explained by the traditional human capital and other variables affecting income.[30] Further support for this finding comes from Cotton and Darity, Guilkey, and Winfrey who found, using 1980 and 1990 Census data, that black Hispanics suffered close to ten times the proportionate income loss due to differential treatment or given characteristics than white Hispanics.[31] Evidently, skin shade plays a critical role in structuring social class position and life chances in American society, even between comparable individuals within minority groups.

Cross-national evidence from Brazil also is relevant here. Despite conventional beliefs in Brazil that race is irrelevant and class is the primary index for social stratification, Silva found, using the 1976 national household survey, that blacks and mulattos (or "browns") shared a depressed economic condition relative to whites, but mulattos earned slightly more than blacks. Silva found slightly greater unexplained income differences for mulattos, rather than blacks vis-à-vis whites. He viewed such unexplained differences as evidence of discrimination.[32] A new study by Telles and Lim, based upon a random national survey of 5,000 persons conducted by the Data Folha Instituto des Pesquisas, compares economic outcomes based upon whether race is self-identified or interviewer-identified.[33] Telles and Lim view interviewer-identification as more useful for establishing social classification and treatment. Their results suggest that self-identification underestimates white income and overestimates brown and black incomes relative to interviewer-identification.

Despite the powerful results on skin shade, some continue to arge that the extent of discrimination is somewhat overestimated by regression techniques because of missing variables. After all, it seems likely that the general pattern of unobserved variables—for example, educational quality and labor force attachment—would tend to follow the observed variables in indicating reasons for the lower productivity of black males.[34] As a result, adjusting for these factors would reduce the remaining black-white earnings differential.[35]

As one might imagine, given the framework in which economists tackle the issue of discrimination, considerable effort has been made to find measures of all imaginable dimensions of human capital that could be used to test the presence of labor market discrimination. This effort has uncovered one variable in one data set for human capital which, if inserted into an earnings regression, produces the outcome that all or nearly all of the black male-white male wage gap is explained by human capital, and none by labor market discrimination. (However, thus far no one has suggested a reasonable missing variable for the skin shade effect.) The particular variable that eliminates evidence of discrimination in earnings against black men is the Armed Forces Qualifying Test (AFQT) score in the National Longitudinal Survey of Youth (NLSY).

A number of researchers have confirmed, with somewhat different sample sizes and methodologies, that including the AFQT scores in an earnings equation virtually will eliminate the racial differences in wages. In the *Journal of Economic Perspectives* some years ago, June O'Neill examined the 1987 sample of men aged 22–29 who had taken the AFQT when they were interviewed seven years earlier.[36] The average AFQT score for African American men was 48 and for white men it was 73.[37] The unadjusted hourly wage ratio for these men was 83 percent. The ratio adjusted for region, schooling, and potential experience was 88 percent. The ratio adjusted for region, schooling, potential experience, and AFQT score was 95–96 percent, close to parity. Similarly, Maxwell looked at a cohort of men six years after leaving school, and found that the inclusion of AFQT scores in a wage regression explained two-thirds of the gap.[38] Ferguson used the 1988–1992 samples of males aged 25–35 years and found that unadjusted gaps in earnings ranged between 13 to 20 percent and that the AFQT score could explain one-half to two-thirds of that difference.[39] Neal and Johnson found that AFQT scores could explain three-quarters of the black-white gap for men and all of the black-white gap for women.[40] Neal and Johnson also found that AFQT's inclusion in log wage equations can completely explain wage differentials for Hispanic males and females.[41]

The conclusion of this body of work is that labor market discrimination against African Americans is small or nonexistent. Using Neal and Johnson's language, the key to explaining differences in African American and white labor market outcomes must instead rest with "premarket factors."[42] These studies have led Abigail and Stephan Thernstrom (1997) in a prominent *Wall Street Journal* editorial to proclaim that "what may look like persistent employment discrimination is better described as employers rewarding workers with relatively strong cognitive skills."

But matters are not so straightforward. The essential problem is what the AFQT scores are actually measuring, and therefore what is being controlled for. There is no consensus on this point. The AFQT scored have been interpreted variously as providing information about school quality or academic achievement,[43] about previously unmeasured skills,[44] and even about intelligence,[45] although the military did not design AFQT as an intelligence test.[46] The results obtained by O'Neill (1990), Maxwell (1994), Ferguson (1995), and Neal and Johnson (1996) after using the AFQT as an explanatory variable are, upon closer examination, not robust to alternative specifications and are quite difficult to interpret.[47]

The lack of robustness can be illustrated by looking at how AFQT scores interact with other variables in the earnings equation. Neal and Johnson (1996), for example, adjust for age and AFQT score in an earnings equation, but not for years of schooling, presumably on the assumption that same-age individuals would have the same years of schooling, regardless of race.[48] However, this assumption does not appear to be true. Rodgers, Spriggs, and Waaler find that white youths had accumulated more schooling at a given age than African American or Hispanic youths.[49] When AFQT scores are both age and education adjusted, a black-white wage gap reemerges, as the authors report:

> estimates from models that use our proposed age and education adjusted AFQT score [show] that sharp differences in racial and ethnic wage gaps exist. Instead of explaining

three-quarters of the male black-white wage gap, the age and education adjusted score explains 40 percent of the gap. Instead of explaining the entire male Hispanic-white gap, the new score explains 50 percent of the gap. . . . [B]lack women no longer earn more than white women do, and . . . Hispanic women's wage premium relative to white women is reduced by one-half.[50]

Another specification problem arises when wage equations are estimated using both the AFQT and the part of the NLSY sample that includes measures of psychological well-being (for "self-esteem" and "locus of control") as explanatory variables. The presence of the psychological variables restores a negative effect on wages to African Americans.[51]

Yet another specification problem becomes relevant if one interprets AFQT scores as providing information about school quality. But since there is a school survey module of the NLSY which can be used to provide direct evidence on school quality, using variables like the books/pupil ratio, the percent of students classified as disadvantaged, and teacher salaries, it would surely be more helpful to use the this direct data on school quality rather than the AFQT scores. In another method of controlling for school quality, Harrison (1972) compared employment and earnings outcomes for African Americans and whites living in the same black ghetto communities, on grounds that school quality would not be very different between them. Harrison found sharp differences in earnings favoring whites.[52]

One severe difficulty in interpreting what differences in the AFQT actually mean is demonstrated by Rodgers and Spriggs, who show that AFQT scores appear to be biased in a specific sense.[53] They show that if AFQT scores are treated as an endogenous variable—rather than being used as an exogenous explanatory variable—and if equations for AFQT are estimated separately for African Americans and whites, controlling for family background, school quality, and psychological motivation, the coefficients for generating AFQT scores differ substantially between African Americans and whites. White coefficients generate significantly higher scores for given characteristics than African American coefficients.

Following the Blinder-Oaxaca approach, Rodgers and Spriggs then create a hypothetical set of "unbiased" African American scores by running the mean African American characteristics through the equation with the white coefficients. When those scores replace the actual AFQT scores in a wage equation, then the adjusted AFQT scores no longer explain black-white wage differences. A similar result can be obtained if actual white scores are replaced by hypothetical scores produced by running white characteristics through the equation with black coefficients.[54] Apparently, the AFQT scores are a consequence of bias in the underlying processes that generates AFQT scores for African Americans and whites.[55] Perhaps AFQT scores are a proxy for skills that do not capture all skills, and thus leave behind a bias of uncertain direction. Or there may be other predictors of the test that are correlated with race but which are left out of the AFQT explanatory equation.

To muddy the waters further, focusing on the math and verbal subcomponents of the AFQT leads to inconsistent implications for discriminatory differentials.

For example, while a higher performance on the verbal portion of the AFQT contributes to higher wages for African American women than for African American men, it apparently has little or no effect on the wages of white women compared to those of white men, according to work by Currie and Thomas.[56] However, white women gain in wages from higher scores on the math portion of the AFQT, but African American women do not. Perhaps this says that white women are screened (directly or indirectly) for employment and pay on the basis of their math performance, while African American women are screened based upon their verbal skills. Perhaps this is because white employers have a greater "comfort zone" with African American women who have a greater verbal similarity to whites. Or perhaps something not fully understood and potentially quirky is going on with the link between these test results and wages.

Finally, since skill differentials have been a subject of such widespread discussion in recent years as an underlying cause of growing wage inequality in the U.S. economy—see, for example, the discussion in the Spring 1997 issue of the *Journal of Economic Perspectives*—it should be pointed out that growth in the rewards to skill does not mean that the effects of race have diminished. If the importance of race and skill increase simultaneously, then a rising skill premium will explain more the increase in intraracial wage inequality than the changes in interracial wage inequality. For example, when Murnane et al. ask whether test scores in math, reading, and vocabulary skills for respondents in the National Longitudinal Study of the High School Class of 1972 and High School and Beyond datasets have more explanatory power in wage equations for 1980 graduates than 1972 graduates, their answer is "yes"—the rate of return to cognitive skill (test scores) increased between 1978 and 1986.[57] However, in these same regressions, the absolute value of the negative race coefficient is larger for the 1980 graduates than it is for the 1972 graduates! So, Murnane et al. confirm that there are increasing returns to skills measured by standardized tests, but their work does not indicate that the rise in returns to skills can explain changes in the black-white earnings gap very well.

The upshot is the following. There is no doubt that African Americans suffer reduced earnings in part due to inferior productivity-linked characteristics relative to nonblack groups. It is important to account for racial skills differentials or school quality differentials. However, evidence based on the AFQT should be treated with extreme caution. Given that this one variable in one particular data set is the only one which suggests racial discrimination is no longer operative in U.S. employment practices, it is far from convincing evidence. Blacks, especially black men, continue to suffer significantly reduced earnings due to discrimination and the extent of discrimination.

DIRECT EVIDENCE ON DISCRIMINATION: COURT CASES AND AUDIT STUDIES

One direct body of evidence of the persistence of employment discrimination, despite the presence of antidiscrimination laws, comes from the scope and dispensation of job discrimination lawsuits. A sampling of such cases from recent years is presented in Table 8.2. As the table reveals, discriminatory practices have occurred at highly visible U.S. corporations often having multinational operations. The suits reveal racial and gender discrimination in employment, training, promotion, tenure, layoff policies, and work environment, as well as occupational segregation.

Perhaps the most notorious recent case is the $176 million settlement reached between Texaco and African American employees, after disclosure of taped comments of white corporate officials making demeaning remarks about African Americans—remarks that revealed an outlook that translated into corresponding antiblack employment practices. Clearly, neither federal antidiscrimination laws nor the pressures of competitive markets have prevented the occurrence of discriminatory practices that have resulted in significant awards or settlements for the plaintiffs.

Another important source of direct evidence are the audit studies of the type conducted in the early 1990s by the Urban Institute.[58] The Urban Institute audit studies sought to examine employment outcomes for young African American, Hispanic, and white males, ages 19–25, looking for entry-level jobs. Pairs of African American and white males and pairs of Hispanic and white males were matched as testers and sent out to apply for jobs at businesses advertising openings. Prior to application for the positions the testers were trained for interviews to minimize dissimilarity in the quality of their self-presentation, and they were given manufactured résumés designed to put their credentials on a par. The black/white tests were conducted in Chicago and in Washington, D.C., while the Hispanic/white tests were conducted in Chicago and in San Diego.

A finding of discrimination was confirmed if one member of the pair was offered the position and the other was not. No discrimination was confirmed if both received an offer (sequentially, since both were instructed to turn the position down) or if neither received an offer. This is a fairly stringent test for discrimination, since in the case in which no offer was made to either party, there was no way to determine whether employers were open to the prospect of hiring an African American or a Hispanic male, or what the overall applicant pool looked like, or who was actually hired. However, the Urban Institute audits found that African American males were three times as likely to be turned down for a job as white males, and that Hispanic males also were three times as likely as non-Hispanic white males to experience discrimination in employment.[59]

Bendick, Jackson, and Reinoso (1994) also report on 149 race-based (black, white) and ethnicity-based (Hispanic, non-Hispanic) job audits conducted by the Fair Employment Council of Greater Washington, Inc. in the D.C. metropolitan area in 1990 and 1991. Testers were paired by gender. The audit findings are striking. White testers were close to 10 percent more likely to receive interviews than blacks. Among those interviewed, half of the white testers received job offers versus a mere 11 percent of the black testers. When both testers received the same job offers, white testers were offered 15 cents per hour more than black testers. Black testers also were disproportionately "steered" toward lower level positions after the job offer was made, and white testers were disproportionately considered for unadvertised positions at higher levels than the originally advertised job.

Table 8.2   Selected Court Cases Providing Evidence of Recent Employement Discrimentaion

Employer	Allegations	Conditions of Resolution	Source
Publix Super Markets (1997) Gender bias in on the job training, promotion, tenure and layoff policies; wage discrimination; occupational desegregation; hostile work environment	Class-action law suit brought by 8 women (with evidence from 200 women) settled at $81.5 million	St. Petersburg Times (February 2, 1997)3	Shoney's International (1993)
Racial bias in promotion, tenure, and layoff policies; wage discrimination; hostile work environment	Victims (black employees numbering in the thousands) awarded $105 million	The New York Times (February 6, 1993)	Brand Services, subsidiary of Waste Management, Inc. WMX Technologies, Inc. (California, 1996)
Employee fired from job solely on basis of race	Plaintiff awarded $7.6 million	The San Francisco Examiner (April 19, 1996) The Wall Street Journal (April 22, 1996)	HBE Corporation (St. Louis, Missouri,1996)
Discriminatory employment practices	Settlement of $5 million	Rocky Mountain News (April 23, 1996)	US Air (1995)
Discriminatory employment practices	Confidential settlement reached among the parties, approximated at $1.18 million for the two black pilots bringing suit against US Air.	Business Journal-Charlotte (April 11, 1994; March 25 and 27, 1995)	Harris Trust and Savings Bank (1989)
Female college graduates hired in clerical positions; males placed in better jobs; salary and training issues also	Bank agreed to pay $14 million in back pay to women and nonwhite minority employees who joined the class-action lawsuit as part of a settlement.	The New York Times (January 11, 1989)	CSX Transportation (1995)

Racially motivated sexual harassment by a supervisor; differential treatment of black and white female employees; termination of plaintiff by supervisor after she filed a complaint.	Jury awarded $3000 in punitive damages against the supervisor and over $500,000 against the company	California Employment Law Monitor (July 31, 1995)	General Motors Corporation (1983)
Gender and racial discrimination charged in employment practices	GM settled at $42.5 million	The Christian Science Monitor (October 20, 1983)	Texaco (1996)
Racially discriminatory hiring, promotion and salary policies	Class-action lawsuit brought by six black current and former employees settled at $176 million.	Inter Press Service (November 20, 1996) The Chicago Tribune (January 3, 1997)	Pitney Bowes, Inc. (1996)
Racially based harassment from colleagues	Verdict awarded plaintiff $11.1 million	Los Angeles Times (September 10, 1996)	USX Corporation (1986)
Discriminatory hiring practices	Corporation ordered to pay $16 million, including interest	American Metal Market (August 6, 1986)	TIMCO, North Carolina Aviation Contractor (1996)
Hostile work environment based upon race and upon gender	Defendant ordered to pay $242,600 for back wages and corrective measures	FDCH Federal Department and Agency Documents (November 20, 1996)	National Car Rental (unresolved)
Hostile work environment based upon race; discriminatory hiring and promotion practices	?	USA Today (July 9, 1997)	

Overall, the Fair Employment Council study found rates of discrimination in excess of 20 percent against blacks (in the black/white tests) and against Hispanics (in the Hispanic/non-Hispanic tests). In the Hispanic/non-Hispanic tests, Hispanic male job seekers were three times as likely to experience discrimination as Hispanic females. But, surprisingly, in the black/white tests, black females were three times as likely to encounter discrimination as black males. The racial results for women in this particular audit stand in sharp contrast with the results in the statistical studies described above.

The most severe methodological criticisms of the audit technique have come from Heckman and Siegelman.[60] At base, their central worry is that testers cannot be paired in such a way that they will not signal a difference that legitimately can be interpreted by the prospective employer as a difference in potential to perform the job, despite interview training and doctored résumés.[61] Intangibles, such as a person's ability to make a good first impression, or the fact that certain resumes may be unintentionally superior to others must be taken into account.

In an audit study consciously designed to address many of the Heckman-Siegelman methodological complaints, Neumark, Bank, and Van Nort examined sex discrimination in restaurant hiring practices.[62] Four testers (all college students, two men and two women) applied for jobs waiting tables at 65 restaurants in Philadelphia. The restaurants were separated into categories designated as high-, medium-, and low-price, according to average cost of a meal. Waiters at the high-price restaurants tend to receive greater wages and tips than their counterparts in low-priced restaurants; specifically, the authors find that average hourly earnings for waiters were 47 and 68 percent higher in the high price restaurant than the medium- and low-priced restaurant, respectively. One man and one woman applied for a job at each restaurant, so there were 130 attempts to obtain employment. Thirty-nine job offers were received.

One interesting twist to this methodology is that three reasonably comparable resumes were constructed, and over a three-week period each tester used a different resume for a period of one week. This résumé switching mitigated any differences that may have occurred because one résumé was better than another. To reduce other sources of unobserved ability—for example, the ability to make a good first impression—the testers were instructed to give their applications to the first employee they encountered when visiting a restaurant. That employee was then asked to forward the résumé to the manager. In effect, personality and appearance were eliminated as relevant variables for the interview decision, if not for the job offer decision.

Neumark et al. find that in the low-priced restaurants, the man received an offer, while the woman did not, 29 percent of the time, and it never occurred that the woman received an offer while the man did not.[63] In the high-priced restaurants, the man received an offer while the woman didn't, in 43 percent of the cases, while the woman received an offer while the man did not in just 4 percent. The difference at high-priced restaurants was statistically significant; women had roughly a 40 percent lower probability of being interviewed and a 50 percent lower probability of obtaining a job offer at high-priced restaurants. Hence, this audit study shows that within-occupation employment, discrimination may be a contributing source to wage discrimination between men and women.[64]

Another way to overcome some of the difficulties of the audit approach is the "correspondence test," which has been used overseas in Britain and Australia, but not (to our knowledge) in the United States. This test involves investigators sending letters of inquiry from prospective "applicants" to employers, where the letters signal the "applicants'" ethnicity by using a name that provides a strong clue about ethnic affiliation. Of course, the letters of inquiry are designed to demonstrate comparable written skills across the hypothetical members of each group and, again, manufactured résumés are submitted with the letters to present comparable credentials to employers.

Riach and Rich report that in the British studies, letters that appeared to be from Afro-Caribbean, Indian, or Pakistani applicants often received replies that indicated that the positions had been filled, while, simultaneously, letters that appeared to be from Anglo-Saxon applicants received responses inviting them to interviews from the same employers.[65] A similar pattern occurred in the Australian audits: Inquires from applicants with Vietnamese or Greek-sounding names met with information that the position had been filled, while Anglo-Saxon sounding "applicants" again were asked to come for interviews. This is impressive direct evidence of discrimination from a powerful test procedure. However, the correspondence test is limited to identifying discrimination at the initial stage of the hiring process. It cannot identify discriminatory practices during the interview stage, at the point of job offer, or the terms of the job offer like the job audit using trained testers.

Yet another interesting direct test of discriminatory practices based on gender can be found in Goldin and Rouse's assessment of the effects of an alteration in audition procedures for symphony orchestras.[66] In the past, juries watched candidates come out to audition; however, many orchestras now have candidates audition behind a screen, so that their identity is unknown. Goldin and Rouse find that hiding the identity of the players behind a screen raises the probability that a woman will be hired by 50 percent. The implication is obvious: Prior to the adoption of the screen on identity there was sex discrimination in the selection of musicians for symphony orchestras.

The direct evidence from the court cases, audit studies, and symphony auditions confirms the persistence of discriminatory practices in employment. The evidence is consistent with the characterization of employer beliefs and actions found in the joint Russell Sage-Ford Foundation Multi-City Study of Urban Inequality (MCSUI), newly reported by Holzer.[67] Employers seem to possess strong racial and gender preferences in hiring. These preferences are the consequence of enduring stereotypical beliefs about expected performance on the job, which leads them to set up a racial/ethnic and gender ranking of potential hires: white men generally preferred over white women (unless the job is female-typed), Hispanics of either gender preferred over African Americans, African American women preferred over African American men.[68] The MCSUI findings suggest the primacy of race/color as a marker for disadvantageous treatment by employers.

THE THEORETICAL BACKDROP

Standard neoclassical competitive models are forced by their own assumptions to the conclusion that discrimination can only be temporary. Perhaps the best-known statement of this position is Becker's famous "taste for discrimination" proposition.[69] If the two groups share similar productivities, under competitive conditions in which at least some employers prefer profits to prejudice, then eventually all workers must be paid according to their marginal productivity. The eventual result may involve segregated workforces—say, with some businesses hiring only white men and others hiring only African American women—but as long as both groups have the same marginal productivity, they will receive the same pay. Thus, discrimination can produce only temporary racial or gender earnings gaps. Moreover, alternative forms of discrimination are separable processes, that is, wage discrimination and employment segregation are unrelated in Becker's model.

Despite the theoretical implications of standard neoclassical competitive models, we have considerable evidence that the Civil Rights Act of 1964 did make a difference in the extent of racial and gender discrimination. It did not, by any means, eliminate either form of discrimination. This may have been a temporary effect, since there is some evidence that the trend toward racial equality came to an abrupt halt in the mid-1970s (even though interracial differences in human capital were continuing to close) and the trend toward gender equality began to lose steam in the early 1990s. Moreover, we believe the forms of discrimination have altered in response to the act. These outcomes suggest that it is not useful to argue that either racial or gender discrimination is inconsistent with the operation of competitive markets, especially when antidiscrimination laws have reduced the impact of discrimination within the market. Instead, it is much more beneficial to examine the market mechanisms that permit or encourage discriminatory practices.

Since Becker's work, orthodox microeconomics has been massaged in various ways to produce stories of how discrimination might sustain itself against pressures of the competitive market. The tacit assumption of these approaches has been to find a way in which discrimination can increase business profits, or in which deciding not to discriminate might reduce profits.

In the customer discrimination story, for example, businesses discriminate not because they themselves are bigoted, but because their customers are. This story works especially well when the product in question must be delivered via face-to-face contact, but it obviously does not work well when the hands that made the product are not visible to the customer with the "taste for discrimination." Moreover, as Madden has pointed out, sex-typing of jobs can work in both directions:[70] "While service occupations are more contact-oriented, sexual preference can work both ways: For example, women are preferred as Playboy bunnies, airline stewardesses, and lingerie salespeople, while men seem to be preferred as tire salespeople, stockbrokers, and truck drivers."

Obviously, group-typing of employment will lead to different occupational distributions between group A and B, but will it lead to different earnings as well? Madden suggests not necessarily:

[C]onsumer discrimination causes occupational segregation rather than wage differentials. If the female wage decreases as the amount of consumer contact required by a job increases, women seek employment in jobs where consumer contact is minimal and wages are higher. Only if there are not enough non-consumer contact jobs for working women, forcing them to seek employment in consumer-contact jobs, would consumer discrimination be responsible for wage differentials. Since most jobs do not require consumer contact, consumer discrimination would segregate women into these jobs, but not *cause* wage differentials. [emphasis original][71]

Perhaps the best of these attempts to explain in a neoclassical framework how discrimination might persist is the statistical discrimination story, which at its base is a story about imperfect information. The notion is that potential employers cannot observe everything they wish to know about job candidates, and in this world of imperfect information, they will have an incentive to seize onto group membership as a signal that allows them to improve the employers' ability to predict a prospective candidate's ability to perform.

However, this model of prejudicial beliefs does not ultimately wash well as a theory of why discrimination should be long lasting. If average group differences are perceived but not real, then potential employers selectors should *learn* that they are mistaken. If average group differences are real, then in a world with antidiscrimination laws, the test for employers is to find methods of predicting the future performance of potential employees with sufficient accuracy that there is no need to use the additional "signal" of race or gender. It seems implausible that with all the resources that corporations put into hiring decisions, the remaining differentials are due to an inability to come up with a suitable set of questions or qualifications for potential employees.

Models of imperfect competition as explanations of discrimination do not solve the problem completely either. The reason for the immutability of the imperfection is rarely satisfactorily explained—and often not addressed at all—in models of this type.[72] Struggle as it may, orthodox microeconomics keeps returning to the position that sustained observed differences in economic outcomes between groups must be due to an induced or inherent deficiency in the group that experiences the inferior outcomes. In the jargon, this is referred to as a deficiency in human capital. Sometimes this deficiency is associated with poor schooling opportunities, other times with culture.[73] But the thrust of the argument is to absolve market processes, at least in the long run, of a role in producing the differential outcome; the induced or inherent deficiency occurs in premarket or extramarket processes.

Certainly years of schooling, quality of education, years of work experience, and even culture can have a role to play in explaining racial and gender earnings differences. However, the evidence marshaled above indicates that these factors taken alone do not come close to explaining the wage differentials and employment patterns observed in the economy. Instead, discrimination has been sustained, both in the United States and elsewhere, for generations at a time. Such discrimination does not always even need direct legal support, and it is not ended by market pressure. Instead, changes in social and legal institutions are needed to reduce it. James Heckman draws a similar conclusion in his examination of a specific sector of employment, the textile industry:

[s]ubstantial growth in Southern manufacturing had little effect on the labor-market position of blacks in Southern textiles prior to 1965. Through tight and slack labor

markets, the proportion of blacks was small and stable. After 1964, and in synchronization with the 1964 Civil Rights Act, black economic progress was rapid. Only South Carolina had a Jim Crow law prohibiting employment of blacks as textile workers, and the law was never used after the 1920s. Yet the pattern of exclusion of blacks was prevalent throughout Southern textiles, and the breakthrough in black employment in the industry came in all states at the same time. Informally enforced codes and private practices, and not formally enforced apartheid, kept segregation in place, and market forces did not break them down.[74]

Nontraditional alternatives to orthodox microeconomics can lead to a logically consistent basis for a persistent gap in wage outcomes. These alternatives can involve breaking down the line between in-market and premarket discrimination that is so often drawn by orthodox economists. The first of these involves a self-fulfilling prophecy mechanism. Suppose employers believe that members of group A are more productive than members of group B on average. Suppose further that they act upon their beliefs, thereby exhibiting a stronger demand for A workers, hiring them more frequently and paying them more.

Next, suppose that members of group B become less motivated and less emotionally healthy as a consequence of the employment rebuff. Notice that the original decision not to hire may have been completely unjustified on productivity grounds; nonetheless, the decision made *in* the labor market—a decision not to hire or to hire at low pay—alters the human capital characteristics of the members of group B so that they become inferior candidates for jobs. The employers' initially held mistaken beliefs become realized over time as a consequence of the employers' initial discriminatory decisions. As Elmslie and Sedo observe in their development of this argument, "One initial bout of unemployment that is not productivity based can lay the foundation for continued future unemployment and persistently lower job status even if no future discrimination occurs."[75]

More broadly, depressed expectations of employment opportunities also can have an adverse effect on members of group B's inclination to acquire additional human capital—say, through additional schooling or training. The effects of the past could be passed along by the disadvantaged group from generation to generation, another possibility ignored by orthodox theory. For example, Borjas writes of the ethnic intergenerational transmission of economic advantage or disadvantage.[76] He makes no mention of discrimination in his work, but a potential interpretation is that the effects of past discrimination, both positive and negative, are passed on to subsequent generations. Other evidence along these lines includes Tyree's findings on the relationship between an ethnic group's status and performance in the past and the present, and Darity's development of "the lateral mobility" hypothesis based upon ethnic group case histories.[77]

More narrowly, the group-typed beliefs held by employers/selectors also can have a strong effect on the performance of the candidate at the interview stage. In an experiment performed in the early 1970s, psychologists Word, Zanna, and Cooper found that when interviewed by "naïve" whites, trained African American applicants "received (a) less immediacy, (b) higher rates of speech error, and (c) shorter amounts of interview time" than the white applicants.[78]

They then trained white interviewers to replicate the behavior received by the African American applicants in the first phase of their experiment, and found that white candidates performed poorly during interviews when they were "treated like blacks." Such self-fulfilling prophecies are familiar in the psychology literature.[79]

A second nontraditional theory that can lead to a permanent gap in intergroup outcomes is the noncompeting groups hypothesis advanced by the late W. Arthur Lewis.[80] Related arguments emerge from Krueger's (1963) extension of the trade-based version of the Becker model, Swinton's (1978) "labor force competition" model for racial differences, and Madden's (1975) male monopoly model for gender differences, but Lewis's presentation is the most straightforward.[81] Lewis starts with an intergroup rivalry for the preferred positions in a hierarchical occupational structure.[82] Say that group A is able to control access to the preferred positions by influencing the required credentials, manipulating opportunities to obtain the credentials, and serving a gatekeeping function over entry and promotion along job ladders. Group B is then rendered "noncompeting."

One theoretical difficulty with this argument that its proponents rarely address is that it requires group A to maintain group solidarity even when it may have subgroups with differing interests. In Krueger's model, for example, white capitalists must value racial group solidarity sufficiently to accept a lower return on their capital as the price they pay for a generally higher level of income for all whites (and higher wages for white workers).[83] In Madden's model, male capitalists must make a similar decision on behalf of male workers.[84]

This noncompeting group hypothesis blurs the orthodox distinction between in-market and premarket discrimination by inserting the matters of power and social control directly into the analysis. This approach then links discrimination to racism or sexism, rather than to simple bigotry or prejudice. It leads to the proposition that discrimination—in the sense of differential treatment of those members of each group with similar productivity-linked characteristics—is an endogenous phenomenon. "In-market" discrimination need only occur when all the earlier attempts to control access to jobs, credentials, and qualifications are quavering.

One interesting implication here is that growth in skills for what we have been calling group B, the disadvantaged group, may be accompanied by a surge of in-market discrimination, because that form of discrimination has become more necessary to preserve the position of group A. There are several instances of cross-national evidence to support this notion. First, Darity, Dietrich, and Guilkey find that while black males were making dramatic strides in acquiring literacy between 1880 and 1910 in the United States, simultaneously they were suffering increasing proportionate losses in occupational status due to disadvantageous treatment of their measured characteristics.[85] Second, Geographer Peggy Lovell finds very little evidence of discrimination in earnings against blacks in northern Brazil, where blacks are more numerous, but substantial evidence of discrimination against them in the southern Brazil.[86] Northern Brazil is considerably poorer than southern Brazil and the educational levels of northern black Brazilians are more depressed than in the south.[87] It is easy to argue that the exercise of discrimination is not "needed" in the north, since blacks are not generally going to compete with whites for the same sets of jobs. Indeed, there is relatively more evidence of discrimination against mulattos than blacks, the former more likely to compete directly with whites for employment. Third, in a study using data for males based upon a survey taken in Delhi in 1970, Desi and Singh find that the most dramatic instance of discriminatory differentials in earnings was evident for Sikh men vis-à-vis Hindu high caste men.[88] On the other hand, most of the earnings gap for Hindu middle caste, lower caste, and scheduled or "out caste" men was due to inferior observed characteristics. Since these latter groups could be excluded from preferred positions because of an inadequate educational background, it would not be necessary for the upper castes to exercise discrimination against them. But Sikh males possessed the types of credentials that would make them viable contestants for the positions desired by the Hindu higher castes.

A final alternative approach at construction of a consistent economic theory of persistent discrimination evolves from a reconsideration of the neoclassical theory of competition. Darity and Williams (1985) argued that replacement of neoclassical competition with either classical or Marxist approaches to competition—where competition is defined by a tendency toward equalization of rates of profit and where monopoly positions are the consequence of competition rather than the antithesis of competition—eliminates the anomalies associated with the orthodox approach.[89] A labor market implication of this approach is that wage diversity, different pay across firms and industries for workers within the same occupation, is the norm for competitive labor markets. In these models remuneration is a function of the characteristics of the individual and the job. The racial-gender composition of the job affects worker bargaining power and thereby wage differentials. In turn, race and gender exclusion are used to make some workers less competitive for the higher paying positions. This approach emphasizes that the major elements for the persistence of discrimination are racial or gender differences in access to better paying jobs within and between occupations.

Whatever alternative approach is preferred, the strong evidence of the persistence of discrimination in labor markets calls into question any theoretical apparatus that implies that the discrimination must inevitably diminish or disappear.

Acknowledgements

We are grateful to Cecilia Rouse, Alan Krueger, Samuel Myers Jr., Rhonda Williams, William Rodgers III, William Spriggs, and Timothy Taylor for exceptionally helpful suggestions and criticisms. Maiju Johanna Perala provided valuable research assistance.

Notes

1 John Donohue and James Heckman, "Continuous vs. Episodic Change: The Impact of Civil Rights Policy on the Economic Status of Blacks," *Journal of Economic Literature* vol. 29:4 (December 1991), pp. 1603–43.

2 Peter Gottschalk, "Inequality, Income Growth and Mobility: The Basic Facts," vol. 11:2 *Journal of Economic Perspectives* (Spring 1997), pp. 21–40.

3 John Bound and Richard B. Freeman, "Black Economic Progress: Erosion of Post-1965 Gains in the 1980s?" in Steven Shulman and William Darity Jr., ed., *Question of Discrimination: Racial Inequality in the U.S. Labor Market* (Middletown, CT: Wesleyan University Press, 1989), 32–49; David Card and Alan Krueger, "School Quality and Black-White Relative Earnings—A Direct Assessment," *Quarterly Journal of Economics* vol. 107 (February 1992): 1, 151–200; Donohue and Heckman, 1603–43; Richard B. Freeman, "Changes in the Labor Market for Black Americans 1948–72," *Brookings Papers on Economic Activity* (Summer 1973), pp. 1, 67–120. Evidence on racial progress in economic status is contingent on the measure selected for consideration. While black-white earnings ratios rose for more than a decade following the passage of the Civil Rights Act, black-white family income ratios have remained in a stable, narrow band between 60 and 64 percent between 1960 and the present. The ratio actually declined below 60 percent during the 1982 recession (Darity and Myers, forthcoming). Moreover, there has been little change in black-white *per capita income* ratios for more than a century. Vedder, Gallaway, and Klingaman (1990) estimated that black income was 59 percent of white income in 1880. Darity, Guilkey, and Winfrey (1996) find that black mean income was about 60 percent of the U.S. mean income in 1880 and 1990.

4 J. Leonard, "Women and Affirmative Action," *Journal of Economic Perspectives* vol. 3:1 (Winter), pp. 61–86.

5 William Julius Wilson, *The Declining Significance of Race* (Chicago: The University of Chicago Press, 1980); Samuel Myers, Jr. and William E. Spriggs, "Black Employment, Criminal Activity and Entrepreneurship: A Case Study of New Jersey," in Patrick L. Mason and Rhonda M. Williams, eds., *Race, Markets and Social Outcomes* (Boston: Kluwer Academic Publishers 1997), pp. 32–42; Stanley Lieberson, *A Piece of the Pie: Black and White Immigrants Since 1880* (Berkeley: University of California Press: 1980).

6 Hector Cordero-Guzman, "Sociological Approaches to Employment Discrimination," unpublished manuscript, University of Chicago, 1990, p. 1.

7 The only significant exception to the help-wanted ads pattern of maintaining a fairly strict sexual division of labor that we could detect was evident in the *Los Angeles Times* employment section of early January 1945, where we found women being sought as aircraft riveters, assemblers, and army photographers. Of course, World War II was ongoing at that stage, and the comparative absence of men produced the "Rosie the Riveter" phenomenon. However, despite wartime conditions, even this temporary breakdown in gender-typing of occupations was not evident in the help-wanted ads for the *Chicago Tribune*, the *New York Times*, or the *Washington Post* at the same time. Moreover, racial preferences also remained strongly pronounced in wartime advertisements of each of the four newspapers.

8 The C. W. Agency, advertising in the *Los Angeles Times* on January 1, 1950, wanted a "Girl Model 38 bust, 25 waist, 36 hips"; "Several Other Types" with physical characteristics unspecified in the advertisement apparently also were acceptable.

9 John A. Williams, *The Angry Ones* (New York: W. W. Norton and Company, 1996), pp. 30–31.

10 Francine D. Blau, M. Ferber, and A. Winkler, *The Economics of Women, Men, and Work*, third edition (Upper Saddle River, NJ: Prentice Hall, 1988), pp. 134–40.

11 Gottschalk, "Inequality," p. 29.

12 Jane Waldfogel, "Understanding the 'Family Gap' in Pay for Women with Children," *Journal of Economic Perspectives*, vol. 12:1 (Winter 1998), pp. 137–56. Waldfogel also

shows differences in the trend of mean earnings for men and women. Examining the hourly wage rate of men and women ages 24 to 45 for 1978, 1988, and 1994, she finds that women earned $10.49, $11.58, and $11.42, respectively. However, the mean hourly wage rates for men were $16.25, $15.68, and $14.95 for 1978, 1988, and 1994, respectively.

13 Blau et al., "The Economics of Women, Men, and Work," pp. 141–184

14 Francine D. Blau and Lawrence M. Kahn, "Swimming Upstream: Trends in the Gender Wage Differential in the 1980s," *Journal of Labor Economics*, vol. 15:1, Part 1 (January 1997), pp. 1–42. Waldfogel (1998) also reports on differences in the trend of mean earnings for men and women. Examining the hourly wage rate of men and women ages 24 to 45 for 1978, 1988, and 1994, she finds that women earned $10.49, $11.58, and $11.42, respectively. However, the mean hourly wage rates for men were $16.25, $15.68, and 14.95 for 1978, 1988, and 1994, respectively.

15 Waldfogel, "Understanding the 'Family Gap,' " pp. 137–156.

16 Mason, Patrick L., "Competing Explanations of Male Interracial Wage Differentials: Missing Variables Models Versus Job Competition" *Cambridge Journal of Economics* vol. 23 (May 1999), pp. 1–39.

17 Waldfogel, "Understanding the 'Family Gap,' " pp. 137–56.

18 Paula England, "The Failure of Human Capital Theory to Explain Occupational Sex Segregation," *Journal of Human Resources*, vol. 7:3 (1982), pp. 358–70; Janice F. Madden, "Gender Differences in the Cost of Displacement: An Empirical Test of Discrimination in the Labor Market," *American Economic Review*, vol. 77:82 (May 1987), pp. 246–51; Mary C. King, "Occupational Segregation by Sex and Race, 1940–1988," *Monthly Labor Review*, vol. 115:4 (April 1992), pp. 30–36.

19 Suzanne M. Bianchi and Daphne Spain, "Women, Work, and Family in America," *Population Bulletin* vol. 51:3 (December 1996), p. 23. The index of dissimilarity (D) is calculated as: $D = \Sigma_i(|f_i/F - m_i/M|)/2{}^*100$, where f_i (m_i) is the number of women (men) in occupation i and F (M) represents the total number of women (men) in the labor force. A value of 100 indicates complete segregation, while a value of 0 indicates no segregation. Hence, a value of 68 percent indicates that two-thirds of women (or men) would have to obtain a new occupation in order to have equal representation in all occupations.

20 Francine D. Blau and Lawrence M. Kahn, "Wage Structure and Gender Differentials: An International Comparison," *Economica*, vol. 63:250, Supplemental (1996), pp. S29–S62.

21 Ibid., p. S30.

22 Ibid., p. S33.

23 Supporting evidence for this position comes from the recent article in this journal by Fortin and Lemieux, who find that that changes in the real value of the U.S. minimum wage can explain nearly one-third of the variation in female wage inequality over the past decade. This is an example of the interrelationship between overall wage equality and the male-female earnings differential. Nicole M. Fortin and Thomas Lemieux "Institutional Change and Rising Wage Inequality: Is There a Linkage?" *Journal of Economic Perspectives*, vol. 11:2 (Spring 1997), pp. 75–96.

24 Blau and Kahn, "Wage Structure and Gender Differentials," p. S48.

25 William Darity, Jr., David Guilkey, and William Winfrey, "Explaining Differences in Economic Performance Among Racial and Ethnic Groups in the USA: The Data Examined," *American Journal of Economics and Sociology*, vol. 55:4 (October 1996), pp. 411–26. The 1980 and 1990 Censuses provide only self-reported information on interviewees' race and their ancestry, which makes it possible to partition the

American population into 50 different detailed ethnic and racial groups, such as Asian Indian ancestry women, Mexican ancestry women, Polish ancestry women, French Canadian ancestry women, and so on.

The explanatory variables were years of school, years of college, number of children, married spouse present, years of work experience, years of work experience squared, very good or fluent English, disabled, born in the United States, assimilated (that is either married to a person with a different ethnicity or having claimed two different ethnic groups in the census), location, region, and occupation. Annual earnings was the dependent variable.

There was no control for the difference between potential and actual experience; hence, to the extent that the gap between potential and actual experience and the rate of return to actual experience varies by race, the results for the female regressions may be less reliable than the results for the male regression.

26 William Darity, Jr., et al, "Explaining Differences;" William Rodgers III and William E. Spriggs, "What Does AFQT Really Measure: Race, Wages, Schooling and the AFQT Score," *The Review of Black Political Economy*, vol. 24:4 (Spring 1996), pp. 13–46.

27 James H. Johnson, Jr., Elisa Jayne Bienenstock, and Jennifer A. Stoloff, "An Empirical Test of the Cultural Capital Hypothesis," *The Review of Black Political Economy*, vol. 23:4 (Spring 1995), pp. 7–27.

28 H. E. Ransford, "Skin Color, Life Chances, and anti-White Attitude," *Social Problems*, vol. 18 (1970), pp. 164–78; Verna M. Keith and Cedric Herring, "Skin Tone and Stratification in the Black Community," *American Journal of Sociology*, vol. 97 (1991), pp. 760–78; James H. Johnson, Jr. and Walter C. Farrell, Jr., "Race Still Matters," *The Chronicle of Higher Education* (7 July 1995), p. A48.

29 Carlos H. Arce, Eduard Murguia, and W. Parker Frisbie, "Phenotype and Life Chances Among Chicanos," *Hispanic Journal of Behavioral Studies*, vol. 9:1 (1987), pp. 19–33.

30 Edward Telles and Edward Murgguia, "Phenotypic Discrimination and Income Differences Among Mexican Americans," *Social Science Quarterly*, vol. 71:4 (December 1990), pp. 682–94.

31 Darity, Guilkey, and Winfrey, "Explaining Differences;" Jeremiah Cotton, "Color or Culture?: Wage Differences Among Non-Hispanic Black Males, Hispanic Black Males and Hispanic White Males," *The Review of Black Political Economy*, vol. 21:4 (Spring 1993), pp. 53–68.

32 Nelson do Valle Silva, "Updating the Cost of Not Being White in Brazil," in Pierre-Michel Fontaine, ed., *Race, Class and Power in Brazil* (University of California-Los Angeles: Center for African American Studies, 1985), pp. 42–55.

33 Edward E. Telles and Nelson Lim, "Does it Matter Who Answers the Race Question? Racial Classification and Income Inequality in Brazil," *Demography*, vol. 35:4, (November 1998), pp. 465–74.

34 Christopher J. Ruhm, "Labor Market Discrimination in the United States" in F. A. Blanchard and F. J. Crosby, eds., *Affirmative Action in Perspective* (New York: Springer-Verlag, 1989), p. 157.

35 For a view that unobservable factors might favor African American male productivity, thereby meaning that the regression coefficients are underestimating the degree of discrimination, see Patrick L. Mason, "Race, Culture, and Skill: Interracial Wage Differences Among African Americans, Latinos, and Whites," *Review of Black Political Economy*, vol. 25:3 (Winter 1996): pp. 5–40.

36 June O'Neill, "The Role of Human Capital in Earnings Differences Between Black and White Men," *The Journal of Economic Perspectives*, vol. 4 (Fall 1990), pp. 25–45.

37 Interracial differences in AFQT scores appear to be more substantial than the interracial differences in the Scholastic Aptitude Test (SAT) and the National Assessment of Educational Progress (NAEP), although whites have higher scores than African Americans.

38 Nan Maxwell, "The Effect on Black-White Wage Differences of Differences in the Quantity and Quality of Education," *Industrial and Labor Relations Review*, vol. 47 (January 1994), pp. 47, 249–64.

39 Ronald Ferguson, "Shifting Challenges: Fifty Years of Economic Change Toward Black-White Earnings Equality," *Daedalus*, vol. 124 (Winter 1994), pp. 37–76.

40 Derek A. Neal and William R. Johnson, "The Role of Premarket Factors in Black-White Wage Differences," *Journal of Political Economy*, vol. 104:5 (1996), pp. 869–95.

41 Similar results emerge from preliminary research performed with the General Social Survey (GSS) that includes a ten-item cognitive skills test called Wordsum (White, 1997). The mean African American score on Wordsum in the GSS sample was 4.72 and the mean white score was 6.21 out of the maximum possible score of 10, a difference similar in magnitude to the racial differences in AFQT scores. In an income equation controlling for age, sex, father's education, mother's education, occupational prestige, and religious affiliation, but not for Wordsum scores, the the coefficient on the race variable is negative and statistically significant. But when Wordsum scores are included, the race variable actually becomes positive in sign and statistically significant! From this standpoint African Americans actually receive a positive racial premium relative to their productivity-linked characteristics, once cognitive skill is controlled via the Wordsum scores. Once again, the interpretation could be advanced that there is no statistical evidence of wage discrimination based upon these findings. But matters are not so straightforward. First, if occupational prestige is used as the labor market outcome to be explained rather than income results change rather sharply. Even with Wordsum scores as an included variable in the prestige equation, the race coefficient remains strongly negative.

42 Neal and Johnson limited their sample to persons 15–18 years of age in 1980. This sample restriction reduces the possibility of exposure to labor market post-secondary schooling discrimination in influencing test outcomes. They also compute age-adjusted AFQT scores, since the interviewees were not all the same age at the time they took the test in 1980.

43 O'Neill, "The Role of Human Capital."

44 Ferguson, "Shifting Challenges"; Maxwell, "The Effect of Black-White Wage Differences"; Neal and Johnson, "The Role of Premarket Factors."

45 Richard Herrnstein and Charles Murray, *The Bell Curve: Intelligence and Class Structures in American Life* (New York: Basic Books, 1994).

46 Indeed, if one uses a measure that, unlike the AFQT, was explicitly designed as a measure of intelligence, it does not explain the black-white gap in wages. Mason (1997 and 1997a) demonstrates this by using in a wage equation an explanatory variable that comes from a sentence completion test given to 1972 respondents to the Panel Study of Income Dynamics (PSID)—a test that was designed to assess "g," so-called general intelligence. Mason (1999b and 1997) finds that the significant, negative sign on the coefficient for the race variable is unaffected by inclusion of the PSID sentence completion test score as an explanatory variable. Indeed, Mason (1997a) finds that although discrimination declined during 1968 to 1973, discrimination grew

by 2.0 percent annually during 1973–91. On the other hand, the rate of return to cognitive skill (IQ) was relatively constant during 1968–79, but had an annual growth rate of 1.6 percent during 1979–91. Rodgers and Spriggs, "What Does AFQT Really Measure," pp. 13–46.

47 O'Neill, "The Role of Human Capital;" Maxwell, "The Effect on Black-White Wage Differences;" Ferguson, "Shifting Challenges; Neal and Johnson, "The Role of Premarket Factors."

48 Neal and Johnson, "The Role of Premarket Factors."

49 William Rodgers III, William E. Spriggs, and Elizabeth Waaler, "The Role of Premarket Factors in Black-White Wage Differences: Comment," unpublished manuscript, College of William and Mary (25 May 1997).

50 Mason finds a similar result when age and education adjusted IQ scores are used. Patrick L. Mason, "Racial Discrimination and the Rate of Return to Cognitive Ability, 1968–1991," unpublished manuscript, University of Notre Dame, 1997; Quote in Rodgers, Spriggs, and Waaler, "The Role of Premarket Factors," p. 3.

51 Arthur H. Goldsmith, Jonathan Veum, and William Darity, Jr., "The Impact of Psychological and Human Capital Wages," *Economic Inquiry*, 1997. Attention to the psychological measures also provides mild evidence that African Americans ceteris paribus put forth more effort than whites, a finding consistent with Mason's (1997a) speculation that there may be unobservables that favor African American productivity. Mason argues that effort or motivation is a productivity-linked variable that favors African Americans based upon his finding that African Americans acquire more schooling than whites for a comparable set of resources.

52 Bennett Harrison, "Education and Underemployment in the Urban Ghetto," *American Economic Review*, vol. 62 (December 1972), pp. 796–812. Card and Krueger (1992) also directly control for school quality. They find that there is still a substantial wage gap left after controlling for school quality.

53 Rodgers and Spriggs, "What Does AFQT Really Measure," pp. 13–46.

54 Systematic racial differences in the structural equations for the determination of standardized test scores also are evident in the General Social Survey data. Fitting equations for Wordsum scores separately for African Americans and whites also yields statistically distinct structures . See Katherine White, "Simultaneity Issues in the Relationship of Income and Intelligence," Undergraduate Senior Honors Thesis, Department of Economics, University of North Carolina at Chapel Hill, 1997.

55 Maxwell reports a coefficient of -0.274 on the race variable in her AFQT regression. This coefficient indicates that race accounts for less than a one percentile difference in the test score gap after adjusting for differences in family background. However, in a private exchange with William Rodgers, Maxwell has agreed that this reported coefficient is incorrect. The true coefficient is -16.89, which indicates that after adjusting for family background race accounts for nearly 17 percentile points of the unadjusted interracial gap in AFQT scores of 24 percentile points. At most, then, Maxwell can account for 30 percent of the black-white difference in AFQT scores.

The Maxwell correction provides additional weight for the validity of Rodgers-Spriggs correction. There are two alternatives. First, it may be argued that AFQT is a proxy for skill but it does not capture all skill. That is, there are other unobserved skills not captured by the AFQT. However, there is no a priori reason to believe that these additional unobserved skills favor a particular group; hence, we do not whether the coefficient on race is biased upward or downward.

Second, it may be argued that there are other predictors of the test that are correlated with race but which are left out of AFQT explanatory equation.

56 Janet Currie and Duncan Thomas, "Race, Children's Cognitive Achievement and *The Bell Curve*," National Bureau of Economic Research Working Paper #5240 (August 1995).

57 Richard J. Murnane, John B. Willett, and Frank Levy, "The Growing Importance of Cognitive Skills in Wage Determination," *The Review of Economics and Statistics*, vol. 77:2 (May 1995), pp. 251–66.

58 Ronald B. Mincy, "The Urban Institute Audit Studies: Their Research and Policy Context" in Michael Fix and Raymond J. Struyk (eds.), *Clear and Convincing Evidence: Measurement of Discrimination in America* (Washington, D.C.: The Urban Institute Press, 1993), pp. 165–86.

59 Michael Fix, George C. Galster, and Raymond J. Struyk, "An Overview of Auditing for Discrimination," in Michael Fix and Raymond Struyk, eds., *Clear and Convincing Evidence: Measurement of Discrimination in America* (Washington, D.C.: The Urban Institute Press, 1993), pp. 21–22. Another audit study conducted independently of Urban Institute in Denver, Colorado found no evidence of discrimination against either African American males or Hispanic males (James and Del Castillo, 1991). It remains unclear whether this result is due to the fact that the Denver labor market is different or because of methodological differences.

60 James J. Heckman and Peter Siegelman, The Urban Institute Audit Studies: Their Methods," *Discrimination in America* (Washington, D.C.: The Urban Institute Press, 1993), pp. 187–258.

61 Some of their criticisms along these lines frankly strike us as ridiculous, for example, concerns about facial hair on the Hispanic male testers used by the Urban Institute.

62 David Neumark, Ray J. Bank, and Kye D. Van Nort, "Sex Discrimination in Restaurant Hiring: An Audit Study," National Bureau of Economic Research Working Paper No. 5024 (1995).

63 Neumark et al., "Sex Discrimination."

64 Burtless (1995) has argued that more than one-half of the rise in male inequality between 1963 and 1989 is attributable to the growth in the unexplained wage variance.

65 Peter B. Riach and Judith Rich, "Measuring Discrimination By Direct Experimental Methods: Seeking Gunsmoke," *Journal of Post Keynesian Economics*, vol. 14:2 (Winter 1991–92), pp. 143–50.

66 Claudia Goldin and Cecilia Rouse, "Orchestrating Impartiality: The Impact of "Blind' Auditions on Female Musicians," unpublished manuscript, Harvard University (June 1997).

67 Harry Holzer, *What Employers Want: Job Prospects for Less-Educated Workers* (New York: Russell Sage Foundation, 1997).

68 Ibid, pp. 77–106. Holzer's conclusions are derived from survey data. He surveyed employers in the Atlanta, Boston, Detroit, and Los Angeles metropolitan areas. This data was coordinated with household surveys of the same cities. The surveys were conducted between May 1992 and May 1994. See also Kirschenman and Neckerman (1991) for detailed confirmation of the presence of this racial hierarchy among Chicago area employers.

69 Gary S. Becker, *The Economics of Discrimination* (Chicago: University of Chicago Press, 1957).

70 Janice F. Madden, "Discrimination—A Manifestation of Male Market Power?" in Cynthia Lloyd, ed., *Discrimination and the Division of Labor* (New York: Columbia University Press, 1975), p. 150.

71 Madden, "Discrimination—A Manifestation," p. 150.

72 William Darity Jr. and Rhonda Williams, "Peddlers Forever? Culture, Competition, and Discrimination," *American Economic Review*, vol. 75:2 (May, 1985).

73 Thomas Sowell, *Ethnic America* (New York: Basic Books, 1981). To address the effects of culture, following Woodbury (1993), Darity, Guilkey, and Winfrey (1996) held color constant and varied culture by examining outcomes among blacks of differeing ancestries. Unlike Sowell's expectation, black males of West Indian and non-West Indian ancestry were being confronted with the same racial penalty iin U.S. labor markets by 1990.

74 James J. Heckman, "The Value of Quantitative Evidence on the Effect of the Past on the Present," *American Economic Review*, vol. 87:2 (May 1997), p. 406.

75 Bruce Elmslie and Stanley Sedo, "Discrimination, Social Psychology and Hysteresis in Labor Markets," *Journal of Economic Psychology*, vol. 17 (1996), p. 474.

76 George J. Borjas, "Long-Run Convergence of Ethnic Skill Differentials: The Children and Grandchildren of the Great Migration," *Industrial and Labor Relations Review*, vol. 47:4 (July 1994), pp. 553–73.

77 Andrea Tyree, "Reshuffling the Social Deck: From Mass Migration to the Transformation of the American Ethnic Hierarchy," in Judith Blau and Norman Goodman, eds., *Social Roles and Social Institutions: Essays in Honor of Rose Laub Coser* (Boulder, CO: Westview Press, 1991), pp. 195–215; William Darity, Jr., "What's Left of the Economic Theory of Discrimination?" in Steven Shulman and William Darity, Jr., eds., *The Question of Discrimination* (Middletown, CT: Wesleyan University Press, 1989), pp. 335–74.

78 Carl O. Wood, Mark P. Zanna, and Joel Cooper, "The Nonverbal Mediation of Self-Fulfilling Prophesies in Interracial Interaction," *Journal of Experimental Social Psychology*, vol. 10 (1974), pp. 109–20.

79 Mark Sibicky and John Dividio, "Stigma of Psychological Therapy: Stereotypes, Interpersonal relations, and the Self-Fulfilling Prophecy," *Journal of Counseling Psychology*, vol. 33:2 (1986), pp. 148–54.

80 Arthur W. Lewis, "The Dual Economy Revisited," *The Manchester School*, vol. 47:3 (1979), pp. 211–29.

81 Anne O. Krueger, "The Economics of Discrimination," *Journal of Political Economy*, Vol. 79:2 (March/April 1963), pp. 481–86; David Swinton, "A Labor Force Competition Model of Racial Descrimination in the Labor Market," *Review of Black Political Economy*, vol. 9:1 (Fall 1978), pp. 5–42; Madden, "Discrimination—A Manifestation of Male Market Power?"

82 Lewis, "The Dual Economy."

83 Krueger, "The Economics of Discrimination," pp. 481–86.

84 Madden, "Discrimination—A Manifestation."

85 William Darity, Jr., Jason Dietrich, and David Guilkey, "Racial and Ethnic Inequality in the United States: A Secular Perspective," *American Economic Review*, vol. 87 (May 1997), pp. 301–5.

86 Peggy Lovell, "Development and Discrimination in Brazil," *Development and Change*, vol. 24 (1993), pp. 83–101.

87 The portion of the gap that can be explained by discrimination is much lower in the high black region of Brazil, the Northeast, than the rest of Brazil. We know of no evidence that suggests that this is or is not true for the U.S. South.

88 A. Singh Dhesi and Harbhajan Singh, "Education, Labour Market Distortions and Relative Earnings of Different Religion-Caste Categories in India (A Case Study of Delhi)," *Canadian Journal of Development Studies* 10:1 (1989), pp. 75–89.

89 Darity and Williams, "Peddlers Forever?;" Howard Botwinick, *Persistent Inequalities: Wage Disparity Under Capitalist Competition*, (New York: Princeton University Press, 1993); Mason, "Race, Competition and Differential Wages," *Cambridge Journal of Economics*, vol. 19 (1995), pp. 545–67; Mason, "Competing Explanations of Male Interracial Wage Differentials: Missing Variables Models Versus Job Competition," *Cambridge Journal of Economics*, vol. 23 (May 1999): 1–39.

CHAPTER 9

RACE, CLASS, AND SPACE: AN EXAMINATION OF UNDERCLASS NOTIONS IN THE STEEL AND MOTOR CITIES

KAREN J. GIBSON

INTRODUCTION

The most fundamental difference between today's inner-city neighborhoods and those studied by Drake and Cayton is the much higher level of joblessness. . . . The loss of traditional manufacturing and other blue-collar jobs in Chicago resulted in increased joblessness among inner-city black males and a concentration in low-wage, high-turnover laborer and service-sector jobs. Embedded in ghetto neighborhoods, social networks, and households that are not conducive to employment, inner-city black males fall further behind their white and Hispanic counterparts, especially when the labor market is slack. The position of inner-city black women in the labor market is also problematic. Their high degree of social isolation in impoverished neighborhoods reduces their employment prospects.—Wilson, 1996, pp. 18, 144

William Julius Wilson first argued that the plight of the underclass is primarily due to class, and not race in his book *The Declining Significance of Race* (1978) and again in *The Truly Disadvantaged* (1987). Although he acknowledges that racial discrimination has played a role in creating segregated neighborhoods, and in "statistical discrimination" practiced by employers, in his latest book *When Work Disappears: The World of the New Urban Poor* (1996), Wilson argues that the combined influence of structural economic change and the flight of the middle class are the key factors in perpetuating the spatially isolated "jobless ghettoes" of the new urban poor.[1] The implication is that because the middle class was able to achieve some success in the labor market and leave the ghetto, race is no longer a barrier; the underclass suffers only because of its isolation as a class of people whose jobs have disappeared.

From an historical perspective, the notion that the nature of black urban poverty in the 1990s was worse than ever before is troubling, especially given the extremes of poverty faced by African Americans in cities during the turn of the twentieth century and the Great Depression. It is even more difficult to accept the notion that class could be more important than race in explaining contemporary black poverty. Has the level of economic progress by the black middle class been so great, since the Civil Rights Movement, to signify that race is no longer a barrier to advancement? If this is the case, then we should expect to find no racial disparity in measures of income, wealth, education, employment, and occupational status between residents of black and white working and middle class neighborhoods. And if class is the cause of black urban poverty, then likewise we should expect to find no racial disparity between poor white and black neighborhoods in the degree of labor market detachment.

Wilson provides little evidence on the status of the black middle class to support his argument. His analysis focuses narrowly on those living in concentrated poverty (census tracts with poverty rates 40 percent and higher) in Chicago's South Side. A pair of sociologists, Douglas A. Massey and Nancy Denton, analyzed black housing patterns in large cities and conclude that race is more important than class in perpetuating the underclass. In their book, *American Apartheid: Segregation and the Making of the Underclass* (1993), they assert that "racial segregation—and its characteristic institutional form, the black ghetto—are the key structural factors responsible for the perpetuation of Black poverty in the United States."[2] They argue that because of continued housing discrimination, the black middle class has been unable to move away from the poor, and live in neighborhoods that offer less in the way of housing and educational services that would enable them to pass their gains on to their offspring. Class is important, but there is a danger associated with the conception that middle-class African Americans have "made it." As Melvin L. Oliver and Thomas M. Shapiro point out in their book *Black Wealth/White Wealth: A New Perspective on Racial Inequality* (1997), in measures of wealth, the racial disparity remains enormous. We are already witnessing a regression in policies that help open up doors in white-collar professions; this misconception that African Americans have "made it" only provides a legitimization for such policies.[3]

I argue that the underclass suffer the compound effects of race and class. Through both housing and labor markets they disproportionately bear the brunt of economic restructuring and the suburbanization of employment. Race is the key factor explaining the racial disparity in labor market attachment, not class. Although some African Americans have been able to escape the oldest and poorest areas of town (especially in Detroit) as Wilson suggests, black middle-class neighborhoods also fall behind their white "counterparts" in terms of unemployment. Middle-class African Americans who live in neighborhoods that are "conducive to employment" and do not lack education or experience continue to face barriers in the labor market. Even when work doesn't disappear, blacks are marginalized within the contemporary urban economy. Wilson's inference in *When Work Disappears*, that that middle class has "made it," is based on an analysis that does not consider racial economic inequality between the entire black and white class strata. In the contemporary age of attack on gains African Americans have made since the Civil Rights and Black Power movements, this is premature.

Isolating the Underclass

The underclass literature carries on the long tradition of characterizing the black poor in terms of a "tangle of pathology"; this dates back nearly a century to studies by W. E. B. DuBois and E. Franklin Frazier through the controversial "Moynihan Report" of 1965, and Wilson's *Truly Disadvantaged*.[4] Wilson attempts to link these behaviors to their "structural underpinnings" in his new book, but the perspective is not without problems because of its elite frame of reference, which compares these behaviors to middle-class values of the majority culture. This set of behaviors consists mainly of weak male labor force attachment, female headed households (which were inherently pathological, according to Moynihan), high rates of welfare dependency, out-of-wedlock births, crime, and low educational attainment. Wilson's focus on the "ghetto-related" behavior of the poor continues in this tradition, ultimately contributing to the perpetuation of the culture of poverty and the blame-the-victim approach, deflecting attention from the high degree of economic inequality in the United States, particularly racial economic inequality.

Although it is important to deal with the plight of those poor in our urban areas, the underclass debate, by focusing on a small segment of the poor who live in concentrated poverty (less than 10 percent of all poor), has distorted our knowledge of poverty. African Americans are disproportionately represented among the poor, but in absolute numbers, there are many more white poor than black. In 1991 there were 17.7 million non-Hispanic white poor, 10.2 million black poor, and 6.3 million Chicano/Latino poor in the United States. The term "inner-city poor" is used to connote the black poor, yet in absolute numbers the numbers of white and black poor living in central cities in 1991 were nearly equivalent, at 6.2 million.[5] The key difference between the non-Hispanic white poor (hereafter referred to as white) and the black poor is that because of residential segregation, the black poor are more spatially concentrated; the white poor are spatially dispersed and hence less visible. A theoretical notion that argues that class is the key to the new urban poverty needs to include an analysis that crosses racial boundaries and truly considers class by incorporating the white poor.

Frustrated by the narrow lens through which contemporary analysts study urban poverty, and intrigued by the challenge of untangling the effects of race and class on the "underclass," I engaged in a systematic comparative analysis of white and black poor, working-class, and middle- to upper-class neighborhoods, using data from the 1990 Census for the Detroit and Pittsburgh metropolitan areas. With the census tract serving as proxy for the neighborhood, the data were probed to explore how neighborhood characteristics differed at low, medium, and high poverty levels. The current study examines both intraracial and interracial differences in labor force attachment, educational attainment, household structure, income, and wealth (as measured by homeownership rates). Intraracial analysis of neighborhood characteristics will show how increased poverty affects predominantly white and black neighborhoods. We can assess both the degree to which whites live in concentrated poverty and the degree to which the black middle class has been able to escape poor communities. Interracial analysis allows us to determine which characteristics are similar and which remain different between black and white neighborhoods of the same class.

Theoretical Framework: Comparing Neighborhood Life Chances

How do the neighborhood life chances compare both intraracially and interracially in terms of education, employment, and household structure? "Underclass" theorists make the claim that life chances are influenced by where a person lives, based upon analysis of racially segregated neighborhoods where educational and employment opportunities are limited relative to nonsegregated neighborhoods. This construct is logically compatible with Weber's notion that the distribution of life chances is influenced by the distribution of resources as determined by the social structure, and that these resources are affected by characteristics such as race.[6] Max Weber defined "life chances" in terms of access to goods and services; they represent the opportunity structure: "It is the most elemental economic fact that the way in which the disposition over material property is distributed among a plurality of people, meeting competitively in the market for the purpose of exchange, in itself creates specific life chances."[7] According to the *Blackwell Dictionary of Sociology*, the term "life chances"was used by Max Weber to describe differences among social classes:

> Weber defined social class in terms of people's access to goods and services, especially as these are distributed through markets. These would include material goods such as food and housing; services such as medical care, police and fire protection, and public education; and cultural products such as art, music, and knowledge. The distribution of life chances is influenced primarily by the distribution of resources such as income and wealth (inherited, earned, and otherwise), occupational skills, and education. Depending on the society, it also is affected by ascribed characteristics such as gender, race, and ethnicity.[8]

In other words, life chances reflect "the opportunities to apply one's talents and efforts" to achieve success.[9] In this study the concept of life chances is operationalized through the use of indicators that measure access to resources or the opportunity structure in four categories: poverty, income, and wealth; educational attainment; labor market attachment; and household structure. These outcomes indicate the level of access to resources that assumes a model of human nature in which people try to do their best within the limits of the opportunity structure or resources available to them. Thus the outcomes are symptomatic of the limits of the structural conditions in the environment. For example, the high-school dropout rate is an aggregation of individual outcomes that indicates the quality of the access to the resource education in that neighborhood. If the dropout rate is high, then access to education is considered poor and the ability to reach one's potential is stymied, and thereby life chances are reduced. The reason for dropout could be due to problems with the school or low aspirations among the students. The purpose here is to measure the level of access to resources, not to engage in a causal analysis to determine why access is or is not present.[10] If there are many dropouts, then access is blocked and the opportunity structure is weak.

The indicators were chosen because they either measure poverty and economic well-being directly or are related to one's ability to achieve economic security. They are measures of socioeconomic status commonly used in social research;

more specifically, they are the key variables analyzed in "underclass" research.[11] The poverty rate, levels and sources of income, home ownership, and home value are measures that indicate achieved economic status and potential for access to more economic resources. Educational attainment, as measured by the high school noncompletion rate (dropout rate) is an indicator of the quality of educational resources in the environment and is strongly related to the degree of labor force participation and chances of finding a job that pays a wage that is above poverty level wage or has upward career mobility. The indicators of labor market attachment such as the labor force participation rate, unemployment rate, and the number of workers in the family, provide information on the level and quality of employment opportunity in a neighborhood environment. Measures of household structure are percentage of female-headed parent households in the tract and percentage of married-couple households. I do not consider female-headed households inherently pathological; rather, gender bias in the labor market and in notions of parental responsibility for children underlie the poverty of women raising children. Also, household structure is closely related to labor market indicators because it affects the number of workers in a household.

CROSS-SECTIONAL ANALYSIS OF TWO METROPOLITAN REGIONS IN 1990

This study consists of a comparative empirical analysis of race, class, and space in two metropolitan regions, Pittsburgh and Detroit. In 1990, the U.S. Census Bureau defined primary metropolitan statistical areas (PMSAs) as areas with more than a million persons, consisting of a "large urbanized count or cluster of counties that demonstrates very strong internal economic and social links."[12] In the Detroit region, the PMSA consisted of Wayne, Oakland, Macomb, St. Clair, Monroe, and Lapeer counties.[13] In the Pittsburgh region the PMSA consisted of Allegheny, Beaver, Butler, Fayette, Washington, and Westmoreland counties. In terms of population size, Pittsburgh was smaller than Detroit, but it was a good case study site because it contained a substantial population of white poor. In 1989 there were about 183,000 white poor, and they comprised three-quarters of all poor. Over two-thirds of all poor lived outside of the central city. Within the central city there were roughly equal numbers of black (37,000) and white poor (36,000).

In Detroit, large numbers of whites concentrated in poverty tracts in the central city as well as many poor whites in the suburbs. About 231,000 white poor comprised 41 percent of all poor. Unlike Pittsburgh, about two-thirds of all poor live inside of the central city; the black poor in the central city far outnumbered the white poor (271,000 vs. 49,000); and there was a large black middle class with political power. The Detroit central city led the nation in the growth of poverty tracts during the 1980s.[14] Both cities were ranked among the most economically distressed cities with populations over 200,000 in 1990: Detroit was second and Pittsburgh was twenty-second.[15] The Pittsburgh region ranked seventh among metropolitan areas with the largest increases in the white population in poverty during the 1980s while the Detroit region ranked first among areas with the largest increase in the black population in poverty during the same period.[16]

Former industrial powerhouses, the Steel and Motor Cities ranked first and second in terms of specialization in one branch of manufacturing industry. Tracing the decline in the automotive and steel industries from the period 1970 to 1990, the impact on employment in each region was substantial but different. The Detroit region suffered not only an absolute loss in manufacturing employment, but a shift in manufacturing and service employment from the city of Detroit to outlying suburban areas, especially to Oakland County, just north of Detroit. Although suburbanization of employment occurred to some degree in the Pittsburgh region, the metro area suffered more of an absolute loss of employment in both the central city and suburbs, as steel mills had historically been located along the river valleys surrounding the city. In fact, according to the 1992 "State of the Region Report" on Southwestern Pennsylvania, while the City of Pittsburgh and much of Allegheny County have recovered from the steel industry crisis of the early 1980s, "other counties of the region, as well as the Monongahela Valley in Allegheny County experienced much less recovery and have been much more negatively affected by the recent recession."[17] In contrast, the City of Detroit is called the "Centrifugal City" because of the loss of both manufacturing and service employment and population to surrounding suburbs.[18]

Detroit's black population concentrated primarily within Wayne County, with 91 percent of the total in the city of Detroit. Another 8 percent lived in Oakland County, and the remaining 1 percent lived elsewhere. In the Pittsburgh region, 83 percent of the black population resided in Allegheny County, primarily in the city of Pittsburgh. Residential segregation was very high in metropolitan Detroit: the index of black-white segregation was 86.7. Blacks made up 22 percent of the regional population; if there were a completely even spread across neighborhoods of black residents (22 percent per tract), then the dissimilarity index would have been 0. Detroit is one of the metropolitan areas which Massey and Denton considered "hypersegregated" because it scored 70 or more on the five dimensions of segregation: unevenness, isolation, clustering, centralization, and concentration (see Table 9.1). Black residents in Detroit clustered around the downtown area or central business district. The Pittsburgh region did not meet all of the criteria for hypersegregation because it failed to score at least 70 on the dimensions of isolation and clustering. The isolation index was 54.1, which means that the average black person lived in a neighborhood that was 54.1 percent black. In terms of clustering, blacks neighborhoods are not highly contiguous, but scattered about in various parts of Allegheny County. Segregation tends to be higher the larger the black population is, and this is the case in Detroit and Pittsburgh.

Table 9.1   Residential Segregation in 1980 Detroit & Pittsburgh PMSAs

	Unevenness	Isolation	Clustering	Central-ization	Concen-tration
Detroit	86.7	77.3	84.6	92.4	84.2
Pittsburgh	72.7	54.1	27.2	81.2	82.1

Source: Massey & Denton, 1993, p. 76.

DATA AND METHOD

The primary data source is the 1990 Census Summary Tape File 3A (SFT3A), which permits analysis of the spatial distribution of the poor within each six-county region. The data is aggregated at the census tract level, and analysis on this spatial scale serves as a proxy for the level of neighborhood. The tract-level statistics represent all persons living in the tract, and care must be taken to avoid the ecological fallacy of attributing neighborhood characteristics to individuals and families residing within. This analysis employs a quasi-experimental design that uses the neighborhoods with low poverty rates as a control and compares their socioeconomic characteristics (measures of life chances) against neighborhoods with concentrated poverty. It is quasi-experimental because the observations are not randomly assigned, as in a true experimental design.

The tracts are categorized into three groups, according to their poverty concentration level: low, medium, and high. "Low Poverty" tracts are those that have poverty rates up to 19 percent, "Medium Poverty" tracts have poverty rates ranging between 20 percent and 39 percent, and "High Poverty" tracts have poverty rates of 40 percent or more. The cutoff points of 20 percent and 40 percent are the same used by the Bureau of the Census to analyze concentrated poverty areas. The tracts are further categorized by race according to the group which comprises at least 60 percent of the tract. This typology of six tract groups facilitates comparative analysis of neighborhood types.

The neighborhood comparisons are designed to untangle the effects of class and race. Poverty concentration can affect life chances because of these interacting factors. The effects of class (income) on life chances are manifested as differences between white neighborhood characteristics when level of poverty changes and differences between black neighborhood characteristics when the level of poverty changes. These can be thought of as class differences. The effects of race on life chances are those differences between white and black neighborhood characteristics when poverty level is held constant. Figure 9.1 shows how the comparison will be made using data from one point in time (1990 census). Class differences appear on horizontal axis and racial differences appear along vertical axis.

The tracts are grouped by race and poverty level in order to compare average socioeconomic characteristics. The set of techniques often used for this type of quasi-experimental design, more frequently in the behavioral sciences such as psychology or education, is analysis of variance (ANOVA).[19] Like a typical quasi-experiment, the low-poverty groups are control groups, and the medium- and high-poverty groups are receiving the treatment: poverty concentration. For example, in a test to see if the homeownership rate in the white medium category is significantly different from the rate in the white low category, if the result is that there is a significant difference, we can infer that the independent variable (poverty concentration) has an effect on the homeownership rate. An interracial comparison of homeownership rates in the medium poverty category that results in no statistically significant difference allows the inference that, when controlling for level of poverty, race does not affect homeownership rates. These two

Average White **Low** Poverty Tract Group Characteristics	Average White **Medium** Poverty Tract Group Characteristics	Average White **High** Poverty Tract Group Characteristics
Average Black **Low** Poverty Tract Group Characteristics	Average Black **Medium** Poverty Tract Group Characteristics	Average Black **High** Poverty Tract Group Characteristics

1.   Income (Class).
     Intra-racial comparison between neighborhoods with different levels of poverty concentration. Differences reveal that income segregation, as defined by level of neighborhood poverty, influences life chances.
2.   Race
     Inter-racial comparison between neighborhoods of the same level of poverty concentration. Differences reveal that race influences life chances, even when poverty level is held constant.

Figure 9.1   Quasi-Experimental Design: Intraracial and Interracial Comparative analysis

examples illustrate in informal terms the method by which I test the hypothesis that concentrated poverty has a negative effect on the life chances of the poor.

RACIAL DIFFERENCES IN THE SPATIAL DISTRIBUTION OF POVERTY

Table 9.2 displays statistics on the census tract distribution in each region by race and poverty level. In Detroit, 94 percent of majority-white tracts fall into the low-poverty category, in contrast to 18 percent of majority-black tracts. The pattern is similar in Pittsburgh, although poverty concentration is slightly higher among whites there, as indicated by relatively greater share of medium poverty tracts (13 percent). Neither region contains more than a tiny fraction of white neighborhoods considered underclass by the 40 percent or more poverty criterion. The spatial distribution of black tracts indicates a small group living in low poverty neighborhoods with rates as low as 13 percent about a third of the regional averages in Detroit (35 percent) and Pittsburgh (39 percent). These were members of the black middle class who had left the "ghetto" and inhabited Detroit's Northwest side, and Pittsburgh's Penn Hills and "Sugar Top" in the Hill District. These comprised 18 percent of Detroit's and 16 percent of Pittsburgh's black neighborhoods (see low poverty categories). The absolute number of black middle class tracts in Pittsburgh was only 7, a much smaller figure than the 49 found in Detroit.

The black working class in both regions lived in the medium-poverty tracts with an average poverty rate of 30 percent, below the regional average. These

Table 9.2 Census Tract distribution by Race and Poverty Level Detroit & Pittsburgh PMSAs, 1990

TRACT GROUP SIZE, POVERTY, RACIAL COMPOSITION, & POPULATION CHARACTERISTICS

Region-Race(> 60%) Poverty Level	Number of Tracts	Percent of All Tracts	Average Poverty Rate	Standard Deviation	Median Poverty Rate	Percent Non-Hisp. White	Percent Black	Average Population
Detroit-White								
Low (0–20%)	778	.94	.05	.04	.04	.95	.02	3912
Medium (20–39%)	42	.05	.29	.06	.28	.80	.11	3281
High (40% and up)	8	.01	.45	.04	.43	.74	.13	3603
Total/Mean	**828**	**1.00**	**.07**	**.08**	**.05**	**.94**	**.03**	**3877**
DETROIT-BLACK								
Low (0–20%)	49	.18	.13	.05	.13	.13	.86	3674
Medium (20–39%)	105	.39	.30	.06	.30	.09	.90	3449
High (40% and up)	115	.43	.49	.08	.47	.08	.91	2893
Total/Mean	**269**	**1.00**	**.35**	**.15**	**.37**	**.09**	**.90**	**3252**
PITTSBURGH-WHITE								
Low (0–20%)	559	.85	.09	.05	.08	.96	.03	3569
Medium (20–39%)	85	.13	.25	.04	.24	.87	.11	2783
High (40% and up)	10	.02	.49	.07	.49	.77	.17	1788
Total/Mean	**654**	**1.00**	**.12**	**.09**	**.09**	**.95**	**.04**	**3439**
PITTSBURGH-BLACK								
Low (0–20%)	7	.16	.12	.04	.14	.18	.82	2285
Medium (20–39%)	18	.40	.30	.06	.30	.16	.83	2166
High (40% and up)	20	.44	.56	.15	.49	.06	.93	1890
Total/Mean	**45**	**1.00**	**.39**	**.20**	**.38**	**.12**	**.87**	**2062**

Source: 1990 Census STF3A

Note: In Detroit's White Medium Poverty group, 3.5% and 4% are Hispanic White and Other, respectively. In Detroit's White High Poverty group, 3.7% and 7.1% are Hispanic White and Other. In Pittsburgh's White High Poverty group, 3.6% are Asian. The rest of the tract groups contained less than 2% of any race other than Non-Hispanic White or Black. Poverty line was about $14,000 for family of four in 1990.

comprise about 40 percent of all tracts in both regions (see "Percent of All Tracts"). In contrast, the medium-poverty tracts for whites had average poverty rates that were much greater than the regional averages (7 percent in Detroit and 12 percent in Pittsburgh). They were relatively poor. Detroit and Pittsburgh had similar proportions of black "underclass" neighborhoods (40 percent) with average poverty rates of 49 percent and 56 percent.

Whites comprised a significantly larger proportion of the residents in black middle- and working-class neighborhoods in Pittsburgh compared to Detroit. And the black high-poverty neighborhoods in both regions were more black than the white high poverty areas were white. In other words, the higher the concentration of poverty, whether in majority white or black neighborhoods, the greater the proportion of blacks in the population. This makes perfect sense since blacks were more likely to be poor in the first place.

Detroit's neighborhoods were more densely populated than Pittsburgh, which had suffered tremendous population loss over the past half-century. It is notable that Detroit's eight white high poverty tracts had double the population of Pittsburgh's ten high poverty tracts, indicating that the incidence of public housing, which concentrated poverty, was relatively greater in Detroit's white "underclass" neighborhoods.

POVERTY, INCOME, AND WEALTH

Table 9.3 displays the findings for six indicators of poverty, income, and wealth. Reading across the table from left to right, one can see intraracial differences between average neighborhood characteristics as the poverty level rises. Median household income, homeownership rates, and median house values decline for both racial groups as the poverty rate rises.

The data reveal that Detroit's white middle- and upper-class neighborhoods had an average poverty rate (5 percent) much lower than the black middle class neighborhoods. This changes at the medium and high poverty levels, where the rates are not statistically different. In Pittsburgh, the opposite occurs: black and white low poverty tracts had similar poverty rates while in the medium and high tract groups the black poverty rate was significantly higher. Whites incomes were higher in Detroit relative to Pittsburgh and this combined with higher residential segregation by race and income resulted in a set of white residential neighborhoods that were much better off economically than any other group.

Home ownership rates and home values were statistically different between black and white middle-class neighborhoods in Detroit, but not in Pittsburgh. Although the homeownership rate was high for blacks at 70 percent, median house value was $40,000 less than whites, on average. There were no interracial differences in home ownership or median house value in the medium- and high-poverty categories for Pittsburgh or Detroit. Thus poverty also affected the ability of the white poor to accumulate wealth in the form of home ownership.

Rates of public assistance receipt increased in both white and black neighborhoods as the poverty level rose, although there was a very different pattern in the "underclass" neighborhoods of Detroit and Pittsburgh. Black and white rates were not different in Detroit, but the black rate was double the white rate in Pittsburgh.

Table 9.3 Average Poverty, Income, and Wealth Characteristics by Tract Group Detroit & Pittsburgh PMSAs

Average Tract Group Characteristic		Detroit PMSA			Pittsburgh PMSA		
Poverty Level Number of Tracts in Group (White/Black)		LOW n=778/49	MEDIUM n=42/105	HIGH n=8/115	LOW n=559/7	MEDIUM n=85/18	HIGH n=10/20
Poverty Rate	W	.05*	.29	.45	.09	.25*	.49*
	B	.13*	.30	.49	.12	.30*	.56*
Number of Poor	W	211*	940	1572	298	696	1109
	B	463*	1036	1390	282	683	878
Median Household Income	W	$42.5*	$18.6	$13.5	$30.5	$16.5	$9.8
	B	$35.4*	$19.0	$11.2	$23.8	$15.2	$9.0
Households With Public Assistance	W	.05*	.21*	.35	.06*	.16*	.22*
	B	.13*	.26*	.40	.15*	.25*	.44*
Homeownership Rate	W	.78*	.49	.39	.74	.54	.20
	B	.70*	.52	.39	.70	.47	.27
Median House Value	W	$87.4*	$29.2	$25.4	$61.4	$35.3	$35.8
	B	$45.7*	$24.3	$19.1	$40.0	$29.6	$23.5

Source: 1990 Census Summary Tape File 3A

*White and Black means statistically different at .05 level.

Note: Poverty threshold was $13,924 for family of four in 1991.

Household Structure

Concentrated poverty was associated with gender and marital status. The incidence of marriage declined in poor neighborhoods, and, related to this, the incidence of single parent households increased as the poverty rate increased (see Table 9.4). The interracial gap in percentage of female single parent households was greatest in the low poverty neighborhoods and decreased as the poverty level rose (with the exception of Pittsburgh's high-poverty neighborhoods, which were of a different nature than Detroit's high-poverty neighborhoods). In other words, poverty made black and white household structure more similar. Actually, logic dictates that a household's marital status precedes poverty and wealth status. The neighborhood had low rates of poverty because there were more married-couple families with two-wage earners residing there. Women earned less than men, and if they had children without the benefit of affordable daycare it is often more economically rational to stay at home rather than work—this is a dilemma that faced both black and white single parents.

Educational Attainment

Average levels of educational attainment declined significantly in neighborhoods where poverty was concentrated (see Table 9.5). Interracial differences in educational attainment at the regional level disappeared at the neighborhood level when poverty was held constant. In Detroit's high-poverty neighborhoods, roughly half of the persons aged 25 years and older had not completed high school, and 2 out of 5 had not in the medium-poverty neighborhoods. Poor white neighborhoods in Detroit had substantially more dropouts than their counterparts in Pittsburgh, which was further evidence of a high degree of class segregation in the Motor City region. Because low educational attainment then more than ever before implied lower earnings, poverty was higher where education was low. This was especially key for the white poor, as evidenced by the relatively large gap between low and medium poverty neighborhoods compared to the black gap. Finally, there was no difference between black and white neighborhood educational attainment as measured by the percentage with bachelor's degrees. When looking down here on the ground, blacks had closed the gaps with their white counterparts when it comes to education. This makes differences in labor market status more difficult to understand.

Labor Market Attachment

Labor force participation rates were much lower in Pittsburgh, where the weak economy had shifted from manufacturing to low-wage service employment (see Table 9.5). More people had simply left the labor market entirely, and those who remained were more likely to be employed in low-wage jobs. In contrast, manufacturing jobs remained a large share of the total in the Detroit region, and more people participated in the labor force, but there was higher unemployment.

Table 9.4 Average Household Structure Characteristics by Tract Group Detroit & Pittsburgh PMSAs

Average Tract Group Characteristic		*Detroit PMSA*			*Pittsburgh PMSA*		
		LOW	MEDIUM	HIGH	LOW	MEDIUM	HIGH
Poverty Level Number of Tracts in Group (White/Black)		n=778/49	n=42/105	n=8/115	n=559/7	n=85/18	n=10/20
% Female Single Parent Households	W	.04*	.14*	.22	.04*	.08*	.06*
	B	.14*	.21*	.25	.09*	.16*	.30*
% Married Family Households	W	.62*	.38*	.35*	.59*	.41*	.16
	B	.42*	.29*	.20*	.40*	.27	.17

Source: 1990 Census Summary Tape File 3A
*White and Black means statistically different at .05 level.

Table 9.5 Average Education and Employment Characteristics by Tract Group Detroit & Pittsburgh PMSAs

Average Tract Group Characteristic		Detroit Pmsa			Pittsburgh Pmsa		
Poverty Level		LOW	MEDIUM	HIGH	LOW	MEDIUM	HIGH
Number of Tracts in Group (White/Black)		n=778/49	n=42/105	n=8/115	n=559/7	n=85/18	n=10/20
% Over 24 Yrs. without H.S. Diploma	W	.20	.41	.52	.21	.33	.37
	B	.22	.38	.48	.30	.37	.43
% Over 24 Yrs. with B.A. Degree	W	.13	.05	.02	.13	.06	.09
	B	.11	.05	.03	.09	.05	.03
Labor Force Participation Rate	W	.67	.56	.50	.60	.50	.46
	B	.66	.55	.46	.58	.49	.41
Unemployment Rate	W	.06*	.14*	.21*	.06	.12*	.16*
	B	.12*	.21*	.32*	.10	.17*	.31*
Unemp. Rate-Females w/Child. <6 yrs.	W	.06*	.22	.41	.06	.20	.53
	B	.18*	.29	.53	.09	.25	.43
Jobless Rate	W	.37*	.52*	.60*	.44	.56	.61*
	B	.42*	.56*	.68*	.47	.59	.71*
% Families with No Workers	W	.11	.26	.32	.17	.27	.30*
	B	.13	.26	.38	.21	.23	.43*
% Families with Two Workers	W	.45*	.30	.23	.41	.30	.30
	B	.40*	.28	.20	.38	.29	.15
% In Low Wage Service Occup.	W	.11	.19	.23	.13*	.18*	.22*
	B	.13	.20	.24	.19*	.25*	.35*

Source: 1990 Census Summary Tape File 3A
*White and Black means statistically different at .05 level.

The most significant finding in the interracial analysis of labor market attachment is that black unemployment was substantially higher than white unemployment, even when educational attainment levels are similar. In Detroit, the rate of unemployment in black middle-class neighborhoods was double the white middle class neighborhood rate; in Pittsburgh, it was 66 percent percent higher. The gap remained significant in the medium and high poverty areas of both regions. In the case of Detroit, the middle class neighborhoods were even further divided into two levels of poverty: less than 10 percent and 10 percent to 20 percent, so there was no interracial difference in poverty levels and black educational attainment was even higher than white, yet the neighborhood unemployment rates were still statistically different. The racial disparity in unemployment rates, regardless of class, provides strong evidence to refute the thesis that class is more important than race in creating the underclass. Ghetto-related behaviors and neighborhoods "not conducive to employment" do not explain the gap in unemployment in middle class black Detroit. Considering the geographic location of the middle class in northwest Detroit, in close proximity to majority-white neighborhoods on the other side of Eight Mile Road in Oakland County where unemployment was low, spatial mismatch theory does not suffice either.

Regardless of race or region, in poor neighborhoods more than half the persons 16 and over were jobless in 1990. The racial gap in joblessness is statistically different in all Detroit neighborhoods; due to the incidence of low wage-employment this is only true in the case of high-poverty neighborhoods in Pittsburgh. Even though many whites work in low-wage service occupations, black workers in Pittsburgh are much more crowded into these occupations.

Along with labor force participation rates, the similarity in percentage of families with no workers between white and black neighborhoods indicates that African Americans have no less a desire to work than their white counterparts. In today's economy, the families that have secured the most financially remunerative attachment to the labor market are those that consist of at least two full-time workers earning a better-than-average wage. Except for a small fraction at the top of the income distribution, most black families need at least two workers to achieve middle class status. Roughly 40 percent of the households in middle-class neighborhoods, black or white, had two workers.

The relationship between the labor market attachment and marital status is important. Because white males continued to have the best attachment to the labor force in terms of employment, occupation, and earnings, they could afford to have their wives remain outside of the labor market. Thus we find in the case of Detroit, that even though 62 percent of the households in low poverty tracts have married couple families, only 45 percent consisted of families with two workers. In contrast, 42 percent of the households in black middle class neighborhoods consisted of married couple families, yet 40 percent of all households had two workers. If black workers had better access to white collar managerial occupations, particularly in the private sector, black middle-class neighborhoods would have become a greater fraction of the total and the

incidence of marriage would have increased. There has always been and continues to be an economic component to the marriage relation. As shown earlier, marginalization from the labor force reduced the incidence of marriage
among blacks and whites; but blacks continued to suffer this burden disproportionately.

The Black Middle Class:
The Myth of "Makin' it"

Between 1943 and 1953, black workers engaged in two major struggles which directly
affected the postwar community building process. One was the struggle of black blue-col-
lar workers for seniority and upgrading in the plants. The other was the struggle of black
white-collar workers to obtain jobs outside of the factories. The latter group was successful
only in finding such jobs in the black community or in government. Black white-collar
workers received more jobs in governmental civil-service and technical positions "than
comparable positions in private business". This meant that while there did exist a pool of
blacks trained and prepared for such jobs, "private employers [were] far more selective on
a racial basis than [the] government." During this period the Detroit Urban League
worked hard and "for the most part silently" to open up jobs for blacks. (Thomas, 1992,
p. 318)[20]

Richard Walter Thomas traced the efforts of the black community in Detroit to
break through discriminatory barriers in blue- and white-collar occupations during
the 1940s and 1950s. Other historians have written about the "struggles in steel"
for equal employment opportunity in Pittsburgh.[21] Both economies were overly
dependent on a single industry and its workers have suffered because of their decline.

Throughout the 1980s, white workers in Pittsburgh continued their shift from
manufacturing and clerical employment to managerial and professional employment. Black workers increased their representation in clerical work, and while
gains were made in managerial and professional specialty work, they are not
enough. Over the decade whites increased the proportion in managerial and professional specialty occupations by 6.2 percent, blacks by 4.4 percent. By 1990, 31
percent of white and 20 percent of black workers were executives, managers, or
professionals.

While African Americans have a long history of struggle to secure access to
good jobs, analysis of the 1990 occupational distribution revealed that opportunities were still blocked, in Detroit and Pittsburgh, especially in private-
sector white-collar employment and skilled blue-collar jobs. Nationwide, only
14.7 percent and 20.1 percent of black males and females were employed in
managerial and professional specialty occupations, compared to 27.5 percent
and 29.9 percent of white males and females. African American workers were
still crowded into lower level service, clerical, operative, and laborer positions.
Substantial gains were made at the management level in public administration
and certain professional fields such as teacher and social worker, but the corporate world was still off limits to many. Legal settlements of racial discrimination cases in the corporate sector became headline news. The executives of
Texaco were caught on tape referring to African American managerial employees as black jellybeans. This was significant not just because of the negative

racial connotation, but because black jellybeans are usually few in number among all the other jellybeans, and therefore it is an accurate metaphor for black representation in the higher ranks of the corporate world. Problems remained in blue-collar employment as well. But because much of the economy is now comprised of white-collar employment, African American representation in the corporate sector is pivotal to the reduction of racial economic equality.[22]

By the early 1990s the black middle class had not attained income parity with the white middle class, and female incomes continued to trail behind male incomes. In 1993 black males 25 years and older with at least a bachelor's degree, had median income of $32,865, compared to $43,063 for non-Hispanic white males; the figures for black and non-Hispanic white females were $26,765 vs. $25,298.[23] Two fifths, or 41.2 percent of white males had incomes of $50,000 or more in 1993, compared to 23.9 percent of black males, 13.5 percent of white females, and 11.5 percent of black females.

Public administration and executive positions were disproportionately occupied by black workers in 1990s Detroit. They succeeded in gaining access to civil service jobs, but did not gain equal access to the private sector; this hadn't changed much since the 1950s, except in some professional occupations. A survey of black and white education and white economic indicators over a fifty-year period in Pittsburgh (Allegheny County) suggests that present day levels of inequality are nothing new. In fact, since the 1970s black median incomes have taken a turn for the worse (see Table 9.6). In summary, while the black middle class may have moved away and made substantial economic gains relative to the past, they still faced racial barriers.

Table 9.6 Education, Unemployment, and Income Ratios for Allegheny County, 1940–1990

Year	Ratio of Black/ White High School completion (25 years +)	Ratio of Black/ White Unemployment Rate (14 & 16 years +)[†]	Ratio of Black/White Median Family Income
1940	.48	1.7*	-
1950	.58	2.3	.68
1960	.59	3.0**	.63
1970	.65	1.8	.63
1980	.81	2.4	.56
1990	.86	3.2	.49

*City of Pittsburgh.
**Figures for males only.
† The labor force includes persons 14 years and older in the 1940, 1950, and 1960 decennial censuses. In 1970 it was changed to include persons 16 years and older.
Source: Census Tract Reports, U.S. Census Bureau

Summary & Theoretical Implications
Intra-Racial Comparison

On the one hand, the conservative explanations emphasizing a racially based culture-of-poverty argument have failed to explain how poor whites who reside in predominantly white concentrated-poverty neighborhoods have exhibited behaviors that are alleged to be culturally specific to African-Americans. On the other hand, liberal scholars have damaged the integrity of their structural arguments by not examining the circumstances of poor whites who inhabit concentrated-poverty communities. (Alex-Assenoh, 1995, p. 16)[24]

Political scientist Yvette Alex-Assensoh pointed out that both liberal and conservative analyses of the "underclass" fall short of providing a rigorous explanation for socioeconomic outcomes associated with concentrated poverty. This analysis clearly demonstrates that unemployment, low educational attainment, and single parent households are associated with poverty concentration, regardless of race. "Underclass" characteristics are not culturally unique to African Americans: the "behaviors" associated with the "underclass" and particularly with the black poor are found among the white poor as well.

However, the white poor were much less likely to live in a poor neighborhood. Only one of three poor lived in concentrated poverty and these neighborhoods comprised a relatively small fraction of the total. Most poor whites lived in neighborhoods with low poverty rates, as 94 percent of the tracts in Detroit and 85 percent of the tracts in Pittsburgh had a combined average rate of about 8 percent. Relative to Detroit however, Pittsburgh had a high degree of concentrated white poverty, especially in declining mill towns along the Monongahela, Ohio, and Allegheny Rivers. Pittsburgh is actually part of Appalachia, and the hills and canyons help create neighborhoods that are socially isolated to a certain degree. The white "underclass" neighborhoods in Detroit were more similar to black "underclass" neighborhoods than they were in Pittsburgh. In Pittsburgh the "underclass" neighborhoods have more nonfamily households comprised of students and single adults 18 to 64 years of age.

Middle-class black neighborhoods comprised a much smaller fraction of all black neighborhoods, but had average poverty rates about one-third of the black regional poverty rate. This evidence supports Wilson's argument that the black middle class had been able to move into neighborhoods that few poor inhabit. Particularly striking in Detroit is the high degree of intraracial segregation by educational level. Poverty affects those who suffer from low educational achievement; the black middle class is well educated.

Black medium-poverty, or working-class neighborhoods, comprised about two-fifths of all black neighborhoods in Detroit and Pittsburgh. There was not much discussion of these neighborhoods in the literature on the urban poor and they need to be studied further. They have the most in common with poor white neighborhoods.

Black high-poverty neighborhoods comprised the other two-fifths of all majority-black neighborhoods in both regions. Public housing projects in large measure accounted for the high levels of poverty concentration in these neighborhoods.

Prolonged marginalization from the mainstream economy, economic restructuring, and housing segregation via the efforts government, bankers, realtors, and private citizens, resulted in neighborhoods with high levels of joblessness in the 1990s.

INTER-RACIAL COMPARISON

Although black and white neighborhoods had very similar rates of home ownership and educational attainment, significant racial disparities remained in rates of unemployment and in the prevalence of single parent households. Race affected life chances. It played a strong role in creating and maintaining the "underclass" and marginalizing working- and middle-class African Americans from the labor market. Much recent empirical research has documented the persistence of housing market discrimination. These findings suggest a need for parallel efforts in the study of labor market discrimination.

We also need to know more about the institutional mechanisms through which employment discrimination operates. Historical studies of black workers in various occupations that shed light on the ways that these workers resisted discrimination and overcame barriers may be helpful to contemporary efforts in this regard.

POLICY IMPLICATIONS

The America in which they lived conceded nothing without a demand. If Afro-Americans expected a share of the nations bounty, then Afro-Americans would have to act in their own interests. (Lewis, 1991, p. 1)[25]

One implication of these findings, for policy, is that there is a need to focus on the demand side of the labor market (employer demand for labor), and not just the supply side (worker skill/education), as much of the literature on poverty and employment suggests. Racial disparities persist even when education and neighborhood conditions are controlled. The private-sector white-collar labor market is problematic and requires systematic policy intervention. I suggest three strategic areas in which policy initiatives may work to open up employment opportunities.

First, private and public sector collaborative, voluntary efforts to include African American workers and reduce occupational crowding and unemployment are necessary. Both individual private sector firms and associations (such as the Chamber of Commerce) should take a proactive role in this regard. One major issue to be dealt with is the problem of information regarding jobs. Acknowledging that part of the problem is not direct discrimination but a result of social segregation, African Americans need to be brought into the informal social networks by which many employers recruit employees.

Second, affirmative action efforts that broaden search, hiring, and promotion procedures remain vital to the reduction of racial economic inequality. Contrary to much public opinion that African Americans no longer need affirmative action programs, the evidence presented here indicates that there is still a very real need for this kind of intervention strategy.

Third, rigorous enforcement of employment discrimination law is necessary. The civil rights of African American and white female workers are continuously violated in the workplaces in Pittsburgh and across the nation. Is the Texaco discrimination case the tip of the iceberg? The Pennsylvania Human Relations Commission produces an annual report that documents cases of employment discrimination by race and gender. These reports reveal that numerous valid complaints are settled every year against employers. But underfunding prevents the commission from processing the full volume of cases it receives annually. This is also problematic for the federal Equal Opportunity Employment Commission, which has recently chosen a strategy of pursuing high profile cases such as Texaco. Enforcement efforts need the active support of government, nonprofit, and private sector interests.

There are some policy implications from this research in terms of education and employment that merit discussion. It is clear from this research that those in concentrated poverty suffer from low educational attainment, which results in marginalization from the labor market. Education for adults and youth is of primary importance on the supply side of the labor market. Even in low-poverty neighborhoods, one-fifth of the population over 25 does not have a high school diploma. Perhaps this is an area in which interracial coalitions can be formed to call attention to this problem and engage government and the private sector in designing policy solutions.

Another major policy implication from this research is that spatial dispersion of the poor would improve their life chances, thus policies which spatially disperse the poor may be a solution. This is being done by HUD now with the Gautreaux experiment in Chicago and with a program called "Moving to Opportunity" in several cities across the nation.[26] However, while dispersal may certainly improve the life chances of the youth who are enrolled in better schools and live in safer neighborhoods, often the educational attainment level of the adult members of the family is also problematic. Dispersion is not going to solve this problem.

Dispersion also does not address the fundamental problems facing the poor wherever they live. Respondents in an evaluation of the Gautreax experiment (a court-ordered public housing desegregation program in the Chicago area) "indicated that lack of transportation, lack of daycare, discrimination, and the higher skill levels that suburban employers expected still presented barriers to obtaining a good job in the suburbs."[27] The evaluation did show that adults had better employment opportunities in suburban nonpoor communities, which improved their level of motivation. However, even though employment was found, it was often at a job with wages too low to bring a family out of poverty.

The point of this is that although the findings do suggest that poverty concentration worsens life chances, the solutions do not necessarily lie in deconcentrating the poor. They lie in changing the socioeconomic status of the poor, regardless of where they live. This does not mean that residents of poor neighborhoods should not be encouraged to move to better surroundings. But policy makers must recognize that simply moving people around does not change their status and that we need to concentrate serious effort on removing barriers to employment.

NOTES

1 William Julius Wilson, *The Declining Significance of Race: Blacks and Changing American Institutions,* second edition (Chicago: University of Chicago Press, 1980); William J. Wilson, *The Truly Disadvantaged: The Inner City, the Underclass, and Public Policy* (Chicago: University of Chicago Press, 1987); William J. Wilson, *When Work Disappears: The World of the New Urban Poor* (New York: Alfred Knopf, 1996), p. 129.

2 Douglas S. Massey and Nancy A. Denton, *American Apartheid: Segregation and the Making of the Underclass* (Cambridge: Harvard University Press, 1993), p. 9.

3 Melvin L. Oliver and Thomas M. Shapiro, *Race, Wealth and Inequality in America* (New York: Routledge, 1997).

4 For a critique of these works, see the introduction to this volume by Trotter, Lewis, and Hunter.

5 Karen Joyce Gibson, "Income, Race, and Space: A Comparative Analysis of the Effects of Poverty Concentration on White and Black Neighborhoods in the Detroit and Pittsburgh Metropolitan Areas" (Ph.D. diss., Berkeley: University of California, 1996).

6 Ralf Dahrendorf, in his book *Life Chances,* discusses the ambiguity in the term chance as it is often construed to mean something purely probabilistic. Dahrendorf explains that Weber's concept means that chance is determined by social structure: "For Weber the probability of sequences of action postulated in the concept of chance is not merely an observed and thus calculable probability, but it is a probability which is invariably anchored in given structural conditions. Thus, chance means probability on the grounds of causal relations, or structurally determined probability." Ralf Dahrendorf, *Life Chances: Approaches to Social and Political Theory* (Chicago: University of Chicago Press, 1979), p. 65.

7 Hans H. Gerth and C. Wright Mills, *From Max Weber: Essays in Sociology* (New York: Oxford University Press, 1946), p. 181.

8 Allan G. Johnson, *The Blackwell Dictionary of Sociology: A User's Guide to Sociological Language* (Cambridge, MA: Basil Blackwell, 1995), p. 158.

9 William C. Levin, *Sociological Ideas: Concepts and Applications,* second edition (Belmont, CA: Wordsworth Publishing Company, 1988).

10 The goal of this analysis is to expand knowledge on a topic (comparative analysis of white and black neighborhood poverty) that is rarely studied. As exploratory analysis, it is beyond description but not at the level of causal analysis. According to Earl Babbie, exploratory techniques are used when little is know of a topic: "Much of social research is conducted to explore a topic, to provide a beginning familiarity with that topic. This purpose is typical when a researcher is examining a new interest or when the subject of study is itself relatively new and unstudied." Earl Babbie, *The Practice of Social Research, Fifth Edition* (Belmont, CA: Wadsworth, 1989), p. 80.

11 Wilson, *The Declining Significance, The Truly Disadvantaged,* and *When Work Disappears.*

12 Technical Documentation, 1990 U.S. Census Summary Tape File 3A, page A-9.

13 In 1991, the U.S. Census definition of the Detroit PMSA was changed to include Washtenaw County (Ann Arbor) and exclude Lapeer County.

14 John Kasarda. "Inner-City Concentrated Poverty and Neighborhood Distress: 1970–1990." *Housing Policy Debate,* 4(3): 243–302, 1993.

15 Sue G. Neal and Harold L. Bunce, "Socioeconomic Changes in Distressed Cities During the 1980s," *Cityscape: A Journal of Policy Development and Research* (1994).

16 William H. Frey and Elaine L. Fielding, "Changing Urban Populations: Regional Restructuring, Racial Polarization, and Poverty Concentration," *Cityscape: A Journal of Policy Development and Research* 1 (2), pp. 1–66.

17 University Center for Social and Urban Research, *The State of the Region Report: Economic, Demographic, and Social Trends in Southwestern Pennsylvania* (Pittsburgh: University of Pittsburgh, 1992).

18 J. Darden, *Detroit: Race and Uneven Development* (Philadelphia: Temple University Press, 1987).

19 Analysis of variance refers to a number of statistical techniques that vary depending on the nature of the data and design of the experiment. The technique tests for the effect of one or more independent variables on one or more dependent variables, as in linear regression. In ANOVA, the independent variable is a categorical (nominal) and the dependent variables are interval variables.

20 See essay in this volume by Richard Walter Thomas.

21 Dennis C. Dickerson, *Out of the Crucible: Black Steelworkers in Western Pennsylvania, 1875–1980* (Albany: State University of New York Press, 1986); Peter Gottlieb, *Making Their Own Way: Southern Blacks' Migration to Pittsburgh, 1916–30* (Urbana and Chicago: University of Illinois Press, 1987); John Hinshaw, *Steel and Steelworkers: Race and Class Struggle in Twentieth-Century Pittsburgh* (Albany: State University of New York Press, 2002).

22 Karen J. Gibson, William A. Darity, Jr., and Samuel L. Myers, Jr., "Revisiting Occupational Crowding in the U.S.: A Preliminary Study," *Feminist Economics* 4 (3) (1998); pp. 73–95. Also see essay by William Darity and Patrick Mason in this volume.

23 Claudette E. Bennet, The Black Population in the United States: March 1994 and 1993. U.S. Bureau of the Census, Current Population Reports, P20-480 (Washington, D.C.: 1995).

24 Yvette Alex-Assensoh, "Myths About Race and the Underclass: Concentrated Poverty and 'Underclass' Behaviors," *Urban Affairs Review* 31 (1): 3–19, 1995.

25 Earl Lewis, *In Their Own Interests: Race, Class, and Power in Twentieth-Century Norfolk, Virginia* (Berkeley: University of California Press, 1991).

26 James E. Rosenbaum, "Changing the Geography of Opportunity by Expanding Residential Choice: Lessons from the Gautreaux Program," *Housing Policy Debate* 6, (1) 1995: 231–69.

27 Lisa Aikman, "Fighting Poverty: Lessons from local Intervention Programs," paper prepared for the SSRC Policy Conference on Persistent Urban Poverty (Washington, D.C., November 9–10, 1993.)

Chapter 10

The Black Community Building Process in Post-Urban Disorder Detroit, 1967-1997

Richard W. Thomas

Introduction

Over the past three decades I have watched the African American community in Detroit suffer through protracted periods of poverty, crime and violence. Because I was born and raised in Detroit, I developed an early interest in the history of the African American community in the city. In 1976 I wrote my dissertation on the Black Industrial working class in Detroit.[1] During the next decade I took students in my undergraduate and graduate courses on tours of the city to observe firsthand the social misery of black neighborhoods as well as the courageous and persistent efforts of blacks to rebuild their communities.

In 1987 I wrote a small monograph for the Detroit Urban League, *The State of Black Detroit: Building from Strength*, which focused on the black self-help tradition in Detroit. Researching this monograph involved interviewing several African American leaders of community-based organizations founded during the first few years after "the 1967 Black Rebellion." These leaders and organizations were dedicated to empowering poor black communities. They were part of a growing network of African-American organizations and institutions involved in what I described in my 1992 book, *Life for Us is What We Make It: Building the Black Community in Detroit, 1915–1945*, as "the black community building process."[2]

As I explained in the book and later in a paper,[3] the black community building process is a conceptual framework for analyzing the black urban experience in industrial Detroit between 1915 and 1945. In my book I defined the black community building process as "the sum total of the historical efforts of black individuals, institutions, and organizations to survive and progress as people and to create and sustain a genuine and creative communal presence."[4]

Rather than exploring all the components of the black community building process discussed in the aforementioned works, I will focus on just one of the components of this conceptual framework: namely, how certain individuals, classes, institutions, and organizations played key or pivotal roles at various stages of the black community-building process during the post-urban disorder period in Detroit and the implications of these roles for public policy. It is my hope that the study of these elements might contribute to our understanding of the efficacy of a given change strategy or change agent at a particular point in time.

For example, during World War I, the black industrial working class was the main catalyst for the process of black community-building, thus setting in motion the economic and social transformation of the larger black community. While other classes, groups, individuals, organizations, and institutions also played roles during this stage of the process, such as the Detroit Urban League, churches, and ministers, the role of the black industrial working class proved pivotal because it was the vital link between industrializing Detroit and the black community building process.[5]

Each stage of the black community-building process in Detroit required creative responses and adaptations to both internal and external conditions. Often times, individuals, classes, institutions, and organizations that had successively shepherded the black community or some segment of it through one stage of development, were either unable or unwilling to do so at another stage. For example, during the World War I period, black churches in Detroit did not have the resources or trained personnel to tackle the complex problems of the migrants as efficiently as the Detroit Urban League. However, several black churches played a key role in the Negro Health Week campaigns.[6] Another example was black ministers who had patiently built relationships with the Ford Motor Company from World War I to the 1930s—relationships that proved vital to the employment of black workers in the Ford plants at that stage of black community building—were unwilling to accept unionization as a viable next step in the community building process. Other groups emerged at other stages of the process, such as protest and political leaders, and black business and self-help advocates, during the 1920s and 1930s. These groups energized the community with new visions of its destiny and demonstrated how each stage of the black community-building process in Detroit required creative responses and adaptations to both internal and external conditions.

Therefore, with the above in mind, this chapter will examine selected aspects of the black urban experience in Detroit between the urban disorder of 1967 and 1997, using one component of the community-building process: how certain individuals, classes, institutions, and organizations played key roles at various stages of the process and what the implications of these roles were for public policy.

The Detroit Urban Disorder of 1967: The Impact on the Black Community Building Process

The urban riots or "black urban rebellions" that rocked many central cities throughout the 1960s were rooted in both the deteriorating state of the urban economy and the relentless institutional racism that effectively kept blacks locked into ghettoes.[7] While the black Detroit ghetto of "Paradise Valley" was almost totally uprooted and shifted to the Twelfth Street area, where it "became the center of the 1967 riot," white workers were escaping to prosperous and grow-ing suburban communities, where many of them fought to keep blacks out.

White suburban officials, such as the late Mayor Orville L. Hubbarb of Dearborn, became famous overnight by promising to keep blacks out of white suburbs. As Grosse Pointe, Bloomfield Hills, Birmingham, and other white sub-urbs developed mechanisms to exclude blacks, Detroit's black ghettoes were forced to accommodate an increasingly impoverished black population.[8]

The housing market for blacks in Detroit was so restricted that in 1957, although representing 20 percent of the population, they received less than 1 percent of the new houses built.[9] This meant that those blacks who could afford to buy new houses were denied the opportunity. Thus, black ghettoes became more crowded.

As a result, during the 1960s blacks were living in "essentially the same places that their predecessors lived during the 1930s—the only difference [was] that due to increasing numbers, they occup[ied] more space centered around their traditional quarters."[10] Ironically, such residential segregation had once created the very conditions that fostered key aspects of the black community-building process such as black self-help activities.[11]

The black population density resulted in decreasing amounts of land available for public recreation. Since the black population was younger than the white, more recreation areas were required for black children. The lack of recreation areas, therefore, meant black "children and youth were growing up in areas in which the conditions were unfavorable for their development as individuals."[12] Lacking the space for fruitful recreation, many black youth took to the streets and to crime.

Poor housing and limited living space produced an unhealthy environment for education and for students and teachers alike. On the eve of the 1967 urban dis-order more than 50 percent of the black students (in black high schools) became dropouts before graduation. Seventy-two percent of all black students went to schools that were 90 to 100 percent black. During the 1966–67 school year, "only 30 percent of the eligible students were assisted by the 11.2 million in title 1 funds earmarked for inner city schools."[13]

As could be expected, these conditions generated a high rate of unemployment among black youth. Most black youth less than 25 years of age experienced a rate of unemployment between 30 and 40 percent.[14] Many of these youth fit the pro-file of the typical rioter during the 1967 disorder. They were teenagers who had lived in Detroit all their lives, had dropped out of school, and were slightly more educated than their peers. And they also had a great deal of racial pride.[15]

In July 1967 Detroit experienced the bloodiest urban disorder in a half cen-tury and the costliest in property damage in U.S. history. When it finally burned and bled itself out, 33 people had been killed, 374 injured, and 3,800 arrested. Close to 5,000 people were homeless, most of them black. More than 1,000 buildings had been burned to the ground. When the total damage was tallied, it soared to $50 million. During the riot, or "rebellion," white police deliberately shotgunned three unarmed black men in the Algiers Motel. Two of the men were shot while lying or kneeling.[16]

While a police raid on a "blind pig" triggered the disorder, the black "rebellion" itself "developed out of an increasingly disturbed social atmosphere, in which typically a series of tension-heightening incidents over a period of weeks or months became linked in the minds of many in the Negro community with a shared network of underlying grievances."[17]

Soon after the riot a staff worker for the Kerner Commissioner reported not being able to find a single black in Detroit who was "happy" concerning conditions in the city.[18] What some people called a "black rebellion" left a bad taste in everyone's mouth. White police feared blacks even more now that they knew how volatile the racial situation really was in Detroit, yet many white police officers continued rubbing salt in the wounds of racial discord. White police officers flocked into the National Rifle Association, using their membership to buy carbines in preparation for the next black rebellion. Private citizens began buying guns in record numbers, and suburban housewives were seen on T.V. practicing shooting handguns. However, some white suburbanites trembled as they heard the Detroit radical black preacher, the Reverend Albert B. Cleage, Jr., give a sermon on the black struggle at a memorial service for those killed in "the rebellion." "We are engaged in a nation wide rebellion," he declared, "seeking to become what God intended that we should be—free men with control of our destiny, the destiny of black men."[19]

BLACK COMMUNITY-BUILDING IDEOLOGIES AND STRATEGIES IN THE WAKE OF THE 1967 URBAN DISORDER

An assorted group of black leaders and organizations emerged and gained increased visibility in the wake of the 1967 urban disorder. From storefront community organizations such as Operation Get-Down, to established old-guard organizations like the Urban League, they all rushed to the aid of their bruised and battered, but far from subdued, community. Their ideologies and strategies for rebuilding the collective body and spirit of the community differed widely, but they were unified in the common belief that the black community had just suffered a major crisis and needed to be healed and empowered.

No matter how segments of the black community chose to describe the great human tragedy of July 1967, whether as an urban disorder or black rebellion, it marked a historic watershed in the black community-building process. To many militant blacks and restless unemployed youth, it was a defining moment in their lives. They refused to allow whites to define what happened during those bloody days in July as a mere "urban disorder." Rather, it was a "black urban rebellion," marking a revolutionary turning point in the lives of the "Black Nation." Black community-building became "Black Nation-Building."

Four months after the urban disorder, two black representatives of the Malcolm X Society, one of many militant black organizations that surfaced during this period, presented to the New Detroit Committee (to be discussed later) a statement calling for "control in black areas under black control." "We speak in the name of the Malcolm X Society, which represents the political side of the Black Revolution. We speak for the militants, not because we control or direct them—we do not—but because we are both part of the same revolution . . . and we therefore understand what the goals of the revolution are, that those goals are not being achieved, and what will happen if they are not achieved."[20] According to the statement, the "simple overriding goal for which black people fought this July [was] control: control of our lives and all those institutions which effect them. We have failed to gain control in the following areas: Police . . . Jobs . . . Housing . . . and economic control."[21]

The Malcolm X Society's statement elaborated on each area of black control. Regarding law enforcement, they wanted police in black areas to be under "black command." It would be unacceptable to have a black in the number three position in the police department if the person could not give "a single order to a line patrolman." If the black community could not get a black police commissioner, then, "the only acceptable approach to black control is the creation of a Board of Commissioners to replace the single Commissioner, with each Commissioner over a district and each Commissioner elected by vote in his District. This is an absolutely essential revision of police power. For the police force must cease to be a white people's army used to oppress black people." Furthermore, the statement continued, "police recruitment must be taken from the Department and placed under normal civil service like the recruitment for other city departments."[22] Significant changes in police recruitment of blacks would have to wait until the next stage of black community building in 1973 with the election of Coleman Young, the first black mayor of Detroit.[23]

Jobs for the black community occupied a central place in the community building ideologies and strategies of both militants and moderates. In fact, jobs had always been central to the black community-building process. The Malcolm X Society was not introducing anything new, other than a more militant ideological spin and policy strategy. "The power of the state must be used to create black employment and full employment, under black supervisors. . . . The notion of black people waiting on the largess of good white people is absurd." A full employment program was needed and should be "time-phased, enforceable and reviewable. Government particularly at the state and local levels, must commit itself to full employment at decent wages at a given time, list the unemployed and the underemployed, match these people with jobs on a compulsory basis, and subject, and subject the entire program to systematic in-process review by a board of black citizens." In addition, "where jobs at decent wages no longer exists, the government must open businesses directly to make such jobs."[24]

In the area of housing, the statement to New Detroit demanded that "a crash program of immediate relief for people in the rebellion area must be instituted. Hundreds are without adequate sanitation facilities, without hot water, without heat, without properly working windows and doors, and, in the case of city welfare recipients, without the means of withholding rent from landlords, since the rent is sent directly to the landlords." On their "must items" list, the Malcolm X Society statement placed housing codes enforcement and minimum housing standards along with "seizure and correction of bad housing." The group assured the New Detroit Committee that they were prepared "to support these charges and needs with specific data." They also expressed their concern that "such farces as the turning of 12th Street [the main site of the urban disorder] into a Boulevard while no concrete housing plans are implemented, must be halted."[25]

Again, many of the above concerns had been voiced before by traditional black organizations with a long and proven history of black community-building. The Detroit branch of the Urban League had voiced these concerns for decades,[26] but now in the wake of the most bloody urban disorder in American history, certain power brokers in the white establishment seemed more interested in the voice of the black militant, if for no other reason than to contain the groundswell of black resentment that caused so much property damage. Therefore, at least for a while, white power brokers and policy makers chose to listen to black militant organizations such as the Malcolm X Society.

The last item in the statement focused on black economic control. "Four million dollars are needed as a start to assist black churches, organizations, and businesses to get their economic projects off the ground between now and March 1, 1968. One-third of the money would be administrative grants; the rest, a revolving loan fund. The money must be made available on a simple and direct basis."[27]

Fortunately for black militants, white power brokers in Detroit were already setting up their own plans to address many of the same problems, and because of their fear of more riots, they were eager to involve black militants. Mayor Jerome Cavanagh and the business community realized that the government needed help in rebuilding the city and that help had to come from the private sector. On July 28, just a few weeks after the riot, the Greater Detroit Board of Commerce, representing "thirty-eight hundred businesses, professional, and industrial interests, asserted that since the riot had made it evident that the 'basic solution' for 'these problems' was jobs, its main response to the disorder would be an effort to cope with unemployment and underemployment in the city's disadvantaged areas." The Board promised to continue its support for the Career Development Center and "announced the formation of a Manpower Development Committee among other initiatives."[28] However, the opportunity for the black militant ideology and strategies for black community-building to be heard came with the establishment of the New Detroit Committee.

The New Detroit Committee was formed on July 27, 1968. According to historian Sidney Fine, "The most significant response of the private sector to the riot was the establishment of the New Detroit Committee." Mayor Cavanagh and Governor George Romney led the way to the formation of the committee by convening a meeting of 160 community leaders to discuss Detroit's "current and future problems." Both men had asked Joseph L. Hudson, Jr., President of the J. L. Hudson Company, which operated Detroit's largest department store, "to assume leadership of a new committee that would mobilize and coordinate the public and private resources necessary to help rebuild Detroit's social and physical fabric." While the composition of those who attended the July 27 meeting reflected a wide range of community representatives, black Congressman John Conyers "complained that 'the voiceless people in the community' were missing. 'I didn't hear anyone off of 12th Street' he declared. 'Anyone poor or black. And that's what triggered this as I understand it.'"[29] Conyers was right on target. The voiceless people in the community needed to be heard and major white leaders agreed. Gradually, the way was being prepared for the grand entrance of black militants and their vision of black community-building.

Mayor Cavanagh was basically concerned about how to "associate the commanding firms in the private sector with the well-being of the city to a degree that had previously been lacking. This, indeed, was the message the riot conveyed to the heads of the Big Three auto companies whom Cavanagh invited to the July 27 meeting." James Roche of General Motors declared that "We didn't do enough. . . . An extra effort is needed." Henry Ford II, agreeing, confessed, "I thought I was aware . . . but I guess I wasn't. This terrible thing has to wake us up." Concerned about the reputation of Detroit as a "model city," Lynn Townsend of Chrysler warned, "We'd better make an extra effort. Detroit is the test tube for America. If the concentrated power of industry and government can't solve the problems of the ghetto here, God help our country." Hudson felt that business leaders in the past had failed the city because they, as Fine explained, "left the city's problems to be solved by government and social workers and had absolved their responsibilities by writing a check. Now, he said, they had to involve themselves personally in the rebuilding of Detroit's social and physical framework."[30]

In order to move forward with the development of the committee, Hudson needed more than the input he had received from the July 27 meeting. He approached Huge White and James Campbell, two leaders of the Detroit Industrial Mission. Hudson trusted White's racial awareness and his understanding of the dynamics of organizations. White and Campbell conveyed their concerns that the new committee not turn into just another blue-ribbon committee. They felt that black militants should be included in the committee "with power and in a way [the militants] consider significantly." More important, they advised Hudson to consult with black community leaders to determine who should serve on the committee. He should, they advised, seek to include leaders of those organizations that the " 'established Negro leadership' was 'out of touch with' like the Inner City Organizing Committee and the WCO (West Central Organization), and men like Cleage."[31]

What followed was a brief involvement of selected black militants, with somewhat vague ideologies and strategies of black community building, on a committee with selected white power elites who had little understanding of the black community but who felt great fear of what alienated and frustrated elements of that community could do to the peace and stability of the city. At a meeting arranged by White and Campbell, Hudson asked the black militants to advise him on the "operation and membership of the new committee." One well-known militant, Milton Henry, expressed the view that black nationalists should be involved in the reconstruction of the city "in a civilized manner." Cleage stressed areas in which cooperation between blacks and the committee was possible. Lorenzo Freeman, a WCO organizer, disagreed with the idea of an interracial committee, saying it was "passé." His ideological position on the issue was clear: White leaders should "unblock" the white community and black leaders should "take care of the black community."[32] In one way this was vintage black-nationalist separatist ideology and strategy for black community-building. While simplistic and out of touch with the complex problems of black community—

survival and progress in a racially polarized and declining industrial city[33]—it was a voice that had to be heard.

The meeting generated other possible black candidates for membership on the committee. Black moderates at the meeting, such as Arthur Johnson and Damon Keith, contributed to this process as well. Finally, the selection of the committee was complete with "three militants among the nine blacks to be appointed to the thirty-nine member committees." Predictably, some people interpreted the inclusion of the three black militants as "blackmail." According to this view the New Detroit Committee was merely "rewarding lawlessness in adding the three militants to the committee." Hudson's response was: "We are responding to complaints against injustices." Later, the committee was accused of seeking "riot insurance" in embracing the militants." In response, Hudson could only comment that there could be no guarantee that another disturbance would not occur. He argued that the voices of the militants had to be heard and that he "hoped that they would 'sensitize' the whites on the committee."[34]

The participation of black militants and moderates on the New Detroit Committee contributed to an already tense conflict between the two camps complicating the process of community-rebuilding across ideological lines. William T. Patrick, Jr., a black moderate, characterized the militants as saying to whites, "Give . . . us what we want or we'll burn your damm house down, whereas the moderates said, Give . . . us what we want because it is the morally correct thing to do."[35] However, the real distinctions were far deeper, more complex, and potentially problematic for the future of black community-building. Never in its recent history had the black community experienced such ideological conflicts over the future of the community.[36]

The black militant community included Maoists, The Republic of New Africa (by far the most extreme of the black nationalist groups, as they advocated the "creation of a separate black nation on U.S. soil and independent black city-states within our big cities"), advocates of self-determination and followers of Malcolm X, including the young black nationalists and students who produced the Inner City Voice, among others.[37] Most of these groups and organizations rejected interracial coalition-building which, had played a vital role in the black community-building process.

On the other hand, the moderates included those who still had faith in integration and in traditional means of community building. The Trade Union Leadership Council (TULC), the Cotillion Club, the Booker T. Washington Businessmen's Association, the Michigan Chronicle, and the Council of Baptist Ministers, among others, had played leading roles in the community building process.[38] Some of these moderate black organizations felt slighted by their exclusion from the committee. The Booker T. Washington Businessmen's Association saw their exclusion from membership as an "affront" to them as an organization. The Council of Baptist Ministers shared the feeling, particularly since, as they viewed it, they spoke for "125 ministers and 150,000 communicants." Some people wrote letters protesting that "grass roots people from the immediate affected community had been excluded." The black newspaper, The Michigan Chronicle, joined in the chorus of complaints by proclaiming that the three black militants selected "did not speak for the "'man on the street.'"[39]

At this stage two major black organizations had emerged out of the ashes of the urban disorder or black rebellion with their own aspirations to play the pivotal role in black community building. The City Wide Citizens Action Committee (CCAC) and the Detroit Council of Organizations (DCO), "took the initiative in seeking to organize the black community after the riot." At their city-wide meeting on August 9, 1967 at the City-County Building, militant slogans of black revolutionary rhetoric held sway. "We must control our community or we won't have a community." Moderate Robert Tindal of the NAACP did not have a chance and was shouted down. Reverend Cleage, who had emerged as the "most influential spokesman for black militancy and black nationalism in Detroit following the riot," declared that "the Toms are out." He was elected chairman of the CCAC. One local magazine commented that the CCAC was "possibly the most broadly based Black Power organization in any city."[40]

Several weeks later the CCAC met to spell out its goals and objectives to "an overflow crowd" and received unanimous approval. Cleage told the gathering that there was no east and no west. "We are speaking for black people all over the city." He reported that a structure would be put together similarly to that of the New Detroit Committee. The gathering learned that "technicians and architects from many parts of the country have offered their services so that the needs of the black community, which has been articulated so many times, can finally be put into action." The CCAC, Cleage explained, was trying to "find out what other organizations are doing . . . and we're not trying to supplant them." Various committees reported on their tasks. The legal committee's responsibility was to be a "nuisance" whenever it saw black people getting unequal justice in the courts. A representative of the legal committee said that the only way to stop unequal justice was to unite. "We are just a part of this total revolutionary picture, all working together." The chairman of the consumer control committee said that the black community must remove the Chaldeans from the community because they were exploiting blacks. He informed the gathering that a price index sheet would be published to show people how the corner store prices compared with prices at major stores. The chairman of the redevelopment committee mentioned that three experts in housing and development would be working with CCAC and that any plan that displaced the black community would not be accepted. Other goals and objectives were also discussed.[41]

Hudson and the New Detroit Committee wasted little time embracing the CCAC. This was consistent with their policy of giving more credence to the militant segments of the black community. This recognition by the committee validated CCAC and no doubt encouraged Cleage to claim that for the first time in the history of the city, blacks had formed an "informal organization" that could speak for the entire community.[42]

The CCAC was basically a black militant organization with a black nationalist self-determination approach to black community-building. However members ranged from "those favoring self-determination or separation," the organization's principle thrust, to those advocating an "all-out war." (Whatever the black nationalist rhetoric, their community-building strategy was mainly funded by nonblack sources. For example, in September the Interfaith Emergency Council contributed $19,000 to CCAC. And the Interreligious Foundation For

Community Development presented the organization with a check for $85,000 because it felt that the CCAC was the first "black organization in the country" that had displayed "unity and determination" in seeking to "control the community" where blacks were in the majority.) Other aspects of CCAC's community building strategy (community control) included opening a store through its Black Star Co-op in December 1967, setting up a black-operated company to produce African dresses, and encouraging teaching of black history, culture, and languages in public schools.[43]

In a few months the CCAC had managed to put forward its ideology and strategy of community building. However, its pivotal role at this stage of community-building would not go unchallenged. Not long after the birth of CCAC and its recognition by Hudson and the New Detroit Committee, another group took to the field with a competing ideology and strategy of black community-building. The black moderates resented the attention the militants were receiving through CCAC as spokespeople for the black community. They held a special resentment for Cleage, who many moderates saw as a "Johnnie-come lately" to the black movement. The moderates, under the leadership of Reverend Roy Allan, President of the Council of Baptist Ministers, formed the Detroit Council of Organizations (DCO). They went after the middle and upper-class blacks connected with the professions, black trade unions, community leaders, and the Democratic party. A few months later, a host of the traditional black organizations that had played significant roles in earlier stages of black community-building joined the DCO. Among these were: the Cotillion Club, the Wolverine Bar Association, the Trade Union Leadership Council (TULC, and the NAACP. It was not long before they were able to claim to be the voice of 29 organizations and 350,000 Detroit Blacks."[44]

Predictably, Cleage accused the DCO of being "the creature of the white establishment, City Hall, and the UAW." Reverend Allen emphasized a key moderate ideology and strategy: "legal and peaceful means" could solve the problems of the black community. The DCO, Allan argued, was not "out of touch" with the rioters and "was not opposed to any black group, and wanted to work with the CCAC. . . ." However, he did characterize some of the CCAC's views and approaches to black problems as "irresponsible." The DCO's ideology and strategy for black community-building was essentially integrationist. It wanted "integrated schools, open housing, the building of low-cost homes for blacks, more blacks on the police force and improved police-community relations, and increased job opportunities for blacks."[45]

Another member of DCO, James S. Garrett of the Cotillion Club, expressed concern for unity among the two organizations, even as he recognized their "fundamental differences." In October, Garrett and Cleage spoke together before the Booker T. Washington Business Association, where they continued a discussion from the previous month. Obviously responding to the growing tension between the two organizations, both men agreed that unity was needed for the benefit of the black community. Garrett argued that in order to achieve unity "there must be efforts on the parts of all groups." He said, "I get a feeling here of antagonism that anything the DCO might propose is going to be knocked down. There are disagreements within each organization, too, but we have got to get together: we are all seeking self-determination." In response to a question concerning what issues DCO and CCAC could work on together, Cleage, speaking for CCAC, said that his organization "would support any black group that makes sense. We're going to love our black brothers in spite of what they might do." Garrett, in turn, suggested that one key program on which both organizations could work would be finding a black in each precinct to help DCO establish a civilian review board. He pointed out that DCO had met to "hear and consider CCAC proposals."[46]

In an article in the *Michigan Chronicle* in December 1967 entitled "Negro Community Must Strive for Unity, Not Division," Garrett attempted to explain the origins, philosophies, and strategies of the CCAC and DCO. He wrote, "The riot in July of this year made a tremendous impact on the Negro community. In essence, it was a great awakening to a vital need, the need to combine efforts to eliminate the cause and correct the conditions that brought about the explosive reaction. There was a sense of obligation and necessity permeating the air to draw closer together and work collectively toward common goals." Garrett commented on how the black community responded to the riot. "Many individuals, groups and organizations made numerous attempts to provide a means in an organized manner to effectively give purpose, substance and form to these aspirations. Some meaningful success has been achieved in this regard." He then listed CCAC as one of the "meaningful" successes.[47]

As a black moderate, Garrett demonstrated admirable generosity in his description of the process of how the militant CCAC came into being. "The City-Wide Citizen Action Committee came into existence following a meeting of people who felt they could best express themselves and pursue their objectives under the leadership and concepts of their own choosing." The Committee immediately set out to deal with grievances and problems in a manner determined as appropriate and necessary. The desire expressed was to bring about radical changes in the black areas for the primary benefit of black people. Accomplishing these objectives meant obtaining control of the areas with respect to business, and social and structural development.[48]

Garrett then turned to the DCO. He explained how the DCO emerged at about the same time as the CCAC. "It brought together organizations, groups and individuals whose ideas and attitudes were similar on methods and approaches for firm establishment of Negro citizens in the economic, social and political life of the whole community." The DCO's main objective was to assemble blacks in order to provide a source "for collective action in an organized fashion by its members and supporters . . . to act as a coordinating organization, to work toward the elimination of discrimination, and to carry out programs that will be basic to the specific needs of the city and the critical problems confronting the Negro community." Garrett acknowledged that both organizations wanted to "improve conditions for Negroes." But this was the beginning and end of what the two organizations had in common. As explained by Garrett, the "CCAC has advocated separatism. DCO does not, but rather endeavors to make Negroes an integral part of the total community."[49] In short, the CCAC advocated a black nationalist, self-determination-approach to black community building, in contrast to the DCO's traditional integrationist approach to black community building.

Whatever their differences, Garrett felt that they were not so "acute" between the two organizations "that they would or should prevent them from finding a way or develop[ing] . . . means to . . . plan together on common objectives. This would seem to be an important effort to make if the Negro community is to have some semblance of total unity." Garrett made a passing reference to another black organization, the Federations of Black Organizations and Individuals, formed earlier by Cleage to embrace both black militants and moderates. Unfortunately, it did not last long. Garrett expressed great concerns that instead of working together both organizations were "pushing farther apart." He cautioned that before matters became too serious, they should think about "why they exist and what was intended to be accomplished for the benefit of the community. Every effort should be made to undo any damage that has been done and to start anew."[50]

Summing up, Garrett then outlined what the DCO would do to cope with this "sensitive situation." The DCO would "cooperate as fully as possible where appropriate and feasible, in programs of groups and organizations whose goals are the same or similar in nature and to dissuade conflict, disunity, competition and confusion between and among organizations operating toward common objectives. . . . Whether these very important groups work together or apart, neither should interfere with the other's efforts to accomplish worthwhile objectives."[51]

Perhaps the CCAC and the DCO might have been able to work out some of their differences over how best to address the problems of the black community during this period if New Detroit had not complicated matters. The white leadership had become awed by the black militants on the committee and their tales of lives in the inner-city: One of the local white papers reported that "there was a hypnotic attraction for these middle and upper-class whites in dealing with the Inner City for the first time."[52] This explains why some of the white leadership were not interested in listening to the DCO; from where they stood, in their "awe" for black militants, the DCO did not represent the "real black" community. As Henry Ford, II put it, "the middle class black is as far removed from what's happening in the ghettoes as we are."[53]

In the next few months relationships among all the parties involved in this post-riot drama shifted back and forth, yet all the while illuminating the complex interplay between New Detroit, black militants, and black moderates in the larger unfolding process of black community-building. In its efforts to formulate policies and programs to address the "urban crisis," New Detroit continued working with and funding some black militant organizations while at the same time funding and supporting moderate groups such as the DCO. The ideological battle over the best approaches to community-building and what roles individuals, groups, and organizations would play at this pivotal stage continued along side of tried and tested moderate organizations such as the Urban League, the practical black nationalists, and community-based organizations such as the Inner-city Sub-Center and Operation Get-Down.[54]

COMMUNITY-BASED ORGANIZATIONS A
COMMUNITY-BUILDING PROCESS: PRA
STRATEGIES FOR THE LONG HAU

INNER-CITY SUB-CENTER

The Inner-City Sub-Center (ICSC) was one of several black community-based organizations that emerged during the post-urban disorder period. The Education Committee of the Association of Black Studies at Wayne State University established the ICSC to serve the needs of ghetto residents. The organization started in a store front on the east side of Detroit in 1967. The Center, as it was called, had a big picture of Malcolm X plastered on the front of the building. Black youth in the neighborhood were immediately attracted to the Center, where they were exposed to black history and culture, as taught by the Center staff. Speakers were brought in for discussion groups to help raise the consciousness of the black youth.[55]

In 1968 the ICSC was incorporated as a nonprofit organization. After receiving a grant from the Youth Opportunity Program in June 1969, the ICSC began operating several programs. At the end of the funding period, the organization received funds from New Detroit, Inc., which funded a one-year cultural-recreation program. The next source of funding for the ICSC came through United Community Services summer grants, Christ Church Cranbrook Grants, and "community support." A big break came in 1972, when New Detroit, Inc. funded the ICSC for a three-year developmental program. During the Fall of 1973, the ICSC moved to the old Thomas Lutheran School on Fischer. This provided the Center more space to expand to include preschool, senior citizen, and adult education programs, and a food co-op. As a result of this program expansion, the Center was able to provide services to more than 2,000 people a year. In 1976 the ICSC reached what they considered "a major turning point in its history," when after a successful campaign, they were able to move to a school building on East Forest.[56]

The restoration of the building was made possible through grants from the City of Detroit's Neighborhood Service Department, the Dayton/Hudson Foundation, the Kresge Foundation, and the Detroit Development Corporation. Additional sources of funding came from United Community Services, the State of Michigan's Neighborhood Education Authority, and the Comprehensive Youth Training and Community Involvement Program (CYTCIP) of New Detroit, Inc. Starting in January of 1982 the United Foundation Neighborhood Area Project funded the Center's Youth Development Program. This funding continued for four years. Finally, in the fall of 1985, the United Foundation admitted the Center into its "family" as a provisionary member. The Center was then awarded funds for its Neighborhood Development Program. In 1986 the Center was serving more than 10,000 community residents a year.[57]

Unlike some traditional black self-help organizations and institutions in Detroit and elsewhere, for which white financial aid often influenced "the Politics" or the basic philosophy of the enterprise, the ICSC emerged at a time when radical black community-based organizations could at least call some of the ots. These community-based organizations came about in the post-urban dis-order and "black rebellion" period of the 1960s. They had more credibility among poor blacks as well as among white funding sources than the older, more moderate black self-help organizations and institutions.[58]

Paul Taylor and David Booker, co-Directors of the ICSC, came out of the rad-ical black movement of the 1960s. Twenty years later (1987) the ICSC had not abandoned its commitment to the cultural values of the movement. In its pro-motional brochure the sub-center's philosophy was stated clearly: "To provide meaningful and relevant programs, services, and activities to the black commu-nity that will serve to raise the level of black consciousness, awareness and under-standing, and promote positive black values, pride, love, and respect among black people.[59]

Consistent with its philosophy, the ICSC developed a system that included the "Seven Principles of Blackness." This is how it appeared in its brochure:

The Sub-Center's Value System
NGUZA SABA
(Seven Principles of Blackness)
1. UMOJA (Unity). To strive for and maintain Unity in the family, community, nation, and race.
2. KUJICHAGULLA (Self-Determination). To define ourselves, name ourselves and speak for ourselves, instead of being defined and spoken for by others.
3. UJIMA (Collective Work and Responsibility). To build and maintain our community together and to make our Brothers' and Sisters' problems our problems, and to solve them together.
4. UJAMAA (Collective Economics). To build and maintain our own stores, shops and other businesses and to profit together from them.
5. NIA (Purpose). To make our collective vocation the building and develop-ment of our communities, in order to restore our people to their traditional greatness.
6. KUUMBA (Creativity). To do always as much as we can, to leave our com-munity more beautiful and beneficial than when we inherited it.
7. IMANI (Faith). To believe with all our heart in our parents, leaders and peo-ple, and the righteousness and victory of our struggle.[60]

The ICSC's impressive range of programs and activities was oriented around the needs of the black community. It housed a senior citizens program that included hot lunches, arts and crafts, field trips, group sessions, counseling, bus transportation, and daily exercise, among other activities. The adult program offered career counseling, an exercise class, sewing, upholstery, and G.E.D. preparation. There was also a hot breakfast program and a self-supporting co-cop store that was a model of economic self-help or "Ujamaa."[61]

In 1987 the ICSC's youth program formed the centerpiece of the organiza-tion. Throughout its history ICSC has focused on the problem of poor black youth, guiding them away from "the streets" to more socially responsible roles in the community. At the Center black youth studied African and Afro-American history and culture; learned African dance and choir; participated in arts and crafts, baseball, basketball, dance, gymnastics, and music; they also learned karate, obtained tutoring and counseling, and participated on a drill team. These youth-oriented programs reflected Taylor's belief that "when it comes down to the most significant thing we do, the main program has always been and always will be the youth program, because it's our contention that consciousness raising for the young folk . . . is the key to the struggle." If "resources get so tight that we had to scrap everything, we would scrap everything but the youth program," Taylor said.[62]

The Ujamaa boutique shop, housed in the Center, was operated by black youth between the ages of 14 and 21, who were members of the Ujamaa Club. They sold clothes and candy, held bake sales, and solicited donations. The youth and the Center divided the profits. The members of the Ujamaa Club met once a week on Thursdays for a couple of hours. As one staff member said, the program was "a self-help program . . . operated by youth."[63] During one of these meetings Paul Taylor gave an inspiring talk to the youth of the Ujamaa Club about how the principle of cooperative economics related to the black community. He started with an introduction to the concept of Ujamaa, explaining that Ujamaa money is used to benefit everyone. Taylor then described what he considered to be the three kinds of young adults "out here." One kind is the person who needs money but does not care how he gets it. "He will hit people on the head, he will break into folks' homes, sell dope on the corner(s), she will sell herself on the street. They will do any and everything because their thing is to get money by any means necessary." There is a second kind of young adult who understands that there are no jobs to be had. But he or she is "not going to break into people's houses, or sell dope on the corner, or sell herself on the street." This young adult will come home from school, talk on the telephone, look at T.V., keep off the corner, and when he or she needs money they will ask their parents or friends. This type of black young adult, according to Taylor, is the majority. "They are not going to do nothing wrong, but then again they are not going to do anything right in terms of try-ing to make some money or resources for themselves." These people will sit around waiting for summer jobs or their parents to give them some money. The third type of young adult, "the ones we are looking for," is not going to sell dope, or rob or sit around talking on the phone and looking at T.V." This kind of young adult is going to put his intelligence to work . . . is going to do some-thing . . . to make some money for themselves." They will baby-sit, shovel snow, mow lawns, go to the store for people. "This young adult might be doing any number of positive kinds of things to make an honest living." This is "the kind of young adult that we are looking for to join . . . the Ujamaa Club."[64]

Taylor then lectured the youth on the importance of the sales industry. "Believe me when I tell you everything is bought and sold . . . most anything that we can look at in this room was bought by somebody and sold by somebody. Unfortunately, historically we as black folk have been the buyers and not the sell-ers. We buy everything and sell nothing . . . This club . . . is designed to teach us some basic principles about sales. We want to become sales people . . . not just consumers . . . and that is really what the club is all about."[65]

The Ujamaa Club used three basic methods to make money. One was by direct sales through which club members approached people to buy merchandise by first explaining to them "what we are and what we are about and asking their support." Members received commissions for each sale. The second method involved group projects. Once a month the Club decided on a collective project to prevent Club members from being "caught up and hung up on . . . individualism. . . ." The profits from the group projects went into the Club treasury and were earmarked for the club's economic/business development programs, which helped to start businesses in the community, such as the Club's Boutique Shop. The goals, according to Taylor, were to "have as many businesses as we can have . . . businesses on each corner . . . We want to be able to control the businesses in our community through cooperative ownership. . . . We are trying to get away from the idea that 'as soon as I get . . . some money I am going to do something else.' . . . We are trying to get to 'we and us.' . . ." The third method was through donations. Taylor believed that when people heard about what the Ujamaa Club was "doing and trying to do," they would make donations to the club. According to Taylor, people would support the club because they were impressed with its objectives and goals and "wanted to see a group of young adults do something positive."[66]

After discussing the three basic methods of generating money, Taylor pointed out to the youth that most of the businesses in their communities were owned by nonblacks or "individualistic blacks. The latter being the opposite of Ujamaa's model of collective ownership."[67] Therefore, they, as members of the Ujamaa Club, should see the establishment of black businesses as community-owned.

In mentioning "nonblacks" Taylor was no doubt referring to the increasing numbers of Chaldean (immigrants from Iraq) store owners in the black community, stemming in large part from changes in the immigration laws of the 1960s and 1980s. Chaldean and other Middle Eastern grocers filled the vacuum in poor black inner-city neighborhoods created by the flight of large supermarket chains in the wake of the 1967 riot. While at the same time providing black inner-city black neighborhoods with basic foods, these "nonblack" store owners created a challenge for community organizers, like Taylor, who were trying to teach black youth the importance of black community business ownership as a key component of community building.[68]

Whatever one might think of the economic philosophy of the Ujamaa Club, it was certainly a vast improvement over the aimless and self-centered materialism of many black youth and adults. In terms of the community it represented, it was a refreshing alternative to those views held by many contemporary black business persons who saw blacks merely as consumers to be exploited instead of members of communities needing social and economic development. Taylor's example of "materialist" black businesses could have easily been a reference to the Motown Record Company, known to most black youth. By 1973, when it left Detroit, Motown was "the most successful black business in the United States, with $40 million in sales."[69] What did its success mean for black community-building in Detroit, however? As Suzanne E. Smith argues, "the false promises of black capitalism originates in the faulty assumption that capitalism can be enlisted to remedy racial inequality. Improving the racial conditions of society has never been capitalism's primary objective."[70]

This was implicit in Taylor's message to black youth, who needed to understand that a successful black-owned company based on the principles of capitalism alone could in fact be a deterrent to the community-building process in the inner-city. For example, as Smith explains so well: "On a more global level, Motown's decision to leave Detroit and the community that nurtured it not only participated in the larger process of the industrialization of the city, but ultimately created the circumstances that leave the company vulnerable to corporate takeovers in years to come."[71] Helping young blacks to see the difference was crucial in the way they viewed their responsibility to the poor and underdeveloped segments of their communities.

Taylor's discussion of the three kinds of black youth was an excellent way of helping young blacks to recognize that they had to take some, if not most, of the responsibility for improving their lives. The third kind of young adult Taylor discussed was the model that all black youth could emulate. The Ujamaa Club represented an excellent first step.

Several years later an interviewer put this question to Taylor: "You've been here twenty-two years. With such a great need do you feel you're on your own?" He replied that his organization had "never reached the goal of total self-sufficiency and self-support. We'd love to reach that goal. By the same token, we pay taxes to this city, we have been pretty law-abiding, and we feel that the government and people in society have an obligation to do some of these social programs." The message was clear: Although the ICSC advocated "self-help," the larger society still had an obligation to contribution to the programs. Taylor continued, "We plan to see to it that they fulfill that obligations. We're not going to give them the notion that all social-oriented programs should be on a self-help basis."[72]

OPERATION GET-DOWN

Located a few miles from the ICSC, Operation Get-Down (OGD) was the home of another black self-help community organization involved in the community-building process. Incorporated in September 1971 as a nonprofit organization,[73] the evolution of OGD as a black self-help community organization was not that different from that of the ICSC. Both organizations were founded by young radical blacks motivated by the spirit of Malcolm X and the black movement of the 1960s, and energized by the militancy of the posturban disorder and black rebellion period. In addition, both organizations used white resources to develop some of their most important community-based programs. Yet, neither organization compromised its commitment to the philosophy of black self-help as a community-building strategy.

OGD owed its existence to a long list of able blacks and whites who contributed to its development. In 1970 the United Methodist Church hired Barry L. Hankerson to work in Detroit as a community developer. Soon after his arrival, Hankerson; a group of young blacks, including the Executive Director, Bernard Parker, Jr.; senior citizens; college students; and families, held a community meeting. Other meetings followed which were held at St. Mark's United Methodist Church. These meetings included weekly leadership classes in which communication skills, problem solving techniques, conflict management and group motivation were taught. Hankerson played a leading role in conducting these classes. Parker also credited a local white minister for teaching him and other young blacks techniques of problem solving, long range planning, and self-development.[74]

In June 1971, the United Community Services Summer Project Fund financed the group's first summer project, which provided services to unemployed, "unoccupied" low income black youth. The group later adopted the language of these youth in naming the organization "Operation Get-Down." "Get-Down" referred to how well one was performing a particular activity, such as: "The brother was really getting down." Several months later, Operation Get-Down was incorporated. The group elected Barry Hankerson as Chairperson, and Bernard Parker and Frances Messinger as Vice-Chairpersons.[75]

From the beginning, OGD viewed itself as a self-help organization. According to one source, "Their guiding principle was self-help, the motivating force and motto was adopted from Malcolm X," who said: "I believe that when you give the people a thorough understanding of what confronts them and the basic causes, they will create their own program; and when the people create a program, you get ACTION!" Much like other community organizations at the time, OGD had to rely upon funding sources outside of its control. As the need for community programs increased and "funding . . . remained elusive," OGD was forced to function one day at a time. These were periods of rejection; their requests for grants were constantly turned down. It seemed that no one was willing to trust this unknown group of people from the east side.[76] But finally they came up with a solution solidly grounded in the black self-help tradition and an excellent example of community building.

This solution involved organizing a fund-raiser for Sickle Cell Anemia, which at the time had not gained much attention as a health problem peculiar to blacks. This approach provided citywide exposure for OGD while addressing a serious health need in the black community. They received support from Dr. Charles Whitten, who was already working with the Sickle Cell Detection and Information Center at Kirwood Hospital. OGD then approached WKBD (channel 50) for air time to produce a telethon for Sickle Cell. The T.V. station refused to go along with the project until OGD came up with 50,000 signatures on a petition. In addition, WKBD wanted OGD to come up with a nationally known personality to host the telethon and five well-known stars to be on the show.[77] After an enormous amount of hard work, OGD was able to meet these requirements. On May 28, 1972 Operation Get-Down's Sickle Cell Telethon was on the air waves. The show was from 6:00 PM to 2:00 AM and Sammy Davis, Jr. and Nipsey Russell were the co-hosts. The nationally known stars were: Muhammad Ali, Gladys Knight and the Pips, the Four Tops, Marvin Gaye, the Spinners, and Stevie Wonder. Other people involved in political, professional, and community life volunteered to provide technical and other assistance. The telethon proved a great success and raised more than $250,000 for the Kirwood Hospital Sickle Cell Detection and Information Center. As a result, OGD gained the needed exposure and "served notice to the City of Detroit that they were a serious and committed organization."[78]

The successful telethon demonstrated the role that a black community-based organization could play in the process of community building. This demonstration probably convinced New Detroit Inc. to not only award OGD a grant, but also purchase a building for the organization. In November 1972 OGD held their first open house. Larry Doss, New Detroit Inc.'s President, was the keynote speaker. OGD extended an invitation to the community to become involved in a range of programs, including Head Start day care, adult education (G.E.D), a youth recreation project, and a community development program. These programs contributed to the reduction of gang violence in the 1970s and improved relationships between the black community and the police on the east side. OGD increased parent and community involvement at Kettering, Burroughs, and A. L. Holmes schools and obtained recreation areas on the east side for youth. The organization also played a key role in the establishment of the Harper Gratiot Multi-purpose Center.[79]

Throughout this early period of growth and development, OGD continued to view itself as a self-help organization. It secured grants from outside sources but never forgot Malcolm's advice about the role of people in creating their own program. As a black self-help organization, OGD tried to rely upon black resources as much as possible. In a 1987 interview, Bernard Parker, who succeeded Barry L. Hankerson as OGD's Executive Director in 1974, said that "there are enough black dollars out here to support black programs; we just have to tap them."[80] OGD used this approach by focusing on black entertainers as a source of financial support. It also raised money through cabarets, dinner sales, and such productions as "Crack Steppin'" and "Rhythmn's Blues" by play writer Ron Milner. Milner had worked closely with OGD over the years in the writing, producing, and touring of several plays. For example, Milner's play, "Crack Steppin'" was created and written with the assistance of some young blacks associated with OGD. They performed in the play, which had a successful tour in Detroit and in other cities. Other plays followed, demonstrating once again how blacks with imagination could build upon strengths within their own community.[81]

By 1976 OGD had evolved into one of the most impressive self-help black community organizations in the nation. While still securing grants "the organization's guiding principle of self-help continued to prevail. . . ."[82] That year the organization moved into a larger facility at 9980 Gratiot. They received a grant from the City of Detroit that enabled them to greatly expand their services and participation. OGD could now serve daily hot meals to more than fifty senior citizens through their Food and Friendship Program. Other services included transportation to and from the Center, field trips, exercise classes, and art and craft classes. An expanded recreation program included basketball and baseball teams, drill team, karate classes, sewing, dance and drama, and preschool.[83]

In 1973 Operation Get-Down started a food co-op. According to *Black Enterprise,* this co-op "has become the nation's largest inner-city food cooperative."[84] Referring again to the teachings of Malcolm X, Parker explained "Malcolm said people who control their food control their minds. . . . If people can control what they are eating, then they control what they are going to eat, how they're going to eat and where they're going to eat. There's power in that."[85]

The food co-op grew out of a 1970 boycott of a store for selling poor-quality food. Fifty families pooled their money and purchased vegetables and produce in bulk at lower prices than at grocery stores. Famous vocalist Gladys Knight contributed $500 to get the project going. Detroit area residents on welfare and social security, and the unemployed received free membership in the co-op. Others paid a membership fee of five dollars a year. Starting as a single small store, the co-op soon expanded to five other sites located in churches and Detroit Neighborhood Service Centers. In 1986 the largest of these sites, located at the SW Center on Grand River, was serving 1,200 people a week.[86]

A hunger crisis existed in Detroit long before it was officially declared so by Mayor Young and Governor Milliken in 1981. Although OGD had been feeding the hungry for years, the hunger crisis in Detroit worsened in the early 1980s. OGD's food co-op led the way in "the battle against hunger." The organization received a grant from the State of Michigan authorizing it to "utilize their cooperative food system to network (and provide) central purchasing and warehousing for many agencies and churches throughout the city." By this time OGD's food co-op had acquired much knowledge about and experience in feeding people. During this period of the "declared" hunger crisis, OGD provided "emergency food not only to their co-op members, but to anyone in need in the City of Detroit."[87]

In 1985 OGD received a grant from New Detroit, Inc., that allowed it to serve senior citizens with food vouchers. Through this arrangement senior citizens obtained fresh food each month from OGD's food cooperative system. That same year the City of Detroit Health Department asked to join OGD's food co-op system so that their expectant parents could obtain fresh food. Clearly, by this time, OGD's food co-op had earned "a great reputation in the food business."[88]

Throughout its history OGD has believed in and operated on the principles of black self-help and building from strength. The food co-op provided the foundation upon which OGD was able to leverage existing resources to develop and attract other resources. The quantum leap in utilizing this building from strength principle occurred when OGD obtained 40,000 square feet of refrigeration and a fleet of semi-trucks, vans, and cargo wagons that provided OGD with the capacity to receive, store, transport, and distribute more than three million pounds of food a year. This capacity and confirmed success explained why OGD received a contract from the Michigan State Department of Social Services to supply food to 22 food shelters throughout Wayne County and a state grant of $748,000 to provide free fresh food to 9,000 families each month through emergency shelters.[89]

Operation Get-Down's commitment to black self-help was not restricted to Detroit and Michigan. The organization also contributed to the economic well-being of black farmers by purchasing millions of pounds of food from them. In addition, Parker shared his expertise on food co-ops with people around the country.[90] The co-op model of black self-help was central to Parker's view of the survival of blacks in the future. "The developments of the co-op is essentially an economic issue," he argued. "It gives us the power to make legitimate economic choices about where to shop and spend our money."[91]

In keeping with its principles of self-help, OGD's food co-op was self-support-ing, a fact that pleased the Executive Director. "Our food co-op now is completely independent. It received no funds from anyone . . . the building (co-op and ware-house facility) on Harper is completely supported through our co-op efforts. Our staff there is completely maintained and supported through the co-op. No federal funds or outside funding goes into that operation . . .," he said in 1987. While Parker understood the general need for outside funding, he explained the poten-tial pitfall of reliance on such funding: " [w]hat happens is that they take . . . (their) grants and they forget about the fund-raising aspects." As a result, the organization dies as soon as the external funding ends.[92]

One of OGD's newest programs, B.I.R.T.H. (Babies' Inalienable Right To Health), developed in September 1985 "as a response to the rate of infant mor-tality and morbidity in the City of Detroit," was run as a pilot during the sum-mer of 1986 and supported entirely by funds raised through various activities. Although B.I.R.T.H. received a $20,000 grant from New Detroit, Inc., in early 1987 for assistance in transporting clients back and forth between the Center and their doctor's appointments,[93] the emphasis was always on self-help.

For years OGD had been requesting membership in the United Foundation family. Finally in 1986 they were accepted as an associate member. The first grant they received enabled them to provide both fresh food and vitally needed nutri-tional counseling to low-income expectant mothers during the summer of 1985.[94] However, this long sought-after membership did not dampen OGD's spirit of self-help. In 1987 OGD was in the process of reopening an abandoned meat processing plant formerly owned by Chicago Beef, a company that had moved out of town. OGD acquired the building, which was completely equipped for meat processing. The plan was to start packaging, labeling, and selling chick-ens and chicken parts to local stores, and then expand to major chains under their own label. To learn about this process, OGD visited Holly Farms' major meat packing operation in Sweetwater, Texas. After the visit, they came away con-vinced that they had what was required to start their operation. As stated by Parker, "the whole idea is to keep generating funds to support our program."[95]

OGD's hope at the time was to be able to duplicate their east side social serv-ices on the west side, for people who did not have transportation to the original facilities, and to do this without relying on government grants. Later perhaps, external grants could be used to "maintain it and increase the services."[96]

The problems of black youth had not been neglected in the expansion of OGD's food co-op and other programs. During the 1985/86 fiscal year, OGD organized and hosted several events aimed at black youth. These included a youth conference at Wayne State University, featuring Kim Fields and Taurean Blacque as keynote speakers, (this attracted more than 350 young adults); a Teen Resources Fair at which 42 youth-oriented human services agencies participated; and the B.I.R.T.H. program already mentioned.[97] Four teenage mothers worked as assistants in this program, which provided expectant mothers on-site meals and prenatal care, which included childbirth education; medical care; childbirth preparation; individual, family, and group counseling; family planning; crisis intervention; and transportation for medical visits and field trips. G.E.D and A.B.E classes, education in daily living skills, home management assistance, and parenting skills were other aspects of B.I.R.T.H.[98]

In January of 1987 the B.I.R.T.H. Program held an all-day orientation covering its prenatal programs. About thirty black pregnant and parenting women participated in a half-day orientation presented by B.I.R.T.H.'s Proejct Director, Veda Sharp. Some young fathers also attended the sessions.[99]

The spirit of service and devotion that permeated the B.I.R.T.H. program was evident in the person of Ms. Henriatta Reaves. B.I.R.T.H. provided the atmosphere of caring that many of the teenage mothers had never experienced. Reaves said, "This is the first time that people really cared about them. . . . We show them a different side of life because a lot of them have come from home environments where there is a lot of violence—physically and verbally."[100] Teenage mothers and expectant mothers in the program interviewed by the author expressed similar feelings about the "caring" environment of B.I.R.T.H. As one young mother said "I came to B.I.R.T.H. because of the staff that is here. . . . You can sit down and talk to them . . . and the people in . . . class you can sit down and talk with them . . . because your parents are not the type who would like to sit down and talk with you about your problems." This particular young mother enrolled in the program on her own. Another young mother enjoyed the program because, in her words, "it is easier to talk to people around my own age than talking to an adult . . . here they [the staff and participants] makes me feel like I am wanted . . . makes me feel that someone cares about me."[101] "The program," she said, "made her a better mother and a better person." "Here I found out it is more than just . . . changing a baby's diaper . . . and cleaning the baby. . . ." As another young mother explained, "to be a parent you have to give the baby love, understand the baby's feelings, and what the baby is going through, too . . . the baby might be depressed because it feels its mother is feeling that way too. Here they care about your feelings . . . and treat you just like you are at home." Another young mother echoed the same: "There are a lot of nice people here . . . they make you feel welcome . . . it is a nice place to be for a person like me."[102]

In response to the author's question, "What are some specific things you want to get out of the program?," several young mothers responded: "To learn how to take care of my baby and get my G.E.D . . . finish my GED . . . finish my curriculum . . . to accomplish something to do with law . . . to be a better mother than I am now because I fly off the handle real easy. . . . I want to be around people where I can learn to control my temper and raise my daughter right, better than I am raising her now." The author then asked these young mothers to discuss their short and long range goals. One wanted to be a computer technician, another aspired to be a nursery assistant and then a registered nurse. Several planned on completing high school. One young mother planned to return to college if she could find a good baby sitter, but first she wanted to find a job.[103]

These testimonies of young black mothers and expectant mothers in the B.I.R.T.H. program cannot help but touch the heart of those who lament problems plaguing black youth in general and black teenage mothers in particular.

The two black women running the B.I.R.T.H. program, Veda Sharp and Henrietta Reaves, were certainly building community by fostering an environment in which teenage mothers and expectant mothers could get the love and care to mend and strengthen their lives and the lives of their children. The B.I.R.T.H. program was one of the vital links in OGD's chain of human services and was one of the best examples of black community-based organizations in the community building process.

By 1991 OGD had become a United Way agency, with close to a $2000,000 annual budget and with a staff of about 70 people. The programs included a health clinic, emergency food programs, a program for pregnant teenagers, a day-care program, an adult education program, an after-school youth program, and a homeless warming center. In addition, OGD operated "a caravan that goes out every night to feed about 400 homeless people." According to Parker, OGD was "the largest community agency of that nature in the nation."[104]

The transition to being a United Way agency enabled OGD to leverage resources to enhance and sustain its community building programs. In keeping with the best traditions of accountability and community-based leadership as the core guiding principles of community-building from the bottom-up, the organization had monthly community meetings in which "people come in and direct us." "They tell us what the problems are and what we should be doing." A fifteen-member board of directors set policies and advisory committees over each program provides daily directions.[105]

In 1990 Parker was elected to the Wayne County Board of Commissioners where he represented the constituency around the OGD community on the east side of Detroit. This was yet another key stage in community-building for both Parker and the OGD. "I ran on my experiences in Operation Get-Down and said that I wanted to take that experience down to government: self-determination and helping people to solve their own problems. My campaign was very grassroots."[106]

As a commissioner, Parker was finally in a position to influence public policy. In his first year in office, Parker opened up the first community office of any Detroit commissioner. Half of his staff were placed in the neighborhood, addressing constituent concerns such as "cutoff of utilities and complaints about tax bills"[107] In 1997 Parker was still involved in projects that contributed to black community-building as well as the betterment of the larger society.

PREVENTING BLACK YOUTH VIOLENCE AND COMMUNITY BUILDING: THE WORK OF SOSAD

In the mid 1980s black teenage violence in Detroit emerged as the major challenge to community-building. Despite great strides in black political empowerment in the city, which had culminated in the election of Coleman Young as the first black mayor of Detroit. The black community was losing the fight for the lives of its black youth.[108] In one sense, the future of black Detroit embodied in its youth was bleak: the black youth population was declaring war on itself, maiming and killing. The larger black community looked on helplessly as the seeds of black tomorrows were destroyed.

More than 300 youth were shot in Detroit in 1986 by other youth, 41 died. As the year ended, the black youth death toll had jumped 32 percent over the 1985 youth death tolls (in that year 32 youth died). By April of 1987, 99 black youth had been shot that year. Ten died.[109]

In the midst of this carnage of black youth, a black mother, Clementine Barfield, whose 16-year-old son was killed in the summer of 1986, founded an organization appropriately named Save Our Sons and Daughters (SOSAD). Ms. Barfield, along with other black parents, "decided to go beyond mourning and began working together to create positive alternatives to violence throughout the community." A little over a year later, SOSAD began to fill a vital role of community-building in the midst of black youth violence.[110] At a time when black youth violence was destabilizing many black neighborhoods, SOSAD moved onto the center stage of the struggle to save black youth.

Barfield initiated a local community-based movement that became a national peace movement, with chapters in Fresno, California; Louisville, Kentucky; and Washington, D.C. SOSAD's approach to youth violence centered around counseling and training in violence prevention, crisis intervention, multicultural conflict resolution, gang redirection, and peer and bereavement support. The organization's Crisis Intervention Program won praises not only in Detroit but across the country "as the model grassroots initiatives used to address the issues of trauma, grief, and conflict." This included counseling for survivors and their extended families and friends and a 24-hour crisis hotline for survivors of homicide and others who had been traumatized by violence.[111]

SOSAD responded to school violence by providing Crisis Response Teams "throughout the community to respond swiftly and meaningfully to crises, as they arise." The increase in black youth violence during the 1980s in Detroit created a demand for these teams to "perform critical incident debriefing and follow-up responses after a tragedy." For example, after children witnessed a homicide or had people close to them killed, SOSAD teams went to their schools and conducted eight weeks of crisis counseling.[112]

In July of its first year (1987) SOSAD sponsored a march described by its founder as "historic for some and a resurrection of hope for others." The mobilization for the march began several weeks earlier with a pre-march youth rally at the state fair grounds. The premarch notices preached out to the public: "Kids Killing Kids" and "Getting to the Root of the Problem." Although only 200 people attended the June 13 pre-march youth rally, some youth asked the organizers if other such rallies could be held each week. SOSAD responded to this request by planning another youth rally two weeks later at the island park, Belle Isle. This pre-youth rally was a big success. As one observer described it: "Even a sudden thunderstorm didn't dampen the spirits of the 500 in attendance." Much of the success of this rally was no doubt due to the participation of "Just Chillin'" Blake & Hines and NU-Boiz, recording artists from Motown.[113]

The build-up for the march stimulated the process of community building around black youth violence, as other black organizations rallied to lend their support to SOSAD's efforts. These included the City Sub-Center, Association of Black Social Workers, Operation ACT, Nation of Islam, East Side Optimists Club, Detroit Urban League, Community Action Program (formerly Operation

Get-Down) along with "countless churches and block clubs all over the city." The organization for the march involved youth volunteers, which certainly provided a healing effect for those youth who had had close relatives killed. Kendra Dixon, Jesse Fair, and Tiki Higgins were three youth volunteers with first-hand knowledge of violence and bloodshed. Kendra's brother Eric had been shot in October 1986. Jesse was lucky to be alive— he had been shot with a .350 Magnum in February of the same year. In their "Special Pre-March Issue" of the SOSAD Newsletter, a writer explained the importance of the march for the entire community: "Now we have organized the July 18, March so that we can bring thousands of Detroiters together to say that Kids Killing Kids must stop. This is not just SOSAD's March: it is a March to preserve our future which is in our children."[114]

After the march, Clementine Barfield commented that SOSAD's "attempt to stop the bloodshed resounded around the world as reporters from Washington, D.C. and London, England marched with us." But Barfield had to concede that SOSAD's voice "was not loud enough here at home because the death toll [was] still rising." Every day, she lamented, "the body count goes higher. The movement for change must rise along with it." Notwithstanding the rising death toll, Barfield claimed that since the organization of SOSAD, "people in Detroit no longer feel so powerless and hopeless. They are beginning to think that something can be done." Writing in the August 18, 1997 newsletter, Barfield informed readers that SOSAD had a "tremendous responsibility because so many people are looking to us for answers." She reported that people calling SOSAD are constantly, asking, "Why aren't you doing something?" They do not "seem to realize," she wrote, "that we are mothers who have lost our children, that we are victims too—and that much is already being done because we have overcome despair and are trying to reach out and help others."[115]

SOSAD's practice of reaching out provided comfort to families of children who had been killed. The June 1987 issue of the newsletter mentioned that SOSAD mothers were continuing this vital role by giving presentations and organizing talks at middle and high schools in the Detroit metropolitan area. In addition, they visited the Maxey Boys Training Camp, a correctional institution and appeared on radio and television programs.[116] Barfield also understood that parents with children in correctional institution had "lost their children, too." She saw the need to make a healing connection between the parents of murdered kids and those parents whose kids murdered kids. "We all have to reach the point where we reach out and touch [each other] with love. We have to teach them love. Society is only showing them the negative aspect. We must show them the positive aspect. If we are going to do real healing, children have to see us coming together." She went on to explain that "the perpetrator is a victim too. Anybody who does these things has no self-esteem. The first thing kids say is that "my life isn't worth much." In an encouraging note to both sets of mothers, Barfield said, "We need to make changes in how we view ourselves and know that we can make changes. Once you feel that, you can do anything. Children will stop killing one another. . . . If we mothers can do it (make changes in how we view ourselves) we feel that everybody can do it."[117]

In addressing the grief of both parents of murdered kids and parents of kids who murdered kids, Barfield was building community at the deepest, most wounded and fractured level. She knew only too well how easy it could be to declare war on the relations and kin of the perpetrator. Instead she chose to use the guiding principles of SOSAD to break the cycle of victim-perpetrator, with love and understanding.

For the next ten years SOSAD gradually emerged as the leading community organization working to prevent youth violence in the black community and to offer comfort for families of slain children. In 1988, SOSAD's programs included prayer breakfasts for families of slain children; conflict resolution; a 24-hour poetry reading entitled, "Words Against Weapons"; "alternatives to violence" exhibits by local artists; among others. Barfield and SOSAD appeared on the television news program 20/20 in September 1988. Sadly, at year end, as Barfield pleaded for no shooting on New Year's Day, 52 kids younger than 17 years old had been killed.[118]

Each year SOSAD went deeper into the trenches of killing, despair and mourning, lifting spirits and building community. The year 1989 was barely two months old before SOSAD hosted still another breakfast for families of slain children, a testimony to the continue ritual of youth killings. In March, it held a "workshop for bereaved persons and those who care for them." Later in the year it organized a rally for volunteers and a dedication ceremony for the planting of a Hope Garden.[119] People needed something to symbolize hope to supplant the constant reminders of the death toll of children.

In 1990 SOSAD sponsored the film "Stop the Madness," a documentary about youth violence. In April the area chapter of Women's Action For Nuclear Disarmament awarded Clementine Barfield the annual Peace Day Award.[120]

Seven years later SOSAD was still working in the trenches and providing comfort for families, but by this time it had grown into an internationally known organization with an impressive track record for its work in preventing violence. As a result of Barfield's efforts and the activities of SOSAD, the peace movement for the prevention of violence began to attract people from around the world: Reporters representing television, magazines, newspapers, and radio from around the United States and Europe found their way to the SOSAD offices. Mothers from SOSAD have appeared on the Oprah Winfrey Show and other national television programs. One of the many promising outcomes of the work of SOSAD is that dozens of college students each year spend their "alternative spring break" with SOSAD "working with school children to build the peace movement."[121] This author attended the Tenth Anniversary Breakfast Celebration on November 13, 1997[122] as a historian; as I witnessed parents crying and carrying pictures of their slain children, however, I realized that I was also the parent of black children and youth now grown, fortunate enough to have been spared the violence that gave birth to SOSAD.

Conclusion and Implications for Social Policy

Since the urban disorder of 1967, the black community in Detroit has explored a wide range of community building strategies, beginning with black militants and white leaders on the New Detroit Committee and black moderates challenging the militants over which ideology and strategy of community-building would prevail. Because of the urban disorder, or as the militants put it, "the black rebellion," a crisis occurred at this stage of community-building. For a while, the moderates had lost their influence among the youth segments of the community. They had also lost credibility with the white leadership class which endorsed the militants' approach to community-building. What ensued was a conflict between two competing ideologies and strategies of community-building.

The 1967 urban disorder traumatized both the traditional black leadership in Detroit and white policy makers, and fueled ideological conflicts between segments of the black community. White policy makers had to confront the social and economic consequences of their past policies, and the traditional black leadership had to face up to their failure to connect sufficiently with the poorer sections of the black community. This leadership also had to confront the painful fact that they did not have any clear vision of community-building before or immediately after the 1967 riot. Thus, they could not contribute to a visionary social policy to guide the black community in the wake of the riot. Few policy makers had a long-term vision of black community-building in economically depressed black neighborhoods. Black militants, who for a while had the ear of influential policy makers, also failed in the end to come up with practical community-building strategies. Few of these militants developed long-term community-building strategies.

Even the late Mayor Coleman Young, who represented a quantum leap in black community building in the political sphere and did his best given the economic circumstances he inherited, tended to view black community-building from the perspective of top-down development.[123] This was hardly visionary social policy.

For the long haul the future of effective community-building during this stage would take place at the neighborhood level. As the problems of urban decline intensified and the social and economic conditions of inner-city blacks worsened, few policy makers had answers. Fortunately, visionary grass-root leaders who had lived through decades of failed social policy and understood some of the inherent limitations of the policy community decided to act on their own. Rather than wait for policy makers to ponder and act, they decided to make a difference. They became change agents.

Paul Taylor, Bernard Parker, and Clementine Barfield emerged at the stage when black and white policy makers had largely failed poor black youth. Their policies had little relevance for the most vulnerable members of the black community. Taylor, Parker, and Barfield went beyond traditional social policies of dealing with the problems of inner-city black youth and developed strategies aimed at saving them. Both Taylor and Parker taught black youth to love themselves as black people and dedicate themselves to building black communities. Their focus was on building self-esteem among black youth, giving them a sense of mission, as a prerequisite to building communities. This was linked to a clear vision of their role in the community building process.

Parker demonstrated best how to develop specific programs targeted to specific segments of the black community. His genius was in crafting self-help programs to give blacks a sense of their own ability to change their conditions.

Parker did this at the same time that he linked self-help and the accessing of external funds to the process of community building.

Though the youth violence of the 1980s was well on its way to seriously crippling the black community, traditional policy makers had few programs to effectively address this dilemma. The problem was not that policy makers did not care, but that their approaches were irrelevant. It took someone out-side of the policy making community to address the issue. That someone was Barfield and the vehicle was SOSAD. Had she and other black parents of murdered kids waited for policy makers to respond, far more kids would have died.

What policy implications can be drawn from the work of these grass-roots lead-ers of community building? One clear implication is that policy makers during this period tended not to be on the cutting edge of community-building in eco-nomically depressed black neighborhoods. They could not always think outside of the box of traditional policy responses to critical problems.

Another policy implication is that policy makers in the field of urban poverty need to spend more time working with and learning from those grass-roots leaders who *are* on the cutting edge of community building in some of the most economically depressed areas of the inner-city. These brave leaders need support from the policy community without losing their unique views of how best to empower poor black communities.

NOTES

1 Richard W. Thomas, "From Peasant to Proletarian: The Formation and Organization of the Black Industrial Working Class in Detroit, 1915–1945" (Ph.D. dissertation, University of Michigan, 1976).

2 Richard W. Thomas, *Life for Us Is What We Make It: Building Black Community in Detroit, 1915–1945* (Bloomington: Indiana University Press, 1992), p. xxi–xiv.

3 Richard W. Thomas, "Community Building: A Holistic Conceptual Framework For Black Urban History, Black Detroit, 1915–1945," 79th Annual Meeting of the Association for the Study of Afro-American Life and History, Atlanta, GA, October 12–14, 1994.

4 Richard W. Thomas, *Life for Us Is What We Make It: Building Black Community in Detroit, 1915–1945* (Bloomington: Indiana University Press, 1992), p. xi.

5 Ibid, p. 35.

6 Ibid, p. 82.

7 National Advisory Commitee Report on Civil Disorders (New York: Bantam Books, 1968).

8 B. J. Widick, *Detroit: City of Race and Class Violence* (Chicago: Quadrangle Books, 1971), p. 143.

9 Ibid, p. 143.

10 Albert J. Mayer and Thomas F. Hoult, *Race and Residence* (Urban Research Laboratory, Institute for Urban Studies, Wayne State University, Detroit, August 1962), p. 2.

11 Thomas, *Life For Us*, pp. 180–227.

12 *A Profile of the Detroit Negro: 1959–1967* (Detroit Research Department of Detroit Urban League, revised December 1967), p. 8.

13 Ibid.

14 Widick, p. 163.

15 *National Advisory Committee Report*, p. 111.

16 *Ibid*, p. 84; Widick, *Detroit*, pp. 166–67, 183.

17 *National Advisory Committee Report*, p. 111.

18 Sidney Fine, *Violence in the Model City: The Cavanagh Administration, Race Relations, and the Detroit Riot of 1967*, (Ann Arbor: The University of Michigan Press, 1989), p. 39.

19 Widick, p. 189.

20 *The Michigan Chronicle*, December 2, 1967.

21 Ibid.

22 Ibid.

23 For a history of pre-1967 black community/police relations, see Mary M. Stolberg, *Bridging the River of Hatred: The Pioneering Efforts of Detroit Police Commissioner George Edwards* (Detroit: Wayne State University Press: 1998), pp. 12, 19–20, 85–86, 149–51. For recruitment of black policemen and the appointment of the first black police chief, see, Wilbur C. Rich, *Coleman Young and Detroit Politics* (Detroit: Wayne State University Press) pp. 212–15.

24 *The Michigan Chronicle*, December 2, 1967.

25 Ibid.

26 Thomas, *Life For Us*, pp. 50–87.

27 *The Michigan Chronicle*, December 2, 1967.

28 Fine, p. 320.

29 Ibid.

30 Ibid.

31 Ibid., p. 321.

32 Ibid.

33 This is the period in which "the economic transformation of the city launched a process of deproletarianization, as growing numbers of African Americans, especially young men, joined the ranks of those who gave up on work." See Thomas J. Sugrue, *The Origins of the Urban Crisis: Race and Inequality in Post-War Detroit* (Princeton, NJ: Princeton University Press, 1996), p. 262.

34 Fine, p. 322.

35 Ibid., p. 376.

36 To my knowledge the only comparable ideological conflicts over the direction of community building occurred between the pro-union and the anti-union (pro-Henry Ford) factions in the black community between 1936–1941. See chapter 8, "Conflicting Strategies of Black Community Building: Unionization vs. Ford Corporate Paternalism, 1936–1941," in Thomas, *Life for Us is What We Make It*, pp. 271–304.

37 Ibid., pp. 371, 376; Jim Ingram, "The Republic of New Africa: Is it a Serious Threat? *Detroit Scope Magazine* (May 31, 1961), p. 20.

38 Several of these "moderate" organizations played key roles in the black community process, see the section on "The Booker T. Washington Trade Association and the Housewives League of Detroit," in Thomas, *Life For Us*, pp. 214–221. For a more recent discussion on the BTWBA, see, *The State of Black Detroit: Building From Strength-The Black Self-Help Tradition in Detroit* (Detroit: The Detroit Urban League, 1987), pp. 27–29; For the Trade Union Leadership Council (TULC), see, Philip S. Foner, *Organized Labor and the Black Worker, 1619–1981* (New York: International Publishers, 1981), pp. 324, 330, 333, 341, 374.

39 Fine, p. 323.

40 Ibid, p. 373.

41 *The Michigan Chronicle*, September 23, 1967.

42 Ibid.

43 Fine, p. 374.

44 Ibid., p. 375.

45 Ibid., p. 376.

46 *Michigan Chronicle*, November 11, 1967.

47 *Michigan Chronicle*, December 30, 1967.

48 Ibid.

49 Ibid.

50 Ibid.; For more information of the Federation for Self-Determination, see Fine, pp. 377–80, 381, 383.

51 *Michigan Chronicle*, December 30, 1967.

52 *Detroit Free Press*, August 11, 1968. Quoted in Fine, p. 376.

53 Fine, p. 376.

54 Fine, pp. 380–82; Progress Report of the New Detroit Committee, April, 1968, pp. 66–72; Community Dissensus: Black Militants and the New Detroit Committee," in Leonard Gordon, ed., *A City in Racial Crisis: The Case of Detroit Pre- and Post-the 1967 Riot* (New York: William C. Brown Company Publisher, 1971), pp. 107–10.

55 "Inner-City Sub-Center, Inc. is About People Helping People" (Brochure); Interview, Paul Taylor, Inner-City Sub-Center, Detroit, Michigan, January 16, 1987; *The Inner-City Sub-Center Project, Inc: 17th Anniversary Souvenir Booklet*, June 27, 1986.

56 Ibid.

57 Ibid.

58 Ibid.

59 Brochure, N. D.

60 Ibid.

61 Ibid.

62 Interview, Paul Taylor, Co-Director, Inner-City Sub-Center, Inc., March 26, 1987.

63 Interview, Gladys Morant, Inner-City Sub-Center, Detroit Michigan, February 16, 1987.

64 Interview, Paul Taylor, Co-Director, Inner-City Sub-Center, Inc., March 26, 1987.

65 Ibid.

66 Ibid.

67 Ibid.

68 See, Mary D. Sengstock, *Chaldean Americans: Changing Conceptions of Ethnic Identity* (New York: Center for Migration Studies, 1999, second edition), p. 99; Gary C. David, "Behind the Bulletproof Glass: Iraqi Chaldean Store Ownership in Metropolitan Detroit," in Nabeel Abraham and Andrew Shryock (eds) *Arab Detroit: From Margin to Mainstream* (Detroit: Wayne State University Press, 2000), pp. 151–153.

69 Suzanne E. Smith, *Dancing in the Street: Motown an the Cultural Politics of Detroit* (Cambridge, MA: Harvard University Press, 1999), p. 255.

70 Ibid.

71 Ibid, p. 256.

72 Paul Taylor, Jr. Part I: "Organization for Survival at the Grassroots," in Robert H. Mast (comp. and ed.) *Detroit Lives* (Philadelphia: Temple University Press, 1994), p. 39.

73 "History of Operation Get-Down." *Operation Get Down's 15th Anniversary Dinner*, November 19, 1986, p. 8 (Brochure).

74 "History of Operation Get-Down," p. 8; Interview, Bernard Parker, Executive Director, Operation Get Down, February 24, 1987, Detroit, Michigan.

75 "History of Operation Get-Down," p. 8.

76 Ibid.
77 Ibid.
78 Ibid.
79 Ibid.
80 Interview, Parker.
81 Ibid.
82 "History of Operation Get-Down," p. 9.
83 Ibid.
84 Lloyd Gite, "Feeding the Masses," *Black Enterprise*, March 1987, p. 16.
85 Ibid, p. 16.
86 "History of Operation Get-Down," p. 9.
87 Ibid.
88 Ibid.
89 Gite, p. 16.
90 Ibid.; "History of Operation Get-Down," p. 4.
91 Gite, p. 16.
92 Interview, Parker.
93 *Operation Get-Down NIA Newsletter*, February 1987, p. 4; Ibid., April 1987, p. 2.
94 "History of Operation Get-Down,", p. 9.
95 Interview, Parker.
96 Ibid.
97 "History of Operation Get-Down,", p. 12.
98 *Operation Get-Down Newsletter*, February 1987, p. 4.
99 *Operation Get Down NIA Newsletter*, March 1987, p. 1.
100 Interview, Henriatta Reaves, B.I.R.T.H. Program, Operation Get-Down, February
    23, 1987, Detroit, Michigan.
101 Ibid.
102 Ibid.
103 Ibid.
104 "Bernard Parker" in Mast, *Detroit Lives,* p. 179.
105 Ibid.
106 Ibid.
107 Ibid.
108 Wilbur C. Rich, *Coleman Young and Detroit Politics,* (Detroit: Wayne State University
    Press, 1989), pp. 91–125; Mayor Coleman Young and Lonnie Wheeler, *Hard Stuff:
    The Autobiography of Mayor Coleman Young,* (New York: Viking, 1994), pp. xv, xxi.
    Some early warning signs of black teenage violence began surfacing ten years earlier
    in the local black press; see: Nadine Brown, "Violence Hits Jr. High Schools,"
    Michigan Chronicle, January 25, 1975; "Tragedy Hits 2 Local Schools: Outbreaks of
    Violence Pose Threats to City Educational System," *Michigan Chronicle*, September
    27, 1975. The 1980s saw the rise of Young Boys Incorporated (YBI), "the most dan-
    gerous youth gang since the Purple Gang." According to two federal indictments, this
    black youth gang was highly organized and "grossed 7.5 million weekly, $400 million
    annually in 1982." See Carl S. Taylor, *Dangerous Society* (East Lansing: Michigan
    State University Press, 1990) p. 11.
109 *The Detroit Free Press*, December 28, 1986; April 21, 1987. The 1980s witnessed a
    wave of black youth violence in central cities throughout the nation. For an example
    of both black youth violence and community efforts to overcome it, see, Joseph
    Marshall, Jr. and Lonnie Wheeler, *Street Soldier*, (New York: Delacorte Press, 1996).
110 Save Our Sons and Daughters (SOSAD) Tenth Anniversary Breakfast Celebration,
    Thursday, November 13th, 1997, brochure, p. 2; *Save Our Sons and Daughters*

(SOSAD) Newsletter, no. 2, June 21, 1987; *Detroit Free Press*, July 18, 19, 1987; September, 7, 9, 1987; November 17, 22, 1987.

111 SOSAD Tenth Anniversary brochure, 1997, p. 2.

112 Ibid, p. 2.

113 *SOSAD Newsletter*, no. 4, August 18, 1987, p. 1; no. 1, June 7, 1987, p. 1; no. 2, June 21, 1987, p. 1; no. 2, July 12, 1987, p. 1.

114 *SOSAD Newsletter*, "Special Pre-March Issue!!!," no. 2, July 12, 1987, p. 1.

115 Ibid, no. 4, August 18, 1997, p. 1.

116 Ibid, no. 1, June 7, 1987.

117 Ibid.

118 Ibid, no. 9, February 5, 1988; no. 10, March 10; no. 11, April 11, 1988; no. 12, May 11, 1988; no. 13, June 17, 1988; No. 16, September 13, 1988; *Detroit Free Press*, December 30, 1988.

119 Ibid, no. 20, January 3, 1989; no. 21, January 6, 1989; no. 24, May 9, 1989.

120 *Detroit Free Press*, January 24, 1990; April 28, 1990.

121 Grace Lee Boggs, *Living for Change: An Autobiography* (Minneapolis: University of Minnesota Press, 1998), p. 214.

122 *Tenth Anniversary Breakfast Celebration brochure,* Thursday, November 13, 1997.

123 For a critique of Coleman Young's Redevelopment Policies, see June Manning Thomas, *Planning a finer City in Postwar Detroit,* (Baltimore, MD: The Johns Hopkins University Press, 1997), pp. 149–76.

PART III

COMPARATIVE PERSPECTIVES

CHAPTER 11

ASIAN AMERICAN LABOR AND HISTORICAL INTERPRETATION

BY CHRIS FRIDAY*

In 1969, the first year of the publication for the journal *Labor History*, the field was still focused on institutions. Those institutions from the National Labor Union to the AFL had long histories of anti-Asian activities. Accordingly, Asian Americans[1] received virtually no treatment even as of the mid-1960s in the scholarly literature. A volume by Philip Taft had but five pages on Chinese exclusion and Foster Rhea Dulles's synthesis had a single sentence on the same subject.[2] Only Philip Foner discussed at length how Chinese exclusion occupied labor debates until the American Labor Union and the Industrial Workers of the World chose to admit Asians. Foner implied that if organized labor had abandoned its racist stance, Asians would have joined in droves. While he did document Asian American union activities in Oxnard, CA, Rock Springs, WY, and elsewhere, his overall treatment of Asian Americans reflected the tenor of the times—attention to exclusion, not to what Asians themselves had done.[3]

Essays on Asian American labor were scarce. *Labor History,* for example, ran no articles concerning Asian Americans until the 1970 appearance of Lamar B. Jones, "Labor and Management in California Agriculture."[4] While an important breakthrough for the journal, Jones took an approach similar to Foner by examining actions taken against workers.[5]

Asian American studies scholars were aware of the problem. In the mid-1960s, Roger Daniels had issued the criticism that most studies focused on anti-Asian activities.[6] In the 1969 issue that is commemorated in this volume, James A. Gross delivered a similar assessment of African-American labor history.[7] Still, African-Americans received much more attention than did Asian Americans. Again, taking the example of *Labor History,* in its first 10 years of publication, 15 articles on "Negro" labor history appeared in the journal (though only four before the 1969 issue).[8] Indeed, some six years before Jones wrote his piece, Gerald Grob had penned an assessment of "Organized Labor and the Negro Worker, 1865–1900."[9]

The dearth of studies on Asian American labor also reflected a preference among those in Asian American studies to publish in journals with a focus on ethnic and racial studies.[10] It took 10 years and a sea change in the field of labor history for another work on Asian Americans to appear in *Labor History,* and within four years the journal published four more articles.[11] However, in the ensuing decade, a second drought occurred and the journal published only one article dealing with skilled white labor's view of the Chinese. Understanding why reveals much about the history and the state of the field.

Until the late 1960s, the few studies that existed addressed Chinese and Japanese, but not other groups.[13] Typical of the early work was Gunther Barth's *Bitter Strength* (1964) which dominated the literature. He wholeheartedly espoused the influential "sojourner" thesis that sociologist Paul Siu had developed more than a decade earlier.[14] Like Siu, Barth claimed that Chinese immigrants had come to the U.S. thinking only to amass sufficient money to return to their homeland as wealthy. In doing so, he argued, they made no attempt to acculturate to American ways and thereby contributed significantly to the anti-Chinese movement.[15] He also believed that the kith and kin networks tightly bound Chinese workers to their "bosses"; particularly because many had indentured themselves to labor contractors to pay for their passage to the U.S.

Barth's adoption and use of Siu's sojourner thesis confirmed a mythic vision of American openness and thrust the responsibility for not assimilating to American culture on the Chinese. His stature as one of Oscar Handlin's students gained him more recognition among historians than earlier authors on Asian American topics.[16] His work became the rallying point, too, for criticism from a new generation of scholars, and for the emergent body of Asian American activists it epitomized what was wrong with academic interpretations.[17]

While there were many calls for research on Asian American activities, the most significant literature of the late 1960s and early 1970s regarding Asian Americans continued to focus on the ways in which European Americans perceived and treated Asian immigrants in the U.S., especially in regard to the anti-Asian movement. Alexander P. Saxton examined the manner in which competition between political parties and white working-class activism joined together in California to push for Chinese exclusion on the national level.[18] Saxton's location of the impetus for exclusion in organized labor foreshadowed later interpretations on the creation of whiteness through the lever of racism.[19] While agreeing that labor contributed to Chinese exclusion, Stuart Creighton Miller argued that the origins of anti-Chinese sentiments emerged with early trading and missionary contacts and were only made worse by press coverage of the Opium War.[20] That longstanding racism, he held, was of far greater import than labor's lobbying for Chinese exclusion.

Others took up the debate over the origins of anti-Asian sentiments,[21] but none so forcefully as Carlos Schwantes, who argued that European American migrants to the West Coast, especially the Pacific Northwest, had notions that the "promised land" would yield up great riches for them.[22] When economic depression and domination by large corporate interests blocked their aspirations for social mobility, workers in the Far West developed an ideology of "disinheritance." They targeted Chinese, and later other Asian immigrants, as the cause of their misfortune.

While labor's public rhetoric confirms that notion, Lawrence Lippin has suggested that skilled white workers might have spouted anti-Chinese sentiments, but did not always take direct action at work.[23] He found that Chinese laborers in San Francisco's harness-making workforce lowered the overall cost of production for some firms thereby allowing them to compete with Eastern and Mid-Western companies. The survival of San Francisco harness making gave continued employment to skilled white workers. In public circles, harness stitchers lobbied with the rest of California labor for exclusion (mechanization or women's labor was also available to replace Chinese); but at work they enjoyed the benefits of poorly-paid Chinese laborers and did not try to remove them.

The debate on the origins of anti-Asian sentiments and the degree to which workers translated them into action will no doubt continue, but they ultimately treat Asian Americans as objects. John Modell's 1969 study of Nisei retail produce workers was among the earliest studies to break free from the focus on anti-Asian activities and from notions of Asian Americans as sojourners.[24] Modell found that during the late 1930s, Nisei formed the "independent" Southern California Retail Produce Workers Union (SCRPWU) in order to lobby with coethnic, first-generation owners of produce strands for better wages and hours. At the same time, the AFL issued a charter to the Retail Food Clerks, Local 770 in competition with the SCRPWU. Local 770 ostensibly opened its books to Japanese Americans, but its key mission was to organize Nisei so as to create an "'American' standard of living for white workers." After three brief years of competition between the two unions, "ethnic solidarity" was not enough to protect Nisei employment and the SCRPWU folded. In its place arose a segregated local under a Teamsters charter. Class unity, denied by a segregated local, eluded Nisei as well. Internment in 1942 effectively ended the issue, and even on their return from the camps, Nisei found little to gain in labor organizations. They had, according to Modell, "achieved no foothold in American labor."[25]

Attempting to counter such notions, Japanese American labor activist Karl Yoneda began to write a series of semi-autobiographical accounts of Chinese and Japanese immigrant labor history.[26] Yoneda was at his best in pointing out Asian American contributions in the field of labor struggles, and he reveled in strikes and radical political action. His own life story added to this particular twist on "contributory" history. Yoneda was born in the U.S., but at the age of seven his father took him to Japan to be educated. Yoneda failed to finish high school and dropped out to participate in the student and labor movements of Taisho Japan. When the Japanese Imperial Army drafted him, he escaped to the U.S. There he worked in various wage-labor jobs and joined the Communist Party. During the last half of the 1930s he was an active organizer among Asian American cannery workers.[27] On the surface, he consistently argued for class solidarity but a careful read of his autobiography suggests how transnational his position was. Throughout his life, he remained connected to social movements in the United States and Japan. He also maintained a commitment, controversial though it sometimes was, to Japanese American affairs.[28] Yoneda's perspective as a participant in the labor movement of the 1930s and his

Japanese-language skills make his accounts invaluable. Unfortunately his tendency to simply list incidents and his discounting of those who held opposing viewpoints sometimes obscured as much of Asian American activities as they revealed.

The personal narrative of Filipino labor activist Philip Vera Cruz offers a rare insight into the history of Filipino agricultural laborers and, like Yoneda's work, confirms the consistent and regular involvement of Asian Americans in the labor movement. His account provides a critical assessment of the relationships between Filipinos and Mexican American unionists in the United Farm Workers (UFW). In the 1960s and 1970s as Mexican American membership in the union overwhelmed Filipinos, questions emerged as to how to continue to represent the very different needs and interests of these two groups. While Vera Cruz remained loyal to the UFW, his portrayal of Cesar Chavez and other Mexican American leaders suggests a somewhat darker story of internal politics and strategic decisions than that typically told about the UFW. Ultimately, the UFW, at least according to Vera Cruz, found it more expedient to represent itself as a Mexican and Mexican American union than one with a more heterogeneous membership that included Filipinos.[29] Scholars are only now beginning to give his life and work greater scrutiny.[30]

Roughly contemporary with the initial publication of Yoneda's first historical writings and Vera Cruz's activities in the UFW are the works of two key historians—Yuji Ichioka and Him Mark Lai. Both had personal sympathies with left-wing politics as well as facility in the Japanese and Chinese languages, respectively, but far surpassed Yoneda in the breadth of their research and interpretations. Language abilities were no small matter. Gunther Barth and others had claimed that the history of Asian Americans would never be known because illiterate workers left no written records in any language. Ichioka, by exploring Japanese-language sources, brought to light the histories of Japanese immigrant socialists and anarchists, coal miners, prostitutes, labor contractors, and railroad workers as well as efforts on the part of the Japanese government to establish a diplomatic link with the AFL on the eve of World War I.[31]

No other labor historian has yet surpassed Ichioka's productivity or ability to mine Japanese-language sources. He has effectively demonstrated that Issei laborers employed ethnic solidarity to protect themselves from attacks by white organized labor.[32] They were not, however, beyond cooperating with those same labor organizations when they stood to benefit. In his study of Chinese and Japanese coal miners at Rock Springs, Ichioka found that in 1907 the United Mine Workers admitted Asian laborers out of necessity to protect the union position. Asian immigrants, he argued, were possible to organize; an important conclusion that helped to temper the "ethnic solidarity" thesis that Modell put forth.[33]

Ichioka has also forcefully demonstrated the range of connections that Japanese immigrants had to their homeland and the significance of those ties to labor activities. In the late 19th and early 20th centuries, Japanese socialists and anarchists, though few in number, played an important role in helping immigrants formulate a radical perspective on their position in the U.S. Nonetheless, affairs in Japan, rising Japanese nationalism among the immigrants, and a concerted effort on the part of the Japanese government to maintain an involvement in immigrant lives, effectively limited the range of the political debate for most Japanese.[34] Only occasional individuals like Yoneda openly espoused left-wing politics and class unity.

Ichioka's research also dealt with Japanese immigrant women, including prostitutes, wives by some arrangement for immigrant men, and wives summoned to join husbands.[35] While authors such as Evelyn Nakano Glenn, Peggy Pascoe, and Valerie Matsumoto would significantly extend Ichioka's interpretations of Japanese American women,[36] his recognition of women's presence and roles was a significant departure from previous studies that completely ignored this aspect of Japanese immigration. Questions of waged labor for Asian American women as well as that of family labor remain largely unexplored.[37]

In addition to his significant interpretive contributions, Ichioka has also been involved in collecting manuscripts for the Japanese American Research Project at the University of California, Los Angeles, many of which are of great value to labor historians.[38] In this respect he and Him Mark Lai have much in common. Lai's contributions to Asian American labor history have come in his exploratory research into Chinese workers' lives, his generosity in sharing his research materials, and his concerted efforts to publicize and make known that availability of Chinese-language sources.[39]

Lai's early research and publications aimed at simply uncovering Chinese American activities, most of which involved the documentation of Chinese employment.[40] More significantly, Lai also took a keen interest in the Chinese Left in the US.[41] Like Ichioka, Lai determined that Chinese national politics had a significant impact on Chinese immigrants.[42] In the milieu of mistreatment and harsh working conditions in the United States and the reform movements of early 20th century China, Chinese immigrants were quite attracted to various socialist doctrines. Beginning in the 1910s, various leftist organizations, ranging from anarcho-syndicalist to Marxist, formed among Chinese immigrants. The difficulty, aside from factionalism among the groups themselves, was that followers of the Kuomintang (KMT), or Nationalist Party, held much of the power in Chinese American communities. Consistently, after the late 1920s, these conservative merchants drove Chinese radicals "behind the scenes" with their "intimidation and threats."[43]

In spite of KMT belligerence, Chinese leftists continued to strive to better their conditions. In the late 1930s, the Chinese Workers Mutual Aid Association (*Jiasheng huagong hezouhui*) emerged to represent Chinese laborers' interests in the San Francisco Bay area and it also successfully established links with organized labor there.[44] When the Mutual-Aid Association met in October 1949 to celebrate its 12th anniversary and the formation of the People's Republic of China (PRC), according to Lai, KMT agents raided the gathering, beat some members of the audience and splashed blue ink (the Nationalist color) on those in attendance. The KMT also publicly threatened the lives of PRC supporters.[45]

In the 1950s, the "Old Chinese Left" faded under pressure from the American Right and the generation of increasingly elderly "bachelor" workers whom they represented retreated to the confines of Chinatown.[46] The "New Chinese Left" that emerged in the late 1960s was largely "American-born" and not from the immigrant generation. Consequently, the new generation developed significantly different concerns focusing first on community social welfare. Still, the splits, Lai argued, remained most significant between Chinese radicals and the bulk of the community who, since the 1950s, increasingly allied themselves with the conservative, business-minded elite.[47]

While Lai and Ichioka explored Chinese- and Japanese-language sources to unearth a "buried past," interest in quantitative method and difficulty in finding or interpreting Asian-language materials led to an explosion in research using the manuscript schedules of the federal censuses. While the ability to document how many Chinese or Japanese were working at a given task in a particular place was helpful, a great many of these works simply described the census data, and few authors were able to make any significant generalizations.[48] Census data was too unreliable, too infrequent to be of any more use than as rough benchmarks and supplements to other types of information.

The expansion of the definition of Asian American was a second major development during the 1970s. These works attempted to recover, as Ichioka and Lai had done, the history of various "forgotten" Asian Americans including Filipinos, Koreans, and East Asian Indians.[49] Most of the works were general in nature and treated workers lives as a subset of the immigrant experience. Of those general studies, Fred Cordova's *Filipinos: Forgotten Asian Americans* (1983) was among the best labor history.[50] In spite of the book's sweeping coverage beginning in the mid-1700s and ending in 1963, Cordova gave good coverage to Filipino involvement in strikes and unionization. His sources were the dozens of interviews that the Demonstration Project for Asian Americans, with which he was affiliated, conducted beginning in the mid-1970s of elderly Filipino men and women in the Seattle area.

Through the 1970s and into the mid-1980s, a small body of literature on Asian American labor began to emerge that moved beyond earlier, highly descriptive studies of Asian Americans in mining, railroad construction, and agricultural labor.[51] Breaking from studies that reinforced the popular imagery of Chinese in the American West's goldmines, Yuji Ichioka's study of Japanese and Chinese immigrant coalminers, discussed above, stood as a distinctive approach and topic.[52] Only Gunther Peck has taken a similar tack by examining labor contracting in the mining region around Bingham, Utah.[53] Peck's analysis of the complex relationship between ethnicity and class involves Asian Americans, but they are not at the center of the study.

Other scholars have examined railroad employment. Paul Ong has demonstrated that Chinese laborers for the Central Pacific Railroad were paid one-third less than white laborers.[54] His findings, based on a quantitative analysis of wage data, ran counter to previous interpretations that the essential quality of Chinese labor on the Central Pacific was that it was plentiful rather than cheap. Yuzo Murayama opened new territory in her study of Japanese railroad hands, largely section crew workers, who at first depended heavily on coethnic contractors to secure their jobs. Having become familiar with the U.S. context within the first decade of their employment, however, the laborers broke the contractors' hold over them. Some managed to leave railroad work for more remunerative pursuits. Those who remained negotiated with the companies directly and wage rates rose.[55] Direct negotiation, though it may have boosted wage rates, ultimately played into the hands of railroad companies in the American West. In the late 19th and early 20th centuries, the companies, as W. Thomas White has noted, quite effectively pitted workers against each other.[56]

Railroads continued to employ Asian Americans in the 20th century, not just as construction and maintenance crews, but also as porters in the cars. Barbara Posadas has explained that beginning in 1925 with the formation of the Brotherhood of Sleeping Car Porters (BSCP), the Pullman Company aggressively recruited Filipinos to combat the BSCP.[57] As other companies had done with the section hands, Pullman used ethnic antagonisms between African-Americans and Filipinos to its advantage until 1937, when the BSCP gained company recognition. Filipinos made the adjustment, in part because the BSCP promised to uphold their seniority in the newly recognized union, but they were inordinately lax in their commitment often falling months, even years, behind in their dues.[58] Taken as a whole, these studies on railroads suggest that at least at certain historical moments, workers were able to resist company coercion.

For agricultural labor, most studies in the 1970s were article-length treatments of various labor conflicts, especially in California. Tomas Almaguer demonstrated, like Ichioka, that Japanese workers could cross ethnic boundaries to pursue class unity, but hostility toward Japanese by the AFL blocked formal entry and recognition of labor organizations that represented Japanese immigrant workers.[59] Howard A. DeWitt helped point out the willingness of Filipinos to organize in the 1930s, but recognized the extreme difficulties they faced because of their weak position as seasonal harvest workers, the historical timing of their organization during the Depression decade, extreme racism, and a tendency toward intra-ethnic factionalism among Filipinos.[60] Peter C. Y. Leung and L. Eve Armentrout Ma also pointed out that Chinese continued to work in California fields well into the 1930s.[61] Like the Japanese but unlike most Filipinos, Chinese connections to coethnic farmers helped them secure jobs, particularly in the Depression.

A handful of articles on California vegetable canneries and Alaska salmon canneries extended the scope of discussion beyond field laborers. Martin Brown's and Peter Philips's various works on California canneries revealed the role technology played in remaking work by displacing laborers and deskilling the production process.[62] Chinese had gained early entry into the canneries by virtue of their availability as a workforce. By the end of the 19th century, though, canners looked to European American women whose numbers had increased dramatically in the last quarter of the century and who could be hired for cheaper rates than Chinese. Vicki Ruiz took up the next transformation in the labor market -from largely Anglo women to the employment of many Mexican American women - and the subsequent drive for unionization among them.[63] Hers is a model study, but does not provide any additional information on Asian Americans. Other than Martin and Brown, then, no other significant work has appeared on Asian Americans, men or women, in California canneries.

Robert Masson and Donald Guimary, along with Robert Nash, have written on Asian Americans in the processing sector of the canned salmon industry before World War II. These studies significantly broadened the academic understanding of Asian American seasonal employment patterns in a labor market that stretched from central California to Alaska as well as adding significantly to the literature on Asian American labor contracting.[64] The stories they tell, however, fall into the near-mythic genre of exploitative contractors and victimized laborers. Only Filipino refusals to bow down to the contractors' oppression and the entry of the federal government during the New Deal broke the contractors' hegemony.

The situation was, as the works by Martin and Brown, and Ruiz on California canneries demonstrate, much more complex. My study of Asian American workers in the salmon canneries assesses the role of technology, shifting power relations within the labor market, and the variety of worker attempts to protect their interests.[65] Exploitation was a part of labor relations in the industry and some Filipinos were militant labor organizers, but collusion within each ethnic group, Chinese and Japanese unionists, and changing company strategies were all a part of the transformation from contract to union labor in the industry.[66]

For scholars seeking to break from straight narrative and contributory histories, Edna Bonacich's theory of "ethnic antagonism"[67] with the addition of the attempt by labor economists David M. Gordon, Richard Edwards, and Michael Reich[68] to apply segmented-labor market theory to the historical transformations of work, have been of great assistance. Mike Hinton, Wing-cheung Ng, and Paul M. Ong have demonstrated how racism relegated 19th century Chinese immigrant workers to the bottom tier of labor—the unorganized and highly volatile secondary sector—and divided workers against each other to the ultimate benefit of company owners.[69] The use of segmented-labor market theory represented a significant shift from interpretations that Chinese "clannishness" and unwillingness to acculturate was the determinant of their economic position.

In the 1990s, segmented-labor market theory achieved a wide acceptance. Richard White in his synthesis of the American West adopted the theory to describe a two-tiered labor market in which people of color (Asian Americans included) are locked into the region's poorest paying, least rewarding jobs. European American workers may start in such positions, but by virtue of their ethnic backgrounds, become eligible for upward mobility providing they can accumulate enough human capital.[70] Like Bonacich, White pointed to racism as the key element in determining where Asian Americans entered into the economy. Ong argues, though, that while racism predated the creation of segmented labor markets, "the spread of the capitalistic mode of production undermined this racial hierarchy by forcing whites and Chinese into a common labor market."[71] European American workers, stung by having to work alongside Chinese, sought to elevate themselves at the expense of the Chinese, as Bonacich theorized and Schwantes demonstrated. Once elevated, as Lippin suggested, white laborers' anti-Asian activities became more rhetorical than real.

Even for those who looked to it as a helpful analytical device found segmented-labor market theory limiting. In the early 1990s, immigration historian Ewa Morawska argues that U.S. firms before 1930 did not operate in true primary and secondary labor markets, but exhibited features of both. She suggested that "an ethnically split secondary internal labor market" existed in most companies and that national origins and ethnicity were the prime determinants of how a person might enter into the economy.[72] Other critics of segmented-labor market theory argued that it too often is used to describe workers as passive subjects rather than agents in their own histories. In some cases, certain workers—like Chinese workers in the salmon canneries—used their position of relative power to establish an "aristocracy of labor" sometimes colluding with labor contractors to protect their jobs from European American women and girls, and members of other racialized groups.[73] Robert M. Jiobu has characterized such activity as the establishment of an "ethnic hegemony."[74] He noted that certain ethnic groups may gain control over some small sector in the economy, including access to jobs, and then negotiate from this position. Ethnic groups are thus able to elevate themselves as a group relative to the dominant, and sometimes hostile, society but tend to jockey with others for position.[75]

Several studies have suggested that labor contractors are the essential negotiators between the minority and majority societies.[76] Examinations of labor contracting by Asian American scholars have been quite extensive.[77] Most of the current literature recognizes the dual nature of ethnic labor contracting; that it is at once exploitative and protective. In many ways, the 1969 ethnic solidarity arguments put forth by Modell still hold sway.[78] The problem with such interpretations is that ethnicity and class are too often treated as constants. Peck's study on labor contracting in Utah mining districts, which involved Asian Americans as well as a host of other ethnic groups, forcefully demonstrates that ethnicity and class were "highly mutable social constructs" that underwent continual revisions.[79]

Careful consideration of such issues was difficult given the fact that most of the work of the late 1970s and early 1980s was article-length. The publication of book-length labor histories on Asian Americans in the mid-1980s remedied that situation. In particular, those on Hawaii's working-class provided one of the fastest growing and most intriguing areas of investigation. Ronald Takaki, Michi Kodama-Nishimoto, Warren S. Nishimoto, Cynthia A. Oshiro, and Edward D. Beechert, produced a powerful combination of works that will continue to stand for years.[80] Takaki explained working-class culture in a fashion inspired by Herbert Gutman. He examined workers' daily lives and showed how their culture provided a basis for their responses to exploitation within the sugar plantation labor system. Takaki only carried the study to 1920 and suggested that laborers had set aside their ethnic differences. Beechert examined a much broader sweep of Hawaiian labor and noted that working-class unity in Hawaii was not easy to achieve.[81] Not until 1946 did plantation workers build a lasting union and not until the eve of statehood did unionization effectively represent a broad sweep of workers in Hawaii. Kodama-Nishimoto, Nishimoto, and Oshiro further developed these themes into more recent times and added even more voices.

Alongside these new studies of Hawaii, Sucheng Chan tackled the Chinese role in California agriculture.[82] Chan's focus was on Chinese agriculturalists as entrepreneurs, but her Herculean work in local county archives allowed her to contest earlier notions of Chinese labor and to reconstruct a more thorough history of their activities. She convincingly argued that Chinese laborers were neither docile, cheap, nor responsible for the rise of agribusiness and land monopolization in California as previous authors had argued.

While Chan's study was remarkable for its depth of research and its interpretive insights, like most studies it focused on the American West. Yet Asian Americans were present and working in other sections of the country. General surveys have some information, but Lucy M. Cohen's volume on Chinese in the American South after the Civil War is the best available discussion of how Southern plantation owners sought Chinese labor, often from Cuba, to replace their "lost" slaves.[83] Chinese ran athwart those plans, however, by refusing to be the docile "coolies" the plantation owners desired. They overtly resisted attempts to make them servile, exploited workers.[84]

A full study of Chinese and other Asian laborers in the pre-World War II South has yet to be done but future scholars will need to consider the possibilities in urban centers as well as in rural sectors in their studies. Tera Hunter's masterful study of black women's labor in the urban South after the Civil War hints at the intersection between the lives of black women and Chinese laundry workers.[85] More studies recognizing these interactions and resulting conflicts will not only shed light on Asian American or African American history, but more broadly on race, class, and gender in American society.

Most of the major works during and prior to the 1980s were historical narratives of particular groups of Asian immigrants and Asian Americans. In response, Lucie Cheng and Edna Bonacich attempted to recast the discussion of Asian immigrant labor before World War II through the use of an extensive theoretical framework.[86] They argued that international labor migration occurred within the development of capitalism and imperialism, which directed cheap labor to the site of development and creates underdevelopment in the sending country. Meanwhile, the immigrants in the receiving country sat in a disadvantaged position as a reserve pool of labor. Ethnic middlemen may emerge as labor contractors or some other petite bourgeoisie, but regardless of their beneficence to their coethnics, ultimately they "participate[d] in keeping immigrant workers in a superexploited position."[87] In the same volume, Bonacich provided a synthesis of Asian immigration, U.S. capitalist development, and the role of Asian labor in the development of Hawaii and California[88] followed by a second section of empirical research by various authors to support their theoretical model. The empirical essays provide a discussion of Chinese, Japanese, Filipino, Korean, and Punjabi immigration and labor.[89]

The separate essays represented some of the earliest efforts to understand the context of Asian emigration and the theoretical section provided a good review of existing theories and welded them into a forceful and holistic model. The volume as a whole, however, demonstrated the difficulties of applying complex historical situations to a sweeping theory that relegated human agency to so much grist for the mill of international capitalism. Ultimately their rigid theoretical framework offered no avenue to address how immigrants and laborers, "play within structures" to make their lives more bearable.[90]

Getting at Asian American laborers' actions and discerning potential motivations is not easy. Renqiu Yu's recent work is an excellent example of how to unearth Asian workers' actions and expressed political beliefs.[91] Yu used numerous interviews of Chinese immigrant men and other more traditional sources to detail the history of the Chinese Hand Laundry Alliance (CHLA) of New York since its origins in 1933. Significantly challenging the notion that Chinese immigrants, especially laundrymen, were "isolated" sojourners[92] caught in a static culture that denied them entry into American ways, Yu details how the CHLA challenged the power elite of New York's Chinatown by organizing the alliance in opposition to the *Guomingdang* or Chinese Nationalist Party (KMT). They denounced old "feudal" customs, embraced democratic practices, and espoused class consciousness while articulating an individualist, rather than collectivist ideology. The CHLA also refused to join with white labor organizations because of their long history of racism.

While Peter Kwong had discussed class conflict within New York's Chinese community between 1930 and 1950, Yu went far beyond that general work.[93] Cut off from U.S. politics with no rights to gain citizenship, Yu's study revealed that Chinese laundrymen were active in the politics of their immigrant community and of their homeland. Between the late 1930s and the end of the 1940s, the CHLA was influential, but KMT and FBI repression as well as political shifts and turns in the newly formed People's Republic of China led to its decline. The CHLA continued to exist and linked up with the "new" Chinese left in the 1960s and 1970s, but it was not at the center of politics in the Chinese community. The CHLA's failure, Yu argued, need not obscure the importance of shifting ethnic identity based on the immigrant experience -an identity that was not necessarily moving toward assimilation and one that was heavily influenced by labor concerns. In portraying Chinese as actors playing within the larger constraints of US exclusion policies and China's struggle to establish a unified polity, Yu significantly alters the notion of sojourners that Paul Siu first articulated in his 1952 study, and which Barth embraced. Perhaps the only weakness of the study is Yu's lack of discussion about women either in China or Chinatown. Did they, as Dirk Hoerder has suggested for European American immigrants, play an important role in keeping the homeland and host country connected?[94] What are the historical constructions of gender and race that are so apparent in service sector jobs?[95]

Those concerns aside, Yu's demonstration of the connection between the "old" left and the "new" left is important. Edna Bonacich has argued that Asian American studies in the 1980s became too focused on the emergence of a middle class, that there was an "erosion of working-class consciousness in Asian American studies in the 1980s and 1990s."[96] She urged scholars and students to recognize three key factors: First, that an Asian American working class remained in place; second, that entrepreneurial activity, so often and mistakenly celebrated as some innate Asian American characteristic, is not individualistic but depends upon unpaid family labor; and finally, she noted that upward mobility is often had at the expense of others in the community.

On many counts, Bonacich was correct and was confirmed by contemporary scholars. Taking on the task of examining contemporary working-class issues among Asian Americans and Pacific Islanders, Dean S. Toji and James H. Johnson, used 1980 census data to argue that these people suffer from inordinately high levels of poverty when the working and jobless poor are considered.[97] According to their data, poverty affected nearly 80% of all Hmong, 50-60% of Cambodians and Laotians, and nearly a third of the Vietnamese in the U.S. Some 10-20% of Chinese, Koreans, East Asian Indians, and various Pacific Islanders live in poverty, while Filipinos and Japanese had comparatively low proportions in poverty at 7 and 6% respectively. In comparison, African-Americans, "nonwhite Hispanics," and Native Americans had poverty rates of 18%, 20%, and 15%, respectively. The general white population had a poverty rate of 6%.

The data demonstrated that not all Asians are among the "model minorities" and issues of economic parity remain quite relevant. Indeed, in his survey of data from the 1980s, Gregory DeFreitas found that Hispanic, Asian, and white workers were equally inclined (or disinclined) to join unions while African-Americans most often sought representation in unions.[98] The propensity of Asian workers to join unions, though, may be on the rise, according to the authors in an important special issue of *Amerasia Journal* that brought together researchers and community activists to reveal for readers the potency of contemporary grassroots labor organization in Asian American communities in spite of the continued disbelief in labor circles that Asians and Pacific Islanders can be organized.[99] The studies of Asian and Pacific Island communities reflect not only the ongoing labor struggles, but also the continual broadening of the definition of Asian American as new immigrants have flooded into the U.S. after 1965 immigration reforms and as political refugees in the context of the Cold War. No longer are the studies simply of Chinese, Japanese, and occasional Filipinos or Koreans. Asian Pacific American communities are diverse, often with competing interests.[100] While readers of *Amerasia Journal* have known for more than two decades that there is much more to Asian America than the "old" Asian immigrants and that Asian Americans sought to contend with abysmal working conditions to this day,[101] this 1992 issue confirmed the importance of working-class history in contemporary Asian and Pacific Island communities and emphasizes the need for further investigation.

The mid–1990s proved to be a watershed in Asian American Studies. The field's traditional base in history and sociology found itself challenged by new developments in critical and cultural studies.[102] No single author so challenged the narratives and social science theory driven works as Lisa Lowe, *Immigrant Acts*.[103] Though not her central focus, Lowe forcefully demonstrates how Asian American and Asian Immigrant workers continue to toil in transnational positions. They creatively engage the political circumstances in which they find themselves, but face immense odds. She is impressed by workers' abilities to find "new modes of organizing and struggling."[104] Some historians are likely to find Lowe's dense prose impenetrable and jargon-filled, but none should ignore the implications of her study: Asian Americans live their working lives in a social and cultural space created between the desire to claim a place within America while remaining connected to emigrant homelands, either by choice or by assumptions that all Asians are "perpetual foreigners." That position necessitates creativity in response, but by no means completely disempowers workers. In short, she offers a means to discern how workers "play within structures."

Lowe's explicit analysis of discourse meshes well with Latin American labor historian Charles Bergquist's earlier call to refocus labor history on four central themes.[105] In 1993, Bergquist argued that labor historians ought to focus on issues of control, gender, globalism, and "postmodernism." In his blueprint for action, he explained that labor historians must continue to focus on issues of control, or that struggle to control not only work places but the communities and countries in which workers live.[106] A focus on politics can reveal coalition building and other searches for democratic practices. Attention to gender moves labor historians away from the misleading dichotomies of men and women, public and private, work and community. Scrutiny of globalism, not just of capitalism, but also of workers and their connections to each other—often cast as transnationalism—will allow American historians to see how Asian Americans exist in larger frameworks. Just as importantly, it will also serve to remind them of the ways in which "free" labor in one place may well be dependent upon coerced labor in another. Finally, the use of "postmodern" modes of analysis will allow researchers to carefully examine the words and actions of workers and their "bosses." In Bergquist's words, it makes it possible to "discover and decenter the social bias in hegemonic discourse and legitimize understandings of the past generated by groups of the oppressed."[107] Indeed, these are the questions Asian American Studies scholars like Lisa Lowe and many others have consistently examined. Labor historians would be well served to not only see Asian American labor in their model, but also to recognize that Asian American labor history can be an important vehicle for decentering the privilege of largely institutional, white and male labor in much the same way that Gary Okihiro suggests can be the case for the whole of American history.[108]

Asian American labor history still has much room for expansion and exploration. Authors like Lowe and Bergquist will challenge researchers looking back to earlier historical periods of the Asian American labor experience. Comparatively little has been done on gender roles. How did constructions of masculinity affect workers behavior? What roles did Asian American women have in waged and family labor? How did sexuality, only recently explored by authors such as Nayan Shah, interact with ideas of race, gender, and class?[109] Examining political ideologies and nationalism needs to be extended beyond Chinese and Japanese first generation immigrants to other immigrant groups and to the second and third generations. How is citizenship defined and used in ethnic, racial, and labor contexts? It will be important for scholars to pay attention to the continual reconstruction of ethnic identity as well as notions of class. In spite of my criticisms of labor history's long-standing institutional focus, I do believe additional examinations of institutions beyond Yu's study of the Chinese Hand Laundry Alliance or mine of the various cannery workers' locals will provide fruitful territory. Moreover, Asian American scholars must not fall victim to the same myopic vision of history that often plagues American historians. They will be well served to look at Asians in the Americas, not simply in comparative context, but by investigating the linkages between Asian American communities in places like Seattle, Washington, and Vancouver, British Columbia, or the U.S. Southwest and the north of Mexico. Shifts and changes in immigration laws, international diplomacy, and multinational corporations will provide the grounds for additional studies, some of which are now emerging in the published literature.[110] Ultimately, scholars in the field will have to have facility in various Asian and Pacific Island languages in order to reveal how the workers themselves understand their positions and how they contend with difficulties. The immigrant press of the late 20th century will be a vital source for future historians.

Writing in the introduction to his 1988 synthesis, Roger Daniels, a long-time scholar in the field of Asian American history, commented that "there exists as yet no dense corpus of scholarly books and articles" on the Asian American experience and in 2000, I made essentially the same argument about Asian American labor history.[111] A central problem in the equation is that the field of labor history seems to have little space for Asian Americans. Since 1994, for example, the two leading journals in the field, *Labor History* and *International Labor and Working-Class History*, have published 261 articles. Six, or a mere 2.2%, of those have had Asian Americans as some aspect of the study. Two were on anti-Asian movements. One was about labor organizing in Vietnam. That left but three articles dealing with Asian American labor history. In comparison, the two leading journals of Asian American Studies, *Amerasia Journal* and *The Journal of Asian American Studies*, published 155 articles in that same time span. Nine were about some aspect of labor history and of those eight were tightly focused labor history studies. While the overall percentage of labor studies in the two Asian American journals was low (5.8%), Asian Americanists are nearly three times as likely to pay attention to labor history issues as labor historians are to Asian American history. This is not just an issue of percentages or numbers. If labor history is to speak to an inclusive past, present, and future, it must be able to contend with the decentering role that Asian Americans play in that history.[112] At present, I remain hopeful, if guarded about the prospects.

NOTES

*The author wishes to thank Alan Gallay, Sucheng Chan, and Katie Walker for their contributions to the original published version of this essay. Joe Trotter deserves much credit for his patience with the author on this updated, revised version. While there are too many people to thank for their individual influences, Valerie Matsumoto and Kevin Leonard have offered regular and consistent friendship and support in my efforts to understand history.

1   I have used the term Asian American in its most general sense in this essay to include Asian and Pacific Islanders, immigrants and U.S.-born including people of Chinese, Japanese, Filipino, Korean, East Indian, Southeast Asian, and various Pacific Islander ancestry.

2   Philip Taft, *Organized Labor in American History* (New York: Harper and Row, 1964), 301–306; Foster Rhea Dulles, *Labor in America*, 3rd ed. (New York: Thomas Y. Crowell Company, 1966), 183.

3 Philip S. Foner, *A History of the Labor Movement in the United States*, vol. I (New York: International Publishers, 1964), 425428, 488–493; *ibid.*, vol. 2 (1955), 58–60, 204–205; *ibid.*, vol. 3 (1964), 269–277, 427428; *ibid.*, vol. 4 (1966), 70, 82, 104, 123–124, 260.

4 Lamar B. Jones, "Labor and Management in California Agriculture, 1864–1964," *Labor History*, 11 (1970), 23–40.

5 Roger Daniels, "Westerners from the East: Oriental Immigration Reappraised," Pacific *Historical Review*, 35 (1966), 375, leveled this critique on the field.

6 Daniels, "Westerners from the East," 375.

7 James A. Gross, "Historians and the Literature of the Negro Worker," *Labor History*, 10 (1969), 538–539.

8 Martha Jan Soltow, comp., "Index to *Labor History:* Volumes 1–10, 1960–1969," *Labor History*, 11 (1970), esp. 544–545.

9 Gerald Grob, "Organized Labor and the Negro Worker, 1865–1900," *Labor History*, 1 (1960), 164–167.

10 *Amerasia Journal*, for example, began publication in 1971 as an outgrowth of the Asian American Studies Center at the University of California, Los Angeles, and to this date has remained one of the key forums for literature on Asian Americans. More recently, the *Journal of Asian American Studies* has provided another outlet for scholarly publication. Other journals include: *Ethnicity, Ethnic and Racial Studies,* and *The Journal of Ethnic Studies.* Sociological journals include: *American Sociological Review* and *Sociology and Social Research.* For a more complete listing, see Hyung-chan Kim, ed., *Asian American Studies: An Annotated Bibliography and Research Guide* (New York: Greenwood Press, 1989) and the annual bibliography in *Amerasia Journal.*

11 Yuji Ichioka, "Japanese Immigrant Labor Contractors and the Northern Pacific and the Great Northern Railroad Companies, 1898–1907," *Labor History*, 21 (1980), 325–350; Jack Masson and Donald Guimary, "Asian Labor Contractors in the Alaska Canned Salmon Industry: 1880–1937," *ibid.*, 22 (1981), 377–397; Ronald Takaki, "'An Entering Wedge': The Origins of the Sugar Plantation and a Multiethnic Working Class in Hawaii," *ibid.*, 23 (1982), 32–46; Barbara M. Posadas, "The Hierarchy of Color and Psychological Adjustment in an Industrial Environment: Filipinos, The Pullman Company, and the Brotherhood of Sleeping Car Porters," *ibid.*, 23 (1982), 349–373; Tomas Almaguer, "Racial Domination and Class Conflict in Capitalist Agriculture: The Oxnard Sugar Beet Workers' Strike of 1903," *ibid.*, 25 (1984), 325–350.

12 Lawrence M. Lippin, " 'There Will not be a Mechanic (sic) Left': The Battle against Unskilled Labor in the San Francisco Harness Trade, 1880–1890," *Labor History*, 35 (1994), 217–236.

13 For a brief discussion of Asian immigrant demography and the scholarly literature concerning their migrations, see Charles Choy Wong, "Toward Research in History and the Social Sciences: The Asian American Experience," in *Asian American Studies*, 3–14, and Shirley Hune, "Pacific Migration Defined by American Historians and Social Theorists up to the 1960s," in *ibid.*, 17–42.

14 Paul C. P. Siu, "The Sojourner," *American Journal of Sociology*, 58 (1952), 34–44, and *idem., The Chinese Laundryman: A Study of Social Isolation*, ed. John K. W. Tchen (New York: New York University Press, 1987). Tchen, "Editor's introduction," in *ibid.*, provides an excellent discussion and critique of the thesis as does Franklin Ng, "The Sojourner, Return Migration, and Immigration History," *Chinese America: History and Perspectives* (1987), 53–71.

15 Gunther Barth, *Bitter Strength: A History of the Chinese in the United States, 1850–1870* (Cambridge: Harvard University Press, 1964), 1.

16 Those earlier works are too numerous to mention. For a relatively complete list, see Kim, *Asian American Studies*, 43–58, and 93–100.

17 The strongest critique came from Linda Shin in her review of *Bitter Strength*, in Emma Gee, *et al.*, eds., *Counterpoint: Perspectives on Asian America* (Los Angeles: Asian American Studies Center, University of California), 36–38. For additional assessments, see Shirley Hune, "Asian American Studies in the First Decade: Trends and Themes; Failures and Revisions, 1960s-1970s," in *Asian American Studies*, 242. On the growth of the Asian American movement, see William Wei, *The Asian American Movement* (Philadelphia: Temple University Press, 1993), esp. 132–168; and Yen Le Espiritu, *Asian American Panethnicity: Bridging Institutions and Identities* (Philadelphia: Temple University Press, 1992).

18 Alexander P. Saxton, *The Indispensable Enemy: Labor and the Anti-Chinese Movement in California* (Berkeley: University of California Press, 1971). Also see Herbert Hill, "Anti-Oriental Agitation and the Rise of Working-Class Racism," *Society*, 10 (1973), 43–54.

19 For example, see Edna Bonacich, "A Theory of Ethnic Antagonism: The Split Labor Market," *American Sociological Review*, 37 (1972), 547–559; and David R. Roediger, *The Wages of Whiteness: Race and the Making of the American Working Class* (London: Verso Press, 1991). For a further extension of Saxton's ideas about race and politics, see his *The Rise and Fall of the White Republic. Class, Politics, and Mass Culture in Nineteenth-Century America* (London: Verso Press, 1990). This debate about whiteness has recently become quite contentious among labor historians. For a perspective on the controversy, see Eric Arnesen, "Whiteness and the Historians' Imagination," *International Labor and Working-Class History*, 60 (2001): 3–32 and the responses to the essay by James R. Barrett and others in that same volume.

20 Stuart Creighton Miller, *The Unwelcome Immigrant. The American Image of the Chinese, 1785–1882* (Berkeley: University of California Press, 1969), ix, 191–192.

21 Gwendolyn Mink, *Old Labor and New Immigrants in American Political Development: Union, Party, and State, 1875–1920* (Ithaca: Cornell University Press, 1986), 71–112, explores the links between organized labor's activities in the anti-Chinese movement and its subsequent lobbying for more general immigration restrictions.

22 Carlos A. Schwantes, "Protest in a Promised Land: Unemployment, Disinheritance, and the Origin of Labor Militancy in the Pacific Northwest, 1885–1886," *Western Historical Quarterly*, 13 (1982), 373–390. Other studies in this genre are listed in Kim, *Asian American Studies*, 111–135.

23 Lippin, "Unskilled Labor."

24 John Modell, "Class or Ethnic Solidarity: The Japanese American Company Union," *Pacific Historical Review*, 38 (1969), 193–206.

25 *Ibid.*, 198 and 206.

26 Karl Yoneda, "One Hundred Years of Japanese Labor in the U.S.A.," in Amy Tachiki, ed. *Roots: An Asian American Reader*, (Los Angeles: Regents of the University of California, 1971), 150–158; and Karl G. Yoneda, *Ganbatte: Sixty-Year Struggle of a Kibei Worker* (Los Angeles: Asian American Studies Center, University of California, 1983).

27 For additional information on Yoneda, see Chris Friday, *Organizing Asian American Labor: The Pacific Coast Canned-Salmon Industry, 1870–1942* (Philadelphia: Temple University Press, 1994), 152–153, 156, 160, 167–68, 181, 257–259. Readers may also find it worthwhile to compare Yoneda's life to the experiences of the Japanese Canadian labor activist in Rolf Knight and Maya Koizumi, *A Man of Our Times: The*

Life-history of a Japanese-Canadian Fisherman (Vancouver, Canada: New Star Books, 1977).

28   I have attempted to address some of these aspects of Yoneda's life in a biographical essay, "Karl Yoneda: Radical Organizing and Asian American Labor," that is forthcoming in a volume on labor biographies edited by Eric Arnesen.

29   Philip Vera Cruz, *Philip Vera Cruz: A Personal History of Filipino Immigrants and the Farmworkers Movement*, ed. Craig Scharlin and Lilia V. Villanueva, foreword by Elaine Kim (Seattle: University of Washington Press, 2000).

30   Dorothy Fujita Rony, "Coalitions, Race, and Labor: Rereading Philip Vera Cruz," *Journal of Asian American Studies*, 3 (2000), 139–162; and E. San Juan, Jr., "From National Allegory to the Performance of the Joyful Subject: Reconstituting Philip Vera Cruz's Life," *Amerasia Journal*, 21 (1995–96), 137–153..

31   Yuji Ichioka, "A Buried Past: Early Issei Socialists and the Japanese Community," *Amerasia Journal*, 1 (1971), 1–25; "Ameyuki-san: Japanese Prostitutes in Nineteenth-Century America," *ibid.*, 4 (1977), 1–21; "Asian Immigrant Coal Miners and the United Mine Workers of America: Race and Class at Rock Springs, Wyoming, 1907," *ibid.*, 6 (1979), 1–24; "An Instance of Private Japanese Diplomacy: Suzuki Bunji, Organized American Labor, and Japanese Immigrant Workers, 1915–1916," *ibid.*, 10 (1983), 1–22; and "Japanese Immigrant Labor Contractors." These articles along with additional primary research and a synthesis of existing literature are included in Yuji Ichioka, *The Issei: The World of the First Generation Japanese Immigrants, 1885–1924* (New York: The Free Press, 1988).

32   Ichioka, "Immigrant Labor Contractors."

33   Ichioka, "Asian Immigrant Coal Miners"; Modell, "Japanese American Company Union."

34   In addition to Ichioka, "Early Issei Socialists" and *idem.*, "Suzuki Bunji, Organized American Labor," see *idem.*, "Japanese Immigrant Nationalism: the Issei and the Sino-Japanese War, 1937–1941," *California History*, 69 (1990), 260–275, 310–311.

35   Yuji Ichioka, "Ameyuki-san: Japanese Prostitutes in Nineteenth-Century America," *Amerasia Journal*, 4 (1977), 1–21; Yuji Ichioka, "America Nadeshiko: Japanese Immigrant Women in the United States, 1900–1924," *Pacific Historical Review*, 48 (1980), 339–357.

36   Valerie Matsumoto, "Japanese American Women During World War II," *Frontiers*, 8 (1984), 6–14; Evelyn Nakano Glenn, *Issei Nisei, War Bride: Three Generations of Japanese American Women in Domestic Service* (Philadelphia: Temple University Press, 1986); Peggy Pascoe, "Western Women at the Cultural Crossroads," in P. N. Limerick, et al., eds., *Trails Toward a New Western History* (Lawrence: University Press of Kansas, 1991), 40–58, and esp. n. 11, 220–221. For similar literature on Chinese women, see Lucie (Cheng) Hirata, "Free, Indentured, Enslaved: Chinese Prostitutes in Nineteenth-Century America," *Signs* (Autumn 1979), 3–29; Judy Yung, *Chinese Women of America, A Pictorial History* (Seattle: University of Washington Press, 1986); and Judy Yung, *Unbound Feet: A Social History of Chinese Women in San Francisco* (Berkeley: University of California Press, 1995).

37   Haya Stier, "Immigrant Women Go to Work: Analysis of Immigrant Wives' Labor Supply for Six Asian Groups," *Social Science Quarterly*, 72 (1991), 67–82, argues that this persists to the present day.

38   For a guide to the bulk of the collection, see Yuji Ichioka, *A Buried Past: An Annotated Bibliography of the Japanese American Research Project Collection* (Berkeley: University of California Press, 1974).

39 Him Mark Lai, "A Historical Survey of the Chinese Left in American Society," in *Counterpoint,* 63–80, for example, has brief, but important discussions of Chinese salmon cannery workers and Chinese hand laundry workers. This is available in a revised and expanded format in Him Mark Lai, "To Bring Forth a New China, To Build a Better America: The Chinese Marxist Left in America to the 1960s," *Chinese America: History and Perspectives* (1992): 3–82. His treatment of the former helped me conceptualize and document Chinese unionists in *Organizing Asian American Labor.* His work on the latter was an important aid to Renqiu Yu, *To Save China, To Save Ourselves: The Chinese Hand Laundry Alliance of New York* (Philadelphia: Temple University Press, 1992). Lai also has handed over many Chinese language documents to researchers like me and his *A History Reclaimed: An Annotated Bibliography of Chinese Language Materials on the Chinese of America,* ed. Russell Leong and Jean Pang Yip (Los Angeles: Asian American Studies Center, University of California, 1986), is an invaluable aid on the order of Ichioka, *Buried Past.* There are few students of Chinese American history who are not in Lai's debt in some fashion.

40 Thomas W. Chinn, H. Mark Lai, and Philip P. Choy, eds., *A History of the Chinese in California: A Syllabus* (San Francisco: Chinese Historical Society of America, 1969).

41 Lai, "Chinese Left."

42 Lai's work, for example, assisted in the creation of the best available study on Chinese and Chinese American politics, see L. Eve Armentrout Ma, *Revolutionaries Monarchists, and Chinatowns: Chinese Politics in the Americas* (Honolulu: University of Hawaii Press, 1990).

43 Lai, "Chinese Left," 68.

44 *Ibid.,* 68–72. For additional information, see Friday, *Organizing Asian American Labor,* 155–156, 158, 174.

45 Lai, "Chinese Left," 72. Shih-shan Henry Tsai, "Chinese Immigration through Chinese Communist Eyes: An Introduction to the Historiography," *Pacific Historical Review,* 43 (1974), 395–408, provides a useful discussion on how politics affect historical writing.

46 Victor Nee and B. de Bary Nee, *Longtime Californ': A Documentary Study of an American Chinatown* (New York: Pantheon, 1973), depicts the lives of some of those bachelors.

47 Lai, "Chinese Left," 75.

48 Such works are usually identifiable by their titles: "The Chinese in or The Japanese in . . . "See Kim, *Asian American Studies,* esp. 65–80.

49 Howard Brett Melendy's two works are instructive on this point: *The Oriental Americans* (New York: Twayne Publishers, 1972) discusses Chinese and Japanese; *Asians in America: Filipinos, Koreans, and East Indians* (Boston: Twayne Publishers, 1977), is self-explanatory. For others that reflect the same trend, see: Gary R. Hess, "The Hindu in America: Immigration and Naturalization Policies and India, 1917–1946," *Pacific Historical Review,* 38 (1969), 59–79; Bong-Youn Choy, *Koreans in America* (Chicago: Nelson-Hall, 1979); and Fred Cordova, *Filipinos: Forgotten Asian Americans, a Pictorial Essay, 1763–Circa 1963* (Dubuque, IA: Kendall, Hunt Publishing Co., 1983).

50 Cordova, *Filipinos.* Howard DeWitt, *Violence in the Fields: California Filipino Farm Labor Unionization during the Great Depression* (Saratoga, CA: Century Twenty One Publishing, 1980), is also an excellent recounting of events involving Filipinos.

51 On railroads, see Alexander Saxton, "The Army of Canton in the High Sierra," *Pacific Historical Review,* 35 (1966), 141–151; George Kraus, "Chinese Laborers and the Construction of the Central Pacific," *Utah Historical Quarterly,* 37 (1969),

41–57. On mining, see David V. DuFault, "The Chinese in Mining Camps of California: 1818–1870," *Southern California Quarterly*, 41 (1959), 155–170; and John P. Eswelt, "Upper Columbia Chinese Placering," *Pacific Northwesterner*, 3 (1959), 6–11. More recent examples include Randall E. Rohe, "After the Gold Rush: Chinese Mining in the Far West, 1850–1880," *Montana*, 32 (1982), 2–19; and Daniel Liestman, "The Chinese in the Black Hills, 1876–1932," *Journal of the West*, 27 (1988), 74–83. For two classic studies on agriculture, see Carey McWilliams, *Factories in the Field: The Story of Migratory Farm Labor in California* (Boston: Little, Brown and Company, 1939); Theodore Saloutos, "The Immigrant in Pacific Coast Agriculture, 1880–1940," *Agricultural History*, 49 (1975), 182–201.

52 Ichioka, "Asian Immigrant Coal Miners."

53 Gunther Peck, "Padrones and Protest: 'Old' Radicals and 'New' Immigrants in Bingham, Utah, 1905–1912," *Western Historical Quarterly*, 24(1993), 157–178.

54 Paul M. Ong, "The Central Pacific Railroad and Exploitation of Chinese Labor," *Journal of Ethnic Studies*, 13 (1985), 119–124.

55 Yuzo Murayama, "Contractors, Collusion, and Competition: Japanese Immigrant Railroad Laborers in the Pacific Northwest, 1898–1911," *Explorations in Economic History*, 21 (1984), 290–305.

56 W. Thomas White, "Race, Ethnicity, and Gender in the Railroad Work Force: The Case of the Far Northwest, 1883–1918," *Western Historical Quarterly*, 16 (1985), 265–284.

57 Posadas, "Filipinos, the Pullman Company, and the Brotherhood of Sleeping Car Porters."

58 For Posadas, the adjustment by Filipinos from an oppositional stance to unionization to union members was a part of the acculturation process. Still, the continued segregation of Filipinos *suggests* that ethnic identity remained strong.

59 Tomas Almaguer, "Racial Domination." For a less optimistic view of the strike and its promise of racial coalitions, see Richard Steven Street, "The 1903 Oxnard Sugar Beet Strike: A New Ending," *Labor History*, 39 (1998), 193–199.

60 Howard A. DeWitt, "The Filipino Labor Union: The Salinas Lettuce Strike of 1934," *Amerasia Journal*, 5 (1978), 1–22.

61 Peter C. Y. Leung and L. Eve Armentrout Ma, "Chinese Farming Activities in the Sacramento San Joaquin Delta: 1910–1941," *Amerasia Journal*, 14 (1988), 1–18. For a very personal look at this topic, see Jeff Gillenkirk and James Motlow, *Bitter Melon: Stories from the Last Rural Chinese Town in America* (Seattle: University of Washington, 1987).

62 Martin Brown and Peter Philips, "The Evolution of Labor Market Structure: The California Canning Industry," *Industrial and Labor Relations Review*, 38 (1985), 352–407, idem., "Competition, Racism, and Hiring Practices among California Manufacturers, 1860–1882," *Industrial and Labor Relations Review*, 40 (1986), 61–74, idem., "The Decline of the Piece-rate System in California Canning: Technological Innovation, Labor Management, and Union Pressure, 1890–1917," *Business History Review*, 50 (1986), 561–601, *idem.*, "Craft Labor and Mechanization in Nineteenth-century American Canning," *Journal of Economic History*, 18 (1988), 743–758.

63 Vicki L. Ruiz, *Cannery Women, Cannery Lives. Mexican Women, Unionization, and the California Food Processing Industry, 1930–1950* (Albuquerque: University of New Mexico Press, 1987). For a continuation of the discussion historically and conceptually, see Patricia Zavella, *Women's Work and Chicano Families: Cannery Workers of the Santa Clara Valley* (Ithaca: Cornell University Press, 1987).

64 Masson and Guimary, "Asian Labor Contractors," idem., "Filipinos and Unionization of the Alaskan Canned Salmon Industry," *Amerasia Journal*, 8 (1981),1–30, *idem.*,

"The Exploitation of Chinese Labor in the Alaska Salmon Industry," *Chinese America: History and Perspectives* (1990), 91–105; and Robert A. Nash, "The 'China Gangs' in the Alaska Packers Association Canneries, 1892–1935," in *Life, Influence and the Role of the Chinese in the United States, 1776–1960* (San Francisco: Chinese Historical Society of America, 1976), 257–283.

65 Friday, *Organizing Asian American Labor.*

66 Also see Arleen deVera, "Without Parallel: The Local 7 Deportation Cases, 1949–1955," *Amerasia Journal,* 20 (1994), 1–25; and Chris Friday, "Competing Communities at Work: Asian Americans, European Americans, and Native Alaskans in the Pacific Northwest, 1938–1947," in *Over the Edge: Remapping the American West,* ed. Valerie J. Matsumoto and Blake Almendinger (Berkeley: University of California Press, 1999), 307–328.

67 Bonacich, "Ethnic Antagonism."

68 David M. Gordon, Richard Edwards, and Michael Reich, *Segmented Work, Divided Workers: The Historical Transformation of Labor in the United States* (Cambridge: Harvard University Press, 1982).

69 Wing-cheung Ng, "An Evaluation of the Labor Market Status of Chinese Americans," *Amerasia Journal,* 4 (1977), 101–122; Mike Hinton, "The Split Labor Market and Chinese Immigration, 1848–1882," *Journal of Ethnic Studies,* 6 (1979), 99–108; Paul M. Ong, "Chinese Labor in Early San Francisco: Racial Segmentation and Industrial Expansion," *Amerasia Journal,* 8 (1981), 69–92.

70 Richard White, *"It's Your Misfortune and None of My Own": A New History of the American West* (Norman: University of Oklahoma Press, 1990), 274.

71 Paul M. Ong, "Chinese Labor in Early San Francisco: Racial Segmentation and Industrial Expansion," *Amerasia Journal,* 8 (1981), 78. Mark A. Johnson, "Capital Accumulation and Wage Rates: The Development of the California Labor Market in the Nineteenth Century," *Review of Radical Political Economics,* 21 (1989), 76–81, in a recent variation of Gunther Barth, argues that Chinese appeared in the secondary sector because they accepted these jobs. They could survive on a lower cost of living and were not acculturated. Therefore, their position in the economy was a result of their acceptance of the jobs and their self-imposed segregation.

72 Ewa Morawska, "The Sociology and Historiography of Immigration," in Virginia Yans-McLaughlin, ed., *Immigration Reconsidered: History, Sociology, and Politics* (New York: Oxford University Press, 1990), 198.

73 Friday, *Organizing Asian American Labor,* esp. 82–103.

74 Robert M. Jiobu, "Ethnic Hegemony and the Japanese of California," *American Sociological Review,* 53 (1988), 353–367.

75 Education, for example, is usually cited as a key reason for Japanese American upward mobility in works like Jared J. Young, *Discrimination, Income, Human Capital Investment, and Asian-Americans* (San Francisco: R and E Research Associates, 1977). Young seeks to demonstrate that Chinese and Japanese have been successful within the capitalist system by increasing their human capital—education, job training, etc. On the notion of racialized peoples fighting for position, see Michael Omi and Howard Winant, *Racial Formation in the United States from the 1960s to the 1990s,* 2nd. ed. (New York: Routledge, 1994). I have attempted to sketch out some of these issues in the context of the American West in Chris Friday, " 'In Due Time': Narratives of Race and Place in the Western United States," in *Race, Ethnicity, and Nationality in the United States: Toward the Twenty-first Century,* ed. Paul Wong (Boulder, Colo.: Westview Press, 1999), 55–101.

76 Sucheng Chan, *This Bittersweet Soil, The Chinese in California Agriculture, 1860–1910* (Berkeley: University of California Press, 1986), 206, notes that labor contractors were the social nuclei of rural California because of their connections to employment opportunities in the region and their ties to China.

77 Among the more recent studies directed specifically to labor contracting, see: William S. Hallagan, "Labor Contracting in Turn-of-the-Century California Agriculture," *Journal of Economic History,* 40 (1980), 757–776; Yuzo Murayama, "Contractors, Collusion, and Competition: Japanese Immigrant Railroad Laborers in the Pacific Northwest, 1898–1911," *Explorations in Economic History,* 21 (1984), 290–305; Patricia Cloud and David W. Galenson, "Chinese Immigration and Contract Labor in the Late Nineteenth Century," *ibid.,* 21 (1987), 22–42. The latter argue that Chinese contracting was not particularly exploitative. For the ensuing debate, see: Charles J. McClain, Jr., "Chinese Immigration: A Comment on Cloud and Galenson," *ibid.,* 27 (1990), 363–378; Patricia Cloud and David W. Galenson, "Chinese Immigration: Reply to Charles McClain," *ibid.,* 28 (1991), 239–247.

78 Modell, "Japanese American Company Union." For more thorough discussions, see John Modell, *The Economics and Politics of Racial Accommodation: The Japanese of Los Angeles, 1900–1942* (Urbana: University of Illinois Press, 1977); Edna Bonacich and John Modell, *The Economic Basis of Ethnic Solidarity: Small Business in the Japanese American Community* (Berkeley: University of California Press, 1980).

79 Gunther Peck, "Padrones and Protest: 'Old' Radicals and 'New' Immigrants in Bingham, Utah, 1905–1912," *Western Historical Quarterly,* 24 (1993), 157–178. Readers will want to review the much more extensive treatment in Gunther Peck, *Reinventing Free Labor: Padrones and Immigrant Workers in the North American West, 1880–1930* (Cambridge, Eng.: Cambridge University Press, 2000).

80 Ronald Takaki, *Pau Hana: Plantation Life and Labor in Hawaii 1835–1920* (Honolulu: University of Hawaii Press, 1983); Michi Kodama-Nishimoto, Warren S. Nishimoto, and Cynthia A. Oshiro, *Hanahana: An Oral History Anthology of Hawaii's Working People* (Honolulu: Ethnic Studies of Oral History Project, University of Hawaii at Manoa, 1984); Edward D. Beechert, *Working in Hawaii a Labor History* (Honolulu: University of Hawaii Press, 1985). Additional and important studies are John Liu, "Race, Ethnicity, and the Sugar Plantation System: Asian Labor in Hawaii, 1850–1900," in Lucie Cheng and Edna Bonacich, eds., *Labor Immigration Under Capitalism: Asian Workers in the United States before World War II* (Berkeley: University of California Press, 1984), 186–210; Miriam Sharma, "Labor Migration and Class Formation among the Filipinos in Hawaii, 1906–1946," in *ibid.,* 579–615.

81 In addition to Beechert, Masao Umezawa Duus, *The Japanese Conspiracy: The Oahu Sugar Strike of 1920,* trans. Beth Cary and adapted by Peter Duus (Berkeley: University of California Press, 1999), offers an incredibly detailed account of the strike. Ultimately, her argument supports those who argue that Takaki was overly optimistic about interethnic cooperation.

82 Chan, *This Bittersweet Soil,* and *idem.,* "The Chinese in Rural California: The Impact of Economic Change, 1860–1880," *Pacific Historical Review,* 53 (1984), 273–307. Chan revised the interpretations of Varden Fuller, "The Supply of Agricultural Labor as a Factor in the Evolution of Farm Organization in California," *Hearings Pursuant to Senate Regulation 266, Exhibit 8762–A,* 76th Cong. 3rd, sess., 1940, 19777–19898; Paul S. Taylor, "Foundations of California Rural Society," *California Historical Society Quarterly,* 24 (1945), 193–228; Lloyd H.

Fisher, *The Harvest Labor Market in California* (Cambridge: Harvard University Press, 1953); Cletus E. Daniel, *Bitter Harvest: A History of California Farmworkers, 1870–1941* (Ithaca, NY Cornell University Press, 1981); and Linda C. Majka and Theo J. Majka, *Farm Workers, Agribusiness, and the State* (Philadelphia: Temple University Press, 1982).

83 Lucy M. Cohen, *Chinese in the Post-Civil War South: A People Without a History* (Baton Rouge: Louisiana State University Press, 1984). For other studies on Chinese in the South, see James W. Loewen, *The Mississippi Chinese: Between Black and White* (Cambridge: Harvard University Press, 1971); and Shih-shan Henry Tsai, "The Chinese in Arkansas," *Amerasia Journal*, 8 (1981), 1–18.

84 Moon-Ho Jung's book manuscript in progress on the role of Asian "coolies" as potential replacements for African American labor in post-Civil War Louisiana sugar harvest and production suggests that race and labor need to be conceptualized in a transnational context as well as in the interplay between national and regional ideas.

85 Tera W. Hunter, *To Joy My Freedom: Southern Black Women's Lives and Labors after the Civil War* (Cambridge: Harvard University Press, 1998), 78–81.

86 Lucie Cheng and Edna Bonacich, eds., *Labor Immigration Under Capitalism: Asian Immigrant Workers in the U.S. Before World War II* (Berkeley: University of California Press, 1984).

87 Lucie Cheng and Edna Bonacich, "Introduction: A Theoretical Orientation to International Labor Migration," in *Labor Immigration Under Capitalism,* esp. 33–34.

88 Edna Bonacich, "Some Basic Facts: Patterns of Asian Immigration and Exclusion," in *Labor Immigration Under Capitalism,* 60–78, *idem.,* "U.S. Capitalist Development: A Background to Asian Immigration," *ibid.,* 79–129, *idem.,* "Asian Labor in the Development of California and Hawaii," *ibid.,* 130–185.

89 The authors and essays are: Liu, "Race, Ethnicity, and the Sugar Plantation"; Sharma, "Labor Migration and Class Formation"; June Mei, "Socioeconomic Origins of Emigration: Guangdong to California, 1850–1882," 219–247; *idem.,* "Socioeconomic Developments Among the Chinese in San Francisco, 1848–1906," 370–401; Alan Moriyama, "The Causes of Emigration: The Background of Japanese Emigration to Hawaii, 1885–1894," 248–276; Linda Pomerantz, "The Background of Korean Emigration," 277–315; Sucheta Mazumdar, "Colonial Impact and Punjabi Emigration to the United States," 316–337, *idem.,* "Punjabi Agricultural Workers in California, 1905–1945," 549–578; Lucie Cheng, "Free, Indentured, Enslaved: Chinese Prostitutes in Nineteenth-Century America," 402–435; Nobuya Tsuchida, "Japanese Gardeners in Southern California, 1900–1941," 435–469; Evelyn Nakano Glenn, "The Dialectics of Wage Work: Japanese American Women and Domestic Service, 1905–1940," 470–515; Sun Bin Yim, "The Social Structure of Korean Communities in California, 1903–1920," 515–548.

90 Morawska, "The Sociology and Historiography of Immigration," esp. 196–212.

91 Yu, *To Save China, To Save Ourselves.*

92 Yu specifically attacks and modifies the sojourner thesis articulated by Siu, "The Sojourner."

93 Peter Kwong, *Chinatown, New York: Labor and Politics, 1930–1950* (New York: Monthly Review Press, 1979). See also *idem.,* *The New Chinatown* (New York: Hill and Wang, 1987).

94 Yuji Ichioka, in a review of Yu's book points out the lack of discussion of women, *Amerasia Journal,* 19 (1993), 163. Dirk Hoerder, "International Labor Markets and Community Building by Migrant Workers in the Atlantic Economies," in Rudolph J. Vecoli and Suzanne M. Sinke, eds., *A Century of European Migrations, 1830–1930* (Urbana: University of Illinois Press, 1991), 98–100.

95 Chan, *Bittersweet Soil,* and Glenn, *Issei, Nisei, War Bride,* have the best discussion of the status of Asians in various service occupations. Scholars of Asian American labor will find instructive guidelines for the study of gender issues in Ava Baron, *Work Engendered: Toward a New History of American Labor* (Ithaca, N.Y.: Cornell University Press, 1991); Patricia Zavella, "Mujeres in Factories: Race and Class Perspectives on Women, Work, and Family," in Micaela di Leonardo, ed., *Gender at the Crossroads of Knowledge: Feminist Anthropology in the Postmodern Era* (Berkeley: University of California Press, 1991), 313; and Karen Anderson, "Work, Gender, and Power in the American West," *Pacific Historical Review,* 61 (1992), 488.

96 Edna Bonacich, "Editorial Forum: Reflections on Asian American Labor," *Amerasia Journal,* 18 (1992), xxiii-xxiv.

97 Dean S. Toji and James H. Johnson, "Asian and Pacific Islander Poverty: The Working Poor and the Jobless Poor," *Amerasia Journal,* 18 (1992), 83–91.

98 Gregory DeFreitas, "Unionization Among Racial and Ethnic Minorities," *Industrial and Labor Relations Review,* 18 (1993), 281–301.

99 In addition to Bonacich, "Reflections," and Toji and Johnson, "Asian and Pacific Islander American Poverty," the authors and articles *Amerasia Journal,* 18 (1992), are: Alex Hing, "Organizing Asian Pacific American Workers in the AFL-CIO: New Opportunities," 141–149; Pam Tau Lee, "Asian Workers in the U.S.—A Challenge for Labor," 95–102; Ramsay Liem and Jinsoo Kim, "Pico Korea Workers' Struggle, Korean Americans, and the Lessons of Solidarity," 19–69; Miriam Ching Louie, "Immigrant Asian Women in Bay Area Garment Sweatshops: 'After Sewing, Laundry, Cleaning and Cooking, I have No Breath Left to Sing," ' 1–26; Lydia Lowe, "Paving the Way. Chinese Immigrant Workers and Community-Based Labor Organizing in Boston," 39–48; Glen Omatsu, "To Our Readers: Asian Pacific American Workers and the Expansion of Democracy," v-xix; Kent Wong, "Building Unions in Asian Pacific Communities," 149–154.

100 Espiritu, *Asian American Panethnicity,* provides a good definition of the tensions inherent in creating an "Asian American" community.

101 Dean Lan, "The Chinatown Sweatshops: Oppression and Alternative," *Amerasia Journal,* 1 (1971), 40–57. For other recent accounts, see Wesley Macawili, "Chinatown Workers Organize," *The Progressive,* Feb. 1994, 14; and Peter Kwong and JoAnn Lum, "Hard Labor in Chinatown: How the Other Half Lives Now," *The Nation,* June 18, 1988, 858; and Peter Kwong, *Forbidden Workers: Illegal Chinese Immigrants and American Labor* (New York: New Press, 1997).

102 One entire issue of *Amerasia Journal* is devoted to this challenge. See *Amerasia Journal,* 21, no. 1–2 (1995).

103 Lisa Lowe, *Immigrant Acts: On Asian American Cultural Politics* (Durham, N.C.: Duke University Press, 1996), 174.

104 *Ibid.,* 175.

105 Charles Bergquist, "Labor History and its Challenges: Confessions of a Latin Americanist," *American Historical Review,* 98 (1993), 757–764. I apologize for the misspelling of Bergquist's name in Friday, "Asian American Labor History."

106 This has long been a theme in Asian American Studies and one that at least some labor historians such as Elizabeth Faue, *Community of Suffering and Struggle: Women, Men, and the Labor Movement in Minneapolis, 1915–1945* (Chapel Hill: University of North Carolina Press, 1991), have successfully embraced.

107 Bergquist, "Labor History and its Challenges," 764.

108 Gary Okihiro, *Common Ground: Reimagining American History* (Princeton, NJ: Princeton University Press, 2001).

109 Nayan Shah, *Contageous Divides: Epidemics and Race in San Francisco's Chinatown* (Berkeley: University of California Press, 2001).

110 For a review and commentary, see Friday, "Asian American Labor History."

111 Roger Daniels, *Asian America: A History of Chinese and Japanese in the United States since 1850* (Seattle: University of Washington Press, 1988), xiv; Friday, "Asian American Labor History."

112 Okihiro, *Common Ground.*

CHAPTER 12

CONVERSING ACROSS BOUNDARIES OF RACE, ETHNICITY, CLASS, GENDER, AND REGION: LATINO AND LATINA LABOR HISTORY

CAMILLE GUERIN-GONZALES

The project of remembering, recovering, and reconstructing the working-class origins of Latinas and Latinos in the United States has been the cornerstone of Latina and Latino scholarship in the twentieth century.[1] At the same time, political, sociological, economic, and anthropological studies by and about Latinos and Latinas that address working-class issues have informed both Latino and Latina labor history in such a way as to create a rather unique interdisciplinary Latino/Latina working-class history. Twentieth-century scholars of Latina and Latino experience have been particularly concerned with explaining and understanding the subordinate position of Latinas and Latinos in U.S. society. Thus, questions concerning political participation, educational attainment, social adjustment, and cultural retention, for example, have been informed to a great extent by the broader issue of economic subordination.

The incorporation of Latinos and Latinas into the U.S. economy and society in 1848 occurred in the midst of the economic transformation of the country into an industrial society. Mexicans, newly conquered, lost most of their land base in a matter of decades and found themselves with few alternatives to entering the nascent wage labor force in the Southwest. They were joined by immigrant workers from Mexico, and became, in the eyes "of most of their Anglo conquerors, indistinguishable from Mexican immigrants—"foreigners in their native land."[2] If one defines Latino history as the history of Latinas and Latinos living within the political boundaries of the United States, Latino labor history has its origins in this period of rapid industrialization.

The first body of scholarship focusing on Mexican American workers appeared in the 1920s and 1930s. David Gutiérrez analyzes this early work in an essay on Mexicans in the history of the American West, in which he argues that these early writings were self-consciously political in nature.[3] These writers, Gutiérrez tells us, set out to write their own history and to gain political equality.[4] The two projects were, he writes, inextricably intertwined and driven by the imperative to explain the impoverished condition of the vast majority of Mexican Americans: "The most important theme unifying this research was these scholars' obvious concern to represent ordinary working-class Mexican Americans and Mexican immigrants as complex, fully-formed, and fully-functional human beings."[5]

The three leading Mexican American intellectuals of the period—Carlos E. Castañeda, George I. Sánchez, and Arthur L. Campa—although not self-identified labor historians, contributed greatly to our understanding of the history of working-class ethnic Mexicans. Castañeda's writings, public addresses, and teaching dealt with labor history tangentially, although he did address the issue of discrimination against Mexican American workers directly in several studies.[6] George I. Sánchez's work, too, contributed to Latino and Latina labor history only indirectly. Sánchez dedicated his life to combating the effects of economic discrimination against Mexican Americans through reform of the public school system, and his scholarship offers important insights into the everyday lives of Mexican American working-class children, as do the writings on the popular culture of Mexican American working people by Arthur L. Campa.[7]

Three other writers of the same generation addressed labor history more directly. Manuel Gamio, a Mexican anthropologist; Paul S. Taylor, an Anglo political economist at the University of California, Berkeley; and Carey McWilliams, an Anglo journalist and freelance writer, are the best known scholars of ethnic Mexican labor history from the 1920s and 1930s. Although a small number of government-sponsored reports documented the participation of Mexicans in the U.S. work force in the early years of the century, Gamio, Taylor, and McWilliams were among the first to analyze Mexican American labor history from the perspective of Mexican immigrants and with the expressed purpose of achieving social justice for Mexican workers.[8]

Mexican Immigration to the United States by Manuel Gamio examines the extent of Mexican immigration in the early years of the twentieth century and the political, economic, and social implications of such immigration for both the United States and Mexico. Its companion publication, *The Life Story of the Mexican Immigrant*, is a collection of personal narratives culled from interviews conducted by Gamio and his research team between 1926 and 1927. Both volumes offer insight into the international tensions immigration provoked, as well as into the ways in which race, gender, and class mediated the experiences of Mexican immigrant women, men, and children.[9]

Paul S. Taylor's studies of Mexican immigration also draw on interviews and personal narratives, as well as on quantitative research, and address issues of race and class. Taylor began writing about Mexican workers in the 1930s and continued doing so into the 1980s. Over those six decades, Taylor produced a large body of work, the most comprehensive of which is his ten-volume *Mexican Labor in the United States*.[10] His field studies on Jalisco, Mexico, and Nueces County, Texas, broke new ground and, along with *Mexican Labor in the United States*, influenced a generation of scholars of Mexican American working-class history.[11] But Taylor's lasting legacy to Latino and Latina labor history is not only his research and published writings but his unrelenting pressure on employers and government agencies to recognize the economic and cultural contributions of Mexican workers to U.S. society. Beginning with his fight against restrictive immigration laws in the 1920s and his opposition to the expulsion programs of the 1930s, Taylor wrote and campaigned vigorously against discriminatory policies in the United States.[12]

The writings of Carey McWilliams also were explicitly political in nature. McWilliams began researching and writing about Mexican workers after working as an American Civil Liberties Union lawyer on cases involving striking Mexican agricultural workers in California. He wrote about the repatriation and removal programs aimed at Mexican immigrants and Mexican Americans during the 1930s and about the strikes in which Mexican workers participated during the same period.[13] His book *Factories in the Field* exposed the industrial nature of agricultural production in California in a way that no other writing had before.[14] Completed in 1935 and published in 1939—the same year as John Steinbeck's *Grapes of Wrath*—*Factories in the Field* created a furor.[15] The work of both Taylor and McWilliams contrast sharply with most of the scholarly and journalistic accounts of Mexican labor written in the 1920s and 1930s by Anglos, which were paternalistic and condescending at best and virulently racist at their worst.[16]

A number of other studies written in the 1930s also helped lay the groundwork for the history of Latino and Latina labor organizing in the United States. Ruth Allen's studies of ethnic Mexican women workers in Texas and Sidney Sufrin's article, "Labor Organization in Agricultural America, 1930–35," documented the labor and living conditions that underlay strike actions in the 1930s.[17] Ernesto Galarza, who published work on Mexican immigrant and Mexican American labor history over a span of 50 years, also focused on working-class unions and protests. Galarza was expressly interested in understanding the economic subordination of ethnic Mexicans in the United States, and his writings on the Bracero Program (1942–1964) are especially important to Latino labor history. Two books in particular— *Merchants of Labor* and *Spiders in the House and Workers in the Field*—helped to publicize discriminatory labor relations in California agriculture and documented the struggle of Mexican farm workers to organize labor unions from the 1940s through the 1970s.[18]

Throughout the 1930s and into the World War II and post-war era, studies by Carlos Castañeda, George I. Sánchez, Arthur Campa, Manuel Gamio, Paul Taylor, Carey McWilliams, and Ernesto Galarza continued to lead the way for students of ethnic Mexican labor history.[19] The most notable addition to this scholarship was Stuart Jamieson's *Labor Unionism in American Agriculture*.[20] Jamieson's study discussed and analyzed union organizing and activism of Mexican immigrant and Mexican American farm workers and, along with Varden Fuller's "The Supply of Agricultural Labor as a Factor in the Evolution of Farm Organization in California" and Lloyd Fisher's *The Harvest Labor Market in California*, analyzed the industrial nature of farming and the factory-like conditions of work for the predominantly ethnic Mexican farm labor force, building on the pathbreaking work of Taylor and McWilliams.[21]

Latino and Latina labor history in this period was dominated by Anglo scholars who sought through their writing either to reform labor relations between Latino and Latina workers and their employers or to aid employers in procuring and allocating Mexican labor.[22] This scholarship included efforts by Charles Loomis, Seldon Menefee and Orin Cassmore, and Pauline Kibbe.[23] A number of studies on Puerto Rican migrant workers in the United States were driven by a similar impulse. These studies included Victor Clark's *Porto Rico and Its Problems*, published in 1930 by the Brookings Institution; Lawrence R. Chenault's *The Puerto Rican Migrant in New York City*; Arthur D. Gayer, Paul T. Homan, and Earle K. James's *The Sugar Economy of Puerto Rico*; and *Labor Conditions in Porto Rico*, a report for the U.S. Department of Labor by Joseph Marcus.[24]

Writers seeking to bring about socially just labor relations, as well as those who sought simply to create a more rational labor system, either ignored Latina workers or mentioned them only in passing. Most scholars superimposed the dominant ideal of a nuclear family, with women occupying a separate sphere outside the work force, onto ethnic Mexicans and Puerto Ricans in the United States. Not only did this obscure women's participation in wage labor but it hid and in the process subordinated and devalued women's reproductive labor. Although several studies written in this period focused specifically on women—for example Ruth Allen's "Mexican Peon Women in Texas," and *The Pecan Shellers of San Antonio*, by Seldon Menefee and Orin Cassmore—these are the exception, rather than the rule.[25] Thus, gender as a category of analysis is either completely absent or subsumed within discussions of race and class in nearly all scholarship on Latino workers written in these years. It took the social and political revolution of the 1960s and 1970s to change this state of affairs, although early Chicano movement scholarship continued to ignore women completely or to subsume them under the category of "family."

Working-class histories during the early years of the Chicano movement focused on farm labor, especially on the organizing drive of the United Farm Workers. Studies by Ernesto Galarza, John Gregory Dunne, Mark Day, Peter Mathiessen, Ronald B. Taylor, and Sam Kushner are the most well-known of this early scholarship on the UFW.[26] The 1965 UFW strike at Delano and the publicity surrounding the grape boycott brought about a renewed interest in earlier labor protests.[27] The 1933 berry-pickers' strike at El Monte was of particular concern to scholars such as Ronald W. López and Charles Wollenberg, who saw it as a precursor to the UFW's fight.[28] The grape strike, the Chicano movement in general, and coalitions among Chicana/o, Puerto Rican, Cuban, and other Latino/a activists opened the way for an unprecedented explosion of scholarship on every aspect of Latina and Latino life. The underlying concern of these studies was the economic, social, educational, and political subordination of Latinos and Latinas in the United States.

Combining a commitment to social justice for *Mexicanos* in the United States with historical scholarship, Juan Gómez-Quiñones led the way in the new Chicano history that emerged during these years.[29] In this tradition, Luis Arroyo examined ethnic Mexican participation in CIO organizing in Los Angeles between 1938 and 1950; Victor Nelson Cisneros looked at the experiences of

workers in Texas in the 1920s and 1930s; and Emilio Zamora, Jr. analyzed socialist labor activity of ethnic Mexicans in Texas in the early years of the twentieth
century.[30]

A number of Latino scholars were particularly influenced by Latin American theorists who developed the concept of internal colonialism to explain relations in
Latin America between native peoples and whites and between native peoples and
mestizos. Pablo González Casanova's "Internal Colonialism and National
Development," Rodolfo Stavenhagen's "Classes, Colonialism, and Acculturation,"
and Julio Cotler's "The Mechanics of International Domination and Social
Change in Peru," published between 1965 and 1968, influenced a generation of
scholars concerned with the social, economic, and political domination of Latinos,
as well as of African Americans, native peoples, and Asian Americans.[31] Carlos
Muñoz, Tomás Almaguer, Mario Barrera, and Charles Ornelas all drew on the
model of internal colonialism in writings and public speeches in the early 1970s,
during the campaign for Chicano studies programs in higher education.[32] Mario
Barrera's *Race and Class in the Southwest* is perhaps the most fully articulated application of the internal colony model to explain labor relations between Chicano
workers and their predominantly Anglo employers.[33]

Not all scholars writing about Chicano labor history subscribed wholly to the
internal colony model. Some, like Richard Griswold del Castillo, drew on a number of theoretical and methodological models, including those represented by
the work of urban historian Stephen Thernstrom, gaining "from each a degree
of direction."[34] Others turned as well to the work of labor historians such as E.
P. Thompson and Herbert Gutman. For example, when Pedro Castillo set out to
analyze "how and why the Chicano emerged and remained as a worker at the
bottom of the class structure," he placed his study firmly within the theoretical
framework of Thompson, Gutman, and Thernstrom.[35]

Similarly, Albert Camarillo, in his book, *Chicanos in a Changing Society*,
expanded on arguments he had posed in an earlier essay, "Chicano Urban
History: A Study of Compton's Barrio, 1936–1970," and used Thernstrom's
work as a framework for examining barrioization and proletarianization of ethnic
Mexicans in Santa Barbara, Los Angeles, San Bernardino, San Diego, and other
communities in southern California.[36] Mario García, too, was strongly influenced by Thompson, Gutman, and Thernstrom, as well as by David Brody's
Steelworkers in America, in developing his analysis of Mexican immigrant workers and their role in the growth of industrial capitalism in the Southwest.[37] *Desert
Immigrants*, by García, examined the experiences of Mexican immigrant workers
within a context of industrial capitalist development and "its need for new
sources of cheap and manageable labor."[38] And Arnoldo DeLeón integrated economic analysis with intellectual history in his cultural and social history of Texas
in the years 1836 to 1900.[39]

Puerto Rican labor scholars in this period were also particularly concerned
with the economic, social, and political implications of immigrant and migratory labor of Latinos and Latinas. Many of these writers turned to the work of
Harry Braverman to explain what they saw as a degradation of the labor
process, and to that of Andre Gunder Frank and other dependency theorists.[40]
In their scholarship of the 1960s and 1970s, they challenged the prevailing

notion that Puerto Rican migration was simply the result of overpopulation in Puerto Rico.[41] For example, Clara Rodríguez looked at Puerto Rican workers who had migrated to New York City in the first half of the twentieth century and analyzed the relationship between industrial capitalist development in Puerto Rico and the colonial ties between Puerto Rico and the United States. Manuel Maldonado-Dennis also examined this relationship in his study of the emigration dialectic. Building on earlier work, Maldonado-Dennis constructed a compelling Marxist analysis of emigration from Puerto Rico to the United States. He laid out, point by point, the connections between the colonial relationship between Puerto Rico and the United States and the development of underdevelopment in Puerto Rico. Felipe Rivera described the consequences of this relationship for Puerto Rican farm workers in the U.S. and linked the experiences of Puerto Rican farm workers with those of ethnic Mexican workers in their drive for unionization and their participation in UFW organizing during the 1960s and early 1970s.[42]

The development of analytical constructs to explain Latino and Latina experiences in the U.S., which emerged from the social upheavals of the 1960s and early 1970s, contributed to a growing, theoretically complex body of scholarship on Latino and Latina workers. Scholars writing about the experiences of Latinas in the work force were at the center of this new labor history. The work of Magdalena Mora, Margarita Melville, Adelaida del Castillo, Rosaura Sánchez, Clementina Duron, and Douglas Monroy was especially important to the project of beginning to recover the history of Chicana workers.[43] Such writers, drawing on a number of theoretical and methodological frameworks, examined the working-class experiences of Latinas. Magdalena Mora grounded her study of the 1975 strike at Toltec Foods in Richmond, California, in Marxist analysis, for example.[44] Historian Clementina Duron built on the work of Ricardo Romo, Victor Nelson Cisneros, and Albert Camarillo, as well as that of Ruth Milkman, in her study of ethnic Mexican women garment workers in Los Angeles.[45] Others drew on the methodologies of social history. For example, Laurie Coyle, Gail Hershatter, and Emily Honig interviewed immigrant Mexican women and Chicanas for their study of the 1972 garment-workers' strike of the Farah clothing company.[46]

Latina labor scholars' integration of gender analysis into their examinations of race and class relations complicated our understanding of the social relations of work. For example, although Vicki Ruiz was influenced by Louise Tilly and Joan Scott, her integration of race and ethnicity into class and gender analysis in her study of women cannery workers in California during the 1930s and 1940s provides insights into the ways in which race and ethnicity mediated both gender and class relations in the work place.[47] Ruiz's study helps us to have a better understanding of the limits and possibilities of gender and class alliances among ethnic Mexican and white women. Margaret Rose's study of ethnic Mexican women's activism in the UFW was also influenced by Louise Tilly, as well as a number of other women's historians.[48] She offers important insights into the sexual division of labor within the UFW and the ways in which this division limits the participation of ethnic Mexican women. Nancy Hewitt focuses on women's union activities and on ethnic, race, gender, and class alliances among women cigar workers that were based on a "Latin" ethnic identity that included both Cubans and Italians. Her examination of the role of patriotism and nationalism among Cuban expatriates and of notions of proper gender behavior in the work place offers a much-needed analysis of the complexities of class and gender relations in this period.[49]

Drawing on a number of methodologies and theoretical models, writers interested in the work experiences of Latinas have produced an innovative and exciting body of work in the 1980s and 1990s. For example, Devra Anne Weber analyzes the use of autobiography and oral history in recovering the history of Mexican women in studies of ethnic Mexican farm workers.[50] Gary R. Mormino and George E. Pozetta's community study of Ybor City includes a discussion of the experiences of Cuban women workers.[51] And, Sarah Deutsch's study of *hispanas* in northern New Mexico and southern Colorado in the late nineteenth and early twentieth centuries discusses the development of a regional community, and how *hispanas* and *hispanos* were able to draw on regional ties to resist integration into a wage labor system.[52]

Resistance to domination in the work place is a central theme in a number of studies on Latina and Latino labor. For example, Rosalinda González analyzes Latinas' unpaid labor as a strategy of resistance.[53] Virginia Sánchez Korrol looks at the ways in which Puerto Rican women workers resisted cultural domination. And Rosalia Solorzano examines struggles for control of the work place in her essay on Mexican immigrant women domestic workers in El Paso and in her research on women working in *maquiladoras* on the Mexican side of the border.[54]

The struggle for control over the work place was a dominant theme in Latino labor history in the 1980s and 1990s. Drawing on the pathbreaking work of David Montgomery, a number of writers explored questions of worker control under industrial capitalism. One of the best of these is David Montejano.[55] Montejano traces the rise of the working class in south Texas within a dialectic pattern of ethnic conflict and accommodation. His discussion and analysis of the social construction of races in the southwest and of the ways in which race and class shaped industrialization in Texas offer crucial insights into ethnic Mexican working-class history, as well as labor history in general. Another labor historian, Yvette Huginnie, also focuses on control over the work place in her study of ethnic Mexican copper miners in Arizona between 1870 and 1920. She, too, expands on the work of David Montgomery by focusing on race and ethnicity, as she skillfully analyzes the racialization of labor relations during the heyday of the Arizona copper industry. Linda Gordon's study of the adoption of white orphans by Mexican copper mining families and the violent response of white residents of the camp to the formation of these interracial families owes a great debt to Huginnie's generosity in sharing her pioneering research on this infamous incident in working-class history, developed in Huginnie's book in progress on race relations in Arizona copper towns.[56] Dennis Nodin Valdez's study of Mexican and Puerto Rican agricultural workers in the Midwest and Zaragosa Vargas's examination of the northward migration of Mexican immigrants and their experiences as urban workers also analyze aspects of workers' control. These works make especially important contributions in their emphasis on proletarianization in a heretofore understudied region of the United States.[57] *Al Norte*, by Valdez, is social history at its best. He uses industrial farming in the Midwest as an "ethnic laboratory" to examine race relations and strategies developed by both workers and employers to control the work place. In it he brings home the exploitative impact of industrial work in a way few writers have succeeded in doing. Zaragosa Vargas sees his own study, *Proletarians of the North*, as completing a sort of trilogy of regional studies of proletarianization and urbanization of Mexican immigrant (complementing Albert Camarillo's study of California and Mario García's of Texas). Vargas draws on labor market segmentation theory, especially the writings of David Gordon, Richard Edwards, and Michael Reich, in his analysis of what he interprets as a transition among ethnic Mexicans from agricultural work to industrial labor in the steel mills and automobile factories of the Midwest.[58]

The importance of community activism and politics to the everyday lives of Latina/o workers is at the center of a number of studies. Two books on Chicano politics by Juan Gómez-Quiñones build on his earlier work on the Chicano working class to offer an exploration of labor protest firmly situated within an analysis of community activism.[59] Gilbert González contributes to this project in his examination of community activism and organizing among Mexican and Mexican American citrus workers living in labor camps in Southern California between 1900 and 1940, *Labor and Community*. His new study of the role of the Mexican government in labor organizing among Mexican nationals in the U.S. adds an important dimension to his earlier work.[60] David Gutíerrez also is concerned with the politics of immigrant and working-class cultures and the construction of ethnic, class, and national identity. His book on ethnic Mexicans, *Walls and Mirrors: Mexican Americans, Mexican Immigrants, and the Politics of Ethnicity in the American Southwest*, is a tightly argued and beautifully crafted study of how Mexican immigrants negotiated citizenship, identity, and class in the United States.[61] New Deal politics in California labor wars contextualize Devra Weber's study of farm workers in depression California. Weber "crosses borders" to look at transnational identities of Mexican farm workers and labor organizers in this pivotal period.[62] My study, *Mexican Workers and American Dreams*, also examines patterns of ethnic Mexican resistance to domination in their mapping of national and ethnic identity on the contested terrain of the American Dream, and analyzes the racial constructions and limitations of the American Dream.[63]

Tomás Almaguer traces the development of racial supremacy in California in his book, *Racial Faultlines*, thereby situating the subjugation of ethnic Mexicans within a larger context of racialization.[64] Susan Johnson studies similar issues from a different vantage point in her work on gender and race relations in the California Gold Rush, in which she also complicates the hierarchically organized opposition between productive and reproductive labor that informs much labor history.[65] Johnson builds on the work of Chicana historians Deena González and Antonia Castañeda in their work on women in nineteenth-century New Mexico and late eighteenth- and early nineteenth-century California, respectively. Together, González and

Castañeda provide a powerful model for considering the meanings and practices of women's work in the context of conquest.[66] Johnson's examination of
race relations among Mexican, Chilean, Anglo, Pacific Islander, Chinese, and
native peoples offers a breathtaking vision of a multiracial world in one part of
the U.S. West. Racial constructions take center stage in Neil Foley's study of
agricultural workers in the Texas cotton industry. His work begins to build a
bridge between Southern and African American history, on the one hand, and
Southwestern and Chicano history, on the other, even as its primary emphasis
is on the racialization of poor whites. He argues provocatively that the real
scourge of the South was not cotton but whiteness itself. The violence of slavery and racism resulted not from economic relations specific to the cotton
industry but rather from a philosophy of racial superiority that savaged not
only African Americans and Mexican Americans but poor whites who could
not live up to the standards of superior whiteness.[67]

A number of studies interrogating constructions of racial, ethnic, and gender
identity among Latinos draw on cultural studies theorists in their analysis of
Latino working-class cultures. George Sánchez, in his book *Becoming Mexican
American*, explores the ways in which Mexican immigrants forged a new cultural identity in the United States as ethnic Americans.[68] Vicki Ruiz's essay,
"Star Struck," also looks at social constructions of ethnic identity. She grounds
her study of identity formation, Americanization, and generational tension in a
superb analysis of popular culture—movie and romance magazines, radio programs, films, newspaper advertisements, popular ballads.[69] And in her pathbreaking book, *From Out of the Shadows*, Ruiz looks at the shop floor as a site
of cultural conflict. There, women's "silk stockings were accessories to unionization," Ruiz tells us, as shared consumerist desires facilitated alliances among
immigrant and American-born *Mexicanas*, as well as between Anglo women
and ethnic Mexican women. Mexican women fought for economic justice and
dignity with courage, intelligence, and style. They embraced the American
Dream, but made it their own and, in the process, created alternative meanings
of the dream for ethnic Mexicans in the United States. Ethnic Mexican women
moved between and among cultures, crossed and recrossed cultural borders—
occupying different positions in the process of negotiating social, political, and
economic space. This process was part of a large repertoire of strategies
Mexican women self-consciously used to navigate multiple terrains. This is
quite different from a process of either "becoming American" or, to use
George Sánchez's term, "becoming Mexican American."

The new Latino/a labor history continues to draw on a variety of disciplines
and methodologies in the project of remembering, recovering, and (re)con-
structing the working-class lives of Latinas and Latinos in the United States. Yet
the scholarship that developed out of the social movement of the 1960s and early
1970s transformed Latino labor history. The student movement made it possible
for a critical mass of scholars to be trained as professional historians, and for their
scholarship to begin to have a home in the academy. But this possibility has yet
to be achieved.[70] The foundation laid by scholars from a variety of disciplines has
made it possible for historians in the twenty-first century to explore new avenues
of intellectual inquiry, to take risks that those responsible for the pick-and-shovel

work of uncovering and beginning to make sense of Latino history often did not have the luxury of taking.

The exciting new work in which Latina and Latino labor historians are engaged is part of a Latino/a Renaissance in music, art, literature, drama, and other areas of Latina and Latino expression. Scholars of Latino/a labor history are engaged in a conversation across disciplines, across time, and across borders. This conversation of remembering and (re)constructing our own history continues in the work of Matt García, whose *A World of Its Own* exemplifies the best of the new scholarship on working-class Latina/o cultures. *Teatro*, music, dance, and youth culture unite with labor and community organizing in a multicultural, multiracial, and multiethnic metropolis in his careful analysis of race relations in the citrus industry of greater Los Angeles.[71] Adrian Burgos's scholarship on labor relations and the "playing" of race in professional baseball leagues reminds labor historians of the multiple and shifting constructions of racial identity among Latinos. Two essays in particular, "The Latins from Manhattan" and "Playing Ball in a Black and White 'Field Of Dreams'" complicate our understanding of the relationship between work and cultural production in the construction of racial identities.[72]

Nancy Raquel Mirabel's study of labor, community, nation, and identity is an elegantly written interrogation of the cultural work of Cuban and Puerto Rican immigrants in New York in the late nineteenth century. She argues that Cuban and Puerto Rican cigar workers and garment workers set out to "build a nation from the outside" that better represented and reflected their diasporic identities. Political activism, labor organizing, and the formation of community organizations united Puerto Ricans and Cubans in a dynamic struggle to create a new vision of nation and identity—a hybrid nation *afuera*, "an Antillean Nation,"—in New York City.[73] Miroslava Chávez explores the changing status of women in California using untapped legel records in her "Mexican Women and the American Conquest in Los Angeles."[74] And Omar Valerio-Jiménez looks at the role of the state in cultural transformation and identity construction in his examination of class and gender differences in the Texas borderlands.[75] Another new study that focuses on identity is Raquel Casas's examination of the relationship between constructions of identity of second generation *Californiana*s and their ability under the law to own and inherit property.[76] And property ownership is at the center of "Translating Property," María Montoya's sensitive, compelling study of the conflict over land in the northern New Mexico in contests over region, ethnicity, and class.[77]

Conflicts over property and ownership of the products of labor is a central feature of Mary Laura Coomes's beautifully crafted comparative study of cinnabar and mercury miners who worked in a California mine in the eighteenth, nineteenth, and early twentieth century. Her study of the different meanings native peoples, *Mexicanos*, and Anglos attached to resources at *Pooyi*, or the New Almaden mine, offers important insights into the ways in which relations of production racialize and engender physical and cultural space.[78] My own project, a comparative study of coal mining communities in northern New Mexico-southern Colorado, Appalachia, and South Wales draws inspiration from what is now an established and flourishing field of Latina and Latino labor history.[79] We occupy borders and borderlands, crossing and recrossing them to create a new, hybrid labor history of Latinas and Latinos that refuses the limits of borders.

NOTES

1 The term Latino encompasses a diverse Latin American-descent population in the United States. I will focus primarily on scholarship by and about people of Mexican, Puerto Rican, and Cuban origin. Following the lead of David Gutiérrez, I use "ethnic Mexican" when referring to both Mexican immigrants and Mexican Americans, and "Mexican American" in reference to Americans of Mexican descent before the Chicano Movement of the 1960s.

2 See David Weber, ed., *Foreigners in their Native Land: Historical Roots of the Mexican Americans* (Albuquerque: University of New Mexico Press, 1973), vi.

3 David G. Gutiérrez, "Significant to Whom?: Mexican Americans and the History of the American West," *Western Historical Quarterly*, 24 (November 1993)4:519–539.

4 Gutiérrez discusses the writings of George I. Sánchez, Arthur L. Campa, Carlos Castañeda, Ernesto Galarza, Jovita González, and Americo Paredes.

5 Gutierrez, "Significant to Whom"?, 525.

6 Carlos E. Castañeda, "Statement on Discrimination Against Mexican-Americans in Employment," unpublished typescript (1947), "Wetbacks: A Preliminary Report to the Advisory Committee Study of Spanish-Speaking People," (1949), cited by Mario T. García, *Mexican Americans: Leadership, Ideology, and Identity, 1930–1960* (New Haven: Yale University Press, 1989).

7 Gutiérrez, "Significant to Whom?", 525–527. See also García, *Mexican Americans*.

8 See Victor S. Clark, *Mexican Labor in the United States*, Bureau of Labor Bulletin no. 78 (September 1908), 417–644; and Frank R. Stone, "Report to the Commissioner General of Immigration on Activities of Labor Agents in Recruiting Mexican Labor," June 23, 1910, Immigration and Naturalization Service Division, Record Group 85, National Archives and Record Service, Washington, D.C. They are the two most in-depth of these studies. Prescriptive literature aimed at an audience of employers appeared in the late nineteenth and early twentieth centuries as well. These studies, though, did not focus specifically on Mexican and Mexican American workers. See, for example, A. D. Shamel, "Housing the Employees of California's Citrus Ranches," *California Citrograph* (February-March 1918).

9 Manuel Gamio, Mexican *Immigration to the United States: A Study of Human Migration and Adjustment* (Chicago: University of Chicago Press, 1930 ; reprint ed., London: Dover Publications, Inc., 1971); *The Life Story of the Mexican Immigrant: Autobiographic Documents* (Chicago: University of Chicago Press, 1931; reprint ed., London: Dover Publications, Inc., 1971). These two volumes are the result of a study Gamio conducted between 1926 and 1927, under the sponsorship of the Social Science Research Council.

10 Paul S. Taylor, *Mexican Labor in the United States: The Imperial Valley*, University of California Publications in Economics, vol. 6, no. 1 (Berkeley: University of California Press, 1928), *Mexican Labor in the United States: Valley of the South Platte, Colorado*, University of California Publications in Economics, vol. 6, no. 2 (Berkeley: University of California Press, 1929), *Mexican Labor in the United States: Racial School Statistics, California 1927*, University of California Publications in Economics, vol. 6, no. 4 (Berkeley: University of California Press, 1929), *Mexican Labor in the United States: Dimmit County, Winter Garden District, Southern Texas,*

University of California Publications in Economics, vol. 6, no. 5 (Berkeley: University of California Press, 1930), *Mexican Labor in the United States: Bethlehem, Pennsylvania*, University of California Publications in Economics, vol. 7, no. 1 (Berkeley: University of California Press, 1931, *Mexican Labor in the United States: Chicago and the Calumet Region*, University of California Publications in Economics, vol. 7, no. 2 (Berkeley: University of California Press, 1932), *Mexican Labor in the United States: Migration Statistics*, I-IV, University of California Publications in Economics, vol. 6, no. 3; vol. 12, no. 1, and vol. 12, no. 3 (Berkeley: University of California Press, 1933–34).

11 Taylor, *A Spanish-Mexican Peasant Community: Arandas in Jalisco, Mexico*, Ibero-Americana, no. 4 (Berkeley: University of California Press, 1933, *An American-Mexican Frontier: Nueces County, Texas* (Chapel Hill: University of North Carolina Press, 1934).

12 See Taylor, "More Bars Against Mexicans," *Survey* 44 (April 1930), 26–27, "Mexicans North of the Rio Grande," *Survey Graphic* (May 1, 1931), 135–140, "The Resettlement Administration and Migratory Agricultural Labor in California," *Plan Age* (June 1936), 26–29, "Refugee Labor Migration to California," *Monthly Labor Review* (August 1938, reprint ed., Washington, D.C.: Government Printing Office, 1938), "Migrant Mother: 1936," *American West* 7 (May 1970), 64–84, "Uprisings on the Farms," *Survey Graphic* 24 (January 1935), 19–22, "Some Aspects of Mexican Immigration," *Journal of Political Economy* 38 (October 1930), 609–615, *The Migrants and California's Future; the Trek to California, the Trek in California* (San Francisco: Resettlement Administration, 1935), *Seasonal Labor on Arizona Irrigated Farms* (Tucson: University of Arizona, 1937), and "California Farm Labor: A Review," *Agricultural History* 42, no. 1 (January 1968), 49–54.

13 McWilliams, "Getting Rid of the Mexican," *American Mercury* 28 (March 1933), 322–324, "Civil Rights in California," *New Republic* (January 22, 1940), 108–110.

14 Carey McWilliams, *Factories in the Field: The Story of Migratory Farm Labor in California* (Boston: Little Brown, 1939; reprint ed., Santa Barbara and Salt Lake City: Peregrine Smith, Inc., 1971).

15 John Steinbeck, *Grapes of Wrath* (New York: Viking Press, 1939).

16 See, for example, Lloyd Fellows, *Economic Aspects of the Mexican Rural Population in California with Special Emphasis on the Need for Mexican Labor in Agriculture* (1929; reprint ed., San Francisco: R & E Research Associates, 1971); Vera Sturges, "Mexican Immigrants," *Survey* 46 (July 1921), 470–471) Charles B. Spaulding, "The Mexican Strike at El Monte, California," *Sociology and Social Research* 18 (August 1934), 571–580; Emory Bogardus, "Mexican Repatriates," *Sociology and Social Research* 18 (November/December 1933), 169–176; Osgood Hardy, "*Los Repatriados*," *Pomona College Magazine* 21 (January 1933) 71–73; Max Handman, "Economic Reasons for the Coming of the Mexican Immigrant," *American Journal of Sociology* 35 (January 1930), 601–611; Robert McLean, "Goodbye Vicente," 66 *Survey* (May 1, 1931), 182–183 and 195–197; McLean, "The Mexican Return," *The Nation* (August 24, 1932), 165–166, and Report of Governor C.C. Young's Mexican Fact-Finding Committee, "Mexicans in California," (San Francisco: California State Printing Office, 1930; reprint ed., San Francisco: R & E Research Associates, 1970).

17 Ruth Allen, "The Labor of Women in the Production of Cotton," *University of Texas Bulletin* 30 (September 1931), "Mexican Peon Women in Texas," *Sociology and Social Research* 16, no. 2 (November-December 1931), 131–142, *Chapters in the History of Organized Labor in Texas* (Austin: University of Texas Publications,

1941); Sidney C. Sufrin, "Labor Organization in Agricultural America, 1930–1935," *American Journal of Sociology*, 43, no. 4 (January 1938), 544–559.

18 Ernesto Galarza, "Life in the U.S. for Mexican People: Out of the Experience of a Mexican," *Proceedings*, National Conference of Social Work, 1929 (Chicago: University of Chicago Press, 1929), 399–404, "Without Benefit of Lobby," *Survey* 66 (May 1931), 181, "Big Farm Strike at the DiGiorgio's," *Commonweal* 48 (June 4, 1948), 178–182, *Farm Workers and Agribusiness in California, 1947–1960* (Notre Dame, IN: University of Notre Dame Press, 1977), *Merchants of Labor: The Mexican Bracero Story; An Account of the Managed Migration of Mexican Farm Workers in California, 1942–1960* (Santa Barbara: McNally Loftin Publisher, 1964), *Strangers in Our Fields* (Washington, D.C.: Joint U.S. Mexico Trade Union Committee, 1956), *Tragedy at Chular: El crucero de las treinta y dos cruces* (Santa Barbara: McNally and Loftin, 1977), "California, the Uncommonwealth," in Renato Rosaldo, et al., *Chicano: The Evolution of a People* (Malabar, FL: Krieger, 1982), 164–175.

19 For example, Manuel Gamio, "Anglosajones y Latinoamericanos en la frontera de Estados Unidos con Mexico," *America Indigena* 10, no. 3 (July 1950), 191–194.

20 Stuart Jamieson, *Labor Unionism in American Agriculture*, U.S. Department of Labor, Bureau of Labor Statistics, Bulletin no. 836 (Washington, D.C.: United States Government Printing Office, 1945).

21 Varden Fuller, "The Supply of Agricultural Labor as a Factor in the Evolution of Farm Organization in California," (reprinted in U.S. Senate, Subcommittee of the Committee on Education and Labor, Hearings on S. Res. 266, Violations of Free Speech and Rights of Labor, 74th Cong., 2d sess., Washington, D.C.: Government Printing Office, 1940), pt. 54, 19777–19898; Lloyd H. Fisher, *The Harvest Labor Market in California* (Cambridge: Harvard University Press, 1953); Clarke A. Chambers, *California Farm Organizations: A Historical Study of the Grange, the Farm Bureau, and the Associated Farmers, 1929–1941* (Berkeley: University of California Press, 1952).

22 See Mario Barrera, "Traditions of Research on the Chicano Worker," paper prepared for the Symposium on Chicano Research and Public Policy, Stanford Center for Chicano Research, Stanford University, March 4, 1982.

23 Charles Loomis, "Wartime Migration from the Rural Spanish Speaking Villages of New Mexico," *Rural Sociology* (December, 1942), 384–395; Seldon Menefee and Orin Cassmore, *The Pecan Shellers of San Antonio* (Washington, D.C.: U.S. Government Printing Office, 1940, reprinted in Carlos Cortes, ed., *Mexican Labor in the United States*, New York: Arno Press, 1974); Pauline Kibbe, *Latin Americans in Texas* (Albuquerque: University of New Mexico Press, 1946).

24 Victor Clark, et al, *Porto Rico and Its Problems* (Washington, D.C.: The Brookings Institution, 1930); Lawrence R. Chenault, *The Puerto Rican Migrant in New York City* (New York: Columbia University Press, 1938), Arthur D. Gayer, Paul T. Homan, and Earle K. James, *The Sugar Economy of Puerto Rico* (New York: Columbia University Press, 1938); Joseph Marcus, *Labor Conditions in Porto Rico*, Report for the U.S. Department of Labor (Washington, D.C.: U.S. Government printing Office, 1919); Azel Ames, "Labor Conditions in Porto Rico," *Bulletin of the Bureau of Labor* 34 (1901); U.S. Department of Labor, "Unemployment in Porto Rico, 1928–29," *Monthly Labor Review* 31, no. 5 (May 1930); U.S. Department of Labor, "Unemployment in Porto Rico, 1929," *Monthly Labor Review* 31, no. 3 (September 1930); U.S. Department of Labor, "Labor Conditions in Porto Rico, 1930," *Monthly Labor Review* 31, no. 35 (December

1930); Walter Weyl, "Labor Conditions in Puerto Rico," *Bulletin of the Bureau of Labor* 61 (November 1905). For a contrasting perspective see Luis Munos Rivera, *Companas politicas 1901–1916* (Madrid: Editorial Puerto Rico, 1925) and Manuel F. Rojas, *Estudios sociales o frutos del sistema* (San Juan, Puerto Rico: Federación Libre Press, 1918); E. Padilla, "Puerto Rican Immigrants in New York and Chicago: A Study in Comparative Assimilation (Ph.D. dissertation, University of Chicago, 1947).

25 Allen, "Mexican Peon Women in Texas," "The Labor of Women in the Production of Cotton," and *Chapters in the History of Organized Labor in Texas,* Seldon Menefee and Orin Cassmore, *The Pecan Shellers of San Antonio* (Washington, D.C.: U.S. Government Printing Office, 1940, reprint ed., Carlos Cortes, ed., *Mexican Labor in the United States,* New York: Arno Press, 1974); Elizabeth Fuller, The Mexican Housing Problem in Los Angeles. Studies in Sociology, Sociological Monograph no. 17, vol. 5 (Los Angeles: Southern California Sociological Society, 1920, reprint ed., New York: Arno Press, 1974); Earl Chapin May, *The Canning Clan* (New York: The Macmillan Co., 1938); Donald Anthony, "Labor Conditions in the Canning Industry in the Santa Clara Valley of the State of California" (Ph.D. dissertation, Stanford University, 1928).

26 John Gregory Dunne, *Delano, The Story of the California Grape Strike* (New York: Farrar, Straus and Giroux, 1967); Peter Mathiessen, *Sal si puedes: Cesar Chavez and the New American Revolution* (New York: Random House, 1969); Mark Day, *Forty Acres: Cesar Chavez and the Farm Workers,* with an Introduction by Cesar Chavez (New York: Praeger Publishers, 1971); Ronald B. Taylor, "The Boycott and the N.L.R.A.," *The Nation* (May 1969), 591–593; Taylor, *Chavez and the Farm Workers* (Boston: Beacon Press, 1975); Sam Kushner, *Long Road to Delano* (New York: International Publishers, 1975); Jaques Levy, *Cesar Chavez: Autobiography of La Causa* (New York: W. W. Norton, 1975).

27 The strike received national attention and received broad coverage in the *New York Times,* as well as the *Los Angles Times,* the *San Francisco Chronicle, U.S. News & World Report.* See also Keith Jones, "A Report from Delano," for a succinct and piercing analysis of the barriers the farm workers and their leaders had to overcome during the strike (typescript copy in author's files).

28 Ronald W. Lopez, "The El Monte Berry Strike of 1933," *Aztlán* 1, no. 1 (Spring 1970), 101–114; Charles Wollenberg, "Race and Class in rural California: El Monte Berry Strike of 1933 *California Historical Quarterly* 51 (Summer 1972), 155–164, "*Huelga,* 1928 Style: The Imperial Valley Cantaloupe Workers' Strike," *Pacific Historical Review* 28, no. 1 (February 1969). See also Jim Dan, "Communists Try to Organize 'Factories in the Fields': Organizing California Migrant Workers in the Great Depression," *Progressive Labor* (February 1969; reprint ed., Boston, MA: New England Free Press, 1969).

29 Juan Gomez-Quinones and Devra Weber, "'Down the Valley Wild': Epilogue, Prologue, Media-Res Still; the Strikes of the '30's," *Aztlán* 1 (Spring 1970), 119–123; Juan Gomez-Quinones, *Development of the Mexican Working Class North of the Rio Bravo: Work and Culture Among Laborers and Artisans, 1600–1900* (Los Angeles: Chicano Studies Research Center, University of California, 1982); Gomez-Quinones, "The First Steps: Chicano Labor Conflict and Organizing 1900–1920," *Aztlán* 3, no. 1 (Spring 1972), 13–49; Gomez-Quinones, "History of the Chicano Labor Movement," *La Raza,* 2, no. 1 (February 1974), 48–52; *Sembradores: Ricardo Flores Magon y el Partido Liberal Mexicano* (Los Angeles: Aztlán Publications, Chicano Studies Center, University of California, 1973).

30 Luis Leobardo Arroyo, "Chicano Participation in Organized Labor: The CIO in L.A.,
    1938–1950, and Extended Research Note," *Aztlán* 6, no. 2 (Summer 1975),
    277–303; Victor Nelson Cisneros, "La clase trabajadora en Texas, 1920–1940,"
    Aztlán, 6, no. 2 (Summer 1975), 239–265; Emilio Zamora, Jr., "Chicano Socialist
    Labor Activity in Texas, 1900–1920," *Aztlán*, 6, no. 2 (Summer 1975), 221–236; see
    also Arroyo, "Industrial Unionism and the Los Angeles Furniture Industry,
    1918–1954" (Ph.D. dissertation, University of California, Los Angeles, 1979);
    Manuel Patricio Servín, "Historical Conditions of Early Mexican Labor in the U.S.:
    Arizona—A Neglected History," *Journal of Mexican American History* (1975),
    43–56; Lorenzo Valdez, "Labor History in the Villages," *El Cuaderno*, 2 (Spring
    1974), 54–63; Erasmo Gamboa, "Chicanos in the Northwest: An Historical
    Perspective," *El Grito* 6, no. 4 (Summer 1973), 57–70; Emilio Zamora, Jr., "Mexican
    Labor Activity in South Texas, 1900–1920" (Ph.D. dissertation, University of Texas,
    Austin, 1983); Lawrence A. Cardoso, *Mexican Emigration to the United States,
    1897–1931* (Tucson: University of Arizona Press, 1980).

31 Pablo González Casanova, "Internal Colonialism and National Development,"
    Studies in Comparative International Development 1, no. 4 (1965); Rodolfo
    Stavenhagen, "Classes, Colonialism, and Acculturation," *Studies in Comparative
    International Development* 1, no. 6 (1965), reprinted in Irving L. Horowitz, ed.,
    Masses in Latin America, (New York: Oxford University Press, 1970); Julio Cotler,
    "The Mechanics of Internal Domination and Social Change in Peru," *Studies in
    Comparative International Development* 3, no. 12 (1967–68), reprinted in Irving
    L. Horowitz, ed., *Masses in Latin America*, (New York: Oxford University Press,
    1970).

32 Carlos Muñoz, Jr., Summary of "On the Nature and Cause of Tension in the Chicano
    Community: A Critical Analysis," *Aztlán* 1, no. 2 (Fall 1970); 99–100; Tomás
    Almaguer, "Toward the Study of Chicano Colonialism," *Aztlán*, 2, no. 1 (Spring
    1971), 7–20; Mario Barrera, Carlos Munoz, Jr., and Charles Ornelas, "The Barrio as
    Internal Colony," in Harlan Hahn, ed., *People and Politics in Urban Society* (Los
    Angles: Sage Publications, 1972), 465–498. See also Robert Blauner, *Racial
    Oppression in America*, (New York: Harper and Row, 1972), especially chapter five,
    "Racism and Culture: Chicano Writing," 162–181.

33 Mario Barrera, *Race and Class in the Southwest: A Theory of Racial Inequality* (Notre
    Dame, IN: University of Notre Dame Press, 1979).

34 Richard Griswold del Castillo, *The Los Angeles Barrio, 1850–1890: A Social History*
    (Berkeley: University of California Press, 1979), 105.

35 Pedro Castillo, "The Making of the Mexican Working Class in the United States:
    Los Angeles, California, 1880–1920," in Elsa Cecilia Frost, Michael C. Meyer y
    Josefina Zoraida Vazquez, compiladores, *El trabajo y los trabajadores en la historia
    de Mexico* (Mexico, D.F. and Tucson, Arizona: El Colegio de Mexico and the
    University of Arizona Press, 1979), 506–517. See also Castillo, "Mexicans in Los
    Angeles, 1890–1920" (Ph.D. dissertation, University of California, Santa Barbara,
    1978).

36 Albert Camarillo, *Chicanos in a Changing Society: From Mexican Pueblos to American
    Barrios in Santa Barbara and Southern California, 1848–1930* (Cambridge, MA:
    Harvard University Press, 1979).

37 Mario T. García, *Desert Immigrants: The Mexicans of El Paso, 1880–1920* (New
    Haven: Yale University Press, 1981), "The Californios of San Diego and the Politics
    of Accommodation, 1846–1860," *Aztlán* 6 (Spring 1975), 69–85; David Brody,
    Steelworkers in America: The Nonunion Era (Cambridge, MA: Harvard University
    Press, 1960).

38   García, *Desert Immigrants,* p. 8.

39   Arnoldo de León, *The Tejano Community, 1836–1900* (Albuquerque: University of New Mexico Press, 1982). See also De León, *They Called Them Greasers: Anglo Attitudes toward Mexicans in Texas, 1821–1900* (Austin: University of Texas Press, 1983).

40   Harry Braverman, *Labor and Monopoly Capital: The Degradation of Work in the Twentieth Century* (New York: Monthly Review Press, 1974); Andre Gunder Frank, *Capitalism and Underdevelopment in Latin America* (New York: Oxford University Press, 1970. See also "Imperialism and the Working Class in Latin America," special issue of *Latin American Perspectives* vol. 3, no. 1 (Winter 1976).

41   Susan C. Scrimshaw and Bernard Pasquariella documented one outcome of this generally accepted theory of over-population in an essay on the sterilization of Puerto Rican women in New York City's Spanish Harlem. Susan C. Scrimshaw and Bernard Pasquariella, "Variables Associated with the Demand for Female Sterilization in Spanish Harlem," *Advances in Planned Parenthood*, vol. 6 (1971). See also J. Mayone Stycos, "Female Sterilization in Puerto Rico," *Eugenics Quarterly* 1, no. 2 (June 1954); and Adelaida R. del Castillo, "Sterilization: An Overview," in Magdalena Mora and Adelaida R. del Castillo, *Mexican Women in the United States: Struggles Past and Present* (Los Angeles: Chicano Studies Research Center Publications, University of California, 1980).

42   Clara E. Rodríguez, "Economic Factors Affecting Puerto Ricans in New York," paper presented at the 1974 Conference on Puerto Rican Historiography, City University of New York, published in History Task Force, Centro de Estudios Puertorriquenos, *Labor Migration Under Capitalism: The Puerto Rican Experience* (New York: Monthly Review Press, 1979), 197–221; Manuel Maldonado-Dennis, *The Emigration Dialectic: Puerto Rico and the U.S.A.* (New York: International Publishers, 1980, c.1976), *Puerto Rico: A Socio-Historic Interpretation* (New York: Random House, 1972); Felipe Rivera, "The Puerto Rican Farmworker: From Exploitation to Unionization," paper presented at the 1974 Conference on Puerto Rican Historiography, published in *Labor Migration Under Capitalism*, 239–264. See also Clara Rodríguez, *The Ethnic Queue in the United States: The Case of Puerto Ricans* (San Francisco: R&E Research Associates, 1973).

43   Magdalena Mora, "The Tolteca Strike: Mexican Women and the Struggle for Union Representation," in Antonio Rios Bustamante, *Mexican Immigrant Workers in the U.S.* (Los Angeles: Chicano Studies Research Center, University of California, 1981), 111–117; Margarita Melville, "Mexican Women Adapt to Migration," *International Migration Review* 12, no. 2 (Summer 1978), 225–235; Rosaura Sánchez, "The Chicana Labor Force," in Rosaura Sánchez and Rosa Martinez Cruz, eds., *Essays on La Mujer* (Los Angeles: Chicano Studies Center, University of California, 1979); Clementina Duron, "Mexican Women and Labor Conflict in Los Angeles: The ILGWU Dressmakers' Strike of 1933," *Aztlán* 15 (Spring 1984):145–161; Douglas Monroy, "La Costura en Los Angeles, 1933–1939: The ILGWU and the Politics of Domination," in *Mexican Women in the United States*, 171–178; see also Mario García, "The Chicana in American History: The Mexican Woman of El Paso, 1880–1920–A Case Study," *Pacific Historical Review* 44 (May 1980), 315–337.

44   Magdalena Mora, "The Tolteca Strike," *Mexican Immigrant Workers in the U.S.*, p. 117. See Magdalena Mora and Adelaida del Castillo, "Sex, Nationality, and Class: La Obrera Mexicana," in *Mexican Women in the United States*, 1–4.

45   "Mexican Women and Labor Conflict in Los Angeles," *Aztlán* 15 (1984), 145–161; Ricardo Romo, "Mexican Workers in the City: Los Angeles, 1915–1930" (Ph.D. dissertation, University of California, Los Angeles, 1975), *East Los Angeles: History*

of a Barrio (Austin: University of Texas Press, 1983); Victor Nelson Cisneros, "UCAPAWA and Chicanos in California: The Farm Worker Period, 1937–1940," *Aztlán* 7 (Fall 1976), 453–477, "UCAPAWA Organizing Activities in Texas, 1935–50," *Aztlán* 9 (Spring-Summer-Fall, 1978), 71–84; Albert Camarillo, *Chicanos in a Changing Society*; Ruth Milkman, "Women's Work and Economic Crisis: Some Lessons from the Great Depression," *Review of Radical Political Economics* 8, no. 1 (Spring 1976), 73–97.

46   Laurie Coyle, Gail Hershatter, and Emily Honig, *Women at Farah, An Unfinished Story* (El Paso: Reforma Press, 1979).

47   Vicki L. Ruiz, *Cannery Women, Cannery Lives: Mexican Women, Unionization, and the California Food Processing Industry, 1930–1950* (Albuquerque: University of New Mexico Press, 1987); Louise A. Tilly and Joan W. Scott, *Women, Work, and Family* (New York: Holt, Rinehart, and Winston, 1978).

48   Margaret Rose, "Women in the United Farm Workers: A Study of Chicana and Mexicana Participation in a Labor Union" (Ph.D. dissertation, University of California, Los Angeles, 1988); "Traditional and Nontraditional Patterns of Female Activism in the United Farm Workers of America, 1962 to 1980," *Frontiers* 11, no. 1 (1990), 26–32.

49   Nancy A. Hewitt, " 'The Voice of Virile Labor': Labor Militancy, Community Solidarity, and Gender Identity among Tampa's Latin Workers, 1880–1921," in Ava Baron, ed., *Work Engendered: Toward a New History of American Labor* (Ithaca: Cornell University Press, 1991); Joan Marie Steffy, "The Cuban Immigrants of Tampa, Florida, 1886–1898" (Master's thesis, University of South Florida, 1975).

50   Devra Anne Weber, "*Raiz Fuerte*: Oral History and Mexicana Farmworkers," *Oral History Review* 17, no. 2 (Fall 1989), reprinted in Vicki Ruiz and Ellen DuBois, eds., *Unequal Sisters: A Multicultural Reader in U.S. Women's History* (New York: Routledge, 1994), 395–404.

51   Gary R. Mormino and George E. Pozetta, *The Immigrant World of Ybor City: Italians and their Latin Neighbors in Tampa, 1885–1985* (Urbana: University of Illinois Press, 1987).

52   Sarah Deutsch, *No Separate Refuge: Culture, Class, and Gender on the Anglo-Hispanic Frontier in the American Southwest, 1880–1940* (New York: Oxford University Press, 1987).

53   Rosalinda M. González, "Chicanas and Mexican Immigrant Families, 1920–1940," in Lois Scharf and Joan Jensen, eds., *Decades of Discontent: The Women's Movement, 1920–1940* (Westport, Connecticut: Greenwood Press, 1983), 59–84.

54   Virginia Sánchez Korrol, "On the Other Side of the Ocean: Work Experiences of Early Puerto Rican Migrant Women in New York," *Caribbean Review* (January 1979), 23–30. See also Altagracia Ortíz, "Puerto Rican Women in the ILGWU, 1940–1950,"paper presented at the Women's Studies Conference, Brooklyn College, April, 1984; and Sánchez Korrol, *From Colonia to Community: The History of Puerto Ricans in New York City, 1917–1948* (Westport, CT: Greenwood Press, 1983); Rosalia Solorzano Torres, "Women, Labor, and the U.S.-Mexican Border: Mexican Maids in El Paso, Texas," in Margarita Melville, ed., *Mexicans at Work in the United States* (Houston, TX: Mexican American Studies, University of Houston, 1988), 75–83. See also, Lionel Maldonado, "Altered States: Chicanos in the Labor Force," in Winston A. Van Horne, ed., *Ethnicity and the Work Force* (Milwauk: American Ethnic Studies Coordinating Committee/Urban Corridor Consortium, University of Wisconsin, 1985).

55   David Montejano, *Anglos and Mexicans in the Making of Texas, 1836–1986* (Austin: University of Texas Press, 1987); David Montgomery, *Workers' Control in America:*

Studies in the History of Work, Technology, and Labor Struggles (New York: Cambridge University Press, 1979); and Montgomery, *The Fall of the House of Labor: The Workplace, The State, and American Labor Activism, 1865–1925* (New York: Cambridge University Press, 1987).

56 Andrea Yvette Huginnie, " `Strikitos': Race, Class, and Work in the Arizona Copper Industry, 1870–1920," Ph.D. dissertation, Yale University, 1991); book manuscript in progress.

57 Dennis Nodin Valdez, *Al Norte: Agricultural Workers in the Great Lakes Region, 1917–1970* (Austin: University of Texas Press, 1991); Zaragosa Vargas, *Proletarians of the North: A History of Mexican Industrial Workers in Detroit and the Midwest, 1917–1933* (Berkeley: University of California Press, 1993).

58 David Gordon, Richard Edwards, and Michael Reich, *Segmented Work, Divided Workers: The Historical Transformation of Labor in the United States* (Cambridge: Cambridge University Press, 1982).

59 Juan Gomez-Quinones, *Chicano Politics: Reality and Promise, 1940–1990* (Albuquerque: University of New Mexico Press, 1992); *Roots of Chicano Politics, 1600–1940* (Albuquerque: University of New Mexico Press, 1994). See also Emilio Zamora's *The World of the Mexican Worker in Texas* (College Station: Texas A&M University Press, 1993) for a discussion of the relationship between ethnic Mexican culture and political action.

60 Gilbert G. González, *Labor and Community: Mexican Citrus Worker Villages in a Southern California County, 1900–1950,* (Urbana: University of Illinois Press, 1994), *Mexican Consuls and Labor Organizing : Imperial Politics in the American Southwest* (Austin: University of Texas Press, 1999).

61 Dave Gutierrez, *Walls and Mirrors: Mexican Americans, Mexican Immigrants, and the Politics of Ethnicity in the American Southwest* (Berkeley: University of California Press, 1995);

62 Devra Weber, *Dark Sweat, White Gold: California Farm Workers, Cotton, and the New Deal* (Berkeley: University of California Press, 1994).

63 Camille Guerin-Gonzales, *Mexican Workers and American Dreams: Immigration, Repatriation, and California Farm Labor, 1900–1939* (New Brunswick, NJ: Rutgers University Press, 1994). This study was informed and enriched especially by the work of Robin Kelley, Stuart Hall, and Lee Quimby. Robin D.G. Kelley, " `We Are Not What We Seem': Rethinking Black Working-Class Opposition in the Jim Crow South," *Journal of American History* 80, no. 1 (June 1993), 75–112, expanded in *Race Rebels: Culture, Politics, and the Black Working Class* (New York: Free Press, 1996); Stuart Hall, "Ethnicity: Identity and Difference," *Radical America* 23, no 4 (1990); and Lee Quimby, *Freedom, Foucault, and the Subject of America* (Boston: Northeastern University Press, 1991).

64 Tomas Almaguer, *Racial Faultlines: The Origin of Racial Supremacy in California* (Berkeley: University of California Press, 1994).

65 Susan Johnson, *Roaring Camp, The Social World of the California Gold Rush* (New York: W. W. Norton, 2000), "Bulls, Bears, and Dancing Boys: Race, Gender, and Leisure in the California Gold Rush," *Radical History Review* 60 (Fall 1994).

66 Deena González, *Refusing the Favor: Spanish-Mexican Women of Santa Fe, 1820–1880* (New York: Oxford University Press, 1999), "The Widowed Women of Santa Fe: Assessments on the Lives of an Unmarried Population, 1850–1880," in *On Their Own: Widows and Widowhood in the American Southwest, 1848–1939,* ed. Arlene Scadron, (Urbana: University of Illinois Press, 1988; reprint ed. *Unequal Sisters: A*

Multicultural Reader in U.S. Women's History, eds. Ellen Carol DuBois and Vicki L. Ruíz (New York: Routledge, 1990, 34–50); Antonia Castañeda, "*Presidarias y Pobladoras*: Spanish-Mexican Women in Frontier Monterey, Alta California, 1770–1821" (Ph.D. dissertation, Stanford University, 1990), "Gender, Race, and Culture: Spanish-Mexican Women in the Historiography of Frontier California," *Frontiers* 11, no. 1 (1990), 8–20.

67 Neil Foley, *The White Scourge: Mexicans, Blacks, and Poor Whites in Texas Cotton Culture* (Berkeley : University of California Press, 1997).

68 George Sánchez, *Becoming Mexican American: Ethnicity, Culture and Identity in Chicano Los Angeles, 1900–1945* (New York: Oxford University Press, 1993).

69 Vicki L. Ruiz, " 'Star Struck': Acculturation, Adolescence, and the Mexican American Woman, 1920–1950," in *Building With Our Hands: New Directions in Chicano Studies*, ed. Adelo de Torre and Beatríz M. Posquera (Berkeley: University of California Press, 1993), 109–129, *From Out of the Shadows: Mexican Women in Twentieth-Century America* (New York: Oxford University Press, 1998). See also Ruiz, "The Flapper and the Chaperone: Historical Memory Among Mexican American Women," in Donna Gabaccia, ed., *Seeking Common Ground: Multidisciplinary Studies of Immigrant Women in the United States* (Westport, CT: Greenwood Press, 1992), 141–158.

70 For example, as of 2002, less than 20 Chicana Ph.D.s hold teaching positions in history departments in the United States, and not all of these are centrally concerned with working-class cultures or labor history. The situation for Puerto Rican and Cuban women historians is even more discouraging. Latina and Latino scholars in the United States shoulder a myriad of political and social responsibilities in addition to their intellectual responsibilities in the academy.

71 Matt García, *A World of Its Own: Race, Labor, and Citrus in the Making of Los Angeles, 1900–1970* (Chapel Hill: University of North Carolina Press, 2001).

72 " 'The Latins from Manhattan': Confronting Race and Building Community in Jim Crow Baseball, 1906–1950," in *Mambo Montage: The Latinization of New York*, eds. Agustín Laó-Montes and Arlene Dávila (New York: Columbia University Press, 2001), "Playing Ball In A Black And White 'Field Of Dreams': Afro-Caribbean Ballplayers in the Negro Leagues, 1910–1950," (*Journal of Negro History* 82, no. 1 (1999), 67–104, see also "Playing America's Game: Latinos and the Performance and Policing of Race in North American Professional Baseball, 1868–1959" (Ph.D. dissertation, University of Michigan, 2000).

73 Nancy Raquel Mirabel, "*De aquí, de allá*: Race, Empire, and Nation in the Making of Cuban Migrant Communities in New York and Tampa, 1823–1924" (Ph.D. dissertation, University of Michigan, 2001).

74 Miroslava Chávez, "Mexican Women and the American Conquest in Los Angeles: From the Mexican Era to American Ascendancy" (Ph.D. dissertation, University of California, 1998).

75 Omar Valerio-Jiménez, " 'Indios Barbaros,' Divorcees, and Flocks of Vampires: Identity and Nation on the Rio Grande, 1749–1894" (Ph.D. dissertation, University of California, Los Angeles, 2001).

76 Raquel Casas " 'In Consideration of His Being Married to a Daughter of the Land': Interethnic Marriages in Alta, California, 1825–1875" (Ph.D. dissertation, Yale University, 1998).

77 María E. Montoya, *The Maxwell Land Grant and the Conflict Over Land in the American West, 1840–1900* (Berkeley: University of California Press, 2002).

78 Mary Laura Coomes, "From *Pooyi* to the New Almaden Mercury Mine: Cinnabar, Economics, and Culture in California to 1920" (Ph.D. Dissertation, University of Michigan, 1999).

79 Camille Guerin-Gonzales, *How Black is Coal?: Appalachia, South Wales, and the American Southwest, 1890–1947* (Urbana: University of Illinois Press, December 2003, forthcoming).

Chapter 13

Ethnic and Racial Fragmentation: Toward a Reinterpretation of a Local Labor Movement

James R. Barrett

Perhaps the most striking characteristic of early twentieth century American working-class history is the extreme diversity in experience. Racial, ethnic, and gender differences; labor market stratification; uneven economic and social development across geographic regions—all meant that various groups of workers experienced class in decidedly different ways. In fact, some historians would argue that this fragmented experience led to a sort of "unmaking" of the American working class in these years.[1]

Starting at the top end of the social structure, other historians have emphasized how the overwhelming power and increasingly sophisticated strategies of corporate executives led to an ideological and organizational integration of the labor movement under the auspices of a pervasive corporate liberal consensus during the Progressive Era. They hold that the strong position of the largest firms in the concentrated market structure of the early twentieth century allowed them to make concessions and to experiment with new systems of industrial relations, forging in the process a new kind of relationship with the more privileged, better organized segment of the working class.[2]

The extent to which we accept either of these formulations is crucial to our understanding the relative importance of the working class experience and, indeed, of labor history in the broader context of American historical development. In their extreme form, the effect of such interpretations can be to read working-class people out of the picture entirely. Thus, the Marxist historian Gabriel Kolko surveyed the wreckage of working-class fragmentation on the one hand and the pervasive influence of the corporations on the other, and concluded that "it is no wonder that workers, the poor, and the oppressed counted for little in determining the fate of the first century of modern American history." Is it even possible to speak of an American working class at all during this era or were American workers, as Kolko concluded, "lumpen people in a lumpen society?"[3]

For all the resistance lately to notions of American exceptionalism, there is still a strong tendency to think about working-class fragmentation in rather abstract theoretical terms and to explain it in relation to broad social forces. What often gets left out in such an approach is history—particular situations and events that are themselves products of the complex interplay between human agency and broader social, economic, and political conditions but which in turn help to shape consciousness and behavior. In trying to explain the course of U.S. labor history and in thinking about problems like periodization, we should reconsider the impact of major historical *events* that have tended to be slighted with social history's emphasis on process and trend.

This article deals with the topical issues of the defeat and decline of local labor movements by considering the case of one of the early twentieth century's strongest, the Chicago labor movement in the era between the turn of the century and the early 1920s. I consider several related problems: First, how and why did organizers build strong labor movements amidst great social diversity? Second, what factors account for the relative decline of a powerful and progressive local labor movement? Third, what is the relationship between the apparent social fragmentation of the working-class population and specific historical events— World War I, the postwar depression, the Red Scare? I argue that it is important to consider the decline of Chicago's labor movement in these years as a comprehensible historical event rather than a historical eventuality.

Throughout the late nineteenth century, Chicago was the center of the radical labor movement in the United States. The great Haymarket upheaval of 1886 and the anarcho-syndicalist movement that provided much of the impulse for it; the Knights of Labor and German American Marxism; independent labor and early socialist electoral politics; even the abortive farmer-labor alliance of the mid-1890s—all took root in the great midwestern industrial metropolis. The epic labor conflicts of the era, notably Haymarket and Pullman, are woven into the labor history of the city. Nowhere were class lines drawn more tightly during the late nineteenth century than in Chicago, where a series of dramatic confrontations in the workplace, the polling booth, and the streets pitted perhaps the best-organized and most militant local labor movement in the United States against some of the nation's largest industrial firms—McCormick, Swift, Armour, U.S. Steel.[4]

But conditions changed for both business and labor between the 1890s and the 1920s. Chicago's economy became a bastion of what labor activists called "federated capital," and many of the city's big businessmen conformed to our image of the corporate liberal, willing to experiment with welfarism and scientific management in the shop and, less commonly, to even sit down with labor leaders at the conference table. Chicago giants like U.S. Steel, International Harvester, National Biscuit Company, and the Big Five meat packers had all achieved a high degree of control in their respective markets by the early years of the twentieth century. With the exception of some of the meat packers, who tended to their capital themselves, all of these corporations were the creations of either the reigning New York financial houses, notably Chase Manhattan and the House of Morgan, or of the Chicago Clearing House comprising an ever-decreasing number of the city's own banks that controlled most large-scale financial transactions. The men behind these corporations were far-sighted enough to have implemented some of the earliest industrial welfare plans in the nation and to have played prominent roles in the Chicago Civic Federation, the model for that ideological and organizational focal point of corporate liberalism the National Civic Federation. Yet they also planned and directed some of the most brutal assaults on organized labor and the rights of working people anywhere in the United States.[5]

If Chicago's businesses showed the earmarks of early monopoly capital, its working-class population exemplified the sorts of divisions historians usually have in mind when they use the term "working-class fragmentation." Already one of the most "foreign" cities in the United States by the 1880s, Chicago experienced a dramatic recomposition of its working-class population in the following generation. Between 1880 and 1930 the size of the city's labor force increased by 600 percent, largely through massive immigration that drew migrant peoples from all around the world into the city's large factories. During these years over 637,000 immigrants poured into the city, as the ethnic composition of the immigration shifted from old immigrant to new. By 1930 Chicago had the largest Polish, Scandinavian, Czech, Lithuanian, and Slovak and the third-largest Italian populations of any city in the United States.[6]

More significant for the fate of the labor movement during these years, however, was the dramatic rise of Black Chicago in the period between 1917 and 1929. A severe labor shortage caused by the decline of immigration, the World War I draft, and a tremendous increase in wartime production opened employment opportunities in the city's factories, while racist violence, floods, and the boll weevil drove an increasingly large number of Black laborers and sharecroppers off the land in the South. With this "Black Diaspora" between 1910 and 1920, Chicago's Black Belt swelled to the point of bursting as its population rose by 148 percent. By 1930 the city had the second largest Black urban population in the United States—a community of 234,000.[7]

The vast majority of these Black and immigrant workers arrived in Chicago with few industrial skills and went to work in the city's giant plants as laborers or machine tenders. Many were not employees in any particular factory, but rather part of a floating population of laborers who shifted from one industry to another in search of work.[8]

Numbers alone cannot convey the social and cultural complexity of such a population. Each of the city's major immigrant groups created for itself a community in the fullest sense of the term, with its own churches, schools, and other cultural institutions; its own business and political leaders; its own values. A similar process of institution and community-building was occurring in the city's Black Belt. On the surface, at least, Chicago's workers were divided—not simply by language but, more importantly, by culture and by worldview.[9]

What did all of this diversity mean for the character of Chicago's labor movement? Notwithstanding theories about the successful integration of the labor movement in these years, even a cursory look suggests that working class organization and class conflict persisted. The city had a larger portion of its laboring population organized into unions and a proportionally higher level of strike activity than any other large city in the United States. At various times, Socialist

Party organization and independent labor politics thrived amidst this bewildering array of races and nationalities. Chicago was the birthplace of the IWW and the Communist Party, and the headquarters of many radical organizations precisely because it continued to be recognized as the heart of the movement.

Certainly the potential for working-class fragmentation was there throughout the early twentieth century. The existence of such a large, heterogeneous population of unskilled laborers consisting of the city's most recent arrivals; the fact that Poles, Blacks, and other newcomers were often first introduced into the labor market as strikebreakers; and the threat that this population represented for the wages and status of the more skilled native-born and old immigrant workers—all of these factors heightened the danger of interethnic and interracial conflict and, under some conditions, inhibited the growth of class solidarity. Often excluded from a wide range of workplaces by white employers and unions, African Americans were in a particularly vulnerable situation. Clearly some employers had interethnic and interracial tension in mind when they consciously recruited their labor forces from a variety of ethnic groups.[10]

It is a mistake, however, to think that workers from these various backgrounds had nothing to do with one another, to conceptualize ethnicity as a solid wall that enclosed each of the various groups. Even if we turn first to residence where ethnic identification meant the most, the fact is that few if any Chicago workers lived in "ethnic ghettos." Neighborhoods *were* often identified as Polish, or Bohemian, or Irish, but most of these and other neighborhoods were quite mixed. Women from the various ethnic communities came into contact with one another in the street, in shops, and at the settlement house—even on the steps of the small tenements, which they sometimes shared with one another. Children played together on the streets and in the alleys. While there were certainly neighborhood ethnic saloons that were primarily Polish or Bohemian or Irish, there were also "daytime" (that is, workplace) saloons that served an ethnically mixed clientele.[11]

Immigrants also rubbed elbows at work and, in the process, they faced many of the same problems, experienced the same sense of grievance. The Union Stock Yards, for example, and the surrounding slaughterhouses and packing plants provided jobs for a bewildering array of more than 40 ethnic groups by 1909. The comparable figure for the South Chicago steel mills in the same year was 28, for International harvester and the rest of the city's farm implement industry, 43, for clothing manufacturers, 35. At work, then, as well as in the community there was some common ground within this diverse population.[12]

In Chicago, this industrial common ground was often a giant factory. The largest plants were the steel mills and packinghouses. By 1900, Illinois Steel, Armour, and the Deering plant of International Harvester all employed between 6,000 and 8,000 workers. Pullman, Swift, Western Electric, and Harvester's McCormick plant each had around 5,000. The demand for supplies during World War I produced even larger plants, labor forces often doubling in the course of the conflict. As early as 1909, about one-third of the city's wage earners worked in plants with more than 500 employees; by 1919, this proportion was more than 40 percent. Such huge industrial plants and the finely integrated production systems within them brought together thousands of workers from diverse backgrounds who might otherwise have had little contact with one another. In count-less ways such plants shaped the lives of the workers who toiled in them and the communities that grew up around them.[13]

Working-class organization flourished amidst Chicago's staggering social diversity. Throughout the early twentieth century and particularly in two distinct eras, 1900–1904 and 1915–1919, Chicago's unusually strong labor movement was built not in spite of but rather on the shoulders of the new immigrants.

By almost any criteria one wishes to apply—level of strike activity, sympathetic strike action, size and scope of trade union organization, evidence of independent labor politics, or community mobilization during strikes—Chicago had a very militant labor movement in these years. Trade union membership soared just after the turn of the century. The high point in the early years was 1903 when union membership doubled, 251 strikes were launched, and a general campaign for shorter hours brought the nine-hour-day to many of the city's industries. By the end of 1903, the Chicago Federation of Labor (CFL) had more than 245,000 members—over half of the city's labor force. Even more impressive than the size of the movement, however, was its scope and composition. Organization extended from the building tradesmen, classic autonomous craftsmen with tight control over the labor market, elaborate work rules, and extensive restriction of output, through thousands of new immigrants in the stockyards and in factories throughout the city to the lowliest immigrant common laborers and a wide assortment of service workers. The Chicago movement also led the nation in the organization of women workers, having drawn in more than 35,000 from 26 different occupations—not only garment and candy workers but also teachers, scrub women, and waitresses. Federation leaders argued convincingly that theirs was the "best organized city in the world."[14]

As this movement crystallized, sympathy strikes became endemic. The tactic was particularly prevalent in the building trades where trouble with one union could bring all the work on a site to a grinding halt. But the linchpins of the sympathetic strike movement in these years were the city's powerful teamsters, an ethnically diverse union of 35,000 with a large number of Poles and almost 2,000 Blacks. The teamsters were often prepared to use their own very considerable bargaining power—the ability to tie up traffic along congested commercial streets—to help other groups of workers. The entry of the teamsters into a conflict also brought the danger of what contemporaries called a "street strike"—that is, one in which crowds were mobilized throughout the city to stop the scab wagons, through violence if necessary. The teamsters' power was particularly obnoxious to the city's large merchants, one of whom prophesied in the spring of 1904 an imminent confrontation between Chicago's increasingly aggressive labor movement and the city's equally class conscious employers. "Some day," he said, "the unions and the business community will have to fight it out to see who owns Chicago."[15]

As the economy dipped and unemployment rose in the summer and fall of 1904, the Chicago Employers' Association launched an ambitious (and quite successful) open shop drive. By July of that year Chicago was convulsed by 92 strikes and lockouts involving 77,000 workers. While unions won in some cases, the net effects of these struggles were negative, particularly in the city's largest factories. Strong organizations at Illinois Steel, International Harvester, and in the packing houses were completely destroyed. The teamsters' union itself was badly beaten in its 1905 strike. The crisis faced by Chicago workers in these years highlights both the high degree of class feeling and the increasing potential for serious racial conflict in the city's working-class communities.[16]

When the Amalgamated Meat Cutters and Butcher Workmen took the packers on in July 1904, it was in the name of the industry's unskilled common laborers, most of them recent Polish, Lithuanian, and Slovak immigrants along with sprinkling of Blacks, for whom the union demanded a set minimum wage. "Perhaps the fact of greatest social significance," John R. Commons wrote, "is that the strike of 1904 was not merely of strike of skilled labor for the unskilled, but was a strike of Americanized Irish, Germans, and Bohemians in behalf of Slovaks, Poles, Lithuanians, and negroes." In the course of the strike *both* the organized labor movement and the city's various ethnic communities rose to defend the packing house workers' movement. The ten thousand skilled men from the allied trades, every craft workers except the stationary firemen and engineers, refused to cross picket lines. Next, the packinghouse teamsters walked out in defiance of their own contracts and the admonitions of their officials. Other teamsters blocked the entrance of police vehicles, and the unionized streetcar men refused to pick up strikebreakers. Waitresses would not serve strikebreakers, and saloonkeepers refused to cash their checks. Thousands of dollars poured into the strike fund from the Chicago Federation of Labor and from dozens of individual unions.[17]

Chicago's South Side ethnic communities rose as one in support of the strike. Although the conflict was relatively peaceful by the standards of the time and place, considerable crowd violence occasioned every effort to introduce scabs into the yards. The Bridgeport Irish were particularly active, but all ethnic and age groups took part in these attacks. A settlement house worker watched a crowd of women and children chasing a Black strikebreaker down the street, yelling, "Kill the fink, kill the fink!" Significantly, both Black and White strikebreakers were hung in effigy from posts throughout the neighborhoods. The most important institutions in Packingtown, the community's ethnic parishes, strongly supported the strikers, as did various immigrant businessmen's associations.[18]

Likewise, the 1905 teamsters' strike was particularly violent and brought widespread community support. The conflict originated in a boycott of Montgomery Ward in sympathy with a garment workers' strike but soon spread to 10,000 teamsters throughout the city. When a racially-mixed group of 5,800 strikebreakers was brought in, violence flowed in the wake of every non-union wagon. Crowds pursued the wagons, hurling bricks and pulling the drivers from their seats.[19] Settlement house worker Graham Taylor was saddened by a pervasive and violent class consciousness that he saw as a form of intolerance.

> It was the disclosure of the intensity and intolerance of class-conscious feeling prevailing not only among those on both sides who were immediately involved in controversy, but as pronouncedly throughout one whole class as the other. Such a discovery came when our non-union neighbors around Chicago Commons became as class-conscious, almost overnight, as were the striking teamsters. When the strike breakers drove the

police-protected coal carts down our avenue, men from the sidewalks, women from the tenement-house windows, and even the little children from the playground, cried with one voice, "Down with the scabs," some of them hurling any missile at hand at the frightened drivers. Then we learned, what most employers fail to discover, that the "solidarity of labor" extends beyond the membership of unions, and that on occasion the class-conscious spirit emerges from the whole working class, expressing the personal claim to the job as inviolate.[20]

As in the Packingtown strike, among the most violent elements in the crowd were the Polish housewives who took a proprietary interest in their husbands' jobs on the lumber wagons. A seasoned teamster and striker described their assaults.

In all the riotous scenes attending the strike there was nothing done even to approach the fierceness of the attacks by these women. The police would charge upon them with drawn clubs, but hesitated when it came to rapping them over the head...Many a time drivers, policemen and bystanders would be compelled to flee pell mell before a mob of these women, flourishing clubs of enormous size.[21] Attacks continued throughout the 100 days of the strike, leaving an estimated 20 people dead and hundreds injured.

The reproduction of class sentiments in the younger generation is suggested by the fact that children harassed strikebreakers delivering coal to their schools and eventually organized their own strike of the "skilled pupils' union" in support of the teamsters. Their unionized teachers and parents clearly condoned the actions.[22]

In spite of such widespread support throughout the city's working-class community, both of these strikes were defeated. It was precisely those organizations in industries with the largest concentrations of unskilled immigrants that were most vulnerable in times of depression. Events in both strikes foreshadowed serious racial conflicts among workers. Although employers found it difficult to find strikebreakers in the city's immigrant neighborhoods, they recruited more successfully in the Black Belt and also imported thousands from various ethnic and racial backgrounds from outside of the city. Chicago's situation as a center for casual and seasonal labor throughout the nation facilitated their efforts. Although strikebreakers in both strikes were ethnically and racially heterogeneous groups, Blacks were singled out for particularly rough treatment.[23]

Much of the organization among recent immigrants, African Americans, and women workers was destroyed in these conflicts and during the following decade. A writer for the *American Federationist* in 1905 called Chicago "the best organized city in the United States for women workers," boasting over 37,000 women unionists to New York's 5,000. But by 1909 the number of organized women workers had fallen to only 10,000 and there was not a single all-female local left in the city. Yet the period 1910–1915 witnessed another upsurge of immigrant labor militancy of which the 1910 and 1915 garment workers' strikes are the most famous. Because the garment labor force in Chicago was more diverse than New York City's, the formation of clothing workers' organizations, notably Sidney Hillman's Amalgamated Clothing Workers of America, is yet another testament to the forces of class cohesion in the midst of extreme ethnic diversity.[24]

As in many other industrial cities around the country, labor organization surged in Chicago during the era of World War I. More than in most other localities, however, this organizing was coordinated and strongly supported by the city's central body. Radicals like William Z. Foster found warm support from the federation's legendary leader John Fitzpatrick who welcomed all who shared his goal of building a powerful labor movement in Chicago. The federation, which William Z. Foster called "the most progressive labor council in the United States," welcomed the Russian Revolution and called for recognition of the new Soviet government; organized opposition within the AFL to American military intervention in the Russian Civil War; organized a Chicago Railway Council as a step toward industrial unionism in that industry; and worked closely with the Women's Trade Union League to educate immigrant working women to the values of the labor movement. The ideas and strategies that were employed to organize the vast open shop steel and meat packing industries were all hammered out in the federation and supported by its constituent unions. John Fitzpatrick, Foster, and others involved in these drives consciously set out to create mass interracial industrial unions, the only sorts of organizations that could successfully organize basic industry in the United States. They dispatched Black and Polish organizers to the yards and steel mills and openly denounced race prejudice among white workers.[25]

Even more than in the earlier period, the union movement was built in large part of "new immigrant" workers. In all the city's major industries immigrants not only made up the bulk of the labor force; they also tended to respond much more enthusiastically to unionization drives than the native-born. William Z. Foster found that the response of Slavic laborers in the South Chicago steel area "compared favorably with that shown in any organized effort ever put forth by workingmen on this continent. Beyond question, they displayed trade union qualities of the very highest type." In the stockyards, ten thousand Polish and Lithuanian were organized within one month at the end of 1917.[26]

1919 was the high point of industrial conflict in Chicago and throughout the U.S. with well over 4 million workers participating in strikes. Most industrialized portions of the country were affected but none more than Chicago. Only New York, a much larger city, had more strikes than Chicago in 1919, and no other city came close. Not only machinists and building tradesmen, but also street sweepers, sanitation workers, bridge tenders—in all almost 5,000 public employees, including 300 fire department engineers, left their work. Boston was not the only city with police labor troubles that year. Three thousand five hundred of Chicago's finest rallied, though they decided against a strike. Hundreds of thousands of other workers voted to go out. By July, a veritable strike fever was sweeping through Chicago's largest plants. Two thousand Polish, Russian, and Lithuanian laborers struck the Corn Products Refinery at Argo, just south of the city, to enforce the closed shop. Seven thousand six hundred mostly immigrant metalworkers left the giant International Harvester plant almost empty, despite a company union, an ambitious welfare plan and other efforts by the company union to contain the walkout. Several thousand more immigrants surprised their employers and the unions by striking the thoroughly unorganized Crane plant. In spite of the sinister presence of hundreds of mounted policemen and national guard, 10,000 butcher workmen struck at the stockyards. When 16,000 carpenters struck to raise their wages to $1 per hour, the Building Construction Employers' Association locked out most of the other trades in the industry, thus halting virtually all construction in the city and throwing another 80,000 men out of work. Towards the end of July the streetcar men prepared to walk out and the Committee to Organize the Steelworkers took a strike vote in the South Chicago mills. By the end of the month, more than 250,000 workers, about one-third of those in industries where there was any labor activity whatsoever, were either on strike, preparing to strike, or locked out.[27]

Not coincidentally, 1919 also brought the most ambitious mobilization of labor's political power since the 1880s. Although independent, union-based labor parties were forming throughout the county, Chicago was the heart of the movement. Organized at the end of 1918 by the mainstream leadership of the Chicago Federation of Labor, the Cook County Labor Party fielded its first slate of candidates in the spring municipal election. Though somewhat disappointing viewed in the abstract, the party's 8 percent share of the vote represented a potential threat to machine politics in the city.[28]

The Labor Party made a particularly strong showing among the new immigrants. John Fitzpatrick, the party's mayoral candidate, was very popular among them as that rarest of birds—an "honest" Irish politician. The star of the party's ticket, however, was the brilliant and charismatic orator John Kukulski who, with deep roots in both the labor movement and the fraternal orders of Chicago's Polonia, had organized tens of thousands of Slavic laborers in the steel and meat packing industries, at the McCormick plant of International Harvester and elsewhere throughout the city. Labor ran strongest "Back of the Yards" in the Twenty-ninth Ward in spite of what was reputed to be the strongest Democratic machine in the city, and within this ward, Labor did best in the densely populated Polish and Lithuanian precincts just west and south of the mammoth Union Stock Yards.[29]

The new immigrants also assumed an increasingly high profile in the Socialist Party. Of the thousands of new members pouring into the party's Cook county branch each year between 1916 and 1920, manual workers represented the overwhelming majority, approximately 80 percent, and the older ethnic groups continued to be well represented. But a decided shift set in as the war progressed. By the war's end, Chicago's Socialist Party was becoming increasingly unskilled and new immigrant in its social composition. The party's strongholds were the heavily immigrant wards, and its foreign language federations, already a significant proportion of membership before the war, mushroomed between 1917 and 1919. The Russian, Yiddish, Hungarian, Lithuanian, and Hungarian federations showed particularly large gains in the period 1917 to 1919. This change reflected the general trend in the party, since the proportion of membership in the language federations jumped from 35 percent to 53 percent of the total during these years. But the language federations constituted a particularly important section of the Chicago membership, given the composition of the city's working class population.[30]

The party's expanding appeal and the shift in its social base were reflected both in election results and also in the city's socialist press. One month before the United States declared war, delegates to the regular meeting of the Cook County Socialist Party resolved "that any member of the Socialist Party voluntarily joining military organizations of any form shall stand expelled from the Socialist Party, declared as traitors of the working class in the Socialist Press and the strongest boycott against them." On April 1, in anticipation of the declaration of war, the Chicago delegates sent a proclamation to the national party demanding "that the Socialist Party of the United States express its most emphatic protest against any declaration of war, and that it continue its work of education of the producing workers, no matter in what country, for the purpose of their emancipation, political and economic." Apparently in response to the party's strong antiwar position, the Socialist vote in the Chicago municipal elections rose from 3.4 percent in 1916 to 34.4 percent in 1917. The number of socialist aldermen rose from one to three and aldermanic contests were close in other wards with socialist candidates losing by a few hundred votes. Shaken by the socialist groundswell, Democratic machine leader Roger Sullivan speculated that the time had come "to amalgamate the Republican and Democratic parties in the nation in a new lineup of conservatives and radicals."[31]

In the decade before World War I, in addition to at least three English-language publications, Chicago had mass circulation Bohemian, German, Italian, Lithuanian, Slovenian, Serbo-Croatian, Slovak, Scandinavian, and Armenian socialist periodicals. For most of the period 1900 to 1918, the city sustained a daily socialist newspaper as well. As on the national level, then, party publications as well as membership and voting figures indicate that Chicago's socialist movement was growing at least through 1917.[32]

Clearly, a process of class formation occurred in Chicago throughout the early twentieth century. It was an ongoing process, most easily discernible in the years just after the turn of the century and during and immediately after World War I. Level of organization, level of strike activity, behavior during strikes, both revolutionary and reformist labor politics—all of these and other indications of class thinking and behavior had grown significantly by 1919. More impressively, the new immigrants—far from being impediments to labor power—seem to have become the backbone of this impressive movement. So, what happened to all of this activity, all these movements?

The problem, of course, was that there were also forces of fragmentation at work—latent in 1900–1904 and 1917–1919; overpowering in the era 1919–1922. Increasingly in these latter years the city's working class community did split along racial, ethnic, and political lines. But fragmentation, when it came, was not simply a product of ethnic and racial diversity. The fault lines within the working class population that we recognize by the terms skill, race, and ethnicity were accentuated by specific events and by the general social and political atmosphere of the so-called Red Scare. Chicago's militant labor movement—the product of painstaking action in the city over decades—did not simply fall apart; it was attacked and destroyed. Between 1919 and 1922 Chicago employers used every weapon at their disposal to crush what they saw as the "tyranny" of the city's unions. The diversity of Chicago's laboring population facilitated this process, but it did not cause it.

Although they were certainly not experienced in this discreet form, it is useful for analytical purposes to distinguish between long-term tendencies toward fragmentation that were largely sociological (ethnic and racial diversity) or environmental in nature (decentralization of industrial manufacturing) from more immediate contingent factors which tended to be economic (depression and high unemployment) or political in nature (the use of injunctions and police force, the Red Scare). The existence of social diversity did present the potential for working-class fragmentation in Chicago. The racial division in the city was particularly critical. Yet there is considerable evidence of class cohesion across ethnic and even racial lines in the period right up to 1919. In the next several years economic conditions, employer and government repression, and other more short-term factors, combined with the sociological characteristics of the working-class population to create a critical conjuncture in the social history of the city. In the post-war years and the early 1920s the conjunction of events with latent divisions in the working-class movement subjected it to extreme pressure. In the course of the early 1920s the movement did indeed splinter—native-born against immigrant; Black against White; skilled against unskilled.

The decisive social division within the working class in Chicago and in other large cities across the country was not nationality but race. It is important to note, however, that in Chicago at least, even this division was successfully bridged at times and to note the specific conditions in which it contributed to a fragmentation of the Labor movement. The Amalgamated Meat Cutters and Butcher Workmen of North America and some of the building trades accepted Blacks during the early twentieth century. During and immediately after World War One, the Chicago Federation of Labor launched an ambitious campaign to integrate the rapidly increasing population of Black workers into the movement and had some success. Because of the large number of migrants who had poured into the industry, the Union Stock Yards became the center for this effort. There were significant gains in the short-run and important individuals, organizations, and institutions in the Black community supported interracial unionism as a strategy for Black workers at least up to the point of the 1919 riot, and in some cases, beyond.[33]

There was a hard-core group of Black union activists—not only among Pullman porters and musicians, but also among building tradesmen and butcher workmen, the largest single group of manufacturing workers in the Black Belt. Although there were certainly exceptions, most of these activists were "northern negroes", many of them born in Chicago or at least having worked in industry for a considerable period of time. In meat packing an estimated 90 percent of these Blacks had joined the union by early 1918, a proportion identical to that for white workers in the industry. This generation of Black workers created the types of institutions commonly associated with stable, maturing working-class communities—unions, co-ops, fraternal groups, and independent political organizations. Local 651 of the Amalgamated Meat Cutters and Butcher Workmen co-sponsored educational meetings with White locals, established and supported a cooperative store, and played a leading role in the Cook County Labor Party and the convention to form a national labor party. Like most other Chicago unions, they passed the obligatory resolutions calling for the establishment of an independent Irish Workers' Republic.[34]

Packing house workers Robert Bedford and Frank Custer may have been typical of this group. Both were skilled, experienced cattle butchers and had been elected floor committeemen by a racially-mixed constituency at the Wilson Packing Company in 1918–1919. They had neither the luxury nor the inclination to forget they were Black; in Chicago, in the summer of 1919, this would have been impossible. When push came to shove, Custer and other union Blacks were clearly "race men." "Supposing trouble starts," he explained, "I am a colored man and I love my family tree, and I ain't going to stand for no white man to come imposing on my color. . . there is going to be a fight." But men like Custer and Bedford also felt a bond with the White unionists. Like so many new immigrants, they concluded that the only hope for change lay in collective action across the color line. Along with their Slavic union brothers, this group had, to use Hobsbawm's phrase, "learned the rules of the game." They were integral to the process of class formation.[35]

The great mass of Black workers, however, most of them recent migrants from the Deep South, stood apart. The question of why most Black workers remained beyond the reach of the labor movement is as complex as it is significant. For some, a deep antipathy toward "the white man's union" rose from bitter experiences with segregation and violence in the south or right in Chicago where an estimated 37 or more of the city's 110 AFL unions either explicitly excluded Blacks or at least refused to integrate them into white locals. Black workers who fell prey on their way to work to the notorious Irish-American gangs; those who'd been excluded repeatedly from jobs by both white unions and employers; those who had seen or heard descriptions of "labor riots" where anyone with a Black face—union or strikebreaker—was beaten; these people greeted progressive white labor's call for an interracial movement with a healthy dose of skepticism. "Unions ain't no good for a colored man," one migrant concluded, "I've seen too much of what they don't do for him." Other migrants seem to have been genuinely convinced of the benevolence of their white employers and most understood their power. They were reluctant to risk all they had gained through migration on the dubious proposition of going up against the giant corporations. It is difficult to do justice to the rather complex psychology of the migrants which is so eloquently displayed in their own letters. To men and women who had lived with brutal racist oppression and grinding poverty in the South, migration to Chicago represented a genuine measure of liberation, and for this they were grateful. As far as the struggle of the classes was concerned, most immigrants concluded that they would sit this one out and see where the chips fell.[36]

Given the very different mentalities of immigrant and black migrant workers, the creation of an interracial labor movement was a difficult enterprise at best, but race relations within Chicago's working class did not take place in a vacuum, and it is a mistake to analyze the impact of even so important a factor as race as an independent variable. Black workers did not develop their attitudes about unions solely on the basis of their own experience nor did the struggle over unionization in black communities occur in a vacuum. Chicago's black middle class fought for the hearts and minds of the migrants, and in this enterprise they drew heavily on the paternalism of the meat packers and other corporations. Employers used various strategies to divide workers along racial lines, and their success in this regard goes some way toward explaining the fragmentation and decline of Chicago labor in the 1919–1921 era. The attitudes and responses of key Black organizations and institutions like the Urban League, the YMCA, and race newspapers to the issue of labor organization were shaped and reshaped by the financial power which the packers and other employers wielded in the Black community. Here again timing and specific strategies were crucial. Organizations like the Urban League were not inherently anti-union, but as the economy dipped and unemployment in the Black Belt rose and as the packers' contributions and those from other large employers poured in, it became increasingly difficult to remain objective on the issue of unions. Having been somewhat ambivalent on the matter up until 1919, the Urban League was decidedly anti-union by 1921, if not earlier. The organization helped to recruit strikebreakers in a number of Chicago area disputes, thereby winning the undying hatred of unionists across the city. In the case of other community institutions, the close relationship with employers was even less ambiguous. A. L. Jackson of the Wabash Ave. YMCA was avowedly anti-union. He received considerable financial support from the meat packers and other large employers and in return sponsored a variety of social organizations aimed at keeping Black migrants out of unions.[37]

In the case of meat packing, employers supplemented this community-focused program of paternalism with a much more aggressive strategy aimed at disrupting interracial solidarity within the plants. While the union was specifically enjoined from recruiting on company time, "race man" Richard Parker's all-Black American Unity Labor Union, which had close financial ties to the packers, solicited openly and seemed always welcome in the plants. At Wilson, and apparently at other houses, a group of Black "non-union agitators" received preferred treatment from foremen and supervisors. According to both Black and white unionists, this group was responsible for much of the workplace racial friction in the weeks preceding the 1919 riot. The labor men claimed that the trouble was over unionism, not race. "I can get along with these colored fellows," smokehouse worker Louis Mihora told federal judge Samuel Alschuler, "We all can get along with them just like brothers, with these fellows that have the buttons." But other white workers, faced with the intransigence of many migrants, embraced the language of racial hate and placed increasing pressure on the non-union holdouts. The anti-union "agitators", on the other hand, insulted and even physically assaulted Black unionists—all with the protection of the packers.[38]

Racial fragmentation was displayed in its most violent form, of course, in the tragic Chicago race riot of July 1919 that claimed the lives of 23 Blacks and 15 whites. The riot shattered the prospects for interracial organization in the meat packing plants, the city's large steel mills, and elsewhere. William Z. Foster and his organizers made efforts to bring black migrants into the steel organizing drive and the Great Steel Strike of 1919. Yet most blacks already in the industry were "extremely resistant to the trade-union program," Foster reported; "those on the outside allowed themselves to be freely used as strikebreakers." As in the stock-yards, so in the steel mills, black migrants seemed "almost immune to the union appeal." In the highly-charged, class-conscious environment of Chicago, there was no greater crime. CFL leaders and black and white union activists fought vociferously against racial thinking, but the cancer spread. Thus, the riot was only the most dramatic manifestation of the race issue. The Ku Klux Klan moved into the city, establishing 20 Klaverns with 100,000 members and another 100,000 in the suburbs, the largest urban Klan concentration in the nation. Competition for housing and political power fed on earlier confrontations between white strik-ers and Black strikebreakers, resulting in chronic racial friction throughout these years.[39]

Historical conjunctions were also crucial to the direction of the labor move-ment's internal politics. Although factional conflict was rife in the Chicago Federation of Labor throughout the era, the heightened sense of patriotism between 1919 and 1922 provided the right wing with a more hospitable climate for their attack on the federation's leadership. As relations between the CFL and the American Federation of Labor deteriorated during the early 1920's as a result of conflicts over the Labor Party campaign and foreign policy issues, the Chicago conservatives grouped around the building trades unions made their move. They established a rival newspaper, *The Unionist,* funded by business advertising and possibly by direct business grants, and carried on incessant snip-ing at the Labor Party, its organ the *New Majority,* and President Fitzpatrick, all part of what it termed a "Bolshevist conspiracy" to destroy the city's labor movement.[40]

This conflict paralleled those raging in several of the federation's constituent unions. In packing, for example, a dual labor council was established which col-lected dues, published its own paper, and competed for the loyalty of immi-grant packinghouse workers with the left-wing led Stockyards Labor Council. Charges and counter-charges of malfeasance and treachery flew among elected labor officials, and some conflicts ended only with beatings and murders. Here and elsewhere, the struggle took on a distinctly nativist quality. The primary division among steelworkers during the great 1919 strike was between the so-called "Hunkies," most of whom remained loyal to the union to the bitter end, and the more "Americanized" old immigrant and native-born skilled men, many of whom remained at work. The ethnic friction that had already existed within the plants was exacerbated by confrontations between foreign-born, "bolshevik" strikers and "patriotic" scabs. In meat packing, too, nativism reared its head. The patriotic faction secured a "100% American" resolution stipulating that all officers, local as well as national, must be American citizens. This clause had the effect of excluding many of the Polish and Lithuanian unionists who had relatively low levels of naturalization even after the war. Many of the organizing strategies that brought the new immigrants into the labor movement in the first place were gradually abandoned. In 1921, for example, the Amalgamated Meat Cutters dropped the various foreign language columns from the union's journal.[41]

During this era of war and revolution, international political events took on greater significance within the context of Chicago's highly ethnic labor force.

The cause of Irish independence and protests over Britain's ruthless suppression of the 1916 Easter Rising garnered significant support from Poles and other peoples from small, subject nations who sought their own independent states. Jews and other immigrants from Eastern Europe, Irish republicans, and Chicago's German American workers all had their own reasons for welcoming the Russian Revolution and the fall of the Czar. The CFL and Labor Party leaders' support for the new Soviet state soon turned into a political liability, however, at the time of Poland's border conflicts with the Soviet Union. A 1920 CFL resolution condemning Poland for its aggression in the Ukraine and supporting the Soviets angered many Chicago Poles. Occurring at a time when Polish-American nationalism was probably at its zenith, the CFL's pro-Soviet tendencies in the midst of invasion and war tarnished the image of its progressive leadership in Chicago's Polonia. The crisis robbed the federation of much of its base among Poles who had generally supported the left up to that point. In its wake, old world prejudices reemerged. The clerical and anti-semitic paper *Narod Polski* not only excused pogroms against Jews and black migrant workers, but also called for a boycott of Jewish-owned businesses in Chicago so that "we will not have any leeches sucking our blood."[42]

By the early 1920s, political factionalism also developed within the leadership of the fledgling labor party movement. This conflict first pitted conservative AFL leaders against Fitzpatrick and the Chicago progressives who had proved quite willing to work with a small but effective group of Communist trade unionists in the city's unions. As part of a more general move against the Chicago, Seattle, and other progressive city labor federations, Gompers cut the CFL's organizing subsidy in April 1923 and threatened to reorganize the body, in part at least due to its cooperation with the Communists. But eventually the Communist and non-Communist radicals also came to blows. Against the wishes of their own trade union activists who prized their relationship with Fitzpatrick and the other Chicago progressives, the Workers' (Communist) Party forced a Farmer-Labor convention in July 1923 that they successfully controlled. Under increasing pressure from Gompers, Fitzpatrick also bitterly resented the radicals' efforts to manipulate him. Anti-communist attacks followed at both the Illinois Federation of Labor and the AFL conventions. Now Fitzpatrick as the Chicago progressives supported the attacks and their coalition with the communists disintegrated. Independent labor politics declined in Chicago and elsewhere during the early 1920s for many reasons, but political factionalism certainly hastened its demise. In the wake of the Labor Party debacle, conservative leaders attacked not only communists but other progressive activists in one union after another.[43]

Such factional conflict within the labor federation was itself a product of the conservative post-war political atmosphere, but the relationship between class fragmentation, the Red Scare, and the American Plan was far more widespread and quite concrete. The Illinois Manufacturers' Association combined with the Chicago Chamber of Commerce, the major packers, and other elements of federated capital to enforce the open shop. Because of labor's strength in certain industries, the results were uneven. In the building trades, for example, a Citizens' Committee declared war on the craft unions, imported 25,000 strikebreakers, hired 700 armed guards, and opened it own employment agency. Here the unions fought back with considerable violence and hung on to reassert their power amidst the building boom of the twenties. It was precisely in those industries populated by new immigrants and Black migrants, however, that the open shop campaign had its greatest success. In basic industry and mass production plants, low incomes and low skill made it extremely difficult to sustain organization in the midst of severe unemployment during the depression of 1920–21. Even then, the young organizations in steel, meat packing, agricultural implement manufacturing and elsewhere might have made it but for rather brutal treatment at the hands of the courts, the police, and private guards.[44]

The state played an active role in industrial repression at both the local and federal levels. Again, the racial divide proved crucial. In the decisive 1921–22 strike in meat packing, which ended effective union representation in the industry for a generation, an Urban League leader estimated that at least half of the 5,000 strikebreakers were Black. The packers enhanced the social divide by favoring non-union Blacks in the early 1920s over union whites. Unions did not simply fall apart during the strikes and lockouts of 1919–1922; they were suppressed through widespread use of sweeping court injunctions and violent police force against virtually any sort of picketing. As in steel mill towns, hundreds of mounted policemen, whom the immigrants referred to as Cossacks, invaded the immigrant neighborhoods "Back of the Yards" to break up picketing and public meetings, at times even pursuing strikers up onto the porches of their wooden tenements. In the Calumet region steel, federal troops intervened to protect strikebreakers.[45]

While employers and police unleashed this legal assault on worker's industrial organization, the state and federal governments turned on the radical political movement. The State's Attorney and federal agents competed with one another in raiding the offices and meetings of the city's radical labor organizations. In the 48 hours following midnight New Year's Eve, 1919, 350–400 labor activists were arrested. The most famous trial, of course, involved the entire leadership of the nascent Communist Party that in Chicago, as elsewhere, found its strongest adherents among eastern European immigrants. Just as important, however, were the arrests of hundreds of lesser known foreign-born radicals who were imprisoned or deported under federal and Illinois sedition laws. In the course of these raids and the subsequent trials, the city's immigrant socialist movement was decapitated, and whatever political space labor had created for itself during the war began rapidly to contract.[46]

An emphasis on long-term processes of social-historical change and a turn away from narrative toward broader structural analyses have been defining characteristics of what used to be called the "new social history." I do not mean to call here for a "return to the narrative." Nor do I share the view that the methods of the new social history have "depoliticized" the field by concentrating on a kind of populist, antiquarian "history of everyday life." On the contrary, it is on the experience of everyday life and the lessons drawn from such experience that successful forms of working class politics have always been based. A narrative social history which concentrates solely on dramatic episodes and social crises not only misrepresents the everyday experiences of immigrant and black migrant workers; it also misses aspects of their lives that can help us to understand their mentalities and thus their roles as active agents in historical change. Nor do I mean to minimize the importance of race, ethnicity, and other social and cultural divisions within the working class during these years in Chicago or elsewhere. On the contrary, all these divisions and particularly the rise of racial conflict made it exceedingly difficult to sustain a strong movement in basic industry. Most broad, structural interpretations of class formation and fragmentation would be difficult to square with the experience of workers in the sort of highly diverse population we find in early twentieth century Chicago and most other large industrial cities of the US in this era.

But a strictly sociological analysis of class formation—i.e., one which explains the history of American workers largely in terms of their ethnic and racial diversity and independent of the major historical events which swirled about them is also insufficient. The growth and decline of a radical working class movement in the United States can only be understood in historical terms by placing a subtle understanding of the myriad worlds of American workers against the historical events of these years. There are cases where the timing of particular events or the combination of events had a dramatic impact on class relations in communities like Chicago. It is at the conjunction of broad social characteristics with historical events that we find our best prospects for explaining the development as well as the defects of American labor.

Yet the fundamental ingredient in historical causation remains human agency. Both the creation and destruction of a powerful labor movement amidst the extreme social diversity of Chicago in these years were conscious efforts on the parts of contending parties, acting within the constraints of a particular time and place. The fact that we end this part of the story with the destruction of such a movement should not obscure the accomplishments of its creators.

NOTES

Earlier versions of this paper were presented to the Illinois History Symposium, The Social Science History Association, and to seminars at Cambridge University, the University of Chicago, Warwick University, and Manchester City University. I would like to thank the respondents and Rick Halpern for their comments.

1 Many labor historians see the early twentieth century as a period of fragmentation, though the way in which such fragmentation is defined and explained varies from one study to another. See, for example, Richard J. Oestreicher, *Solidarity and Fragmentation: Working People and Class Consciousness in Detroit, 1877–1900* (Urbana, 1986), 222–233; *idem*, "Industrialization, Class, and Competing Cultural Systems: Detroit Workers, 1875–1900" in Hartmut Keil and John B. Jentz, eds., *German Workers in Industrial Chicago, 1850–1910: A Comparative Perspective* (DeKalb, Illinois, 1983), 52–69, which stress cultural fragmentation during the "new immigration"; David Montgomery, "Labor and the Republic in Industrial America, 1860–1920," *Le Movement Sociale*, 110 (1980): 201–215, which deals with ideological fragmentation; David Brody, *Steelworkers in America, the Nonunion Era* (New York, 1969); and John Bodnar, *Immigration and Industrialization: Ethnicity in an American Mill Town* (Pittsburgh, 1977), Chapters One and Two, both of which stress social fragmentation and psychological distance between the new immigrants and an earlier generation of old immigrant and native born workers. On labor market stratification, see David M. Gordon, Richard C. Edwards, and Michael Reich, *Segmented Work, Divided Workers: The Historical Transformation of Labor in the United States*

(London and New York, 1982), esp. 127–162. My own research has emphasized a significant degree of class cohesion in the midst of extreme racial, ethnic, and skill diversity. See James R. Barrett, "Unity and Fragmentation: Class, Race, and Ethnicity on Chicago's South Side, 1900–1922," *Journal of Social History*, 18 (Fall 1984), 37–56; Caroline Waldron and James A. Barrett, " 'We Are All Brothers in the Face of Starvation': Forging an Interethnic Working Class Consciousness in the 1894 Bituminous Coal Strike," *Mid-America* 83 (Summer 2001): 121–154.

2 James Weinstein, *The Corporate Ideal in the Liberal State* (Boston, 1968); *idem*, "The IWW and American Socialism," *Socialist Revolution*, 1 (1970), 3–42; Ronald Radosh, "The Corporate Ideology of American Labor Leaders from Gompers to Hillman," *Studies on the Left*, 6 (1966), 66–68; *idem*, "Labor and the American Economy: The 1922 Railroad Shop Crafts Strike and the 'B&O Plan' " in Jerry Israel, ed., *Building the Organizational Society: Essays on Associational Activities* (New York, 1972); Gabriel Kolko, *Main Currents in Modern American History* (New York, 1977), 80–83, 176–177. See also, Martin J. Sklar, *The Corporate Reconstruction of American Capitalism, 1890–1916: The Market, the Law, and Politics* (Cambridge and New York, 1988), especially 435, 436.

3 Kolko, *Main Currents in Modern American History*, Chapters Three and Five. (The quotes are on pages 99 and 173.)

4 Richard Schneirov, *Labor and Urban Politics: Class Conflict and the Origins of Modern Liberalism in Chicago, 1864–1897* (Urbana, IL, 1998); Paul Avrich, *The Haymarket Tragedy* (Princeton, 1984); Kenneth Kann, "Working Class Culture and the Labor Movement in Nineteenth Century Chicago" (Ph.D. diss., University of California at Berkeley, 1978); Bruce Nelson, *Beyond the Martyrs: A Social History of Chicago's Anarchists, 1880–1900* (New Brunswick, NJ, 1985); Hartmut Keil and John B. Jentz, eds., *German Workers in Industrial Chicago, 1850–1910: A Comparative Perspective* (DeKalb, 1983); Hartmut Keil "German Radicalism in the United States from the 1870s to World War One," in Dirk Hoerder, ed. *"Struggle a Hard Battle": Essays on Working-Class Immigrants* (DeKalb, 1986), 71–94; "The German Immigrant Working-Class of Chicago, 1875–90: Workers, Labor Leaders, and the Labor Movement," in Dirk Hoerder, ed. *American Labor and Immigration History, 1877–1920s: Recent European Research* (Urbana, 1983), 156–176.

5 Donald F. Tingley, *The Structuring of a State: The History of Illinois, 1899–1928* (Urbana, 1980), 16–37; Weinstein, *The Corporate Ideal in the Liberal State*, Chapter One and passim; Robert Ozanne, *A Century of Labor-Management Relations at McCormick and International Harvester* (Madison, 1967), Chapters Two and Four; Stuart Brandes, *American Welfare Capitalism 1880–1940* (Chicago, 1976).

6 David J. Hogan, *Class and Reform: School and Society in Chicago, 1880–1930* (Philadelphia, 1985), 3; John Allswang, *A House for All Peoples* (Lexington, 1971), 17–22.

7 Allen Spear, *Black Chicago: The Making of a Negro Ghetto, 1890–1920* (Chicago, 1967), 129–166; William M. Tuttle, *Race Riot: Chicago in the Red Summer of 1919* (New York, 1970), 74–107; James R. Grossman, *Land of Hope: Chicago, Black Southerners, and the Great Migration* (Chicago, 1989); Hogan, *Class and Reform*, 3. For the increasingly large proportion of laborers and other unskilled industrial workers in the city's Black population, compare the tables in Spear on pages 30–33 and 152–154.

8 US Immigration Commission, *Reports* (Washington, DC, 1911), vol. 13, Part 11,213, 216; vol. 26–27, 307–308; Chicago Commission on Race Relations, *The Negro in Chicago* (Chicago, 1922), 166–168; Grossman, *Land of Hope*, 181–207; David J. Hogan, "Capitalism and Schooling: A History of the Political Economy of Education in Chicago, 1880–1930," D.Ed. dissertation, University of Illinois, Urbana-Champaign, 1978, 76.

9 Edward Kantowicz, *Polish-American Politics in Chicago, 1888–1940* (Chicago, 1968); various essays in Peter d'A. Jones and Melvin Holli, eds. *Ethnic Chicago: a Multicultural Portrait* (Grand Rapids, MI, 1995); Victor Greene, *For God and Country: The Rise of Polish and Lithuanian Ethnic Consciousness in America, 1860–1910* (Madison, 1975); Spear, *Black Chicago*, 167–200; Humbert Nelli, *The Italians in Chicago, 1880–1930* (New York, 1970), especially, Chapters Four and Six. On the persistence of strong ethnic subcultures well in the 1920s, see Lizabeth Cohen, *Making a New Deal: Industrial Workers in Chicago, 1919–1939* (London and New York, 1990), 53–158.

10 Nell, *Italians in Chicago*, 78; Ethelbert Stewart, "The Influence of Trade Unions on Immigrants," US Bureau of Labor, *Bulletin Number 56* (Washington, DC, 1905); Grossman, *Promised Land*, 210, 217–18, 225, 230; Rick Halpern, *Down on the Killing Floor: Black and White Workers in Chicago's Packinghouses, 1904–1954* (Urbana, IL, 1997), 30–31, 36–37, 39; Alma Herbst, *The Negro in the Slaughtering and Meat Packing Industry in Chicago* (Boston, 1933), 16–17; Tuttle, *Race Riot*, 108–156; Sterling Spero and Abram L. Harris, *The Black Worker* (New York, 1931; reprinted, New York, 1968), 128–146; R. R. Wright, Jr., "The Negro in Times of Industrial Unrest," *Charities*, 15 October 7, 1905), 69–73; Hogan, "Capitalism and Schooling," 152–161; James R. Barrett, *Work and Community in 'The Jungle': Chicago's Packinghouse Workers, 1894–1922* (Urbana, 1987), 166–67, 172–74, 258–60. On the situation of African American strikebreakers more generally, see Warren C. Watley, "African American Strikebreaking from the Civil War to the New Deal," *Social Science History* 17 (1993): 525–558.

11 *Hull House Maps and Papers* (Boston, 1895), maps; Dominic Pacyga, "Chicago's Ethnic Neighborhoods: The Myth of Stability and the Reality of Change" in *Ethnic Chicago: A Multicultural Portrait*, Melvin G. Holli and Peter d'A. Jones, ed., 604–617; Nelli, *Italians in Chicago*, 25, table on 33, 40–47; Barrett, "Unity and Fragmentation," 45; Thomas Philpott, *The Slum and the Ghetto* (New York, 1978), *passim.*; Kathleen Conzen, "Immigrants, Immigrant Neighborhoods, and Ethnic Identity: Historical Issues," *Journal of American History*, 66 (1979), 603–615; Madeline Powers, *Faces Along the Bar: Lore and Order in the Workingmen's Saloon, 1870–1920* (Chicago, 1998); Perry Duis, *The Saloon: Public Drinking in Chicago and Boston, 1880–1920* (Urbana, 1983), 178, 181–182, 185–187; E. C. Moore, "The Social Value of the Saloon," *American Journal of Sociology*, 3 (July 1897), 1–12.

12 Barrett, "Unity and Fragmentation," 44–45; Ozanne, *Century of Labor-Management Relations at International Harvester*, 192 Table 4 (percentage of blacks employed at International Harvester); U.S. Immigration Commission, *Reports*, part 11, *Immigrants in Industry*, vol. 76, 505–506, Table 88, vol. 73, 433–434, Table 143.

13 Daniel Nelson, *Managers and Workers: Origins of the New Factory System in the United States, 1880–1920* (Madison, 1975), 7–9; Hogan, "Capitalism and Schooling," 56–60; Barrett, *Work and Community in 'The Jungle,'* 19, 56–7. See also Cohen, *Making a New Deal*, 13.

14 *Chicago Record Herald*, March 26, 1903, 2 (quote); Ibid., December 27, 1903, 6; *The Economist*, Sept. 5, 1903, 299; all in Bessie Louise Pierce Papers, Box 86A, Chicago Historical Society; Theodore Glocker, *The Government of American Trade Unions* (Baltimore, 1913), 24; Georg Leidenberger, "Working-Class Progressivism and the Politics of Transportation in Chicago, 1895–1907," Ph.D. dissertation, University of North Carolina at Chapel Hill, 1995, 44–112; Dorothy Richardson, "Trade Unions in Petticoats," *Leslie's Illustrated Monthly Magazine*, 1904, 489–500; Marjorie Murphy, *Blackboard Unions: the AFT and the NEA, 1900–1980* (Ithaca,

1990); Dorothy Sue Cobble, *Dishing It Out: Waitresses and Their Unions in the Twentieth Century* (Urbana, IL, 1991), 66–67; Meredith Tax, *The Rising of the Women: Feminist Solidarity and Class Conflict, 1880–1917* (Urbana, IL, 2001), 91; Kathryn Hinchliff, "Together we won and together at last as we learn our own might, we will win the great fight: Women and Trade Unions in Chicago, 1903–1917," B.A. Thesis, Univeristy of East Anglia, 2002.

15 William English Walling, "Can Labor Unions Be Destroyed?" *The World's Work*, December 1905, 6955 (quote). On the situation in the building trades, see E. L. Bogart, "The Chicago Buidling trades Dispute," *Political Science Quarterly*16 (1901): 114–141; Royal E. Montgomery, *Industrial Relations in the Chicago Building Trades* (Chicago, 1927); William Haber, *Industrial Relations in the Building Industry* (Cambridge, 1930), Chapter Two; on the teamsters, John R. Comons, "The Teamsters of Chicago." In John R. Commons, Ed., *Trade Unionism and Labor Problems* Boston, 1905), ; Steven Sapolsky, "Class Conscious Beligerents: The Teamsters and the Class Struggle in Chicago, 1901–1905," Seminar Paper, University of Pittsburgh, 1974, in the author's possession; Steven Piott, "The Chicago Teamsters' Strike of 1902: A Community Confronts the Beef Trust," *Labor History*, 250–267; Georg Leidenberger, "Working-Class Progressivism;" and for the rank and file teamster's perspective, "The Chicago Strike: A Teamster," Independent, reprinted in *Plain Folk: The Life of Undistinguished Americans*, David M. Katzman and William M. tuttle, Eds. (Urbana, 1982), 117–123.

16 *Chicago Tribune* July 31, 1904, clipping in Pierce Papers, Box 86A. On the Chicago Employers' Association and its offensive on the unions, see Isaac Marcosson, "Labor Met by Its Own Methods," *The World's Work* 7 (January 1904), 4313–4314; and idem, "The Fight for the Open Shop," Ibid., December 1905, 6955–6965.

17 Barrett, *Work and Community in 'The Jungle'*, 203–223; John R. Commons, "Labor in the Slaughtering and Meat Packing Industry" in Commons, ed. *Trade Unionism and Labor Problems*, 245. See also David Brody, *The Butcher Workmen: A Study in Unionization* (Cambridge, MA, 1964), Chapter Two.

18 Barrett, *Work and Community in 'The Jungle'*. See also, Dominic Pacyga, "Villages of Packinghouses and Steel Mills: The Polish Worker on Chicago's South Side, 1880–1921," Ph.D. dissertation, University of Illinois, Chicago, 1981; Howard B. Myers, "The Policing of Labor Disputes in Chicago: A Case Study," Ph.D. dissertation, University of Chicago, 1929, 540–546.

19 Tuttle, *Race Riot*, 121–122; Georg Leidenberger, "Working-Class Progressivism," 165–196: "The Chicago Strike," 116–117, 119–123; Spero and Harris, *The Black Worker*, 132; Sapolsky, "Class Conscious Belligerents," 15–23; Myers, "Policing Labor Disputes in Chicago," Chapter Ten.

20 Graham Taylor, *Chicago Commons Through the Years* (Chicago, 1936), 118.

21 "The Chicago Strike," 121.

22 *Ibid.*, 116–117; Tuttle, *Race Riot*, 120–123. Chicago had experienced strikes by elementary school children in working class neighborhoods, usually in support of their own demands, at least as early as the turn of the century. See Murphy, *Black Board Unions*, 7–11.

23 *Ibid.*, 112–124; Spero and Harris, *The Black Worker*, 130–133. On the problem of the casual labor situation in Chicago, see Carlton Parker, *The Casual Laborer* (New York, 1920), Chapter Two; Grace Abbott, "The Chicago Employment Agency and the Immigrant Worker," *American Journal of Sociology*, 14 (1908), 289–305; and Alice Solenberg, *One Thousand Homeless Men* (New York, 1919), 7–8.

24 Tax, *Rising of the Women*, 91–2, Lizzie Swank Holmes, "Women Workers of Chicago," *American Federationist*, 12 (August 1905), 509, quoted in *Ibid.*, 91.

In addition to the clothing workers' strikes, there was also another major strike at International Harvester. (See Ozanne, *Century of Labor Relations at International Harvester*, 104–115) On ethnic solidarity in the 1910 and 1915 garment workers' strikes, see Nelli, *Italians in Chicago*, 80–85; "Chicago at the Front: A Condensed History of the Garment Workers' Strike," *Life and Labor*, 1 (January 1911), 4–13; Clara Masilotta, "We Can't Make Our Living: Girl Tells of Life in Chicago's Garment Shops," *Chicago Daily Socialist*, November 21, 1910; Amalgamated Clothing Workers of America, *Documentary History, 1914–1916* (Chicago, 1922), 17–48, 95–108. See also John R. Commons, et. al. *History of Labor in the United States* (New York, 1935), IV, 304–307, 315–317; Youngsoo Bae, *Labor in Retreat: Class and Community Among Men's Clothing Workers of Chicago, 1871–1929* (Albany, NY, 2001), especially 131–160; Hinchliff, "Women and Trade Unions," 12–23.

25 John Keiser, "John Fitzpatrick and Progressive Labor" (Ph.D. diss., Northwestern University, 1965), 11–19 and passim; David Brody, "John Fitzpatrick," *Dictionary of American Biography*, supp. 4, ed. John Garraty (New York, 1974), 279–280; William Z. Foster, *American Trade Unionism* (New York, 1947), 20–21; James R. Barrett, *William Z. Foster and the Tragedy of American Radicalism* (Urbana, IL, 2000), 171–201.

26 "Strikes and Lockouts in the United States, 1916, 1917, 1918, 1919," *Monthly Labor Review*, 10 (June 1920), 1509. On wartime organizing, see Barrett, *Work and Community in 'The Jungle'*, Chapter Six; Pacyga, "Villages of Packinghouses and Steel Mills," 276–334; Ozanne, *Century of Labor-Relations at International Harvester*, 113–131; Brody, *Steelworkers in America*, 214–230. For the Foster quote and for his contrast between native-born docility and immigrant militancy in the South Chicago steel area, see William Z. Foster, *The Great Steel Strike and Its Lessons* (New York, 1920), 200–201.

27 Montgomery, *Workers' Control in America*, 97–99; Graham Taylor, "An Epidemic of Strikes at Chicago," *The Survey*, 42 (August 2, 1919), 645–646; Tuttle, *Race Riot*, 139–142; Richard Schneirov and Thomas J. Suhrbur, *Union Brotherhood, Union Town: The History of the Carpenters' Union of Chicago, 1863–1987* (Carbondale, IL, 1989), 98; Cohen, *Making a New Deal*.

28 Keiser, "John Fitzpatrick and Progressive Unionism," 127–128; James Weinstein, *The Decline of Socialism in America, 1912–1925* (New York, 1969), 221–229; Eugene Staley, *History of the Illinois State Federation of Labor* (Chicago, 1930), Chapter 22; David F. Simonson, "the Labor Party of Cook County, Illinois, 1918–1919," M. A. Thesis, University of Chicago, 1959; Roger Horowitz, "The Failure of Independent Political Action: The Labor Party of Cook County, 1919–1920," Bachelor's Essay, University of Chicago, 1982; Tingley, *The Structuring of a State*, 109–110; Andrew Strouthous, *U.S. Labor and Political Action, 1918–1924* (New York, 2000), *passim*.

29 Strouthous, *U.S. Labor and Political Action*, 68–69. On Kikulski, see Barrett, *Work and community in 'The Jungle'*, 196, 207, 225, 241. Precinct-level voting returns are available in the Cook County Board of Election of Commissioners, Reports, City of Chicago, Municipal Reference Library. See also, Kantowicz, *Polish American Politics*, 141–143.

30 Michael K. Rosenow, "Divided They Fell: The Cook County Socialist Party and the Decline of Socialism in America, 1917–1921," BA Honors Thesis, University of Illinois at Urbana-Champaign, 2000, 31–45. Recruitment lists for the Cook County branch of the Socialist Party are available at the University of Illinois, Chicago. I am just beginning a quantitative analysis of the party's social base (occupation, ethnicity, neighborhood) in the city. On the rising proportion of the Socialist Party national

membership in language federations, see Nick Salvatore, *Eugene V. Debs, Citizen and Socialist* (Urbana, 1982), 285.

31 Minutes of the Cook county Delegate Committee Meeting, March 11, 1917, Minutes of the Cook County Delegate Committee Meeting, April 1, 1917, Cook County Socialist Party Records, University of Illinois at Chicago Library, Special Collections, both quoted in Rosenow, "Divided They Fell," 24, 24–25. *Chicago Daily News Almanac and Year-Book for 1917*, Ed., James Langland (Chicago 1917), 623–624. While the Chicago numbers tended to be higher, the Socialist electoral success was mirrored in numerous other industrial cities and towns. See Weinstein, *Decline of Socialism*, 145–159, Sullivan quoted, 157–158.

32 On the party press in Chicago, see Jon Bekken, "Working-Class Newspapers, Community, and Consciousness in Chicago, 1880–1930," Ph.D. dissertation, University of Illinois at Urbana-Champaign, 1992, especially chapters 1, 3, and 6, and nationally, Weinstein, *Decline of Socialism*, 84–93, 94–102.

33 Tuttle, *Race Riot*, 124–137; Barrett, *Work and Community in 'The Jungle'*, 250–253; James R. Grossman, *Land of Hope: Chicago, Black Southerners, and the Great Migration* (Chicago, 1989), 229–239.

34 Cayton and Mitchell, *Black Workers and the New Unions* (Chapel Hill, NC, 1939), 242; Brody, *Butcher Workmen*, 85; Spero and Harris, *The Black Worker*, 271; *Butcher Workman*, 4 (October 1918); *New Majority*, March 15, April 16, August 2, 1919; Forrester B. Washington, "Chicago Negroes Launch Cooperative Store," *Life and Labor*, 8 (July 1919), 184; George Haynes, *The Negro at Work During the World War and During Reconstruction* (Washington, DC, 1921), 75; Strouthous, *U.S. Labor and Political Action*, 60–61; Broadside for the "Colored Club" of the Cook County Labor Party, Graphics Collection. Chicago Historical Society; Rick Halpern, *Down on the Killing Floor: Black and White Workers in Chicago's Packinghouses, 1904–54* (Urbana, 1997), 52, 57–58.

35 Custer quoted in Records of the Mediation and Conciliation Service, RG280, Case 33/864. Box 43, Federal Records Center, Suitland, Maryland. On Bedford, Custer, and other black activists, see Barrett, *Work and Community in the The Jungle*, 208–210; E. J. Hobsbawm, "Custom, Wages, and Workload in the Nineteenth Century," in Hobsbawm, *Labouring Men: Studies in the History of Labour* (London, 1968), 345.

36 Spear, Black Chicago, 36–41, 160; Tuttle, *Race Riot*, 112–124, 145–146, 153, quote, 127. The black migrants' own mentalities and their suspicions of "the white man's union" are best developed in Grossman, *Land of Hope*, especially 210–219. See also, Barrett, *Work and Community in the Jungle*, 217–219.

37 On the hostility of the Urban League, the YMCA, and black professional and religious leaders to unionization, see Barrett, *Work and Community in the Jungle*, 210–214, Grossman, *Land of Hope*, 208–245; Halpern, *Down on the Killing Floor*, 52, 59–61; Chicago Commission on Race Relations, *The Negro in Chicago* (Chicago, 1921); Alma Herbst, *The Negro in the Slaughtering and Meat Packing Industry* (Boston, 1932), 52; Sterling Spero and Abram L. Harris, *The Black Worker* (New York, 1931; repr, New York, 1974), 268.

38 Barrett, *Work and community in the Jungle*, 214–218, quote, 214–215. For the struggle at the Wilson plant, see the detailed testimony of Robert Sobyro (109–148), Robert Bedford (1148–192, 220–243), Frank Custer (258–299), William Bremer (193–220), William Ghee (243–258), Frank Guzior (302–348), and Austin "Heavy" Williams (429), Records of the Mediation and Conciliation Service, RG 280, Case 33/864, National Archives, Suitland, MD. Box 42 and for similar problems at the Hammond and Armour plants, 8–39 and 54–58, Ibid. See also the testimony of Jack Johnstone and Joseph Hodges, Box 46, Ibid.

39 William Z. Foster, *The Great Steel Strike and Its Lessons* (New York, 1920), 205, 206; David Brody, *Labor in Crisis:the Steel Strike of 1919* (Philadelphia, 1965), 162; Bruce Nelson, *Divided We Stand: American Workers and the Struggle for Black Equality* (Princeton, 2001), 164–168; Kenneth Jackson, *The Ku Klux Klan in the City* (New York, 1967), 239; St. Clair Drake and Horace B. Cayton, *Black Metropolis: A Study of Negro Life in a Northern City* (New York, 1962), vol. 1, 79–80; Tuttle, *Race Riot, passim*; Chicago Commission, *Negro in Chicago*, passim.

40 On the tensions between the CFL and the AFL, see McKillen, *Quest for a Democratic Diplomacy*, 119–121, 196–197, 204 and on the factionalism and nativism in the Chicago labor movement Barrett, *Work and Community in the Jungle*, 227–230.

41 On racialized ethnic tensions in the steel industry and the 1919 strike, see James R. Barrett and David R. Roediger, "Inbetween Peoples: Race, Nationality and the 'New Immigrant' Working Class," *Journal of American Ethnic History* 16 (Spring 1997), 3–43 and on factionalism in meat packing, Barrett, *Work and Community in the Jungle*, 224–227, 228–229.

42 McKillen, *Quest for a Democratic Diplomacy*, 186–190, quote, 188.

43 James R. Barrett, *William Z. Foster*, 136–143; Strouthous, *U.S. Labor and Political Action*, Chapter Six; McKillen, *Chicago Labor and the Quest for a Democratic Diplomacy*, 193–213.

44 Tingley, *The Structuring of a State*, 209–224; Barrett, *Work and Community in the Jungle*, 255–262; Brody, *Labor in Crisis*; Grossman, *Lord of Hope*, 224–225.

45 *Ibid.*

46 Robert K. Murray, *Red Scare: A Study in National Hysteria* (New York, 1955), 215–217; William Preston, *Aliens and Dissenters: Federal Repression of Radicals, 1903–1933* (Cambridge, MA, 1963). Tingley, *The Structuring of a State*, 209–224.

CHAPTER 14

IS RACE THE PROBLEM OF THE 21ST CENTURY?

ALAN DAWLEY

Is the color line going to be the problem of the 21st century?[1]

Listening to the conversation of the past decade, one would think so. Liberals deplored the division of America into two nations, one black, one white, while conservatives complained that race-based affirmative action undermined a color-blind society. Even those who claimed, against a mountain of evidence, that progress had all but eliminated racial inequality were forced to do battle on racially defined terrain.[2] Cultural studies of whiteness, black culture, Afrocentricity, and residential segregation all flourished.[3] So did studies putting race at the center of urban decay, national politics, American exceptionalism, the American dream, and labor history.[4] Even those radical scholars who called for "the abolition of whiteness" did their part to swell the tide by insisting that racial identity be taken as a fundamental category of social organization.[5]

The media also resounded with racial themes. In controversies where African Americans were involved, events were commonly rendered as racial melodramas. Witness the Clarence Thomas/Anita Hill hearings and the O. J. Simpson murder trial where race was put at the forefront, even though other factors—sex, gender, politics, class—may have been more important.[6] Similarly, when well-intentioned liberals, such as President William Jefferson Clinton, sought to address social injustice through a national conversation, what did they propose as the topic? What else? . . . race.

The recent conversation is part of a long-standing American preoccupation. Even as new cultural approaches repudiate old biological thinking, there are eerie echoes of earlier eras—the 1920s, when ethnic and nationality groups were defined as races; the Gilded Age, with its Darwinian belief in a global competition of races; the antebellum years when northern and western states wrote race into their constitutions. Looking back on generations of race thinking, it seems as if America is as obsessed with race as Ahab was with the great white whale.

Yet the recent resurgence is noteworthy for reversing the trend of the post-World War II decades when racial discourse appeared to be in decline, both in the social sciences and in Western society at large. Ashamed of the horrors perpetrated under the myth of Aryan supremacy and hoping to curry Cold War favor with the emerging nations of Africa and Asia, elites in Europe and North America seemed ready to repudiate the legacy of racial reasoning that had wreaked such havoc from the beginnings of European conquest through slavery time to Jim Crow.

From all quarters, an assault was mounted that left the fortress of biological determinism in ruins. Attacking the belief that genetic ancestry was a fixed predictor of social behavior, a new breed of biologists stressed wide variation in intelligence and physical appearance within broad population groups and shook their fingers at the artificial and sometimes dishonest invention of so-called races.[7] Even sociobiologists shied away from anything that smacked of genetically determined races. Best known for the idea of *herrenvolk* democracy, Pierre van den Berghe accepted a genetic base for kinship that predisposed people to support members of their own "ethny." But he took pains to warn that genetic differences have not been shown to bear "any functional relationship with the *social* attribution of racial characteristics nor with relative positions of dominance and subordination." Inequalities were the result of "socially ascribed significance." Biology was not destiny.[8]

Among anthropologists, the idea of biological determinism had long been under fire. Picking up where Franz Boas and Ashley Montague had left off, post-war anthropologists turned their backs on the racial constructions of an earlier generation and raised so many questions about the scientific validity of the concept of race that, eventually, the American Anthropological Association saw fit to repudiate it. Instead, ethnographers tried to get inside the lifeworlds of street corner men and welfare mothers and in general rejected any notion that culture and behavior were expressions of inbred racial characteristics. In a parallel vein, sociological investigations of social stratification and economic dislocation produced evidence of growing class distinctions among African Americans and seemed to justify the view neatly captured in the title of William Julius Wilson's landmark 1978 study *The Declining Significance of Race*. Under relentless assault from the sciences and social sciences alike, Social Darwinism collapsed; the once-respected "science" of eugenics came to be seen as a fraud; and entire races— Nordics, Alpines, Mediterraneans—miraculously became extinct.[9]

The overthrow of racial Darwinism by the 1960s opened the way for two strikingly different approaches to diversity. One was to boil down racial classifications to a simple bi-polar difference between whites and everybody else. In the American context, that meant, first and foremost, the black-white divide, as indicated in the widespread discussions of "the crisis in black and white," "black skin, white masks," and being black "in white America." To make this division work, there had to be a more or less homogeneous white community, which, in turn, required the thorough assimilation of second and third generation European immigrants, who were fast losing their identity as separate "races," anyway. In the Black Power climate of the late 1960s, radical scholars debunked myths of equal opportunity by contrasting the avenues of advancement open to white Europeans with the obstacles faced by African Americans. In the wake of the 'Sixties, the burgeoning fields of black studies and black history emphasized black resistance to slavery, segregation, and other forms of racial oppression. The bi-polar model of racial division and resistance to oppression was carried over into the emerging fields of Amerindian and Asian history and, eventually, "white" was counterpoised to "peoples of color" in general.[10]

Meanwhile, others were moving in a quite different direction toward ethnic pluralism. Rejecting the idea that European immigrants had melted down into a homogeneous glob of whiteness, a new breed of immigration historians in the 1960s and 1970s set out to recapture the Old World roots—Polish, Italian, Jewish, etc.—of American ethnic groups. Responding to sociological cues regarding cracks in the melting pot, they emphasized differences brought over from Europe and many-sided conflicts among Catholics, Jews, Wasps, and African Americans. The model of ethnic pluralism, with its emphasis on wide variation in the ways immigrants adapted to harsh conditions, was readily transposed to the writing of Chicano history. In its overall impact, ethnic history widened the gap between group experience and biology, especially when attention focused on the social ecology of urban life and social practices built around kin and community. The idea that social and cultural influences took precedence over blood lines is what allowed the Darwinian races of yesteryear to metamorphose into ethnic groups in the first place.[11]

Transposing the ethnic model to African-American history proved more difficult. Since African Americans had suffered like no other immigrant group starting with their involuntary arrival, the invisible walls around the black ghetto were always higher than those around Little Italy or Polonia. Even so, studies of kinship, culture, and tradition tended to highlight the ethnic, as opposed to the racial, side of African-American community life. Once group experience was linked directly to social and historic practices, rather than biological or in-bred cultural traits, it even became possible to treat race as a special form of ethnicity in which phenotypes played a prominent role marking differences that were social and historical in nature. That allowed African Americans to enter ethnic history as one among many enclaves or sub-cultures within the urban working class.[12]

To its supporters, the shift from race to ethnicity contained a liberating potential. In the American context (unlike the Bosnian or Rwandan), ethnicity loosened the linkage between identity differences—us/them—and power inequalities—who/whom. That is because ethnic privileges were not inscribed in legal and political institutions the way racial privileges had been from slavery through Jim Crow. Detaching identity from power allowed everyone to relax. The national community could become more inclusive and pluralistic; local communities could enjoy lower barriers between groups, weaker taboos against inter-group sex, and reduced resistance to neighborhood integration. All in all, the healthy effect was to break apart the racial monoliths—white majority, black minority—that had loomed so large in American history.

Another development that chipped away at the monoliths was the historicization of race. Postwar historians began to write about race as an "idea" that had changed radically over time and as an "image" that existed more in the mind than in any physical reality.[13] This trend was fostered by comparative studies of white supremacy in the United States, Latin America, and South Africa. After travelling a good way along this path, some even began to question whether race had any permanent basis in social life at all. George Fredrickson, following Max Weber, posited the inevitability of some kind of status hierarchy, but left open the possibility that race would become less important in assigning positions on the totem pole. Pointing to the success of the civil rights movement, he noted that blacks were no longer categorically relegated to lower-caste status, with the result that "opportunities for the construction of class and the deconstruction of race may now exist to an unprecedented degree. . . ."[14]

By the end of the 1970s, many scholars were calling racial explanations into question. Instead of being the answer to questions of inequality—the explanation for slavery, status hierarchy, or urban poverty—race had become a central question itself, something that needed to be explained. What accounted for shifting patterns of race relations? Why did social relations come to be defined in racial terms in the first place? Intellectual developments found parallels in polling data which registered a steady decline in overt prejudice among whites and in the Great Society's unprecedented civil rights legislation and universal social welfare programs. For a brief moment, it seemed possible that the great whale might finally be harpooned.

Over the next two decades, however, race returned with a vengeance. Optimism about racial integration and economic equality gave way to pessimism. Despite obligatory multiculturalism in television and magazine ads—what might be called *virtual* integration—the fact was that real segregation, intense racial passions, and invidious representations of difference persisted. The present moment is a good time to reconsider race as an analytical category. How has cultural theory shaped understanding? Is it possible to recognize the special role of racial division in American history without accepting that America is, therefore, somehow exceptional? At what point does race become an alibi, an excuse for failing to examine class and other aspects of inequality?

II. THE TURN TO CULTURE

Recent revisions of American history are preoccupied with race to a degree not seen for decades. Just when the color line was being breached at countless points—employment, politics, TV advertising—there was a resurgence of color distinctions, red, white, black, brown, and yellow. Everyone from multiculturalists to the Bureau of the Census adopted the multiracial pentagon arising out of the five great diasporas—the original migration from Asia followed millennia later by influxes of Euro-Americans, African Americans, Latinos, and Asians. Although the diasporas were often discussed in cultural terms, the impact of race was evident in scholarly battles over the fate of the Poles, Greeks, Jews and other Euro-American ethnics who arrived as fodder for American industry between the 1880s and the 1920s. In a bizarre and confusing process, they entered an Alice-in-Wonderland world of ever-changing racial classifications where they could be dark Sicilians one minute and white Europeans the next.[15]

To race historians, however, what counted most in the long run was the black-white polarity. Initially, conflicts between "us and them" may have pitted Irish against Italians and Poles, but increasingly these rivalries were melted down in the crucibles of race hate toward blacks. Southern and eastern Europeans may have started out as "in-between peoples"—neither black nor white—but, like the Irish before them, they eventually found their way into the melting pot of whiteness.[16]

Race was also used to explain an increasing array of historical developments. Although the distressed condition of rust-belt cities, such as Chicago and Detroit, can be traced back to industrial decline and federal policies that steered resources toward the suburbs, distress was manifested first and foremost in racial ways. Not only were hardships born disproportionately by African Americans, but working class Euro-Americans whose prospects were not that much better often blamed black victims for troubles all around. Issues of social reproduction—education, dating, mating, housing—became flashpoints of racial polarization, as ex-peasant white ethnics sought to preserve the sacred space of their Catholic parishes against outsiders and to hand down their petty patrimonies to the next generation.[17]

Racial boundaries were commonly enforced through violence. Where restrictive covenants and red-lining were not enough to defend neighborhood turf, there were mob actions, race riots, and violent rampages against black residents. In their own street-fighting way, white ethnics in the North recapitulated the grisly rituals of lynching, night-riding, rape, and vigilantism that were so much a part of white supremacy in the South. Even though white ethnics lost most of their battles for urban turf, they won the race war by regrouping in the suburbs, leaving the urban landscape in the North at the end of the twentieth century even more segregated than the South.[18]

Given the multitude of ways that race shaped the experience of African Americans, North and South, much of the writing on African American history inevitably hinges on race matters. Even when business or professional success brings a modicum of privilege, continued denigration inspires racial "rage." Just as the life of W. E. B. DuBois is said to be "the biography of a race," so the collective experience of the Great Migration is said to find its meaning through the category of race. Although acknowledging class influences, a major study of the migrants asserts, "Black workers from the South ultimately rejected union appeals because they analyzed the situation in racial rather than class terms."[19]

More surprising is to find race at the forefront in labor history. Vituperative critics are wrong to say that earlier labor historians ignored working class racism.[20] To the contrary, ever since the 1960s, labor historians and economists devoted considerable attention to racial division among wage earners. In some cases, they treated it as a reflex of economic competition designed to protect craft privilege and "the American standard of living" against low-wage, unskilled labor; in other cases, they treated it as a pernicious structure imposed on workers from above by racist employers and demagogic politicians. Either way, race was recognized as a powerful wedge that split the labor market, segmented the labor process, and divided the labor movement.[21]

In hopes of repairing that damage, optimists searched the record of the Knights of Labor, the Industrial Workers of the World, and the United Mine Workers for instances where the intrinsic logic of class solidarity had prevailed over the extrinsic wedge of racial division.[22] Wedded to a progressive account of labor's development, they drew contrasts between the hidebound American Federation of Labor—with its segregated member unions, nativist support for immigration restriction, and endorsement of anti-Chinese agitation—and the more enlightened Congress of Industrial Organizations, with its "culture of unity" exemplified in the slogan "black and white unite and fight."[23] Progress was evident in the CIO's healing of bitter divisions hanging over Chicago packinghouse workers ever since the 1919 race riot and in the organic links between the races forged by the CIO even in southern bastions of segregation such as Memphis and Birmingham. Under favorable circumstances, these studies suggested, industrial unionism demonstrated that the logic of class could point toward solidarity, not racial division.[24]

The most stunning impact of the cultural approach was to turn that formula on its head. Focusing on the cultural construction of identities, labor historians increasingly came to emphasize the importance of race in the everyday lives of working people, black and white. Building on the work of Alexander Saxton, historians of nineteenth century minstrelsy, notably, David Roediger and Eric Lott, showed how "whiteness" was a prominent aspect of popular and working class culture. For the great bulk of white working people, they argued, all the virtues associated with the producing classes—freedom, independence, self-discipline—were coded white. Conversely, all the vices associated with degraded labor—servility, dependence, hedonism—were coded black or yellow. Similarly, in an imaginative unmasking of a seemingly fixed racial identity, Noel Ignatiev showed "how the Irish became white." Within a generation of their arrival in the United States, he argued, they had adopted a white identity in hopes of escaping from the stigma of being an inferior race, in the process incorporating white supremacy into working class life. The most radical assertion was the idea that *racial identity arose directly from class experience*. Far from pointing toward transracial solidarity, the logic of class was now said to point in exactly the opposite direction toward racial polarization.[25]

Polarization played out in very different ways for African Americans. From Marcus Garvey's race pride to Malcolm X's black power, according to Robin Kelley, "black working people struggled to maintain and define a sense of racial identity and solidarity." In Kelley's view, everything from gangsta rap to petty theft contributed to an "infra-politics" of everyday resistance to a form of oppression in which class and race are inextricably intertwined, but where overt expressions of resistance normally demonstrated "the centrality of race in the minds and experiences of African-Americans."[26]

Whether or not they accepted the cultural approach, more and more labor historians made race their first priority. Reconsidering his own account of transracial success in the 1930s, Bruce Nelson came to focus, instead, on the deep attachment of (white) industrial workers to assumptions about white men's jobs at white men's wages, privileges they were ready to defend through "hate strikes." Although some historians went so far as to abandon labor subjects altogether, shifting their categorical sights from class to race, others, following Saxton, continued to link race matters to class division. Michael Goldfield, for example, sought to explain the whole sweep of American politics in terms of shifting coalitions built around white supremacy which succeeded at every critical juncture—the Revolution, Reconstruction, the New Deal—in dividing and conquering the working class.[27]

Such interpretations were given a boost by the idea of "racial formation." Michael Omi and Howard Winant proposed a model of social development in which they assert that race in the United States should be treated as "a fundamental *organizing principle* of social relationships." Conceived as rebuttal to conservative ideas about ethnic pluralism and color-blind individualism, the idea of racial formation was also an attack on a reductionist tendency among historical materialists to treat race as a spin-off of class. Instead, they argued, racial formation was a separate, parallel process that operated according to its own dynamic. Following in these footsteps, Tomas Almaguer concluded after an examination of inequality in nineteenth century California that the social order was "a hierarchy of group inequality in which race, not class, became the central stratifying variable." Almaguer remained enough of a materialist to posit the "intersection" (a much-used but little examined concept) between racial ideologies and class structures based in material interests. But his priority was clear.[28]

The idea of racial formation had strong affinities with studies of racial identity. The study of identity began long before historians took the turn toward culture. It had its roots in psychological interpretations which posited a dialogue between Self and Other that led to the creation, not just of different identities, but of a rank order among them. In one view, the origin of racism in North America was seen to be the consequence of psychic mechanisms in the English mind that placed "white over black." In Freudian views, white racism originated in psychic repression of bodily urges and resulted in rage toward the racial other, whether on the Indian frontier or in the Deep South.[29]

The study of identity received a huge boost from discourse theory. For help in overthrowing biological determinism, cultural historians turned to postmodern philosophers who repudiated what Cornel West calls "racial reasoning" in favor of cultural explanations that stressed the malleability of group difference. Theories of representation were also highly influential in showing how signs and symbols of dominance and subordination were inscribed in the human body. In these views, skin color, hair texture, and other phenotypical features were a kind of text whose meaning needed to be deciphered. Michael Foucault's ideas about discourse were especially influential in this regard. Stuart Hall, for example, may have retained the view that "events, relations, structures do have conditions of existence and real effects outside the sphere of the discursive." However, following Foucault, Hall began to lay greatest stress on discourse: "This gives questions of culture and ideology, and the scenarios of representation—subjectivity, identity, politics—a formative, not merely an expressive, place in the constitution of social and political life." In practice, discourse analysis moved away from the concept of ideology, which had located race within a matrix of specific material conditions, socioeconomic structures, and political institutions, and instead emphasized the primacy of cultural forms in the constitution of social organization.[30]

Poststructuralism pushed that point to the hilt. In a widely followed debate over the languages of class, Joan Scott took Gareth Stedman Jones to task for clinging to a concept of class as an objective structure, instead of seeing it as a cultural construct, that is, an identity "through which people established, interpreted, and acted on their place in relation to others." According to Scott, language and discourse determine identities, which, in turn, work on the social

environment to constitute social relations and social organization: "These relations to others—of subordination or dominance, equality or hierarchy—constituted social organization." For poststructuralists like Scott, systems of meaning
came to occupy the same place once held by metaphysical ideas in Hegelian philosophy, and putting discourse first inverted Marx in the same way that Marx had
inverted Hegel. Instead of social being determining social consciousness, it was
now the other way around.[31]

At its best, the cultural critique of historical materialism showed how classical
Marxism was so tightly bound to political economy—production/consumption,
interest groups, factory labor, state power—that it slighted social reproduction
and cultural forms of power. Gender and women's history felt the impact of discourse analysis far more than studies of race and class. Yet with or without
Foucault, cultural critics took social historians to task. They showed how (white)
working people and (some of) their historians were encumbered with hidden
assumptions about lost independence, debased citizenship, and emasculation that
were, in the end, consistent only with the experience of (some) white men.[32]

In addition, the cultural approach bristled with insights, for example, on masculinity and the New Negro, black domestics and working class values, and the
wellsprings of neo-conservative attacks on welfare mothers.[33] Overall, cultural
history revealed startling connections between class experience and racial identity
that had been invisible in much earlier social history. Indeed, it embodied a tragic
vision of American history in which the relentless racialization of other workers
by workers themselves sprang from a noble motive—to escape from oppression.
For whites, that meant throwing off the burden of class; for blacks, the double
burden of class and race.

But the turn to racial identity has been a mixed blessing. The more identity
became an object of study, the more race returned to its former status as the
thing that explained other things, more of an answer than a question. Indeed,
racial division has been put forward once again as the answer to Sombart's classic question "Why is there no socialism in America?" and as the explanation for
a litany of related failures—the weakness of a class conscious labor movement, the
absence of a labor party, and Uncle Sam's skinflint social policies. In broader
terms, race is said to be the key to American exceptionalism, the thing that
defines the United States and makes it different from all other countries.
According to Toni Morrison, the key to American national identity is the forging of white solidarity across the Mason-Dixon line in a cultural dialogue that
counterposed American civilization to African savagery: "It was this Africanism,
deployed as rawness and savagery, that provided the staging ground and arena for
the elaboration of the quintessential American identity."[34]

It is hard to avoid associating this turn of events with a pervasive sense of
defeat.[35] The turn to cultural explanations occurred at a time when the capitalist economy chalked up unprecedented conquests, the labor movement suffered
relentless decline, civil rights and other social movements became almost mori-
bund, and systemic alternatives to the free market collapsed everywhere from
Moscow to Managua. In the thickening atmosphere of defeat, beacons of interracial hope grew increasingly dim. For historians whose scholarship was intended
to contribute to the transformation of society itself, this souring experience

shook their progressive faith to the foundations, raising deep doubts about the very categories used by social historians to apprehend the past: society, experience, agency, transformation, revolution.

Sometimes the retreat from class was cast in terms of American exceptionalism, as if peculiar circumstances, including the acute racial dilemma, had somehow diverted the United States from the true path of History which, until 1991, still ran through the Soviet Union to a glorious socialist future. It was clear, however, that Europe and the United States were on the same track and that the "forward march of labor" had halted on both sides of the Atlantic well before the triumph of Margaret Thatcher and Ronald Reagan.[36] The fact was that by the 1980s, there was a loss of confidence all around in material factors, economic interests, and class-based explanations of social development. Instead of the long anticipated general crisis of capitalism, it was bureaucratic socialism that went into shock. As cultural historians put more distance between themselves and their materialist past, even lifelong rebels against vulgar economism, such as E. P. Thompson, came to be characterized as avatars of orthodoxy, class was converted into a wholly linguistic category, and—the final insult—Marx himself was treated as a forerunner of deconstruction.[37]

The irony of identity was that what started out as an advance in class analysis ended up as a retreat. In the initial stages, race had been seen as an ideological expression of a class divided society. By the end, race was hoisted over class as a key determinant in the construction of reality. Oddly, that contributed to a similar situation at the end of the twentieth century that had prevailed at the beginning: ruling myths of individualism and equal opportunity—restored to center stage by free market ideologues—stood alongside racial explanations for the stubborn reality of inequality. By a strangely circuitous route, race was returning to its former place as a fundamental social fact, a historical given, an analytical first principle. The difference was that instead of discredited notions of biology, now the foundations of racial analysis were seen to lay in culture—identity, representation, discourse. Starting out with the intention of destroying biological determinism, cultural studies ended up putting cultural essentialism in its place.

III. THE LIMITS OF CULTURE

The ascendancy of cultural approaches to race has brought the perennial American dilemma to the fore. As in Gunnar Myrdal's classic 1944 formulation, once again, racism—rather than corporate wealth, elite control, or upper class privilege—is seen as the major contradiction to the promise of liberty and equality embodied in the American creed. Once again, race becomes the prime explanation for inequality in a society founded on the self-evident proposition that all men are created equal. Furthermore, to focus on race as the *American* dilemma is to foster notions of American exceptionalism. Instead of being one case of the general problem of inequality in capitalist democracies, America becomes unique because of its race problem.[38]

It is not my intention to minimize the crimes committed in the name of race. There is no doubt about the reality of racism and its countless victims in

Amerindian genocide, slavery, white supremacy, Western colonialism, and the Holocaust. In fact, precisely because the stakes are so high, it is all the more important to be scrupulous in identifying the limits of any approach, including the cultural one. Some of the limits arise within the framework of poststructuralism—inconsistencies and complexities that weaken or disable the identity model of race. Others are apparent only from the outside, appearing as blind spots or evasions that suggest the need for other approaches. The question is whether it is possible to recognize the reality of race—as cultural construct, lived experience, or ideology—without reifying it. Is it possible to pursue the great white whale without being swallowed up by it?

One problem internal to cultural studies is the unresolved contradiction between the us/them analysis of difference and the who/whom analysis of domination. In some ways, racial differentiation is but one case of the process of defining *difference* between us and them, a process which, for Jacques Derrida, is hard-wired in human language and thought. In other ways, racial distinctions are arrayed along a who/whom hierarchy of *domination*, which, for Foucault, is a built-in feature of discourse. The result is to pin poststructuralists on the horns of a dilemma: how to embrace race as difference among equals without also embracing race as domination. After almost two decades of elaborately exfoliating analysis, even the most sophisticated cultural treatments remained pinned on the same horns.[39]

A related problem has to do with the asymmetry of racial identities. When the black radicals of the 1960s issued their call for "black power," it was a call to resist the unjust authority of white police and political institutions. Can the same be said when skinheads or para-military militiamen proclaim white power? By the same token, "black" is a thick description in which color serves as a vehicle for bundling together ethnicity, folkways, popular culture, and historical memory in rich and complex ways. "White," on the other hand, is a very thin description, which boils down to one thing—being on top of somebody else. Black culture has rendered immeasurable contributions to world civilization. Would not the world be better off if whiteness was abolished?

Even in their bold call for the abolition of whiteness, cultural approaches unintentionally wind up refurbishing the twin peaks of the black-white monolith. The assumption of uniformity in white identity obscures the many ways oppressed groups exploited cracks and contradictions in the dominant group to their own advantage. For instance, even in the heyday of segregation after black men were shunted to the sidelines by disenfranchisement, black leaders were able to turn the Progressive era discourse of improvement to the betterment of the African American community, when black women stepped into the public sphere to enlist elite white support for schools, public health, and other forms of racial uplift. To take another example, nothing is more unexpected in the heyday of Jim Crow than the kind of cooperation that developed between black and white dockworkers in New Orleans or the interracial unionism of Alabama coal miners. Although these instances were anything but textbook cases of racial harmony—everyone involved seems to have rejected the incendiary idea of "social equality"—cooperation of this sort is simply not predicted in bi-polar models of racial identity.[40]

Having illuminated race as a cultural construct that changes over time, cultural history comes up short in explaining the reasons behind these historical ups and downs. The fall and rise of Chinese Americans is a case in point. Given the sorry history of degradation epitomized by the 1882 Chinese exclusion act, who could have predicted that after the 1965 revisions in immigration law, the Chinese (and Koreans) would be touted as "model minorities?" What accounts for this remarkable turn-about? Is it a case of increasing acceptance of racial diversity? Or of the declining significance of race? Either way, it probably has a lot to do with the middle class skew of recent immigrants and their relative economic success, to the point where the median family income of Asian Americans (Chinese among them) is higher than whites. Changes in world affairs also played a major role in lifting Chinese lights when the extraordinary boom in Asian economies gave China greater influence in world affairs than at any time since the advent of European imperialism. Were the same happy boost in wealth somehow to befall African Americans at the same time as the African economy boomed and African states began to bid for great power status, is there any doubt that the status of African Americans would rocket skyward?

One unsavory tendency of cultural studies has been to let the upper classes off the hook.[41] Where are the studies of whiteness among the middle and upper classes to compare in richness and bite with those of urban workers? Why do some otherwise sophisticated discussions of race and class leave corporate elites, saturated in racial privilege, out of the equation? Unfortunately, history "from the bottom up" boomeranged as too much of it never got out of the social world of the lower classes. Perhaps the effect is unintended, but the retreat from the critique of institutional power is not likely to be remedied by "recentering" labor history on non-white workers. It is one thing to turn a monochromatic picture of American workers into a polychromatic one. But it is another to marginalize the European-American majority and to focus, instead, on racial minorities as some kind of vanguard.[42]

Further complications arise with the very category of identity. The trouble is that there are so many: race, class, gender, nation, ethnicity, religion, age . . . identities multiply almost without limit. When DuBois posed the problem of "double consciousness" at the beginning of the twentieth century, little did he realize he was opening the door to triple, quadruple, and more. In spinning out the permutations, it did not take long to recognize that identities are both multiple and multiplex. (The subject of multiplex identities will be considered later on.) They are *multiple*, in so far as actual individuals and social groups are composites of many attributes at once—mother, citizen, consumer, etc.—which derive from different roles, pull in different directions, and make it hard to bundle social identities together in any single category. All people, individually and collectively, are hybrids of multiple social practices, cultural traditions, and ethnic customs. No group, not even African Americans, the most racialized of all, is merely the sum total of its racial attributes.

The treatment of Americans of Mexican descent illustrates the difficulty. Mexican Americans have been categorized in every conceivable way—a people, an ethnic group, a national minority, a race. No wonder one scholar calls Mexican Americans an "ambivalent minority," and census data (1990) disclose that about half self-identify as "white," half as "other race," and a handful as "black," reflecting the contradictory experience of both assimilation and racial discrimination, combined with the admixture of red, white, and black in *La Raza*. The U.S. census has done its bit to confuse things. Having always counted Mexican-Americans as white, the Census Bureau decided by 1930 that they were, in fact, a "colored race." But then in subsequent decades, the Bureau reversed itself again and restored Mexicans to the white column, added the category Hispanic, and, most recently, allowed people to pick multiple categories.[43]

Taking account of somersaults like these, some postmodernist critics have decided race is, in reality, an "illusion." Pitting multiplicity against essentialism, whether biological or cultural, Anthony Appiah decries the genetic fallacy that ascribes a specific culture to individuals of a given biological descent group or a culturally-constructed racial identity. The notion that blacks have jazz while whites have Shakespeare is not only "a bad deal" for both, it is simply untrue. Instead, Appiah embraces the Enlightenment principle of individual choice in a pluralist environment to argue that individuals "make up selves from a tool kit of options made available by our culture and society." Not limited to a single racial identity, individuals actually are a composite of plural and complex identities.[44] In a similar vein, Werner Sollars contends for the elevation of "consent," or free choice, over "descent," while David Hollinger calls for a "postethnic" America where individuals will be free to choose their affiliation. In what amounts to a kind of motto for this approach, Hollinger notes, "Racism is real, but races are not."[45]

The emphasis on free choice, however, seems naive in the face of institutional constraints and imposed representations—stereotypes, social expectations, constructed identities. If advocates of free choice know about constraint, then why do they so often leave out the coercive framework within which individual choices must be made? For example, a highly influential study of "ethnic options" manages to keep class out of the equation by including only 2 questions among the 83 posed to interview subjects that pertain to such things as wealth, income, occupation, or status.[46] The result, whether intended or not, is to reinforce the exceptionalist bent of American social science and to replicate myths of individualism in a classless society, the very ideological environment that led to the heightened consciousness of race in the first place.[47] Instead of harpooning the white whale, cultural studies is now in danger of being swallowed by it.

IV. REVISIONS

The fact that race has been a central preoccupation of American history does not make racial inequality a uniquely *American* dilemma. European powers, too, have their own versions of race-based inequality owing to the legacy of slavery and colonialism. Nor is race the sole dilemma in America. Inequality takes complex forms in which class, status, wealth, gender, and state power are all part of the equation. In the framework of complex inequality, it is possible to see race as an ideological element linked to specific economic arrangements in an ever-changing socio-political environment.

Viewing race as ideology has been one of the main contributions of social history. Well before poststructuralism came on the scene, social historians were rethinking the connections between culture and economy. Using Antonio Gramsci's idea of hegemony, they treated culture as a species of ideology which always remained a constituent element of a complex, unequal social order subject to the pressures and coercions of what Gramsci called "relations of force" and E. P. Thompson, using the image of iron filings arrayed between magnetic poles, called a "field of force." Instead of hanging attitudes and beliefs on the scaffolding of economic structures, they viewed cultural practices as part of the economic scaffolding itself. On this point, the contributions of poststructuralism were welcome in emphasizing the ways economic practices are structured by signs, symbols, and forms of representation.[48]

These ideas emerged in arguments within, and increasingly, arguments *with* Western Marxism. The ambivalent relation to Marxism is evident in debates over class. In classical Marxism, class is defined as a social relation keyed to the extraction of surplus from actual producers by owners of property and wielders of power. Whether surplus is rendered up through a mode of production based on slavery, feudalism, or the capitalist market, class is a matter of give-and-take—some give, others take.[49]

While accepting that, at bottom, class has to do with the transfer of wealth from those who create it to those who accumulate it, revisionists objected to the classical view because it slighted or completely ignored vast spheres of social life outside of production. Revisionists wore many stripes from feminist to institutionalist. Some were Marxists, many were not. They belonged to no single school, but they revitalized the practice of historical materialism in examining patterns of complex inequality where the mechanisms for separating the dominant and subordinate included family inheritance, education, and other aspects of social reproduction; status display, taste, and other aspects of consumption; moral attitudes about the undeserving and the undesirable; social myths and other consensual aspects of authority; law, the military, and other coercive institutions of the state. As this suggests, the original impulse of social history was not to study the history of the bottom, however worthy that may be, but to study the history of the whole "from the bottom up."

In the 1970s and 1980s, this impulse had been refracted through the prism of American pragmatism to illuminate understanding of race as an ideological component within a field of complex inequality. Instead of using race to explain other things—slavery, poverty, backwardness—historians such as Edmund Morgan and Barbara Fields set out to explain race itself as a consequence of other factors, though none the less real for being a consequence. Reacting against the idea that Africans were enslaved because light-skinned Europeans saw dark-skinned Africans as racial inferiors, Morgan, among others, pointed out that plantation slavery began as a particularly cruel method of producing tobacco, sugar, rice, and cotton, not as a system of producing white supremacy. Likewise, Fields ridiculed the idea that "Europeans seeking the 'ultimate' method of segregating Africans would go to the trouble and expense of transporting them across the ocean for that purpose when they could have achieved the same end so much more simply by leaving the Africans in Africa."[50]

Expanding that idea to American society as a whole, Fields argued that race became powerful in a capitalist society only because it provided a way of reconciling the contradiction between egalitarian values and class inequality: "Racial ideology supplied the means of explaining slavery to people whose terrain was a republic founded on radical doctrines of liberty and natural rights. . . ." Pushing the analysis beyond the Civil War, Eric Foner, Ira Berlin, and the Freedom History Project showed how the racial politics of Reconstruction operated in a context of class conflicts arising from industrialization. Far from the thing that explained other things, the very division of society into racial categories was the thing that most needed explaining.[51]

Similarly in labor history, Alexander Saxton argued that native white workers seized upon Chinese immigrants in nineteenth century California as an "indispensable enemy" against which they forged their own cohesive identity *as workers* in order to do battle with capitalist employers. Always concerned with the permutations of political power, Saxton went on to argue that consciousness of being white was the main bridge linking Euro-American workers to the shifting political coalitions that ruled the country. In a society divided by class, Saxton warned, democracy could only wind up being restricted to the racially elect *herrenvolk*. Similar analysis can be found in political sociology, where racism is sometimes treated as a means of shoring up hierarchy in a class-divided society, and in comparative histories of the impact of race on capitalist development.[52]

These historians helped raise understanding of race to a level of sophistication never before attained. Unlike the earlier generation of Progressive historians (DuBois excepted), who had either slighted race (Beard) or treated it in essentialist terms (Dunning, Phillips), the race-as-ideology scholars pulled off the astounding feat of putting race at the forefront, while, at the same time, treating it as a consequence of deeper social and economic forces. Closely tied to developments in society at large, their work drew inspiration from the civil rights and black power movements and strongly suggested that minimizing social and economic inequities was the best way of reducing the burden of race.

Despite the current pessimism in that regard, analysis of complex inequality is going forward. Some of the more innovative treatments appear in social histories of everyday life among African Americans. Instead of treating blacks (or whites) as the sum total of their race relations—in other words, instead of defining African Americans in terms of the white Other (and vice versa)—these studies look at actual social worlds of people with multiple identities. Whether the stress is on wage labor or the split between work-based and home-based strategies of improvement, they assess the lifeways and struggles of laboring communities. Within that frame, a focus on the family and community roles of African American women upends older assumptions about the separation of home and work, since for the largest women's occupations—domestics, service workers, and agricultural laborers—work usually took place in and around the household. In addition, looking at the ways domestics negotiated their conditions of employment after Emancipation, refusing to be "slaves" to their mistresses, expands the field of vision for studying class formation at the grass roots.[53]

The study of women shades over into gender. From its advent in American historical writing in the mid–1980s, gender was closely linked to discourse theory, as the followers of Foucault showed how the discourse of feminine/masculine helped constitute the nexus of inequality in all its many facets. Virtually every historical landscape that had been mapped out by class was re-mapped by gender.[54] As in the reaction against class analysis, gender analysis, too, was subject to many doubts, feuds, and disappointments. But it took its place alongside older categories—social reproduction, sexual division of labor, sexuality, etc.—in actual historical practice.

The South has been an especially fertile ground for bringing all these topics into the equation. In a region where white women's chastity was the symbolic lynchpin of social order, both economic structures and class relations have been shaped in fundamental ways by the often violent defense of her honor against mythic assaults upon race purity. Prohibiting the sexually promiscuous mixing of the races was a commonly heard justification for keeping the textile industry, with its high numbers of female employees, lily white, and for maintaining segregation in bi-racial work places, such as laundries and tobacco factories. Whether or not trade unions favored "social equality"—and they often went to great lengths to show they did not—they could never escape the charge that they would bring about race mixing, with all its connotations of sexual transgression. The South's race/gender ideology was thus one the most potent obstacles to labor organization anywhere in the country.

Approaching race as ideology has born fruitful conclusions in a number of southern cases. One study of the Ku Klux Klan treats gender and racial purity as parts of a complex ideology buttressing the social order of the New South, which rested on the backs of a racially divided working class. The importance of gender is also highlighted in the unusual case of inter-racial unionism among Alabama coal miners, whose solidarity across the racial divide may have been enhanced by the absence of women from the mines. Adding another ethnic element to the mix, the case of South Florida cigar makers shows how working class women, black and Latina, politicized domesticity in ways quite different from middle class Anglo reformers, and, in the process, generated resistance to Anglo capitalists.[55]

From the local to the global, complex inequality involved a racialized class structure. Since W. E. B. DuBois is invoked in almost ritual fashion on "the problem of the twentieth century," it is worth noting the evolution of his ideas beyond his oft-quoted aphorism about the color line. Like many of his fellow progressives, DuBois entered the battle against laissez-faire as a reform Darwinist, believing in the upward "striving" of races as the vehicle for human progress. It was not long, however, before he came to regard racialized *classes* as the prime movers of history. In the midst of World War I, he wrote, "the world today consists, not of races, but of the imperial commercial group of master capitalists, international and predominantly white: the national middle classes of the several nations, white, yellow, and brown, with strong blood bonds, common languages, and common history; the international laboring class of all colors: the backward, oppressed groups of nature-folk, predominantly yellow, brown, and black." As Thomas Holt summarizes the point, "Class was 'racialized' in this hierarchical scheme; capital ruled, but the capitalists were white." As a cultural construction—a fiction—linked to European expansion in the modern epoch, race was so thoroughly bound up with European capitalism that one could not attack one without attacking the other.[56]

If anything, a global perspective is even more apt at the end of the twentieth century. With the rise of high-roller capitalists in eastern and southern Asia, money is not as white as it used to be. At the same time, capitalist development is shifting peasants into urban-industrial settings, generating extreme polarizations between multicultural elites and the polyglot poor, and deepening class divisions within ethno-racial groups. It can be debated whether these changes mark the declining significance of race on a global scale, or merely a shift in its impact. But either way, it is hard to see the color line as *the* problem—the single overriding issue—of the century to come. To get a handle on complex inequality at the global level will require imaginative, new ideas and methods that expand the angle of vision from the working and dependent classes to take in the wider web of class relations, specific forms of capitalist economy and state institutions, complex social formations, and the changing historical circumstances in which all these are played out.

Some of the most interesting work in this regard is going on at the borderlands. Having taking insights from cultural studies on board, social historians are investigating spatial and social zones of interaction where the developed North meets the impoverished South around the globe. One of those borderlands runs along a band from Florida and the Caribbean through New Orleans and the Gulf of Mexico out along the border between Mexico and the United States to the Pacific Ocean. Picking up where Frederick Jackson Turner left off, the new approach treats the frontier as a zone of engagement rather than a barrier and emphasizes the mutual impact of peoples on both sides to produce the hybrid "mestizo America." In the more highly developed work, cultural interaction takes place in the context of economic change (the advent of agribusiness, coal mining, and railroads) which transformed Chicano peasant villagers into migrant laborers and domestics. Working in the businesses and homes of Anglo owners, Chicanos were subjected to discrimination and segregation, which were justified in terms of supposed innate Anglo superiority. In contrast to more brittle schemes of class analysis keyed to the means of production, this supple analysis incorporates aspects of social reproduction and cultural practices to show how the us/them differentiation of Anglo and Chicano helped to determine the who/whom vertical axis of economic and political power.[57]

The treatment of race as ideology acquired a new lease on life in the borderlands. In a leading example, David Montejano contends that "Mexican" is an ethnic (or national) designation on some occasions and a racial one on others, depending on the way struggles for power are played out within changing social formations. Using what he calls a "relaxed" class analysis that is close to the position being argued in this essay, Montejano argues Mexicans were deemed a race "whenever they were subjected to policies of discrimination or control." Thus during the economic transition to large-scale agribusiness, Mexican immigrants were subjected to labor coercions and Jim-Crow-style segregation that heightened their identification as a race *in order to* bring about their subordination as laborers. By contrast, after World War II, greater economic diversity, social integration, and political influence undermined explicitly racial forms of subordination.[58]

Treating race as ideology implies that identities should be seen as *multiplex*. That is to say, social attributes work on and through one another—racial identity affects status, status shapes gender, and so on. In a white supremacist, bourgeois society, dark skin comes to represent lower class status, and, conversely, "money whitens." Thus to be a Mexican resident of the American southwest was to be caught up in a vicious cycle, where being deemed a racial inferior—a "greaser"—created the substandard "Mexican wage," which helped create the poverty-stricken *barrio*, whose unkempt appearance only confirmed the inferiority of Mexicans in the eyes of privileged Anglos. A similar cycle was at work in the formation of immigrant enclaves and black ghettoes in the urban-industrial North, while the presumed docility of women made them fitting recruits to wage labor in the early stages of industrialization. If identities are multiplex, then issues of us/them are always bound up with the question of who/whom.

Much can be learned in other settings by applying the borderlands idea. Taking a leaf from Montejano's book, the racialization of southern and eastern European immigrants around the turn of the nineteenth century begins to make sense in terms of changes in the socioeconomic environment. Surely, the spread of an urban-industrial way of life, the rise of American empire, and the Wasp elite's anxiety about maintaining wealth and position had a lot to do with making the period from the 1890s to the 1920s the most race-conscious in American history, as indicated by the ascendancy of racial Darwinism, Jim Crow, Asian exclusion, eugenics, and race-based immigration restrictions. We should be careful to avoid the anachronism of reading back contemporary bi-polarities into a multipolar past. Thus during World War I, being white and civilized did not exempt the highly regarded Teutons from being transformed into "the Hun" and, as such, being made the targets of *racial* hatred fomented by Anglo-American leaders from Woodrow Wilson on down. Something similar happened in World War II, where government propaganda was careful to distinguish between branches of the "yellow races"—the Chinese, who were our friends, and the Japanese, who were pilloried in the most vicious racist terms. In should be added that the wartime experience highlights the importance of the institutional power of the state in shaping racial identities.[59]

All of this adds up to an argument for treating race within a larger framework of power and meaning that changes over time. One of the most compelling statements along these lines comes from Thomas Holt in a set of essays on "the problem of race in the 21st century." Seeking to update DuBois, Holt contends that "the meaning of race and the nature of racism articulate with (perhaps even are determined by) the given social formation of a particular historical moment." In contrast to the postmodernist claim that cultural identities determine structures of power, Holt retains a degree of materialism in defining "social formation" as "all the interrelated structures of economic, political, and social power, as well as the systems of signification (that is, cultural systems) that give rise to and/or reflect those structures." It is not only DuBois but the tradition of historical materialism that is carried forward here.[60] Surely, treating race as an ideological component within a nexus of complex inequality is a more fruitful method than one which puts race first, or which poses a choice between race *or* class, or which assumes individual freedom to shop at the identity boutique for whatever ensemble looks good in the mirror. By the same token, class analysis is enriched by taking social reproduction and cultural methods on board. To return to a pure-and-simple economic concept of class—whether Weberian conflict of interest in the market, or Marxist conflict within a mode of production—would be to repeat the mistake cultural historians were trying to correct in the first place. Given that class has complex origins, including some rooted in social reproduction, it is hard to see occupational difference as *the* key to understanding class relations, as some have argued. Given multiple and multiplex identities, it is also hard to see economic self-interest, pure and simple, as the basis for "common dreams." Given the continuing significance of race, "Class-conscious work must be anti-racist, not race-blind to address the construction of race."[61]

So long as people continue to think and act in racial terms, then "race" will remain part of the historical reality—a fictional part, to be sure—that scholars have to address. Whether race will retain the central place it acquired in the 1990s is another question. At the very least, the (usually unstated) assumption that individuals or groups can be studied as if they were the sum total of their racial attributes—whether biological or cultural—will have to give way in the face of multiple and multiplex identities. Cultural studies moved in that direction with its embrace of the categorical trinity "race, gender, class," but it remains trapped in a discursive box of its own making. To move forward, it will be well to remember that history is made by real people adapting social practices and ideological forms to changing economic structures and material conditions in which questions of "us" and "them" are always bound up with questions of "who/whom." Such a re-affirmation of the promise of social history might just foster a deeper conversation about social injustice in the twenty-first century than one centered primarily on race. Instead of restating the American dilemma, it might offer the hope of transcending it.

NOTES

1 Thanks to Tom Sugrue for valuable suggestions and to readers Ira Berlin and Gary Gerstle for useful criticism.

2 Andrew Hacker, *Two Nations: Black and White, Separate, Hostile, Unequal* (New York, 1992); Stephan Thernstrom and Abigail Thernstrom, *America in Black and White: One Nation, Indivisible* (New York, 1997); Dinesh D'Souza, *The End of Racism* (New York, 1995); Liberals, too, have to fight on racial terrain, Jim Sleeper, *Liberal Racism* (New York, 1997); Orlando Patterson, *The Ordeal of Integration: Progress and Resentment in America's 'Racial' Crisis* (Washington, D.C., 1997).

3 Matthew Frye Jacobson, *Whiteness of a Different Color: European Immigrants and the Alchemy of Race* (Cambridge, MA, 1998); Grace Elizabeth Hale, *Making Whiteness: The Culture of Segregation in the South, 1890–1940* (New York, 1998); Noel Ignatiev, *How the Irish Became White* (New York, 1995); David Roediger, *The Wages of Whiteness* (London, 1991); Eric Lott, *Love and Theft: Blackface Minstrelsy and the American Working Class* (New York, 1993); Paul Gilroy, *The Black Atlantic* (Cambridge, MA, 1993); Douglas Massey and Nancy Denton, *American Apartheid: Segregation and the Making of an Underclass* (Cambridge,MA, 1993).

4 Michael Goldfield, *The Color of Politics: Race and the Mainsprings of American Politics*
   (New York, 1997); Randall Kennedy, *Race, Crime and the Law* (New York, 1997);
   David Shipler, *A Country of Strangers: Blacks and Whites in America* (New York,
   1997); Thomas Sugrue, *Origins of the Urban Crisis: Race and Inequality in Postwar
   Detroit* (Princeton, NJ, 1996); Jennifer Hochschild, *Facing Up to the American
   Dream* (Princeton, NJ, 1995); Ellis Cose, *The Rage of A Privileged Class* (New York,
   1993). Race has become a staple of debate in the field of labor history, where review
   essays include Eric Arnesen, "Whiteness and the Historians' Imagination,"
   International Labor and Working Class History, 60 (Fall 2001), 3–33; Eric Arnesen,
   "Up From Exclusion: Black and White Workers, Race, and the State of Labor
   History," *Reviews in American History* 26 (1998): 146–174; Herbert Hill, "The
   Problem of Race in American Labor History," *Reviews in American History* 24
   (1996): 180–208; Alan Dawley and Joe Trotter, "Race and Class," *Labor History* 35
   (Fall 1994): 486–494.
5 David Roediger, *Towards the Abolition of Whiteness* (London, 1994); Michael Omi
   and Howard Winant, *Racial Formation in the United States: From the 1960s to the
   1980s* (New York, 1986); Tomas Almaguer, *Racial Fault Lines: The Historical Origins
   of White Supremacy in California* (Berkeley, 1994).
6 Toni Morrison, ed., *Race-ing Justice, En-gendering Power: Essays on Anita Hill,
   Clarence Thomas, and the Construction of Social Reality* (New York, 1992).
7 Stephen Jay Gould, *The Mismeasure of Man* (New York, 1981); The rise, fall, and
   reassertion of biological influences are traced in Carl Degler, *In Search of Human
   Nature: The Decline and Revival of Darwinism in American Social Thought* (New
   York, 1991).
8 Pierre van den Berghe, *The Ethnic Phenomenon* (New York, 1981), 31, italics in original.
9 Carol Stack, *All Our Kin* (New York, 1974); Elliot Liebow, *Talley's Corner: A Study
   of Negro Street Corner Men* (Boston, 1967); Elazar Barkan, *The Retreat of Scientific
   Racism: Changing Concepts of Race in Britain and the United States Between the
   World Wars* (New York, 1992); Degler, *In Search of Human Nature*; William J.
   Wilson, *The Declining Significance of Race* (Chicago, 1978).
10 Charles Silberman, *Crisis in Black and White* (New York, 1964); Frantz Fanon, *Black
   Skin, White Masks* (New York, 1967); Martin Duberman, *In White America* (Boston,
   1964); Stokley Carmichael and Charles Hamilton, *Black Power* (New York, 1967);
   Stanley Lieberson, *A Piece of the Pie: Blacks and White Immigrants Since 1880*
   (Berkeley, 1980).
11 Herbert Gutman, *Work, Culture, and Society in Industrializing America* (New York,
   1976); Irving Howe, *World of Our Fathers* (New York, 1976); Nathan Glazer and
   Daniel Moynihan, *Beyond the Melting Pot* (Cambridge, MA, 1963); Josef Barton,
   Peasants and Strangers (Cambridge, MA, 1975); David Gutierrez, *Walls and Mirrors:
   Mexican Americans, Mexican Immigrants, and the Politics of Ethnicity* (Berkeley,
   1995); George Sanchez, *Becoming Mexican-American: Ethnicity, Culture and
   Identity in Chicano Los Angeles, 1900–1945* (New York, 1993).
12 John Bodnar, Roger Simon, and Michael Weber, *Lives of their Own: Blacks, Italians,
   and Poles in Pittsburgh, 1900–1960* (Urbana, IL, 1982); Lizabeth Cohen, *Making a
   New Deal* (New York, 1990); Kenneth Kusmer, "African American in the City Since
   World War II: From the Industrial to the Post-Industrial Era," *Journal of Urban
   History* 21 (May 1995), 458–504.
13 Discussions of race as an idea include Thomas Gossett, *Race: The History of an Idea
   in America* (New York, 1983); Michael Banton, *The Idea of Race* (Boulder: Westview
   Press, 1977); Richard Hofstadter, *Social Darwinism in American Thought*, rev. ed.

(Boston, 1955; orig. 1944); George Fredrickson, *The Black Image in the White Mind* (New York, 1971).

14 George Fredrickson, "Reflections on the Comparative History and Sociology of Racism," unpublished paper delivered 1992, p. 13, in possession of the author; Herbert Klein, *Slavery in the Americas: A Comparative Study of Cuba and Virginia* (Chicago, 1967); Carl Degler, *Neither Black Nor White: Slavery and Race Relations in Brazil and the United States* (New York, 1971); George Fredrickson, *White Supremacy: A Comparative Study in American and South African History* (New York, 1981); Fredrickson, *Black Liberation: A Comparative History of Black Ideologies in the United States and South Africa* (New York, 1995); John Cell, *The Highest Stage of White Supremacy: The Origins of Segregation in South Africa and the American South* (Cambridge, Eng., 1982); Anthony Marx, *Making Race and Nation: A Comparison of the United States, South Africa and Brazil* (Cambridge, 1997).

15 The best work on the nativist response to immigration remains John Higham, *Strangers in the Land* (New Brunswick, NJ, 1955); the fact that race is not treated as a fundamental category points to the waning of race thinking in the postwar period.

16 James Barrett and David Roediger, "Inbetween Peoples: Race, Nationality and the 'New Immigrant' Working Class," *Journal of Ethnic History* 16:3 (Spring 1997), 3–44; this article draws on Robert Orsi, "The Religious Boundaries of an Inbetween People: Street *Feste* and the Problem of the Dark-Skinned 'Other' in Italian Harlem, 1920–1990," *American Quarterly*, 44 (September 1992).

17 Arnold Hirsch, *Making the Second Ghetto: Race and Housing in Chicago, 1940–1960* (New York, 1983); Thomas Sugrue, *Origins of the Urban Crisis: Race and Inequality in Postwar Detroit* (Princeton, NJ, 1996); John McGreevy, *Parish Boundaries: The Catholic Encounter with Race in the Twentieth-Century Urban North* (Chicago, 1996).

18 Paving the way for recent studies, an older literature stimulated by the riots of the 1960s looked at "ecological warfare" over jobs, housing, and patronage; William Tuttle, *Race Riot: Chicago and the Red Summerr of 1919* (New York, 1970); Elliott Rudwick, *Race Riot at East St. Louis* (Urbana, 1964). On segregation, see Douglas Massey and Nancy Denton, *American Apartheid: Segregation and the Making of an Underclass* (Cambridge,MA, 1993).

19 Ellis Cose, *The Rage of a Privileged Class* (New York, 1993); David Levering Lewis, *W.E.B.DuBois: Biography of a Race, 1868–1919* (New York, 1993); James Grossman, *Land of Hope: Chicago, Black Southerners, and the Great Migration* (Chicago, 1989), 7, 210.

20 Herbert Hill, "Myth-Making as Labor History: Herbert Gutman and the United Mine Workers of America," *International Journal of Politics, Culture and Society* 2 (Winter 1988); Hill, "The Problem of Race in American Labor History," *Reviews in American History* 24 (1996): 180–208.

21 Edna Bonacich, "A Theory of Ethnic Antagonism: The Split Labor Market," *American Sociological Review* 37, no. 5 (1972), 547–559; racism and labor market competition are discussed in Paul Ong, "Chinese Labor in Early San Francisco: Racial Segmentation and Industrial Expansion," *Amerasia* (1981) 8 (1): 62–92; Paul Frisch, " 'Gibraltar of Unionism': Women, Blacks and the Anti-Chinese Movement in Butte, Montana, 1880–1900," *Southwest Economy and Society* 1984 6(3), 3–13; David Gordon, *et al.*, *Segmented Work, Divided Workers: The Historical Transformation of Labor in the United States* (Cambridge, Eng., 1982).

22 Herbert Gutman, "The Negro and the United Mine Workers of America: The Career and Letters of Richard L. Davis and Something of Their Meaning: 1890–1900," in *The Negro and the American Labor Movement*, ed. Julius Jacobson (New York, 1968);

James Green, "The Brotherhood of Timber Workers, 1910–1913," *Past and Present*, 60 (August 1973).

23   Contrast the critical treatment of the AFL in Gwendolyn Mink, *Old Labor and New Immigrants in American Political Development: Union, Party, and State, 1875–1920* (Ithaca, NY, 1986) with the favorable treatment of the CIO in Lizabeth Cohen, *Making a New Deal*. See also Horace Cayton and George Mitchell, *Black Workers and the New Unions* (New York, 1939).

24   Rick Halpern, *Down on the Killing Floor: Black and White Workers in Chicago's Packinghouses, 1904–54* (Urbana, IL, 1997); Roger Horowitz, *"Negro and White, Unite and Fight!": A Social History of Industrial Unionism in Meatpacking, 1930–90* (Urbana, IL, 1997); Michael Honey, *Southern Labor and Black Civil Rights: Organizing Memphis Workers* (Urbana, IL, 1993), especially chs. 4 and 5. See also Daniel Letwin, *The Challenge of Interracial Unionism: Alabama Coal Miners, 1878–1921* (Chapel Hill, 1998); Bruce Nelson, *Workers on the Waterfront: Seamen, Longshoremen, and Unionism in the 1930s* (Urbana, IL, 1988).

25   Noel Ignatiev, *How the Irish Became White* (New York, 1995); Theodore Allen, *The Invention of the White Race* (New York, 1994); David Roediger, *The Wages of Whiteness* (London, 1991); Eric Lott, *Love and Theft: Blackface Minstrelsy and the American Working Class* (New York, 1993).

26   Robin D. G. Kelley, *Race Rebels: Culture, Politics, and the Black Working Class* (New York, 1994), 5; Kelley, " 'We Are Not What We Seem,': Rethinking Black Working Class Opposition in the Jim Crow South," *Journal of American History* 80 (June 1993), 75–112; Kelley, *yo' Mama's Disfunktional! Fighting the Culture Wars in Urban America* (Boston, 1997).

27   Bruce Nelson, "Class, Race and Democracy in the CIO: The 'New' Labor History Meets the 'Wages of Whiteness,' " *International Review of Social History* 41 (1996), 351–374; the shift to race is evident in two publications by Nick Salvatore, *Eugene V. Debs: Citizen and Socialist* (Urbana, 1982) and *We All Got History: The Memory Book of Amos Weber* (New York, 1996); Goldfield, *The Color of Politics*.

28   Michael Omi and Howard Winant, *Racial Formation in the United States: From the 1960s to the 1980s* (New York, 1986), 66, ital. in original; Tomas Almaguer, *Racial Fault Lines: The Historical Origins of White Supremacy in California* (Berkeley, 1994), 12.

29   Winthrop Jordan, *White Over Black: American Attitudes Toward the Negro, 1550–1812* (Chapel Hill, NC, 1968); Richard Drinnon, *Facing West: The Metaphysics of Indian Hating and Empire Building* (New York, 1990; orig. 1980), xxv–xxviii; Joel Williamson, *The Crucible of Race: Black/White Relations in the American South Since Emancipation* (New York, 1984).

30   Cornel West, *Race Matters* (Boston, 1993), ch.2 "The Pitfalls of Racial Reasoning;" Stuart Hall, "The New Ethnicities," in James Donald and Ali Rattansi, eds., *"Race," Culture, and Difference* (Newbury Part, CA, 1992), 253–254; for an earlier emphasis on the "dialectic between conditions and consciousness," see Hall's 1980 essay "Cultural Studies: Two Paradigms," in Dirks, Eley, and Ortner, eds., *Culture/Power/History*, 520–538.

31   Joan Scott, *Gender and the Politics of History* (New York, 1988), 59; William Sewell, Jr., "A Post-Materialist Rhetoric for Labour History," in Patrick Joyce, ed., *Class* (Oxford, 1995), 174–182, inverts Marx's inversion of Hegel.

32   See Dirks, *et al.*, *Culture/Power/History*, especially, Geoff Eley, "Nations, Publics, and Political Cultures: Placing Habermas in the Nineteenth Century," 297–335; Gareth Stedman Jones, *The Languages of Class* (Cambridge, Eng., 1983); Nell Painter, "The New Labor History and the Historical Moment," *International Journal of Politics,*

Culture, and Society 2 (Spring 1989); a representative collection of cultural approaches in a variety of fields is Lynn Hunt, ed., *The New Cultural History* (Berkeley, 1989).

33 Sharon Harley, "When Your Work Is Not Who You Are: The Development of a Working-Class Consciousness among Afro-American Women," in Frankel, *Gender, Class, Race, and Reform*, 42–55; Robin Kelly, *yo' Momma's Disfunktional!*.

34 Morrison quoted in Richard Delgado and Jean Stefancic, *Critical White Studies: Working Behind the Morror* (Philadelphia, 1997), 84.

35 Terry Eagleton, "Where Do Postmodernists Come From?" *Monthly Review* 47 (July-August 1995), 59–70.

36 Eric Hobsbawm, *The Forward March of Labour Halted?* (London, 1981).

37 Joan Scott, *Gender and the Politics of History*; a useful guide to the cultural turn is Patrick Joyce, ed., *Class* (Oxford, 1995); Jacques Derrida, *The Specters of Marx*.

38 Gunnar Myrdal, *An American Dilemma: The Negro Problem and Modern Democracy* (New York, 1944); on exceptionalism, see Michael Kammen, "The Problem of American Exceptionalism: A Reconsideration," *American Quarterly* 45 (March 1993), 1–43; Ian Tyrell, "American Exceptionalism in an Age of International History," *American Historical Review* (October 1991), 1031–1072; Rick Halpern and Jonathan Morris, eds., *American Exceptionalism? U.S. Working Class Formation in an International Context* (New York, 1996).

39 Gail Bederman, *Manliness and Civilization: A Cultural History of Gender and Race in the United States, 1880–1917* (Chicago, 1995); Howard Winant, *Racial Conditions: Politics, Theory, Comparisons* (Minneapolis, 1994).

40 Glenda Gilmore, *Gender and Jim Crow: Women and the Politics of White Supremacy in North Carolina, 1896–1920* (Chapel Hill, NC, 1996); Eric Arnesen, *Waterfront Workers of New Orleans: Race, Class, and Politics, 1863–1923* (Albany, 1988); Arnesen, "Up From Exclusion," 157; Daniel Letwin, *The Challenge of Interracial Unionism: Alabama Coal Miners, 1878–1921* (Chapel Hill, 1998).

41 A related point about the need to examine employer discrimination and structural inequality is found in Tomas Sugrue, "Segmented Work, Race-Conscious Workers: Structure, Agency and Division in the CIO Era," *International Review of Social History* 41 (1966), 389–406.

42 Michael Goldfield, "Race and the CIO: The Possibilities for Racial Egalitarianism During the 1930s and 1940s," *International Labor and Working-Class History* 44 (Fall 1993), 1–32, and responses 33–63; Roediger, "What if Labor Were Not White and Male? Recentering Working-Class History and Reconstructing Debate on the Unions and Race," *International Labor and Working-Class History* 51 (Spring 1997), 72–95.

43 Peter Skerry, *Mexican Americans: The Ambivalent Minority* (New York, 1993); Earl Shorris, "Racism and Racismo," *Latinos: A Biography of the People* (New York, 1992), 146–171.

44 Anthony Appiah, "Illusions of Race," *In My Father's House: Africa in the Philosophy of Culture* (New York, 1992), 28–46; Anthony Appiah and Amy Gutmann, *Color Conscious: The Political Morality of Race* (Princeton, 1996), 90, 96; Appiah, "The Multicultural Misunderstanding," *New York Review of Books* 44 (October 9, 1997): 30–35. For a parallel argument "against culture" in Middle Eastern studies, see Lila Abu-Lughod, *Writing Women's Worlds: Bedouin Stories* (Berkeley, CA, 1993), 9–13.

45 David Hollinger, *Postethnic America: Beyond Multiculturalism* (New York, 1995), 39; Werner Sollors, *Beyond Ethnicity: Consent and Descent in American Culture* (New York, 1986).

46 Mary Waters, *Ethnic Options: Choosing Identities in America* (Berkeley, 1990), 175.

47 Dorothy Ross, *The Origins of American Social Science* (Cambridge, 1991), 22–52; Gary Gerstle, "Liberty, Coercion, and the Making of Americans," *Journal of American History*, 84:2 (September 1997): 524–558.

48 Gwynn Willians, "Gramsci's Concept of Egomania," *Journal of the History of Ideas* 21 (October-December, 1960), 586–99; Perry Anderson, "The Antinomies of Antonio Gramsci," *New Left Review*, 100 (January 1977), 5–80; Raymond Williams, *Marxism and Literature* (Oxford, 1977); E. P. Thompson, "Eighteenth Century English Society: Class Struggle Without Class?" *Social History*, 3 (May 1978); postmodernists such as Frederick Jameson attempt to connect new understandings of culture to capitalist totality; for a thoughtful and readable contribution along these lines, see David Harvey, *The Condition of Postmodernity* (New York, 1989).

49 Classical analysis can be found in Maurice Dobb, *Studies in the Development of Capitalism* (New York, 1947); for a revisionist analysis of modes of production based on kin, tribute, and capitalism, see Eric Wolf, *Europe and the People Without History* (Berkeley, 1982).

50 Barbara Fields, "Slavery, Race and Ideology in the United States of America," *New Left Review* 181 (May/June 1990), 95–118; quotes on p. 99; Edmund Morgan, *American Slavery/American Freedom: The Ordeal of Colonial Virginia* (New York, 1975); the many studies by Eugene Genovese, especially, *Roll, Jordan, Roll: The World The Slaves Made* (New York, 1974).

51 Fields, "Slavery, Race, and Ideology," 114. The paradox of racial inequality emerging from egalitarian ideology is compared to the Hindu caste system in Louis Dumont, *Homo Hierarchicus: An Essay on the Caste System*, trans. M. Sainsbury (Chicago, 1970); Eric Foner, *Reconstruction: America's Unfinished Revolution, 1863–1877* (New York, 1988); Ira Berlin, et al., eds., *Freedom: A Documentary History of Emancipation* (New York, 1982)

52 The pioneering nature of Saxton's work is evident in the publication date of *The Indispensable Enemy: Labor and the Anti-Chinese Movement in California* (Berkeley, 1971); Alexander Saxton, *The Rise and Fall of the White Republic: Class Politics and Mass Culture in Nineteenth Century America* (London: Verso, 1990), 13–18; on political theory, see Thomas D. Boston, *Race, Class, and Conservatism* (Boston, 1988); David T. Wellman, *Portraits of White Racism* (Cambridge, Eng., 1993) 2nd. ed. On capitalist development, see Stanley Greenberg, *State and Race in Capitalist Development: Comparative Perspectives* (New Haven, CT, 1980).

53 Joe Trotter, *Black Milwaukee: The Making of an Industrial Proletariat, 1915–1945* (Urbana, IL, 1985); Joe Trotter, *Coal, Class, and Color: Blacks in Southern West Virginia, 1915–32* (Urbana, 1990); Earl Lewis, *In Their Own Interests: Race, Class, and Power in Twentieth-Century Norfolk, Virginia* (Berkeley, 1991); Tera Hunter, *To Joy My Freedom: Southern Black Women's Lives and Labors after the Civil War* (Cambridge, MA, 1997); Jacqueline Jones, *Labor of Love, Labor of Sorrow: Black Women, Work, and the Family from Slavery to the Present* (New York, 1985); for a perspective on the black middle class, see Susan Smith, *Sick and Tired of Being Sick and Tired: Black Women's Health Activism in America, 1890–1950* (Philadelphia, 1995).

54 Nicolas B. Dirks, Geoff Eley, and Sherry B. Ortner, eds., *Culture/Power/History: A Reader in Contemporary Social Theory* (Princeton, 1994); Joan Scott, *Gender and the Politics of History* (New York, 1988); examples of gender re-mapping include Mary Blewett, *Men, Women, and Work: Class, Gender, and Protest in the New England Shoe Industry, 1780–1910* (Urbana, 1988); Kathleen Brown, *Good Wives, Nasty Wenches, and Anxious Patriarchs: Gender, Race, and Power in Colonial Virginia* (Chapel Hill, 1996).

55 Nancy MacLean, *Behind the Mask of Chivalry: The Making of the Second Ku Klux Klan* (New York, 1994); Dan Letwin, *The Challenge of Interracial Unionism*; Nancy Hewitt, "Politicizing Domesticity: Anglo, Black, and Latin Women in Tampa's Progressive Movements," in Noralee Frankel, *et al.*, eds, *Gender, Class, Race, and Reform in the Progressive Era* (Lexington, Ky., 1991), 24–41. See also, Dolores Janiewski, *Sisterhood Denied* (Philadelphia, 1985); Glenda Gilmore, *Gender and Jim Crow: Women and the Politics of White Supremacy in North Carolina, 1896–1920* (Chapel Hill, NC, 1996).

56 Thomas Holt, "W. E. B. DuBois's Archeology of Race: Re-Reading 'The Conversation of Races,' " Michael Katz and Thomas Sugrue, *W. E. B. Dubois, Race and the City: The Philadelphia Negro and its Legacy* (Philadelphia, 1998), 71–73.

57 Richard White, *The Middle Ground: Indians, Empires, and Republics in the Great Lakes Region, 1650–1815* (New York, 1991); Gary Nash, "Mestizo America," *Journal of American History*; Sarah Deutsch, *No Separate Refuge: Culture, Class, and Gender on an Anglo-Hispanic Frontier in the American Southwest, 1880–1940* (New York, 1987).

58 David Montejano, *Anglos and Mexicans in the Making of Texas, 1836–1986* (Austin, TX, 1987), 4–9; David Gutierrez, *Walls And Mirrors: Mexican Americans, Mexican Immigrants and the Politics of Ethnicity* (Berkeley, 1995).

59 Higham, *Strangers in the Land*; John Dower, *War Without Mercy: Race War in the Pacific* (New York, 1986).

60 Thomas Holt, *The Problem of Race in the Twenty-First Century* (Cambridge, 2000), 22.

61 Erik Olin Wright, *Class Counts: Comparative Studies in Class Analysis* (Cambridge, Eng., 1997), 24–25, 29–37; Todd Gitlin, *The Twilight of Common Dreams: Why America is Racked by Culture Wars* (New York, 1995); Michael Tomasky, *Left for Dead: The Life, Death and Possible Resurrection of Progressive Politics in America* (New York, 1996); the quote on anti-racism is from Martha Mahoney, "Segregation, Whiteness, and Transformation," Richard Delgado and Jean Stefancic, eds., *Critical White Studies: Working Behind the Mirror* (Philadelphia, 1997), 657.

Index